Chimes of Change
and Hours

Views of Older Women
in Twentieth-Century America

Books by Audrey Borenstein

Custom: An Essay on Social Codes, a translation of *Die Sitte* by Ferdinand Tönnies (New York: The Free Press, 1961)

Redeeming the Sin: Social Science and Literature (New York: Columbia University Press, 1978)

Older Women in Twentieth-Century America: A Selected Annotated Bibliography (New York: Garland Publishing, Inc., 1982)

Chimes of Change and Hours: Views of Older Women in Twentieth-Century America

Chimes of Change
and Hours

Views of Older Women
in Twentieth-Century America

Audrey Borenstein

Rutherford • Madison • Teaneck
Fairleigh Dickinson University Press
London and Toronto: Associated University Presses

Associated University Presses, Inc.
440 Forsgate Drive
Cranbury, NJ 08512

Associated University Presses Ltd
25 Sicilian Avenue
London WC1A 2QH, England

Associated University Presses
2133 Royal Windsor Drive
Unit 1
Mississauga, Ontario
Canada L5J 1K5

Library of Congress Cataloging in Publication Data

Borenstein, Audrey, 1930–
  Chimes of change and hours.

  Bibliography: p.
  Includes index.
  1. Middle aged women—United States—Social
conditions. 2. Aged women—United States—Social
conditions. I. Title.
HQ1426.B685 1983   305.2′44′0973   82-48159
ISBN 0-8386-3170-3

Printed in the United States of America

for Shari and Jeff
and all young people everywhere
to light you on your way

Henceforth, from the Mind

Henceforth, from the mind,
For your whole joy, must spring
Such joy as you may find
In any earthly thing,
And every time and place
Will take your thought for grace.

Henceforth, from the tongue,
From shallow speech alone,
Comes joy you thought, when young,
Would wring you to the bone,
Would pierce you to the heart
And spoil its stop and start.

Henceforward, from the shell,
Wherein you heard, and wondered
At oceans like a bell
So far from ocean sundered—
A smothered sound that sleeps
Long lost within lost deeps,

Will chime you change and hours,
The shadow of increase,
Will sound you flowers
Born under troubled peace—
Henceforth, henceforth
Will echo sea and earth.

—LOUISE BOGAN

Contents

Acknowledgments

Grateful acknowledgment is made herewith to Farrar, Straus and Giroux, Inc., for permission to reprint the poem "Henceforth, from the Mind" from *The Blue Estuaries* by Louise Bogan; to Macmillan Publishing Co., Inc., and to A. P. Watt, Ltd., for permission to reprint the lines from *The Countess Cathleen* from *The Variorum Edition of the Plays of William Butler Yeats*, Russell K. Alspach, ed., to Everyman's Library, J. M. Dent and Sons, Ltd., for permission to quote the lines from *Of the Nature of Things* by Lucretius, a metrical translation by William Ellery Leonard; and to the Beinecke Rare Book and Manuscript Library of the Yale University Library for access to the Edith Wharton "Notebook, 1924–1934" (Quaderno dello Studente) in the Yale Collection of American Literature.

For their contributions to the preparation of this work, I am deeply grateful to the Rockefeller Foundation for the Humanities Fellowship in support of my research project, "the older woman as seen through literature and social science," awarded for the academic year 1978–79,

to Doris B. Albrecht, Librarian, Kristine Mann Library, C. G. Jung Foundation; Professor Judith T. Gatlin, Director of Career Programs at Furman University; Professor Barbara Kirshenblatt-Gimblett, Folklore and Folklife Department of the University of Pennsylvania; Professor Corinne A. Krause, Project Director of the Women, Ethnicity and Mental Health Project; Elinor Langer, writer and biographer; Erminie Lantero, writer and editor; Ruth Limmer, writer and editor; Professor Elaine Scarry, Department of English at the University of Pennsylvania; Professor Jo O'Brien Schaefer of the Department of English at the University of Pittsburgh; Professor Mary Sohngen, Department of English at Miami University; Harriett Straus, Librarian of the New York State Supreme Court, Third Judicial District Law Library; and Professor Kathleen Woodward, Department of English at the University of Wisconsin at Milwaukee, and Director, Center for Twentieth Century Studies at the University of Wisconsin at Milwaukee, for graciously sharing papers or bibliographies with me,

to Harry R. Moody and the members of the staff of the Institute on Humanities, Arts, and Aging, Brookdale Center on Aging, for encouragement of my research endeavors,

to Professor Harry Keyishian, Chariman of the Editorial Committee of Fairleigh Dickinson University Press and to Julien Yoseloff of Associated University Presses for their generous assistance in the preparation of this manuscript for publication and for their many kindnesses, to Grace Marie Aldrich, Rosa Cabrera, Joan de la Cova, Phyllis Crawford, Helen Fein, Irma Goldknopf, A. V. and Minetta Goyne, Gail Hartigan, Florence Michels, Regina deCormier-Shekerjian and Harriett Straus, for the gift of their friendship,

to the nine older women artists for their oral histories,

and to Walter Borenstein, for his love and his faith and his moral sustenance.

—AUDREY BORENSTEIN
New Paltz, New York

Introduction
This Most Faint Neglect

> LEAR: Thou but rememberest me of mine own conception: I
> have perceived a most faint neglect of late; which I have
> rather blamed as mine own jealous curiosity than as a
> very pretence and purpose of unkindness: I will look
> further into't.
>
> —*King Lear,* Act 1, scene 4

In her Introduction to *America Through Women's Eyes,* a book first published in 1933, Mary Beard proclaimed that "the most striking and significant tendency of contemporary social thought" was the movement to unify every aspect of life. She believed herself to be writing as one in the vanguard of an intellectual revolution, crossing the threshold of a period of reconstruction more far-reaching even than the Renaissance. "Economic man" and "political man" were fading at last, she wrote; for too long a time, these phantoms had been taken to be the moving forces of contemporary history. She pointed to the writings of Benedetto Croce, the works of the German cultural anthropologists, and the founding of the Social Science Research Council in the United States as signs of the shaping of a new perspective, one that would encompass and at the same time transcend the limited "specialisms" of the various intellectual disciplines. And in her view this confluence had been given official, concrete expression in the report by President Hoover's Committee entitled *Recent Social Trends,* since here the various divisions of social thought had been brought together to focus on the subject of American civilization. That the National Council of Women, representing five million members of all its component organizations, called for the conference at Chicago in 1933 on "Our Common Cause—Civilization," was a further indication to her that this revolution in social thought was already under way. The divisions of thought—she named politics, economics, war, art, education, literature, and feminism as examples—were no longer to be seen as separate and self-contained spheres of life, no longer to be isolated from one another. Her contemporaries were abandoning the notion of culture or civilization as an assemblage of items "in a basket called history," for they saw that this conception has no correspondence with the reality of a society in the process of development. Indeed, notions such as these were recognized as obstacles to an understanding of civilization and to the designing of social policies for its

13

conservation and advancement. There is no way, she wrote, that the intellectual climate of the nineteenth century could ever be restored: "That age has passed and the new epoch has opened."[1]

Nearly fifty years after Mary Beard wrote these words, this vision she presaged of an intellectual revolution that would unify all aspects of life, floats up from the page as a mirage—and a reproach. Specialisms breed subspecialisms shamelessly. The fragmentation of knowledge and the partitioning of human community along deeply drawn lines of every imaginable affiliation and persuasion have become our most common condition. The worlds of thought flee ever further away from one another. Philosophers and artists, those in the various intellectual disciplines of the natural sciences and the social sciences and those in the literary world, when they are on speaking terms at all, talk past one another in tongues that defy the genius of the most gifted translator. The vital center did not hold; and the closing decades of the twentieth century are haunted by Yeats's augury of the dread "second coming" that might follow this chaos. Each self, ever more sealed from others, suffers its own anarchy of selves, dismembered as the human community has been dismembered, into quarrelsome factions of gender and generation, of race and religion and nationality, of social class and occupation and political belief. Though Mary Beard spoke on the side of the angels, she spoke far too soon. Today, one must lay to rest the ghosts not only of "economic man" and "political man," but of a host of phantom species found in that double mirror of self and society in the past half-century. Yet this is the task that must be undertaken by those who would build a bridge between the "specialisms." These bridges—ethnobotany, psychohistory, sociobiology, biophysics, bioethics—are expressions of the essential unity of all aspects of life. Artists and thinkers who give form to this take their chances in a world where every preserve is jealously guarded against trespassing. That is what interdisciplinary study is all about.

This book is a venture into interdisciplinary study. It is a book about aging, about women's aging, in twentieth-century North America. It is a book about older women as seen through social science and literature, and as seen in life by themselves and others. It represents a bridge between the oral and written traditions in our society . . . between American studies, social gerontology, and women's studies . . . and, over-arching these, between the humanities and the social sciences. It gathers between its covers a conspectus of social facts and imaginative field studies by social scientists engaged in gerontological research; insights into women's later years drawn from works in analytical psychology and from older women's oral histories, personal documents, and fiction; and an exploration of older women's creativity—a combined research and literary project of my own. Both a writer and a social scientist who has a fascination for the possibilities of the second half of life, I set out in quest of what social scientists and writers have to offer one another, and what both have to offer social gerontology, beyond recitations of statistical litanies and phrases from Cicero's *De Senectute*. The spirit guiding this work is the ambition to draw the demographer and the poet, the analytical psychologist and the essayist, the social gerontologist and the memoirist, the economist and the fiction writer, the oral historian and the literary critic into a symposium on memory, on wisdom, on the creative imagination, on freedom and responsibility in the second half of women's lives—on the many meanings of the passage of time for women in the twentieth century in the United States.

This book is a response to a call from many quarters for a work about older women as seen through social science and literature. National organizations and projects focusing on older women include the Displaced Homemakers Network, the Gray Panthers National Task Force on Older Women, the NOW National Older Women's Rights Committee, the National Action Forum for Older Women, the Older Women's League, the Older Women's League Educational Fund, and PROJECT HAVE Skills and PROJECT ACCESS. The designation of "older women" as women over the age of forty was made by the founders of the National Action Forum for Older Women, by the authors of *Uncharted Territory*,[2] by the participants of the 1973 Michigan conference on older women,[3] by sociologist Ruth Jacobs in her book on older women,[4] and by many social gerontologists addressing the issues and concerns of women in later life. Some have called attention to the need for further study of older *women*, who until now "have not been the focus of most major research efforts in gerontology."[5] Others have pointed to the need for research into the meaning of the women's liberation movement for *older* women,[6] or remarked the lack of attention given to middle-aged and older women at the inaugural conference for the first International Women's Year in 1975 and in succeeding sessions held throughout the year.[7] Myrna Lewis and Robert Butler raise the question in an article, "Why Is Women's Lib Ignoring Old Women?"[8] Still others have suggested that *middle-aged* women have been neglected by social scientists—in her study of American housewives, sociologist Helena Znaniecki Lopata writes that gerontologist Bernice Neugarten had made this observation. Most women in American society, Lopata remarks, are "treated as rather valueless" once they have "produced at least one child and reared it to pre-adulthood. Thus, most women are left in a situation similar to that of retired men, for thirty or more years of their lives."[9] Finally, the need for *literary* explorations of aging has been declared both by gerontologists and by those in the humanities engaged in research and teaching courses on aging. In his Pulitzer Prize–winning work, *Why Survive? Being Old in America*, Robert Butler reflects that, although the arts illuminate old age in important ways, there are not very many art forms—novels or poems or films—in which older persons are central subjects. Among the few exceptions to this in literature, Butler mentions the works of Cervantes, Balzac, Proust, Joyce, Mann, and Tolstoy.[10] In none of these are there any materials to be mined by those in search of women's experience of aging—to say nothing of the American woman's experience of aging. Indeed, in her discussion of "Old Age in Historical Societies," Simone de Beauvoir remarks that "old age is as much a woman's concern as a man's—even more so, indeed, since women live longer. But when there is speculation upon the subject, it is considered primarily in terms of men."[11] Tillie Olsen has documented the neglect of American women of letters by literary critics and scholars. Thus, she found, among other examples, that "In Alfred Kazin's 317 page *Bright Book of Life,* forty-three concern women writers. They are segregated into one chapter, not for purposes of illumination, discovery, or because of similarities in theme or style—legitimate reasons for grouping and a different matter from segregation—but simply because they are women."[12] And in a paper presented at the 1978 Modern Language Association meeting's Special Session on Perspectives on Aging, Charlotte Goodman reported that she had found that most of the readily available literary works about old age concern the experience of male protagonists. Goodman observed that works such as Katherine Anne Porter's "The Jilting of Granny Weatherall" and Tillie Olsen's "Tell Me a Riddle" ought to be read in conjunction with those written by male authors about male characters, for a balanced perspective on aging. But works by and about men—"Death in Venice" and "The Death of Ivan Ilych" are prominent examples of this—are the ones traditionally included in anthologies and listed in course syllabuses.[13]

It may not be too much to say that the 1980s could become the decade of older women as "Growing Numbers: Growing Force" in the United States. In October of 1980, the White House Mini-Conference on Older Women adopted this as the title of its convention in Des Moines, Iowa.[14] Work sessions addressed fifteen topics that were divided into three clusters—insuring adequate income, health concerns of older women, and quality of life and the impact of aging. About 200 women participants stayed on after this conference, at their own expense, to found the Older Women's League, an outgrowth of the Older Women's League Educational Fund founded by Tish Sommers and Laurie Shields, and named Sommers as the first president of OWL. One year after the Des Moines meetings, the third White House Conference on Aging met in Washington, and for the first time one of its fourteen committees, Committee no. 11, focused on "Concerns of Older Women: Growing Numbers, Special Needs."

If the 1980s are to be remembered as the decade of older women as "growing numbers, growing force," the 1970s may be seen in retrospect as a time of confluence of two major movements for social reform in the United States, the women's movement and the movement for age equality. All through the 1970s there were signs of the recognition by social observers of the breadth of the sociological category "older women" and of the profound implications this has for social policy. This was evinced by the greater attention given to older women in the media, particularly in the latter half of the decade; by the establishment of the NOW Task Force on Older Women in 1974, the National Action Forum for Older Women in 1978, and the National Task Force on the Older Woman of the Gray Panthers in 1979; by the appearance of *Prime Time,* a newsletter for women over forty earlier in the decade, and, in 1978, by the appearance of the periodical *Broomstick;*[15] and by numerous conferences and workshops convened, and networks and task forces established throughout the decade. A pioneering conference, "Women: Life Span Challenges," was held in Ann Arbor, Michigan, in 1973.[16] It is clear that the proliferation of interests addressed by these activities attests to issues and concerns of profound social and economic significance in the United States in the last decades of the twentieth century.

The sociological perspective on aging focuses on the ways demographic, social, economic, and historical changes combine to make the "older woman" a very timely subject in late twentieth-century North America. In the first chapter of this book, the consequences for women in general and for society as a whole of the growing numbers and proportion of the elderly and of the increasing sex differential in life expectancy are examined. And the implications of social facts—and some fictions—about the living arrangements of the elderly, and about poverty, work, leisure, retirement, and widowhood are discussed. Sociologists have contributed many outstanding studies to the field of social gerontology. Of these, a number of observational studies are reviewed, in order to explore the varieties of experience and circumstance of older women in contemporary America. Underlying the search for what is the case—the changing relationships of older women to family, neighborhood, community, and society, and the changes in women's lives as they grow older—is the search for what *ought* to be: for the humanistic sociologist, every inquiry leads ineluctably to the moral horizons of the discipline. Social facts and field studies are not ends in themselves. Rather, they are means of arriving at an understanding of the nature of the good society—of the possibilities of life on this earth. The challenges of aging, the losses and the triumphs of the second half of life, the changing meanings of private affection and universal love over the life course, the chances for freedom and moral responsibility and creativity in the later years—these humanistic concerns inspire the study of *Four Stages of Life* by Marjorie Fiske Lowenthal and her associates,[17] Robert Butler's *Why Survive? Being Old in America,* and Maggie Kuhn's impassioned criticisms of the prevailing social arrangements.[18] To explore them fully requires an appreciation of their *meanings* for people. For this, one must look under the social terrain, into inner life.

To live is to change, and change again: women's "change of life" is but one of many thresholds crossed in the course of human life, though it is on this threshold that the subject of this book begins. There are very few cultures in which rites of passage are prescribed for women in menopause—and none where menopause is given the attention given the menarche. Doubtless, this is a reflection of a feature of human societies everywhere and in all times (though there are always exceptions): supreme value is placed on the perpetuation of the species and the continuation of the human group. As ever greater numbers of women live far beyond the childbearing years, the absence of cultural definitions of the meaning and purpose of those years becomes an issue that can no longer be ignored. Older women as a collectivity, however else each may differ from the other, have in common this spiritual quest for a raison d'être in the second half of life. The approach of the analytical psychologists—Jungian psychology—is unique in the attention it gives to midlife and later life. It is unique as well for the appeal it had from the beginning for women disciples[19] and for those of artistic temperaments and inclinations. Although I have never been in Jungian analysis or, indeed, in any other, I found insights into the inner lives of older women in the works of analytical psychologists that I could not find elsewhere. Among these were two imaginative interpretations of rites of passage for women at a "turning point" in life. Through analytical psychology, a woman's passage along the life course is seen as a striving for wholeness, for the realization of Everywoman in her inner life. From this standpoint, the spiritual significance of the "change of life" is that, at this turning point, a woman feels called to develop those talents which had been neglected in her youth and early womanhood. For choices must always be made, and youth is the time when one makes them. That these choices need not be fatal for women, that in the second half of life a woman may truly change her life—this is the unique contribution of analytical psychology to an understanding of the inner life of older women. In meeting the challenge of life's turning point, the call to individuation, a woman is seen as an initiate in the mystery play of life. In encountering the "radiant diversity" of the archetype of the Feminine, and in seeing herself as Everywoman, she encounters her possibilities for further growth. The approach of the analytical psychologists is exceptional for its illuminations of the relationships of older women to lovers and friends, daughters and mothers; for its explorations into the mythological and religious significance of Wisdom—Wisdom as Woman; and for the attention it gives to creativity and freedom in the lives of older women.

Stereotypes of older women pale before the vividness and power of the primordial images of the archetype of the Feminine. And they shatter when those who believe in them encounter the flesh and blood people of whom they are less than the most threadbare caricatures. In their oral histories, in the "grandmothers' tales," in the life stories and reflections of women in the later years of life, the voices of older women living in the United States today are heard. With the finest intentions and with unassailable logic, one may deliver a spirited rebuttal to the claim that older women are asexual or ugly, or passive, or aggressive, or uncreative or devouring—that they are, whether scorned or pitied, to be shunned. But no argument against these stereotypes is as persuasive as an attentive reading of transcripts of oral histories of older women, as "listening" through reading the words transcribed from tape onto the printed page to older women's "first-person stories."

In the nineteenth century, the social sciences—and sociology, in particular—and the social novel came into their own. Up until that time, Beauvoir remarks, the upper classes spoke only of themselves when they wrote about the meaning of the later years of life.[20] Since then, writers and social scientists alike have spoken for people of every circumstance, so that our understanding of aging is no longer limited to the experience of "the eupatrids, the highly-privileged." But since the late 1940s, with the inception of the oral history movement, those from whom we might not otherwise have heard speak for themselves—indeed, so much so that the researcher today suffers from an embarrassment of riches of source materials. Countless pages of transcripts of tape-recorded oral histories have been gathered over the past thirty years, and every day, hundreds of pages are added to the treasuries of first-person stories. Thanks to the vibrancy of the oral history movement, the researcher must make selections from a wealth of materials that is truly appalling.[21] The choice of oral histories for this book was guided by an appreciation of the varieties of social and cultural worlds there are in the United States—a country that is a veritable paradise for the cultural anthropologist, the folklorist, and the cultural historian. Only a series of encyclopedias would be spacious enough to reflect them all; and I wanted to write a book one could hold in one's hands, not a set of volumes that would require the support of several sturdy podiums. And even those encyclopedias would not do, since every oral history is a story told in a distinctive voice, as well as by a member of some chorus. In my selection of "first-person stories," I wanted to balance accounts by women who live in the country with those by women who live in the city, accounts by women in the South with those by women in the North, those of the foreign-born with those of the native-born; I read oral histories of women of a variety of racial and religious and ethnic identities. I wanted to know what a diversity of women had to say about growing older as well as about what they remember of the early decades of this century. I was especially sensitive to regional differences, which, strangely enough, have never been given the attention they deserve by sociologists in the United States. Character, circumstance, place, time, and human destiny—of these, works of sociology *and* works of literature are made. A central concern of the sociologist is circumstance, while that of the fiction writer is character. However, a keen historical sense and a fascination with the question of what this life is for—these inform the finest works of sociology as well as of literature; and that the same cannot be said of the sense of place is curious, indeed. Many writers seem to know by instinct that place is as indivisible from character as historical time. In many enduring works in American literature, place is breathed through the very pores of a character, and becomes itself a living presence. But the great American sociological work on regional differences is yet to be written, and whoever undertakes it will have few signposts along the way.

Old people need listeners, confessors even: the need to reminisce may be as urgent in later life as the need for food, for love. Even if no one listens, anthropologist Barbara Myerhoff writes, one tells one's story "aloud, to oneself, to prove that there is existence, to tame the chaos of the world, to give meaning. The tale certifies the fact of being and gives sense at the same time."[22] The old people in *Number Our Days* told their stories for the sake of finding some sense of continuity, some coherence in their lives; they needed to rescue the past from the oblivion more fearful than death itself. Reminiscence was "a major developmental task" for them, a means of putting their lives together. In the United States, a good listener is hard to find. So many people are going to confession to one another; so few have the time or the patience to listen. The cruelty of this indifference to a vital need of older people, and the incalculable loss to the culture that is a consequence of it, have been remarked by many gerontologists.

Oral histories are a unique source of information, cross-reference, and documentation for those engaged in a variety of research objectives. Yet they are far more than records of events and actions and social facts. Indeed, they are a broth of fact and fiction, as every human life may be said to be. To remember is to give form to all that is summoned to consciousness. In commenting, in filling in the spaces, and in infusing memories with feeling, the story-teller becomes author and myth maker of her or his life. The transformation of all that has been experienced into meaning for one's own life and for the lives of others is a creative act. In weaving a retrospective, an old person creates designs of experiences, dreams and reflections. To give sense and form to all that the memory restores is creative work in the same way that sculpture is, or writing a novel, or composing a sonata. The interpretive art of remembering makes the past a work of imagination and desire. The humanistic gerontologist who is alive to this finds in oral histories a rich resource of insights into the many meanings of the life review and of memorial consciousness. Oral histories offer at once a feeling for an earlier time and place, *and* for the remembering mind of an old person. They tell of the way things seemed to be for particular people when they were younger, and of the way they experience their lives as they are now.

Literary perspectives on women's aging are shaped by the study of many genres. Among these are personal documents—autobiographies, diaries, journals, letters, notebooks, memoirs—and drama, essays, fiction, and poetry. Bernice Neugarten has emphasized the importance of seeing the aging process as a continuum,[23] and the personal documents kept by women—in particular, autobiographies, and memoirs—are a means of achieving this perspective. A woman's autobiography can be (although it by no means always is) an occasion for a long backward look upon her life, for seeing it steadily and seeing it whole. In writing her life, a woman may come to terms with it, and know what she can accept of her past and what she will never accept. In the confrontations and judgments of autobiographical writing, a woman may see all her earlier selves as a part of one another and of the woman she is still becoming, and may understand the ways that others have become a part of all she feels herself to be. When one is older, one begins to apprehend the unfolding of a lifeway; the younger person has only intimations of this. In writing one's life, one comes upon the character who was coming into being over the passage of the years. In autobiographies, biographies, and memoirs, the life course perspective is given tangible form and expression. These genres are literary journeys in quest of patterns and the ways these enter into a broader design.

Each personal document has its own insights to offer. In many, events, thoughts, actions, and feelings are recorded as though time were linear. But in some, linear time is apprehended as a mirage, and the life is written out of the experience of time's vagrancies and circularities. Each story is its own, and cannot be compressed into another's. Since there are as many "Americas through women's eyes" as there are American women, and since most of these Americas are yet to be written or recorded, a study of women's views on aging ought to include the works of women in a variety of occupations and professions. That, at least, is a beginning. For one's calling may have as fateful consequences for how one experiences aging as one's parentage or birthplace or choice of mate. Life stories are records of the passage of the years. Diaries, journals, and notebooks are books of days, of hours. In these conversations with the self, and in the conversations with another in letters, there are perceptions and revelations about the many meanings of growing older that can be found in no other source. Whether these are in long passages, in asides, or in sudden illuminations, there are disclosures—about how old parents are seen through the eyes of a daughter grown old herself, about the feelings one has for grown children when one is very old, about love and friendship and work and caring for the world at the last of life, about the workings of memory, about older women remembered as mentors or models of how to be or how *not* to be, about how marriage or the family or war or religion or education are seen by women at the far side of life. These offer a unique contribution to an understanding of women's aging from within, and a source of materials complementary to social scientific studies and works of fiction.

One of the discouraging features of personal documents—particularly of autobiographies and memoirs—as well as of oral histories, is that they so often run on and on. Another is that no one of them may be taken as representative of another. Selection is imperative, and interpretations must be made: the use of personal documents is an art by more than half. These are challenges that must be met, and they are serious. But what is even more serious than this is that life stories can be—and sometimes clearly are—self-serving. Writing or tape-recording one's own history can be taken as the occasion for writing an apologia. Each of us makes our own life, though some are given far more materials and freedom for the task; each of us invents the self—and probably never more imaginatively than when we are giving an account of our lives. Therefore, every personal document, and every oral history, is in part a work of fiction.

The further one moves toward the making of fiction in telling one's life, the more consciously one invents and rewrites it, the more the life story turns into a short story—or a novel. There may be a turning point, although few would be certain of where to fix it, when a memoir, oral or written, turns into a work of imaginative literature. And there are insights into women's aging in works of fiction that cannot be found in any other source. In fiction, an older woman may write of the older woman she longed to become—or dreaded she might one day be. In the multiple mirrors of short stories and novels, unforgettable older women are seen—Eudora Welty's Phoenix Jackson of "A Worn Path," Katherine Anne Porter's Granny Weatherall—whose stories tell us something about our lives we had forgotten; in the lamps of fiction, little worlds are illuminated—Ruth Suckow's Iowa, Sarah Orne Jewett's Maine. Here, older women's lives may be perceived with all the senses. In stories by and about women in later life—women of various times and places in this century and in this country—concreteness and life are given to the conditions described by the social scientists and the reflections expressed in oral and written personal documents. Solitude and loneliness (they are not at all the same) and poverty, and the physical changes that come with aging; the older woman's concern for ancestry and generation, and her wanderings of body and mind and spirit— all these come true through works of fiction about particular lives of particular women. In these, we find some truths about the meaning of our own.

Of the many American women of letters who chose to write about aging in their fictions, there are those in this century who have returned to the theme of growing older, not only in their novels and stories, but in essays or personal documents as well. They write about aging in their autobiographies, diaries, essays, fiction, journals, letters, or notebooks; and aging is a theme in biographies about them and in critical studies of their works. Therefore, it is possible to explore their views on aging as they themselves explored the subject, in an interplay of genres. Each of these writers had her own way of seeing this many-faceted subject; each spoke of aging in a distinctive voice.

Rejuvenation was an article of faith for Gertrude Atherton. Aging, she thought, ought to arouse a woman's fighting instincts. It seemed natural to her that one would want to begin life over again at any age, and she believed that it was never too late to do this. For Atherton, it is not aging that matters, but the attitude a woman takes toward growing older.

Ellen Glasgow wrote movingly of "the inevitable change and fall of the years." Still, she believed that she lived her fullest, richest years after the age of sixty. With aging, she wrote, there is a failing of elasticity, of resilience; there is a keen edge to disappointments once the age of expectancy has passed. Yet, old age frees one from the entanglements of personalities. In Glasgow's fictions she portrays the patient hope of the old for an Indian summer of happiness, the old person's calmness, and old people's need to be needed. Time moves as a living force through the lives of her characters; and in their thoughts, the past arrives in visitations of astonishing radiance and clarity.

Time's passages, woman's maturity, change . . . all these recur as themes in the life and work of Zora Neale Hurston. When she was seven, she saw "vision pictures" of her future that she likened to stereopticon slides. They were previews of her fate of motherlessness and homelessness, and they came true. The hour of her mother's death was the hour that began Hurston's wanderings—spiritual wanderings, in time, not space. In *Their Eyes Were Watching God,* an older woman loves a younger man in the face of the fear that she might become Time's fool. In *Seraph on the Suwanee,* a woman learns to change herself when her life changes, when her children are grown and all the familiar things are fading.

For May Sarton, growing older is an adventure in change and growth, a striving towards completeness, a test of moral courage. An old woman can meet the neglect and indifference of society with a rebellious spirit. Age does not diminish the power to attract and to be attracted. An old woman still cares about what happens to the world—perhaps more passionately than she did when she was young. Solitude has great gifts; but one must fight continually for the peace that is needed for dedication to one's calling. There will always be interruptions, even in late life. And the old quarrels are never settled, and the mourning for parents is never done. But with aging, there is a joy in encouraging the efforts of young people, and an exhilarating freedom from conventions. There is a growing toward the light.

Edith Wharton's fictions were her progeny—so she wrote of them in letters to her friends. In the connections between her life and work, she reflected on what the generations owe one another. A woman in middle age is in a limbo between daughterhood and motherhood, a pilgrim in search of a sense of continuity. It is too late then to make certain changes; yet the chance for renewal beckons—the possibility for late bloom, as the bloom of witch hazel in autumn. Growing older, grievous losses must be borne—the death of beloved friends, the recognition that one's time is passing. There comes a time when one must deliver the world into the hands of the next generation. And one knows at last that life is incomplete. But in spite of it all, an old woman may still be eager for life, curious about it, still—a celebrant to the last.

"Ever since the Renaissance," Leo Lowenthal writes, "modern man has perpetuated the idea that he carries an infinity of possibilities within himself; their realization is always within reach, at least in his phantasies and dreams."[24] And this is a book about possibilities—about the possibilities of life for women at what May Sarton calls life's meridian. Social scientific studies of older women are concerned with the conditions of their lives, with the needs and problems of older women in contemporary society, and the designing of ameliorative policies and programs. Literary works by and about older women complement the works by social scientists by mirroring societal attitudes toward aging, and by illuminating the inner lives of those who have "come of age." But life is so large, so immense and so various, that the reach of scholars and writers always exceeds the grasp. People in books, Louise Bogan wrote, are "paper people . . . , who have one agony to endure, *one* set of toils to fight clear of, in their lives." They are "figures that breathe print and the air of the paragraph and the page," and when one is fully mature, one ought to undertake "the task . . . to fix on paper the bizarre, disordered, ungainly, furtive, mixed elements in one's life."[25]

As I sought them in social facts and fictions, in social science and in literature, so I sought them in life—older women who are seekers, who are conscious, creative beings. The sociological issues and problems attendant upon a society in which a growing proportion of the population live far into later life are serious and of great moment. How shall they be provided for, how can their needs—for an adequate income, for places to live, for companionship—be met? For there must be bread first, then roses. But the spiritual, intellectual, and emotional needs—for meaningful work, for contributing to the community and the society, for love, for the chance to express the gifts each person is given—these needs are as vital as material needs. Indeed, they cannot be separated from one another except in theory. What is life without some sense of purpose and accomplishment, some way of continuing to grow? What is life without friendship, without love? There must be bread *and* roses. Because they respond to this, programs such as Elderhostel have met with great success. Martin T. Knowlton, founder of Elderhostel at the University of New Hampshire, puts the matter succinctly: "The single most pervasive need of retired people is to see themselves as significant people." Elderhostel was designed as a growth experience; and in its fifth year, in 1979, 13,000 elderly people participated in the program on 233 campuses in 38 states. The 1978 annual report forecast a growth to all 50 states by 1981, and, by 1983, to about 400 colleges with nearly 60,000 participants.[26] If there has been less written about the aging of women than about the aging of men, there has been almost nothing written on the subject of women's spiritual, intellectual, and emotional needs in later life, and on the subject of creativity in older women's lives. There is the stubborn notion that woman's need to be creative is gratified by giving birth to human babies. There is also the stubborn notion that older people are uncreative. These biased and insupportable views may account for the silence about the many forms of creativity in the lives of older women—a silence broken by the last chapters of this book. If every work in gerontology is in essence a work of advocacy, this book is written in advocacy of the possibilities of later life for women.

In search of the truth of a thing, one comes upon small and shining truths that are often contradictory and always complex. In my own meditation on women's second half of life in the last chapter of this book, I write about these things, and about the chances there may be that the small bridge built here might hold. When I was an undergraduate student in the 1950s, the subject of aging was given no more attention than one class hour—if even that—in a social problems course; I doubt that the subject fared much better in courses in the humanities. Today, gerontology has "come of age." It has been estimated that about 1,300 colleges and universities around the country—perhaps five times the number in 1973—now offer at least one course in gerontology, and that 30 or 40 offer programs with career training in the field.[27] Historian David Hackett Fischer notes that the psychologist G. Stanley Hall was the first American scholar to give sustained and serious attention to the subject of gerontology; but his book *Senescence,* published in 1922, "fell dead from the press."[28] According to Fischer, it was not until the late 1940s that social gerontology began its rapid growth in the universities—since then, it has "managed to institutionalize itself"—and he rightly names Bernice Neugarten as the pioneer of the discipline. No body of theory has been created, in his assessment—the controversies over "activity theory" and "disengagement theory" are fading, as he remarks—and Fischer doubts that the field will ever be a theoretical discipline. It appears to him that it has been most constructive in its attack on the myths that befog the subject of aging about the weakness of the aged, in its opposition to age prejudice, and in its sharpening of the awareness in our society that old age is a social problem. He perceives a second generation of social gerontologists appearing in the 1960s and 1970s; and their objective is "not merely to improve the condition of elderly people in American society, but to balance the requirements of the old against those of the young."[29]

During the 1970s, too, gerontology has attracted the attention of growing numbers of humanists, and Walter G. Moss writes that in the United States this is "thanks largely . . . to the encouragement of the National Endowment for the Humanities and its state-based programs."[30] David D. Van Tassel suggests that the need for a stronger voice from the humanities in every area of gerontology has long been evident in "the frequent use of fiction, poetry, and philosophy in courses and programs in gerontological education." Van Tassel names Joseph Freeman, M.D., a founder of the Gerontological Society and an internist, as "most prominent in calling for formal recognition of this need." It was Freeman who presented the motion passed by the Council of the Gerontological Society that established its Ad Hoc Committee on Humanism and the Humanities in Gerontology.[31] W. Andrew Achenbaum finds that the "unprecedented effort during the past five years to promote gerontology in the humanities represents a most auspicious development." Achenbaum calls attention to the pioneering projects supported by the National Endowment for the Humanities, and to the vital contributions that scholars and teachers from the humanities can make to research in gerontology, among them adding new and vital dimensions to what we know about old age, offering different perspectives and generating novel insights, and drawing our attention to the values, both explicit and implicit, in our assumptions about older people. In helping gerontologists bring their message to the public, transmitting discoveries across "disciplinary fiefdoms," gerontologists from the humanities can demonstrate the advantages of a multidisciplinary approach to research in aging, and "evoke the humanist and nurture the humaneness in all of us."[32] Stuart F. Spicker, Kathleen M. Woodward, and David D. Van Tassel write that the subject of aging is too vast . . . to be left solely to social and physical scientists." The humanities have a vital contribution to make to the field: "Until we know what we have been, we cannot know what we can become."[33] In the same spirit, David Hackett Fischer recalls the wisdom of Robert L. Heilbroner's remark, that the future is "the growing edge of the present."[34] Fischer reminds us that, "we are not merely witnesses to our history, but its agents and even its authors" (197).

Research on "the older woman as seen through literature and social science" has led to the discovery of many interconnections between the works of scholars in the social sciences and the humanities. Examples from recently published works are the literary references in Arlie Russell Hochschild's *The Unexpected Community* and Zena Smith Blau's *Old Age in a Changing Society*, and the many references to Erik H. Erikson's theory of ego development in *A Feast of Words*, Cynthia Griffin Wolff's literary study of the works of Edith Wharton. In many commentaries on women's oral histories, there is an interweaving of social scientific with literary works. And in two very different kinds of books—*Four Stages of Life* and *What the Woman Lived: Selected Letters of Louise Bogan 1920–1970*—there are references to the insights of the works of analytical psychologists into the inner lives of older women. Indeed, in numerous publications from the 1920s to 1980, references to Jungian psychology appear in a wide variety of works. Gertrude Atherton, Ellen Glasgow, and May Sarton all wrote about Jung in their personal documents, and these are but three examples of women of letters who did so. The Jungian approach is also mentioned in a number of works by anthropologists, psychologists, and sociologists published over the past half-century. An example from the 1930s is Grace Elliott's lucid and comprehensive *Women After Forty*, a work of such rich scholarship and breadth of vision that it transcends the "disciplinary fiefdoms." An example from a 1980 publication is the paper by Carol Boellhoff Giesen and Nancy Datan on "The Competent Older Woman" in *Transitions of Aging*.

In Mary Beard's day, there were certainly exchanges between scholars in the various "specialisms." The bibliography of Grace Elliott's *Women After Forty* evinces an omnivorous reader. Among the books Elliott consulted are Mary Austin's autobiography, *Earth Horizon*, Pearl Buck's *The Mother*, Cicero's *De Senectute*, Malinowski's *Sex and Repression in a Savage Society*, and Hall's *Senescence*. Elliott read works by Jung *and* Freud, by Ernest Jones and Otto Rank, by Adler and Buhler, by Ferenczi and Havelock Ellis; she read the works of J. B. Watson and she read William Hocking's *The Meaning of God in Human Experience*. And fifty or more years ago in this country, there were women of letters who were very much interested in developments in the social sciences. Edna Ferber acknowledged a debt to a classic work in sociology which she read when she was working on her novel *American Beauty*. "The incidental reading was an education," Ferber recalled. "Two enormously fat blue-bound volumes entitled *The Polish Peasant in America* were alone more absorbing and exciting than any fiction I'd read in years."[35] For some, the exchanges were more than incidental. Although it is doubtful that any American woman of letters of that time moved with greater ease between the worlds of social science and literature than did Zora Neale Hurston—a writer who bridged the oral and written traditions, the heritages of folklore, anthropology, and literature—the record suggests that there may have been a strong interdisciplinary spirit abroad at Columbia University. Both Margaret Mead and Ruth Benedict wrote poetry, and in Mead's book about the work of Ruth Benedict she remarks that when she held an assistantship under Ogburn's direction she "filled his office with working poets," among them Louise Bogan.[36] In 1922, Bogan did cataloguing work for Ogburn, who was then professor of sociology at Columbia. Through the years, Bogan was *au courant* with developments in social science. Indeed, she provided "an introduction, some advice . . . and some literary references" for Ann Rogers, a teacher of sociology and an author, when Rogers was gathering materials for *A Cookbook for*

Poor Poets and Others.[37] But in reading Bogan's letters I found intimations of a change in the poet's attitude toward Mead and her work[38] that later I came to see as a paradigm of the growing distance between the two worlds of literature and social science over the past fifty or sixty years in this country. Although they are often talking about the same things, social scientists and writers almost invariably talk past one another. Sometimes it is worse than that, and the disdain that is very high on the one side[39] is matched by a distrust that is very deep on the other.[40] Yet explorations in the study of aging lead to convergences of thought again and again.

One of the motifs of Achenbaum's history of old age in America since 1790 is the divergence between the rhetoric and realities of growing old. Achenbaum shows that there is no necessary consonance between the *perceptions* of the value and functions of old people and their *actual social position*. He maintains a critical distinction between the intellectual and social history of old age in the U.S., and avers that ideas about the old have a life of their own.[41] The approach of this study of "the older woman as seen through literature and social science" attests to the cogency of this point of view. This approach discloses the complex and protean relationship between facts and fictions, images and realities, illusions and truths about older women and women's experiences of aging, and hence the relativity of interpretations of what has been thought and said on this neglected subject.

This approach also suggests that the "most faint neglect" of the subject of older women is due to much more than chance. The subject attracts and repels women as well as men. In the face of an aging woman, one may see a resemblance to a kinswoman—a mother, an aunt, a grandmother—who, for good or for ill, was once a strong influence on one's life, and powerful emotions of love or dread or pity or guilt or resentment are aroused. In the face of an aging woman, one may see primordial images. Their fascination for these images has carried artists, classical scholars, mythologists, and analytical psychologists far below the surfaces of society in their explorations of the psyche. On the face of an aging woman, one may see something of one's future inscribed—a portion of one's fate. To study it closely and reflectively is to begin to understand something of the destiny of the human race.

How should the gift of extended life be received? How might the second half of life be lived with love and dignity and a sense of purpose? Where are older people in the Good Society? What are the possibilities of later life? These are the essential concerns of a humanistic gerontology. In this book they are addressed from the point of view Mary Beard took during an earlier time of troubles in this century:

> If civilization—the great society of today—is to continue, then the problem becomes one of making the huge superstructure of economics and politics function for the essential purposes of life and at the same time of maintaining a sound and creative community life at the basis. In this effort, which engages the best talent of the time, women are sure to be involved from beginning to end, in thought and in action.[42]

Notes

1. Mary R. Beard, "Introduction," *America through Women's Eyes*, Mary R. Beard, ed. (New York: Greenwood Press, Inc., 1976), pp. 1–2. Throughout this book, North America is designated by the abbreviated term *America*.

2. Marilyn R. Block, Janice L. Davidson, Jean D. Grambs, and Kathryn E. Serock, *Uncharted Territory: Issues and Concerns of Women over Forty* (College Park, Md.: University of Maryland Center on Aging, 1978.) *Uncharted Territory* was produced under a grant from the Administration on Aging, U.S. Department of Health, Education and Welfare. The curriculum guide is made up of fourteen modular units, with topics on menopause and sexuality, widowhood and death, continuing education, and ethnic and racial variations of older women, among others; and the work includes an annotated filmography and bibliography.

3. *No Longer Young: The Older Woman in America* (Ann Arbor, Mich.: The Institute of Gerontology, University of Michigan–Wayne State University, Occasional Papers in Gerontology No. 11, 1975.)

4. Ruth Harriet Jacobs, *Life After Youth: Female, Forty—What Next?* (Boston: Beacon Press, 1979).

5. *Uncharted Territory*, Introduction, p. 3.

6. Juanita Kreps, *Sex in the Marketplace: American Women at Work* (Baltimore: The Johns Hopkins Press, 1971), p. 107.

7. Jon A. Hendricks, "Women and Leisure," in *Looking Ahead: A Woman's Guide to the Problems and Joys of Growing Older*, Lillian E. Troll, Joan Israel and Kenneth Israel, eds. (Englewood Cliffs, N.J.: Prentice-Hall, Inc., 1977), p. 115.

8. Myrna I. Lewis and Robert N. Butler, "Why is Women's Lib Ignoring Old Women?" *Aging and Human Development* (1972) 3(3):223–31.

9. Helena Znaniecki Lopata, *Occupation: Housewife* (New York: Oxford University Press, 1971), p. 41.

10. Robert N. Butler, M.D., *Why Survive? Being Old in America* (New York: Harper and Row, 1975), p. 419.

11. Simone de Beauvoir, *The Coming of Age*, trans. Patrick O'Brian (New York: Warner Paperback Library, 1973), p. 134.

12. Tillie Olsen, *Silences* (New York: Delacorte Press/Seymour Lawrence, 1978), p. 187.

13. Charlotte Goodman, "Despair in Elderly Women: Katherine Anne Porter's 'The Jilting of Granny Weatherall' and Tillie Olsen's 'Tell Me a Riddle,' " M.L.A. Special Session, Perspectives in Aging, New York, December 1978.

14. *Growing Numbers, Growing Force. A Report from the White House Mini-Conference on Older Women* (The Long Report) (San Francisco: Western Gerontological Society, and Oakland: Older Women's League Educational Fund, 1981). The week before this conference, the issues and concerns of older women were discussed at a briefing given by population organizations to the U.S. Department of Health and Human Services Secretary's Advisory Committee on the Rights and Responsibilities of Women, and reform of the Social Security system was a major topic.

15. *Prime Time* has ceased publication. *Broomstock*, a periodical supporting *Options* for women over forty, began publication in 1978 at the San Francisco Women's Centers.

16. See note 3 above. The Work Group Reports were published in 1974. Note also that in 1978 there was a special session on older women at the annual meeting of the Gerontological Society, and in that same year, the National Institute on Aging and the National Institute of Mental Health cosponsored a conference on "The Older Woman: Continuities and Discontinuities."

17. Marjorie Fiske Lowenthal, Majda Thurnher, David Chiriboga, et.al., *Four Stages of Life: A Comparative Study of Women and Men Facing Transitions* (San Francisco: Jossey-Bass, Inc., 1975).

18. Dieter Hessel, ed., *Maggie Kuhn on Aging: A Dialogue edited by Dieter Hessel* (Philadelphia: The Westminster Press, 1977).

19. Jung's "first, most enthusiastic, and most fanatic disciples" were women, Paul J. Stern reports, and "In Zurich medical circles, these overly rapturous devotees were tagged with the

inevitable label, 'Jung-Frauen.'" Paul J. Stern, *C. G. Jung: The Haunted Prophet* (New York: George Braziller, 1976), p. 63.

20. Beauvoir, *The Coming of Age*, pp. 317–18.

21. Roddy reports that during the Depression, writers—some of whom became famous throughout the world since that time—"were employed by the federal government to capture, in oral histories of the unemployed, the folklore and folk fantasy of America; a monumental 180,000-page collection of Americana that has since been gathering dust on Deck 19 of the Library of Congress." Joseph Roddy, "The Treasure on Deck 19," *RF Illustrated, The Rockefeller Foundation* (September 1978) 4(2):1. Since then, eighty of the accounts gathered through the Federal Writers' Project were arranged and annotated by Ann Banks, and published in *First-Person America*, ed. and with an Introduction by Ann Banks (New York: Alfred A. Knopf, 1980).

22. Barbara Myerhoff, *Number Our Days* (New York: E. P. Dutton, 1978), p. 271.

23. See Walter G. Moss, "Aging in Humanistic Perspective," in *Humanistic Perspectives on Aging*, Walter G. Moss, ed. (Ann Arbor, Mich.: The Institute of Gerontology, University of Michigan—Wayne State University, 1976), p. 2.

24. Leo Lowenthal, *Literature and the Image of Man* (Boston: The Beacon Press, 1957), p. 59.

25. Ruth Limmer, ed., "From the Journals of a Poet," *The New Yorker* (January 30, 1978) 53 (50):47.

26. Ron Winslow, "Elderhostel: A Growing Chain," *New York Times*, September 9, 1979, Education, p. 11.

27. Robert Lindsey, "Gerontology Comes of Age," *New York Times*, January 8, 1978, Education, p. 11.

28. This was in marked contrast to Hall's development of the modern idea of adolescence, which, Fischer writes, "rapidly caught on." David Hackett Fischer, *Growing Old in America* (New York: Oxford University Press, 1977), pp. 141–42, n. 36. On p. 193 of this book, Fischer names Hall as the first American scholar to show a sustained interest in social gerontology.

29. Ibid., pp. 194–95.

30. Moss, "Aging in Humanistic Perspective," p. 1.

31. David D. Van Tassel, Preface, *Aging and the Elderly: Humanistic Perspectives in Gerontology*, Stuart F. Spicker, Kathleen M. Woodward and David D. Van Tassel, eds. (New Jersey: Humanities Press, Inc., 1978), p. vi.

32. W. Andrew Achenbaum, Preface: From the Historian's Perspective, *Images of Old Age in America: 1790 to the Present*, W. Andrew Achenbaum and Peggy Ann Kusnerz, eds. (Ann Arbor, Mich.: Institute of Gerontology, The University of Michigan–Wayne State University, 1978), p. vii.

33. *Aging and the Elderly*, Editors' Foreward, p. vii.

34. Fischer, *Growing Old in America*, p. 196, n. 1. Hereafter, reference to this book will be cited in the text by page number.

35. Edna Ferber, *A Peculiar Treasure* (New York: Literary Guild, 1939), p. 343.

36. Ruth Limmer, ed., *What the Woman Lived: Selected Letters of Louise Bogan 1920–1970* (New York: Harcourt Brace Jovanovich, Inc., 1973), p. 5, n. 2.

37. Ibid., p. 325, n. 1.

38. Compare what she wrote Ruth Benedict in 1928 about Mead's *Coming of Age in Samoa* with what she wrote May Sarton in 1955 about Margaret Mead in ibid., pp. 37, n. 2, and 294.

39. It would be difficult to match Hortense Calisher's. "In the zoo of the social sciences," she wrote, "is where the musk-glands of humanity are removed—for study. A novel doesn't study—it invents. Inevitably, it represents." Hortense Calisher, *Herself* (New York: Arbor House, 1972), p. 63. In this, her autobiography, she declares herself to be "an enemy of any who look at literature topically" (p. 365) and says she has not changed her view that "sociology is for the simple-minded" (p. 18).

40. In her book about life during the post–World War II years and the years of the McCarthy witch hunt, poet Helen Bevington tells an anecdote that rivals others I have heard for evincing this distrust. A professor of sociology who had been invited to join a discussion group said to the

students, "If I were the father of a son, I'd rather have him be a ballet dancer than a poet. In either case I'd disown him as a pansy." Helen Bevington, *The House Was Quiet and the World Was Calm* (New York: Harcourt Brace Jovanovich, Inc., 1971), p. 74.

41. W. Andrew Achenbaum, *Old Age in the New Land: The American Experience Since 1790* (Baltimore: The Johns Hopkins University Press, 1978).

42. Mary R. Beard, Introduction, *America Through Women's Eyes*, p. 8.

Chimes of Change and Hours

Views of Older Women in Twentieth-Century America

Part 1

1

Older Women in a Changing Society

> Perhaps today more than ever we need dreams and visions
> of what is possible, unconstrained by sex or age. We need to
> influence current change in preparation for our future. We
> need to build into our daily lives what Robert Merton calls self-
> fulfilling prophecies. And we need to see some of these
> prophecies become social realities.
>
> —MATILDA WHITE RILEY,
> "Old Women"

During the Centennial Year (1955) at Michigan State University, a conference on the potentialities of women in the middle years was convened by the School of Home Economics of that institution. At this conference, Bernice Neugarten presented a report on the Kansas City Study of Adult Life and an analysis of responses to a TAT stimulus picture of four figures—a young woman, a young man, an older woman, and an older man—and led a discussion about the implications of the finding that middle-aged women perceived the older woman in this picture in a positive light.[1] In speaking about the changing roles of middle-aged women in society, Robert Havighurst cited evidence that after the age of 45 or 50, women surpass men in health and intellectual vigor. Havighurst contrasted the roles of women in 1850 and 1950, and suggested that the middle years are potentially the best years of their lives for women who are able to use their freedom, and that the major task of middle age is emotional and intellectual expansion. And Lawrence K. Frank addressed the question of ways to discover and cultivate an individuated self, which he believed to be a new prospect for mature women in the 1950s. Reporting that at the Cold Spring Institute for college men and women over the age of 60, people in their later years were engaged in a process of self-discovery through creative activities, Frank observed that there are not very many people who can undertake this task alone. He remarked that there were at that time very few agencies or organizations with services available to women undergoing the process of individuation. Furthermore, he noted, neither high schools nor colleges offered programs for women designed so as "to give them some orientation to their whole life careers, to help them develop in youth the resources and the awareness of latent capacities upon which, in these middle years, they can draw."[2]

In retrospect, this conference may be seen as a symposium well ahead of its time, and its participants as remarkably prescient. Although the "graying of America" and the emergence of older women as "a majority within the minority" of the elderly in the United States are two interrelated demographic trends that have been developing over the course of the twentieth century, they were remarked by few social observers before the 1970s. It was not until that decade that social scientists in a number of disciplines entered into the lively exchange of ideas and research endeavors focusing on the age-sex category "older women" that is bringing this term into common currency. The midpoint of the twentieth century, 1950, marked the first time in any decennial census that women of all ages outnumbered men of all ages in the United States.[3] Throughout the entire course of this century, the sex ratio—the number of males for every 100 females—has been declining. This decline is most apparent at the higher levels of the age-sex pyramid. At the turn of the century, in 1900, the sex ratio for all elderly (those aged "65 and over") was 102.1; it declined almost by one-third, to 69.3, in 1975, International Women's Year. And the sex differential in mortality rates is especially marked among the age category "75 years and over." One-third of elderly men are over the age of 75, but among elderly women, slightly more than 40 percent have passed their seventy-fifth birthday. Demographers predict that this discrepancy between the numbers of elderly women and the numbers of elderly men in the population of the United States will widen in the coming years. In a report on the elderly in the U.S. in the 1980s, sociologist and demographer Beth J. Soldo observes that this prediction "has significant policy implications because older women have quite different social and economic resources. Far more older women are widowed, live alone, and on less income than older men."[4]

Women aged 65 and over have constituted a larger share of the female population in every successive decade since the turn of the century. In 1900, 4 percent of the female population were in this age category; in 1975, this had increased threefold, to 12 percent. The "aging" of the female population, combined with the sex imbalance among the elderly, which reflects higher male mortality over the entire life course, are trends that have been unfolding over the decades of this century. Yet it was only during the past ten years that the issues and concerns of older women were joined to the issues and concerns of the elderly in the United States. If the 1970s are remembered as a time of renaissance for the women's movement as well as for the movement for age equality, they may also be seen, perhaps more clearly in retrospect than at the present moment, as a time of confluence of these two major movements for social reform. There were intimations of this confluence at the conference on the potentialities of women in the middle years held at Michigan State University. The participants in that symposium viewed middle-aged women from the life-course perspective. Implicit in the very choice of the theme of that conference and in the observations made in individual sessions was the recognition that for a woman to think of herself as an "older woman" only at the age of 65 (if even then) is to cast a quarter of a century of her life—the years from age 40 to age 65—into a kind of limbo. A woman who defers giving thought to the subject of aging until the seventh decade of her life fails to perceive the vital connection between her circumstances, experiences, and perspective when she is in her forties and fifties and early sixties, and her life and thought during the years (which may amount to another full quarter of a century) that follow. When women in their forties and fifties look ahead as well as backward, they affirm this vital connection. And the shaping of social policy from the life course perspective, which enhances awareness of the continuity of life and of the interdependence between the generations, will follow from this affirmation.

Women and Aging: A Confluence of Issues in the 1970s

Gerontology is the study of older persons and of the processes of aging. By its very nature, it is a multidisciplinary field of study, which encompasses aspects of medicine (geriatrics), biology, psychology, sociology, economics, political science, and anthropology, as well as aspects of the humanities, of law, and of architecture, literature, and the fine arts. Social gerontology is the subdiscipline of gerontology that focuses on the non-physical aspects of aging. One of its founders, Clark Tibbitts, named its central concerns as "the developmental and group behavior of adults following maturation" and the "social phenomena which give rise to and arise out of the presence of older people in the population."[5] In the biological sense of the word, aging may be said to begin at birth. Psychological aging, which encompasses changes in psychological processes with aging and the awareness of growing older varies considerably from one person to another. But aging is a social as well as a biological and psychological process. Through the perspective of social gerontology, older people are seen in their relationships with one another and with those of other age strata, within the living context of ongoing social change.

In the United States, the age of 65 was adopted in 1935 as the official designation of the age of entrance into the "elderly" segment of the population. In order to facilitate implementation of its program, the Social Security Administration selected this chronological marker (which was borrowed from Bismarck, who proposed it as the calendar age for eligibility for pension benefits) as the simplest means of assessing eligibility for receiving Social Security benefits. Since that time, official definitions of "the elderly" have been modified. The Social Security Administration chose age 62 for optional eligibility for reduced benefits for retirement of women in 1956, and this same participation was offered to men in 1961. In 1973, with the signing into law of the Older Americans Comprehensive Services Amendment to the Social Security Act, optional retirement age was reduced to sixty.[6] However, while the chronological age used to define the focus of study of many research projects and publications, as well as of many programs and conferences for and about older persons has shifted from 65 to 60, and later even to age 55, almost all the available official data about "the elderly" are based upon the official designation "65 years and over." For this reason, those in search of information about older people as defined by a marker other than the calendar age 65 must make adjustments in the data available for examination. Furthermore, the data in publications in which the age of 65 is used to designate the elderly must be transposed by the reader if they are to be interpreted correctly. This is because statistics present a static ("cross-sectional") view of whatever feature of the social landscape has been chosen for study. But society, like the self, is forever coming into being, forever changing. An appreciation of this is not won easily because of the very human tendency to see the present as fixed, unchanging. But by its very nature, the composition of "society" is protean. In any census year, the age distribution or any other feature of a population provides no more than a cross-sectional view. Time flows continuously past these points crystallized by the enumerators. They are no more than approximations of social realities, still-lifes of an ever-shifting socioscape. They serve as no more than reference points from which the outlines of the shapes of many futures may be divined.

Until very recently, women over the age of 65 in the United States have been concealed within the generic "he" or "older person" named as the subject of statistical reports and studies of "the elderly." Therefore, the fact that elderly women comprise the majority of the subjects of many publications in social gerontology has escaped the attention of those who consult them. Marie Marschall Fuller and Cora Ann Martin compare the neglect of the topic of older women with the neglect of 59 percent of a tribe by an anthropologist who also fails to note sex and age differences among its peoples. They attribute this neglect to a number of factors, among them to the search for universals in social science, which may bias perception, to the focus of most theories on only one phase of the life cycle, to the age bias in research samples, to the fact that the norm for statistical analysis is male, to the sex bias in language, and to the preponderance of older men in positions of power in scholarly circles, perhaps among those who are theorists and researchers as well as professors. They also suggest that this neglect may be attributed to social factors: the visibility of older women is limited by transportation and living patterns in our society, and it is only in fairly recent times that older women have been present in such large numbers in the population.[7]

Whatever the factors contributing to this neglect, older women are certainly over-represented in social gerontology publications about a broad range of topics, although their titles do not reflect this fact. For example, 79 percent of the applicants to Victoria Plaza were women.[8] Rosemary Redmond reports that the Legal Protective Services for Adults Component of the Older Americans Legal Action Center investigates cases of financial exploitation involving older persons, and that, since 1976, about 78 percent of the clientele in this category have been women.[9] Elinor Waters and Betty White, in describing the program of group counseling offered since 1972 by the Continuum Center for older persons who are affiliated with various community centers in the metropolitan Detroit area, report that about 80 percent of the clientele are women.[10] In his ethnographic study of a retirement community in California, Jerry Jacobs found that single women outnumber single men at a ratio of about three to one.[11] And the late anthropologist Jules Henry, in part 3 of *Culture Against Man*, which is about three hospitals for the aged, reported that at "Tower" Nursing Home, women outnumbered men at a ratio of four to one.[12] Of course, the preponderance of women among the participants of programs for the elderly and the fact that women are disproportionately represented in the samples of research studies about older persons in the United States are a clear reflection of the fact that women are the "majority within the minority" of North Americans over the age of 65. But, as the paucity of gender-based data attests, this is not commonly recognized. Nor do those who shape social policy make it a practice to acknowledge that the majority of those who are affected by their decisions concerning the elderly citizens of this country are women.

If social scientific data focusing on elderly women are limited, so that information about them must be extrapolated from the statistics, data focusing on middle-aged women, the *future* majority within the minority, are virtually nonexistent. It is only during the past decade that publications on the subject of middle-aged women in the United States have begun to appear in significant numbers, indicating that their authors are pioneering a new and important field of study. Examples of this are publications by sociologists Pauline Bart, Ruth Jacobs, and Lillian Rubin, by anthropologist Estelle Fuchs, by psychologists Nancy Datan and Lillian Troll, and by the staff members of the Center on Aging at the University of Maryland, Marilyn R. Block, Janice L. Davidson, Kathryn E. Serock, and Jean D. Grambs, who broadened the definition of "older women" to include women who are middle-aged.[13] Information about middle-aged women, which is now being gathered by researchers engaged in a variety of projects, ought to be of particular interest to policymakers, for, as Tish Sommers has observed, the middle years are crucial in a woman's life cycle. Sommers points out that a situation in which displaced homemakers—women who have experienced a sudden personal and economic dislocation because of divorce or widowhood and departure of grown children from the home—are left to "sink or swim" and in which they are paid exploitive wages for work in exploitive jobs, simply lays the foundation for more costly welfare and social services at a later time in their lives.[14]

Just as there is no consensus about when a person is "elderly" or "old," so there is no common agreement about the age at which one enters midlife. In proposing that a distinction be made between the "young-old," or those in the U.S. aged 55 to 75, and the "old-old," or those who are aged 75 and over, Bernice Neugarten writes that despite the fact that chronological age is not a satisfactory marker, it is an indispensable one. In her view, our perceptions of the life cycle and the periods of life have been refined, and it is now commonly recognized

> that persons no longer move abruptly from adulthood—the period of full commitment to work and family responsibilities—into old age, but that they go, instead, through a relatively long interval during which family responsibilities are diminished, work continues, even though specific work roles may change—for example, women reentering the labor market in their 40s and 50s—and physical vigor remains high.[15]

It is only in the past few decades that middle age became a clearly delineated phase of the life cycle. Indeed, Neugarten has suggested that it is likely that a further refinement in our perception of the second half of life is now in the making. This is the phase of the "young-old," and a major life event—retirement—marks the passage from middle age to this phase of the life cycle. Retirement, Neugarten suggests, is as meaningful a marker for the age category of the "young-old" as the departure of grown children from the home is for the category of the middle-aged.

In their publication on older women, Marilyn R. Block and her associates discuss the difficulties of arriving at a precise chronological definition of this age-sex category. Like Neugarten, they conclude that meaningful markers for any phase of the life cycle are major life events or "milestones." They point out that it is in their forties that many women experience physiological and social changes that "predicate . . . the direction of the aging process."[16] For this reason, the definition of "older women" as women aged 65 and over is too narrow: it excludes the major life events that occur during the preceding twenty years. Therefore, for Block and her associates, the chronological age at which women are seen as "older" women is 45. While the precise age designating women in midlife or older women varies from one study to another, there has been a growing consensus in the 1970s that "older women" are women over the age of 40.[17] Thus, two generations of women are encompassed in the term, and it does not so much matter that a woman is age 43 or 46 or 49 as that she is experiencing changes in her life that are milestones, and that "predicate . . . the direction of the aging process." Whether this change in the definition of "older women" initiated or followed from the changing social and economic conditions of women's lives throughout the twentieth century in this country, or whether the material and ideational aspects of culture are inseparable and influence one another in equal measure, is an issue of long-standing controversy in social philosophy. Marxists perceive changing consciousness as the consequence of changes in material culture; those inclined to Max Weber's sociology ascribe a greater role to ideas in influencing the course of social change than Marxists do. While both Max Weber and Émile Durkhiem acknowledged that ideas arise from social conditions, both thinkers differed from Marx in their perception "that ideas can also influence the course of events: they can become 'detached,' as it were, from the social conditions in which they originally arose and can then have an independent effect on social action."[18]

However ideational and material culture may have interacted to bring about the confluence of the movements for gender and age equality in the United States, the signs of change appeared early in the decade of the 1970s. In 1973, the title chosen for the Twenty-sixth Annual Conference on Aging sponsored by the Institute of Gerontology in Ann Arbor, Michigan, was "Women: Life Span Challenges."[19] Throughout the decade, organizations of older women and advocacy projects and publications advancing their collective concerns were founded. Among these are the Displaced Homemakers Network, the Gray Panthers National Task Force on Older Women, the NOW National Older Women's Rights Committee, the National Action Forum for Older Women, and the Older Women's League Educational Fund; through OWLEF, a number of Gray Papers and other resource materials of special interest to older women have been published to promote social action and research. Toward the end of the decade, in 1978, a special session on older women was incorporated into the agenda of the annual meting of the Gerontological Society. In that same year, the National Institute on Aging and the National Institute of Mental Health co-sponsored a conference on "The Older Woman: Continuities and Discontinuities." And in 1979, older women and the rural aged were chosen as topics of special interest at the first West Virginia University Gerontology Conference.[20]

In the first year of the new decade of the 1980s, the concerns of older women were made public at the White House Mini-Conference on Older Women, "Growing Numbers: Growing Force," which was convened in October in Des Moines, Iowa. The 400 participants in this conference included men as well as women, and people ranging in age from their twenties to their seventies, as well as representatives from a variety of ethnic and racial groups. Some of those who attended the conference were disabled; the majority had personally experienced the combined effects of ageism and sexism. The conference, which opened with a Speakout, had work sessions that addressed fifteen topics, divided into three clusters—Insuring Adequate Income (topics were Social Security, pensions, employment and training, means-tested programs, and midlife planning for aging), Health Concerns of Older Women (the cost and delivery of health care, medical research and training, the image of growing older female, long-term care and alcohol and drug abuse), and Quality of Life and Impact of Aging (the demographics of aging, the family, older women alone, housing, and older women as victims of violence and fear). There was also a panel discussion on minority women at this meeting.[21] About 200 women stayed on an extra day after the conference, at their own expense, to establish the Older Women's League, an outgrowth of the Older Women's League Educational Fund which was founded by Tish Sommers and Laurie Shields. Sommers serves as the first president of the Older Women's

League. She and Shields stated that one of a number of priority issues for
OWL is the improvement of access to health-care insurance for older women:
about four million women in the United States between the ages of 45 and 65
are not covered by health insurance, a fact that Sommers has termed "a
national disgrace" for they are in a "no woman's land between menopause and
Medicare." One year after the convening of the White House Mini-
Conference on Older Women, in 1981, the third White House Conference on
Aging met in Washington, and for the first time one of the official committees, Committee No. 11, focused on "Concerns of Older Women: Growing
Numbers, Special Needs." Tish Sommers, who delivered the keynote address
at the first meeting of this committee on November 30, stated in an interview
that the primary problems of aging are overwhelmingly *women's* problems,
citing the 1980 median income figure for women in the U.S. aged 65 and
over, which was $4,226—just $176 above the official poverty level.[22] Near the
close of the four-day conference, Sommers stated that she believed the delegates had addressed the "bread and butter issues," particularly Social Security
and health care, and added that she thought the best part of the work of the
committee was "that we got rid of two myths: that women can't work together,
and that older women are timid."[23]

   In a workshop held in June 1972 at the University of Oregon, Alice J.
Kethley stated that she considers aging to be a challenge, a natural phenomenon and a privilege—not a morbid topic, not a disaster. Kethley affirmed the
need for knowledge about the entire life course and for the acceptance of the
worth of people of all ages, an acceptance that ought to be reflected in our
attitudes and in our actions.[24] Older women's need for a positive self-image is
undeniable, and the fashioning of this image is one of the most challenging
tasks to be accomplished by those who would combine the movements for sex
equality and age equality in a common cause. Because self and society are
indivisible, the self-image of an older woman has collective as well as individual features: the reflexive self interweaves a composition of character with
circumstance. And it is through the special lighting of the social scientific
perspective that the collective aspects of this self-image are revealed. Gerontologist Matilda White Riley writes that it is her conviction that the thirteen
million women in the United States who are sixty-five years of age or older,
most of whom have raised families, many of whom are

> well educated, some of them with previous labor force experience . . . , all of
> them born before World War I and hence with a long perspective on the
> 20th century—have more to offer to society than society is ready to receive,
> and more to offer to themselves than they believe possible. Yet most . . . are
> no longer accepted in positions of prestige outside the home. Many are
> deprecated, patronized, sometimes even feared. A majority are widowed,
> and 40% live entirely alone. They are doubly disadvantaged because they
> are *old* and because they are old *women*. There is something wrong with the
> social arrangements of our time that leave so many persons at such loose
> ends simply because of their age and their sex. Surely it is our collective

responsibility to restructure these social arrangements, and our individual responsibility to prepare ourselves for our own old age.[25]

Riley believes that the social sciences have the potential for providing guidelines for making rational decisions about the issues involved in the numerous current proposals for social change that will affect the lives of women as they grow older. And she foresees a time when many older women will distinguish themselves in the creative and performing arts, and will make significant contributions to the economy and the political life of this nation.

A humanistic gerontology is a prefiguration of possibilities for older people—possibilities of freedom for spiritual growth and for wisdom, and of the chance for the expression of creativity and social service in the second half of life. But a variety of researches by social scientists have brought into bold relief the distinctive features of a collective portrait of older women, not only as "a majority within a minority" but as "the fastest-growing poverty segment in the country." For older women to realize the possibilities of later life for creative expression and social service, they must be free from want. For the promise of humanistic gerontology to be fulfilled, there must be a transformation of social arrangements as much as of individual consciousness. Therefore, the features of the collective portrait emerging from researches in the social sciences ought to be examined closely. These researches are the source of guidelines for the formulation of a social policy that is just, and therefore sound—since, ultimately, its soundness is not only measured but proven by its justice.

Older Women: A Demographic Portrait

Among the varieties of older women in the United States are grandmothers in all their ethnic and racial and religious diversity. There are wives and mothers whose lives are closely intertwined with those of their husbands and grown or almost-grown children, and there are displaced homemakers and never-married women whose closest ties may be with friends or with those with whom they work, rather than with kin. There are great numbers of daughters in their forties and fifties and, increasingly their sixties, who are primary caretakers for their own aging mothers or mothers-in-law. There are middle-aged and elderly wives who are primary caretakers for ill or disabled husbands, and many of these are the main providers for children or for divorced children's families. There are older women living in single-family dwellings; there are others living in apartment buildings and trailer courts and retirement communities, and still others living in extended care facilities. There are affluent "cosmopolites," and there are "shopping bag ladies." Some older women are not quite fifty; others are in their eighties—or older. Researches in demography depict the growing presence of all these varieties of older women in the population in a collective, statistical portrait. In order to perceive the social and economic issues arising from this growing presence of older women in the population, the demographic portrait must be examined first.

A demographic portrait is an abstraction; persons and groups can only approximate it to a greater or lesser degree. Thus, if the age of 45 is taken as the chronological marker designating "older women," there were over 22 million women aged 45 to 64, and another more than 13 million women aged sixty-five and over in the United States in 1975, International Women's Year. By this reckoning, nearly one of every three women in the United States was an "older woman." Of the other age segments demarcated by the Census Bureau, the youngest—girls under the age of fifteen—constituted 24 percent of the total female population, young women aged 15 to 24 comprised 18.2 percent, and those aged 25 to 44, 24.9 percent of all women in the United States in that year.[26]

Of the two generations encompassed by the term *older women,* one is officially defined as "elderly." In International Women's Year, the eldest of these women were those born during the last decades of the nineteenth century, and the youngest in 1910. This group includes women who were infants or children or young women during the time of World War I, and women who were marrying and bringing up their children during the 1920s and the years of the Great Depression. More than half their numbers are widowed now, and whether their work histories were stable or erratic, very few of them are still in the labor force. Of the second generation of "older women" in International Women's Year, the eldest were born in 1911 and the youngest in 1930. This generation includes women who were infants during World War I, and women who were born during the 1920s and in 1930, at a time when the birth rate in this country was declining from the higher levels of the preceding decades—from over 30 births per 1,000 population before World War I to a low of 17 per 1,000 population during the Great Depression. These women are daughters of parents whose families were smaller, on the average, than those of earlier generations. Therefore, now that they are middle-aged, they have fewer siblings with whom to share caretaking responsibilities for aging parents than their *own* parents would have had if these filial responsibilities had devolved upon *them* in great numbers (which did not happen because the mortality rate was still very high early in the twentieth century.) Middle-aged women today belong to a birth cohort that is unique in that the measure of filial devotion is taken of so many of them. The extent of caretaking responsibilities for aging parents in our society which, in the majority of cases, are assumed by daughters and daughters-in-law of aging women, is an effect of the changing birth rate during the first three decades of this century. Soldo shows the consequences of alterations in fertility for those of the older generation:

Cohorts who experienced the Depression during their childbearing years
. . . have the lowest *completed* fertility of any observed so far in this century.
In old age the survivors of these cohorts (those born roughly between 1900
and 1910) have smaller families on average to rely on than those born only
ten to 20 years earlier or later. Such unique life histories shape the old age
experience of the cohorts now 65 years of age and older and help to differentiate them from those who will be old 10, 20, or 40 years from now.[27]

Ultimately, the fact that each birth cohort has a distinctive life history has an
effect upon the interrelationships of the generations. Women who were married during the 1940s and 1950s—and most of them were—are mothers of
the postwar "baby boom" cohort. The ranks of these women, the middle-aged
women of today, are thinner than those of the cohort born around the turn of
the century and those of the cohort born after World War II. People born
between 1925 and 1945 are members of a generation born between two much
larger cohorts—those of their parents and those of their children. Women
who are middle-aged today were born at a time when the birth rate was as a
trough between the two peaks of the 1900s and the 1950s. The fact that so
many of them are confronted over and over again with the choice betweeen
fulfilling responsibilities to their parents and their children is a clear example
of a private trouble caused by sociological (specifically, demographic) factors.[28]

From a distance, society may be perceived as divisible into age strata, wend-
ing their way upward through the age-sex pyramid in an inexorable process
of cohort succession. This is the perspective of the sociology of age
stratification proposed by Matilda White Riley in a symposium of the Gerontological Society held in Toronto on the eve of the 1971 White House Conference on Aging.[29] In this paper, and in another appearing in the third volume
of the series on *Aging and Society*, Riley considers how age, as Karl Mannheim
would have phrased it, "locates" a person in the social structure, just as social
class may be said to do. A person's world-view is shaped in part by her or his
age, and Riley recommends that *cohort-centrism*, or the view of a stage of life
from the unique point in historical time in which one happens to find oneself,
ought to be added to the lexicon of social science terminology.[30] The sociology of age stratification is instructive for many reasons, two of which are
especially germane to this study of older women. One is that it suggests that
chronological age affects the sense one makes of experience—including the
experience of growing older itself. Another is that it illuminates one of the
processes of social dynamics, cohort succession, and in so doing it contributes
to every woman's appreciation of the value of the life course perspective. This
perspective and a knowledge of history should inform the reading of statistical data. For example, by the 1990s, which are almost upon us, the survivors
of the more than 27 million women who were aged 25 to 44 in International
Women's Year will all have entered the second half of life. The youngest of
these are among the post World War II "baby boom" daughters. In 1975, that

large birth cohort included all those in the age segment 15 to 24 and the youngest in the age segment 25 to 44. (These are two of the age categories officially adopted by the Census Bureau for presenting data about the age distribution of a population.) In the 1990s, the members of the "baby boom" generation will be moving toward middle age. During the third decade of the twenty-first century, in 2025, even the very youngest in this birth cohort will be celebrating their sixty-fifth birthdays.

Over time, each birth cohort "ascends" the age-sex population pyramid, and because cohorts vary in size, they alter its shape: it is a "pyramid" in name only. Cutler and Harootyan provide a graphic depiction of the changing proportions of the elderly from the turn of the century to 1970. They show that in 1900 the pyramid did, indeed, resemble a triangle. But in 1940, because of the lower fertility during the post–World War I economic depression years, it began to take on the shape of a pear. And in 1970, it was "pinched" at the base (ages 0–4), in the middle (because of the smaller birth cohorts from the late 1920s to the end of World War II), and at the apex (those aged 70–74), so that it was shaped less like a pyramid than like an hour glass.[31] Soldo also points to the changing shapes of the "pyramid" in 1910, 1940, 1960, and again in 1980. She observes that the birth rate had declined by 1940, but that the potential reductions in the relative size of the younger age categories were counterbalanced by their improved survivorship, that the birth rate remained low throughout the 1940s and the relative number of the elderly increased thirty-seven percent during that decade, but that the "baby boom" of the 1950s broadened the base of the population pyramid for 1960, and contributed to the slowing of the "aging" of the U.S. population at that time. However, the rapid "aging" of our national population by 1980 was stimulated by the combined effect of the aging of the large birth cohort of 1900–1910 and the small size of the cohorts born during the late 1960s and throughout the 1970s.[32]

In predicting the *future* absolute and relative sizes of the elderly, demographers take three basic processes into account—fertility, mortality, and migration. Fertility, so to speak, "sets the stage" for the size of any birth cohort.[33] The high fertility of the late nineteenth and early twentieth centuries accounts in part—but only in part—for the extraordinary presence of the elderly in our population today. In *absolute* (and rounded) numbers, those aged 65 and over increased more than eightfold—from about 3 million in 1900 to about 25 million in 1980—over the course of the twentieth century, whereas the total U.S. population increased only threefold, from nearly 76 million in 1900 to about 226 million in 1980. The elderly age segment also increased over the twentieth century *in proportion to* the other age segments of our population. In 1900, the elderly constituted only 4.1 percent of the total population; in 1980, about 11.2 percent of our national population was aged sixty-five and over. Census Bureau projections are that there will be nearly 30 million elderly in 1990, about 32 million in the year 2000, 35 million in 2010, 45 million in 2020, and 55 million in 2030. Predictions of the absolute numbers of the future elderly are easier to make than forecasts of the relative size of this age segment in the decades ahead, and this is because its relative size is contingent upon future birth rates. If the birth rate increases slightly to 2.1, which is replacement level, about 12 percent of the population will be elderly in the year 2000, nearly 16 percent in 2020, and 18 percent in 2030. On the other hand, if fertility declines to 1.7 (below-replacement level), nearly 13 percent of the population will be elderly in the year 2000, 18 percent in 2020, and 22 percent in 2030. But if fertility increases to 2.7 (above–replacement level), then the "graying of America" will be slowed somewhat, and there will be about 11.3 percent elderly in the year 2000 (roughly the same proportion as there was in 1980), 13 percent in 2020, and 14 percent in 2030. Soldo predicts that the U.S. population will continue to be ranked among the demographically old nations of the world in the decades to come, regardless of the fertility assumption upon which demographers base their predictions.[34] However, as she points out, the growth of the elderly population between 1980 and 2030 will not be steady or uniform. A decline in the "growth rate" of the elderly will become apparent in the 1990s, when the members of the smaller birth cohorts of the Great Depression era turn 65. But after 2010, when the members of the postwar "baby boom" generation begin to enter the ranks of the elderly, there may be a "senior boom" in the United States. Whether this will come to pass depends not only upon changing birth rates, but upon the future course of mortality and migration.

Women over the age of 65 in the United States today are members of a cohort that is remarkable for its longevity. Riley observes that the average lifetime rose in this country "from four decades among cohorts born in the mid-nineteenth century to an estimated seven decades among those born in the mid-twentieth—a situation apparently unparalleled in human history."[35] The improvement in average life expectancy over the course of the twentieth century has been dramatic: in round numbers, it increased from 47 at the turn of the century to 73 years in 1980. What is not commonly recognized is that this improvement reflects a dramatic decline in the mortality of infants and young children over the course of the twentieth century in the United States. It is often and mistakenly thought that it reflects an extension of the life span, which is the maximum number of years of life that members of a particular species may attain, and which has been estimated to be about 120 years for *Homo sapiens*. The heavier the toll of lives in infancy and childhood, the lower average life expectancy will be. This is because life expectancy represents the average length of life attained by those of a given birth cohort.[36] Although the birth cohorts of the late nineteenth and early twentieth centuries were unusually large, the dreadful toll taken by infant and child mortality depressed their size as they moved forward in time. It is the decline in infant mortality that has been identified as the single most significant factor in reducing the general death rate in this country since 1900, and that at the same time has been cited as the major factor in contributing to the unparalleled improvements in life expectancy in the twentieth century.[37]

Once the first year of life has passed, the age-specific death rate for any birth cohort declines sharply, and it only gradually increases as those in that cohort approach the later stages of the life cycle. Of those babies born in 1900, only four of every ten could expect to survive to the age of 65; in 1980, more than seven of every ten were expected to reach their sixty-fifth birthday. Although these facts may be familiar to many, two further facts are not so widely known. One is that the greater increase in average life expectancy at birth appears to have been achieved during the first half of this century. The rate of improvement slowed between 1950 and 1970. Then it "picked up again between 1970 and 1978 when the gain was 2.4 years—almost as much of an improvement as there was between 1950 and 1970."[38] Whether this trend will continue during the years ahead depends upon many factors, chief among them the infant mortality rate. This statistic compresses grim facts about poverty and illegitimacy that document the inequalities of social class in the United States that characterize our society to this day.[39] The second fact that must be taken into account in assessing the improvements in life expectancy accurately is that life expectancy at age 65 (age-specific life expectancy) has not improved much more markedly between 1950 and the late 1970s than it had between the turn of the century and 1950. In 1900, the average 65-year-old (both sexes combined) could look forward to another 11.9 years of life. In 1950, life expectancy at age 65 had increased by two years to 13.9, and in 1978, it had increased 2.2 years—from 13.9 to 16.1 years. For those aged 65, this is only a gain of 4.2 years over the entire course of the twentieth century. In contrast to this, the gain in average life expectancy at birth increased by *26* years from the turn of the century to the beginning of the 1980s.[40]

Migration works interdependently with fertility and mortality in determining the size of any age segment of a population. Although anyone contributes only once to the death rate, a person can migrate many times in her or his life, and a woman can contribute many times to the birth rate. Migration and fertility are to some extent a matter of individual choice. This is why estimates of the future size and composition of a population are always provisional.[41] Throughout the history of this country, immigration has had the effect of lowering the median age of our national population. Between 1881 and 1930, at least 27.5 million immigrants, most of whom were between the ages of 15 and 39, came to the United States. In their essay on the demography of the aged, published in 1975, Cutler and Harootyan wrote that, although immigration to the U.S. continues, the numbers have decreased over the past half-century. Given a statutory ceiling of about 400,000 immigrants, they conclude that "(with some legal exceptions in times of war or special international crises), *the population projections into the twenty-first century are minimally affected by immigration*" (44).

But the 1970s, the very decade during which this essay was published, "may be remembered as the decade of the immigrant," since it was one when our country "absorbed more than four million immigrants and refugees and perhaps twice that number of illegal aliens, more new residents than in any decade in its history. So many have arrived that if current immigration and fertility rates remain the same, the nation's population will double in 100 years."[42] Although a flood of young immigrants to the United States during the coming decades cannot affect the *absolute* numbers of near-future elderly, it can certainly and very radically affect the *relative* size of this age segment of the national population. Therefore, migration must be weighed as carefully as fertility and mortality in projecting demographic trends for the 1980s and beyond.

Predictions about the age composition of the U.S. population beyond the year 2030, which are made chiefly on the basis of assumptions about the birth rate,[43] shade into prophecy. Yet predictions about a much more immediate future are as much informed by imagination as by the most sophisticated techniques of quantitative analysis. There are myriad possibilities ("scenarios") that might be imagined. But, unless it is predestined by forces beyond human understanding or control, the future is seeded by human action and social interaction in everyday life at the present moment. The birth rate might soar at the end of this century because of a radical change in cultural mentality (there might be a revival of pronatalist norms), or because of a shift from the pattern of neolocal residence to multigenerational house- holds (there is a positive correlation between a high birth rate and a joint family residence pattern in societies around the world), or because of an acceleration of the immigration rate of the 1970s. Hence, the "gerontology boom" or "senior boom" projected upon the screen of the second decade of the twenty-first century may never come to pass. Whether it does depends upon family patterns, which in turn are inextricably bound up with the for- tunes of the national economy, and upon social policy that is in the making at this very moment. For example, a highly restrictive immigration policy could contribute to this "senior boom." And it is noteworthy that some of those who recommend a restrictive immigration policy are the very same people who express grave concern about the solvency of the Social Security system. They base their apprehensions upon the projected increase in the old-age depen- dency ratio after 2010. But this *would* probably increase if there were a closing of the gates to immigrant workers, if the birth rate continues to be low, and if most workers retire by the age of 65. A variety of measures might be taken to conduce to balancing the numbers in the working population—who are pay- ing into the Social Security system that supports the recipients of benefits— with the numbers in the retired population. When the old-age dependency ratio is high, the objective of policy intervention is to increase the number of people in the working or supportive population. This, however, presupposes the availability of employment opportunities. Thus, issues concerning the demography of aging are interconnected with issues concerning the formula- tion of social and economic policy.

The "aging" of the female population in the United States,[44] combined with the sex differential in life expectancy, have many significant social and eco- nomic consequences—for older women themselves and for the society in which so many more elderly women than elderly men are widowed and live alone and on low incomes. In 1980, the life expectancy for all men in the United States was almost 70 years, and for all women it was over 77 years.[45] The sex ratio has declined steadily from 1910, when there were 106.2 males for every 100 females, to 94.9 in 1975, International Women's Year. This change in the sex ratio over the course of the twentieth century has been most evident for those aged 65 and over. In 1900, there were 102.1 males for every 100 females in this age group. By 1975, the sex ratio for the elderly was 69.3. This steep decline is attributed by many to the growing discrepancy between the mortality rates of men and women over the life course, that is, to a discrepancy that becomes ever more marked at the later ages of life:

> The number of survivors of the heavy immigration that occurred during the first quarter of this century, when male immigrants were more numerous than female immigrants, has dwindled. The "mortality" factor has in fact produced an increase in the proportion of women among persons surviving to successively older ages. Approximately 53 percent of all women 65 years and over in March 1975 were widowed, and this fact has profound implications for social and economic policy.[46]

The preponderance of elderly females in the population of this country is, as Soldo observes, "a relatively recent phenomenon," for only half a century ago, the sex ratio was 100.7, or nearly equal. However, "after 1930 women began surviving longer than men as maternal mortality and deaths from infectious diseases dropped rapidly and chronic diseases became the leading causes of death."[47] The decline has been continuous, although not uniform: the sex ratio was 89.7 in 1950, 82.9 in 1960, and 72.2 in 1970. The discrepancy between the numbers of elderly women and elderly men is expected to widen because of the projected increases among those aged 75 and over (the "old-old"), among whom the sex imbalance is especially marked. The sex ratio for those aged 75 and over is 56 men for every 100 women. Whereas about one-third of the elderly male population are over the age of 75, slightly more than 40 percent of the elderly female population are "old-old." As Dr. Robert Butler, director of the National Institute on Aging, has observed, "The problems of old age in America are largely the problems of women."[48] An assessment of the policy implications of this fact requires a study of the social and economic issues appertaining to the demographic portrait of older women.

Older Women: Social and Economic Issues

In the early 1970s, it was observed that one word—*poor*—describes the economic and legal status of older women, that the single poorest category of people in the United States consists of 7.5 million widows and single women, half of whom were then living on incomes of less than $1,888 a year, that old age—especially for women living alone—usually means living in poverty, and that women who lived by the norm of being devoted wives and mothers become economically and legally helpless when they are older. The precept that issues from these observations was that the need to find some way to redistribute societal income to women who have contributed to the family—and to redistribute it in these women's own names—is compelling.[49]

This collective portrait of older women in the United States is no less representational in the 1980s than it was a decade ago. Only one month before the convening of the 1981 White House Conference on Aging, U.S. Representative Geraldine A. Ferraro, Democrat of Queens and a member of the House Select Committee on Aging, depicted older women as "the fastest-growing poverty segment in the country." In one of the keynote addresses of the conference "A Time for Changes and Choices: A Conference for Midlife and Older Women," sponsored by the New York City chapter of the National Organization for Women, Ferraro outlined the "bleak" statistical portrait of older women in the United States today: "Two out of every three older Americans living in poverty are women. Sixty per cent of unmarried women over age 65 have no income other than Social Security. Nearly half of the five million older women who live alone have yearly incomes of $3,000 or less."[50]

More than half of the elderly women in the United States are widows, and the older a woman is, the more likely it is that she is widowed. The incidence of widowhood in the total population of the male elderly is far less marked than that for their female counterparts. Fewer than 4 of every 10 women over the age of 65 are married, whereas 8 of every 10 elderly men are married. For every male over the age of 65 who is unmarried, there are 4 elderly unmarried women—women who are widowed or who have never married. An even greater sex differential is apparent in statistical data on the marital status of the "old-old," those aged 75 and over: 69 percent of women over the age of 75 are widowed, as compared with only 23 percent of their male counterparts. The fact that widows outnumber widowers for every age segment of the national population and that the older the age segment the higher will be the ratio of widows to widowers, has been attributed to the sex differential in life expectancy, the tendency men have to marry women who are younger than they, and the higher remarriage rate of widowers as compared with that of widows.[51] Differences between the living arrangements of elderly women and elderly men reflect differences in marital status between these two groups. A much higher percentage of elderly men than of elderly women live in a family household, and although most elderly people who live in a family setting reside with their spouses, the percentage of elderly men living with their wives is much higher than that of elderly women living with their husbands.[52] Again, the contrast is even stronger for the "old-old": nearly 43 percent of women over the age of 75 live alone, whereas only about 18 percent of men of that same age group do, and nearly 18 percent of women aged 75 and over, in comparison with 6.7 percent of the men of that age group, live in the household of a relative who is not their spouse.[53]

From the 1960s to the mid-1970s, there has been an increase in the number of persons aged 65 and over who are living alone and maintaining their own households. Also, there has been a decline in that same time period in the numbers of those living with relatives other than their spouses. The multigenerational family living under one roof, which has never been the norm in this country, was even less customary at that time than it had been before.[54] Whether this is a sign of a continuing trend toward solitary living on the part of the elderly—most of whom are women—is a matter of conjecture. Bernice Neugarten states that the four- and five-generational *family* will be the norm by the year 2000, but that whether the trend toward separate *households* will continue remains open to question. She observes that even in 1970 it was apparent that the older a person was, "and the sicker, the more likely he would be living with a child," and that of all persons aged 75 and over, one of five women and one of ten men was living with a child. "It usually goes unnoted," she remarks, "that at present for every older person in an institution, there are nearly three others living with a child."[55] In the future, Neugarten suggests, family members will probably want to have more options in the settings and type of care available for an aged relative whose health is failing. But whether there will be a fragmentation of the family with regard to the *parent-caring* role, as there has been up to now with regard to its *child-rearing* role, remains to be seen. In Neugarten's view, the effect of "the energy problem" on residence patterns is difficult to predict. There could be "more massing of persons in metropolitan areas" and there could be "more doubling-up of families." She thinks that it is likely that there will be "more doubling-up of unrelated older persons for mutual care and companionship," and she reports an increase in residence-sharing between an older person and her or his "old-old" parent. It is possible that this pattern of residence-sharing may become more common, moreover, "if a more effective system of supportive social and home health services appears and if it leads to a decrease in the rate of institutionalization" (340).

The correlation between widowhood, living alone, and low income or poverty status is well documented. The National Council on the Aging reported that, in 1974, of elderly women who live with their spouses, 8 percent were below the poverty level, but that, of elderly widows, 24 percent were poor.[56] A publication on mature women workers reported that "of all poor unrelated women aged 14 and over who lived alone, 81 percent were 55 years and over."[57] And the report *Older Women: The Economics of Aging* cites Census statistics for 1977 indicating that, while 8 percent of elderly women living in families were below the poverty level, 28.4 percent of all elderly women living alone or with non-relatives lived in poverty. The conclusion in *Fact Book on Aging* that elderly black women in the United States are "the poorest of the poor" is supported in *Older Women: The Economics of Aging*, in which it is reported that 60.8 percent of black elderly women living alone or with non-relatives were living in poverty.[58]

Employment. In International Women's Year, 12 million women aged 45 and over had jobs or were looking for work, and of these, 56 percent were within the 45 to 54 age category. That year (1975), more than 660,000 mature women workers (5.5 percent of all mature women in the labor force) were unemployed. A total of 509,000 additional mature women were on involuntary part-time work schedules. Classified as "employed," they were working part-time only because they could not find full-time jobs.[59]

Although increases in labor force activity have been especially pronounced for married women, mature married women are *still* less likely to be working than are mature women who are widowed, separated, or divorced. These women encounter a number of obstacles when seeking entry or re-entry to the labor force:

> They often find employers unwilling to credit their previous work experience or their activities during the period they were out of the labor force as evidence of future potential. Consequently, with rusty or outmoded job skills, little or no recent experience, inadequate counseling, or a lack of job contacts, they frequently must settle for low-skilled and low-paying jobs which require little or no specialized training, and which afford limited opportunity for upward mobility. [1]

Differences in labor force participation rates of older women on the basis of their marital status reflect the difficulties married women experience in the search for paid employment. Whereas 50 percent of the *married* women aged 45 to 54 were in the labor force in 1975, 69 percent of *formerly* married women, and 76 percent of *single* women of those ages were employed. The corresponding figures for women aged 55 to 64 were 36, 53, and 60 percent, respectively. For women aged 65 to 69, the statistics were that 10.5 percent of the married women were in the labor force, 16.9 percent of the formerly married had paid employment, and 28.4 percent of single women were working. And for women aged 70 and over, 4 percent of the married women were in paid employment, 4.9 percent of the formerly married were working, and 9.5 percent of the single women of this age group were in the labor force (6).

Of all women in the United States over the age of 65, about eight percent are still in the labor force. Although official unemployment rates for the elderly are low (in 1978 they were 3.8 percent for whites, 7.1 percent for black men, and 4.8 percent for black women), they do not include would-be workers who became so discouraged about their employment prospects that they gave up the active search for a job. " 'Retirement' for the 'discouraged older worker,' " as Soldo observes, "is simply a more socially acceptable description of a long period of unemployment."[60] There was an increase in the percentage of women over the age of 65 who were employed between 1940 and 1960. Most of these women probably worked "because their retirement incomes were inadequate and their children and relatives had full financial commitments of their own." This may have been especially the case for "elderly black women, who had a higher percentage of employment than their white counterparts." In 1975, it was reported that after 1960, as more women reaching retirement age became eligible to receive their own retirement benefits, the trend toward employment of women over the age of 65 had softened.[61] The percentage of all elderly men aged 65 through 69 who were employed in 1975 was 33.3, and for men over the age of 70, it was 14.9; corresponding figures for women of these two age groups were 14.6 and 5.2. About 5 percent of the men between the ages of 65 and 75 were out of work in 1970, and between 5 and 7 percent of the women aged 65 to 75 were unemployed. These men and women consider themselves to be an active part of the labor force. Nearly 11 percent of women aged 75 and over who wanted to work were unable to find employment, and it is possible that employers' attitudes may be a significant contributing factor: "A Department of Labor study found that physical incapability was the most common reason mentioned by employers for not hiring the elderly despite the fact that 70 percent of those so responding had no factual basis for their attitude" (13).

Although the 1970s will be remembered as a time of renaissance of feminism, it was apparent before the close of the decade that the disparity between women's and men's earnings was growing wider. The median earnings of year-round, full-time women workers over the age of 65 were 72 percent that of their male counterparts in 1970; by 1977, this had fallen to 57 percent of men's earnings. Elderly men's median income rose from $10,540 to $13,815, and elderly women's from $7,622 to $7,838. As for the age group 55 to 64, while earnings for year-round, full-time male workers increased from $14,156 in 1970 to $15,669 in 1977, those for year-round, full-time women workers increased from $8,533 to $8,846 in that same time period. However,

> The widest differential between male and female workers was in the age group 45 to 54, ages at which men's earnings peaked ($17,029 in 1977), and women increased their participation at entry and re-entry levels. Women's incomes peaked ($9,543 in 1977) at a much earlier age—25 to 34—which reflects women's dead-end careers and lack of labor force mobility.
>
> Low earnings among mature minority women are considerably more prevalent than among White women.[62]

The factors that contribute to depressing the earnings of mature women workers are occupational segregation, the combined effects of ageism and sexism, and late or forced entry or re-entry into the labor market. All this is exacerbated for mature minority women workers, who experience discrimination as well. Despite the fact that they are more strongly attached to the labor force than their white female counterparts, black older women have lower wages than black older men, white older women, and white older men (15).

In 1978, most of the 1.1 million women and 2 million men who were still in the labor force after the age of 65 were working in low-paying, white-collar and service jobs.[63] When they retire, their incomes will be reduced by one-third to one-half the amount they receive while they are still employed. The single largest source of income for people aged 65 and over is income from employment, i.e., income from earnings. If one or more members of a family headed by a person aged 65 and over are employed, the family income is substantially greater than if no member of the group is in the labor market. On retirement, earnings are displaced by Social Security as the major source of income for families whose head is aged 65 or over.[64] For some, retirement means a deepening of the poverty they have known all their lives. Others experience poverty for the first time when they retire.

Retirement Income. Social Security benefits, which had never been intended to provide full financial coverage for the elderly, have become the economic mainstay for 9 of every 10 people in our society over the age of 65, and those who receive no other income are very likely to be living below the poverty line. In 1978, one in seven (14.3 percent) of the elderly in the United States had incomes below the poverty level. It is probably superfluous to add that poverty rates were higher for elderly women than for elderly men, higher for elderly nonmarried individuals than for elderly still-married people, and higher for elderly blacks than for elderly whites (about 4 of every 10 elderly black women have incomes below the official poverty threshold).

On the surface, this "14.3 percent" appears to represent a slight improvement of the economic status of the elderly over that which obtained earlier in the decade, when 15 percent of the elderly population were classified as "poor," and 25 percent as "near-poor." However, in 1978, adding the "near poor" to the 14.3 percent living in poverty

> sums up the financial status of the elderly more realistically and raises their poverty rate to 23.4 percent (all persons living below 125 percent of the poverty level). In other words, nearly a quarter of today's elderly are officially classified as poor or very close to it. This translates into 5.4 million older Americans with incomes below the official poor-plus-near-poor threshold of $4,896 a year for older couples and $3,895 for older individuals living alone or with nonrelatives. According to Mollie Orshansky, Social Security Administration designer of the poverty level formula, these official figures would be still higher if they included the "hidden poor"—elderly people whose sparse incomes force them to live with younger relatives.[65]

The Supplemental Security Income program, instituted in 1974 to guarantee a minimum income for the elderly, pays a maximum of $208 a month for an individual and of $312 for a couple with no other income, and Soldo reports that about 11 percent of the elderly now depend in part on public assistance programs, mostly the SSI program (23). Since over 14 percent of the elderly had incomes below the official poverty level in 1978, this means that there are considerable numbers of people over the age of 65 in the United States who are eligible to receive SSI benefits, but who are not using the program.

The moral question of distributive justice is at the core of all social policy, and the integrity of government statistics is always somewhat problematic.[66] There is widespread agreement that chronological age is a wholly unreliable index of physical, social, creative, and intellectual capacity for performance. Some advocates of reform of the Social Security system recommend that the

age for entitlement to benefits be raised and that the benefits of those electing
to retire early be reduced so as to provide incentives for older workers to
remain in the labor force. But this presupposes the availability of employment
opportunities for older workers, and that presupposition is wholly unwarranted. As of this writing (December 1981), the unemployment rate in the
United States is 8.9 percent, and blue-collar workers, so many of whom are
older workers and who did not have the educational opportunities enjoyed by
their younger counterparts, are the most adversely affected by high unemployment. In practice, raising the age for entitlement to benefits and reducing
the benefits of those electing to retire early will impose a hardship on great
numbers of older workers in the United States today. In particular, these
measures would condemn the unskilled and semiskilled and those in poor
health—people who have been economically deprived all their lives—to an old
age of misery and destitution.

It is the perception of those in the Reagan administration and their sup-
porters that the Social Security system is "hard-pressed" and threatened with
insolvency, a perception that originates in an economic philosophy according
to which it would be anathema to take those very measures—combining the
assets of the three trust funds, allowing inter-fund borrowing whenever
needed (in 1981, it was decided to permit this, but only for 1982), strengthening the system with funds from general revenues—which would ensure the
soundness of the program that is vital to the economic security of millions of
Americans. And it is the perception of growing numbers of elderly people
that the Reagan administration, which is postponing decisions for changing
the Social Security system until after the 1982 congressional elections, plans to
make further deep cuts in entitlements. A bipartisan 15-member commission
was appointed by President Reagan on December 16, 1981, to study the Social
Security system and to submit a report and recommendations at the end of
1982. It is doubtful that any major changes will be made in the program
before 1983, and these changes may be postponed during that year because
candidates for the 1984 elections will have entered the race by that time, and
may find it expedient to defer the issue.

Only a few years ago, gerontologist Erdman Palmore observed that data
from the National Center for Health Statistics and from the Census Bureau
indicate that the relative status of the aged in health, income, occupation, and
education is rising and probably will continue to rise for the rest of the twentieth century, that factors accounting for improvements are the slowing in
rates of change for the younger cohorts and the increase in government and
private programs to improve the status of the elderly, and that since present
programs are having beneficial effects, these data justify their continuation or
expansion.[67] During this past year, some of these programs have ceased to
exist, and, while the future of many others is uncertain, it depends to a great
extent on the success of the present administration in convincing the elector-
ate that the Social Security system is in a "crisis" situation. Women, especially,
will be affected by whatever modifications of the system are made: two-thirds

of all recipients of Social Security benefits are women. And the greater burden of the cuts made in social programs during the first year of the present administration are being borne by women.[68]

Atchley is doubtless quite right in stating that "the explosion of benefits and programs for the elderly that occurred from 1965 to 1979 is very unlikely to occur again."[69] But that "explosion," which was long overdue, has hardly resulted in affluence for elderly Americans. A report issued by the House Select Committee on Aging cited "an ominous trend" toward an *increasing* percentage of America's elderly receiving total income that is below the official poverty line. According to this report, 15.1 percent of the elderly were living under the poverty line in 1979, the year for which the latest figures are available. Thus, the steady decline from 25.3 percent in 1959, the year when the first study was made, reached its lowest figure (over 14 percent) in 1978 and then began an upturn. Recent figures from the Census Bureau "demonstrate the last half-decade was not a statistical quirk; rather it was an indication of an emerging and increasing trend." The finding of this report, which contradicts the notion that social programs for the aged are excessively generous, was that the elderly "received inadequate support, on the whole, from Social Security, welfare and private pension plans and encountered difficulty supplementing their income in the private job market." The elderly, who are between 10 and 11 percent of the national population but over 13 percent of those living under the poverty line, "stacked slightly above" the poverty threshold "to a degree unparalleled by any socioeconomic group in the U.S."[70]

As is fairly well known, major changes were made in the Social Security program in 1972, and since July 1975 automatic cost-of-living increases ("escalator" benefits) have been included in Social Security benefits. These increases are to be made in June of every year that the Consumer Price Index shows an increase of 3 percent or more for that year. These adjustments have not kept pace with inflation. Soldo reports that in July 1979, benefits were increased by 9.9 percent, whereas the inflation rate for the preceding twelve months had been 12.6 percent. Furthermore, she notes, "these annual adjustments are not retroactive and the elderly do not receive 'catch-up' checks to compensate them for their year-long loss in purchasing power."[71] Merton C. Bernstein, Coles Professor of Law at Washington University and author of *The Future of Private Pensions*, points out that proposals for change in the Social Security system made by the Reagan administration in the spring of 1981

are advertised as necessary to save cost-of-living adjustments (COLA), which are under attack as unduly favoring retirees (scheduled for an 11.2 percent increase this year) over working people (who averaged 8 percent last year). But the average employed person, with much higher income, obtains dollar increases roughly three times what COLA grants Social Security beneficiaries. Moreover, COLA underestimates the costs of medical care and heating, which the elderly use more heavily than the general population.

Apparently some politicians do not know about, or disbelieve, two recent national polls in which the majority said they would willingly pay higher payroll taxes for better Social Security benefits.[72]

In April 1981 it was reported that the average retired worker's monthly Social Security check would be raised to $374 from $337 in July, because of the 11.2 percent cost-of-living increase. This increase would be based upon the (April 23) release of the Consumer Price Index for March, which reflected the 11.2 percent inflation rate from the first quarter of 1980 to the first quarter of 1981. The *maximum* monthly benefit for workers retiring in 1981 at the age of 65 would then rise to $752.90 from $677, and the *minimum* from $153.10 to $170.30. The *average* elderly couple's benefit would rise from $576 to $640; the *average* aged widow or widower's check would increase by $35, from $313 to $348 a month. The *maximum* federal SSI payment would rise from $238 to $264.70 for individuals, and from $357 to $397 for couples. Most of the states supplement these welfare payments for some or all recipients. However, "some of these welfare recipients may find themselves gaining no ground. More than half also get regular Social Security, and when those benefits rise welfare checks frequently drop. Some persons could also lose their eligibility for other types of welfare."[73]

Except for a very small minority of affluent Americans, the relative economic situation of people in the post-retirement years diminishes throughout the remaining years of their lives. Bernstein has reported that, on the average, Social Security benefits in 1981 replace only 42 percent of pre-retirement income. Reducing these benefits further would consign even greater numbers of elderly widows, who are already overrepresented in poverty statistics, below the poverty threshold. The income of most elderly Americans is fixed. Their purchasing power, meager as it is, is eroded by inflation, and as the years after retirement go on, whatever assets they have are depleted. When there is an urgent need for money, they have little remaining—in the form of savings accounts or insurance policies or property—upon which they might draw. Furthermore, while the needs of elderly people do amount to less than those of younger Americans, they do not amount to 58 percent less—which is the reduction in average income after retirement. Indeed, some expenses— among them, food, housing, and medical care—actually increase between middle age and old age. For many old people, who are more susceptible than the young to both cold and heat, fuel costs are too heavy a burden to be borne. And the elderly still must pay a substantial portion of their bills for health care. Medicare health insurance pays less than 43 percent of the health care bill of the average person over the age of 65. Thus, the very areas for which expenses are most likely to increase as a person grows older are the areas most severely affected by inflation.[74]

The elderly population of the United States is, as Erdman Palmore observes, the most heterogeneous of any society in the world, and he suggests this may be one reason why programs and policies have not been as effective as their designers envisioned they would be.[75] Certainly, the composition of the category "aged 65 and over" is exceedingly diverse in terms of age as much as of any other measure, for it spans a range of thirty to thirty-five years of life.[76] But from the standpoint of income adequacy, it can be stated with confidence that the older a person is in this broad age span, the lower is his— and more often, *her*—median income. Although cost-of-living increases have been applied to modify the harsh effect of inflation, little adjustment has been made for the overall increases in real income since 1935. Atchley has shown the lower Social Security pension payment of beneficiaries aged 95 and over as compared with that of beneficiaries at age 65, and he remarks that this is compounded because extreme old age drastically increases the need to buy services.[77] In the United States, the older the age segment of the female population is, the higher the percentage will be of those who have low incomes. That many older women in this nation are economically disadvantaged is due in part to the fact that they are *women*, who, as a collectivity, have a lower income than men, and in part to the fact that they are *older*—for the elderly, as a collectivity, are overrepresented in poverty statistics. Those who are most disadvantaged among the elderly population are "unrelated individuals," and the majority of these are widows. Very few women over the age of 65 in the United States today receive income from pensions. Karen W. Ferguson, a lawyer and director of the Pension Rights Center, which is a nonprofit organization in Washington that is largely funded by private groups, stated that "low pensions or lack of them are the main cause of women's poverty." In an address to a forum of the New York County Lawyers Association which was attended by 100 lawyers, most of whom were women, Ferguson cited figures depicting a collective economic portrait of elderly women in the U.S. today:

> Some 85 percent of married women outlive their husbands; only 9 percent of women over 65 receive corporate pensions while 25 percent of men do; half the women over age 65 and living alone have less than $1,000 in savings; even with the help of Social Security payments averaging $3,645 a year, about half the women alone are well below the poverty level.[78]

More than six of every ten elderly women in the United States today have incomes solely from their Social Security checks.[79] The Social Security system is more than their "safety net"—it is their lifeline. Any modifications in the system will have an immediate and direct effect upon their lives. This fact is a stubborn one, and no proposals made in the name of balancing the budget or re-ordering priorities in the interest of national security can sequester it.

Social Security. The Social Security program, which was established in 1935, and under which monthly benefits were first paid in 1940, was designed with the assumption that in the typical family in the United States, one marriage partner (the wife), as a lifelong unpaid homemaker, is financially dependent upon the other marriage partner (her husband), who is the sole provider of economic support for his spouse and their children. Therefore, basic protection was provided for workers in jobs covered by the program, and supplementary protection was provided for these workers' wives and widows as dependents. The dependent spouse does not pay into the Social Security system, because household work is not defined as covered employment by the program. Therefore, a woman cannot receive Social Security protection unless she is married to a worker employed in a job covered by the system, and is thereby entitled to supplementary benefits that are keyed to her working partner's taxable income, *or* has paid into the system herself as a worker in a job covered by the program. Thus, while in general the financial security of older men in retirement is contingent upon their work history only, that of older women is more complex because in many cases it is contingent upon both their work history and their marital status (and ultimately to the relationship between them.)

During the 1970s, there was much public debate about the combined effects of the dramatic increase in women's labor force participation rates since the end of World War II and of the marked increase in the rate of divorces per 1,000 population over the past three decades upon the traditional division of labor in the American family. If this division of labor between one lifelong unpaid homemaker and one lifelong paid worker who is the sole provider of the family income was ever representative of social reality (and historical, documentary, and literary textual materials on the Great Depression show it to be so grossly oversimplified as to amount to a distortion of social reality during the 1930s) it contradicts the proliferation of and changes in family and work patterns in the United States today. Indeed, it is now fairly common knowledge that millions of women in this country are combining paid market work with unpaid home work in myriad patterns, and that marriage is an *interdependent* relationship between equal partners whose services—whether rendered as paid workers or as unpaid homemakers—are of equal value as contributions to the economy and well-being of their individual families and of the society as a whole. Public debate about the Social Security system and the changing roles of women and men intensified throughout the decade, and in 1979 a report on this subject was transmitted to the Congress. This report was mandated by the Congress under the Social Security Amendments of 1977 (P.L. 95-216) in order to study proposals to eliminate dependency as a factor in entitlement to spouse's benefits and to eliminate sex discrimination under the program.[80]

This report explores two options for changing the Social Security system—earnings sharing and establishment of a double-decker benefit structure—inasmuch as both these options would address the issues that arise from the present system of providing dependent's benefits. Earnings sharing would provide for the equal division of total annual earnings of a married couple between the spouses for each year of the marriage. Under this system, each spouse would have protection in his or her own right that could be added to any protection acquired as a covered worker while unmarried or from other marriages. The double-decker benefit structure would replace the present system with a two-tier benefit structure. The first tier would be a flat-rate benefit that would be payable regardless of marital status or work in jobs covered under the system. The second tier would be an earnings-related benefit payable to everyone who had worked in a job covered by Social Security. In addition to a discussion of the provisions and costs of these two comprehensive options selected for study because they would deal with a number of the issues that have been raised, would allow for retention of certain fundamental features of the present program, and could be designed to provide benefits, and result in long-range costs, which approximate those under present law, the report also includes a discussion of the potential effects of these options on people reaching the ages of 62 to 64 in the year 2000, a discussion of limited options (among them protection for homemakers in their own right), gender-based distinctions in the law and proposals to elimi-nate the differences in treatment of men and women, and issues concerning the public pension offset provision enacted as part of the 1977 Social Se-curity amendments and possible modifications of and alternatives to this provision.[81] The report does not contain recommendations for legislative changes.

As it was originally conceived, the Social Security program was designed to meet the objectives of both equity and adequacy. The principle of equity is served in that benefits are scaled to past earnings, and a high earner receives a higher basic benefit than a low earner receives. At the same time, the principle of social adequacy is served in the case of low earners, "who have less margin for reduction in income, under a weighted benefit formula that produces benefits that replace a higher portion of their preretirement earnings." The principle of adequacy is also served by the provision of dependent's and survivor's benefits for the families of workers in jobs covered by the program. The tension between the two principles, which are often inconsistent, has obtained since the inception of the program: changes that improve adequacy may reduce equity, and changes that improve equity may reduce adequacy. An "appropriate balance between these two goals is often a source of con-troversy."[82]

Most of the issues raised in the first chapter of the HEW report turn on the fact that the majority of married women have protection under the Social Security program as dependents of their husbands. As the program now operates, a woman is entitled to receive benefits as a dependent wife or widow or ex-wife of a covered worker. She is also entitled to receive benefits as a covered worker in her own right. However, she is not entitled to receive both benefits in full. If she is entitled to both a dependent's and a worker's benefit, she receives an amount that is equal to the higher of the two benefits. In other words, she receives her worker's benefit plus the amount, if any, by which the spouse's benefit exceeds the worker's benefit. This is known as the dual enti-tlement provision.

Adequacy concerns arise because of the gaps and the inadequacies in the protection provided for homemakers as dependent spouses. The substantial contributions that spouses who are not employed may make to the family and community through home work and care for children and other dependent family members may preclude or reduce their participation in the paid labor force, and thus prevent these persons from obtaining primary protection as workers. For the vast majority of older married or formerly married women in the U.S. today, the fulfillment of home work and caretaking responsibilities precluded the possibility for full-time and uninterrupted market work. Furthermore, inasmuch as dependent's benefits are based on a proportion of the worker's benefit and are payable only under certain conditions, homemakers may have inadequate income protection under the Social Security system. As it now operates, the level of retirement benefits is tied to the record of earnings from paid employment. The five lowest-earning years are disregarded, and earnings for the remaining working years—over a 23-year period for those reaching retirement age up to 1991, and over a 35-year period after that year—are averaged. Benefits are based on indexed earnings during this averaging period. The purpose of this is to assure that a person who has worked in a covered job or jobs and paid Social Security taxes for many years receives a higher benefit than a short-time worker: earnings are averaged over the period the worker reasonably could be expected to have worked in covered employment. This method of computing benefits generally results in higher amounts of benefits for workers who have had a longer period of work in covered employment. The system works to the distinct disadvantage of women who have sacrificed their opportunities for steady market work, or the pursuit of a career, in fulfilling home work and caretaking obligations. At retirement age, the level of benefits to which these women are entitled as workers is severely reduced because of a market work record of long periods of zero earnings interspersed with limited earnings from part-time work or full-time employment in low-paying jobs. Married women workers receive substantially lower benefits than men workers because they often spend time out from market work, or work part-time in the labor force, in order to perform home work or caretaking tasks (which tends to reduce their average lifetime earnings, and hence their benefit amounts) *and* because average wages for women are lower than those for men. (The average worker's benefit for women retiring in November 1978 was $215, whereas it was $325 for men.)

A widowed homemaker under the age of 60 cannot receive widow's benefits unless she is either at least 50 years old and disabled, or is caring for children. The period of time elapsing between widowhood and eligibility for widow's benefits is known as "widow's gap"—the period of time when a widow has no Social Security protection. Under a very recent (1981) ruling, widows will lose benefits when their youngest child turns 16 rather than 18: under the budget reconciliation bill that President Reagan signed into law on August 13, 1981, Congress enacted legislation that ends a parent's benefits when the youngest child turns 16, unless the child is disabled. (Children will continue to receive benefits until age 18.) This ruling takes effect immediately for those parents who become eligible after August 1981, and for those eligible before September 1, 1981, it will take effect in September 1983. Most of the persons affected by this new ruling are widows.[83] Furthermore, since the amount of a widow's benefit is related to the standard of living that obtained at the time of her late husband's death rather than to that which obtains at the time she is entitled to receive it, it is likely that she will receive benefits based upon outdated earnings if she reaches the age of 60 a number of years after she is bereaved. Thus, by the time many widows are eligible to receive survivor's benefits, which are based on their late spouse's earnings indexed up to the year of his death, these benefits will have decreased in value.[84]

Adequacy issues also appertain to divorced and disabled homemakers. Until January 1, 1979, women divorced after less than twenty years of marriage did not qualify for Social Security benefits through their ex-husband's earnings; since that date, a woman who is divorced after *ten* years of marriage may receive these benefits. But a benefit that is half the amount of her former spouse's may not be adequate to support a divorced homemaker living alone, since that benefit was intended to be a supplement for a married couple. Furthermore, a divorced homemaker (who may be older than her former spouse) is not entitled to receive even this 50 percent of his worker's benefit until he is 62 years old and retires. Should he continue to work after the age of 62, she cannot receive benefits until such time as he retires. There are also gaps in disability protection for unpaid homemakers. A requirement for eligibility is five years of covered employment out of the ten years preceding the onset of disability, and even though a married woman may have spent many years in paid market work, if she has left the labor force for a period of five years or longer she is not entitled to protection. Once that protection is lost, she cannot regain it until she has accumulated five years of covered work. Yet the loss of a homemaker's services and the medical expenses incurred as a consequence of her disability may impose a severe financial hardship upon her family. Widows who become disabled before they reach the age of 50 also do not have disability protection.[85]

Equity concerns are underscored by the dramatic and unprecedented increase in the labor force participation rate of married women since the end of World War II.[86] Here, the focal point of concern is the relative worth of benefits provided to a dependent spouse receiving benefits through a paid worker and the benefits provided to spouses who have earned them as workers on covered jobs. From an equity standpoint, the system works to the advantage of women who have remained at home and couples who have earned an income from the husband's work alone. The protection a woman receives as a dependent spouse cannot be added to the protection she acquires as a paid worker. A married woman worker is entitled *either* to the benefits she has earned through working at a covered job *or* to benefits to which she is entitled as a dependent spouse, whichever is higher. Thus, an employed woman may receive no benefits or only slightly higher benefits when she retires than she would have received as a dependent who had never worked on a covered job: the money she pays into the system is not returned to her in benefits.

Furthermore, from the standpoint of equity, the treatment of two-earner couples as compared with that of one-earner couples is perceived to be unfair. This issue arises because of the payment of dependent's benefits to spouses who never worked in covered jobs or who worked for very low pay. Because of the method by which averge monthly earnings are indexed, it can happen that a two-earner couple receives lower total benefits than a one-earner couple with similar earnings, since the spouse's benefits are not generally payable to the two-earner couple. Similarly, the larger the proportion of the couple's earnings that was earned by one spouse, the higher the benefit for the aged survivor will be. Just as in the case for couples, the survivor of a two-earner couple generally receives a lower benefit than the survivor of a one-earner couple with comparable earnings. In addition, the system works to the advantage of couples with a dependent spouse as compared with single workers: it provides greater protection for married couples of whom one partner is either not a paid worker or is low paid than for single workers, even though all workers pay Social Security taxes at the same rate. Since the spouse is entitled to a benefit, a one-earner couple receives benefits that are one and one-half times the benefit of a single worker.

Informed public debate on the policy options available for serving the principles of adequacy and equity, and ultimately on the means of striking a balance between them, can only take place if the values implicit in various proposals for change are made *explicit*. Unless people are aware of the philosophy underlying recommendations for reform of the Social Security system, upon which the economic security of millions of Americans depends, the processes of decision-making and policy intervention will be guided not by collective wisdom but by the influence of rich and powerful private interest groups. In their review of the HEW report, Tish Sommers and Laurie Shields point out that since 1939, when the *adequacy* principle was introduced, to serve the social purpose of making adequate provisions for retirement or disability, most changes in the Social Security system were made so as to liberalize benefits, that is, to "make the system more *adequate* for widening circles of beneficiaries." However, in recent years the system has been challenged from the standpoint of *equity*. Sex inequities have been attacked by both men and women, "and minorities have pointed to their shorter life expectancy which results in lessened benefits." But on the whole, most of the pressure during the past few years "has been in the direction of containment or reduction of benefits." The changing old-age dependency ratio has provoked intense debate about the future economic stability of Social Security, and "the general shift of mood toward austerity in government spending has made the huge social security expenditures a target."[87] The reductions in Social Security introduced by the Carter administration in January 1979 in the proposed federal budget prompted the formation of the coalition known as Save Our Security (SOS), headed by Wilbur Cohen, former secretary of HEW. SOS, which "functions to mobilize political pressure whenever current benefits are endangered," is a coalition of the major organizations of elderly Americans, and a broad spectrum of political, religious, labor, educational, ethnic, disabled, and women's groups, among them the Older Women's League Educational Fund. In this Gray Paper published by OWLEF, Sommers and Shields study the economic circumstances of older women today, discuss the reasons why older women are overrepresented in poverty statistics, and identify the positive and negative features of the two comprehensive options, Earnings Sharing (Option #1) and Double-Decker Benefit Structure (Option #2), from the viewpoint of the constituency of older women. They also alert the reader to "new myths" about the changing roles of men and women in the United States, and discuss ways of protecting the interests of older women as shifts in policy occur (2). It is their conviction that older women ought to be involved as individuals and through their organizations in discussions about Social Security. This is not only because they have such an important stake in any modifications in Social Security legislation. It is also because "they have a responsibility to younger women to ensure that benefits are not eroded for those coming along" (17).

One positive feature of both options is that they address the issue of the family as an economic unit. Every homemaker knows that each marriage partner makes an economic contribution to the family. Even so, from the standpoint of policy, the idea of the sharing of earnings credits between spouses is revolutionary. Replacing benefits derived from the husband's earnings with shared benefits "would be a giant step toward recognition of homemaking as work, with the corollary that these workers are entitled to the cushions that other workers enjoy" (8). Another positive feature of the concept of shared earnings, which is central to Option #1 but also included in Option #2, is that it does accommodate the diversity of women's current work patterns. Sommers and Shields also note that Option #1 in particular has positive features for divorced women, that sharing credits between spouses could work as a disincentive to discarding older wives, that the ideas of inheritance of credits in lieu of dependency benefits and of the "adjustment period" for widows below retirement age have some merit, and that Option #2, which provides a minimum floor of benefits for every disabled and elderly citizen (a provision of some European systems), could, depending upon its adequacy, "eliminate the need for SSI, with its demeaning and costly means-testing machinery." Furthermore, this provision would change the principle of benefits for retirement and disability as a function of insurance to a right that is available to all (9).

The negative features of these options are the price of the positive features, and are projected in Appendix H of the HEW report, entitled "Estimated Changes in Benefit Amounts for a Retirement Cohort in the Year 2000 Under Earnings-Sharing and Double-Decker Options." Under Option #1, the average combined benefit amount for retired couples would be about six percent lower than that under present law, and average benefits for widowed persons would be similar to amounts under present law; under Option #2, the projected average for all women is three percent lower, and that for men 3 percent higher than that under present law. Hence, neither option provides a cushion for old age or disability. This, of course, is the logical consequence of the necessary compliance of the capable and committed staff members with the instructions they were given to analyze "all proposals for remedying sex inequities within the straightjacket of social security expenditures" (10). Had they been instructed to study all proposals within a broader framework of possibilities (the most obvious of these is the strengthening of the system with general revenues), the cushion for old age or disability could have remained in place as a fundamental premise of all proposals for changing the system. But limited to this interpretation of the congressional mandate, it was inevitable that the staff members' calculations would show lowered benefits for some groups in order that benefits for other groups be increased.

Sommers and Shields also note the apparent confusion between "equal treatment for men and women" (which was the subject mandated for this study) and equal treatment between women working in covered jobs and women who are dependent homemakers:

> This may reflect the bias of career women who have been in the forefront of social security reform efforts as well as pressures by male policy makers, who often attempt to pit women against each other. Both options improve the benefits of working women, not at the expense of men, but of homemakers, except in the case of divorce. This may have resulted from assumptions that one-earner families were generally better off financially. In fact, the impact of both options on low income, single earner families would be financial disaster.[11]

The authors of this Gray Paper also point out that under both plans, benefits for the dependent homemaker widow would be terminated when her youngest child reaches age 7, and the age at which she would become eligible for benefits would be raised from 60 to 62; therefore, "the widow's gap would become a chasm." Furthermore, neither plan provides for the reduction of the number of years used to compute the Average Indexed Monthly Earnings, so that women would still be penalized for the years they were out of the labor force. Finally, the problem of poor older widows, which they perceive to be the most pressing problem under the Social Security system, is not addressed directly by either Option.

While they recognize that the HEW report offers a constructive opportunity for a critical review of the Social Security system, Sommers and Shields caution that advocates of social change, who may have the finest of intentions, ought to consider very carefully the practical consequences of their proposals, and to make a careful distinction

> between the letter and the substance of equality. For example, the equity questions addressed in both comprehensive plans appear to be between the sexes, but in reality the prime thrust is to improve benefits of employed women, married or single, vis à vis dependent homemakers. The effect is a

more equal sharing of poverty among women, who would continue to reach that state either on their own or through widowhood.[12]

As Sommers and Shields observe, any "reform of consequence" of the Social Security system is going to cost money. Unless there is an infusion of general revenues into the fund, or at least a provision for borrowing between the three trust funds, "reform" can only consist of taking benefits away from some groups of women and giving them to other groups of women.

Older women are well advised to "choose their strategies carefully and build strong alliances," for the economic security of millions of women in the second half of life is now being strongly threatened by powerful interests whose representatives depict the current problems of the system—problems that are mainly due to the fact that the system relies on the payroll tax *and* that there is at present a high unemployment rate—as amounting to a "crisis." Examples of budgetary cuts recommended by the Carter administration, reflecting the climate of "austerity" in regard to social programs that prevailed throughout the late 1970s and that probably contributed to the election of Ronald Reagan in 1980, include eliminating the lump sum death benefit of $255, phasing out Social Security benefits for post-secondary students, eliminating the minimum benefit for low-wage workers, limiting the number of work years that may be disregarded in computing benefits, and eliminating benefits to a surviving parent when a minor child reaches the age of 16. All these proposals represent a major challenge (Sommers and Shields maintain they represent the *first* challenge) to the principle of adequacy. Many of them also violate the principle of equity, because they would have a much harsher impact on women than on men. And those who would pay the highest price for thus "reforming" the Social Security system are elderly widows living alone and in poverty.

In the spring of 1981, President Reagan recommended all the budgetary cuts proposed under the previous administration, and other reductions as well. Protest from the general public and from a number of organizations was strong, and as a consequence of this, Reagan withdrew some of these proposals. One of his recommendations, that the minimum benefit be eliminated, was signed into law in the summer of 1981, but legislators reversed themselves, probably because of public protest, and restored the $122 monthly benefit in December. However, except for members of religious orders who take vows of poverty, no new recipients of this minimum benefit will be accepted after December 31, 1981. Thus, the restoration applies only to the 3 million current recipients and to those who retire in November and December of 1981 at the age of 62 or above, if they are eligible to receive it.[88] Other reductions in the Social Security System—widows will lose benefits when their youngest child turns 16, instead of 18; most retirees will have to wait an extra month beyond their sixty-second birthday to qualify for benefits; benefits for college students will be phased out gradually, and will be discontinued after April 1985—were included in the fiscal 1982 budget reconciliation bill signed by President Reagan on August 13, 1981.

In discussing the long-standing objections to Social Security on the part of the Right, Christina Long quotes John Myles, a visiting scholar at Harvard who has researched this subject extensively, and who states that the threat of Social Security inheres in the fact that it is "the most important nonmarket mechanism for the allocation of income in the American economy." Myles contends that "the fact that Social Security works efficiently, with minimal red tape and broad public support, is a continuing challenge to the supposed superiority of marketlike institutions." Christina Long adds to this the point that, in contrast to pension funds,

> Social Security monies are not available for capital formation.
> In recent years pension funds have become an increasingly important source of capital formation in the U.S. In 1978 they owned 25 percent of all equity capital and were projected to own 50 percent by 1985. The financial community is well aware of the potential of pension monies to aid in the "re-industrialization" of America.
> The easiest way to increase these funds is to encourage the expansion of private pension plans. If this is to happen, Social Security must be restrained, and preferably cut back.
> However, the market has never been able to provide adequate retirement protection for the public at large, which is one of the basic reasons Social Security was first instituted. Any cuts in Social Security, in favor of private pensions, will inevitably be at the expense of the worker.[89]

Merton Bernstein reports that less than half the private work force is covered by private pensions. Benefits from private pensions and from state and local government retirement programs are low—the average payment is lower than the average Social Security benefit—and only a minority of participants receives them. Moreover, "they provide little or no benefits to survivors. They do not index benefits fully—if at all. Many are in precarious financial shape. These second-rate programs cost the U.S. Treasury $15 billion last year in lost taxes."[90]

When the focus of the issues and concerns of older women is shifted from age 65 to age 45, whether the question is one of health care benefits, or the special problems of divorced wives of military and governmental employees,[91] or private pension benefits of widows of men who died before reaching retirement age,[92] or the needs of displaced homemakers for job retraining and counseling,[93] one conclusion appears to be inescapable. That is that unless the interests of older women as a collectivity are protected, many "mature women" of today are destined to become the "old women" of tomorrow who will live in poverty and dependency. Millions of women now in their forties and fifties have worked all their adult lives at two jobs—in the labor force and in providing personal family care. They find in midlife that they are freed from responsibilities for child caretaking only to assume primary responsibility for caretaking of a disabled husband or an aged parent—or their working daughter's small children. Young women today, to whom these problems may seem very remote, will be the "mature women" of the twenty-first century.

They, in turn, may read their collective sociological fate in the lives of their mothers—unless those of all the generations unite in a common cause. That cause is the formulation of a social policy guided by the life course perspective. This perspective reveals the relatedness of all the generations to one another, and the indivisibility of guardianship of the lives of those yet to be born and of the lives of the very old who are still on this earth. Joining the awareness of the continuity of life to an appreciation of the living present as an inheritance and a trust is the truest expression of filial piety—of daughterhood.

Older Women: Toward a Social Policy for the Future

Demographic studies document the growing presence of older women in the national population and the fact that women constitute a "majority within the minority" of the elderly citizens of this country. Economic data document the fact that the elderly are in general a low-income group, and that unmarried older women account for 72 percent of all poor elderly persons.[94] The most compelling issue to be addressed by social policy is economic security in later life,[95] an issue that encompasses matters relating to the employment and the retirement of older women in the United States.

Until World War II, married women followed a worklife pattern of entry into the labor force ("in moderate numbers") during the early years of their marriages, and then withdrawal for childbearing. The women who quit their jobs "did not return even after children were in school or had left the home permanently." During the war, however, women of every age "were called upon to fill jobs that traditionally had gone only to males." The opportunities for work and the wages they were paid surpassed those which women had ever been offered up to that time. Widespread acceptance of working wives on the part of the American public was fostered by these wartime conditions.[96] Viewing women's worklife patterns in the context of historical change over the twentieth century, Juanita Kreps reflects that the generations of women who were young during the first half of this century set a working pattern that "posed little threat to marriage and family formation, or to intrafamily care of small children." Indeed, citing a report on the "working girl" of 1888, Kreps notes that going to work was instrumental in finding a husband in those days, and that this in turn made it possible for women *not* to remain very long in the labor force: employment stimulated marriage, as this report suggested. It is possible that this is the reason for the marked decline in the numbers of women working after age 25 in earlier decades. This is in sharp contrast to the contemporary work patterns of women. Today, increases in the supply of female labor are drawn more and more from the pools of women who are wives and mothers, as well as from the pools of older women.[97]

In the past, many women withdrew from the work force to care for their small children. Today, the "drop-out" rate for women aged 25 to 35 is much lower than it used to be, and Kreps predicted in her book, published in 1971, that it would probably continue to decline.[98] A longitudinal analysis (an analysis over time) of the market activity of cohorts of women born since the beginning of the twentieth century reveals that if women in the 1906–15 birth cohort (who were aged 65 to 74 in 1980) are followed throughout the life course, they exhibit a labor force participation rate that is characteristically low. For each cohort of women succeeding them—women born from 1916 to 1925, from 1926 to 1934, and from 1935 to 1944—the labor force participation rates have continued to increase. In general, "the older the cohort of women, the smaller their investment in market-related human capital, the larger their families, the more rural their setting, and the less permanent their attachment to the labor force."[99]

But a "low labor force participation rate" certainly does not mean a life of leisure. On the contrary, most of the women born in the late nineteenth and early twentieth centuries have been working for most of their lives—and working very hard. Most of those who were born and raised in rural areas had heavy chores to do since the time they were young girls. They completed far fewer years of formal schooling than their daughters, and the hours they did spend in school were preceded and followed by hours of work in the house and around the farm buildings that was labor, indeed—though it was never recorded in any official employment statistics. Some remained in the country, hiring themselves out as domestics; many more migrated to nearby towns and cities and took what jobs they could find in factories or mills or other people's houses. With little formal education and few skills, they earned the lowest of wages. When the Depression came, many of them lost their jobs. Married to men who were out of work and on relief for long periods of time, and mothers of small children, they "scraped along," taking in ironing or sewing or whatever other work there was to be had, and sharing their meager resources with relatives and neighbors. If life was hard in the country, it was no easier for those living in towns and cities whose husbands had gone "on the road" in search of work. It was not until World War II that these women found the job market opening opportunities for them. By then, they and their husbands were older—members of a generation of women and men who had been born too soon to be offered the educational opportunities that became available to many of their children and many more of their grandchildren. The Social Security system, which began paying benefits in 1940, represented a pledge of economic security in their old age to these women and men— economic security for couples for so long as they lived, so that they need not fear becoming an economic burden to their children, and economic security for the surviving spouses, for so long as they would live. Most of these surviving spouses are women—the elderly women in the United States today.

Elderly women who grew up in America's cities, or who are emigrés from Europe, worked as hard as those who grew up in the country. When they were still children themselves, they helped their mothers or aunts with younger children. They helped with the work of doing the laundry and cooking and cleaning in homes that doubled as boardinghouses. Many of them had to leave school after the eighth grade because their families needed their help at home, or needed the wages they could bring home from factory jobs. Some helped their fathers and brothers in family businesses. After they married, many kept boarders, just as their mothers had done, and many worked alongside their husbands in family businesses. Among their numbers are many foreign-born, who had to overcome language and cultural barriers in their search for market work. Like their counterparts born in America's rural areas, these women worked all their lives—although much of that work will never be found in official employment statistics. An oral history study of 75 women of Italian, Jewish, and Slavic ancestry, who were born either in Europe or in the United States to immigrant parents, between the years 1886 and 1910, "documents a great variety of work done by married women that is totally absent from the census data." Corinne Azen Krause found that both first- and second-generation women of all three ethnic ancestries were alike in "concern for the family. This was the primary motivation for work in any breadwinning capacity."[100]

Today, these women—from the country and from the city, both the native-born and the foreign-born—are the majority of America's elderly. The older they are, the more likely it is that they are living in poverty, drawing the minimum Social Security benefit as the surviving spouse of a worker whose own employment record reflects the limitations of educational opportunities, which in turn foreclosed his chances for job advancement during the years when he was in the "prime of life." That these women lived work-filled lives is not recorded in any statistics. The way they are recompensed for the work they did—bringing the next generation into the world and raising them while helping to run boardinghouses, helping out with family businesses, taking in work, interspersing years of zero earnings with years of work for low wages in factories and mills and in domestic labor in the homes of those more fortunate than they—*is* recorded, in poverty statistics, and is a national disgrace. Their lives are proof enough and more of the injustice that is done to women by the continued refusal to recognize household work as covered employment under the Social Security system.

If there is one prediction about which forecasters of the national economy agree, it is that hard times are upon us. With continuing inflation and the unemployment rate, which was 3 percent at the end of the Korean War, now at 8.9 percent (in December 1981) and expected to continue to rise, older women who are looking for work find themselves in a situation in which their employment prospects are bleak and their Social Security entitlement benefits are threatened with further reductions. As Virginia R. Allan has remarked, the reasons that older women work are much the same as those which account for why men work and why younger women work: they need the money—for college educations for their children, for providing care for aging parents, or to help pay the mortgage on their homes, "or to ensure an adequate retirement income." The need to work is even more compelling for single women who are self-supporting and who may be supporting dependents, and for women heads of families, many of whom are divorced, separated, or widowed. "In the light of their needs," Allan stated, "it is tragic indeed that mature women workers are, for the most part, economically disadvantaged." In her view, the problems of older women workers ought to be addressed within the framework of education and training, since these "determine not only what jobs women hold and what they earn but are a deciding factor in the question of whether or not they work at all." Allan thinks it is certain "that lack of training for the kind of work a woman would like to do accounts for much of the 'hidden' unemployment among older women."[101]

Recognizing the widespread need for education, training, and counseling, older women themselves began the work of building support systems for one another in the 1970s, through displaced homemakers networks. Displaced homemakers are older women "displaced" from a lifetime of homemaking by separation, widowhood, or divorce, or because of some overwhelming financial emergency—for example, some are married to men who lost their jobs; some are caretakers of an aged parent forced into dependency because of failing health. Finding themselves without means of support, displaced homemakers must turn to the labor market in search of paid employment, and their marketable skills are either rusty or outmoded. The term *displaced homemaker* was coined by Tish Sommers, who, with Laurie Shields, co-founded the Displaced Homemakers Network, which now operates out of 400 centers throughout the United States, and who took part in the drafting of legislation to assist women between the ages of 35 and 65 who are separated, divorced, or widowed, or who are married to men who are disabled. A provision of that legislation was the establishment of 50 multipurpose centers across the country, patterned after the centers for displaced homemakers in Oakland, California, and in Baltimore, Maryland. Self-evaluation sessions, job counseling, advice about credit, legal and housing matters, job referrals, and emotional support were to be provided at these centers. Furthermore, they were to refer women in need of assistance beyond these services to the appropriate agencies that are available in their local communities.[102]

The meaning of "displaced" is forcible exile—a harsh term, Sommers concedes, but one that accurately depicts the situation in which these women find themselves. In 1979, Barbara H. Vinick and Ruth H. Jacobs provided the *conservative* estimate that there were between 3 and 4 million displaced homemakers in the United States.[103] Their numbers well may increase in the years ahead. These women, who find there is no place for them in society, are faced with every conceivable crisis: "They are usually unemployed, unskilled, ignorant of money and credit matters, isolated, ill-equipped to care for themselves and, often, have no money." Cynthia Marano, who directed the center in Baltimore, observed that many women who come there have been very dependent upon their husbands all their married lives. "They may not know how to balance a checkbook." The problems they encounter, Marano said, may be legal in nature—involving loss of custody of children or an inequitable divorce settlement. Or they may have to do with housing—a woman "may be forced to sell a house because she can't keep up with the payments or she may have to move closer to the city and she's afraid she won't find an apartment because she's unemployed." A widow, living on a meager insurance policy and an even smaller pension, remarked that she had no idea she would ever experience such difficulties. Her husband, she said, took care of all the family's financial matters. "When you're married," she reflected, "you don't think about retirement or taking care of yourself." Sharon Howe, legislative aid to Representative Yvonne Braithwaite Burke, who co-sponsored displaced homemakers legislation with Senator Birch Bayh, noted that "everyone thinks there's someone out there helping these women," but that "the hard truth is that there isn't. These women fall through the cracks of every financial assistance program there is."[104]

In a paper published in 1974, Tish Sommers discussed the many difficulties women encounter in their efforts to re-enter the labor force in midlife. She pointed out that there is a virtual "blackout of services or benefits" during the middle years of a woman's life, and she indicated the ways that age discrimination is applied differently to men than to women. She challenged the values of our society because of the failure to recognize the vital contributions that homemakers and volunteer community workers make to the quality of life of our nation. "Through feminist efforts, Office of Federal Contract Compliance (OFCC) guidelines consider a refusal to rehire after child bearing discriminatory," she observed. "Why not then after child rearing?"[105] Sommers pointed to the confluence of issues in the movements for age equality and sex equality, and suggested that the displaced homemakers may form a spearhead in fusing feminism with the activism of America's elderly.

Education, training, and counseling for mature women who seek entry or re-entry into the labor market at midlife are preventive measures. Their combined effect would be the reduction of poverty and dependency in old age. Yet funding for these as for all social programs was either drastically reduced or abolished entirely during the first year of the Reagan administration, at a time when women and men of all ages are experiencing the harsh effects of the rising unemployment rate. The conclusion of a Harris poll conducted in 1978 was that more than half today's employees would prefer to continue working past "normal" retirement age.[106] And it has been predicted that the labor force participation rates of women will continue to grow in the future, whereas those for older men will continue to decline.[107] It is not that older men elect early retirement given the choice—early retirement "may conceal a rise in actual unemployment among older men, who would prefer to continue working but find no employment opportunities."[108] In any case, it was predicted (with the caveat that "projections are dangerous") that the labor force participation rate of older women will show a marked increase from 1960 to 1990, while that for older men will show a decline: from 1960 to 1990, the number of working women aged 45 to 64 will have increased by *63* percent, but in the case of men of those ages by only *14* percent. And among those aged 65 and over, there will be a *46* percent increase among females and a *minus* 12 percent for males. That prediction was made in 1973, when women as a collectivity were seen as no longer the "temporary tourists" in the labor force that they used to be, but as becoming full-time, year-round workers who appear to take less advantage of optional early retirement than is commonly supposed.[109]

Predictions of women's growing attachment to the labor force are extrapolated from the unprecedented expansion of the female labor force after World War II and from the increase in recent decades in the numbers of women who remain in the labor force during their childbearing and child-rearing years. It is logical to conclude that if these trends continue there will be less need for policy intervention on behalf of returning women in the years ahead. However, these present and future trends presuppose that jobs exist in plentiful enough supply that older women who are returning to the labor market will be able to compete successfully for them. But the social reality, as everyone knows, is quite otherwise. With the unemployment rate high and very likely to rise further, there is increasing competition for jobs not only between women and men, but between younger and older workers of both sexes, and between men and men and women and women. The number of two-income families in the United States declined by about 600,000 in 1981,[110] and doubtless it will decline further. And in some families, it will be the wife who will be able to obtain a job or hold a job she has already secured, rather than the husband; in other families, both spouses may patch together a family income from a variety of temporary or part-time jobs; in still others, the husband may find work, but not his wife. There are many possibilities of what the consequences of the current dislocations of the economy will be for both individual men and individual women, whatever their age and whatever their marital status.

Tish Sommers and Laurie Shields have warned of the dangers of some "new myths," one of which is that dependency is no more than a "transitional problem" because of women's growing attachment to the labor force. More than 50 percent of married women are not in the labor market; the number of entry-level jobs is declining; provisions for child care are wholly inadequate. "Dependency is a condition which women will have to deal with for the foreseeable future."[111] Dependency may also be a condition with which many *men* may have to deal in the years ahead—unemployed fathers of small children, who remain at home temporarily or permanently to care for them while their wives are working (paternity-leave programs have been established in the U.S. at the American Telephone and Telegraph Company, Procter and Gamble, CBS Inc., the Ford Foundation, the Security Pacific Bank in California and the New Jersey Bell system, and the first man working for New Jersey Bell to participate in the program is one of many fathers who are the subjects of an international study of male parenting now being conducted by the Father-hood Project of the Bank Street College of Education in Manhattan[112]), and unemployed, ill, or disabled older male workers whose female relatives are supporting them with their income from market work. The provision of Social Security credits for home work, a measure that would be beneficial for both women and men all along the life course, is long overdue. Under this "limited option," as described in the HEW report, homemakers would receive credits based on an imputed dollar value for their unpaid services in the home, and these credits would replace the current system of dependent spouse's benefits inasmuch as

> a homemaker would acquire her own earnings credits, thereby becoming entitled to a benefit in her own right.
> This approach would eliminate the problem of duplicative protection for women who are homemakers for part of their lives and paid workers for part of their lives. It would also serve to fill any gaps in their social security protection resulting from leaving the paid labor force to perform unpaid homemaker or childcare services. Protection for divorced and disabled homemakers would be increased because homemaker credits could enable their survivors to get benefits and would help them meet the recency of work test for disability benefits.[113]

As noted in the HEW report, a dollar value would have to be set for home work, and to be equitable among homemakers, this value would have to be adjusted based on the time and the effort each homemaker spends performing these services; adjustments might have to be made for homemakers who are employed part- or full-time as well. However, from an administrative standpoint, adjustments on an individual basis would not be feasible, and it would appear necessary to provide a uniform credit, or perhaps two or three alternative amounts, for all homemakers. The amount that is selected might to some extent depend on the way homemaker credits would be financed, and the HEW report identifies three mechanisms for financing homemaker credits. One would be to require homemakers to pay Social Security taxes on the imputed value of their services, or to make this protection an optional decision for each family. A second alternative—which would not disadvantage homemakers in families with low income—would be to finance the additional benefits that would be payable on account of homemaker credits through general revenues—an approach that, as the report notes, could be seen as unfair to paid workers in covered jobs who are required to pay Social Security taxes. A third mechanism, to which—as noted in the report—paid workers would doubtless object, would be to finance the cost of the additional benefits by increasing the Social Security taxes of paid workers. While providing credits for home work would recognize that it has an economic value to both family and society, "it would represent a significant departure from the traditional basis of the social security program under which benefit rights are derived from actual earnings in covered employment" (106).

Wilbur Cohen, former secretary of HEW, recommended amending the Social Security law to recognize household employment as covered employment under the system as one of a number of changes he proposed at the

Twenty-sixth Annual Conference on Aging in Ann Arbor in 1973. He suggested that the homemaker be required to pay a Social Security contribution as a self-employed person, and that each homemaker be allowed a choice of three or four possible alternatives of base values upon which the premium would be paid. While the constitutional lawyers will have to work out the details, Cohen stated, some version of this proposal ought to be considered:

> If household work were considered covered employment under Social Security, every woman would have a right to protection. Her coverage would not depend on her husband's coverage. Neither would it depend on marriage at all. If the woman is married, her coverage would not end with divorce. This change would also solve one of the most perplexing problems of Social Security: the question of the unmarried woman with very low earnings who may spend many years at home caring for her aged parents.[114]

If reparation cannot be made to the mothers of the past, this amendment of Social Security legislation could be made as a gift in their memory to the mothers of small children today and to middle-aged women who may need to take a long period of time out from market work to care for an ill or disabled aging parent or spouse or child. There are women who will not accept discontinuity in their working lives for *any* reason, and there are women who do not expect to have anyone immediately dependent on them. For these women, the choice between "home work" and "market work" is not an issue. But the rest are recompensed for years of providing personal care for family members with an official work history marking those years "zero earnings." Thus are millions of old women in our society today recompensed for their labors, that they comprise "the fastest-growing poverty segment in the country."

Work in the United States is becoming ever more concentrated in the middle years of life, "leaving youth free for education and training and old age for retirement. Both nonworking periods call for heavier transfers of income which are of necessity drawn from the earnings of the middle age group." And both use non-working time that could be spread out over the worklife.[115] Time for market work and time free from market work could have been allocated differently; changes could have been made in the direction the system was taking, directly after the end of World War II. If they had been, men would have been more available for work at home during critical times in the life cycle of the family. As it is now, both "industry practice and government policy bias the individual's time-allocation decision toward working continuously until the mid-sixties, then consuming leisure full time for the rest of life."[116] Juanita Kreps and Robert Clark suggest that "if at age 20 one were given 45 years of work and 10 years of nonwork time, and then allowed to allocate his time as he wished, he probably would not elect to work straight through to age 65 and then retire."[117] And in *Why Survive? Being Old in America*, Robert Butler makes a spirited call for flexibility in spacing the phases of learning and labor and leisure all along the life course.[118] It is instructive that two panels of scientists, one convened to study the problems of youth and the other the problems of elderly people, came independently to the recommendation that work ought to be spread more evenly over the life course.[119] A social policy for the future should have as its first premise the recognition that the possibilities of human life for productive work and for learning and for creative leisure are manifold, and ought to be extended to every person at every age of life.

Social policy has a visionary edge, and it is right that this is so, since it is the work of imagination as well as of reason. However, there is a grave danger that those who love the future overmuch, as many North Americans are said to do, may become so enchanted with their visions of the imagined worlds of tomorrow that they neglect or wish away the issues and concerns of the immediate present. Glowing accounts of the world-to-come can be very useful to those who wish to preserve the world-as-it-is. History has taught that some of the harshest cruelties inflicted on human beings are committed as much in the name of those yet to be born as in the name of the dead, and that the doctrine that some of the present generation must be sacrificed, whether for the sake of those who preceded them or for the sake of those who will follow them, is as cynical as it is evil. Elderly people in the U.S. are in general a low-income group. Their economic security is utterly dependent upon the strength of the Social Security system. No matter how noble-sounding its rhetoric or radiant its vision of the future, a social policy based upon a perversion of these ineluctable facts would be a perversion of social justice itself.

Among the major policy and program recommendations that were adopted by the 1981 White House Conference on Aging are that benefits paid to current recipients should not be reduced, that payments under the SSI program should rise to the poverty line and be made independent of the recipient's assets, that the money cut from federal spending for human services in 1981 should be restored, and strict standards of accountability should be applied to any increases in defense spending, and that Congress should appropriate general fund revenues to bolster the Social Security fund, if this becomes necessary. (This is done routinely in the Western European countries.) In addition, the Number One recommendation of the New York State Conference on Aging was that federal, state, and local governments should plan, finance, and facilitate the implementation of a continuum of services to meet the needs of the elderly, including both those who live in the community and those who are institutionalized. These services should be tailored to individual needs, and delivered without regard to race, religion, sex, national origin, physical or mental disability, or source of payment.[120]

Policymakers in modern industrial societies must of necessity work with statistical data, and these are notorious for their manipulability. Furthermore, perception is unfailingly selective, and the pressures to conform to the dominant mentality of the day are very powerful. Journalistic accounts can be moving renditions of social facts. They can reveal the human being concealed in the thickets of statistics. They can translate the abstractions of social science into a language that is vivid and arresting because of its concreteness. They can awaken consciences that have fallen asleep, and trouble those who would direct the attention of the public elsewhere:

One of the women who attended the conference, "A Time for Changes and Choices: A Conference for Midlife and Older Women," which was held just one month before the 1981 White House Conference on Aging, was Celia Wong, aged 79, a former librarian. Mrs. Wong came to the conference because she had been widowed recently, and wanted to learn as much as she could about Social Security. She said that her Social Security payment is her sole source of income and that she is unable to live on it: "I've been trying to find a job, but no one will hire someone my age. I don't qualify for food stamps, so I wind up buying tired vegetables, food in dented cans and outdated cold cuts. I'm one step away from picking garbage cans." Mrs. Wong stated that she could not use the bathroom in her house because she could not afford the cost of repairing the plumbing. Therefore, she uses showers at Grand Central Terminal, and a toilet in the nearest subway station. She observed that the life experience of the elderly once was thought to be of value, "but today it's considered worthless. Sometimes I wonder why they don't put us on ice floes, like they do in Alaska."[121]

How We Live: Older Women as Seen in Sociological Studies

The United States is a multiracial, multinational, multiethnic society, and each of the varieties of subcultures has its own norms and traditions. Yet the perimeters of these social and cultural worlds are indistinct because of the interchange of customs and beliefs between people who move across these unseen boundaries: in time, we may earn the appellation "pluralistic society." However, for the present it remains true that there are marked cultural differences among our older population, and this fact must be taken into account in the study of older women in the United States today. For example, the peoples included in the category "Asian-Americans" are exceedingly diverse in history, language, religion, and cultural traditions, and this is reflected in the population characteristics of each group: the sex ratio of Chinese-Americans is unique in that it is strongly skewed in the direction of males, and this skewing increases with age so that there are about three men for every woman over the age of 65.[122] Another example is that the elderly comprise only 4 percent of the Spanish-American population; the exception is the Cuban population, among whom 8.6 percent are aged 65 and over. There is also an important difference in life expectancy statistics for the general population of the United States and the subpopulation of Spanish-Americans, among whom "females do not outlive males . . . because their lower socioeconomic lifestyle exposes females to greater risks than females of other racial and ethnic groups." Furthermore, Mexican-American women continue to bear children at a much later age than their Anglo-American counterparts. It has also been reported that "extended family care is a myth for the majority of those of Spanish origin" and that Spanish-American women are three times more likely to live alone than in someone else's household.[123]

Except for the work of Jacquelyne Johnson Jackson, who is the author of numerous publications on older black women in the United States,[124] racial and ethnic differences among older women are not the direct focus of sociological studies, but a by-product of investigations into other research areas. Thus, findings about the living arrangements of older women in a particular community may or may not be representative of those of older women throughout our society. Nonetheless, these researches are very valuable contributions to the study of the varieties of older women in the United States. An outstanding example of this is the work of sociologist Helena Znaniecki Lopata, who has published a number of books and articles on widowhood, most of them based on her studies of Chicago-area widows. Lopata found marked ethnic differences in the living arrangements of her research subjects. She reports that all the Greek women lived with married children, and stated that this was a cultural tradition. Other findings were that half the Polish widows lived alone, and that 76 percent of the Germans, 77 percent of the Italians, and 78 percent of the British lived alone. Lopata concludes that, in general, the lower a woman's socioeconomic status and the stronger her ethnic affiliations, the more likely it is that she would live with her children after she was widowed.[125] An important study by historian Corinne Azen Krause also represents a very valuable contribution to the study of ethnic differences among older women. Krause's oral history study of three generations of Jewish, Italian, and Slavic-American women in Pittsburgh found a much higher percentage of Slavic grandmothers than of Italian and Jewish grandmothers sharing a home with a married daughter (36 percent as compared with 12 percent and 8 percent, respectively). Krause's study also shows that the fact that a woman lives apart from her grown children does not necessarily mean that there is psychological distance between the two households. She found that 88 percent of the grandmothers see their grown children at least once a week, and that almost half see at least one adult child every day. She also found that over 80 percent of the mothers (the middle generation of this three-generation sample) see the grandmothers at least once every week, and that slightly over 30 percent see them every day. The differences between *ethnic groups* were that Slavic and Italian women were more likely to see their mothers every day, whereas Jewish women were more likely to visit them weekly. The differences between *generations* suggest "greater mobility and a trend toward living independently" for this particular group of women. Krause found that one of every three daughters (the youngest of the three generations) see their mothers less than once a week.[126]

Krause's finding of differences in visiting patterns among women of the three generations suggests a stronger emotional attachment between middle-aged daughters and their elderly mothers than between young adult women and their middle-aged mothers. It is possible that this finding reflects the changing patterns of intergenerational relationships between women all along the life course. Young women and their middle-aged mothers often grow apart in their search for separate identities, and then grow closer again when the daughters are middle-aged and their mothers are elderly. Difficult as it is, the material and emotional dependence of an elderly woman on her middle-aged daughter may be more easily accepted than the material and emotional dependence of a young woman on her middle-aged mother, since young adulthood is the time for achieving independence. Furthermore, the female life cycle is such that many middle-aged women are likely to feel they have more in common with their elderly mothers than with their grown daughters. The marital status of a middle-aged woman may also be an important factor influencing her relationship with her elderly mother. Sarah Matthews cites evidence that the pattern of "old mothers living with their single, divorced, or widowed adult offspring is a fairly common occurrence" in the United States.[127] The financial status of grown children and their aging mothers is another important factor that must be taken into account in studying the living arrangements of older women.

Sociological studies have the virtue that they present facts about social reality that show some widely held commonsense assumptions about that reality to be fictions. One of these fictions is that grown children in the United States abandon their aging parents. This fiction, which amounts to a wholesale condemnation of the members of one generation for violation of the Fourth Commandment, ignores the fact that, because of improvements in life expectancy, the multigenerational family is becoming a common feature of our society. Neugarten estimated in 1972 that one of every three 60-year-olds in this country still had a living parent.[128] It also ignores the fact that many elderly people are childless. For example, Jackson reports that in 1970, one of every four older black women had never given birth.[129] Finally, it equates separate residence with abandonment. But of the three out of four elderly people who have at least one living child, it has been estimated that four of every five have seen one of their children within the past week, and that over 60 percent reported seeing a grown child either that day or the day before.[130] Ethel Shanas finds the myth that the elderly in the U.S. today are alienated from their families, especially from their grown children, reminiscent of the Hydra—every time it is slain by fresh evidence to the contrary, new adherents spring up among the mass media, writers for the popular press, researchers, and even the elderly themselves. Family, Shanas writes, is not coterminous with "household," and nothing in the definition of family as a group of people to whom the elderly are related by blood or marriage implies that this group must live under the same roof. Surveys taken in 1957, 1962, and 1975 indicate that in the U.S., the family is the primary basis of security for adults in later life, that older parents do see their adult children often, that the modified extended family—siblings, nieces and nephews, and other primary relatives of kin beyond the nuclear unit—is the dominant family form for old people and is very much alive, and that family help in providing long-term care for the elderly persists, despite the alternative sources made available since 1975.[131]

Sociological and historical researches also contradict the assumption that there is a cause-and-effect relationship between the industrialization of a society and the change from an extended family form to an "isolated nuclear family pattern."[132] Indeed, the very notion of the pervasiveness of such a "pattern" came under the fire of sociologists of the family during the 1950s, when publications of their studies revealed networks of mutual aid between the generations that were very active. Evidence of continuity between the generations continues to accumulate, and a "modified extended family" has come to be seen as prototypical—at least of the samples studied.[133] Nonetheless, as Beth Hess observes, "the absence of three-generation households has been held responsible for every contemporary social problem from religious intermarriage to the status of old people." If households had more persons in previous eras, she writes, "they were as likely to be lodgers, apprentices and servants as they were to be kinfolk."[134] Barbara Laslett presents evidence supporting the conclusion that an extended kinship structure was not in any way characteristic of a large proportion of households in this country, and that while after the decline of apprenticeship the proportion of non-kin residents in the household may have been reduced, "an alternate source was to be found among boarders and lodgers." This was particularly true of the growing urban centers of the United States. Furthermore, Laslett found that boarding was a widespread practice until well into the twentieth century (by 1930, 11.4 percent of all families in urban areas kept a lodger, and perhaps because of the effect of the Great Depression, the figure was still as high as 9 percent in 1940). Only after the middle of this century, Laslett reports, has it happened that household composition became restricted to the nuclear kin group.[135] But the *extended* group before that time consisted of servants, apprentices, boarders, and other non-kin residents.

When the poet Jorge Manrique wrote in "Coplas por la muerte de su padre" that any time in the past was better than the life we have now, he may have been reflecting on the way that memory mingles with desire, for the past is as much a work of the imagination as the future. Anne Foner advises against a romantic view of the family of the nineteenth century, pointing to potential sources of conflict and tension that were more common in the past, among them the indeterminacy of the timing of the transition to full adulthood, and cohort differences among family members. In her judgment, "there has been an overly roseate picture of age relations in the 19th-century family in some works" and "commentary on the modern family abounds with lamentations." Foner concludes that three-generation households were nearly as uncommon in the late nineteenth century as they are in the late twentieth, but that what does appear to be different is that few old people lived alone in the earlier period, and that of these it is likely that fewer still were elderly women. "Living alone," she observes, "appears to be a modern development."

Furthermore, it was far more likely that widowhood would coincide with the time at which the youngest child married in the nineteenth century than it is today.[136] Historian David Hackett Fischer reports that, in the late colonial period, "seeking" children surrounded many a parent until the end of life. At that time, there was neither an early retirement from work, nor release from domestic responsibilities. It was normal for childrearing to go on until the parents' death. Few old people lived alone, but scarcely any lived in three-generation households. Those who did usually had taken in a widowed son or daughter. Therefore, in a three-generation household, "it was more often the young who were in some way dependent upon the old than the old upon the young."[137]

Historical and anthropological records dispel the myths that the old always fared better in the past or in an extended family system in other societies. "To be a poor widow in early America," Fischer writes, "was not to be venerated." A complaint of Increase Mather was that there were children apt "to despise an *Aged Mother*." If a woman were poor, widowed, *and* base-born, she was treated most contemptuously. Neighbors actually drove some of these women away because they were afraid there would be an increase in the poor rates. "The legal records of the colonies contain many instances of poor widows who were 'warned out' and forced to wander from one town to another."[138] The status of poor older women in other societies where reverence for the aged is part of the cultural tradition is not much different from that of poor widows in the colonial period in this country. In Rattan Garh, a village in India, 60 women over the age of 50 were interviewed, and it was found that patterns of family organization are quite at variance with ideal norms. Older women, especially those of a low socioeconomic position, occupy a very tenuous status in old age, and their difficulties are neither new nor the consequences of outside forces.[139] And there is a dark underside of extended family organization in those societies where it is still the norm. We hear, Robert A. Le Vine writes,

> of the frequency of suicide among the desperate young married women of traditional China seeking to escape from their tyrannical mothers-in-law. From North India it is reported that young wives develop hysterical seizures when marital obligations force their return to residence with their husbands' families. Assassins are hired to help settle internal family quarrels in Egyptian villages. Fraternal tensions within domestic groups are extremely widespread from China to West Africa, and in Africa the prevalence of polygyny results in divisive quarrels between the paternally connected sons of different mothers.[140]

Contemporary social arrangements have not always been the way they are now, as Fischer reminds us, although our memories are so short that we imagine they have, and we think that the way things are is "rooted in some deep, organic structure of our being."[141] But there are at least as many fictions and myths about contemporary social arrangements as there are about those of the past and those in other societies. It is the task of the sociologist to distinguish fiction from social fact and myth from social reality, and a variety of research methods are available as guides in this endeavor. Two works, both published in 1979, are of special interest because they focus on older women in present-day American life. In *Life After Youth*, Ruth Jacobs develops a typology of older women—nurturers, unutilized nurturers (including displaced homemakers), re-engaged nurturers, chum networkers and leisurists, careerists (employed and unemployed), seekers, faded beauties, doctorers, escapists and isolates, and advocates and assertive older women. Jacobs presents these types as "constructs for analytical purposes," which indicate the roles that are available to most older women today. She recommends a social climate, a social policy, and a social concern more favorable to older women, and advises women to be change agents rather than change victims.[142] In *The Social World of Old Women*, Sarah Matthews reports the findings of a social psychological study conducted in the 1970s in which she used participant observation, interviewing, and archival research. Her subjects are widows aged 70 and over, all of whom have children, yet all of whom are living alone. Matthews takes the reality-constructionist perspective on identity, and uses exchange theory and labeling theory to clarify the meaning of "oldness" to the social actors she interviewed. Matthews argues that old age is a socially constructed category. She finds that self-identity and self-presentation are problematic for old women, and discusses strategies (which are not always consciously planned) that may be adopted in encounters with others and with the self. She believes that settings are a vital component in maintaining self-identity: there are newcomers and residents in settings, and each role has consequences for self-identity. Matthews found that the elderly widow's children are of paramount importance to her. However, from the perspective of exchange theory, it appears that the *quality* of relationships is affected adversely by the low status of old women, who have a weak power base from which to demand treatment as equals. To protect self-identities in a senior center where they are defined by the staff as "postadults," these elderly women used confrontation and role distance. While Matthews found that all the strategies used to maintain acceptable self-identities lead to greater social isolation, she suggests that two forces in society today—the Gray Panthers and the women's movement—may increase the visibility of options available to elderly women.[143]

It is probably true that every member of a society makes sociological observations from time to time. However, what may be true of particular family relationships or of life in a particular community may or may not be characteristic of families and communities in the United States. The tendency to project impressions about family and community life that are formed on the basis of personal experience onto the broader canvas of society is a very human one. For this reason, the most thoroughly trained and seasoned social observer must confront the challenging and complex problem of establishing evidence to support general statements about social reality made on the basis of a research project. Since the 1960s, a number of sociologists have been conducting research studies of the living arrangements of older Americans in specific localities or "settings." The reliability of generalizations about the way older Americans live that are drawn from the findings of individual studies remains problematic. However, each of these studies has valuable insights to offer precisely because aspects of aging are explored in the context of the geographic and social worlds that the elderly research subjects inhabit. While some are concerned with elderly men and women, others focus directly on older women.

Joyce Stephens's *Loners, Losers, and Lovers* is about old people living in a single-room-occupancy slum hotel, "the Guinevere," in an American city.[144] During the period of her research, an experience that "dealt a lethal blow to the myth of scientific objectivity," 371 of the 524 rooms were occupied, and 108 of these were rented by aged tenants. Most of the elderly tenants lived in sleeping rooms. Their average rent was $20.59 a week. There were 97 men living at the Guinevere, and only 11 women. The average age was 67, and the mean length of residence was nine years. Many had moved there from hotels nearby; shuffling from one hotel to another was quite common in the area. Many former residents of the Guinevere, who are even more disadvantaged, could be found in hotels in the neighborhood.

Stephens reports that the old people at the Guinevere "are unanimously hostile and suspicious toward nursing homes," which they see as "the tangible expression of society's rejection of old people." They speak of the two nursing homes in the area as "playpens." One resident refers to nursing homes as "the final humiliation." Institutionalization is a specter—"a reminder of the catastrophic consequences of loss of personal determination." To move to a nursing home is to succumb to dependency, to physical and mental failure (12). Stephens writes of the ferocity with which the privacy of the rooms is guarded at the Guinevere, of the pervasiveness of gossip (the source of vendettas of many years' standing), and of the absence of loyalties. She found that the belief of the tenants that it could happen that a person could be ill for a long period of time and perhaps even die without anyone either knowing or caring about this "is an accurate appraisal," and that suspicion was "institutionalized." Just as every social world has its mystique, there was a mystique at the Guinevere—that a certain "type" lives in hotels. For this reason, all had their face-saving maneuvers, and the most favored of these was the remaking of one's personal history. On the rare occasions when an account is offered, the listeners are expected to pretend that they believe it. At the Guinevere, people die alone in their rooms, and more often than not, the maid discovers the body. The threat of violence is ever-present.[145]

The old people at the Guinevere carry a burden of losses that has grown heavier with the years. They are lonely and isolated, not because old people are inevitably so, but because they are willing to pay this price for the sake of preserving the independence that means so much to them. The women have not learned so well as the men how to live in the tough and hostile world of the

SRO hotel. They sometimes talk about prestige and about family relationships they claim were theirs in earlier times. They try to make quasi-family relationships with the men, but they are rebuffed and mocked. "Sixty-year-old men," Stephens writes, "do not want sixty-year-old women" (86). As time goes on, they become even more inaccessible and forbidding than the men. "But once we get past their chilly exterior, we find vulnerable and unbelievably lonely people" (83). Stephens perceives these women to be more vulnerable than the men, to have less success in coping, and to remain unreconciled to their status. She found that one of their favorite and familiar stories has the theme of the solicitous care they could still receive from their families—that all they need to do is to make a telephone call, and the relative will come for them and take them home and care for them. "There is no viable basis for these daydreams: children are gone or dead, grandchildren are uninvolved or . . . have actively avoided and refused to have anything to do with these women" (81–82). Even so, they continue to tell the story, although none of their listeners believes it. Although the men do not want them, the women see other women as potential rivals; their friendships with one another are easily broken. Stephens found that the men "keep up with the times," but the women tend to live in the past. Both the men and the women at the Guinevere are alienated solitaries because that is what is required in order to survive in their world. Stephens presents a moving portrait of the women who live in this little world in which there are almost nine times as many males as females: "One cannot help being struck by the poignant appearance of these taciturn and suspicious ladies, with their wigs that don't fit and their veiled hats that, like banners, put forth a brave front" (88).

In contrast to "the Guinevere," the majority of the 43 elderly residents of "Merrill Court," a small apartment building near the shore of San Francisco Bay, are women. In her book about Merrill Court, *The Unexpected Community*, Arlie Russell Hochschild writes of the residents as "widows." Although the 43 people included 35 widows, three couples and two single men, the widows created the moral atmosphere of this "unexpected community."[146] These women, conservative and fundamentalist people from Oklahoma and Texas and other parts of the Midwest and Southwest, were neither isolated nor lonely. They did not talk about "communal living" or "alternatives to the nuclear family," yet that is what they improvised. Theirs was a vibrant community of old people, one they made to work "as a mutual aid society, as a source of jobs, as an audience, as a pool of models for growing old, as a sanctuary, and as a subculture with its own customs, gossip, and humor" (xiv). Most of these women were born in farmhouses; on the average, they had seven siblings, of whom a number "were lost to typhoid epidemics, and had long since been quietly buried in the backyard." They still quilt and darn—skills their mothers taught them. They learned when young "to refill the gas lanterns, to heat bricks to keep the beds warm . . . , to grind coffee, stoke the fire, put up vegetables . . . , and retrieve the pail of milk hung in the well to keep cool." But today, when they are old, "they buy their chickens frozen and

wear Woolworth's drip-dry dresses" (8). Many worked in the fields or factories
when they were children. They remember their earlier selves "as little rapscal-
lions finding fun in a life of work." They were taught the work ethic, and they
were taught to be thrifty. Most of them married young and kept on working—
some even after the children came—as cooks and maids, as waitresses or
factory hands. In the early 1940s, most of them came to California looking for
well-paying jobs in the shipyards. After the war almost all of them were laid
off. They found jobs in factories after this, or at lunch-counters or in laundries; a few went north to farm. "After several trips back East, where wages
were lower, the climate harsher, and things no longer the same, they returned
to California, where most of their children have remained, multiplied, and in
a modest way, prospered" (10).

The widows of Merrill Court are, Hochschild observes, like most elderly
Americans—poor. To qualify for public housing, those who were single had
to have incomes under $2,800 a year, and those who were married, under
$3,000.[147] Although many had lived at one point or another in their lives with
children, most of them preferred to live independently. Hochschild found
that family life matters very much to them. They say they want relationships
with grown children to be "good," and this seems to be contingent upon a
generational autonomy. In general, those who were closest to their kin were
among the most active members of the Merrill Court community. Most of the
residents had been widowed within the five-year period before they met for
the first time in 1965. From an informal gathering around the coffee machine
in the recreation room at Merrill Court, they transformed themselves into a
"beehive of activity," with Service Club meetings, bowling, a morning workshop, twice-weekly Bible study classes, monthly birthday parties, and visits to
the four nursing homes nearby. For these visits, they brought donations of
sweets and soda, and a five-piece band—including a washtub bass—to play for
the "old folks" there. Their band also provided entertainment for Vietnam
war veterans at a recreation center close by. As their community came into
being, so did customs about "our way" of doing things. In time, they came to
see one another as sisters engaged in the common task of building a world.
Hochschild shows that in "doing" for one another and in transforming "free"
time into a productive "workin' in," the widows of Merrill Court created a
sororal community that never could have come into being in an institution.

The sororal bond among old-age peers may be invisible to most people who
come into contact with them in the world outside their communities. The
widows of Merrill Court had dealings with peddlers who came to the building,
for whom they learned how to "play dumb," with managers of local business
enterprises, and with robbers who preyed on them when they went shopping
or to the bank to deposit their monthly pension checks. They had dealings
with the police, and the staffs of the recreation department, the social welfare
department, and the housing authority. (Hochschild notes that most of the
lower-level personnel in the welfare and housing bureaucracies are middle-
aged women—the widows' "sociological daughters." As these jobs are filled

more and more by men—"sociological sons"—the nineteenth-century pattern of the son's assuming responsibility for the aging parent re-appears in a contemporary guise.) To outsiders, they might be perceived as potential and actual victims of crime and exploitation. To those in the commercial sphere, they were a collectivity—"you ladies" or "you folks over there." As "senior citizens" in a welfare state, they were seen "as welfare recipients, beneficiaries of good works and charity, other people's 'poor dears,' and they felt the stigma of that" (125). But just between themselves they could be equals, and were free to speak of matters they felt to be taboo in the presence of even (and sometimes perhaps especially) a beloved daughter. When the young were not watching, they felt free to give in to the impulse to dance or sing. When they were together, they shared thoughts about premonitions and apparitions and dreams, about dying and mourning. Outsiders could not know of their thoughts and feelings about these things because their very presence would have inhibited the widows from expressing them.[148]

Hochschild sees the subculture at Merrill Court as something of a "rear-guard counter-culture" and in many ways more of a counter-culture than those formed by young people (24–25). She writes that there are times in life when a person especially needs and searches for social siblings. One of these times is before marrying and having a family of one's own, and another is after one has raised one's children. Again, one of these times is just before entering the labor market, and another is after retirement. She believes that "the times are ripe for the sibling bond, and for old age communities such as Merrill Court." For different reasons, she suggests, both adolescence and old age are farthest away from the American Dream. But old age is its "underside." Even so, friendships among age peers in youth may be the source of friendships between age peers in later life. She writes of the widows of Merrill Court that "the comradely social bonds of their past work in the shipyards, at the lunch counter and in the laundry have become, in part, a model for social bonds in retirement."[149]

Living in an "independent household" (as about 80 percent of elderly Americans do) does not predestine an older woman to social isolation. In her study of widowhood in Chicago, Lopata states that a number of factors account for the varying degrees of isolation among the widows who were interviewed, among them the woman's age, her financial status, her and her deceased husband's educational and occupational status, her racial, religious, or nationality status, and her own assessment of her health. Lopata found that for about two of every three widows included in the study, friendship was a very important part of life.[150] She reports that friendless women or those with few friends are negative not only about friendship but about the world in general, and that many of these women are poor. Once their lifetime associations with those in the kin group or neighborhood are broken by death, they are left quite isolated. They are suspicious of strangers and acquaintances and do not know how "to convert mere contact into a primary relation." Some never had strong friendships; others drifted away from friends because of "financial or health problems." Lopata writes that the disengagement of these widows is the result of a passive adjustment to their circumstances, and she suggests that this is typical of people who have been brought up to accept whatever befalls them. It is not that these isolated widows *chose* to be alone; interviews with them "indicate a very painful history of the withering of the friendship relations and strong hostility toward the environment for not providing resources for continued engagement" (215–16).

Nearly one of five of the widows in Lopata's study had no living children, and they were social isolates. However, the mere fact that she had living children did not redeem a widow from social isolation. Some had frequent contacts with their grown children—women in the "upper-lower class," mothers of several children, who saw at least one of them quite often, and women of the "upper-middle" or "upper class," who had a high average contact with all her children "but a relatively low frequency with any one." Even so, in all the socioeconomic groups demarcated in this study, there were widows who said they wished they had more direct contacts with grown children. Many remarks in the interviews hinted at dissatisfaction with the location, amount and quality of contact with grown children not sharing the mother's home. Some widows were bitter because they felt grown children neglected them; "others offer complex rationalizations with undercurrents of resentment for infrequent contact" (134). Lopata found that women isolated from living offspring were isolated from other people as well. She points out that mothers are expected to continue to focus on their "family of procreation" even after they are widowed and the grown children have left home; the children, however, are not expected to focus on *them*. She states that this is an issue for older widows, especially for those who were brought up in patriarchal families. These women had been taught to venerate older family members, and they expected that they in turn would be venerated when they grew old. They gave their children more attention than they had received from their own parents, and they feel ambivalent "toward their offspring, who focus downwardly and 'neglect' the older mother in favor of their own children and grandchildren" (152). Lopata also uses the concept of "time-distance" in interpreting visiting patterns between family members. She remarks that "Gary, Indiana may seem a great distance from Chicago to a widow who does not drive and is dependent upon the cheapest available transportation" (125).

This study of widowhood in the Chicago area discloses the variety of "urban widows," the relationship between social class and the possibilities of re-engagement after widowhood, and the complexity of the issue of the social isolation of older women who live alone.[151] Widows who gave up their active involvement with voluntary associations did so because they could not afford the cost of membership, or because of poor health, or because they had moved too far away to be able to keep up with the activities of these groups. Transportation presented a serious obstacle to many of them; Lopata reports that not one woman in the study stated that transportation service is provided by the voluntary associations to which she belongs or formerly belonged. A number spoke of their fear of going out alone at night in the city. There is also the matter of pride in personal appearance; some could not afford to dress as they thought they should to attend organization meetings. Lopata writes, "The stigma of appearing old or disfigured, or of not being able to hear what is going on, to walk fast enough, and do the work involved in being active is enough to wither motivation" (248). She also found that some of these widows never belonged to any organizations. One woman stated in her interview that she had never had the education she felt was necessary to join any group.

Certainly, Lopata identified widows who do have the resources needed to cope with the great change bereavement brought to their lives. She also identified widows whose lives go on much the same as they had before their husbands died because they are part of a thriving ethnic community. Widow-hood does not shatter these women's world of "houses, streets, and shops," and the rest of Chicago or of the country or the wider world is not part of their thinking or their identity. Lopata also identified women who are wealthy "cosmopolites." But her sample also includes widows who do not even know the names of their own neighborhoods, much less a working history of the city of Chicago. She found that these women do not understand how Chicago is organized or know what facilities it might offer them. Older widows who grew up in rural areas, villages, or small towns are apt to feel bewildered, lost, and frightened in the city. Most of the European-born widows moved from one place to another and from one job to another in the course of their lives. They experienced upheaval in their private worlds, in their neighborhoods, and in the wider urban community, and some of them see Chicago as a city of mystery and danger. Another type of urban widow is the social isolate, and Lopata writes that the "downwardly mobile Chicago area widow who becomes isolated, though not yet frequent among the older population, will probably increase in proportion with the years to come" (266).

The central thesis of Lopata's recently published book on support systems of widows "is that family background in urban living, generally leading to better formal schooling, is the necessary precondition to voluntaristic engage-ment in a modern urbanized society."[152] In this report of eight years of reading, research, and writing about widows in the metropolitan Chicago area, Lopata states that her sample includes more affluent widows than are present in the Chicago population, and that younger widows are overrepre-sented because of over-sampling of remarried women and of mothers of dependent children. She also states that the black widows are less represented than the whites, and that the Mexican and Puerto Rican widows are probably greatly underrepresented.[153] However, although the 82,085 widows do not include the highly disadvantaged, they do include "a sufficient number of the very poor to rule out an extreme bias" (57). Indeed, Lopata found that, of the widows who responded to questions about income, approximately 44 percent were living on incomes at or below the official poverty cutoff level. In her judgment, most of the older urban widows were socialized for a different way of life than that which they are now experiencing, and she does not think that younger generations of women will have to face many of the problems encountered by older widows in the city today. In fact, she writes that there are many ways in which the cohorts of women over the age of 60 are unique. However, she does not in any way imply that this would be a justification for neglecting them. The major problem "is that these women do not have sufficient contact with people who will listen to them and try to meet their needs as they define them, not as the observer defines them" (384). Lopata also recommends flexibility in work schedules through the adoption of flextime and other alternatives. She reports that the circumstances to which many of the widows have had to adapt may seem appalling to observers of contemporary life. And she concludes, "There are many ill, hungry, isolated, limited, non-involved widows who do not seek help, and to say that they are in that state voluntarily is no excuse for inadequate societal services, particularly those linking the person to existing resources" (386).

That there are remedies for the social isolation of older women is also the conclusion of a study of disaffiliation in New York City published under the title *Women Alone.*[154] This book is a report of the last two years of the Columbia Bowery Project, which was conducted between 1963 and 1970. "Disaffiliation" refers to people who live alone, are not employed, and are not members of any voluntary association. One reason that middle-aged and elderly women were selected as the focus of this study is that a majority of disaffiliates are women. Another is that there are so few studies of social isolation as it affects the lives of *women*, who—despite the fact that they outnumber men in the later stages of life—have not received the attention that men have been given by researchers in the sociology of aging and related areas of study.[155]

Women Alone is an analysis of interviews with 383 middle-aged and elderly women, including residents of three census tracts in Manhattan (each treated as a separate research site, and each consisting of a very mixed population within which the women were a minority), and 52 clients of a shelter for homeless women. The obstacles to be overcome in reaching reclusive women living in fear—difficulties compounded by the protective attitudes of hotel managers, doormen, and social workers—were awesome.[156] While interviews with these women provide information that is statistically reliable and that represents a valuable contribution to sociological theory, Theodore Caplow observes that these research findings

> are also unbelievably sad. Here are the lifestyles of the people for whom the metropolitan environment is least rewarding: elderly women living alone in dreary little rooms in huge shabby buildings without economic security or emotional response or personal recognition, without the gratification of

familiar pleasures or the excitement of new experiences, and without the elementary protections that ought to be offered by a civilized community [xvi].

While some of the isolation of the older women in Manhattan was voluntary, it was compounded by the well-founded fear in which they live, and by their poverty, and by poor health. Bahr and Garrett found that much of their social isolation is protective: fear, poverty, and poor health hold them back from taking advantage of the opportunities the city has to offer. They conclude, "The constricting social networks of these women represent a failure of delivery of social and human services, of democratic representation, and of governmental responsibilities to the disadvantaged" (133). Many of these women were dissatisfied with their lives, yet they could not see any way to break out of their isolation. Their collective portrait is one of "a decline in involvement, accompanied by a sense of futility and personal insecurity" (38). But because their condition is attributable to factors in their present lives rather than to their social backgrounds, it is remediable. There are other women living in the same neighborhoods who do get out and around the city "without having to risk their lives in the process," as the subjects of this study would have to do. More affluent women "can afford to use cabs and to live in apartments with high security," and therefore they can "go out alone and return and not ever be without a 'guardian' cabdriver or doorman" (37). Bahr and Garrett recommend that employment opportunities be made available to older women, and suggest that since most of the women interviewed for this study wanted to live in better housing, holding part-time jobs might be made a condition of acceptance into better-quality housing. They point out that this would resolve both the housing problem and the problem of isolation from social (work) groups. They also recommend that church groups or community agencies or volunteer groups provide (free) escort services for each housing establishment in the neighborhood. This would mean that a woman could have an escort available to take her out and to accompany her home without having to suffer the loss of face that is associated with the open admission of dependency or fear.

Every urban community has its own distinctive character. In a report on older women who live in SRO hotels in Seattle, Maureen Lally suggests that those she interviewed "may not have felt as personally threatened by crime or violence as other SRO populations" and that "this may reflect a comparative freedom of the Seattle downtown area from advanced stages of urban decay found in larger and older cities."[157] But her study shows that fear of crime and violence are not the only personal costs of social isolation, and that poor health can be the close companion of solitary living for women of severely limited financial resources. Lally cites evidence that social isolation is correlated with mortality. She concludes that those who have a restricted social network are physically more vulnerable than those who have the support a more extensive network provides, and that the high prevalence of health problems that she found among the women she interviewed may be directly related to their social isolation.

If the personal costs of social isolation are high, the social costs are no less so: *Woman Alone* documents the appalling waste of human talent in our society. Nearly two decades have passed since the Columbia Bowery Project was initiated. Although the names of people and programs have changed, the essential story it tells has for too long been part of our world-taken-for-granted. The researchers report that many of the women with whom they spoke are gifted people who have interesting experiences and who could make positive contributions to the lives of others. But this is impossible so long as they remain socially isolated. They have more freedom than many other people in our society, yet they are among the least likely "to take advantage of the range of activities" offered by the city of New York.[158] Consequently, their lives—and ours—remain impoverished. This can be said not only of New York, but of Chicago and Seattle and all other urban communities, and not only of older women who live alone at the very edge of respectability, but of street people as well. In *Women Alone,* Caplow reflects that homeless women are "something of a sociological mystery."[159] But that study concluded that even those at the Women's Shelter, who were especially problem-ridden, could be assisted through intervention programs. And in 1981, with the publication of *Shopping Bag Ladies,*[160] a collection of first-person stories with over 100 photographs, something of the "sociological mystery" of homeless women is unraveled. These oral histories provide documentary evidence of damaged lives and of human courage. They also attest to the waste of the giftedness of those whose presence among us has for so long gone unremarked.

Shopping bag ladies are an apposite subject for writers of naturalistic fiction, and also for satirists, who present social types as embodiments of societal conditions they intend to criticize through their literature. In a society that exalts youth and beauty and affluence, they may be seen as the Jungian shadow of our collective life. But they represent an extreme on the continuum of the fates of older women. Although this may be the very reason why they appeal to social critics and to writers who traffic in pathos or exotica, it may also explain why they do not dominate the popular image of older women in the United States. Interestingly enough, however, those at the *other* extreme of the continuum—wealthy dowagers who live in retirement communities—*are* part of that popular image. Sociological research has shown this to be wholly unwarranted, statistically speaking. (The prevalence of this social fiction is a worthy subject for research in itself, but one that remains unexplored.) In the United States today, about four of every five elderly persons live in "independent households." Only a minority live in independent households headed by a person *under* the age of 65. Most live in single-family houses that they own—houses that are, in general, older homes, of relatively low value, and in need of renovation or repairs (about one of every five households of elderly *rural* Americans is lacking in complete plumbing facilities). Of the majority of American elderly who live independently, only a very small percentage live in planned retirement communities. These are usually homogeneous in social class, racial and ethnic composition, and by definition in age composition. Moving to retirement communities appears to "self-select" older people amenable to living in an age-homogeneous milieu. This homogeneity fosters social interaction and the formation of friendships. Since members are drawn from the ranks of managerial and professional groups in many of these places, they are people accustomed to moving. And, unlike the isolated women in Lopata's study and the "women alone" in New York City, they have the social skills that are needed to make new friends in later life. Atchley reports that for most people who live in retirement communities, the move did not result in greater isolation from grown children, and that these communities provide normative support for those who want to concentrate on "leisure roles."[161]

Atchley concludes that retirement appears to have little impact on migration, since most elderly Americans "stay put" after they retire, and most of those who *do* move change residence for reasons other than a search for "retirement living." Only a minority who move cross county lines, and only one-fifth of these cross state lines as well. It appears to be a myth that retirement brings massive migrations in its wake, and Atchley doubts that migrations after retirement will ever become the norm in our society. Even so, retirement communities attracted considerable attention in the 1960s and the 1970s—from developers, from the media, and from sociologists. Jerry Jacobs reflects in his study of "Fun City" that the retirement-age population of this country has increased by 538 percent since 1900. But, as George and Louise Spindler observe in their foreword to his book, only the relatively affluent can afford to see it as an alternative style of living.[162] Later life is a time for age segregation in very few societies on this planet earth; moreover, age segregation of the elderly creates social and psychological problems of its own. Fun City is not all that different from the popular image of American middle-class society in general, with its wide streets and spaced houses, each with its separate lawn—*and* with its lack of public transportation facilities. (Fun City was studied before the OPEC shocks of the 1970s, when the sources of energy upon which this life-style is utterly dependent may have seemed to many to be inexhaustible.) To the Spindlers, the segregation of the elderly in America's Fun Cities "reflects the nomadic and fragmented character of American social and . . . familial life." The people who live inside the houses "are separated from each other and lonely, like the people in ordinary suburban communities, but the weakness of old age makes some of them even lonelier" (vi).

Fun City's ideal culture is "an active way of life." There are a great many planned activities and clubs, but only 200 to 300 people—the *same* people—participate in them on any given day, and only an estimated 300 to 400 people—probably even less than this number—can be seen in or around the Shopping Center area. Except for this "visible minority" who engage in planned or informal activities, the inhabitants of Fun City—the "invisible majority" or the other 5,500 residents—live in relative isolation; a mailman estimated that 25 percent of them never leave their houses. Outside the Town Hall–Activities Center area, the Civic Hall–Golf Club area, and the Shopping Center, a complex in a space of about six square blocks where the visible minority congregate, a sense of "eerie desolation" pervades the "community." Its architecture is "gray-on-gray," and so is the quality of social relationships.[163] Fun City is located about ninety miles southeast of a large metropolitan area. It is isolated from urban life, and most of its inhabitants are isolated from the hub of its *own* life, the Activities Center. Although many told Jacobs they came there for "security," Fun City has no police department, no fire department, no mayor, and no major medical facilities of its own. Houses, streets, and sidewalks are immaculate—and deserted. "There is only the yellow flicker of lamp lights, mixed with eerie white lights of TV screens shimmering through the drawn drapes, to indicate the presence of Fun City's inhabitants" (10–11).

It appears to be a general pattern that newcomers join clubs, are active for a while, and then, because of faltering interest or failing health, "drop out"— although on paper they are still "members" of organizations. One woman, a Fun City pioneer, told Jacobs how depressing she found the place to be when she and her husband first came there, and she remarked how much she and others accomplished in eight years in organizing clubs and activities. "You get out of a place what you put into it," she said (28–30). However, Jacobs observes, she was part of the visible minority of active residents, most of whom are women. Of the unseen majority, some would like to be active, but for some reason are unable to be. Others are quite deliberately *in*active. Ironically, the blasé attitude so adaptive for life in urban areas (from which most Fun City residents were recruited) is adaptive for life in Fun City as well. Mrs. O. told Jacobs in so many words that few residents are equipped to cope with Fun City's isolation. "Not everyone is a Thoreau," Jacobs writes, nor did most of these people live at Walden Pond. Residents must draw on inner resources, and few seem to have cultivated inner resources. Intellectual and artistic pursuits are virtually nonexistent; watching TV is a major leisure-time activity. One woman worked hard to present a positive image of Fun City to Jacobs—and wept in the process.

At Fun City, good neighbors are made by building good fences. Why, then, did these people come to live there? Because it was "safe." Yet there are no police, crime is underreported, and people do not *feel* safe. Because it is "healthy." Yet many have arthritis or rheumatism and cannot use the air-conditioned facilities, so they become "shut-ins." Fun City has no emergency or in-hospital facilities. Ambulance service is expensive. Transportation is a burning issue for many residents because they do not drive. Promises were not kept; transportation was guaranteed to people when they signed the papers, but 1,500 persons are without it. There is only one bus a day for those who need to go to the three major medical facilities in larger cities within a radius of thirty miles.

They came, residents told Jacobs, because there is "plenty to do" at Fun City. Yet most do nothing. They came because the place is "well situated." But few can use the freeways that make desert, beaches, and mountains accessible. They came to be closer to grown children's families, but for many this did not work out as well as had been expected. Furthermore, Fun City was supposed to be a cross-section of America. But there are no blacks there, no ethnic minorities, not even people from white "middle America," although many from each of these groups could afford it (46). Most households—2,238 of 2,992—are comprised of one male, one female (not necessarily married to one another); the next largest category—504 women—live alone. Interviews disclosed that the shopping was a disappointment, and that many avid golfers drive to a nearby retirement community to play because they found the course at Fun City mediocre and the expense far more than the "minimal cost" they had been promised.

Despite their disenchantment, many Fun City residents stay on. Jacobs attributes this in part to inertia and to the fact that it is much more difficult for older people to move again. Also, husbands and wives see things differently, and many live in a place because the will of one or the other prevailed. In an interesting interview with a couple, Jacobs reports that a Mrs. B. said Fun City seems "unnatural" to her, "Because youth needs age and age needs youth." Her husband remarked that sixty or seventy years of that was enough, that he was "glad to get out of it." The town, she persisted, is "unnatural . . . there is no such thing as old, old age, and nothing but." For her, this "isn't normal." Mr. B. regretted that he had to disagree. The town, he said, is "open," and they see children every weekend. But his wife replied, "You see, as if either they are little animals unusual to us or we become the zoo to them" (65). Some people cannot abide life in an age-segregated community. One woman spoke to Jacobs of how she had to overcome her feeling of "repulsion" at being surrounded by old people. "This is a retreat," she said. "It's sort of a false paradise. . . . We're not of the world and yet do we want to be?" (66)

In a brilliant and profound essay on the fate of old people in the Israeli kibbutz, the late Yonina Talmon reflected on "the over-emphasis of planning" typical of revolutionary societies. People assume all human problems can be resolved by comprehensive social reorganization. "Sooner or later," Talmon wrote, "they learn that social planning cannot cure all ills."[164] In his book about Fun City, Jacobs argues that "disengagement" of the old (as he interprets the term) is neither inevitable nor beneficial either for older people or for society. He believes that there is no one ideal retirement setting for all elderly people, and that the trend toward age-segregated, geographically isolated, and culturally homogeneous retirement settings ought to be reversed. Since about 70 percent of the total population of this country live in urban-metropolitan areas, "some effort should be made to integrate retirement communities into existing urban settings."[165] Thus, retirement communities could be reconstructed within "natural" environments. While Talmon's note of caution about the limitations of social planning ought to be appended to every social policy (for even in paradise there would be those who would find reasons for being discontented, and even the most perfect social arrangements cannot address the compelling needs of inner life), Jacobs' recommendation is well taken. Age-segregated "communities" are not true communities, and people who do not participate in public life are apt to forget their responsibilities as members of the human race.

However, age-segregated housing for the elderly has eloquent and compassionate defenders. The fact that older people with limited financial resources are vulnerable to becoming socially isolated has been well documented. Irving Rosow presents evidence that working-class people are "locality-centered," and therefore dependent upon their immediate environment for opportunities for making social contacts that might lead to new friendships.[166] Zena Blau believes that friendship is especially important in later life when ties to family and the workplace have become attenuated. "It is the *dispersion* of older people in the general community," she writes, "that promotes their social isolation." Since a working-class woman's social life probably was limited to her circle of kin and neighbors long before old age, she could be more isolated by widowhood than affluent older women. Her meager financial resources limit her even further in her chances for forming new friendships: "No matter how modest her social activities are, they usually cost money—the carfare required to pay visits, the refreshments offered to a guest, the price of a movie ticket."[167] Lopata makes the same point in her books about Chicago-area widows.

In some respects, the case for age-concentrated housing for the elderly is a strong one, since so many elderly are poor or "near-poor." But if dispersion results in social isolation, this is sometimes because of the serious problems afflicting the neighborhoods and communities where many older people live. Ultimately, these areas must be transformed if true community life is to come into being. Yet the same can be said of some areas where the elderly live in age-*concentrated* housing, as Stephens's study of the Guinevere attests. A comparison of research findings on this question exemplifies the complexity of the relationship between living arrangements and social isolation. For example, Lally and her associates' study of older women in the SROs in Seattle and Stephens's study of the people at the Guinevere suggest that there is a positive correlation between residence in an SRO and social isolation. However, in her book about the tenants of "problem" SROs, Joan Hatch Shapiro reports that in this "survival culture" made up of "a series of interlocking near-groups," within a world of "walled-off villages for society's rejects," a complex and profoundly social community life was discovered.[168] Shapiro also found that in every building, all the active leaders and organizers except one person were black, and all except one were women. She suggests that the racial differences in the effectiveness of mutual aid systems and in active participation in the recreational programs may be due to differences in socialization. The black women grew up in the rural South in an extended family system, moving from one kin-group member to another throughout childhood; the downwardly mobile middle-class whites, most of whom were elderly Irish, Italian, and Jewish single people, had an orientation that was "small-town" and "primary family." Thus Shapiro's study points to the importance of the ethnic and racial composition of an elderly population in influencing the quality of the peer-group relationships they create. It also points to the importance of differences between the sexes in the ways elderly people relate to one another. A number of studies of communities of older people report that the women are more gregarious than the men, and that older women in general appear to have more inner and social resources than do older men. One example of this is Sheila Johnson's study of the mobile-home park "Idle Haven" in California. Johnson found that overall, women were much more active in the park's formal and informal activities than the men were, and she also found that the women were decidedly easier to interview than the men.[169] Certainly, both Hochschild's and Stephens's studies suggest that the sex ratio of a population of older people does have some relationship to the quality of their communal life. Life at Merrill Court and life at the Guinevere might have been very different if in the case of the former the majority of residents were men, and if in the case of the latter they were women. However, sex and racial and ethnic composition are not the only variables that social gerontologists take into account in their analyses of social isolation in later life. Marital status is one of a number of other factors that must be considered, also. Sheila Johnson found that at Idle Haven, women who entered the park as widows had a much more difficult time making friends, and were far less active in park activities than married women or those who were widowed after they moved there.

In her definitive review of research developments on this subject, Frances Carp remarks the enormous influence that Rosow's landmark study has had on the field of gerontology, and specifically states many reasons why the generalization from that study, that total age segregation in housing is an ideal for the elderly, is unwarranted.[170] Carp writes that the various definitions of "older person" have in common only that all record this status as decremental, and this implies the provision of living environments to compensate for losses. Ambiguous and variable definitions of "older person" and of "housing and living environments," and constant shifts in the living environments and populations of older persons all contribute to the difficulties encountered by anyone who attempts to make valid general statements about the subject. Only three of every one hundred older persons participate in Housing and Urban Development programs, and the extent and nature of the needs of the remaining 97 percent are unknown. The lives of only a very small fraction of the older population are affected by federal subsidized low-cost housing and retirement communities. It is clear that if there is genuine commitment to providing adequate living environments for elderly Americans, the United States confronts a problem of considerable magnitude. Of special importance in assessing the situation of older women is Carp's observation that the greater numbers of older women, and their attraction to public housing, have the consequence that these living situations are "saturated" with older females, while elderly men gravitate toward old hotels and rooming houses. This, in turn, creates a tendency toward sex as well as age stratification. She presents a strong case for the importance of recognizing the varieties of "older persons" in the United States, and the need for a technology of communication between researchers—architects, planners, policymakers, and others—and those who implement research findings. The United States, Carp observes, was slow to undertake the task of housing its elderly citizens, compared with the response to this need in other industrialized nations. In her judgment, "The longer experience in other Western countries calls into question the wisdom of constructing disproportionate amounts of age-specific housing" (261).

The question of how we live encapsulates the question of how we ought to live, and there is no single answer to this question. As with everything else in life, the resolution of a problem fosters the development of new problems. In Maggie Kuhn's dialogue with the students in the Advanced Pastoral Studies Program at the San Francisco Theological Seminary, she was told by them that

> Asians believe it is shameful to send older persons away to a home; but, in effect, when they move out of their neighborhoods, the older people become isolated from their friends. When they're really too old to live alone, they have to move away from communities in which they've lived all of their lives and go to live with their children in order to retain their sense of dignity. Many times their children resent having to care for them and only do it because it is their duty. The parents become demoralized and give up living. Isolated from former friends and familiar surroundings, they have nothing to look forward to. They die lonely—and their children are relieved.[171]

The students stated that they wished they could promote retirement centers for Asians in Hawaii, because they thought that perhaps "even a facade of congeniality" might be preferable to the present situation. They observed that people often attempt to fashion the present and the future from the past:

> The WASP type of people who've gone through the Depression and want a nice safe place to be in their declining years opt for this playpen-type community because of what their past has been. Asians want the family image to stay intact, so they operate out of the past and also dehumanize the human experience.[172]

An Eden for the old, whether built on a desert or in a jungle, is a false paradise, as Jacobs's Fun City attests. But to be uprooted from all that is familiar for the sake of saving face is not much of an alternative.

Another possibility is that boarding and lodging be revived. Tamara Hareven has proposed that the earlier pattern be reversed, and that elderly people move in with young families. Noting that one-member households increased by almost 60 percent during the 1970s, and that more older people are living alone today than ever before in our history, Hareven stated that she believes people are coming to see the limitations of an over-emphasis on privacy, and to understand the isolating effect that family privacy has upon the elderly. She suggested that the presence of elderly persons in a household could foster the intergenerational relationships that benefit the young as much as the old. "Anticipating her critics," however, Hareven acknowledged "that government supervision would be needed to avoid exploitation of the elderly's labor and welfare benefits."[173] This proposal has considerable merit as a corrective for privatism and selfishness, the ills attendant upon an age-graded society. But in view of the exploitation of the elderly by profiteers in the nursing home industry, which led to the movement for federal regulations of these facilities, the need for government supervision cannot be overstated. And at this moment, the prospects for a strong and coherent federal role in this area as in others appear to be quite dim. In December 1981, President Reagan proposed extending the concept of federal "deregulation" to the nursing home industry. If this comes to pass, the responsibility for government supervision would devolve upon the states. Given the considerable variation in regulatory standards and patterns of reinforcement among the states, and the mobility of people in our society, elderly men and women who do not have family support systems—the very people who are most likely to be in nursing homes and most likely to be boarders and lodgers in other people's households—are vulnerable to exploitation. This was precisely what the movement for federal regulation of the nursing home industry was intended to correct. Thus, federal "deregulation" would result in state government supervision of these establishments, and the fate of an old person living in one of them would depend on the accident of geographic location. Furthermore, the policy of federal "deregulation" breeds divisiveness. With limited state funds and fierce competition between groups representing a wide variety of interests and programs, this social change—at this particular moment in our national history— could have the opposite effect of that which was intended.

It is only during the twentieth century that the gift of longevity was extended to so many, and the demographers have shown that the profound question of how this gift is to be received is an especially compelling one for women. And it was only during the decade of the 1970s that the movement for age equality was joined to the movement for sex equality. In that decade, social gerontologists were exhorted to explore the symbolic world of older women inductively,[174] and to include women in their research samples.[175] It was during the 1970s also that sociologists included middle-aged women ("women of a certain age"[176]) in their discussions of "older women." The collective portraits of older women that emerge from the agendas of social action groups and the publications of researchers may be taken as a call for transformations in our social arrangements—transformations that would follow from the recognition of the wholeness of life, of the indivisibility of work and play and learning and of childhood, youth, maturity, and old age. They may also be taken as a sign of a transformation of the consciousness of feminists. Until now, the great social movement of feminism has been, above all else, a declaration of our common sisterhood. Henceforth, it may be a declaration of our common daughterhood as well. In our society, the lives of older women have been such that they were most free to be true sisters to one another in childhood and in youth, but then not again until late maturity. There is another bond, older even than the sororal bond, that unites women at these same stages in life. Perhaps childhood's end comes with the awareness that the reconciliation of our responsibilities as daughters with our responsibilities as sisters is a lifelong task. This is an awakening to a higher consciousness, and it is the source of understanding what it is that the generations owe one another.

Notes

1. Findings of the study of the collective role images of husbands, wives, sons, and daughters, as these emerged from the various projections of respondents to this picture included in the Thematic Apperception Test, are reported in Bernice L. Neugarten and David L. Gutmann, "Age-Sex Roles and Personality in Middle Age: A Thematic Apperception Study," in Bernice L. Neugarten, ed., *Middle Age and Aging: A Reader in Social Psychology* (Chicago: The University of Chicago Press, 1968), pp. 58–71. This paper, and the book reporting on the Kansas City Study of Adult Life, Elaine Cumming, and William H. Henry, *Growing Old: The Process of Disengagement* (New York: Basic Books, Inc., 1961) are discussed in chapter 2.

2. Lawrence K. Frank, "Problems and Opportunities in the Maturation of Women: The Interpersonal and Social Aspects," in Irma H. Gross, ed., *Potentialities of Women in the Middle Years* (East Lansing, Mich.: Michigan State University Press, 1956), p. 118. Frank, author and lecturer, was formerly the director of the Caroline Zachry Institute of Human Development.

3. U.S. Department of Commerce, Bureau of the Census, Current Population Reports Special Studies, *A Statistical Portrait of Women in the U.S.*, Special Studies P23, No. 58 (Washington, D.C.: U.S. Government Printing Office, 1976), p. 3.

4. Beth J. Soldo, "America's Elderly in the 1980s," *Population Bulletin* 35, no. 4 (Washington, D.C.: Population Reference Bureau, Inc., 1980): 12.

5. As quoted in Robert C. Atchley, *The Social Forces in Later Life: An Introduction to Social Gerontology*, 3rd ed. (Belmont, Calif.: Wadsworth Publishing Co., Inc., 1980), p. 6.

6. Leon Bouvier, Elinore Atlee, and Frank McVeigh, "The Elderly in America," *Population Bulletin* 30, no. 3 (Washington, D.C.: Population Reference Bureau, Inc., 1975): 3–4.

7. Marie Marschall Fuller and Cora Ann Martin, Preface and Introduction, in Marie Marschall Fuller and Cora Ann Martin, eds., *The Older Woman: Lavender Rose or Gray Panther* (Springfield, Ill.: Charles C. Thomas, 1980), pp. vii–x, xi–xv.

8. Frances Merchant Carp, *A Future For the Aged: Victoria Plaza and Its Residents* (Austin, Tex.: The University of Texas Press, 1966.)

9. Rosemary Redmond, "Legal Issues Involving the Older Women," in Fuller and Martin, *The Older Woman*, pp. 228–33.

10. Elinor Waters and Betty White, "Helping Each Other," in Lillian E. Troll, Joan Israel, and Kenneth Israel, eds., *Looking Ahead: A Woman's Guide to the Problems and Joys of Growing Older* (Englewood Cliffs, N.J.: Prentice-Hall, Inc., 1977), pp. 184–93.

11. Jerry Jacobs, *Fun City: An Ethnographic Study of a Retirement Community* (New York: Holt, Rinehart and Winston, Inc., 1974.)

12. Jules Henry, *Culture Against Man* (New York: Vintage Books, Random House, Inc., 1963).

13. Publications by these social scientists are listed in the bibliography. The work by Marilyn R. Block, Janice L. Davidson, Jean D. Grambs, and Kathryn E. Serock, *Uncharted Territory: Issues and*

Concerns of Women Over Forty (College Park, Md.: University of Maryland Center on Aging, 1978) was published in a revised edition as Marilyn R. Block, Janice L. Davidson, and Jean D. Grambs, *Women Over Forty: Visions and Realities* (New York: Springer Publishing Co., Inc., 1981).

14. Tish Sommers, "On Growing Older Female: An Interview with Tish Sommers," in Fuller and Martin, *The Older Woman*, pp. 31–34.

15. Bernice L. Neugarten, "Age Groups in American Society and the Rise of the Young-Old," *The Annals of the American Academy of Political and Social Science* (September 1974) 415:190.

16. Block, et al., *Uncharted Territory*, p. 3.

17. At the Twenty-sixth Annual Conference on Aging held in Ann Arbor, Michigan, in 1973, it was decided that "older woman" would be defined as "any woman past menopause." *No Longer Young: Work Group Reports* (Ann Arbor, Mich.: The Institute of Gerontology, University of Michigan–Wayne State University, 1974), p. ix.

18. Ian Robertson, *Sociology*, 2nd ed. (New York: Worth Publishers, Inc., 1981), p. 597.

19. The work group reports were published as cited in note 17, above, and the papers were published in *No Longer Young: The Older Woman in America* (Ann Arbor, Mich.: The Institute of Gerontology, University of Michigan–Wayne State University, Occasional Papers in Gerontology No. 11, 1975).

20. These papers were published in Nancy Datan and Nancy Lohmann, eds., *Transitions of Aging* (New York: Academic Press, Inc., 1980).

21. *Growing Numbers, Growing Force. A Report From the White House Mini-Conference on Older Women* (The Long Report) (San Francisco, Calif.: Western Gerontological Society, and Oakland, Calif.: Older Women's League Educational Fund, 1981). This report includes the national Older Women's League agenda.

22. This committee was not included in the original plans for the White House Conference on Aging, but was added as a result of an intensive letterwriting campaign that was led by the Older Women's League, and after twenty of the twenty-one women in Congress signed a letter urging conference officials to add a committee on the concerns of older women. Judy Klemesrud, "Older Women: No Longer 'Invisible,'" *New York Times*, December 2, 1981, pp. C1, C8–C9.

23. Judy Klemesrud, "For Older Women, Parley Raises Hope," *New York Times*, December 5, 1981, p. 52. Klemesrud reports that many of the other thirteen committees at the conference were divided by charges that their memberships had been "stacked" with conservative delegates who were appointed by the Reagan administration "at the last minute," but that "the women's committee went about its work in a fairly peaceable manner and adopted forty-seven resolutions—many of them diametrically opposed to the Reagan Administration's policies." For example, the committee voted that cost-of-living increases in Social Security benefits be granted twice a year rather than once, that the one-third reduction in benefits for women who live with relatives or others be eliminated, and that women receive credit under the system for the years they devote to child care responsibilities. "The only major discord came," Klemesrud reports, "when a group of delegates tried to get the proposed Federal equal rights amendment placed on the committee's agenda." Although the chairperson, Josephine Oblinger, a Republican member of the Illinois House of Representatives, ruled that the subject was "not germane" to the concerns of older women (Oblinger said she had voted in favor of the amendment in the Illinois legislature), she was overruled on December 2, when committee members voted 87 to 20 "to approve a recommendation to use 'the full leadership of the Federal Government' to ensure passage of the E.R.A." Ibid.

24. Alice J. Kethley, "Women and Aging: The Unforgivable Sin," in Jean Ramage Leppaluoto, Joan Acker, Claudeen Naffziger, Karla Brown, Catherine M. Porter, Barbara A. Mitchell, and Roberta Hanna, eds., *Women On the Move: A Feminist Perspective* (Pittsburgh, Pa.: Know, Inc., 1973), pp. 39–45.

25. Matilda White Riley, "Old Women," *Radcliffe Quarterly* (June 1979), p. 7.

26. U.S. Department of Commerce, Bureau of the Census, *A Statistical Portrait of Women in the U.S.*, p. 5.

27. Soldo, "America's Elderly in the 1980s," p. 6.

28. The irony—that this book is being written by a member of that generation who will be

elderly at a time when being elderly may not attract so much attention as it does today, when our parents are old, nor so much as it may again by the second decade of the twenty-first century, when our children will be old—has not escaped me.

29. Matilda White Riley, "Social Gerontology and the Age Stratification of Society," *The Gerontologist* (Spring 1971, Part 1) 11(2): 79.

30. Ibid., p. 81. See also Matilda White Riley, Marilyn Johnson, and Anne Foner, "Age Strata in the Society," in *Aging and Society*, volume 3: *A Sociology of Age Stratification*, Matilda White Riley, Marilyn Johnson, and Anne Foner, eds. (New York: Russell Sage Foundation, 1972), p. 419.

31. Neal E. Cutler and Robert A. Harootyan, "Demography of the Aged," in Diana S. Woodruff and James E. Birren, eds., *Aging: Scientific Perspectives and Social Issues* (New York: D. Van Nostrand Co., 1975), pp. 35–38.

32. Soldo, "America's Elderly in the 1980s," p. 10.

33. Cutler and Harootyan, "Demography of the Aged," p. 40.

34. The projections of the absolute numbers and relative size of the elderly age segment of the U.S. population are derived from Soldo, "America's Elderly in the 1980s," pp. 7 and 10. It should be noted, however, that most Western European nations have higher percentages of elderly in their populations than does the U.S., and that in Austria, East Germany, West Germany, and Sweden, the proportion of those aged sixty-five and over has already passed 15 percent. Ibid., p. 8.

35. Riley, "Social Gerontology and the Age Stratification of Society," p. 84.

36. Riley calls attention to the fact that infant mortality weighs heavily in life expectancy statistics, and that the data she provides concerning the difference between the average length of life of those born in ancient Rome or medieval Europe and of the elderly in the U.S. today are based upon hypothetical rather than actual birth cohorts. Ibid., p. 84n.

37. Cutler and Harootyan, "Demography of the Aged," pp. 40–41.

38. Soldo, "America's Elderly in the 1980s," p. 15.

39. As sociologist Ian Robertson observes, "The great majority of the nation's preventable childhood deaths occur among the impoverished." Robertson, *Sociology*, p. 257. A study released by the Worldwatch Institute on December 12, 1981, entitled "Infant Mortality and the Health of Societies," reports that the infant mortality rate in the nation's capital rose to the highest of that in any city in the United States. Citing Washington, the Soviet Union, and Brazil as examples of "the paradox of low survival rates for newborn children in areas with relatively high incomes," the report studies infant mortality rates as a "social indicator" that may well reveal conditions which are concealed or obscured in gross national product or per capita income. The report states that the infant mortality rate reflects "not simply per capita stocks of food, clean water, medical care and so forth, but the actual availability of such amenities to all segments of a population." Research findings were that the infant mortality rate rose in Washington in the year 1979 to 1980 to 24.6 deaths per thousand from 22.2. But even this "all-time low" rate recorded for 1979 was higher by far than the infant mortality rate for all of the United States that year, which was 13. The report states that "the persistence of high death rates among the very young even in wealthy surroundings should act as a red flag to policy makers, signaling that beneath the surface of economic progress something is seriously wrong" and that a rising infant mortality rate "signals the entrenchment of a dual society." "Infant Mortality Highest In Capital," *New York Times*, December 13, 1981, p. 37.

40. These statistics are derived from Soldo, "America's Elderly in the 1980s," pp. 15–16. In Alex Comfort's view, "The patching-up of single age-dependent conditions is . . . both costly and of limited usefulness in producing further years of full-quality life." He states that it is possible that physical aging may be postponed in the future "not by removing single diseases, but by integral interference with a rate mechanism." Alex Comfort, "Aging: Real and Imaginary," in Ronald Gross, Beatrice Gross and Sylvia Seidman, eds., *The New Old: Struggling for Decent Aging* (Garden City, N.Y.: Anchor Press/Doubleday, 1978), p. 78.

41. For the points made here, I am indebted to Cutler and Harootyan, "Demography of the Aged," p. 37. Hereafter, reference to this essay will be cited in the text by page number.

42. John M. Crewdson, "New Administration and Congress Face Major Immigration Deci-

sions," *New York Times*, December 28, 1980, p. 1. The issues addressed in this news report—the disarray into which the immigration control system has fallen, and the debate concerning the establishment of controls over illegal immigration, and statutory ceilings on legal immigration— are beyond the scope of this book about older women. Nevertheless, it ought to be remarked that the size, and therefore the perceived significance, of every age segment of the population is related to that of every other.

43. Up to the year 2030, projections depend mainly upon plotting the future course of mortality, which is the most stable of the three demographic processes, as Soldo points out. She suggests that the future course of immigration, which is unpredictable, also plays a role, but she states that this role is minor. Soldo, "America's Elderly in the 1980s," p. 7.

44. The rise in median age over time is one indicator of the aging of the female population; another is the increase in the numbers and proportions of women in the older age segments of this population throughout the twentieth century. Although changes in the median age of all women in the U.S. have not been continuous or uniform, it increased from 22.4 to 30 years between 1900 and 1975, and it is anticipated that it will continue to rise in the years to come. Depending upon fertility, the median age of the female population will be between 33.1 and 38.2 in the year 2000. Furthermore, in every successive decade since 1900, women aged 65 and over have constituted a larger share of the total female population of this country. This increase, which *has* been continuous, was from 4 percent in 1900 to 12.1 percent in International Women's Year. U.S. Department of Commerce, Bureau of the Census, *A Statistical Portrait of Women in the U.S.*, pp. 3–6.

45. Soldo, "America's Elderly in the 1980s," p. 3. On this page, Soldo also points out that only half a century ago, life expectancy for men in the U.S. was 58, and for women it was 62; on pp. 11–12, she presents statistics on differences within the elderly population on the basis of race as well as of sex.

46. U.S. Department of Commerce, Bureau of the Census, *A Statistical Portrait of Women in the U.S.*, p. 4.

47. Soldo, "America's Elderly in the 1980s," p. 11.

48. As quoted in ibid.

49. Kate O'Neil, Recorder, "Economic and Legal Status," in *No Longer Young*, pp. 57–61.

50. Judy Klemesrud, "Improving the Self-Image of Older Women," *New York Times*, November 2, 1981, p. B9. In concluding her summary, Congresswoman Ferraro urged the participants "to inform their elected officials of the problems older women face and to support legislation that would help them."

51. *Fact Book on Aging: A Profile of America's Older Population*, Charles S. Harris, Research Coordinator (Washington, D.C.: The National Council on the Aging, Inc., 1978), p. 19. Soldo notes that, in 1978, nearly 17 of every 1,000 elderly men remarried, whereas only 2 of every 1,000 elderly women remarried. This reflects the very different size of the pool of eligible mates for elderly men and elderly women. See Soldo, "America's Elderly in the 1980s," p. 26.

52. *Fact Book on Aging*, p. 20.

53. These statistics are provided by the Census Bureau for 1976, and are tabulated in Soldo, "America's Elderly in the 1980s," p. 26.

54. *Fact Book on Aging*, p. 21.

55. Bernice L. Neugarten, "The Aged in the Year 2025," in Fuller and Martin, *The Older Woman*, pp. 339–40. Hereafter, reference to this article will be cited in the text by page number.

56. *Fact Book on Aging*, p. 47.

57. U.S. Department of Labor, Employment Standards Administration, Women's Bureau, *Mature Women Workers: A Profile* (Washington, D.C.: U.S. Government Printing Office, 1976), p. 12.

58. *Older Women: The Economics of Aging* (Washington, D.C.: The Women's Studies Program and Policy Center at George Washington University in conjunction with The Women's Research and Education Institute of the Congresswomen's Caucus, 1980), pp. 12, 49.

59. *Mature Women Workers*, pp. 2–3. Hereafter, reference to this publication will be cited in the text by page number.

60. Soldo, "America's Elderly in the 1980s," p. 19.

61. Bouvier, et al., "The Elderly in America," p. 13. Hereafter, reference to this publication will be cited in the text by page number.

62. *Older Women: The Economics of Aging*, p. 15. Hereafter, reference to this publication is cited in the text by page number.

63. Soldo, "America's Elderly in the 1980s," p. 19.

64. *Fact Book on Aging*, p. 55.

65. Soldo, "America's Elderly in the 1980s," p. 21. Hereafter, reference to this publication is cited in the text by page number.

66. See Clyde H. Farnsworth, "Reliability of U.S. Data," Washington Watch, *New York Times*, November 30, 1981, p. D2, and Philip Shabecoff, "Overhaul Is Urged In Jobless Figures," *New York Times*, July 16, 1978, p. 19.

67. Erdman Palmore, "The Future Status of the Aged," in Fuller and Martin, *The Older Woman*, pp. 323–31.

68. See Tish Sommers, "Cuts to Hit Women Hardest," Moving Right Along, *The Gray Panther Network*, July/August 1981, p. 9.

69. Atchley, *The Social Forces in Later Life*, p. 292.

70. Warren Weaver, Jr., "House Unit Finds Aged Getting Poorer," *New York Times*, May 2, 1981, p. 10. Early in 1980, Representative Claude Pepper, chairman of the House Select Committee on Aging, reported that 14.6 million elderly in the United States had incomes under $5,999 and over 16 million had incomes under $6,999—64 percent and 70 percent, respectively, of the total elderly population in America. Claude Pepper, Letter, *New York Times*, February 29, 1980, p. A30.

71. Soldo, "America's Elderly in the 1980s," p. 24.

72. Merton C. Bernstein, Letter, *New York Times*, May 17, 1981, p. 22E.

73. "Social Security Benefits to Be Raised 11.2% in July," *New York Times*, April 24, 1981, p. A18.

74. See *Fact Book On Aging*, pp. 60–65, and Soldo, "America's Elderly in the 1980s," pp. 23–24. Soldo reports that most of the victims of the heat wave of the summer of 1980 were elderly persons living in housing that did not have air conditioning, and that in households in which the head is aged 65 and over, "the median expenditure for all home fuels increased from $397 in 1975 to $651 in 1979—a 64 percent increase in just four years." Ibid., p. 24.

75. Erdman Palmore, "United States of America," in Erdman Palmore, ed., *International Handbook on Aging: Contemporary Developments and Research* (Westport, Conn.: Greenwood Press, 1980), p. 435.

76. See Soldo, "America's Elderly in the 1980s," p. 5.

77. Atchley, *The Social Forces in Later Life*, p. 140.

78. Elizabeth M. Fowler, "Women Without Pensions," Consumer Saturday, *New York Times*, November 21, 1981, p. 12. For a discussion of older women and pensions, see *Older Women: The Economics of Aging*, pp. 18–26.

79. This was one of the points made by Tish Sommers in her keynote address to the Committee on the Concerns of Older Women on the first day of the White House Conference on Aging. Judy Klemesrud, "Conference on Aging Views Older Women," *New York Times*, December 1, 1981, p. A28.

80. U.S. Department of Health, Education and Welfare, *Social Security and the Changing Roles of Men and Women* (Washington, D.C.: U.S. Department of Health, Education, and Welfare, 1979).

81. It is noted in the Introduction that any significant revision of the Social Security program is complicated by the fact that 6 million public employees are not covered by it, and that—unless coverage is universal—the options must be re-examined with a view toward avoiding the anomalous effects of a system whereby one spouse has protection under a public pension system that is based on non-covered employment. Ibid., p. 6.

82. Ibid., p. 12. Unless otherwise indicated, the discussions of issues related to adequacy and equity are based upon chapter 1 of this report.

83. Christopher Connell, "Quietly, Congress cuts $2 billion in SS benefits," *Poughkeepsie (N.Y.) Journal*, August 23, 1981, p. 7A.

84. *Older Women: The Economics of Aging*, p. 20.

85. Separated and divorced homemakers, many of whom are not supported by their spouses or former spouses, are in an especially critical situation. "In some cases, these women become disabled before having the opportunity to get a covered job (or to work long enough to be insured for benefits) after the separation or divorce occurred and may not be eligible for benefits under the Supplementary Security Income program." Ibid., p. 19.

86. This discussion is based on *Social Security and the Changing Roles of Men and Women*, pp. 28–33.

87. Tish Sommers and Laurie Shields, *Social Security: Adequacy* and *Equity for Older Women*, Gray Paper No. 2 (Oakland, Calif.: Older Women's League Educational Fund, 1979), p. 1. Hereafter, references to this publication will be cited in the text by page number.

88. Warren Weaver, Jr., "House Votes to Keep Minimum Retirement Benefit," *New York Times*, December 17, 1981, p. B16.

89. Christina Long, "Social Security: The Right On the Rampage," *Gray Panther Network*, November/December 1981, p. 6.

90. Merton C. Bernstein, Letter, *New York Times*, May 17, 1981, p. 22E.

91. See Tish Sommers, "My Health and Yours," and TASKFORCE Reports: "Who Cares about Older Women. . . ," *Gray Panther Network*, September/October, 1979, pp. 4, 7.

92. See "Widows Would Be Aided Under Pension Law Change," *New York Times*, February 7, 1979, p. A16.

93. Leslie Bennetts, "Displaced Homemakers: Struggling With Insecurity," *New York Times*, June 15, 1979, p. A16.

94. The latter figure, reported in Sommers and Shields, *Social Security: Adequacy* and *Equity For Older Women*, p. 3, n. 7, is derived from the HEW Report.

95. Victor Kassel, a geriatric physician, addresses another compelling issue, that of the low sex ratio of the elderly population, and recommends the institutionalization of polygyny for those aged 60 and over. Among the advantages of this system are the opportunities it would provide for widowed women to remarry, and the chance to establish meaningful family groups again in late life, the sharing of resources for health care and domestic responsibilities, and the fostering of opportunities for sexual expression in old age. Victor Kassel, "Polygyny after 60," *Geriatrics* (April 1966) 21(4):214–18.

96. Juanita Kreps and Robert Clark, *Sex, Age, and Work: The Changing Composition of the Labor Force* (Baltimore: The Johns Hopkins University Press, 1975), p. 10.

97. Juanita Kreps, *Sex in the Marketplace: American Women at Work* (Baltimore: The Johns Hopkins University Press, 1971), p. 14.

98. Ibid., p. 30.

99. Kreps and Clark, *Sex, Age, and Work*, pp. 10–12.

100. Corinne Azen Krause, "Italian, Jewish, and Slavic Grandmothers in Pittsburgh: Their Economic Roles," *Frontiers* (Summer 1977) 2(2):18–19. Krause reports that of the three ethnic groups of grandmothers, Italian women were least likely and Slavic women most likely to be employed outside their homes. See pp. 19–27.

101. Virginia R. Allan, "Economic and Legal Status of the Older Woman," in *No Longer Young*, pp. 25–26. On p. 28, Allan provides information about legal restrictions against discrimination in employment on the basis of age and sex. Juanita Kreps observes that the middle-aged woman's needs have been, for the most part, ignored. For her critical discussion of continuing education for older women, see Kreps, *Sex in the Marketplace*, pp. 88–89.

102. Elizabeth Pope, "Divorce, Death of Husbands Make Millions 'Displaced' Homemakers," *The Sunday Freeman* (Kingston, N.Y.), January 1, 1978, p. 16.

103. This figure is cited in *Older Women: The Economics of Aging*, p. 5, n. 7.

104. Pope, "Divorce, Death of Husbands Make Millions 'Displaced' Homemakers," loc. cit. The Displaced Homemakers' Bill, sponsored by Burke and Bayh, was introduced as an amendment to

106 *Chimes of Change and Hours*

the federal manpower funds in January 1978. A displaced homemakers' bill was passed by the Maryland State Legislature in 1976, patterned after the first displaced homemaker legislation instituted in California. See the discussion on displaced homemakers in Marilyn Block, et al., *Uncharted Territory*, pp. 138–39.

105. Tish Sommers, "The Compounding Impact of Age on Sex," in Ronald Gross, Beatrice Gross, and Sylvia Seidman, eds., *The New Old*, p. 131. This paper was originally published in 1974, in the Fall issue of *Civil Rights Digest*.

106. "Retirement," *Family Weekly*, April 22, 1979, p. 42. This poll was sponsored by Johnson and Higgins, an employee benefit consulting and actuarial firm.

107. Kreps and Clark, *Sex, Age, and Work*, p. 64.

108. Ibid., p. 60. See the section on "Unemployment: Measured and Real," pp. 60–64.

109. Harold L. Sheppard, "The Status of Women, 1993–1998: Financial Aspects," in *No Longer Young*, pp. 108–9. Note that Sheppard makes the important point here that these statistics belie the popular notion that women work mainly to earn "pin money." This notion is as stubborn as it is erroneous, and has been argued by those of a variety of persuasions throughout the course of the twentieth century.

110. These figures were provided by Secretary of Labor Raymond J. Donovan, who presented them as one of the effects of the 1980 "economic slowdown" in "Ask Them Yourself," *Family Weekly*, November 29, 1981, p. 3.

111. Sommers and Shields, *Social Security: Adeqaucy* and *Equity for Older Women*, p. 15.

112. The Fatherhood Project "is analyzing the effect of new practices such as paternity leave, custody-mediation services and company-sponsored educational policies on men's participation in parenthood." Glen Collins, "Paternity Leave: A New Role for Fathers," *New York Times*, December 7, 1981, p. B18.

113. *Social Security and the Changing Roles of Men and Women*, pp. 104–5. Hereafter, reference to this publication will be cited in the text by page number.

114. Wilbur J. Cohen, "Social Security: Next Steps," in *No Longer Young*, p. 99.

115. Kreps and Clark, *Sex, Age, and Work*, p. 55.

116. Ibid., pp. 79–80. See the proposals for change on p. 80.

117. Ibid., p. 4.

118. Robert N. Butler, *Why Survive? Being Old in America* (New York: Harper and Row, 1975), p. 384.

119. Matilda White Riley and Joan Waring, "Age and Aging," in Robert K. Merton and Robert Nisbet, eds., *Contemporary Social Problems*, 4th ed. (New York: Harcourt Brace Jovanovich, Inc., 1976), pp. 400–01.

120. This information was obtained from a memorandum sent to me as a Senior Citizen Advocate from Stanley Fink, Speaker of the Assembly, State of New York, about the 1981 White House Conference on Aging.

121. Klemesrud, "Improving the Self-Image of Older Women."

122. Richard A. Kalish and Sam Yuen, "Americans of East Asian Ancestry: Aging and the Aged," *The Gerontologist* (Spring 1971, Part II) 11(2):38.

123. Block, et al., *Uncharted Territory*, p. 179.

124. Jackson is also the author of *Minorities and Aging* (Belmont, Calif.: Wadsworth Publishing Co., 1980), in which she discusses Black American women and men, American Indian women and men, Asian American women and men, Hispanic American women and men, and Anglo-American women.

125. Helena Znaniecki Lopata, *Widowhood in an American City* (Cambridge, Mass.: Schenkman Publishing Co., Inc., 1973), pp. 109–10.

126. Corinne Azen Krause, *Grandmothers, Mothers and Daughters: An Oral History Study of Ethnicity, Mental Health, and Continuity of Three Generations of Jewish, Italian, and Slavic-American Women* (New York: The Institute on Pluralism and Group Identity of the American Jewish Committee, 1978), pp. 148–50.

127. Sarah Matthews, *The Social World of Old Women: Management of Self-Identity* (Beverly Hills, Calif.: Sage Publications, Inc., 1979), p. 125.

128. Neugarten, "Age Groups in American Society," p. 192. This proportion is expected to increase because the numbers of the "old-old" are growing faster than those of the "young-old."

129. Jacquelyne Johnson Jackson, "Older Black Women," in Lillian E. Troll, Joan Israel, and Kenneth Israel, eds., *Looking Ahead: A Woman's Guide to the Problems and Joys of Growing Older* (Englewood Cliffs, N.J.: Prentice-Hall, Inc., 1977), p. 152.

130. Atchley, *The Social Forces in Later Life*, p. 351.

131. Ethel Shanas, "Social Myth as Hypothesis: The Case of the Family Relations of Old People," *The Gerontologist* (February 1979) 19(1):3–9. See Louis Harris, et. al., *The Myth and Reality of Aging in America* (Washington: The National Council on the Aging, Inc., 1975) for general comparisons of fact and fiction about aging in America.

132. See, for example, Sidney M. Greenfield, "Industrialization and the Family in Sociological Theory," in Meyer Barash and Alice Scourby, eds., *Marriage and the Family: A Comparative Analysis of Contemporary Problems* (New York: Random House, Inc., 1970), pp. 9–27. Barbara Laslett reports she finds "good demographic reasons to believe that the nuclear family form was predominant *before* the advent of industrialization, at least in western Europe and America." Barbara Laslett, "The Family as a Public and Private Institution: An Historical Perspective," *Journal of Marriage and the Family* (August 1973) 35(3):481. (Italics mine.)

133. Gerald R. Leslie, *The Family in Social Context* (New York: Oxford University Press, 1967), pp. 322–37.

134. Beth B. Hess, "Family Myths," *New York Times*, January 9, 1979, p. A19. Hess writes that there is little evidence to support the notion that three-generation households "were psychologically sounder, healthier, or . . . better than the contemporary model." In her view, one of the strengths of the contemporary family may reside in the independence of adult generations its structure implies and the mutual respect that this independence fosters.

135. Laslett, "The Family as a Public and Private Institution," pp. 485–86.

136. Anne Foner, "Age Stratification and the Changing Family," in John Demos and Sarane Spence Boocock, eds., *Turning Points: Historical and Sociological Essays on the Family* (Chicago: University of Chicago Press, 1978), pp. S344–62. Foner reminds her readers that the nineteenth century, too, was shaken by great upheaval and social change, that the family itself is in a continuous process of change, and that "the tendency to refer to the 19th century (or the 20th century) as a whole obscures the differences among families starting out at various periods throughout the century." Ibid., p. S358.

137. David Hackett Fischer, *Growing Old in America* (New York: Oxford University Press, 1977), p. 56. See also p. 57, continuation of n. 62, in which Fischer discusses differences in residence patterns among western, central, and eastern European countries. Jan Stehouwer has suggested that the type of household arrangement in western Europe, in which the first generation moves into the household of the second, may be more urban than rural in origin. "The lack of public care for the aged, the absence of medical care, and the very unattractive institutions for the aged a hundred or even only fifty years ago," he writes, must have figured very prominently in decisions to form three-generation households in urban areas. Jan Stehouwer, "Relations Between Generations and the Three-Generation Household in Denmark," in Meyer Barash and Alice Scourby, eds., *Marriage and the Family: A Comparative Analysis of Contemporary Problems* (New York: Random House, Inc., 1970), pp. 173–74.

138. Fischer, *Growing Old in America*, pp. 62–63.

139. William H. Harlan, "Social Status of the Aged in Three Indian Villages," in Bernice L. Neugarten, ed., *Middle Age and Aging: A Reader in Social Psychology* (Chicago: The University of Chicago Press, 1968), pp. 473–74.

140. Robert A. Le Vine, "Intergenerational Tensions and Extended Family Structures in Africa," in Meyer Barash and Alice Scourby, eds., *Marriage and the Family: A Comparative Analysis of Contemporary Problems* (New York: Random House, Inc., 1970), p. 145.

141. Fischer, *Growing Old in America,* p. 37. Fischer also points out that if one had low status in early America (as poor elderly widows did), one had far less protection than those who have low status today. Ibid., p. 60.

142. Ruth Harriet Jacobs, *Life After Youth: Female, Forty—What Next?* (Boston: Beacon Press, 1979).

143. See note 127.

144. Joyce Stephens, *Loners, Losers, and Lovers: Elderly Tenants in a Slum Hotel* (Seattle, Wash.: University of Washington Press, 1976.) On page 96, Stephens states that sociologists should study specific populations of the elderly "in their natural settings." The locale of Stephens's study is identified as Detroit in Maureen Lally, Eileen Black, Martha Thornock, and J. David Hawkins, "Older Women in Single Room Occupant (SRO) Hotels: A Seattle Profile," in Fuller and Martin, *The Older Women,* pp. 304–16. Hereafter, references to *Loners, Losers, and Lovers* will be cited in the text by page number.

145. During the first two months of Stephens's field work, there was an armed robbery, there were three beatings; "a woman was thrown out of a sixth-floor window, a tenant was gunned down by police officers in the lobby, a recently released mental patient threatened tenants with a loaded gun," pimps roughed up at least six elderly tenants, and there were fights in the bar. Ibid., p. 49.

146. Arlie Russell Hochschild, *The Unexpected Community: Portrait of An Old Age Subculture* (Berkeley, Calif.: University of California Press, 1973). Hereafter, reference to this book will be cited in the text by page number.

147. In the 1950s, special public housing for the elderly was developed in the state of California. Merrill Court was completed in 1965. It was funded by federal, state, and county governments, and by a private donor after whom it was named. Ibid., p. 15. Hochschild notes that HEW provided over a million dollars in grants for experimental cooperative or communal living arrangements for the elderly, experiments already undertaken in Philadelphia, Kansas City, Honolulu, Syracuse, New York City, and Washington. Ibid., p. 150.

148. For a discussion of Hochschild's methodology, see page 142 (her Notes), and pages 3–6 in the text.

149. Ibid., pp. 17, 70–71, xiii.

150. In Lopata's opinion, "The social role of friend does not have strong ideological support for adults in American society." Lopata, *Widowhood in an American City,* p. 215. Lopata, Hochschild, and Stephens are all strongly critical of the assumption of intrinsic processes of aging that they believe to be implicit in disengagement theory. This theory, which is developed in Elaine Cumming and William H. Henry, *Growing Old: The Process of Disengagement* (New York: Basic Books, 1961), is discussed in chapter 2. Hereafter, all references to *Widowhood in an American City* will be cited in the text by page number.

151. Of the respondents, 41 percent live in single-family detached dwellings, 2 percent in single-family attached structures, 16 percent in the "two flats" of Chicago's older workingman's neighborhoods, 18 percent in buildings with ten or more units, and the remainder in apartments with from three to nine households. Boardinghouses and retirement hotels with units that do not have separate cooking facilities were omitted from the study. Ibid., p. 223.

152. Helena Znaniecki Lopata, *Women as Widows: Support Systems* (New York: Elsevier North Holland, Inc., 1979), p. 285.

153. Ibid., pp. 57, 297, n. 1. Hereafter, reference to this book will be cited in the text by page number.

154. Howard M. Bahr and Gerald R. Garrett, *Women Alone: The Disaffiliation of Urban Females* (Lexington, Mass.: D.C. Heath and Co., 1976).

155. Ibid., p. 3. Bahr and Garrett note that the fact that elderly men have been much more studied than elderly women is "a situation that is self-perpetuating in the sense that researchers tend to study populations about which a fund of empirical knowledge already exists." Ibid., p. 4.

156. In Appendix A, on Data Collection, it is noted that there were many reasons given for

refusing to admit interviewers, and that one factor contributing to their inclination to refuse to see the researchers "was the habitual isolation and privacy of some of the women. After many years of being ignored, a sudden confrontation with a stranger who wants to ask questions can be an alarming incident." Ibid., p. 148. It is also reported that many women refused to reveal their age and that, at the Women's Shelter, male interviewers were much more successful in persuading the women to talk with them than were the female interviewers (pp. 149, 163). Hereafter, references to this book will be cited in the text by page number.

157. Lally, et. al., "Older Women in Single Room Occupant (SRO) Hotels," p. 308.

158. Bahr and Garrett, *Women Alone*, p. 133.

159. Theodore Caplow, "Foreword," *Women Alone*, p. xv.

160. Ann Marie Rousseau, *Shopping Bag Ladies: Homeless Women Speak About Their Lives* (New York: The Pilgrim Press, 1981).

161. Atchley, *The Social Forces in Later Life*, pp. 178–79, 327–28.

162. George and Louise Spindler, "Foreword," in Jacobs, *Fun City*, p. vi. Hereafter, all references to this publication will be cited in the text by page number.

163. Jacobs notes that "garden apartments" were under construction at the time of his study, intended as "an intermediate setting for residents, somewhere between the home owners and apartment dwellers . . . and those who can no longer care for themselves and who reside in the adjacent nursing home. With the completion of these apartments a full range of living accommodations will be available to the resident to meet his every need, from early retirement to death." Ibid., pp. 1–2. In some ways, he states, Fun City resembles other "total-institutional" settings— except that in Fun City, the isolation is self-imposed (2–3).

164. Yonina Talmon, "Aging in Israel, A Planned Society," in Bernice L. Neugarten, ed., *Middle Age and Aging: A Reader in Social Psychology* (Chicago: The University of Chicago Press, 1968), p. 466.

165. Jacobs, *Fun City*, p. 83. For an excellent discussion of theories of aging, see ibid., pp. 72–84.

166. Irving Rosow, *Social Integration of the Aged* (New York: The Free Press, 1967). Hochschild, in *The Unexpected Community*, pp. 137–40, discusses Rosow's work in the context of her analysis of Merrill Court as a "forecast of things to come."

167. Zena Smith Blau, *Old Age in a Changing Society* (New York: New Viewpoints, A Division of Franklin Watts, Inc., 1973), pp. 94–96. See also p. 88. Blau finds Rosow to be the shining exception among researchers in his interest in the *nature* of the filial bond, rather than in the number of contacts elderly parents have with grown children. For Blau's discussion of "intimacy at a distance" as "a euphemism for pseudo-intimacy," see pp. 50–56.

168. Joan Hatch Shapiro, *Communities of the Alone: Working With Single Room Occupants in the City* (New York: Association Press, 1971), pp. 124, 23.

169. Sheila K. Johnson, *Idle Haven: Community Building Among the Working-Class Retired* (Berkeley, Calif.: University of California Press, 1971). Idle Haven may be seen as the working-class counterpart to Fun City. In Johnson's opinion, even if mobile-home parks such as Idle Haven disappear in the near future, the needs of those to whom they appeal are not likely to disappear.

170. Frances M. Carp, "Housing and Living Environments of Older People," in Robert H. Binstock and Ethel Shanas, eds., with the assistance of Associate Editors Vern L. Bengston, George L. Maddox, and Dorothy Wedderburn, *Handbook of Aging and the Social Sciences* (New York: Van Nostrand Reinhold Co., 1976), pp. 258–59. Carp states that her own study of Victoria Plaza *(A Future For the Aged)* is often mistakenly cited as support for age segregation in housing the elderly, whereas it "has no data on age segregation *vs.* age integration." Ibid., p. 260. Hereafter, reference to Carp's "Housing and Living Environments of Older People" will be cited in the text by page number.

171. Dieter Hessel, ed., *Maggie Kuhn on Aging: A Dialogue Edited by Dieter Hessel* (Philadelphia: The Westminister Press, 1977), p. 45.

172. Ibid. Kuhn, founder of the Gray Panthers, sees today's elders as "society's futurists" who

"ought to be doing future testing of new instruments, new technologies, concepts, ideas, and styles of living." There are those among the elderly today, she says, who have the freedom to experiment, and who have nothing to lose, who "would like to swim against the tide of fierce economic competition and try other kinds of arrangements whereby work gets done and common tasks are shared." Kuhn speaks of how this might be facilitated by putting together a skill bank in a religious congregation: "Who knows, out of such modest, small experiments some new knowledge and economic systems might emerge." Ibid., p. 80.

173. Hareven, founder of *The Journal of Family History*, outlined her proposal at a session of the White House Conference on Families in April 1980. "Boarding House Concept Proposed to Provide Homes for Elderly," *New York Times*, April 17, 1980, p. C14. Government regulation is also necessary if boarding homes are not to become "psychiatric ghettoes." See Edward A. Gargan, "As 'Psychiatric Ghettoes,' Boarding Homes Get More Dangerous," *New York Times*, February 8, 1981, p. 6E.

174. Diane Beeson, "Women in Studies of Aging: A Critique and Suggestions," *Social Problems* (October 1975) 23(1):52–59.

175. Barbara Payne and Frank Whittington, "Older Women: An Examination of Popular Stereotypes and Research Evidence," *Social Problems* (April 1976) 23(4):488–504.

176. Lillian Rubin adopted this phrase as the title for her book about issues and concerns in the lives of 160 women interviewees aged 35 to 54. Lillian B. Rubin, *Women of a Certain Age: The Midlife Search For Self* (New York: Harper and Row, 1979).

2
Women in the Second Half of Life

Often it happens people are so caught by the new things they
learn in the journey into the unconscious that they immediately want to give it to the world or make a system. It is
natural but not wise, for it is easier to attempt to save others
than oneself, and so put the problem of redemption outside.
—Rix Weaver,
The Old Wise Woman—A Study of Active Imagination

When human life is seen steadily and seen as whole, transitions from one
phase of the life course to another are understood as "passages," each the
crossing of a threshold. In religion and mythology, the journey through time
is a pilgrimage, a procession from one station to the next. Face and form,
spirit and intellect, status and role in the societal world and value in the
cultural world, emotions and moral character—all are shaped and altered
and, finally, transformed in the odyssey of growing older. Aging is an experience of body and mind, of social self and spirit, of feeling and thought—and
these are indivisible. Their unity is as essential as the unity of the childhood
and youth, maturity and old age of a human life. Yet no people anywhere on
earth in any period of history has ever achieved perfection in expressing this
fundamental unity. In one culture, the mind is exalted, in another the body,
in a third the soul, in a fourth the social arrangements. In our own, the
biological and social aspects of aging are given close attention, and for this
reason the changes in soul and spirit and mind are taken by many to be of
secondary importance, or even as wholly determined by changes that are
physiological or sociological in nature. The quarrel over which of these aspects of the human condition is transcendent is the oldest quarrel in the social
sciences. Whatever their other differences may be, anthropologists and
economists, political scientists and sociologists are all of the opinion that social
and cultural realities are things in themselves that cannot be reduced to the
realm of the psyche. For their part, psychologists, who may disagree about
every other issue, agree that inner life is not a mere emanation of the social
and cultural arrangements. The only dissenting opinion among their ranks is
that of the behaviorists, who focus on observable actions and thus are not
concerned with inner life or personality development and change.

Reality is always a matter of definition, of perspective—ultimately, perhaps, of inclination. In this chapter, the inner life of older women is perceived as a thing-in-itself, not as an epiphenomenon of other forces. But since inner and outer reality are indivisible, both are interwoven in these pages—as they are in life. The possibilities of the second half of life are defined here as freedom, creative expression of unique and individual gifts, and fulfillment of the sense of responsibility that is felt all the more keenly by people as they grow older. Since the Renaissance, these have been thought to be within the reach of humanity. But "humanity," almost without exception, has been taken to mean *men*—and *young* men at that. This quest for the chance older women in the United States may have for personality growth and creativity and productivity in later life is guided by the Renaissance vision of what human life could be. Inside cultural forms and under sociological surfaces, older women are seen as aspiring to freedom, to the discovery and expression of creativity, and to the chance to leave a legacy for future generations. If this conception of older women is radical, it is long overdue. Views of older women in other times and places provide a broad field of vision within which the possibilities of older women in this particular time and country may be explored.

Older Women in Cross-Cultural Perspective

One of the great gifts of the study of anthropology is liberation from the notion that one's own way of life is the only one that is possible for humanity, that it is a "natural" expression of what it means to be human. In learning about other cultures, one comes upon myriad interpretations of the meaning and purpose of human life and social organization. One moral lesson of the principle of cultural relativism is tolerance, and this is instruction of no mean substance. But it is not the only one. Learning of another way of life alters one's perspective in a fateful way. It creates distance—moral distance— between the observer and "home." It reveals the "world-taken-for-granted," so that what was once so familiar now appears somewhat strange, as the sound and structure of the native tongue to one who is mastering another language.

Anthropologist Estelle Fuchs writes that, as her career went along, it be- came ever more clear to her that the various social roles having to do with romantic appeal, with economic and political power, and with other spheres of life that have been assigned to older women in different times and places "contrasted sharply with the constricted view of female middle age prevalent in this society."[1] In her inquiry into women's "second season," Fuchs found that the demarcation of middle age varies from one society to another, that in our own there is no consensus about when one may be said to be middle-aged, and that age is much more a matter of social status and role than of birth date. While menopause may be "the station stop of old age" in some societies, there are others in which there is no concern about it, "and femininity and activity go on and on" (2). In some societies, women are taught to anticipate that they will experience difficulties at this time in their lives; in others, there is not even a word in the vocabulary for "menopause." In some societies, menopause is a stigma; in others, women have been given positions of honor and authority in later life. Fuchs concludes from her cross-cultural study, "There is nothing natural about the woman at menopause being either incompetent, unnecessary, unlovely, or unwanted and depressed" (60).

Anatomy does not have to be destiny. The most stubborn and powerful prejudices succumb before cross-cultural analysis—even the notion that women are sexually attractive and desirable to men only when they are young. The traditional Lovedu, a Bantu people of southern Africa, did not live as if they believed this to be the case. For these people—as, indeed, for most people throughout the world, over the generations in human history—marriage had much broader social significance than the forging of a sexual and economic bond between two individuals. Marriage was the occasion for definition and social control of the relationship between groups of people. It was a very serious matter, indeed, for what was at stake was the perpetuation of the society itself. The norm in these societies was arranged marriage, rather than free choice of mates. Among the Lovedu, it was the custom for marriages to be arranged between persons of similar ages. For these people, it was acceptable for spouses to seek sexual adventure outside of marriage, and it was not the unmarried, but the married who had lovers. "Significantly," Fuchs reports, "it was the *older* women who frequently had their liaisons with the young married men, and these men sought their adventures with women who might well be their mothers or grandmothers." Among the Coast Salish of the Pacific Northwest, too, it was not at all uncommon for young men to be engaged in romantic courtships with post-menopausal women (8–9). Of course, sexual liaisons between younger men and older women are not unknown in the United States, in spite of the prejudice against this in many circles. But its relative rarity is attested by the attention it receives when an alliance of this nature is made known in a community or to the public in general. Many people believe that it is unnatural, and this may be why the satire in the film *Harold and Maude* was so effective. One of the features of the Oneida community of Perfectionists that made it such an extraordinary utopian experiment was that no distinction was made between men and women in encouraging sexual liaisons between younger and older members by the principle of "ascending fellowship."[2]

The prejudice against romantic and sexual attachments between younger men and older women is ancient, and Fuchs suggests that one of the major reasons for this is the value placed upon women's ability to procreate. Until only very recently in human history, rates of infant and maternal mortality were very high in most societies, and life expectancy correspondingly low. It may not be too much to say that continuation of the human group was the first law of life for most people around the world. It is only in our own time, Fuchs reflects, that so many millions of women may expect to live one third of their lives beyond the childbearing years. "And with that much time left," she adds, "it is illogical to connect sex only with childbearing."[3]

Although many are still haunted by Victorian morality, there are others who are able to make a clear distinction between the ability to procreate and the ability to enjoy sex. Sex, as the Abkhasians see it, brings pleasure and good health, and, like a good wine, improves with age. Fuchs provides impressive evidence to support her contention that women's sexual interest and activity do not inevitably decline with aging. Many women experience a resurgence of sexual interest in midlife. She refers to the research findings of a study conducted at Duke University that linked the availability of an interested sex partner to the continuation of sexual activity into old age. Thus, it is probably the decline in the sex ratio rather than the decline in sexual interest that accounts for the corresponding decline in sexual activity that many women experience as they grow older. It is practice that keeps one young sexually, according to Masters and Johnson, and Fuchs observes that the Nzakara, who live on the Ubangi River in eastern Africa, are in full agreement with this, for they "have no room for single women. They believe that a woman who no longer has a husband immediately becomes old!" (13) The old beliefs die hard, however, even in our own society. Fuchs cites a study by Diana Scully and Pauline Bart in which it was found that half the 27 gynecology textbooks surveyed, published between 1943 and 1972, instruct that men's sex drive is stronger than women's, that women are interested in sex for procreation and not for recreation, "and that most women are frigid and do not enjoy intercourse" (14). Although evidence is accumulating that supports the view that menopause does not mean the end of sexuality for women who are healthy and who have the opportunity for continuing sexual activity, many continue to associate the end of childbearing with the end of sexuality and of femininity. Fuchs reports that "rural women in Jamaica speak of the loss of their 'health of flowers'" and of their practice of turning away from the world at that time, and of going into "community and religious service." She also reports that many Moslem women may expect to be divorced and to have their places taken by younger wives, "with no further opportunity of intercourse." And the Tiwi women who live on Melville Island, which is north of Australia, "know that their opportunity for sexual intercourse decreases markedly at the end of their childbearing period," although they think the menopause is induced by the cessation of sexual intercourse, rather than the other way around (15).

Although Fuchs's research confirms the absence of rites of passage for menopause in other cultures, she notes that there are many indications made to women in the U.S. that menopause marks a transition to a new status—a passage that, given our celebration of youth, is a descent. She does not accept Doris Lessing's negative view of midlife as this is expressed in her novel *Summer Before the Dark;* to Fuchs, the very title of this novel implies "morbid anticipation." This attitude toward menopause and later life "can and does induce states of hypochondriacal depression. For many women, anxiety and anticipation can produce a legion of complaints, many of which have no organic basis in the biological facts of menopause but, rather, arise out of fear" (57). As for the biological facts of menopause, not very much is known. Fuchs remarks the sparseness of solid research on the physiology of older women; in its absence, traditional and prejudiced attitudes prevail. The menopause, she writes, is a major life event for every woman who survives into middle age. Yet the medical attention given to it is slight, indeed, when compared with that given to the health concerns of younger women. Fuchs quotes Sonja M. McKinlay and John B. McKinlay of the Harvard University Medical School and Department of Sociology, Cambridge, who observe that in Western cultures, the menopause is a "stigmatizing event in a woman's life marking the end of her social usefulness—procreation" and that "this attitude has been perpetuated in the cursory consideration given by the medical profession to the relief of any accompanying uncomfortable symptoms."[4]

Menopause is seen as a milestone in those cultures in which it is recognized as a significant phase in the life course. Therefore, it is only imperfectly understood if it is studied in isolation from the social and cultural context in which a woman experiences a "change of life." Social scientists have presented impressive evidence in support of the idea that the very definition of a bodily state as a symptom or a problem is as much a matter of social and cultural as of biological processes.[5] Fuchs reports that women who live in a South Wales mining town believe that the hot flushes women experience during menopause are good for a woman, and are embarrassed and apologetic if they think they are "not very good at it." On the other hand, some native village women in Jamaica interpret hot flushes in terms of witchcraft or spirit possession, and a woman in Jamaica might take herbal baths or drink herbal tea to relieve this symptom.[6] Mental "symptoms" of menopause, too, are subject to social and cultural definition. Fuchs refers to a critique of Freudian and psychoanalytic interpretation of the difficulties of menopause that was written by sociologist Ernest Becker. In Becker's view, the social system that consigns menopausal women to a very constricted range of life choices or opportunities, and not some repressed libidinal urge in women or the reappearance of a castration complex, accounts for their midlife depression. If menopausal depression is socially and culturally induced rather than fated, it can be treated and perhaps even prevented by the creation of new social roles and life-chances for older women.

There are cultures in which older women are given a measure of freedom that is denied to younger women. Only when she can no longer bear children and only when she is free from childrearing responsibilities can a woman begin to command the respect that comes with authority. Thus among the Tuareg, "the blue-painted people of the North African desert," older women may assume positions of high status equal to those which men have as their due. Yet a Tuareg woman must pay a heavy ransom for her freedom, and that is the price of her sexuality and motherhood, symbol of her femininity. Fuchs perceives a resemblance between the situation of the Tuareg older woman and the nineteenth-century schoolteacher in rural America who could maintain her position of respect and authority only so long as she remained a spinster. Women today, she comments, refuse to accept the idea that sexuality and motherhood must of necessity conflict with positions of high status.

Self and society—they are intertwined. Where menstrual taboos are very strict, where there is fear of defilement by menstruating women, menopause grants women a freedom they had not known since they were children. In many cultures, a woman's status improves when her sons are grown. Among the Greek Sarakatsani, a woman's power and privileges increase when her married son assumes his father's place as head of the household, for it is he who will give her support and comfort in her old age. A woman of the Coniagui of Africa rejoices when her son marries and brings his wife home to live. There, ties of blood are much stronger than affinal ties. This is in clear contrast to our own society, in which it is taught that one should leave one's parents and cleave to one's spouse. Discouragement of attachment between mother and son is not unique to our culture: the traditional peoples of Algeria teach that men must beware of women because they are troublemakers, a divisive force in the *ayla* of four generations of kin who share a common residence. Still, women may come out of seclusion after menopause, and are free to wander outside the enclosed household. Fuchs finds interesting parallels between some women in the U.S. and traditional Greek women for whom the period of life between the ages of 45 and 60 is fraught with emotional problems. These women expect and are expected by others to be irritable, troublesome, and emotionally unbalanced at this time in their lives, and physically ill into the bargain. For many this becomes a self-fulfilling prophecy. Traditional Greek society is male-dominated: men prefer to marry women much younger than themselves, and a very high value is placed on women's procreative powers. Traditional women were confined to the home, subordinated to the control of their husbands and male kin, and expected to be virgins when they married. Menopause is greatly feared; many women deny it to themselves and to their husbands. Because their husbands are so much older, widowhood is imminent for many women at this time in their lives, and menopause is a sign that a woman is becoming old and dependent upon her grown children. Fuchs writes that because these women's lives have been invested in their children and their femininity in traditional roles, they seem to be coming to an end. At this time in their lives, many women withdraw from active engagement with the world around them and give their energies to the church, and in this they resemble the older women in Jamaica. But she also observes that women in the United States are not much different from Greek women or others who deny the fact of menopause, and she observes, "Injections, pills, rest cures, hydrotherapy," and "our responsiveness to estrogen replacements" are all sought after by older women in order to delay or to stave off the effects of biological changes that are inevitable (171).

A cross-cultural perspective on women's second half of life illuminates the possibilities there may be for older women, and the relationship between improved or high status for older women and their mental health. In her study of women's changing status at midlife in a variety of cultures around the world, Pauline Bart reports that among the Burundi, as a woman's social status changes from childhood to adolescence to wifehood and motherhood and then to the status of mother-in-law and grandmother, she progresses toward ever greater independence and power.[7] She found the Lovedu the society most favorable to middle-aged women. Among these people, there is a complacent acceptance of the end of childbearing, "since all Lovedu men and women always have something more to learn to do; and after childbearing, women have more influence, a fuller life, and greater rewards." On the other hand, among the Samoans, where women aged 45 to 55 do most of the heavy work on the plantations, "menopause may be marked by some temporary instability, food finickiness, and whims" (6). Where age is valued because the elders are thought to be repositories of wisdom, a woman's status improves as she grows older. Indeed, in the two societies where women's status declined at midlife—those of the Marquesan and Trobriand Islanders—woman's power was thought to reside not in her knowledge or craftsmanship but in her sexual attractiveness. Where women in the childbearing years are thought to be potentially contaminating, a woman's status may improve at menopause. And if a woman is thought to be asexual after menopause, her status may improve at midlife. Thus, the Arunta of Australia call older women "woman father." Once menstrual and incest taboos are lifted, Arunta women are granted freedom "to come and go and speak with whomever they please" (7). Bart concludes from her survey of these cultures that the characteristics of cultures in which women's status declines at menopause are those in which the affinal ties are stronger that consanguineal ties, in which there is a conjugal-natal family unit that is not embedded in an extended family system, in which sex is seen as an end in itself, there is a weak mother-child bond, the grandmother and mother-in-law roles are not institutionalized, menstrual taboos are minimal, residence patterns isolate women from extended family members, and youth is valued over age. Our culture exhibits all these characteristics but one, she remarks, and that is that in the United States, the mother-child bond is strong, though it is not reciprocal.

A cross-cultural perspective on the status of older women is instructive not only because it documents the variety of ways of life and world-views in cultures throughout the world and in human history, but also because it provides a clearer understanding of the human consequences of a system in which the conjugal-natal unit is isolated. Throughout *The Second Season*, Fuchs calls attention to the price many older women in our society must pay for freedom and individualism. Divorced and widowed women in the United States today may be cast adrift. In the absence of the supports an extended family system provides, they must create support networks of their own. And grown children may turn to their mothers when *they* are divorced, seeking financial aid or asking them to become mothers all over again to the grandchildren. There are older women, too, who lose contact with beloved grandchildren because of the divorce of a grown son or daughter. And there are also many older women today who despair of ever *becoming* grandmothers.

Many older women who have had little or no experience in the labor market are thrown upon their own resources in later life. Because of "no fault" divorce, many older women who have no property or money in their own names, and no joint account with their spouses, may find themselves "financially stranded." In other societies, older women were protected from such eventualities. Moslems and Hebrews allowed women to keep their dowries. Even in Greece today, where the dowry custom still obtains, "the law states that if the dowry has not been signed over to the husband, which is not the usual case, at divorce the woman retains rights to that dowry and can take it with her."[8]

> The old order changeth, yielding place to new,
> And God fulfils himself in many ways,
> Lest one good custom should corrupt the world.

So did King Arthur give solace to Sir Bedivere in Tennyson's *Morte d'Arthur*. There are good customs. Fuchs finds wisdom in the tie-breaking ceremonies performed by widows and widowers in other cultures. She reports that a study of death customs in 78 societies around the world revealed that widowed people were much more likely to remarry in societies in which these customs are followed. In our own time and society, she suggests, perhaps more widows and widowers would remarry "if they were encouraged to dispose of the goods of the deceased and to move to a new home. But many aspects of our culture interfere with this" (247). Divorced women experience even more difficulties than do widows. Indeed, they find themselves in a kind of limbo in society after they are divorced. Widows who do break away from traditional modes of life will find much company among divorced women. In Fuchs's view, it is possible that women who are single may reach "levels of competency, friendship, and sharing with others unknown before in their lives" (248).

Customs cannot be transplanted from one culture to another, since every aspect of culture is related to the whole. Nor is it possible to restore the past, which is itself in part a work of the imagination and of desire. Nonetheless, the existential dilemmas of a particular time and place cannot be fully appreciated without a sense of history and an awareness of cultural diversity. At the same time, every age has its own spirit, and it is not enough to invoke traditional customs and norms in interpreting contemporary life and the existential dilemmas experienced by those who live it. Even those phrases adopted in very recent decades to describe the condition of older women are losing their applicability and usefulness. The "empty nest" syndrome, thought to be an affliction of women in midlife, ought to be redefined. For many older women, "mothering" goes on rather indefinitely, in the form of providing economic as well as emotional support to children long since grown. Just as some older women may want their grown children to remain dependent upon them, there are others who believe that they ought to be independent. And many women in both groups may find that their expectations are not met.

Furthermore, the "empty nest" syndrome is not germane to the study of many older women who have been employed for years, and whose domestic responsibilities do not change very much when the youngest child leaves home, because grown children may leave home and return, leave and return again. As Fuchs astutely observes, a far more serious issue for many older women than the departure of grown children from the home is the growing social isolation of an aging parent, who may become more dependent upon an older woman's time and attention just when her own children are becoming *inde*pendent. As seen from the angle of vision of this perceptive observer, the psychology of contemporary older women is far more complex than the phrase "empty nest" suggests. In the second half of life, many women must mediate between their own and others' needs for personality development, between husbands and grown children, between the expectations of those of older and younger generations, and between traditional and contemporary world-views.

A cross-cultural perspective on older women reveals the many-sided relationship between social and cultural realities and the possibilities women may perceive to be open to them in the second half of life. An exploration of this relationship in twentieth-century America provides valuable insights for sociologists as well as for psychologists, since collective life is the work of people's definitions and interpretations of social and cultural realities. Social gerontologists have found that stage in life is a much more useful criterion than chronological age in the formulation of principles of adult development.[9] In 1975, the research findings of an imaginative study of people at four stages of life was published.[10] Two thresholds that are crossed in the second half of life are demarcated in this study. The first is the post-parental stage of life and the second is the retirement stage. *Four Stages of Life* is a seminal work in which Marjorie Fiske Lowenthal and her associates address the issue of the possibilities for adult development for a sample of people representative of a broad segment of the population of the United States in the late twentieth century.

Older Women in Passage: A Social Psychological View

Even though adult development encompasses many more years than child development, personality growth and change in the early years of life were studied long before the psychological changes experienced by people in the second half of life. Furthermore, the appealing theories of self-actualization have been for the most part "drawn from studies of Harvard students, upper-middle-class patients, and other talented and privileged individuals—including, perhaps, a measure of introspection about the talented and privileged selves of the authors themselves" (x). In *Four Stages of Life,* the appealing self-actualization theories were put to the test through a study of people the authors believe to be representative of "mainstream Americans living in similar contexts" (224). The work is all the more unusual in that it is written from a life course perspective, and reviews an analysis of personality change in adult life that addresses sociological concerns.

The 216 people in this sample, most of whom are Caucasian and from the middle-and lower-middle class, were studied at four pre-transitional stages of life. They are high school seniors, men and women who had been married less than one year and had not yet started a family, middle-aged parents whose youngest child was a high school senior, and older persons planning to retire within two to three years. These people, who live in the central city of a large metropolitan area, are blue-collar, white-collar, and middle-range professional or managerial workers. They include policemen and firemen, nurses and schoolteachers, small businessmen and minor executives, housewives, civil servants, craftsmen, and sales personnel. While they are not leaders in their community, they may be said to represent the center of community life. Yet very few were as involved in organizational life or in cultural and civic activities as those "whose ancestral roots are more firmly middle class." In their use of leisure time, these people are strongly family-centered. Leisure activities were described as "radio listening, reading, household chores, shopping, visiting, being visited, and helping others." Only a few mentioned dancing, physical exercise, picnics, solitary games, or playing a musical instrument as leisure pursuits (6).[11]

When people are in passage, when they are experiencing critical changes in their lives, it is likely that they have a keener awareness of themselves and their world than during the years lived at one or another stage of life. While these people were in the process of self-assessment and life review, particularly those at the third stage, they did not seem able to see very far ahead. Nearly twice as many of them had a circumscribed rather than a growth-motivated approach to life, and this did not have an adverse effect on their well-being. Indeed, it was found that the simplest were the happiest and the most likely to perceive themselves as being fulfilled.

It appears that complexity of personality is maladaptive for older people, and the authors of *Four Stages of Life* suggest that this may be owing to the closing off of avenues for self-expression in our society. A closer look at the preoccupations and concerns, the fears and hopes of the older women in this study reveals the need for transformation of social institutions if society is not to find itself with ever-increasing numbers of "frustrated, self-deprecating, or even self-hating late-middle-aged and older people whose personal way out of their dilemmas may be to adopt the sick role, thus wreaking a legitimate if not deliberate revenge on a society that has denied them any challenging alternatives" (245). A closer look at the older women in *Four Stages of Life* also reveals the changes in women's self-image and world view as they grow older—changes that may signify a psychological transformation in the second half of life.

There were significant differences between older women at the third and fourth stages of life. When they spoke of the stress in their lives, women at the post-parental stage focused on their children much more than women at the pre-retirement stage. Furthermore, many women at the third stage of life seemed to be in despair about their marriages. Women at the pre-retirement stage were not so distraught. In general, they appeared to be more accepting of themselves. The middle-aged women, who were in a more critical period in life than those in any other group, wanted to be more introspective and persevering and more reserved and poised; one-third wanted to be more imaginative. They seemed to be shifting attention away from family members and onto themselves and the wider society. Pre-retirement women were like them in their concern for a social persona, but seemed to be closer to realizing this objective. And they "were unique in their focus on assertiveness and competitiveness" (78). On the whole, middle-aged women did not feel they were in control of their lives. There was a relationship between internal control and planning for the future, but for those who *did* speak of changing their lives, the sense of control had negative connotations. Women at this third threshold "may be disconcerted at finding themselves, perhaps for the first time in their lives, facing a life stage in which their destinies are to some extent in their own hands" (209).

Women, especially older women, were more likely than men to say that they were depressed. Women at the third stage of life foresaw a marked decline in their lives in the coming five years. They said they had positive feelings about the prospect of their youngest child leaving home. At the same time, they were "preoccupied with relishing the last year of the parenting period" (213). Most of these women felt that childrearing was their primary task in life, and that ambition for personal achievement is incompatible with meeting the responsibilities of raising a family. Only about one of every five women named personal achievement or self-fulfillment as the major purpose of life, and most of these were either in higher occupational ranks, or were widowed or divorced or had precarious marriages.

A family-centered life shields the older women from the pressures of the outer world. The more family members there were to be concerned about, the less threatening the future appeared to be to an older woman. Women who were more enterprising, or perhaps newly ambitious, at the fourth stage of life seemed likely to dissipate their energies and gifts within the family. They lacked role diversity. Many were as bored with their jobs as the men were, and the only road they perceived to be open to them was to become more dominant in the family. Older women who were married to men characterized as "stress-avoidant" were likely to find their role conflicts resolved, or perhaps suppressed, because their husbands' need for nurturance supplants that of the children who have left home. "These are the women whose husbands will begin to complain (as some already are complaining) about their wives' becoming too bossy, and whose children may complain about interference." That older women fail to resolve the developmental crisis that occurs in middle age, that the simplest people appear to age most comfortably, that the less gifted seem the most likely to survive, and that women at the fourth stage of life tend to express renewed energies at the expense of personal development, by a growing dominance over others in the family, is wasteful from both the individual and the societal standpoint. Furthermore, all this bodes ill for family life, and for the attitudes younger people are likely to form about aging on the basis of the behavior of such "role models." The developmental needs of both women and men who are gifted seem to be frustrated by traditional sex-role stereotypes as well as by social and economic constraints. While most of the people in this sample were found to be in excellent or moderately good health at the time they were interviewed, "many were almost obsessively preoccupied with health-related issues, perhaps for sheer lack of other outlets" (243–4).

The women in *Four Stages of Life* had impressive employment histories. Over half the women at the third and fourth stages of life were working. Those at the fourth stage of life who were working at the time of the study included four widows and four divorcees. Despite their work histories, few of the women were strongly committed to their jobs. Among these few were women for whom retirement was perceived as a major transition in life. And these women, most of whom were widowed, divorced, or single, were among the minority at any of the four stages of life who had a wholly negative attitude toward their principal transition. "The potential vacuum in their lives, the lack of interpersonal and other kinds of resources of some of these women," Lowenthal and Pierce observe, "supports our . . . thesis that retirement may often be more traumatic for women than it is for men" (205). For most of the women in this study, however, work roles were not so important as their roles as wives, mothers, and homemakers. Such was the case for most women at the fourth stage of life, even though half had work histories as stable as those of the men. The time these women had taken out from the labor force for childbearing was not very different from the time the men had taken out for education or military service or the search for an occupation through which they might build a career. Even so, the working women of this sample

> were satisfied with the financial rewards, the increased affluence that their contribution made to their families' style of life. They would pass up chances for advancement if advancement meant increased obligations and a possible drain on the energy they could direct to their family responsibilities. Since they never really strived for success in their work role, there is no lowering of sights as there was for men. Women's liberation may be changing the stance of some women toward their careers, but we doubt if it will have any immediate effect on the segment of the population being studied here. [20]

Middle-aged men perceived work as a major area of stress in their lives, and one of every three men at the fourth stage of life perceived work as a stressful area, despite the fact that these men were to be retired in only two or three years. Fewer than one-fifth of the older women reported work-related stresses, even though three-fifths of the women in the two later life stages were working. Work simply did not have the meaning for older women that it had for older men. Family and health were the major worries of the older women—the health of others and their own. Most of these women were parents, and all those who did have children felt great responsibility for them and for their aging parents as well.

Because of the significant increase in numbers of women in the labor force after the third stage of life, there was a convergence of the life-styles of men and women. Even so, women's perspectives on the family, leisure, and work differed from those of the men. Most men thought of their family roles in economic terms. Only a few men at the third stage of life named the post-parental stage as the principal change that would be taking place in their lives. Most of them singled out retirement instead, even though this was much more remote in time than the departure of their youngest child from home. When women at the third stage of life spoke of the changes that were imminent, most of them talked about their children. Those who spoke of retirement talked about their husband's retirement and not their own. At the third stage, women's focus was strongly familial, whereas the men seemed to be obsessed with building security for the time when they would be retired. They had been deeply scarred by the experience of the Great Depression when the role of the man as chief breadwinner and provider for his family had been profoundly shaken.

At the fourth stage of life, older women were more likely than those at the post-parental stage to speak of the major transition before them as their own retirement, rather than their husband's. And at this stage, as would be expected, the men thought retirement was the most crucial change they would be experiencing in the near future. But even though about one-fourth of these men still had children living at home, none of them gave primary emphasis to the post-parental stage of life they would soon enter. Women at the fourth stage of life who still had children living at home, however, were more like women at the third stage of life than like the men or women about to retire. For example, the psychological transformation that takes place in the second half of life for some people, whereby men give greater recognition to feelings and women to instrumentality, may be deferred for those women whose children are still living at home. It was found in *Four Stages of Life* that the self-concept of "pre-retirement" women who still had children living at home was far less positive, especially with regard to interpersonal relationships, than that of older women whose children were grown and gone. In sum, critical life reviews[12] may be undertaken most often by women at the completion of the family cycle, and by men at the completion of the work cycle. Indeed, it appears that the major change in values experienced by men comes at the time of retirement, and by women at the time when they are married. Older women who have "low family investment" are women who endorse values culturally defined as "male." For these women, retirement is likely to be far more critical than life events related to the family.

Older women had more disturbances than younger women or than the men at any of the four stages of life, and these were attributed by most of them, at least in part, to menopause. But it was thought that the distress of women at the post-parental stage may be due not so much to the menopause or to the coming departure of the youngest child as to these women's feelings about their relationship with their husbands. Many seemed despairing of the future of their marriages. Indeed, they were the most pessimistic of all the groups in the study about this. They sensed a growing dependency on them on the part of their husbands. It appears that they were not altogether mistaken about this. Judging from the middle-aged men's responses to questions on projective tests, they *did* appear to have a strong need for nurturance. In any case, marital dissatisfactions may crest during the period of time immediately preceding the "post-parental" stage of life. A decline in sexual interest and activity is remarked by both husbands and wives, a decline for which men assume direct responsibility and which women attribute to their husbands' failings. The marriages of couples at the third stage of life seem to be in a much more critical period than those at the fourth stage. Perhaps, if the marriage survives this "midlife crisis," the relationship may improve in time, and sexual interest and activity may be re-awakened. This happened in some cases: about one-third of the oldest group of people reported increasing sexual satisfaction. Those who spoke of *negative* change accounted for this in terms of a change in attitudes and feelings, if they were women, and in terms of a decline of interest in and frequency of intercourse, if they were men. In general, the men's sense of self-worth was more critically linked to sex than women's.

Many more couples may expect to live together a full quarter of a century after the youngest child leaves home than has ever before been the case in human history. Even as recently as the nineteenth century, "there was less likelihood of either parent reaching the postparental stage because of higher mortality, later age at marriage, and more numerous and widely spaced children."[13] A crisis in the marital relationship at the threshold of the post-parental stage of life may serve as the occasion for a re-assessment and redefinition of the relationship between husband and wife. Again, at the time of retirement, people may become preoccupied once more with their marriages. This is precisely what was observed in *Four Stages of Life.* At the pre-retirement stage, there was renewed interest in the personality of the spouse.[14] Husbands and wives evinced

> an underlying worry that the years of work and family, with the relatively independent roles for men and women, have left them without a common basis for their life together after retirement. Women have been absorbed in the problems of others, men in those of work; and life becomes empty for them both unless they have inner resources as well as constructive outlets in a broader community. [23]

The parent-child relationship, like life itself, ought to be seen over the entire life course rather than in one or another interval of time, and this is the perspective taken in *Four Stages of Life.* The older women and men in this study looked back to the years when the children were little as a time of great happiness in their lives. Perhaps the pleasures of these retrospectives were enhanced by memories of their own youth, and the joys of their present life as grandparents. Many seemed nostalgic for a relationship with children that was free of conflict. Having teen-aged children in the household was especially trying. That they were disruptive to the marriage was a recurrent theme in some interviews. Both women and men said they looked forward to the grown children's departure from the home. Even though they came into conflict with their children, parents had very positive feelings about them— although there were more positive feelings at the fourth than at the third stage of life. But conflict with and over teen-aged children came between husbands and wives. It is difficult, perhaps ultimately impossible, to reconcile being a spouse with being a parent. Paul Bohannan has remarked that in the United States, many perceive an antithesis between the two roles: being a parent is seen as interfering with the spouse's capacity to give and receive love and attention from the other. Bohannan has also suggested that an adolescent may revive the remembered *Sturm und Drang* of the parents' own adolescence, and that the presence of teen-agers in the house may bring the parents' unresolved oedipal problems to the surface. It is instructive that Freud thought that women reactivate unresolved oedipal problems in midlife. When this happens, the husband becomes the focus of conflict; he is the projected image of the woman's father. In *Four Stages of Life,* the middle-aged women who were characterized as "self-defeating," and who were very depressed about their poor marriages, appeared to support Freud's thesis.

Given the impressive evidence of the need for nurturance on the part of many older men in *Four Stages of Life,* it is just as likely that men reactivate unresolved oedipal problems in midlife as that women do. And it may be, as many have suggested, that the presence of grown sons and daughters in the household may re-awaken old resentments, old jealousies and rivalries. A man may project his mother onto his wife; a woman may project her father onto her husband. When this happens simultaneously, the battle is joined— between the daughter who still lives in the grown woman and the son who still lives in the grown man. In some instances, the marriage cannot withstand the force of these projections. In others, the projection is accepted, and the relationship is redefined in these terms. This is what took place in some marriages at the fourth stage of life in this study: an older woman consented to become her husband's mother, to play the role of nurturer (and scold, too, probably), rather than continuing the journey to individuation. This is a refusal of freedom.

Both men and women at the fourth stage of life had a heightened sense of humanitarian and moral purpose. The men expressed this in terms of wanting to leave a legacy for humanity, of wanting to make a contribution to society in some tangible form. The women expressed this in more personal and religious terms. They felt the need to care for others, to be kind and useful to them, and to help them. But these needs and desires were not translated into any concrete change to be made in their lives. The few who spoke of plans they had for the future were thinking of taking short trips after retirement, not preparing for a new way of life. Again, there is an inner sense of the need to explore, to extend the self. Again, there is a refusal of freedom.

Tracing the failures of the people in this study to discover and express the unique gifts each person is given is a work of circularities: each stage is seeded with the dilemmas of the next. Women at the third stage were despairing. Their "pretransitional profiles" protrayed them as people living lives of "not very 'quiet' desperation," whereas the middle-aged men were stoic and re-signed. (219). The distress of these women was all the more acute if they thought their children were taking a direction different from that followed by their parents. Many seemed to long for personal growth and for breaking free of the confines of the family. The more complex a woman appeared to be, the more desperate she was—about her marriage, her children, her own future. The years ahead looked bleak. Women at the third stage of life did not feel themselves to be in control; they were drifting into the time that lay before them. They said outright that they were unhappy; they reported more psy-chological symptoms than people in the other age groups; they felt themselves wanting in the very areas where the middle-aged men felt themselves to be strong. Men had a heightened sense of orderliness at this stage, but women of absent-mindedness. Men rejected self-pity, but the women gave in to it. Mid-dle-aged men who felt a sense of hopelessness were fighting against the feel-ing they had reached a plateau in their careers. But the women who felt this seemed to be looking for something more profound—perhaps for a raison d'être. Like the newlyweds (both men and women), women at the third stage of life expressed existential despair. And, like the newlywed *women*, they were the most ready to acknowledge that they had thought about committing suicide. Perhaps what women at these two stages of life have in common is that they must rebuild their lives around the presence or absence of other people. In marriage, there is "a kind of 'death' of the former social self," particularly for women who have no other major commitments. When the children leave home, a woman must find her *self* again, rebuild her identity. For these women, "self" was interwoven with others. They worked, but were not committed to their work. When newlywed, they had narrower social hori-zons than their husbands, and seemed to resent the man's involvements out-side the home: "They were in love, and nothing else seemed to matter" (217). They fully expected to become mothers, and knew their lives would change radically when they did. They seemed to be trying to make the most of their chances for personal growth before the children came. At midlife, they had to pick up those threads again.

In Freud's view, a woman's psychological development may be arrested early on in life, exhausted in "the difficult development to femininity." To Freud, and in our own time to Erik Erikson, psychoanalytic theory seems to have little to offer so far as developmental stages of women are concerned (215–16). While the younger women in *Four Stages of Life* were found to have a "distressing resemblance to the prototypes illustrating Freud's theory of an early and abrupt halt in the development of young women," there is also evidence that women at the third stage may be experiencing a change that eluded theorists of classical psychoanalysis. It eluded them not only because of their view of women, but because of their view of the family life cycle as well. Both views were narrow. Perhaps they did not see much chance for further personality development in the second half of women's lives because at the time they were writing, the post-parental stage of life was very brief. A human potential movement or a movement for self-actualization in the late nineteenth and early twentieth centuries could attract very few people in the second half of life—and even fewer of these would be women.

The horizons of women and men at the third stage of life were narrow, although for different reasons. The men, who were looking ahead to retirement with apprehension, were preoccupied with their jobs and with financial security. Some were making an all but desperate effort to be promoted, in order to provide for a higher retirement income. These claims upon their attention and energies may explain why their civic and religious activities were more nominal than real. As for the women, even though so many of them were working, their wages were used to supplement family income and much of their time, attention, and energy were given over to family-related matters. Their concerns were the lives of others, even in their ideas and uses of leisure time. All across the life course, the men thought of leisure in terms of *play*, and the women in terms of *sociability*. At the third stage of life, men make selective use of leisure time because of work considerations, and women because they are accommodating their husbands. Women have few roles or activities outside the family. Thurnher perceived some striking resemblances between women at this stage and the high school girls who reported high retrospective change, and she suggests that similar psychodynamic processes may be at work. For both the eighteen-year-old girls and the middle-aged women, the awareness of approaching a critical life passage is very intense: the former looks ahead to beginning maternal tasks, and the woman at the third stage is nearing the threshold that is crossed when they are completed. Thurnher writes that Freud did not dismiss the role of the social structure entirely in accounting for the constriction of life women may experience at middle age, and she reports that many of the women who expected there would be a change in their values in middle age had a positive self-concept and also had been exposed to considerable stress in their lives. In her view, women at the third stage of life are not likely to envision the chance for change in their lives or feel the need for it unless they have some confidence that they can shape the conditions under which they live, or unless they have a burning desire to compensate for past frustrations.

In the second half of life, women and men may experience a psychological transformation. According to Jungian theory, a change in perspective and action and personality is an expression of striving toward wholeness. Older people who are aware and accepting of the many-sidedness of the self search for ways to experience and express those possibilities that were not realized in the first half of life. In a society where women are nurturant and passive in childhood and youth and early adulthood, wholeness would demand instrumentality and assertiveness in the second half of life. Conversely, where men are competitive and assertive in the first half of life, wholeness would demand that they become more expressive in the second. In *Four Stages of Life*, evidence was found that supports Jung's view. For example, women at the third stage of life had negative perceptions of their mothers and positive perceptions of their fathers. One interpretation of this is that middle-aged women may be experiencing the need for a new direction in their lives—a need to acknowledge the instrumental and active aspects of their personalities, that is, the masculine component of the psyche. Again, it was found that women appear to "hit their stride" by the fourth stage of life, at which time it appears that they have resolved problems having to do with competence, independence, and interpersonal relations. The pre-retirement women perceive themselves to be more assertive, and less dependent and helpless than they had been when they were younger. Perhaps this enhancement of a feeling of effectiveness exacts its psychic cost, since these women seem to feel more constrained than the women at the other three stages of life. Nonetheless, in this heightened sense of effectiveness, as well as in a feeling of competence, women at the fourth stage of life resemble middle-aged men more than the men in the pre-retirement group. And women at the fourth stage were unique in their focus on assertiveness and competitiveness. It was the researchers' impression that many of them were sublimating any needs they may have felt for mutuality and reciprocity, and that they were bossy and assertive, "perhaps defiantly," and at the same time indulging their husbands' needs for physical comfort. Therefore, they sustained a sort of reversal in role reciprocity in the marriage, and this may have been accomplished by sacrificing their personal development. Jung believed that the psychological transformation that may take place in the second half of life has the consequence that women recognize and are responsive to needs for instrumentality and incisiveness, and men to needs for expressiveness of feeling, and support for this thesis in *Four Stages of Life* is quite explicit. The question as to why these shifts occur is raised. Neither Jung nor Freud was wholly oblivious to the relationship between the development of the personality and the sociocultural milieu, the researchers reflect, and it is possible that these shifts take place at points of transition between *social* stages of life. In any case, the self-concept of women at the fourth stage of life is highly distinctive. It may be that at this time in women's lives, the traditionally valued attributes are in the process of redefinition.

The authors of *Four Stages of Life* state that they concur with the conclusions arrived at by Bernice L. Neugarten and David L. Gutmann in their analysis of a TAT study of age-sex roles and personality in middle age. Neugarten's and Gutmann's purpose was to explore the use of projective techniques in the study of adult age-sex roles in the family.[15] The picture from the Thematic

Apperception Test, designed to evoke the feelings and preoccupations of people in regard to family roles, is a representation of four stimulus figures, a young woman and an old woman, and a young man and an old man. The sample for this study was comprised of 131 people in two age categories, 40 to 54, and 55 to 70, almost all of whom were native-born Protestants of northern European ethnic backgrounds, who grew up in the Midwest. The study was an inquiry into the collective role images of husbands, wives, sons, and daughters, based upon the projections of the respondents.

Nearly all the subjects of this study saw the picture to be a representation of the two-generation family. Those aged 40 to 54 saw the figure of the old man as dominant. Those aged 55 to 70 perceived him as passive. The old man seemed to be a symbol of "the ego qualities of the personality: the rational rather than the impulsive approach to problems, concern over the needs of others, reconciliation between opposing interests, cerebral competence" (64). In contrast, the figure of the old woman (who was seen as the key figure in the family, and very often as the protagonist in a oedipal struggle) represented the impulsive and self-centered qualities of the personality. Most older respondents saw her as the "most feeling, demanding, and aggressive figure, as the other figures tend toward greater passivity, colorlessness, and conformity" (69). They told stories in which the old woman seemed to represent "the breakthrough of impulsivity."

This study was cross-sectional, that is, a sample of people were studied at one point in time. Therefore, it suggests *but does not document* a shift from dominance to passivity of the ego and the ascendancy of impulse life with aging. Age changes are often inferred from studies of age differences. But that is to take liberties with cross-sectional data. Age changes can be documented only from a study of changes of the same sample of people over a period of time. It is possible that, as people grow older, their ego controls decline in the face of forceful pressures from impulse life. But this can be investigated only through longitudinal analysis. Nevertheless, the fact that role definitions of the old man and the old woman vary consistently with the age of the respondent, and the fact that younger respondents tended to see the old man as dominant, while older respondents tended to see this figure as submissive, are arresting and provocative.

The idea that the role of the old man changes from dominance to submissiveness and the role of the old woman from subordination to authoritativeness, is in keeping with the psychological transformation in the second half of life described by Jung. It is also consonant with the research findings of *Four Stages of Life*, and with Gutmann's cross-cultural investigation of aging among the Highland Maya.[16] What are the implications of these research findings for role behavior? Neugarten and Gutmann write that when a person fills a "real-life role," she or he must resolve tensions between personal needs and social expectations. It is the ego's task to organize the affective components of the personality into a pattern of behavior that is socially acceptable as well as personally expressive. But when a person is presented with the TAT picture, something else is asked of her or him than to act in the actual family setting, and that is "to breathe vitality into a representation of family life." To do this, the ego must distribute components of the self among the figures in the picture, rather than integrate the aspects of the self into a coherent pattern. While this division of the components of the personality makes the TAT technique valuable for the clinician, it imposes certain qualifications on its applicability to the study of social roles. When a person describes the role of the old man or the old woman in terms of only one or a few aspects of the self, the projected aspect tends to be expressed in an exaggerated way. Therefore, there is some stereotyping in the descriptions of the roles. This means that the role analyst has a difficult task, because the role patterns one endeavors to describe may have been distorted into extremes in serving as foci for conflicting aspects of the personalities of the interviewees. For this reason, the data of the role analyst "are the affective connotations of role behavior, those which people limit and modify in real life."[17]

Neugarten and Gutmann caution that the findings of their study should be interpreted with care when they are examined with a view to application to actual role behavior. In responding to the picture, a person is given the means for describing any of the figures *(which are projections of aspects of the self)* in a more unitary way than human experience permits different aspects of the personality to be. Then, too, the collective role images do not refer to the day-to-day realities of the role of any of the figures. These data yield centrality rather than the complexity of role behavior as people experience it. In many of the stories, especially in those told by men, the old woman is seen as a figure who is all-knowing and wrathful. These accounts of the old woman are projections of the aggressive energy of the storytellers themselves:

> Women who live in a social environment cannot act purely from un-mediated primitive impulse. They would soon be hospitalized, institutionalized, or dead. What we are being told in such accounts is that older women's behavior in the family expresses, for those respondents preoccupied with such issues, a central quality of free aggression. [70]

Even so, the consistency with which the old woman, not the old man, is described in terms of impulsivity, aggressiveness, and hostile dominance cannot be explained by chance: "The assumption seems warranted that there is something common to the actual role behaviors of older women that elicits this consistency in respondents' fantasies" (70). The conclusion of this study that women appear to become more tolerant of their aggressiveness and egocentricity and men of their nurturant and affiliative impulses as they grow older corresponds with the observations made of many pre-retirement women in *Four Stages of Life*. At the fourth stage, women characterized as "newly ambitious" who were married to men of the "stress-avoidant" type find that the need for nurturance on the part of their grown children is supplanted by their husbands' need for mothering. In accepting this situation, they may resolve (or suppress) their role conflicts, but only at great loss to themselves as well as to society—*and* to harmonious family life. Some of their husbands were already complaining that their wives were becoming too bossy. Some of the grown children found mothers at the fourth stage of life interfering too much with their lives.

The source of Neugarten's and Gutmann's paper is the Kansas City Study of Adult Life, which was conducted in the 1950s. The report of findings of the Kansas City Study appeared in the book by Cumming and Henry entitled *Growing Old: The Process of Disengagement.*[18] Disengagement means that aging is an inevitable and mutual withdrawal that results in decreased interaction between the aging person and the social systems to which she or he belongs. When the aging process is complete, the equilibrium that existed in middle life between the person and society "has given way to a new equilibrium characterized by a greater distance and an altered type of relationship" (14–15). It is important to emphasize that one of the postulates of the theory is that *"because the abandonment of life's central roles . . . results in a dramatically reduced social life space, it will result in crisis and loss of morale unless different roles, appropriate to the disengaged state, are available"* (215). The ability to disengage was the factor found to have the greatest bearing on morale. Indeed, those with the highest levels of morale were found to be at the beginning and end stages of the process of disengagement; those with the lowest morale were at the stages of transition. There is striking agreement between this finding and the findings in *Four Stages of Life.* In *Growing Old,* a group of ten women who were "fully engaged," that is, married women under the age of sixty-five "who have not yet experienced a reduction in object cathexis," had relatively low average morale: "These findings may indicate that these women would like more freedom from their home responsibilities and the opportunity for different types of social interactions, such as might be found in the later stages of disengagement" (137).

Cumming and Henry write that it appears that, as they age, men retreat gladly from active mastery, whereas women "in their new freedom, achieve a kind of activity that is a counterpoise to their life experience." They report that those who work with recreation groups for the elderly have assured them that older women love to "be on the move." They enjoy taking bus rides and going on outings, simply for the pleasure of moving around. Older men, on the other hand, prefer activities that are "useful" or "educational." The elderly man who is disengaged "is a thoughtful, reflective, perhaps somewhat opinionated 'wise man,' while the disengaged older woman is an active, carefree, perhaps even frivolous 'girl' " (158).

Growing Old suggests that disengagement is more difficult for men than it is for women in our society. The modern industrial world does not make use of the accumulated wisdom of men. This is thought to create an important asymmetry in old age. Old men assume honored roles in more traditional socities. But in the United States there is no wise old man as the male counterpart to Mary Worth, the wise old widow of the comic strips. It is modern science that is responsible "in a very real sense for the asymmetry which makes ours, in old age, a woman's world" (160).

If women have the psychological potential to age better than men, this may be unrealized in all too many lives. In *Four Stages of Life,* the people are, on the whole, unable to use their energies and gifts in creative, gratifying, and productive ways. Yet the women are more complex than the men, more attuned to the complexities of personalities—their own, their children's, their friends'. If age change were inferred from the age differences found in this study, it appears that a man's self-image becomes more crystallized as he grows older, whereas the woman's is wavering—uncertain and filled with ambiguities. This sensitivity to the complexity of human personality makes women more accessible than men to others, and means they are more likely than men to form strong and rich friendships, and to have confidantes and to be confidantes of others. These capacities mean much in later life, and in this as in other researches, Lowenthal has shown how having even only one close friend or confidante can help an older person weather the sorrows of retirement, of widowhood, and of diminishing social activity. Regardless of calendar age or socioeconomic circumstances, many more women than men have intimate friendships. Furthermore, a man's only confidante is likely to be his wife, whereas a woman's is just as likely to be a woman friend as to be her husband. Because of this, widowhood may be more grievous for a man than for a woman. This may explain, at least in part, why many widowed men feel an intense need to remarry.[19]

In spite of all these advantages, it appears that the older women in *Four Stages of Life* had fewer resources than did the older men for coping with severe stress.[20] And it is in the second half of life—at the "third stage," for many—that women come to a crossroads. At this time there is a tide, the tide of which Brutus spoke in *Julius Caesar:*

> Which, taken at the flood, leads on to fortune;
> Omitted, all the voyage of their life
> Is bound in shallows and in miseries.
>
> [Act 4, scene 3]

For so many, it is "omitted." For so many, there is a failure of nerve—a refusal to meet the challenges of chance and change.

The fault is in the stars, the social arrangements. But it is in older women themselves, as well. At least, if older women are seen from the perspective of Renaissance humanism, this must be so. Progress, perfectibility, possibility—these are translatable into the lives of individuals as much as into the shape and direction of social institutions. There is an article of faith of humanism that seems to have been lost among the others, and that is that one is responsible for one's own destiny. The world is unintelligible if it is seen as wholly unrelated to our experience of it; at the same time, we cannot know ourselves if we ignore society, culture, and history. But many look outside themselves *exclusively* to find the source of their condition. When changes are proposed, they are phrased in terms of altering the social arrangements. The proposals may be well taken; they may be long overdue. But they are not enough.

Throughout *Four Stages of Life,* there is a sensitivity to all that lies beneath the surfaces of the social arrangements. There is a steady attentiveness to the reality of inner life. Life has its pleasures and its regrets; the sense of gratification about one's self and world rises and falls all along the life course. Yet people tend to look upon present reality in the most favorable light—or at least, to *say* that they see things this way. And perspective does broaden as one grows older. Furthermore, even given this "youth-obsessed society," it does not happen that the self-concept of people becomes completely negative as they grow older.[21] Societal conditions are not all; one must weigh other considerations along with them in the study of adult development. It is possible that people may "disengage" from society, may withdraw from an inward commitment to human relationships as a means of defense against the feeling that others are pulling away from *them.* Older people have been found to have less "ego energy" than the young, and this may be a response to their abandonment by others, a means of shielding themselves from indifference or neglect. The cause of psychological or inner disengagement cannot be known from cross-sectional analysis; it can only be revealed through a study of the changes that take place over the entire life course. In *Four Stages of Life,* it was found that the older people had lower levels of emotional experience. But, because this, too, was a cross-sectional study, there is "no way of assessing whether the lower levels of emotional experience . . . are due to indifference, to lack of opportunity, or to an intrinsic developmental process."[22] An awareness of the close intertwining of self and society deters the social psychologist from making facile or dogmatic assumptions about psychological development in the second half of life. It is entirely possible that the segregated sex roles characteristic of the world in which these people lived, and of the social world of the people Neugarten and Gutmann studied in the Midwest in the 1950s, may account for the psychological transformation observed in later life, whereby women seemed to give increasing emphasis to "masculine" and men to "feminine" components of the psyche.[23] In a society in which men were assigned nurturant and expressive roles, and women were assigned assertive and instrumental roles, a psychological transformation in later life might be in the opposite direction than that taken by people socialized in the United States. In either case, social and cultural realities would account for the direction the psychological transformation takes, but not the fact of the transformation itself. In an ideal society, one could express instrumentality and assertiveness *as well as* nurturance all along the life course. But all societies have their imperfections, and there are possibilities for further growth of the human spirit that are not realized because these flaws in the social arrangements are mistaken for immutable expressions of "human nature." Perhaps it is the central task of those in the second half of life to explore these questions. This is what Jung has suggested:

> A human being would certainly not grow to be seventy or eighty years old if this longevity had no meaning for the species to which he belongs. The afternoon of human life must also have a significance of its own and cannot be merely a pitiful appendage to life's morning. The significance of the morning undoubtedly lies in the development of the individual, our entrenchment in the outer world, the propagation of our kind and the care of our children. This is the obvious purpose of nature. But when this purpose has been attained . . . shall the earning of money, the extension of conquests and the expansion of life go steadily on beyond the bounds of all reason and sense? . . . Culture lies beyond the purpose of nature. Could by any chance culture be the meaning and purpose of the second half of life?[24]

The transformation of our social institutions would follow from our taking a life course perspective on every sphere of societal life. The disaffection of older people in the United States so clearly apparent in *Four Stages of Life*, a study conducted *before* Watergate, before the (first) energy crisis, is ominous, given the ecological and social and political changes on the horizon. Even more ominous are the signs that the younger generation of these people seem to be destined to repeat the lives of those who are older, among whom the simplest seemed to be aging most gracefully, and the least gifted seemed likeliest to survive.[25] Until such time as this social transformation becomes a reality, and people come to terms with maturity and aging and mortality, there ought to be educational programs for middle-aged and elderly people, including the poor and ethnic minorities; serious exploration of the possibilities of establishing a voluntary retirement age; the development of training facilities for a second career in all fields; and a campaign by industry and the mass media to combat a mindless celebration of youth. Educational opportunities and preventive mental health programs to those cohorts of people who are now old are not enough. The most compelling need is for a life course orientation in all our social and educational institutions. The offerings of television are no more than "tranquilizing or escapist consolations." Age segregation is a trend that must be reversed. Society must be transformed if there is not to be an unconscionable waste of social resources and a large population at risk from the perspectives of both mental and physical health.[26]

The transformation of the self would follow from the adoption of a life course perspective on every aspect of one's life—family, work, friendship, responsibility to community and society. It would follow from the acknowledgment that, while one may strive to live life fully, one cannot hope to live it all at once. Thus, whatever is deferred by the choices made in youth and early maturity will be the task to be undertaken in later life. This is a difficult and perilous mission, because, as Jung has remarked, the nearer we approach midlife and the more deeply we are entrenched in our personal attitudes and social positions, the more it seems as if we have found the right attitudes, "the right course and the right ideals and principles of behaviour. For this reason we suppose them to be eternally valid, and make a virtue of unchangeably clinging to them." What is overlooked is that those accomplishments rewarded by society "are won at the cost of a diminution of personality. Many—far too many—aspects of life which should also have been experienced lie in the lumber-room among dusty memories." In midlife, there are signs that "a significant change in the human psyche is in preparation." The change is not conscious and striking, at first, and it can take many forms, as a waning of interests and inclinations that eventually are replaced by others, or a hardening and rigidity of convictions and principles. Jung thought that these and other manifestations he describes are most clearly apparent in people who are rather one-sided. He also believed that they may be delayed by the fact that a person's parents are still alive: "It is then as if the period of youth were unduly continued. I have seen this especially in the cases of men whose fathers were long-lived. The death of the father then has the effect of an over hurried—an almost catastrophic—ripening."[27] This significant change at midlife may be heralded by an intense awareness of mortality. In *The Second Season*, Fuchs writes that many women experience this as menopause approaches: "Almost inevitably a reassessment of one's life is in order. The dreams unfulfilled, the things still undone, the clash between the reality of life and the desires for other things and ways, the children unborn, the lovers unloved, the talents undeveloped."[28] If this life review coincides with menopause, then menopause may be said to be a milestone in a woman's life. But the biological events do not in and of themselves foretoken psychological transformation. Menopause may or may not be the occasion for this. The death of one's mother may be, or the marriage of one's grown daughter . . . or the loss of a beloved friend. Whatever the occasion, the "milestone" is a turning point, a *spiritual* climacteric.

"Change of Life": Psychological Interpretations

In the midst of the Great Depression, at a time when most people in the United States were concerned with very material matters, Grace Elliott's book *Women After Forty* was published. While Elliott addressed issues in psychology and religion, she was not entirely wanting in social awareness. She criticized an economic system that celebrates private initiative and competitiveness—values that are inappropriate for the second half of life. She remarked the limited opportunities for responsible participation on the part of older women in political, religious, and civic life. She thought that women whose lives had centered upon the home and family in the first half of their lives ought to be provided with both the opportunities and incentive for adult learning and development. Furthermore, she found historic religion to be at fault in fostering the repression of ego values rather than their fulfillment, and in its other-worldliness. In her view, religious teaching that prevents its followers from living fully in the present sustains and promotes immaturity. In her concern for the meaning and purpose of life beyond youth, her observations have a curiously contemporary ring: The capacity of the human being

> to transform energy from its purely procreative channels to the creative union with other lives in all of the aspects of personality is the foundation for the human and cultural achievements of life, almost half of which is lived after the procreative functions have ceased. The direct satisfaction of sex desire on the human plane is incidental to the achieving of this larger unity, and is incomplete unless this is attained.[29]

Elliott's definition of the last half of life was that it begins between the ages of 35 and 50, when a woman acknowledges that her youth is past. Up to the age of 35 or 40, a woman may more easily "deceive herself about the denial of her fundamental needs and desires" (20–21). An unmarried woman of this age may have been so involved in other matters that she found it possible to conceal a sense of inadequacy in her love relationships even from herself. But by the age of 35, she becomes fully aware that there are very few years remaining to her in which she might still become a mother. For some women, this may be a crisis: "Single life becomes for the first time intolerable." A woman in this situation "must seek romantic and sexual adventure before the chance is gone forever" (21). If a woman has neglected her love needs up to this age, they may now assume an exaggerated value for her. For a married woman, there is a crisis around this age also. Whereas the single woman has neglected her love relationships, the married woman has probably disregarded interests outside the circle of the family. In midlife, she may perceive that her desire to be recognized as one who can contribute in her own way to the life of the community may soon be unattainable. A married woman who initiates a divorce at the age of 40 may be expressing the effort "to lay hold, 'now or never,' of something that may for her, as for her unmarried sister, soon be gone forever" (22). The crucial factor in the capacity to live life fully is not marital status, not "external relationships," but the development of inner faculties. While she did not discount the conditions of life entirely, Elliott found them to be much less important than a person's attitude toward them.

In the first half of every person's life, some potentialities are sacrificed for the sake of realizing others. The married woman has neglected the need for individual development and achievement. The unmarried woman, no matter how much vocational gratification and recognition she has received, no matter how successful she may appear to be, needs intimate and gratifying personal relationships. The bitterness that some women feel in midlife toward all that earlier gave them a sense of fulfillment—whether this be their growing families or their relationships to husband and children, or continuing vocational or professional advancement—may be a manifestation of reaching this turning point in life. "When one area of life is given exclusive attention," Elliott observed, "and, as a result, has to furnish more than its legitimate satisfactions, there is likely to come a time when there is an exaggerated

revulsion against it" (23–24). In the first half of life, choices must be made—
and they are fateful. There is a narrowing of interests and activities. After one
has found a vocation and a mate, and worked out an approach to life, one may
have the illusion of fulfillment, of having reached the place where the romantic novels end, leaving the characters to "live happily forever after." But not
everyone marries, Elliott wrote, and of those who do, few can even deceive
themselves that they are living in this forever-after. "It is in the 'ever-after,'
which comprises the years of maturity as well as of later life," she wrote, "that
the question as to the meaning of life is of prime importance" (9). Jung had
said that those who refuse to recognize that the "afternoon program" of life
must be different from that of life's morning may become transfixed in time—
eternal adolescents, ever gazing backward. Many people take their lives apart
during a midlife crisis. They divorce, or change jobs, or move to another
community. But the source of their restlessness and discontent lies within. In
projecting it onto others—a spouse, or children, or the workplace—there is a
refusal to take responsibility for the need for inner change and development:

> For Jung, the individual who will not face this change in his own need is
> likely to project the inner irritation, arising from that desire, to his mate or
> to his job, and make the issue one which leads to divorce or resignation
> instead of to a maturing of his own personality. Merely to gain a divorce
> usually means a false and impossible attempt to reattain with a different
> person the satisfactions of a stage which should be outgrown. Merely to
> resign his job because of irrational irritation is to fail to find the leads the
> irritation should reveal for the next stage of development.[159–60]

The task of the second half of life is to find and develop those capacities
which have not yet been realized. Since people make different choices about
personal relationships and vocations in youth and early maturity, the direction of learning and development in later life cannot be the same for all
women. Thus, if a married woman identified herself completely with her
family, an unmarried woman may have identified herself completely with her
job. She may have allowed herself to become fully absorbed by her work,
neglecting other aspects of life. Her identification with her work may have
been so extreme that "to criticize it is as provocative of difficulty as to criticize
her married sister's children" (26). In either case (and these are only two
examples of a variety of cases), the need to move forward is felt urgently at
midlife, because of the sense that the direction of life is changing. To resist
this compelling urge is to risk becoming mired in the past. Elliott cites cases of
radical reversal of interest and activity following the crisis of realization that
certain potentialities have been neglected. One woman, who had been a social
worker until the age of 38, gave up her job at that time and began to study
painting: "She said that she had to do it to save her soul" (25).
    When the family was the unit of production in society, it provided a woman
with the chance for creative expression of many facets of her nature, and with
a dignity of position in the community. "There was always opportunity for

recognition of her craftsmanship or of her administrative ability, in the fact that her products were items of social comparison." But vocational opportunities within the family are limited or nonexistent in an industrial system of production (40–42). Very few women are successful in both marriage and vocation because the attitudes in society are biased against this, and also because both family and work are absorbing and exacting pursuits. The conflict between these two worlds, between the demands of sex and the demands of ego, "is potentially more fundamental with woman than with man because of the heavier demands sex makes on her whole organism. Woman's approach to vocation has always been divided while man's has been single" (33). As women's lives come to resemble those of men, as women become more individual and more differentiated culturally, they become ever more resistant to those instinctive abilities that incline toward the unities of life. But it is for a sense of the unities of life that the second half of life is lived.

Elliott's study had begun with work with adolescent girls that led to the discovery that the mother's problems in middle age were often a major factor in the girls' difficulties. This research led to a growing awareness of the relationship between the problems of adolescence and the problems confronted in later life, and to the conviction that the passage to middle age is as critical as the passage from childhood to adolescence. Western civilization is built on values of the individual ego and personal achievement. These are the concerns of youth. In maturity and old age, gratifying pursuits are those that broaden sympathies and interests, and deepen the awareness of relatedness to all humanity. True maturity is reached when one has outgrown the slavish and narrow pursuits of ego demands. Individuality is no more than the means to the enhancement of experience. Social interdependence and social identification are fundamental to later life. In Elliott's view, one can take creative responsibility for life only to the degree that one can yield to the forces of life that act upon one, and upon which one is dependent. One can find life only by losing it. She is critical of modern education for its failure to acknowledge the circularity of life, and for its silence about the later years. Ideally, one ought to be educated all through life in relatedness to nature and to humanity. Elliott calls attention to Jung's comment that, after thirty years of experience with patients from many countries, it was his judgment that a psychoneurosis is the suffering of a person who has not discovered the meaning of life for him or her. Of all Jung's patients over the age of 35, there was not one whose problem was not fundamentally that of finding a religious outlook on life, and no one who did not find this was cured. This search for the meaning of life and the religious sense of life is a search for the universal through the particulars of an individual's life. It is a striving toward wholeness through knowledge not only of the personal unconscious, but of the collective unconscious—of that which is universal and timeless.

Many older people experience difficulties with aging because they have too much time to think about themselves. One cannot spend all day at play, or all one's time traveling and attending lectures and the theatre: "This is not living;

but marking time till death comes. We can see women condemned to that kind of life growing into hypochondriacs, busybodies, or petty tyrants, a burden to themselves and to others" (44). Useful occupations and interests are the only antidote to the problems of aging. As every phase of life is linked with every other, aging is defined in terms of frustration and defeat by those who fail to meet the challenge of midlife. A woman who has never known what it is to be carefree as a child will inevitably encounter difficulties when she is expected to assume the responsibilities of adulthood. In the same way, a woman who has never met the responsibilities of adult life, who has never become mature, cannot grow old. Elliott mentions the case of a woman in her sixties who resisted the thought of growing old, who tried "to prolong the period that should be passing." In her efforts to "keep up with younger people she is failing to develop her own inner resources. She will never make a grand-mother since her continued absorption in her own ego makes it impossible for her to enter into the lives of little children" (71).

To refuse to change when the direction of life is changing is to deny both self and society the creative contributions that only older people can make. Very few young people, Elliott wrote, enjoy the security that is necessary if one is to be truly radical. She was not convinced by the posters she saw around her that proclaimed the intention of "flaming youth" to build the society anew. Older people must participate in the work of social reconstruction if it is to become a reality. Many young people have too much at stake in the status quo to take the great risks that must be taken for this task. Only those who have lived long enough to be able to take the chances that must be taken can dare to undertake reconstruction of society. "Older women," Elliott wrote, "are needed for the new work of the race" (50).

To work for social reconstruction in later life, and for the creative and productive expression of unique gifts for the sake of making a contribution to the life of culture and humanity, one must be free from preoccupation with narrow ego concerns. This freedom is won when there is a consciousness of life as circular rather than linear in its forward flow, a consciousness of the ways the phases of life and the generations are joined to one another. It is difficult for one imbued with the spirit of Western civilization to arrive at this level of consciousness:

> As we come to the last stage, we become aware of the fact that our civiliza-tion really does not harbor a concept of the whole of life, as do the civiliza-tions of the East: "In office a Confucian, in retirement a Taoist." In fact, it is astonishing to behold, how (until quite recently and with a few notable exceptions) Western psychology has avoided looking at the range of the whole cycle. As our world-image is a one-way street to never ending prog-ress interrupted only by small and big catastrophes, our lives are to be one-way streets to success—and sudden oblivion.[30]

The absence of signposts, of culturally shared understandings of the meaning of the whole of life, of rites of passage symbolic of this meaning through which the pilgrimage through time is guided—all this is felt keenly at midlife. Those who are extraordinarily sensitive and introspective feel it much earlier, when in a sudden blaze of awareness the spell of enchantment that is youth is speared open and the existential quest is revealed. But it is especially acute at midlife. Else Frenkel-Brunswik, who worked with Charlotte Buhler at the Psychological Institute of the University of Vienna, wrote that there are psychological phases in human life, just as there are biological phases, and that these are marked by turning points that "usher in, in very short time, parallel and permanent changes in many fields of life."[31] The biological curve of life is seen as divisible into five phases, the third and middle period lasting from ages 25 to 45, and surrounded by two periods of ascent and descent. The transition to the fourth phase "is marked by psychological crises, just as in the biological development crises also appear at this time (menopause.)" There is a proclivity for change; there is discontent, restlessness, even complete negation. Many people take trips for rest or recuperation in their late forties, and this is interpreted as "renewal of unrest, showing itself in an intensified wanderlust, and a frequent change of residence." There are fleeting inclinations to daydreaming and loneliness, and toward retrospection—which reappears at the age of sixty. "A high point in the destruction of one's own creative work . . . is to be found at the beginning of this period." Everything points to a crisis, although "factual dimensions, such as the specific activity in one's profession or creative work, are still comparatively numerous." All that is related to independent creative work may very well culminate at this time in life. Social activities may undergo a change in direction, a movement "into a new field, since, although the general sociability lessens, the more philanthropic activities begin first at this time." (81).

A particular point in time, a particular place in the world, a culture pattern and a web of social relationships—these are mediums through which the human condition is experienced and expressed. In Austria, these things were felt by many people in their late forties. In the United States, another age interval might be found to be marked by the most frequent number of cases of "midlife crisis." Calendar age does not matter. What matters is the experience, and what is made of it. What precipitates the crisis varies from one social group to another, from one woman to another, even. And a preoccupation with that diverts attention away from what ought to be explored—that is, the nature of the crisis itself. Thus, many of the members of the Spiritualists of Swansea, known for their seances and other means of reaching for communication with the spirit world, are middle-aged women. And many of the messages sent by the Spirit could be interpreted as having to do with the menopause. But the symptoms of menopause were not perceived in physical or medical terms. Rather, they had to do with a sense of uncertainty and a lack of direction in life. These "symptoms" could appear at any time in a woman's life after the age of 24, so obviously they could not be correlated with the end of the childbearing period or the cessation of the menses. Menopause, defined by the Spiritualists as a cultural or social rather than as a biological event, "could occur at any time a woman experienced a sense of change accompanied with uncertainty concerning the direction of her life." When this was experienced, women sought enlightenment from the "spirits."[32]

In a study first published in 1963 on the attitudes toward the menopause held by a sample of women of various ages who had, in general, attained a rather high educational level, it was found that only 4 of 100 women in the menopause age-category 44 to 55 selected the multiple-choice response "Not being able to have more children" as the worst aspect of the "change of life." The panic at the "closing of the gates" described by Helene Deutsch in her discussion of motherhood in *The Psychology of Women*—a panic felt at the ending of the loss of reproductive capacity—was not borne out by these data. It was concluded that this loss, which Deutsch suggested may arouse the desire to have another child, "is not an important concern of middle-aged women at either a conscious or unconscious level."[33] But every woman is different from every other in so many ways. There have been women all through human history to whom motherhood has meant very little. There have been others for whom nothing else in life could ever mean so much. One writer reflects that very often, when she has difficulty coping with her three children, she passes by the portrait of her maternal grandmother at the top of the stairs in her house, and longs to ask her how she managed her nine. The last had been born when she was aged forty-nine.

> My three children were, each one, a planned self-indulgence. Now I know that it's time to move past childbearing to the next stage of life. Intellectually I'm ready, but lately, passing babies in supermarkets . . . , I find myself wishing I had another.
>
> That is a dangerous thought for someone who is 38 years old.

Each child is a wonder and a joy, "But where is the one who was supposed to be just like me. . . ? Every child turns out to be not the clone that each parent expects." Though every pregnancy "speeds up the ruin of the mother's body, leaving the fingerprints of mortality in stretch marks and varicose veins," and though the longing for the youngest to be old enough to go to school is a daily refrain, a woman sees someone's baby—"and your arms start to ache." The mother of ten children, told that her health was in danger and that she would have to have a hysterectomy, finally accepted this and underwent the operation. Afterwards, at a party for her husband, who was "an important man," this woman "was nearly in tears because she could never have another child." The writer who witnessed this at a time before she was married thought of the woman's depression as pathetic and silly. She thought then that to give birth to ten children was irresponsible. She still thinks this—"but now I understand how she felt. I'm still having trouble giving up the babies I'll never have."[34]

Men do not have to give this up at midlife; men can go on fathering children into old age. This way of experiencing rebirth in the second half of life is not denied to them. For women, there is truly a "closing of the gates," and some will suffer deeply because of this. Some will experience the panic

Deutsch described. Procreative powers must be transformed into creative powers. Almost nothing is known of the existence of rites of passage in cultures around the world that guide women in this task of transformation. One report was published in the 1930s of rites that appear to have been performed by women who lived in small, obscure islands of the Hellenic archipelago in ancient times.[35] The ceremonies were intended only for women who had arrived at the age when they could no longer bring children into the world. It was thought that at this time in their lives, the spirit or god who presides over reproduction was about to undergo defeat. Even though objects belonging to Attic cultures have been found on these islands, this ceremony is not derived from the worship of Pan and his satyrs, but was intended to placate some force or being more primitive than Pan. Women performing these rites affirmed the power of this force and asked its consent to its death in them, since it would be resurrected in their children. Their mourning was as for the death of an immortal. There are few tangible traces of these rites. Of the material remains of the ceremony of mourning, there are a number of "mutilated stele. . . , on which it is still possible to distinguish a miniature table-like altar, with a tiny bier upon which is laid a plant resembling our common Jack-in-the-Pulpit. . . . Beside the bier stands the figure of a mourner" (6). The celebrants undertook a journey into time, and prepared themselves for this by purifying and sharpening their senses. They sought what was essential to the material and spiritual concerns of their daily lives. In their journey into the past, they remembered standing at "the shore of the great ocean of feeling that moves between men and women" (17). They remembered their feelings when their childhood ended. To enhance their memory, some women sought the society of young girls. They observed them in silence, and contemplated Woman as an incarnation of the past and the future.

On their journey, women remembered love and marriage, and later came to "the place in the abysm of time where a woman met the image of the child." Even a very young girl may meet this image. "The touch of a baby sends a startling current along her senses, she is obsessed by it, held as in a kind of magic, an ancestral charm" (24). Women who could see beyond the present, and who could put the past in order, would now have to walk through a narrow and painful place, if they wanted to continue their journey into the future:

> The past had held moulds of life, inherited forms; the dying or withdrawal of the daemon had been the signal for the re-visiting of the past. In the past the hierarchic figures, the Maiden, Lover, Child, the House, had moulded the stuff of life. At this age, with the withdrawal of the daemon, came a freedom from moulds, and the way was opened to liberty, but the path was surrounded with danger. [28]

To be free, now, the celebrant must come to terms with an image that only the most gallant could meet. This was the image of the Old Woman.

Whether these rites were actually celebrated at one time, or whether they are wholly imagined, they are a rare expression of the inner journey of women when their youth is past. They are meant to light her way. Therefore, Leonardo da Vinci's *La Sainte Anne* was chosen for the frontispiece of this book. In the painting,

> Saint Anne holds the Virgin on her lap, while the Virgin stretches out her hands to the smiling Christ Child, the newest flame of life. Child, mother and grandmother are all smiling, but there is a peculiar knowledge and power in the smile of Saint Anne, and behind her is a landscape which contains not only breadth and length and height and depth, but another dimension, Time. This dimension, Saint Anne . . . knows both forward and backward. [9–10]

Although it may once have been common knowledge that the plan of life is divisible into phases, this is no longer the case. Today, many people are confused about what psychological time of day it is for them. Today, there are no mystery rites belonging to collective life. Today, there is no common agreement about the meaning of the life cycle, or about the patterns described by the life course. Wanting communal rites of passage, each person must undertake the journey with a few chosen companions or guides—or alone. In the opinion of the late Linda Fierz-David, contemporary woman, "self-sufficient, outwardly well-adapted" as she may be, is as much in need of initiation as her counterpart who lived in the centuries before the Christian era.[36] When a woman today feels herself to be in danger of being overtaken by the sterility of a life that is "merely adapted," she has no mystery cult to which she might resort for guidance. Unless she finds psychological understanding, she is utterly alone. Fierz-David, a docent at the Jung Institute in Zurich up to the time of her death in 1955, interpreted the fresco series of the Villa of the Mysteries in Pompeii from the standpoint of Jungian analytical psychology.[37] She thought that the fact that the Villa was outside the city wall suggested that the cult may not have been officially recognized. In writing of this, Fierz-David remarked the privacy and solitariness of initiation of the contemporary woman, who must go into inner life to perform the rite of passage, rather than beyond the city wall.

In her text, Fierz-David compared the Villa itself, "a *casa muta*," with the Liber Mutus. There is no agreement among scholars as to the meaning of the frescoes. Indeed, many maintain that their meaning cannot be known. Kerenyi had told Fierz-David personally as well as in lecture that the most diverse versions and traditions of the Dionysus myths may be consulted in interpreting the frescoes. At the time they were painted, Hellenism was a mixture of many myths. In her view, the two figures of Dionysus and Ariadne in the frescoes personify the central symbol of the Self and of becoming a Self, uniting the opposites of the masculine and the feminine in the *conjunctio*. The room itself, with this central symbol, forms a great mandala comprised of many small mandalas. Just beyond the narrow entrance is a consecrated circle. The walk through the chamber from one mandala to the next is made in the form of a *circumambulatio*. As it leads to the goal, new meaning is continuously unfolded. All this is suggestive of the symbolism of individuation.

In analytical psychology, individuation means the realization of wholeness, or the experience of all the aspects of the Self. The way of individuation is, like all initiations, an experience of suffering, an ordeal wherethrough an earlier self is extinguished. The Roman woman who made the journey from fresco to fresco read the nature and meaning of her life through the language of mythological truth. Her experience was different from that of the contemporary woman. In antiquity, the unconscious and the conscious were not sharply distinguished from one another: there was a continuous flow of legend and myth into the world-view. Ideas about the psychic needs of women that had been formed in classical antiquity were modified in the Renaissance, the Reformation, and the Counter-Reformation. In the modern era, they underwent further modification by the medical guides of the human soul. As natural science usurped the place once inhabited by the gods, the inner meaning of the life of the world was lost. Religious experience could manifest itself only in dreams. For Fierz-David, dreams are the most eminent Dionysian manifestation for people in the contemporary world. And the Apollonian examination of dreams, the methodical analysis of dreams, is a practice that developed from the scientific attitude toward experience. A mystical winnowing basket or *kista mystika* appears in the frescoes, in which the divine content is hidden. The Roman woman interpreted the meaning of the divine content through the application of mythological symbols that were known by the educated people of that time to represent human experience. The modern woman is in a very different position. She needs an experienced person to serve as her guide in interpreting the meaning of the divine content of the *kista mystika*. This experienced person is the analyst, the medical guide of the human soul. And the *kista mystika*, which appears in the fresco as the vessel of divine content, is the dream. With the guidance of the analyst, the contemporary woman interprets the symbols that appear in the mystical winnowing basket, the dream, in search of their religious and mythological significance. In contemplation of the pattern of the fate of Dionysus and Ariadne, or of Phaidra, who forgets her origin as the daughter of Pasiphaë, or of Medea, who falls into the error of mistaking consciousness for the entirety of the autonomous spirit, the initiate experiences her own fate as a woman and as a creature of nature carrying within herself a particle of the divine.[38]

Fierz-David interpreted the frescoes of the Villa of the Mysteries from the standpoint of analytical psychology. From this standpoint, women are seen as governed by the principle of Eros, or relatedness. Their life flows between them and all that is near to them. That is why women tend to build high walls of opinion around themselves; they feel the need to separate themselves from objects. The symbol of Eros is the weaver's loom, at which the three daughters of Minyas remained rather than respond to the call of Dionysus. The weaver's loom spins countless threads of relatedness to entangle others. Ultimately, the weaver, too, becomes entangled in these threads. If a woman goes on weaving these threads of relatedness at the cost of her own soul, a powerful counter-current will arise in her. And if she remains unconscious of this, it will manifest itself "in a Maenad-like aggressiveness which kills in order to cut threads and break chains." Mythological stories tell of women who kill children. And there are "real-life" stories of women who maim or kill children by their Maenad-like aggressiveness (92–93).

The initiate to the mysteries, like all initiates everywhere, runs a grave risk. While she must subdue relatedness, she must not lose it entirely. If she does, she will be nothing but a ghost to herself and to others ever after this, since Eros is the source of the life-flow for her. There is a moment of epiphany for the initiate at the Villa, and for the contemporary woman who undertakes the way of individuation. This is the moment when a woman's consciousness actively takes part in the event that is being contemplated. At this moment of epiphany, there is a reawakening of the divine in the mortal. The human being meets the spiritual reality with the highest powers of her consciousness.

There is a turning point in life that marks the beginning of the striving toward psychic wholeness. Without realization of wholeness, one is unprepared to meet death. The turning point is symbolized by the summons of the cry of the Dionysian mask of terror, and by the number four—four in the afternoon that is about to turn into evening. When contemporary women arrive at this turning point, they do not have a collective mystery cult through which they can follow the rites of passage. Today, the way of individuation is a private undertaking. Unlike her Roman counterpart, today's woman embarks on a lonely journey in the discovery that she is Everywoman, in her encounter with the selves left undeveloped, the aspects of femininity she has not yet realized in her own life—her "shadow," or neglected side. The cry of the "mask of terror" heralds introversion and transformation. If a woman refuses to heed it, spiritual death ensues. Inner development is arrested; there is a withering of the psyche. A woman will have no more problems or tasks to be met. But then, after this, she will project all danger of death and all terror on the world outside herself. But the woman who heeds the summons, who becomes at this moment an initiate into the spiritual meaning of her life, will learn, as every initiate learns, to face her own danger, rather than projecting it outside herself. Jung had taught that it is dangerous to ignore the active, living spiritual nature of the unconscious. From the standpoint of analytical psychology, a spiritual development is seen to be possible for modern women, a development that resembles the initiation way portrayed symbolically in the Pompeiian fresco series. A modern woman can be driven out of the relatedness that is natural to her, and out of the affairs she is engaged in, by "the terrifying spiritual call of the turning point of life." At this time, she may fall into a "depression," that is, "into the suffering and the darkness of a Katabasis" (138).

To Fierz-David, the myths of the feminine figures that originated in the family of the great old Helios are symbols of levels of the development of femininity. She did not think it at all unusual that a woman in the contemporary world might undergo a phase in development when a man is felt to be a disturbing presence in her life, and when she may resist the presence or influence of a particular man, or of men in general. Women are different from one another. Some forget their consciousness and its activating powers, and they experience their femininity in a passive way. Others are like Medea. They project their own powerful emotions upon men. In interpreting the figures in the frescoes in terms of what they represent in women's condition, Fierz-David found that the figure of Ariadne portrayed

> the way to the goal, which flows into death . . . a situation where conscious-ness and especially everything personal, that women take as so surpassingly important, no longer play any role at all. It is really this condition which women long for when they can occupy themselves so intently with the problems of death, with the remembrance of those who have died, or with ideas about the life after death. Something in them always longs to find itself where nothing personal plays a part any more. That is Death, whom they already forebodingly greet in the transitoriness of the world, for some-thing in them senses that then the wine will begin to flow. [163]

On the way to spiritual development, the initiate undergoes a condition of being forsaken, an acknowledgment that the past is dead—a condition re-sembling the Naxos of Ariadne, in which she renounces her wishes, her long-ings, her strivings. In this way, she parts from everything that is personal. In the course of her spiritual development, a woman arrives at the ninth fresco, where relationships are seen as means of knowing the self, and are no longer taken quite so personally. She has seen that consciousness is relative, and variable. She has learned composure. At the tenth fresco, she contemplates the figure of the Domina, who, in Fierz-David's view, represents *Mnemosyne*, Remembrance. To Fierz-David, the psychological meaning of Memory is a concentration upon what is essential. If a woman can remember what she has learned, she will no longer be subject to blind fate.

The gift of impersonality, which Ellen Glasgow thought to be the great gift age offers to women, and of the ability to concentrate on what is essential in all things, which May Sarton perceives as a goal of the second half of life—these gifts are not easily won. The passage from one phase of the life cycle to another, the experience of a critical change, a turning point, may begin with depression. In exploring the problems of the feminine as these are revealed in fairy tales, Marie-Louise von Franz interprets depression as an initiation, intended "to re-connect one with the divine principle."[39] A common motif in fairy tales is that of the woman who is cured only after she accepts the fact that she must spend a period of time in isolation. Whereas the male hero in fairy tales must accomplish some deed, which usually involves the undertaking of a longer journey, the woman must withdraw for a time. She experiences the unconscious as isolation, and this precedes a return to life. The occasion for this depression, this initiation, may be the death of a woman's mother, or the departure of her grown daughter from the home. When her mother dies, a woman—whatever her calendar age may be—realizes she can no longer be identical with her:

> Therefore the mother's death is the beginning of the process of individuation; the daughter feels that she wants to be a positive feminine being, but in her own form, which entails going through all the difficulties of finding that. Here the archaic mother-daughter identity is broken off and the feminine human being realizes its weaknesses. Again and again it is the great problem in feminine psychology. Women, even worse than men, tend to identify with their own sex, and to remain in this archaic identity. [149]

Again, when her grown daughter leaves home, a mother may find that she "can not get to her own work and creativity." The archaic identification of mother with daughter and daughter with mother is so fundamental that a very great effort must be made for them to separate, and for each to become fully conscious of her own personality. "The mother must take back all her projections on the daughter and become individual herself, and that is very difficult for all women" (151). Much has been written about mothers who devour their sons. But many women are much more entangled with their daughters than with their sons. In these cases, what has happened is that the mother has projected a symbol of the Self onto her daughter. Because the daughter represents the Self for her, she is unable to get out of the projection. "The mother having to pull away from the daughter is always a problem of the second half of life, for it arises only when the daughter is that age" (152).

In becoming an individual, a woman must free herself from unlimited pity. Women's tendency to indulge in excessive maternal pity is portrayed in the fairy tale of Briar Rose and in Apuleius's story of Amor and Psyche. A woman's pity is easily aroused by those who are helpless or in difficulty. But pity can be destructive if it is excessive; it can condemn the one who is pitied to infantilism. A woman must control the maternal instinct, since some objectivity and detachment are needed "to see what is really good for the other person." Excessive maternal pity is often felt for the wrong people. A woman is in danger of attaching herself to that which cannot be changed. In a way, she may actually live off this attachment. This happens with the martyred wife of the alcoholic, and with the maternal woman who loves to mother young men as misunderstood geniuses. The moment in woman's individuation when she must free herself from unbounded pity is critical. The highest value for women, and the essence of femininity, is the need for relatedness,

> but a bit too much of it makes it negative because it makes that dependent clinging which men fear so much in women, and which is . . . a great evil by which women who establish relatedness so easily destroy all the good they do. If their eros—which means genuine interest in the other person and in establishing relationship, . . .—gets the least bit too dependent, . . . it is already on the downward grade into the devouring aspect of the female. If one is attentive to one's relationships, it is infinitely difficult to find the right balance.[40]

Many older people are apathetic. They seem to have lost the élan vital—or, perhaps, they have never known it. The absence of a desire to live may be genuine; it may be a consequence of the feeling that vitality has begun to fade, or of illness or the coming of old age, or even of a very real need to retire from life. But apathy is also seen in those who remain unaware of the darkness of their own nature, who believe themselves to be completely good. Once this destructive darkness is penetrated, and the wish for death surfaces, a counter-reaction will occur, and a person will have the desire to live again.[41]

In striving toward wholeness, the darkness of one's nature is revealed. This is the "shadow," or the unlived part of the personality. People in analysis have been said to engage in "veritable witch hunts and shadow hunts." Acceptance of the shadow demands strength and courage. Through love, it can be redeemed. If a person has "cherished a resplendent ego," then humility is the price to be paid for finding the unrealized part of the personality. This is the sacrifice that must be made in striving toward wholeness. On the other hand, if one has lived on a level lower than that of which one is capable—if one has been running away from life by doing this—one may have even more difficulties than a person who must learn to accept humiliating truths about herself or himself. This is because the realization of potential for creative activity places one under the obligation of working to developing it more fully.[42]

The shadow can contain good elements as well as bad ones. In either case, shadow qualities ought to be known, if one is to accept responsibility for the way these qualities affect other people, as well as for the way they affect the self. To find the shadow, one should notice the qualities in other people that arouse anger or irritation. Something in one's own nature may resemble such qualities, and once this is discovered, the projection of it on another will be withdrawn. Only those qualities of which one is unconscious are projected. One who carries her or his own dark shadow qualities and sets other people free from projections of them may be truly said to be integrated.[43]

Youth and the "prime of life" are given over to ego development. The second half of life ought to be given over to spiritual growth. To live for decades beyond the childbearing period without any purpose to one's life is to receive years of life as a burden rather than as a gift. In the record of her analysis, Anna Hope Gould Robinson reflected that age 60 is rather late in life to have certain insights into oneself, but that any time that one "comes awake" is good. She saw herself as an older woman who wanted to understand herself before the time came to "shuffle off this mortal coil." Robinson experienced seven months of aimless wandering, six months of loneliness in the desert, two months coming to terms with the masculine component (the animus) of her personality, and two in contact with the aspects of her femininity that represent intuition, feminine warmth and understanding, and feminine persistence and determination. She recorded her dreams of a child struggling for ascent, and her feelings of inadequacy in her efforts to care for this child. Through her individuation experience, she learned that the ego is only one part of the psyche, and that, while wholeness cannot be achieved without it, the ego cannot dominate the search. She learned that one is given four faculties—thinking, feeling, sensation, and intuition—and that wholeness means the use of all four equally; it means the sacrifice of the faculty that had up to then been "arrogant." Through wholeness, one is brought to the highest creative point in experience. Robinson found that an older woman comes to understand that conformity is no longer essential in her life. It is not the purpose of her life, as it may well have been when she was younger. She learned that a woman begins to mature only when she steps down from a pedestal, since women on pedestals are consumed either by pride or by self-pity. Through the way of individuation, Robinson experienced the feminine psyche in all the diversity of its aspects. She understood herself to be Everywoman, not only Madonna and Great Mother, but Gypsy and Black Witch, as well. She thought that perhaps the Black Witch may be buried the deepest in women, because women work so hard to incarnate the social ideal of what Womanhood ought to be.[44]

Wisdom: Insights from Analytical Psychology

Jung has shown that those who explore the hidden depths of the psyche will come upon "primordial images, pictures of racial experience, archetypes, ancient powerful forces." Unseen and unknown, these forces influence human action and human character. Those who embark upon the way of individuation learn that the ego is not the center of the psyche. In forming relationships to the inner figures, a new center of consciousness emerges. This new center, known as the Self, has a non-personal quality. It transcends personal wishes and personal needs.[45] When Robinson recognized the figures of her inner life, and created relationships with them, she began to discover the Self. In this way, she became free of a life in nature, dominated by collective impulses, and of a life dominated by the ego—by personal impulses.

As one grows older, integration has more and more to do with recovering an inner value than it has to do with forming some adaptation to the outer world.[46] To become whole is to realize one's uniqueness, one's identity as distinctive from collective identity in a family or a work group or a community or nation. In individuation, the ego finds and establishes a relationship with the objective psyche; it accepts its containment within a more comprehensive psychic whole. When an individuation process is successful, the Self replaces the ego as the center of the personality. For women, the way to individuation is followed by exploring the feminine.

Through the approach of analytical psychology, the feminine is explored as a distinct category of being, and as a form of perception that is inherent in every woman and every man, as well as in all cultures. The originality of this approach is that it does not confine the feminine to women only, that the nature of the feminine is explored through the language of symbol and myth, and that it takes as its premise the idea that the achievement of personal wholeness is possible only through a complete awareness of contrasexuality.[47] Hence, the feminine refers to a psychic reality for men as well as for women, and it is expressed in a variety of social and cultural patterns.

The feminine principle is *sub specie aeternitatis*. It cannot be thought away by reducing it to biology or to culture. The psychic representation of the contrasexual elements in man is the anima, the "inner woman."[48] She may take many forms. She may be hetaira or companion, or Sophia, the incarnation of divine Wisdom. She may be nurturing mother, mediatrix, *femme inspiratrice*, White Goddess, muse. In her dark aspects, she may be the Terrible Mother, the devouring female, the wicked witch who is seen as young Siren or as a withered crone. In symbolic imagery, the figures of women range "from harlot and seductress to divine wisdom and spiritual guide." When a man projects the anima, he "falls in love." When his ego is identified with the anima, he behaves as an inferior woman. "With full psychological development, the anima leads the man to the full meaning of human relationship and provides him an entrance to the deeper layers of the psyche, the collective unconscious."[49] The anima personifies the feminine principle in man—the principle of Eros, which pertains to love and relatedness.

A woman's nature, too, is contrasexual. In striving toward wholeness, she works to reconcile her masculine and feminine components. The masculine element in a woman's psychology, the animus, takes myriad forms. It personifies the masculine principle in women, the principle of Logos, which pertains to consciousness and rationality. The "inner man" may take the form of a young lover, a companion and friend, a wise old man, a divine bringer of light. In his dark aspects, he may be a terrifying figure who preys upon a woman, threatening to rend or to destroy her. The animus may also be—as it was for Robinson—a committee of men sitting around a conference table with a woman. When a woman projects the animus, she "falls in love." If she becomes identified with the animus, she will behave as an inferior man. A woman who is possessed by her animus "is more interested in power than in relatedness."[50]

The psyche of both women and men is an interweaving of both masculine and feminine components, the former representing focus, division, and change, and the latter representing acceptance, awareness of the unity of all forms of life, and readiness for relationship. The one is "focused consciousness" and the other is "diffuse awareness." If the one represents head, the other represents heart. When things are approached from one, the other appears so absurd that it may be repudiated. People who use one or the other approach exclusively are not able to communicate. A person is in conflict when both inner voices clamor to lay claim to the truth. "It is a real dilemma. I offend my head or I offend my heart."[51]

M. Esther Harding writes of the price that is paid in women's advance to conscious development. This is "an unavoidable inner conflict" a woman experiences "between the urge to express herself through work, as a man does, and the inner necessity to live in accordance with her own ancient feminine nature." Woman has always needed to reconcile the dual aspects of her nature, just as man has. But a "modern note" is sounded when this inner need is expressed in practical life. Women today who are at all aware of themselves as conscious persons experience this conflict between the masculine and feminine principles that rule from within, not now and again, but at every turn. A one-sided life is simply not enough for them. Western civilization has placed a very high value on the objective realm, the realm of Logos. As a consequence, both men and women have neglected the feminine component of human nature. But inner life, with its broth of dreams and musings, of myth and poetry and fantasy, is as real, as true as consciousness. In meeting this conflict between the opposing principles of Eros and Logos, women need to make contact with subjective material that was defined by scientists of the nineteenth century as mere superstition or moodiness.[52]

Ulanov calls attention to Jung's perception of the correspondence between psychic material and the universal motifs found in religion and mythology, and to his hypothesis that the psyche is *sui generis*, and not to be identified either with the body or with consciousness.[53] In a culture shaped in accordance with masculine values, consciousness itself is expressed in masculine terms. Therefore,

> this sense of otherness frequently comes in images associated with the feminine, such as female figures who tempt one against one's will, or who are helpful sisters, or who are wise women full of secrets. Although masculine images fulfill this same purpose for women, the lack of ease of women with each other, their bewilderment about their own feminine reality, and their eagerness to trace their discomfort to centuries of male domination—all suggest that even for females, images of the feminine hold a much needed contact with contents and perspectives that they want to make part of themselves. [19]

In Ulanov's judgment, Jung's presentation of the feminine is both limited in quantity and uneven in quality. Furthermore, his observations were sometimes inaccurate, and he glossed over certain profound truths. In spite of these and other flaws which account for the absence of a precise definition of the feminine in his works, she believes he has made an original contribution to an understanding of the psychology of the feminine. Personifying the psyche so as to meet it on its own ground, in its own language of vivid images and symbols, in its expression through dreams, poetry, painting, and sculpture, one receives it through the heart and senses and imagination, rather than through the mind only. Through dreams and myth, storytelling and art, a desire is expressed—a desire Jung thought to be religious in nature—to create and hold "a meaningful relationship between the personal self and the transpersonal source of the power and meaning of being."[54]

From the standpoint of analytical psychology, striving toward wholeness is seen as far more than an objective chosen by the conscious mind. It is experienced as an imperious command from the psyche. Rix Weaver finds that if one misses the significance of the unconscious, "it comes up again with greater force and sometimes changes its mode of expression until understood."[55] Jung perceived that the child who appears in dreams is the being who paves the way for a change of personality. The figure that emerges from a synthesis of conscious and unconscious elements "represents the strongest, the most ineluctable urge in every being, namely the urge to realise itself" (101). This compelling need governs the second half of life, when the spiritual quest for the meaning of one's life is undertaken.

In striving toward wholeness in a society that is ruled by Logos, in a culture in which feminine values have fallen into limbo, a woman turns to what Weaver calls "the nature side." Because this is the side that has been rejected by Western civilization, it is the "shadow side." Feminine and masculine poles of being are archetypes, constellations of feelings, images, and behavior patterns and possibilities. Weaver calls them the "sleeping dominants of the unconscious" that "are not filled out with personal memory images but go beyond into ancestral inheritance" (138). The archetypes of the collective unconscious are psychic structures. In and of themselves, they have no form. It is the creative artist who makes them into figures, who gives them forms—who makes them visible.[56] These forms vary according to the nature of the artist and the historical time and cultural place in which they appear. The archetype of the Great Mother, for example, may take on various styles, although it always keeps its identity. Through time, and in the various cultures of the world, the primordial archetype has been divided into many different goddesses, and this has led to the founding of individual cults.[57] Sophia, the Virgin Mary, the Wise Old Woman, the Terrible Mother, the good witch and the wicked witch—all are images and personifications of the archetype. In his exhaustive inquiry into the archetype of the Great Mother, Neumann expresses the hope that his mode of presentation will intimate "the radiant diversity of the archetypal reality."[58]

Poets and artists have always known of this radiant diversity. A force that is ageless because it is eternally present in the collective unconscious as well as in the personal unconscious, the Great Mother may appear as a protecting and nurturing mother, but also as a mother who ensnares and devours. In other personifications, she is a witch who has the power to work magic for either good or evil, as the priestess of death mysteries as well as the goddess who presides over vegetation mysteries. She may be represented as Hecate as well as Demeter, as Sophia as well as Lilith. In a schematic representation of the archetype, Neumann locates four polar points—The Good Mother, the Terrible Mother, the seductive young witch (the negative anima), and the Sophia-virgin (the positive anima.) Each of these four poles exerts a strong psychic attraction for the ego (Schema III, p. 83).

The archetype holds a powerful fascination for consciousness.[59] Its energy far surpasses that of the ego. As a consequence, the ego may be overwhelmed by it. When this happens, the archetype takes hold, consciousness disintegrates, and the ego is lost. The lower poles are experienced as negative because they are so vulnerable to this. The positive poles are less vulnerable because they contain a consciousness-promoting component, and this protects consciousness and the ego from a fatal fascination. It is at the polar points that consciousness loses its faculty for differentiating, for discerning the difference between what is positive and what is negative. When consciousness comes undone, a phenomenon can shift into its opposite. Distress and loneliness, emptiness and madness can thus be precursors of inspiration and vision. They can "manifest themselves as stations on a road leading through danger to salvation, through the extinction of death to rebirth and new birth." The converse of this is also possible: inspiration and ecstasy, both positive, may be the forerunners of the eclipse of the ego in possession and madness.[60] Though each pole of the archetype is an end point, it is also a turning point. The closer the ego approaches any one of the poles, the greater the chance that it may pass beyond it to its opposite. The archetype is paradoxical in its very nature. The fact that in their extremes the opposites can shift into one another is at the basis of many mystery rites, rites of initiation, and occult doctrines.

An archetype is non-human; it is blind force. In experiencing it, a person is in danger of becoming possessed by it. If a woman experiences the manifestation of the Wise Old Woman in her unconscious, for example, her ego may be so inspired by her utterances that she may identify her ego completely with this figure. This condition is known as "inflation." The Wise Old Woman has the woman's ego in its grasp; it fills her with itself, so that she is truly possessed. In forfeiting her awareness of her separateness from the archetype, the woman surrenders her ability to discriminate. In this way, she loses her freedom—her human qualities. The danger of inflation is more clearly seen when there is negative rather than positive inflation, that is, when one is possessed by the chaotic or even demonic aspects of nature. It is the task of analysis to keep the ego separate from the archetype. It is only when a person recognizes and transforms the powers of the unconscious that they can become positive qualities in psychic life.[61]

The Wise Old Woman, the ancient one, is also a witch. Hers is a divine but also a sinister character. She is "a nature being who weaves the web of life and uses people in a remarkable way."[62] The spindle is the symbol of the Wise Old Woman and of the witch. Wisdom is an active force in realizing and materializing: "Wisdom is weaving the world from the nature of God. This is an archetypal situation underlying the feminine principle, for in life it seems a woman's lot to be busy bringing something about" (46). When Wisdom appears as an ancient, she takes the form of the Wise Old Woman. When she appears in the form of a young woman, Wisdom may take the name of Sophia. In mythology, the figure of Sophia or the Cumaean Sibyl are symbols of the Wise Woman. In history, this archetype is symbolized by women who choose to devote themselves to what they perceive to be the emerging Zeitgeist.[63]

Sophia has been named as the first wife of Yahweh, a "feminine pneuma" and "his intimate playmate from all eternity."[64] Wisdom has also been named as "the Eros of God, the feminine principle."[65] Whether personified as an ancient or as a young virginal Sophia, Wisdom is alchemical power, the principle of transformation. The paradoxical archetype may appear as the good witch—as Glinda, in the tale of the Wizard of Oz—and as the wicked witch, a destructive force.[66] What is often overlooked is the polyvalence of the archetype:

> Isis, both in the form of Nature and in the form of Moon, had . . . two aspects. She was the creator, mother, nurse of all, and she was also the Destroyer. Her name Isis means ancient, and she was also called Maat, which means Knowledge or Wisdom. Isis is Maat, the *ancient wisdom*. This means the wisdom of things as they are and as they always have been, the innate, inherent capacity to follow the nature of things both in their present form and in their inevitable development in relation to each other. It is the wisdom of instinct. To the philosophers of Hellenistic times she was The Wisdom, The Sophia.[67]

In exploring the feminine aspects of divinity, Erminie Lantero notes that an early rabbinic commentator came to the conclusion that Adam had been androgynous and was later separated into male and female. She finds a parallel myth of original androgyny in the *Symposium* of Plato, in which "a lost state of wholeness" is symbolized. Lantero points to the impressive evidence from archaeological researches "that from Paleolithic times, from the Mediterranean lands to the Indus Valley, the ultimate source of life was felt to be maternal." She provides examples of personifications of the maternal principle, among them the triune goddesses who symbolize the stages of feminine life—the Maiden, the Mother, and the aging Hag-Witch, as corresponding to the crescent, full, and waning phases of the moon. Her study, which she is careful to say ought not to be taken as a recommendation for "a relapse into polytheism," is an inquiry into the manifestations of the feminine principle in divinity throughout history.[68] The Virgin Mary, "the first divinized *human*," came to be "the mediator between the whole Trinity and mankind, Mother of all Christians and archetype of the Church." There is another version of the female mediating principle between God and man in post-Biblical Judaism. This is the Shekinah. "The abstract noun *sh'kinah*, literally 'indwelling,' does not appear in the Bible but the related verb does." In the first few centuries A.D., "Aramaic versions of the Old Testament introduce the word 'Shekinah' . . . as a reverent circumlocution for God." The Shekinah experience came into full flowering in the movement of Kabbalism (24–25). Lantero writes, "Sophia, Spirit and Shekinah may be seen as somewhat different but overlapping bands of the total spectrum of Divinity as immanent in the universe and in man." In Sophia, the cosmic aspects predominate. In Spirit and Shekinah, the experiences of inner life and human relatedness have the ascendancy. There is a deeply felt need in our culture for a Mary figure and a Sophia figure, since wisdom and compassion, knowledge and love have lost their essential unity (29–30).

Only the woman can transform, since "in her body that corresponds to the Great Goddess, is the caldron of incarnation, birth, and rebirth."[69] And Wisdom is transformative. It is one aspect of the dual character of the Feminine. While the *elementary* character is that aspect which tends to hold fast to all that is born from it, to encircle it as an eternal substance, as the Great Round or the Great Container, the *transformative* character, dynamic in contrast to conservative, impels toward activity and change. In the development of the psyche, the elementary character dominates the transformative. But gradually, the transformative character wins independence from and ascendancy over that which is unchanging. It is imperative that one recognize that *both* characters of the Feminine have a positive and a negative aspect. The positive aspect of the elementary character is manifested in nurturance and protection of whatever was born from it. The negative aspect is manifested in the ensnaring tendencies of the Terrible Mother. The transformative character, too, may be negative, destroying that which it brings forth, enticing that which it sets in motion to be drawn into fatal encounters. These two characters of the Feminine interpenetrate and combine in many ways.[70]

Know thyself, the philosopher counseled. This is the central task of the second half of life. For an older woman to know herself, she needs to be aware of the archetypal dynamism that underlies her own femininity. It is not only she herself who will be the beneficiary of this knowledge, but all those with whom her life is interrelated. The more completely a woman knows herself, the less inclined she will be to stereotype women or to accept the stereotypes of women that others may try to disseminate as truths. The more completely she knows herself, the less likely she will be to identify completely with one social role or persona, whether this be as mother, housewife, or career woman. The more completely she knows herself, the more likely she will be to experience herself as Everywoman, not just one "kind" of woman. If a woman can accept the many and contending forces within herself, she will "enrich her life, her relation to others, and her contributions to her society."[71] Knowledge of Self brings one into the "now"—"more fully in life, more acutely aware. The 'now of immortality' brings things into the present, into Tao." Past and future are "enfolded in the 'now.' This coming together means also a preparation for death." Self-knowledge is not knowledge of the ego, but of the relationship of the ego to the objective psyche—of the comprehensive psychic whole of which the ego is only a part.[72]

All women, whatever the differences in their individual fates, are daughters. All have known through experience with another woman something of the nature of the Feminine. All women have lived out some part of the divine drama between Demeter and Persephone (Kore). And every woman may experience "a central transformation, not so much by becoming a woman and a mother, and thus guaranteeing earthly fertility and the survival of life, as by achieving union on a higher plane with the spiritual aspect of the Feminine, the Sophia aspect of the Great Mother."[73] It is possible for a goddess to be a Good Mother of the kind in whom the elementary character predominates. It is also possible for a goddess to be a Terrible Mother in whom the transformative character predominates. So far as the situation of the ego and consciousness are concerned, it matters very much, indeed, which of the characters is the prevailing one. The Good Mother can be associated with an infantile ego. An example of this is the witch in the story of Hansel and Gretel. Her house is made of gingerbread and sweets. Through it, she entices little children whom she intends to devour. The converse of this is the Terrible Mother who inclines toward the transformative character. The Terrible Mother may drive a woman to positive development, as Aphrodite drives Psyche onward in Apuleius's tale. "Bad" and "persecuting," she sets development in motion; she promotes individuation. Here, Aphrodite as Terrible Mother is the guiding Sophia, who keeps sending Psyche "on her way."[74] Rejection can be positive. It releases the young when they are grown. It can express "a part of the transformative character that permits living creatures to arrive at their natural development."[75]

Spiritual transformation means a fundamental change of personality and consciousness. A symbol of this is a child emerging from the darkness of the womb, a child who is a light-bringer who impels toward personality change and realization of the Self. To distill wisdom from suffering is to learn how to separate that which is personal from that which is transpersonal. This is the essential meaning of a "change of life." The child who emerges from an initiation rite is a symbol of the birth of a new individuality that takes the place of the ego. This child represents the ability to begin anew, "even after disaster and failure . . . with new values and a new understanding of life."[76] Sophia, as the highest form of the feminine spirit-self, "is a wisdom relating to the indissoluble and paradoxical unity of life and death, of nature and spirit, to the laws of time and fate, of growth, of death and death's overcoming."[77] There is a tragic aspect to growth and transformation, the aspect of transience—the death of a person "is as nothing in view of the unchanging abundance of renascent life." But there is also a heavenly aspect to the Great Round, which "embodies not only a transformation downward to mortality and the earth, but a transformation upward toward immortality and the luminous heavens."[78]

Freedom and Responsibility in Women's Later Life

The power of cultural traditions and beliefs in interpreting human experience and in shaping world-view is undeniable and must be respected. However, it must never be forgotten that the way people fare in other societies around the world is an exceedingly difficult question to explore and that the answers to it must always be very tentative for just this reason. Leo Simmons's conspectus of the status and treatment of the elderly in 71 non-Western societies is the most authoritative and comprehensive cross-cultural survey on this subject available to researchers.[79] Yet Simmons is quite explicit about the limitations of his research procedures and of the sources of his information. He writes that available information is imperfect, that reports are conflicting, that the sources are imprecise, that classifications are oversimplified and may be arbitrary as well, and that subjective judgments are inescapable: all this, he cautions his readers, jeopardizes scientific objectivity. Even so, he believes that his study "represents a more reliable approximation to objective analysis than earlier, less well-controlled procedures" (13). He comments that his study is faulted by insufficient information also. "Ethnographers were not careful in reporting all relevant information on the status and treatment of the aged." Furthermore, they did not categorize this information in a way that would make it useful for other researchers. And the entire subject has been much neglected. "Every grain of available information had to be culled from scattered sources, and even then the picture was often very incomplete for a given tribe" (19). Simmons also remarks that he thinks that 71 tribes are too few a number to justify complete reliance on any one statistical coefficient, although he believes that much greater confidence may be placed in the general trend of large numbers of coefficients that have bearing on any major hypothesis.

Simmons's book is about both elderly women and elderly men, and therefore information about women must be winnowed from chapters that do not have any necessary emphasis on sex differences. His method was to select 109 physical and cultural traits and to list them in three groups—habitat, maintenance, and economy; political and social organization; and religious and miscellaneous beliefs and practices. He tested correlations between these in order to discover general trends. Then he drew correlations between these trends and the various traits found to be associated with the status and treatment of old people. He is careful to state that in particular societies there could be "glaring exceptions" to any general trends for which his correlations are taken as evidence. Also, the age at which a man or woman is thought to be "aged" or "old" is a matter of social and cultural definition. This further qualifies any comparative judgments one may be tempted to make about the status and treatment of "aged" women in these 71 societies and our own. With these caveats clearly issued, certain findings may be found to be suggestive.

While Simmons did not find sex differences in the treatment accorded elderly men and women so far as customs regarding food sharing with the aged are concerned, he did find some striking sex differences regarding property rights, prestige, and political and civil activities. He found that old women have acquired significant property rights in far fewer of these societies than have old men, but that the severity of the climate and the inconstancy of the food supply appear to have been equally detrimental to their success in acquiring them at all. He also reports that old women have shown a relative advantage over old men in the control of property rights among food collectors, hunters, and, to a lesser extent, among fishers whereas old men appear to have been at considerable advantage over old women among farmers, and even more so among herders. This means that, as the economy became more highly developed, men gained an advantage over women in the possession of property. Also, the property rights of old women show greater variations than those of old men, and appear to be more strongly influenced by the prevailing type of social organization. Simmons's chapter on prestige reports that old women apparently gained more prestige in simpler societies with food-collecting, hunting, and fishing economies, and again observes that their social position appears to have been better among farmers than among herders. However, if either sex loses respect in old age, it is much more likely that old women experience this age-related forfeiture. Simmons also found that in most of these societies, aged men were "overwhelmingly favored" over aged women in important political and civil offices. However, the old women often performed important functions in rites of initiation.

So far as general activities are concerned, Simmons reports that midwifery has been much more often the domain of elderly women than of elderly men. He also found that the domestic authority of old women has followed more irregular trends than that of their male counterparts. Old women wielded considerable power over family affairs in the simpler societies "and where the mother-family has prevailed," but the men are dominant in herding societies and in "patriarchal" systems. As seen in cross-cultural perspective, old women appear far less prominently than old men as family leaders; even so, Simmons writes, women have had a greater advantage in this regard than they have had in opportunities to marry men younger than themselves. His conclusion from an examination of all the coefficients is that it appears that old men and women have fared about the same in both matrilineal and patrilineal societies in the matter of family care and support, but that both sexes appear to have fared somewhat better in patrilineal societies.

Simmons's cross-cultural study may serve as a valuable reference for an analysis of older people's status in a modern, industrial society such as our own since it provides insights into the relationship between aspects of social organization and the fate of the elderly. For example, he suggests that

> In a sense it may be claimed that persecution for witchcraft has been a risk accompanying the practice of shamanism by the aged, for individuals might bring it upon themselves whenever they failed to produce socially approved results as reputed magicians and wonder workers. Witchcraft, so viewed, is shamanism gone awry. This may explain in part why old women have been more frequently persecuted as witches than aged men; perhaps they have not been so successful in shamanism and in defending themselves against accusations of witchcraft. [230–31]

However, these insights reveal the perimeters of the range of possibilities to which an older woman may aspire in her social and cultural world; they cannot tell us how she experiences the changes in her life as she grows older, nor her perception of those perimeters. Ultimately the study of women in the second half of life is *trans*cultural, since it leads to an exploration of what may be experienced by older women in all cultures and at any time in human history.

In their reflections on the climacterium, both Theresa Benedek and Helene

Deutsch write of the potential it has as a *developmental* phase in women's life cycle. Benedek cites evidence that in many cultures, women who are about to lose their propagative powers and sexual attractiveness enjoy enhanced power and prestige, and she states that much of the exaggerated fear of menopause some women have appears to be culturally determined. Benedek believes that motherhood plays an important role in a woman's development, and that her personality will be sustained during the "change of life" by the accomplishments of her reproductive period—not just by having children, but by the total developmental achievement of her personality. Benedek discusses the climacterium as a period of intrapersonal reorganization in women. In comparing it with the oedipal phase, she states that the cessation of biological growth affects further intrapersonal integration—a transmutation of growth—and that it releases new energies for socialization and learning.[80] Deutsch, who states that the climacterium "is indeed critical," writes that she does not doubt "that the mastering of the psychologic reactions to the organic decline is one of the most difficult tasks of woman's life."[81] Her essay is as rich in clinical materials as in insights, and reveals an appreciation of how much "individual manifestations of the climacterium . . . greatly depend upon the given woman's personality" (456–57). While some women experience a strong urge to become pregnant and to experience motherhood again, others who until that time were wholly absorbed by "the reproductive function" may turn to occupations outside their homes, and those who had shown "any sort of creative urge or skill" before they married and had children "dig up and revive long buried interests—interests that flowered for a short time during prepuberty but were lost in the conflicts of puberty." Deutsch observes that many women, especially those who had artistic aspirations, gave up this type of activity when they married. "Such women shun, as though in a phobia, the piano, palette, or whatever the instrument of their former interests is, because of a dark feeling that they must 'choose.' Apparently they fear that their artistic sublimations will endanger the emotional experience of marriage." In this passage in her essay, Deutsch recalls others in which she pointed out the inner connection between the erotic experience of woman and her creative achievement, and she states that this explains "why, in a phase of heightened activity and of simultaneous threat to eroticism, the urge to creation is renewed." It is Deutsch's judgment that "the urge to intellectual and artistic creation and the productivity of motherhood spring from common sources, and it seems very natural that one should be capable of replacing the other" (458). During the preclimacterium—between the ages of 40 and 50, broadly speaking, although it is difficult to define the age range exactly—there is a thrust of activity and a return to an old psychic attitude, and Deutsch writes that there are a number of motives that set this in motion. Deutsch perceives that, among other emotions, this thrust of activity "also expresses woman's protest, her assertion that she is not merely a servant of the species, not a machine for bearing children, that she has higher brain centers and a complicated emotional life that is not restricted to motherhood" (459).

The study of women in the second half of life is a daedal undertaking, a work of relatedness, an exploration of the interconnections between the biological life cycle, culture, historical experiences, and women's oral testimony about the way they experience the "change of life." This is precisely what Nancy Datan, Aaron Antonovsky, and Benjamin Maoz achieve in their brilliant work *A Time to Reap*.[82] This is a comparative study of middle-aged women of five ethnic groups in Israel that represent points on a continuum ranging from traditionalism to modernity. The "modern" are the immigrant Jewish women from Central European countries, the "traditional" are the Israel-born Moslem Arab villagers, and the "transitional" are the Turkish, Persian, and North African women. All these women were born between 1915 and 1924 and were in their childbearing years during World War II and the Israel War of Independence, yet they made different decisions about family size. This study found that the new freedoms of the modern woman, the generational continuity of the traditional women, and the dislocations of the transitional women are all part of the experience of the passage to middle age—expressed in different ways in different cultures, but potentially present in all of them. The most remarkable finding was that women from all five subcultures were very similar in their feelings about menopause and the loss of fertility. Despite wide variation in control of conception and in fertility history—whether these women had borne only one or two children or fifteen—all of them welcomed the "change of life" and the loss of their ability to bear children. Datan and her associates remark that this affirms a natural rhythm in the life cycle, and that it represents a rediscovery of the wisdom of the passage in Ecclesiastes that teaches there is a season for all things. Menopause, like every other phase of the life cycle, is not a time of loss or of liberation so much as a time of change—of transition. "Transition brings change, and with change comes the unknown." But in the broadest sense of the word, all middle-aged women in the world today are in transition.

To realize the possibilities of later life, a woman must declare herself free to create the sense of that life. This is an awesome responsibility, and, as *A Time to Reap* affirms, the process of change is costly and it is painful. There is this paradox that the forces that oppose a woman at the same time set her free. "They are in themselves an incentive, for only by collision with life does one know that one lives. . . . Existence . . . means suffering."[83] Granted many years of life of freedom from service to nature, to the bearing and rearing of children, women must accept the responsibility of freedom. They must find what is exceptional in themselves, and transform this into a contribution to the life of the world.

There are many older women who refuse this freedom, who spend their later years obsessed with health, mourning their lost youth. They lay waste their hours, pursuing the narrow ego demands for attention, prestige, wealth, adulation. This is a capitulation to the forces of the culture of the "Nacirema," who devote a considerable portion of their time and energy to ritual activity to enhance the appearance and health of the human body.[84] Many Nacirema equate pleasure and comfort with *physical* well-being. For them, aging is "the gravest, most mortal of insults." Their later years "seem to move in a decreasing spiral, centered around their growing preoccupation with the state of their bodies."[85] Because of the double standard applied to aging, Nacirema women suffer more than the men in this culture as they grow older. "Even young women feel themselves in a desperate race against the calendar." Physical attractiveness counts more heavily in a woman's life than in a man's. Nacirema women pay more penalties than men for "the normal changes that age inscribes on every human face." In this culture, women's sexual market value declines steadily with the years. The model woman's face is Garbo's— the mask without lines, "perfection."[86] In the last pages of Ramón del Valle-Inclán's *Sonata de Invierno*, the Marquis of Bradomín says to his beloved María Antoinieta, "There are some men who prefer to be a woman's first love. I would always prefer to be her last." If this is a rare sensibility for a man anywhere in the world, it would be rarer still for a man of the Nacirema culture. All these cultural forces oppose the older woman's will to meet the challenges of later life. They are aspects of a culture that developed under the dominion of "a dynasty of scientific materialism." But even in this culture there are irruptions of the ancient mystery play called life, and the landscape is peopled "with familiar yet fantastic forms: gurus, shamans, wandering bards, exorcists." From the perspective of all human history, the "years of our rational, scientific enlightenment seem a brief moment in the morning of consciousness." For a woman to become fully conscious and aware, to meet the challenges of culture and of inner life, she needs to be both wakeful and imaginative. The mode of consciousness that is emerging in our time is one that is Janus-faced. With one pair of eyes, things will be seen "not as we wish or fear them to be, but as they are." With the other turned inward, myth will reveal itself as the wellspring "of our highest creativity as well as of our worst delusions, and the secret is all in how it is tended."[87]

If, as has been remarked, little attention has been paid to the biological and social needs of the older woman in the United States, it is even more remarkable how little has been thought or written about her spiritual and intellectual, her artistic and her creative needs. Jung is unique among psychologists for the depth of his explorations into the second half of life.[88] From the standpoint of analytical psychology, the second half of life has a purpose distinctive from that of the years of youth and early maturity. "Life is more than eating, sleeping and pleasure. . . . Those . . . years when the world is no longer the great challenge . . . offer the time of the inner challenge."[89] Rather than following a gradual ascent to the zenith of power and then a gradual descent in the later years, a woman's life curve may more closely resemble the pattern of the seasons: "The autumn of a woman's life is far richer than the spring if only she becomes aware in time." The "change of life" is not an ending, but a change in life's direction.[90] Contemporary older women have been called "pioneers" and the "advance guard" in charting new courses of aging and new uses of freedom in the second half of life.[91] To accept the responsibility of this freedom, they must meet the challenge of spiritual as well as cultural forces that obstruct positive development.

Jung had observed that the youth of men is unduly prolonged if their fathers are long-lived. Today, there are millions of women in their fifties and sixties whose mothers are still living. It is exceedingly difficult for middle-aged women to become fully mature when they are still daughters. Many middle-aged women are overprotective of their aging mothers. Shielding an aging woman too much deprives her of the solitude that very old people need for reviewing their lives and for becoming fully conscious of past mistakes and wrongs so that they may learn to forgive themselves. "To forgive oneself is a very difficult thing to do, but perhaps it is the last task demanded of us before we die. . . . Impersonal forgiveness . . . is Agape as distinct from personal Eros." The old need to grieve and to prepare themselves for death. It may be fear as much as genuine love and affection that underlies the middle-aged woman's mothering of her own aged mother. Too much kindness is false; self-sacrifice that is excessive breeds resentment. In extreme cases of "role reversal," the middle-aged daughter is refusing to meet the claims her own life makes upon her. Development is impossible for both if the daughter swaddles her aged mother as an infant-ancient, and the mother behaves like a spoiled, demanding child.[92]

Adult development is very difficult for a woman whose aged mother will not set her free, for a woman whose aged mother has projected herself on her, identified with her, and who lives vicariously through her daughter's life. There is a great distance between many middle-aged women and their elderly mothers, a distance that may never be so great again as it is today, when such a high proportion of the elderly are foreign-born and have completed very few years of formal schooling. Many of these old women have no life of their own. They do not read much.[93] Confined to a narrow social and psychological space, they lean on their daughters for constant care and devotion. Some are so identified with their grown daughters they give the impression that their lives are interchangeable—"that a sort of transmigration of the soul had occurred."[94] Some of these elderly women live very close to the unconscious. Some of them are worse than poor "role models" of aging; they are impossible. And inner life affects all those around an old person. "The old who are frustrated and resentful because they have omitted to become in life the persons they should have been, cause all in their vicinity to suffer."[95] Middle-aged daughters of such women must teach themselves how to be better. One said,

> If a woman over fifty finds something she enjoys doing, her kids will know that the life of their mother is not over. This example is better than anything she can tell them. Besides, we have all seen our own mothers, who did not develop interests outside of the home, and we have felt the burden of guilt they thrust on us for not spending more time with them. Communication was difficult, because we had less and less in common with them as we grew in experience. We moved into a world of increasing complexity which they had not dealt with. We don't want to be like them. We don't want to burden our kids with guilt for our own emptiness. Having a mother who is herself independent and self-sufficient . . . emotionally and intellectually . . . fosters independence in kids.[96]

"Menopause is not a disease," Vidal Clay writes. "It is an opportunity for growth."[97] Elizabeth Janeway writes that the women's movement offers older women the chance to take themselves seriously and that it is important to take full responsibility for one's life: "Responsibility and dignity go together." The women's movement also brings the isolation imposed by age grading to an end. And older women can offer younger women an overview of what their lives have meant to them.[98] For women, a crucial developmental task in the second half of life is the recognition of the patterning of the mother-daughter bond through the generations, and the fulfillment of the responsibilities this recognition brings to light.

Beyond the figures of human mother and daughter are the archetypal psychic energies radiating from this ancient bond, symbolized by the figures of Demeter and Persephone, of Aphrodite and Psyche. In striving toward wholeness, women in the second half of life seek to reconcile themselves not only with their particular, earthly mother, but with the principle of the Feminine.[99] Because so many older women today are far more conscious than their aged mothers, they cannot look to their mothers for guidance. Whereas their mothers accepted traditions uncritically, these grown daughters must find the courage and strength to become pathfinders for their children.

Over half a century ago, in *Women After Forty*, Grace Elliott observed that the problems of the daughter are reflections of the problems of her mother. Elliott also observed that, on the threshold of the second half of life, women feel impelled to change because they sense that the direction of life is changing. Whatever has been sacrificed in the first half of life, which is the time when critical choices must be made, will become the vocation of the middle and later years. Thus, the woman who has neglected to form gratifying personal relationships for the sake of her individual development and achievement will turn *toward* that from which her married sister who has lived for and through her family is, at midlife, turning *away*. This insight from analytical psychology is as apposite today as it was in the 1930s. In her recently published book *Unfinished Business: Pressure Points in the Lives of Women*, Maggie Scarf reports on research by Wendy Ann Stewart on women in their thirties who, "no matter which way they'd gone, . . . the decade of the thirties had found most of them moving in a completely opposite direction."[100] Women who had committed themselves to the traditional maternal role when they were young "were restive" by their early thirties and wanted to return to the world and its marketplace. They "wanted to discover suppressed and only dimly realized parts of the self—to get in touch with . . . their competitive, assertive, aggressive, 'masculine' strivings" (which, of course, was far from easy to do.) On the other hand, with only one exception, Stewart found that the women who were "career-oriented" had "reached a certain internal turning point" at about the age of 30, and were leaving the marketplace and "plunging themselves into marriage and motherhood with astonishing and complete absorption" (221).

Scarf believes that depression has everything to do with stage of life: "To be depressed is, very simply, to be stopped short in one's life" (7). She believes that individuation, "the work of becoming autonomous," is crucial for personality development (152). She notes that research on personality change in middle age suggests that for both men and women, there is a tendency to begin to confront "cross-sex" issues. The word "middlescence" seems to Scarf to convey the sense of the re-emergence of issues focusing on identity that confront the adolescent, and in her view the changes required of women in middlescence are more radical than those demanded of men. Most women "face the entire problem of creating an identity of their own, far later in life than do most men" (41). Depression in middle-aged women, she states, is not biological, but psychological; it is not somatic, but spiritual. Scarf concludes from her study that there is no scientific evidence to support the notion that the hormonal decline of the middle years causes the depressions of the female climacteric. Rather, these depressions have to do with a loss of emotional relatedness. The context of most depressions in women, she states, is "the loss of emotional relatedness" (86). Women perceive the menopause as "the most shocking of biological markers" not only because it means that they cannot have children ever again, but "because of the threat attached to the loss of sexual attractiveness." For some, aging inflicts "a narcissistic injury" (410). To age is to lose the young, sexually appealing woman one was. But there is more to it than that: "People who respond to the facts of their physical aging with great surges of shock, grief, and fear, may not only be mourning the lost self that 'used to be' . . . but be limited in their capacity to relate to others" (412). Indeed, Scarf has concluded that women are far more vulnerable to depression than men because women's nature is "inherently interpersonal, interdependent, affiliative" (527). Women's relatedness begins at birth. All through women's lives, they are "powerfully invested in their affectional relationships," their inner lives are intertwined with the lives of others (529). It is possible, she suggests, that we feel that to be alone is to be threatened with annihilation because there was a time in human evolution when to be left alone—especially for an infant or a young child—was to be sentenced to death. "A tendency to form and maintain powerful emotional attachments might have been bred into the human female genotype" (97).

A woman who is depressed is a woman who has lost an important emotional relationship; the catalyst of depressive episodes in a woman's life is the loss of a love-bond. Women are not prepared to be left alone. Yet as women grow older, love-bonds are broken. To age is to suffer losses. To live to a great age is to be a survivor. Women are taught to nurture and to be affiliative. Yet, "Rupture and disintegration are not exceptions; they are cultural norms." And there will come a time in their lives when "most women will have to learn that they can *be*, even in the absence of a strong emotional bond. They are going to have to learn to survive 'aloneness' in the same way that men sometimes have to learn they can *be*, even in the wake of a failure" (536–37).

For many women—perhaps for most of us—the first love-bond is the bond between mother and daughter. The separation of mother from daughter may be archetypal for every woman. It is the loss of that love-bond—whether through death or enforced separation or rejection—that sends a woman "on her way." The acceptance of this loss may be a task for one woman when she is eighteen, and for another when she is in later life. For Margaret Garvey, the oldest woman in Scarf's book, the intense struggle to separate Self from the parent was still a task to be completed in her sixties (104). Margaret Garvey had become depressed because she was afraid that the unresolved problems in the relationship she had with her dead mother were about to re-appear in her relationship with her own middle-aged daughter.

The mother-daughter bond extends through time, backwards and forwards, uniting the generations. In Leonardo da Vinci's cartoon for *St. Anne,* twin figures of the feminine may be discerned. Eternally young, they might, like Demeter and Persephone, be called "the goddesses." Yet Mary, who leans forward to clasp her child, may be seen as representing the elementary, eternal character of the Feminine, and the smiling St. Anne as dwelling "in the spiritual, transformative realm of Sophia." It is St. Anne who enfolds both Mary and the child in her arms. In the transcendence of the Sophia-Spirit-transformative over the elementary maternal character is the symbolic expression of an archetypal situation characteristic not only for Leonardo da Vinci, but for all people.[101] The boundless deeps and the mystery of the psyche, impelling Leonardo to continuous change, were the gifts of the Renaissance to modern consciousness.[102] On her inner journey, the older woman encounters the Feminine in all its "radiant diversity." On the way, she may find personifications of maiden, daughter, mother, and sister, of the Baba Yaga and the Wise Old Woman, of the Shekinah and Sophia. In weaving the design of her own life, she serves as both instrument and incarnation of the transformative power of Sophia, of Wisdom. Although this odyssey is undertaken out of her own compelling need for self-knowledge, the consequences may reach far beyond her life into the lives of others, perhaps even into the life of the world.

Notes

1. Estelle Fuchs, *The Second Season: Life, Love and Sex—Women in the Middle Years* (Garden City, N.Y.: Doubleday Anchor Press, 1977), p. vii. Hereafter, reference to this book will be cited in the text by page number.

2. See chapter 2, "The Oneida Community," in William M. Kephart, *Extraordinary Groups: The Sociology of Unconventional Life-Styles* (New York: St. Martin's Press, 1976), pp. 52–106.

3. Fuchs, *The Second Season,* p. 19. Hereafter, reference to this book will be cited in the text by page number.

4. Ibid., p. 138. Fuchs quotes a passage in which the McKinlays write that ineffective treatment such as aspirin or sleeping pills "prescribed with little sympathy by predominantly male physicians has now been replaced with estrogen treatment." Ibid. Fuchs has serious reservations about estrogen replacement therapy. Although the McKinlays may have been excessively harsh toward the medical community in chastising them for not evaluating the effects of estrogen, which was done, "albeit belatedly," she writes, "alternative treatments to estrogen therapy appear to have been given only cursory attention." Ibid. For her discussion of estrogens, see the listing in the Index, p. 287.

5. See Irving Kenneth Zola, "Culture and Symptoms: An Analysis of Patients' Presenting Complaints," in *Perspectives on the Social Order: Readings in Sociology,* H. Laurence Ross, ed. (New York: McGraw-Hill Book Co., 1968), pp. 65–82.

6. Fuchs, *The Second Season,* pp. 124–25. Hereafter, reference to this book will be cited in the text by page number.

7. Pauline B. Bart, "Why Women's Status Changes in Middle Age: The Turns of the Social Ferris Wheel," *Sociological Symposium* (Fall 1969) 3:6. The ethnological data on the Burundi were not derived from the Human Relations Area Files, which served as Bart's source of information about 30 societies representative of the 8 culture areas of the world. In addition, Bart studied material about 6 selected societies from ethnographic records. See pp. 2 and 10–13. Hereafter, reference to this article will be cited in the text by page number.

8. Fuchs, *The Second Season,* p. 244. Hereafter, reference to this book will be cited in the text by page number.

9. See Robert C. Peck, "Psychological Developments in the Second Half of Life," in *Middle Age and Aging: A Reader in Social Psychology,* Bernice L. Neugarten, ed. (Chicago: The University of Chicago Press, 1968), pp. 88–92.

10. Marjorie Fiske Lowenthal, Majda Thurnher, David Chiriboga, et al., *Four Stages of Life: A Comparative Study of Women and Men Facing Transitions* (San Francisco: Jossey-Bass, Inc., 1975). Hereafter, reference to this book will be cited in the text by page number.

11. The people in this sample were found to be more like the working-class East Londoners who migrated to the suburban "estates," described by M. Young and P. Willmott in *Family and Kinship in East London* (New York: Free Press, 1957), and like the Levittowners studied by Gans, than the middle class.

12. Robert Butler's paper on the life review is the classic work on this subject. See Robert N. Butler, "The Life Review: An Interpretation of Reminiscence in the Aged," in *Middle Age and Aging,* pp. 486–96. In a personal communication with Butler in 1970, the authors of *Four Stages of Life* found that he has extended his view of the applicability of the process of the life review to *any* period of crisis or transition along the life course (130).

13. Anne Foner, "Age Stratification and the Changing Family," in *Turning Points: Historical and Sociological Essays on the Family,* John Demos and Sarane Spence Boocock, eds. (Chicago: The University of Chicago Press, 1978), p. S355.

14. Lowenthal et al., *Four Stages of Life,* p. 25. Hereafter, reference to this work will be cited in the text by page number.

15. See Bernice L. Neugarten and David L. Gutmann, "Age-Sex Roles and Personality in Middle Age: A Thematic Apperception Study," in *Middle Age and Aging,* pp. 58–71. Hereafter, reference to this article will be cited in the text by page number.

16. See David L. Gutmann, "Aging among the Highland Maya: A Comparative Study," in *Middle Age and Aging,* pp. 444–52. Gutmann concluded from this cross-sectional, cross-cultural study that in both the United States and the Mexican province of Chiapas, men move through three ego stages in which there are libidinal, defense, and cognitive shifts "towards explicitly oral definitions of pleasure and pain, simplistic defensive tactics of denial and projection, and subjectivity of thinking" (452).

17. Neugarten and Gutmann, "Age-Sex Roles and Personality in Middle Age: A Thematic Apperception Study," p. 69. Hereafter, reference to this article will be cited in the text by page number.

18. Elaine Cumming and William E. Henry, *Growing Old: The Process of Disengagement* (New York: Basic Books, Inc., 1961). This book, an outstanding contribution to social gerontology, is remarkable for its lucid and forthright discussion of the possibilities of sample bias. Respondents were chosen precisely because they enjoyed physical and economic well-being, so that research results would not be invalidated by the ill health or poverty of the subjects. Hereafter, reference to *Growing Old* will be cited in the text by page number.

19. See Marjorie Fiske Lowenthal and Clayton Haven, "Interaction and Adaptation," *American Sociological Review* (February 1968) 33(1):20–30.

20. Lowenthal et al., *Four Stages of Life,* p. 152.

21. See *Four Stages of Life*, pp. 86, 133, 175, and 62.

22. Ibid., p. 90. Disengagement is mentioned in *Four Stages of Life* on pp. 11, 12, 92, 115, and 237. The data from *Four Stages of Life* do not support the inverted U-shaped curve of engagement implicit in Cumming and Henry's formulation. Lowenthal et al. call attention to the fact that their study is an inquiry into age *differences*, and not age *change*. For a criticism of disengagement theory as culture-bound, see Arnold M. Rose, "A Current Theoretical Issue in Social Gerontology," in *Middle Age and Aging*, pp. 184–89.

23. Lowenthal et al., *Four Stages of Life*, pp. 74–75.

24. Carl G. Jung, *Modern Man in Search of a Soul*, tr. W. S. Dell and Cary F. Baynes (New York: Harcourt, Brace & World, Inc., 1933), pp. 109–10.

25. There were few signs of changes in sex roles and attitudes toward growing older on the part of the adolescents and young adults interviewed for this study. These young people, who may be representative of a broad segment of the population of young people in this country, were family-centered and male-dominant in the life-style they pursued and in the one they saw in their futures. When they spoke of their hopes for themselves in later life, they talked about financial security, comfort, and freedom from job and parental responsibilities. Lowenthal et al., *Four Stages of Life*, p. 244. Freedom, one can only wonder, for what? However, many college and university students—regardless of socioeconomic background—appear to have views that are different, and more in keeping with a life course perspective (244–45).

26. Ibid., pp. 241–45.

27. Carl G. Jung, *Modern Man in Search of a Soul*, pp. 104–5.

28. Fuchs, *The Second Season*, p. 58.

29. Grace Elliott, *Women After Forty* (New York: Henry Holt and Co., 1936), p. 195. Hereafter, reference to this book will be cited in the text by page number.

30. Erik H. Erikson, *Insight and Responsibility* (New York: W. W. Norton and Co., Inc., 1964), p. 132.

31. Else Frenkel-Brunswik, "Adjustments and Reorientations in the Course of the Life Span," in *Middle Age and Aging,* p. 81. Hereafter, reference to this article will be cited in the text by page number.

32. Fuchs, *The Second Season*, p. 58.

33. Bernice L. Neugarten, Vivian Wood, Ruth J. Kraines, and Barbara Loomis, "Women's Attitudes toward the Menopause," in *Middle Age and Aging*, p. 200.

34. Joan Gage, "Hers," *New York Times*, September 13, 1979, p. C2.

35. Catharine Cook Smith, *A Graft from the Golden Bough* (New York: The Dial Press, Inc., 1937). Hereafter, reference to this book will be cited in the text by page number.

36. Linda Fierz-David, "Psychological Reflections on the Fresco Series of the Villa of the Mysteries of Pompeii," tr. Gladys Phelan (Zurich, unpublished manuscript, 1957). Fierz-David reports that the Villa was unknown until 1910. Her manuscript is deposited in the Kristine Mann Library of the C. G. Jung Foundation in New York City.

37. Rather than studying the frescoes in the Villa from the point of view of archaeology or aesthetics, Fierz-David experienced "the psychic reality radiating from them," and it is this kind of intense experience which is the central concern of psychology. Heinrich Karl Fierz, Preface, "Psychological Reflections on the Fresco Series of the Villa of the Mysteries in Pompeii," (Zurich: n.p., 1966). In her Introduction to the manuscript, M. Esther Harding writes that the series is meant to portray the psychological reality of certain mythic events as these might be represented by a person undergoing a deep psychological experience—one in which the background material and drama are activated. Ibid., p. 1. Hereafter, reference to this manuscript will be cited in the text by page number.

38. Ibid., pp. 59, 22. In Fierz-David's judgment, only those women who had fought and suffered as the Empress Livia had, and only those who were well-born and well-educated, were initiated. But not all those who were eligible for initiation went through the experience. Nor does every woman in the contemporary world who has the means and the education for the undertaking choose to take the way of individuation. Ibid., pp. 8, 31.

39. Marie-Louise von Franz, *Problems of the Feminine in Fairytales—Lectures Presented as a Seminar*

at the C. G. Jung Institute, Winter Semester 1958–59 (New York: Spring Publications, Analytical Psychology Club of New York, Inc., 1972), p. 125. Hereafter, reference to this book will be cited in the text by page number.

40. Ibid., p. 191. In his interpretation of Apuleius's tale from the standpoint of analytical psychology, Erich Neumann perceives Psyche's actions as expressions of a rite of initiation. When the tower forbids Psyche to give in to her feelings of pity, this represents the insistence on "ego stability" that is made in every initiation. For men, ego stability is shown by the endurance of pain or hunger or thirst, and in women by resisting pity. Erich Neumann, *Amor and Psyche: The Psychic Development of the Feminine,* tr. Ralph Manheim (New York: Pantheon, Bollingen Series LIV, 1956), pp. 112–13.

41. von Franz, *Problems of the Feminine in Fairytales,* p. 185.

42. Rix Weaver, *The Old Wise Woman—A Study of Active Imagination* (London: Vincent Stuart Ltd., 1964), p. 11.

43. Irene Claremont de Castillejo, *Knowing Woman: A Feminine Psychology* (New York: Harper and Row, 1973), pp. 29–30.

44. Anna Hope Gould Robinson, "The Evolution of an Idea," 2 vols. This unpublished manuscript, deposited in the Kristine Mann library, is subtitled, "A personal research project in Analytical Psychology." Copyright Rosamond Robinson Jaqua, 1976.

45. M. Esther Harding, *The Way of All Women* (New York: G. P. Putnam's Sons for the C. G. Jung Foundation for Analytical Psychology, 1970), pp. 23–24.

46. Ann Belford Ulanov, *The Feminine in Jungian Psychology and in Christian Theology* (Evanston, Ill.: Northwestern University Press, 1971), p. 71.

47. Ibid., pp. 13, 141.

48. Edward F. Edinger, "An Outline of Analytical Psychology," *Quadrant* (Summer 1968) 1:5.

49. Ibid.

50. Ibid.

51. Castillejo, *Knowing Woman,* p. 15.

52. M. Esther Harding, *Woman's Mysteries—Ancient and Modern* (New York: G. P. Putnam's Sons, 1971), pp. 11–12.

53. Ulanov, *The Feminine in Jungian Psychology and in Christian Theology,* p. 18. Hereafter, reference to this work will be cited in text by page number.

54. See ibid., pp. 17, 24, 95, 12.

55. Weaver, *The Old Wise Woman,* p. 5. Hereafter, reference to this book will be cited in the text by page number.

56. Erich Neumann, "Art and Time," in Erich Neumann, *Art and the Creative Unconscious (Four Essays),* tr. Ralph Manheim (New York: Pantheon, Bollingen Series LXI, 1959), p. 82.

57. Neumann, *Amor and Psyche,* p. 116.

58. Erich Neumann, *The Great Mother: An Analysis of the Archetype,* tr. Ralph Manheim (Princeton, N.J.: Princeton University Press, 1963), p. 93. Neumann writes that "early mankind" and "matriarchal stage" are not archaeological or historical facts, but rather "psychological realities whose fateful power is still alive in the psychic depths of present-day man." Ibid., pp. 43–44. See also his discussion of psychohistory on p. 89. Hereafter, reference to this book will be cited in the text by page number.

59. Neumann, in his essay on "Art and Time," writes, "As magnets order a field of iron filings, so do the archetypes order our psychic life." "Art and Time," p. 124.

60. Neumann, *The Great Mother,* p. 76.

61. Weaver, *The Old Wise Woman,* pp. 7–8.

62. Ibid., p. 118. Hereafter, reference to this book will be cited in the text by page number.

63. Ulanov, *The Feminine in Jungian Psychology and in Christian Theology,* p. 208. Of the four structural forms of the feminine described by Jung's disciple Toni Wolff, Ulanov observes that the Amazon and Mother types are offered the widest possible range in our culture, whereas in antiquity, in the Middle Ages, and in the Renaissance, cultural support was given to the Hetaira and Medial types. Ibid., p. 207. In her positive aspect, the Medium can inspire others to become

conscious of the psyche. If a medial woman does not have a strong ego, she may be used by the objective psyche as an agent sowing confusion or destruction. Ulanov refers to witches and fortune-tellers who do not distinguish between their own ego and the powers of the unconscious. Since it is the negative aspect of things that is usually not permitted by the environment to come into consciousness, it is this which is activated and developed by the medial woman who has a weak ego. Thus, "medieval witches in large part represented the unacceptable heresies and evils of their times." Ibid., pp. 208–9.

64. Carl G. Jung, *Answer to Job*, tr. R. F. C. Hull (London: Routledge and Kegan Paul, 1954), p. 49. In this passage, Jung writes that Lilith is the Satanic correspondent to Sophia, and Eve corresponds to the people of Israel, with whom Yahweh is legitimately united.

65. Weaver, *The Old Wise Woman*, p. 48.

66. Ulanov, *The Feminine in Jungian Psychology and in Christian Theology*, p. 279.

67. Harding, *Woman's Mysteries—Ancient and Modern*, p. 184.

68. Erminie Huntress Lantero, *Feminine Aspects of Divinity* (Wallingford, Pa.: Pendle Hill Publications, 1973), pp. 5–7, 31. Hereafter, reference to this publication is cited in the text by page number.

69. Neumann, *The Great Mother*, p. 288.

70. Ibid., pp. 24–29.

71. Ulanov, *The Feminine in Jungian Psychology and in Christian Theology*, pp. 210–11. Harding also writes that recognition of the forces in the unconscious has great potential benefit for Western civilization. Harding, *Woman's Mysteries—Ancient and Modern*, pp. 8–9.

72. Weaver, *The Old Wise Woman*, p. 98.

73. Neumann, *The Great Mother*, p. 319. In this section on Spiritual Transformation, Neumann discusses "the woman's experience of herself and the Eleusinian mysteries." Ibid., pp. 305–25.

74. Ibid., p. 38; Neumann, *Amor and Psyche*, p. 128. In the *Golden Ass*, the story of Eros and Psyche is told to a young girl by an old woman, and Neumann finds that the tale, told "the young bride by way of consolation, is an initiation into the feminine destiny of development through suffering, for it is only after misfortune and suffering that Psyche is reunited with her beloved." He finds that the fact that this old woman comes from Thessaly, "the land of witches and of Hecate . . . , broadens the background and gives us a glimpse of the matriarchal mysteries in their mythical depth." Ibid., p. 147.

75. Neumann, *The Great Mother*, p. 66.

76. Harding, *Woman's Mysteries—Ancient and Modern*, p. 154. Ulanov observes that the cultural repression of the feminine principle makes it very difficult for women to differentiate their own feminine nature. In discussing Toni Wolff's insights into this matter, Ulanov cites Wolff's comment that the relative absence of feminine symbolism in the Godhead of Protestantism and Judaism "contributes to the estrangement of Protestant and Jewish women from their deeper natures." Ulanov, *The Feminine in Jungian Psychology and in Christian Theology*, pp. 315–16. On this point, see also Jung, *Answer to Job*, p. 169.

77. Erich Neumann, "The Moon and Matriarchal Consciousness," in Erich Neumann, *Fathers and Mothers: Five Papers on the Archetypal Background of Family Psychology*, trans. Hildegard Nagel (Zurich: Spring Publications, 1973), p. 56.

78. Neumann, *The Great Mother*, pp. 53–54.

79. Leo W. Simmons, *The Role of the Aged in Primitive Society* (New Haven, Conn.: Yale University Press, 1945). Hereafter, reference to this publication will be cited in the text by page number.

80. Theresa Benedek, *Psychosexual Functions in Women* (New York: The Ronald Press Co., 1952). Chapter 13, pp. 352–72, in this collection of studies in female sexuality is entitled "Climacterium: A Developmental Phase."

81. Helene Deutsch, M.D., "The Climacterium," Epilogue, *The Psychology of Women, A Psychoanalytic Interpretation*, vol. 2: *Motherhood* (New York: Grune and Stratton, 1945), p. 456. Hereafter, references to this essay will be cited in the text by page number.

82. Nancy Datan, Aaron Antonovsky, and Benjamin Maoz, *A Time to Reap: The Middle Age of Women in Five Israeli Subcultures* (Baltimore: The Johns Hopkins University Press, 1981).

83. Weaver, *The Old Wise Woman*, p. 72.

84. "Nacirema," of course, is "American" spelled backwards. See Horace Miner, "Body Ritual among the Nacirema," *American Anthropologist* 58 (June 1956):503–5.

85. Robert C. Peck identifies *Body Transcendence vs. Body Preoccupation* as one of the critical psychological tasks to be met in old age. Robert C. Peck, "Psychological Developments in the Second Half of Life," p. 91.

86. Susan Sontag, "The Double Standard of Aging," *No Longer Young: The Older Woman in America* (Ann Arbor, Mich.: The Institute of Gerontology, University of Michigan–Wayne State University, 1975), pp. 31–39.

87. Stephen Larsen, *The Shaman's Doorway: Opening the Mythic Imagination to Contemporary Consciousness* (New York: Harper and Row, 1976), pp. 1–4.

88. Elliott, *Women After Forty*, p. 143; Lowenthal et. al, *Four Stages of Life*, pp. 215–16, 43.

89. Weaver, *The Old Wise Woman*, p. 94.

90. Castillejo, *Knowing Woman*, pp. 149–52. For an analyst's account of how two groups of women worked to balance the relating or Eros side and the achieving or Logos side of the self, see Katherine Bradway, "Hestia and Athena in the Analysis of Women," *Inward Light* (Spring 1978) 61 (91):28–42.

91. Fuchs, *The Second Season*, p. 64; Jon A. Hendricks, "Women and Leisure," in *Looking Ahead: A Woman's Guide to the Problems and Joys of Growing Older*, Lillian E. Troll, Joan Israel, and Kenneth Israel, eds. (Englewood Cliffs, N.J.: Prentice-Hall, Inc., 1977), p. 115. For a recent study of the problems and prospects of 160 women aged 35 to 54, see Lillian B. Rubin, *Women of a Certain Age: The Midlife Search for Self* (New York: Harper and Row, 1979).

92. Castillejo, *Knowing Woman*, pp. 161–64.

93. Two comprehensive surveys on book reading and book readers were made in 1978, one by Yankelovich, Skelly, and White, commissioned by the Book Industry Study Group, and the other by the Gallup Organization, commissioned by the American Library Association. Among the findings are that 60 percent of all book readers in the United States are under age 40, and 75 percent are under age 50. "Who Reads in the United States?", *Coda: Poets and Writers Newsletter* (September/October 1979) 7(1):6.

94. Arlie Russell Hochschild, *The Unexpected Community: Portrait of An Old Age Subculture* (Berkeley, Calif.: University of California Press, 1973), p. 100. Hochschild finds a resemblance between this identification and the "altruistic surrender" described by Anna Freud in her book *The Ego and the Mechanisms of Defense*. Hochschild suggests that altruistic surrender "is probably more evident among the old whose own life . . . is relatively uneventful." Since the grandmothers at Merrill Court do have eventful lives, and still exhibit characteristics of altruistic surrender, Hochschild concludes that this identification is remarkably powerful. See ibid., pp. 101–11 for a discussion of the meaning of altruistic surrender "for what it says about the grandmothers and about *other* socially deprived groups," of the connection between identification and envy, and of the major conditions in society that may engender altruistic surrender. Hochschild believes that the subculture of Merrill Court provides an alternative to vicarious living.

95. Castillejo, *Knowing Woman*, p. 161.

96. Irene Thorson as quoted in Luree Miller, *Late Bloom: New Lives for Women* (New York: Paddington Press, Ltd., 1979), pp. 197–98.

97. Vidal S. Clay, *Women: Menopause and Middle Age* (Pittsburgh, Pa.: Know, Inc., 1977), p. 120.

98. Elizabeth Janeway, "Breaking the Age Barrier," *Ms.* (April 1973) 1(10):50–51, 53, 109–11.

99. Neumann, *Amor and Psyche*, p. 131.

100. Maggie Scarf, *Unfinished Business: Pressure Points in the Lives of Women* (Garden City, N.Y.: Doubleday and Co., Inc., 1980), p. 223. Hereafter, all references to this book will be cited in the text by page number.

101. Erich Neumann, "Leonardo Da Vinci and the Mother Archetype," in Erich Neumann, *Art and the Creative Unconscious*, pp. 59–60.

102. Ibid., p. 61.

3
Voices from Oral Histories: Self-Portraits of Older Women

> Sometimes I just wonder if there was times like that. I know they was, but th'way it is nowadays, so many ol' cars an'ever-'thing to go anywhere y'want t'go. . . . We went over to the old home place one time. It looked so different, though—everything gone. I said I wished I just had one little rock from that old chimbley.
>
> —FLORENCE BROOKS, *Foxfire* 3

Oral histories, like autobiographies, are life stories told by those who live them. These reminiscences, whether published or unpublished, breathe life into the sociological category of "older women," and have a concreteness that makes them quite distinctive from both sociological and psychological documents. By definition, they are source materials for the historian. But the ever-shifting focus of many oral histories, which are, after all, records made by older persons engaged in the act of remembering, may serve to frustrate and even defeat the purposes of historical research even as they fascinate the philosopher whose special subject is Memory.

Whatever their virtues and limitations, oral histories are a powerful antidote to stereotypy. Every human life is exceptional in some way; the most ordinary-seeming person has an extraordinary quality. To understand this is to begin to learn where to look, and how to ask the right questions. Storytelling is like weaving. Each thread can be dyed a different color, and from a handful of threads a thousand patterns, a thousand lives can be woven. In one of these is the essential truth of how the weaver experienced her life. To impose a design upon the life of another is to do violence to that other's truth. This is risked every day in serving the myriad interests of social scientific inquiry, of historical or legal or medical fact-finding, of literary scavenging.

Oral histories are a broth of reminiscences and restorations of a personal as well as a collective past, and of revelations about growing older. Oral histories of older women in the United States have been gathered by people of divers persuasions and intentions. Among these are interviewers working with photographers on creating a documentary, social reformers, linguists, feminists and folklorists, genealogists and geriatric counselors, cultural anthropologists,

171

regional historians, and those engaged in studies of racial, religious, and ethnic minorities. But because oral histories are protean, just as human life is protean, they elude the specific focus of research.[1] They have a way of redefining the occasion for recording the recollections. There is an unexpectedness in the air during oral history interviews: people have a way of saying something about one aspect of their experience while seeming to be talking about another. Furthermore, because the very act of conscious and deliberate reminiscing calls forth a host of things "forgotten," because remembering seeds the memory, oral histories are discoveries as much as *re*discoveries. In reviewing their lives, some people exclaim that they had not suspected until then that there was a pattern there, that in the very act of recording, the sense of the life was revealing itself, unfolding before the reflective mind. In creating an oral memoir, one works as a sculptor, releasing a form from its hiding-place.

Like autobiographies, oral histories are primary sources of material on the subjective aspects of aging, for both are in most cases the work of people in middle or later life. In many ways, they may fairly be said to be the oral counterparts to autobiographies. Although they belong to the oral tradition because they are told aloud to another or are recorded by the oral author on tape, they cross over into "print culture" the moment they are transformed from tape recordings into typewritten transcripts. Thus, the distinguishing characteristics of the oral tradition—the laughter, the pauses, the silences, the accents—are destined to become symbols—bracketed words, ellipses, deliberately misspelled words—on the typewritten page. They are like the stage directions given by a playwright of a script. In transcription, the auditory elements of the oral history recording are transformed into textual materials. The extent to which the reader recreates the recording depends upon the imaginativeness of that reader and the sensitivity, skill, and integrity of the editors of the tape. Oral histories are *meant* to become documents; in many instances, they are collected as sources of documentation and testimony. They are meant to be transformed into historical or social scientific or literary documents. It can even be said that they are meant to become autobiographies, since part of the *raison d'être* of the oral history movement was to create source materials to take the place of written documents (diaries, journals, letters, memoirs) that people may have been more in the habit of composing before telephones, mass-produced greeting-card verses, and television screens lured them away from the writing desk. The term *oral history* is often used interchangeably with *oral memoir,* and written memoirs or autobiographies that are "told to" an amanuensis, whether in person or in a series of tape-recording sessions, are indistinguishable from oral memoirs.

In the study of older women as seen through social science and literature, oral histories are as indispensable (and inexhaustible) as autobiographies. Both offer insights into the subjective aspects of aging and a sense of the continuity of life ("the life course perspective") that are rarely found in any other resource materials. But these insights must be culled or distilled from books that are hundreds of pages long and from oral history transcripts that are of the same length as a monograph, and sometimes a novel. To read a memoir in search of inside views on aging is an editorial enterprise in itself. And this material has already passed through the hands of editors, and was, in the raw, no more than an intimation of all the memoirist thought and felt about this matter of growing older. Furthermore, some lives engage the reader's or listener's attention more than others, or sustain it longer than others do, and it is useless to deny this. As if these were not challenges enough, there is also the consideration suggested in the first paragraphs of this chapter, that thoughts and feelings about aging, and the look of life to one who is on the other side of it are often inextricably interwoven with recollections of experiences and events. Then, too, some people are so gifted in evocations of something from the past that they weave a spell around the listener or reader. Thus, at the very moment when a stunning revelation might be made about the workings of memory, the chance is missed because attention has been drawn away from remembering to what is being remembered. Paradoxically, the most talented memoirists seduce their audience into forgetting one of the major reasons they are attending the performance. In any case, the very telling of one's life story reveals at least as much about the ways of remembering and about the moral attitude and quality of feeling of the memoirist as it does about a recollected event or experience. The researcher who reads oral histories, for whatever purpose, is confronted with this moral dilemma: How does one separate one thread from another without unraveling the essential design? What justification could there be for undoing the design that another human being is weaving of her life? Every research project in social science is in essence a moral enterprise, and although there are no final resolutions for these questions, they cannot be evaded by the morally responsible scholar.

In writing her autobiography, a woman works at her own pace, except in those rare instances in which someone or some unusual circumstance imposes a deadline upon her. The woman recording her oral history may keep her own hours and establish her own rhythms of work, at least in part; but in many cases, probably in the majority of them, these are imposed upon her. Because of this, written memoirs may read smoothly and unhurriedly and convey a meditative mood, whereas oral memoirs may leave the reader with the impression of a woman whose brisk, even breezy style of speech reflects a personality that is lively or shallow or impulsive, and a life that was lived without much self-communion. While it is probably true that people inclined to introversion prefer written forms of record-keeping and communication (diaries, letters) to oral ones (dictaphones, telephones), and that, given the choice, an extrovert would rather tape-record or dictate her memoirs than sit down and write them out, the choice of mode of presentation is not always left to the individual, and no one writes exactly as she or he speaks. Therefore, a memoir may leave certain impressions that are utterly false, precisely because it happens to have been written or oral, as the case may be. There is another, very vital difference between autobiographies and oral memoirs, and that is the presence of the interviewer or research team and the occasion for recording the life story. These affect what will go into the making of the oral history transcript even more than the real or imagined public of the writer affects what she decides to put down upon the manuscript page. Each of us has a persona for every person we know and every person we imagine, and every encounter, as the symbolic interactionists have shown, has surprises for each of its participants. Thanks to this unpredictability in encounters and situations, and this mysterious chemistry between any two people that is always quite distinctive, we know that we are flesh and blood and not "paper people" or part of a percentage point rounded off by a statistician. And since we never really know exactly what we are going to do or say or think or feel, we are constantly engaged in self-discovery—even, sometimes especially, during an oral history interview. It is probably true that if a woman has something to say about growing older, she will manage to say it in spite of the researcher's prodding questions about the Depression or World War II or about what it is like to be a Midwestern farm wife or a Jewish grandmother or a black woman in the South or an American Indian woman in the Southwest, or, indeed, an older woman anywhere in twentieth-century America. And if a woman does not want to talk about aging and mortality, she will manage not to discuss it, no matter what questions are put to her. As Sherna Gluck observes, every oral history interview is collaborative—a transaction between the person doing the interviewing and the person being interviewed. She believes that it is intellectually dishonest to underestimate or to deny the interviewer's collaboration in the memoir that is being created through this transaction, and that a concerted effort ought to be made "to maintain a balance between what we, as feminist historians, think is important and what the women we are interviewing think was important about their own lives."[2] Gluck makes the important point that there is a trust implicit in the tape-recording of an oral history, a trust that either party could violate.

Oral histories may represent a bridge between the social sciences and the humanities. They are histories of local, regional, or national significance as told by a witness; they are grist for the mills of many specialists in anthropology and psychology as well as sociology. They are treasure troves for folklorists as well as gerontologists. At the same time, the record of a human life has all the makings of drama, of short stories, of a novel, of poetry, and of the familiar essay. At a 1978 Modern Language Association Special Session on Perspectives on Aging, Diana Hume George spoke of her experiences while employed as a CETA worker for the Chautauqua County Office for the Aging. Chautauqua County, which she said may be described as on the borderline of Appalachia, was one of the first in this country to conduct a comprehensive study of its population aged 60 and over. George called for an interdisciplinary approach to the study of aging and of older people. She suggested that interested students ought to be directed to projects related to CETA for which they may qualify, and that students in the humanities ought to be included along with students in the social sciences in internship programs. She recommended community involvement and field work on the part of students in the humanities to supplement their traditional academic program of reading and thinking. And she argued persuasively for a focus on aging in the study of art, poetry, fiction, and drama in humanities classes.

George concluded her presentation with the recommendation that a creative writing approach be adopted in teaching aging as a theme in humanities courses. This approach, she said, lends itself very well to integration with field work. Sociologists and cultural historians, she told her audience, are not the only people who can claim competence with tape recorders, or the ability to cultivate a "keen memory for conversations." She found tapes of conversations with the elderly to be "superb raw material for poetry, short stories, songs, and drama." If humanities courses are to be more than "watered-down sociology," she remarked, they ought to maintain firm roots in aesthetics and work with the transformation of this raw material of conversations and oral histories into literary art. She found that the voices of old people echo in her own poems, "and the rhythms of their speech and the off-hand aptness of their metaphors." A humanities perspective on aging ought to involve people in "doing the slow work of keeping this generation of older Americans alive in creative ways."[3]

In the hundreds of pages of oral histories that were read in preparation for the writing of this chapter, there are materials from which social scientific and literary documents may be fashioned, and because of this, oral histories are seen as raw materials for artists as well as scholars. But they are more than that. Every oral history is a work of tracery that has an immediacy and vividness all too easily lost when it is transformed into a work of art or scholarship. Even on the pages of the transcript, the human voice comes through, telling the story of a particular human life as seen and experienced by the narrator. This record is true to life in a way no other form can be. It has an authenticity all its own. There is a reality here that comes out and stands. All uses of it can be no more than imitations.

The population of the United States is so various in composition, and the twentieth century a time so close to us as to seem more chaotic and cataclysmic than earlier centuries, that any selection from oral histories of older women in twentieth-century America can only suggest the varieties of time and place encompassed in this study. When these memoirists were children and young women, differences between rural and urban life in the United States were much more striking than they are in the last decades of this century. So, probably, were regional differences, and ethnic, nationality, racial, and religious differences among people. Furthermore, there are many more foreign-born older women in the population of the United States today than there will be among the generations of older women of the future. Finally, since the inception of the oral history movement at Columbia University in 1948 under the direction of Allan Nevins,[4] there has been a multiplication of depositories of transcribed reminiscences, an expansion of the acquisitions for these archives, and a diversification of research interests promoting oral history collections, such that there exists in the United States today a veritable feast of memoirs. Selections from this massive memory bank for the materials in this chapter were made with a profound respect for the varieties of "older women" in America and for the diversity of focus and methods of memoir-collecting in the oral history movement.

Just as an individual oral memoir is kaleidoscopic and shifting, a wandering of the remembering mind through times and places visited, so are all the hundreds of thousands of pages of transcripts of oral histories of older women in twentieth-century America a panoramic motion picture of this century and country as seen through innumerable lenses, from innumerable angles of vision. As witnesses of history, older women have only very recently been asked what they have seen, and their observations bring new and unsuspected aspects of events and social conditions out of the shadows into which most human lives are consigned. As older persons, they offer glimpses into the experience of aging. In life stories there is counsel, there are warnings, and secrets may be told. Sometimes life stories are confessional, at other times instructional. They show how long the road can be, and how little can be seen of what lies beyond each hill that must be climbed. They tell young people who read them, just as the elders used to tell the young people gathered around the campfire, that there *are* hills, and that the sense of a life will change and change again as it is lived out, and that nothing is final, perhaps not even death. They show that life has a way of moving outward in ever-widening circles, and that there is an unfolding inward, too. Oral histories are a mixing of attitude and emotion, of fact and fiction and fantasy. They are so formless and open as to tempt the creative artist, to delight the soul of the humanist and to make even the most stout-hearted ideologist have troubled dreams. The same could be said of any human life.

The Light on the Hill: Two Older Women in the South

There are older women whose movement along the life course is guided by an unwavering commitment to the loftiest ideals of human association. Some of these women trace the roots of this extraordinary sense of social responsibility to childhood. Others discover it in themselves in early adulthood, or even later than that. Whenever it is discovered, it is a revelation of purpose and direction, and life thereafter becomes the unfolding of a destiny, the action of one who knows what it is she was meant to do. The passion for social justice, the faith in human sisterhood and brotherhood, the readiness to make sacrifices of ego expansion for the sake of others, and the sense of human fellowship that extends in ever-widening arcs from family to neighborhood to community and thence outward—these are gifts not given to everyone. These two women, whose portraits were drawn for an issue of *Southern Exposure* on women in the South,[5] Sallie Mae Hadnott and Anna Mae Dickson, appear to experience middle age not as a crisis, but as the fullness of the tide. They appear to see their lives as links in the chain that joins those generations which are gone to those which are yet to come into being.

In 1976, when she was fifty-six years old, Sallie Mae Hadnott was interviewed by Margaret Rose Gladney, at her home in one of the few black sections of Prattville, an antebellum cotton-mill town located ten miles northwest of Montgomery, Alabama. Gladney also interviewed her with her daughter, Nitrician, in Washington, D.C. She introduced her article on Mrs. Hadnott by stating that her entire life has been an engagement in a spirited battle against racial discrimination and poverty.[6]

With her second husband, whom she met through the church choir, Mrs. Hadnott raised eight children. Until her notoriety as a civil-rights activist made it impossible for her to find work, she had held a variety of part-time jobs. In the mid-1960s, she organized the Autauga County chapter of the NAACP out of a room she and her husband added to their three-room house as a meeting place for the blacks in the community. It was there that she raised her large family and worked on a campaign to register black voters. She was a leader in the community long before the civil-rights movement: her daughter remembers her as having been "*the mother of the neighborhood,*" a woman whose sense of social responsibility "*just grew within her.*" (22, 20). She had always been opposed to people's mistreatment of one another. For years, she had been advising neighbors about legal and business matters. And she addressed political issues in the speeches she made at church and other meetings.

Mrs. Hadnott ran for office twice, in 1968 for county commissioner, and in 1970 for secretary of state on the National Democratic Party of Alabama ticket. She was also the name plaintiff in the Supreme Court case *Hadnott* v. *Amos,* which ruled that the names of blacks could be entered on the ballot as members of the NDPA. Although she was unsuccessful in both races for public office, she said that she felt, "*I done very well, and that was saying to me right then that if you left a light on the hill that some younger person is gonna be inspired later on to come on and pick this torch up and keep it moving*" (22). Two of the Hadnott children chose to be among the first black students to integrate Autauga County High School when the "freedom of choice" plan for school desegregation was implemented in 1965. Because of this, Mrs. Hadnott was invited several times to testify before the U.S. Commission of Education in Washington on the education of poor children and ways of improving federal programs of education. In 1970, Walter Mondale visited the Hadnotts, where, in their kitchen and yard, he heard black children from all over the county tell of their experiences of having been threatened, beaten, and some of them even expelled by teachers and administrators of their schools.

Her passion for social justice has roots buried deep in Mrs. Hadnott's childhood. One day she had been sent to help her grandmother, who was ill, and when she was rubbing her grandmother's back she saw scars larger than her hand and asked about them. Her grandmother told her that once she had forgotten to get the kindling wood for her boss, and he had put live coals down her back to "teach me a lesson that I wouldn't forget" (20). The child promised her grandmother then that when she grew up she would not take it and would pay back for what had been done to her. Whenever she has a chance to do something for good, Mrs. Hadnott said, she feels as though she is keeping that promise.

Mrs. Hadnott grew up with her five brothers at a time when opportunities for formal education were all but nonexistent. She remembers her mother, who died when she was about eleven, cooking food for white people and being given the scraps for her children and herself. She remembers having to go out on the steps or the back porch to eat those scraps, and her keen sense of how unfair this was. They used to have to make do with peas and sweet potatoes "when hardship was on," and to learn how to do without (19). She remembers, too, how unfair it was that white children rode the school bus while black children had to walk out and back to school on the muddy roads. At seventeen, she dropped out of school. She had had to wear her brother's shoes, and the children had teased her about the way the soles flapped. But if she had known then what she knows now, she says, she would have put those shoes on and continued going to school. She recalls that she had said she wanted to go to Tuskegee, but that it was not possible for her to do so. Her family could not afford it.

A school breakfast program for the poor children of Autauga County is one of the objectives Mrs. Hadnott is working to achieve, and another is getting black women on the police force. She also believes that, now that blacks serve on juries, workshops ought to be held every month for the purpose of educating jurors about their responsibilities. Gladney writes that even though Mrs. Hadnott has worked hard to see to it that blacks have the doors of opportunity opened to them, it is not enough for her just to see blacks take the places of whites in positions of leadership in the community. Rather, Mrs. Hadnott believes that both whites and blacks who are community leaders ought to be responsive to the needs of the whole community. She is critical of whites who want only to work with blacks who are "yes-men," and of blacks—especially elected black officials—if they do not assert their rights. When she was asked, as president of the Autauga County chapter of the NAACP, to host a Sunday morning show on a local radio station, she let it be known that she intended to speak her mind, and that if this was not wanted, they should get someone else for the broadcast. "The preachers said we was dominized and the educators said we was crazy," Gladney quotes Mrs. Hadnott as saying, "But . . . If it was anything for justice," she wanted her children to have the same thing that the others had for *their* children.

In the course of a year-long study of Grimes County, an area of small towns and farms seventy miles northwest of Houston, Wendy Watriss interviewed more than one hundred people from all parts of the community. One of these was Anna Mae Dickson, "a black woman, a maid, born in a rural East Texas county 55 years ago."[7] Mrs. Dickson, who has worked as a cook, babysitter, and housemaid since the age of thirteen, is one of a number of black women who emerged as community leaders with the rise of the civil-rights movement and the integration of schools and public agencies in the county. Watriss reports that in recent years Mrs. Dickson has become president of a PTA that is newly integrated, and also "a spokesperson for the black community." There is constant activity in the small home Mrs. Dickson and her husband recently built. All day long the telephone rings. Mrs. Dickson's callers are "women seeking aid on home demonstration programs for underprivileged children, a school benefit, an immunization clinic, a church project" (77). In addition to this, Mrs. Dickson provides meals for several families, plans meetings, and cares for grandchildren. And she also works as a cleaning woman and caters weddings that sometimes include 1,000 guests.

Like Mrs. Hadnott, Mrs. Dickson believes fervently in the value of education. She never completed her high school education, but she insists upon this as a minimum for her children. She has encouraged both her children and grandchildren "to reach high—not to think about what somebody else is doing but about what should be done." She has taught them that "the only way to do it is to start within yourself first. And then your family. And then just spread out!" (81) Watriss reflects that the life of Mrs. Dickson "might go unnoticed in the framework of the modern struggle for women's rights, yet it is a significant example of how one woman survived 40 years of domestic servitude and was able to turn that experience to the service of her family and her community" (76). Watriss shows how remarkable an achievement this transformation is, for it was an accomplishment of a black woman who grew up in a time and place when the possibilities for leadership in the black community were severely limited, and the chances for realizing a wider public role were virtually nonexistent. Mrs. Dickson's life story is not marked by dramatic climaxes, but is a record of "the day-to-day effort to survive and maintain her sense of self-respect in a world which consigned her to a position of servitude" (77).

Mrs. Dickson grew up during the 1930s and 1940s, chopping and picking cotton for 75 cents a day and helping her grandmother wash and iron for a living, and raise hogs and vegetables. Her upbringing was very strict and, in its own way, sheltered; although her grandmother and great-grandmother had been midwives, she was told at home that babies came out of tree stumps. She says children did not know how hard their lives were at that time. They thought nothing of walking three miles back and forth to go to school. When she was seventeen, Mrs. Dickson finished the ninth grade at the county school and went to town to attend the only black high school in Grimes County. She stayed with an aunt in Navasota because there was no money for bus fare for daily travel back to the country, and she worked in a café to earn pocket money. But halfway through the tenth grade, she decided to get a full-time job so she could buy the clothes she felt she needed. She had wanted to become a secretary but there was no chance for this. Black women could not work in the stores, either, in the late 1930s. Nor could she remember having seen any black registered nurses working in the hospitals. All that was available for her was a job nursing other people's children, combining baby-sitting, cooking, and housecleaning. In 1938, she was working for $2.50 and $3 a week; by the late 1950s, she earned between $10 and $12 a week. She suffered many personal indignities which she endured because she needed the work. Sometimes she was angry with herself for having dropped out of school. She had the feeling she was leading two lives. She worked all day in houses with fine floors, and all she had were little patches of linoleum. She worked for people who had more hot running water than they needed, and at home she had to haul and heat water to do her dishes. But self-pity was useless. She had to earn a living.

There was a turning point in Mrs. Dickson's life. She had gone to Houston in 1942 and worked there for three years in a boardinghouse where she earned $13 a week. But she lost her job when she separated from her husband after becoming pregnant with her second child, and she went home to have her baby. She reached a critical point, and felt dread for the life that she was living. After that, her only thought was to help others and to work with her own people. She became a member of her church again in 1950, and found her talents for organization through her work in the Baptist missionary society. She learned she was an effective speaker, and extended her activities from the church into the community. She directed home demonstration programs for black girls, helped establish one of the first clubs in the county to raise funds to support school athletics, served as president of the PTA at three schools, assisted in rodeos, health programs, and the organization of a volunteer fire department, and says that the more active her life is, the happier she feels. When her children tell her to slow down, she tells them back that she is not yet ready to die.

Both blacks and whites in Grimes County, a place where black activism was very limited in the 1950s and 1960s, and where many blacks still do not want to work with whites in community activities, regard Mrs. Dickson as a leader. She believes that blacks should maintain ties with the white community and that blacks ought to be represented in community organizations. Although she thinks that conditions for women and for blacks have improved, she does not have illusions. Watriss writes that Mrs. Dickson perceives a need for blacks "to stand up for their rights," but that she does not have "patience with those she sees as an embarrassment to her race or an impediment to long-term progress" (80). Mrs. Dickson believes that one ought to take time to learn facts before taking any action, and she says that she does not mind beginning at the bottom, and that she wants to show progress in anything that she undertakes. The objective of all her efforts is equal opportunity. She sees reason to hope for change, especially for the younger people around her. She has learned after forty years of working as a domestic that no one ever knows what is in another person's mind. She speaks of an inner strength that makes a person endure and persevere. There are times when people are not aware of what they are doing. "What did I know when I went to Navasota from the countryside?" A person goes along thinking about other matters and suddenly becomes aware of what is happening—she made the analogy of driving a car and suddenly discovering you have gone far past the speed limit. She thinks this is what we do with our lives, that we let them go. "We follow the gang. We don't think about how precious our life is or what we can do with it." She reminded Watriss that an old slave woman who was being whipped said that no one could know what was in her heart. There is "something inside of you," Mrs. Dickson said, that no one can ever take away from you (81).

This "something inside" is encapsulated—some would say it is mutilated, or even crushed—by statistics, and if the realities of hardship elude quantitative description, those qualities of the human spirit with which hardship is sometimes met—courage and perseverance—defy it entirely. Responses to interview questions may take the shape of a moral lesson that is far more commanding and lasting than the most sophisticated arrangement of "data." Oral histories of people who are of a low social and economic status can provide empirical evidence of the realities of social deprivation, of sociological plight. They may be collected by the social scientist, photographer, filmmaker, or journalist in the interest of conveying the reality of experience of individuals selected as representative of a social class or stratum for whom they speak. In this sense, they have a collective character. At the same time, these oral histories inform the emotions as much as the intellect, and they offer an inside view of a particular life. In *this* sense, each has an individual character that marks it as a work of literary expression rather than as a social scientific document. Whatever uses are made of the stories of these two women, they are eloquent testimony on how the second half of life can be lived with a sense of purpose and dedication by older women who have other things on their minds than wealth or public recognition or declining beauty or the loss of youth. Their community service is given in a spirit reminiscent of that which inspired the artists who created the paintings inside the Paleolithic caves and left them unsigned as a legacy for the future.

The Way Things Were: Remembering the Great Depression

Oral histories of older women tell stories without which history itself remains only half-told. In her Epilogue to *Making Do,* a book about how women survived the Great Depression, Jeane Westin remarks that history is falsified when women's experience of it is left unrecorded.[8] Westin was in search of answers to questions that remained to be asked, especially about women of the 1930s. She wanted to know how they lived, and what they thought about the condition of their lives at the time. She interviewed 160 women, who ranged in age from 47 to 91. Most of them were in their sixties and seventies when Westin spoke with them.

Westin's book is subdivided into four sections—on "the lady of the house," "growing up female in the thirties," "woman's work," and "women influencing the world about them." She prefaces each section with a historical sketch of social conditions prevailing in the 1930s. These sketches flesh out statistics about average annual income, the birth rate, the divorce rate, enrollments in colleges across the country, the changing fortunes and composition of the labor force, and women's participation in religious, political, and civic organizations at that time. These descriptive passages are followed by vignettes in which individual women speak of their recollections. Among the stories are those of Bertha Norton, a Maidu-Wintu, of Marion Conrad, interviewed at age 85, a nutrition expert and author of books on food allergies, of Constance Chang, whose grandmother came to America on a sailing schooner as a "picture bride" for a marriage arranged by a broker, and Mary Tsukamoto, who told Westin that, because she is Japanese, her memory of the 1940s is sharper than her recollections of the 1930s. There are also the stories of Monette, who spoke of herself as one of the "Southern dames," and who took a pseudonym because her family in New Orleans would be shocked at what she had to say about being a "Deep South" girl at Southern Louisiana University in the early 1930s, and Clarice Rodda, the wife of a California state senator, whose father was an immigrant from Ireland who, as a widower with six children, made great sacrifices for his children's education. Westin also spoke with Nina Parr, who told her that you have not experienced the Depression unless you experienced it in Oklahoma; Margaret Marks, founder of the Arms of Mercy Feeding programs in Del Paso Heights, California, who was called "Mama" by thirty-one foster children and countless hungry people, although she had never had a baby of her own; and Frances Ridgway, now head nurse at a university medical school hospital, who worked for ten years as a domestic to earn her tuition to nursing school. When Westin called a senior citizens housing office in a county in southern California to ask for the name of a Mexican-American woman who might remember the Great Depression, she was given Lupe Renaldo's name. Renaldo described an adolescence, Westin remarks, "that made Cinderella sound like a carefree teen" (198–99). Westin also spoke with Genora Johnson Dollinger, head of the Women's Emergency Brigade during the Flint, Michigan Sit-down strike at the General Motors plants in the winter of 1936–37. Dollinger, who recently retired from her work with the American Civil Liberties Union, is a sculptor in her spare time. She said she can still see "those wonderful women . . . a vision of them, marching down Chevrolet Avenue" (310).

Women's memories of the Depression were of times when nothing was wasted. A 1930s cook recalled, "When we cleaned out a bowl we said we'd 'hoovered it'—that meant we'd scraped out every last bit" (38). They remembered hocking engagement or wedding rings, and hoboes asking for something to eat, sometimes offering to work for the food and sometimes not. They remembered sharing. Kathryn Haskell Perrigo told Westin that there was more than hard work to the Depression. On "big" Saturday nights, people used to square dance to their own music. And they always brought their babies with them for social gatherings. She remembered entire big beds filled with wriggling babies that had chairs stacked around them to protect the infants from falling out. She remembered how often the women used to visit one another, and that they almost always had some kind of work in their hands while they talked. "We talked about everything," she said, "we poured our hearts out. We didn't worry about psychiatrists—we were each other's psychiatrists" (52).

The 1930s were a time when it was difficult to keep the family together. Fathers looked for any kind of work that would bring in a few shekels. Sometimes there was no work to be found, and children were farmed out to live with relatives, because the parents were "under." Some women remembered fathers who deserted their families, others, the threat of having water and electricity turned off because of unpaid bills, still others, of being forced to go on relief, which was a terrible disgrace. Those were times of restrained behavior, times when many young girls had to discover the "facts of life" for themselves and had to endure the consequences of ignorance and innocence. Many clung to their jobs as if they were, in Margaret O'Donnell Paladino's words, "life rafts." "I did not spout obscenities at the boss or go on strike," she said. "I did everything possible to keep the axe from falling" (211). A typing teacher recalled how she endured the sexual harassment of her boss in silence. "You can put up with a lot to go on eating," she told Westin (209). Many women had ambitions for higher education, but family and work responsibilities made it impossible for them to realize these. Even after their children were grown and had left home, few women returned to college or went to graduate school. It was too expensive, and, Mary Ann Page Guyol said, "it just wasn't done." The League of Women Voters, a true democracy in action, was "the only game in town" for women who were not employed. It "became our university, our graduate school . . . just everything" (282). Guyol, retired public relations director for the National League, said that the LWV played a major role in changing the climate of opinion in the United States from isolationism to internationalism.

Many of the women Westin interviewed spoke of the differences between the 1930s and the 1970s in America. Doris Lemaster said people had more time then, and that television is "the ruination of the American home. There's no family life as we knew it" (19).[9] Mary Grace McKenna Monahan said "you didn't go on relief without working" during the Depression. "It wasn't a handout" (27). Although she does not remember those times as having brought out the goodness in people, she thinks that the next Depression, which she feels is inevitable, "will be even harder on the unemployed than the thirties were. I remember my mother would sit those poor folks out on the sun porch and feed them. Not today. . . . Today if you get a knock on the door, you're too scared to let them in" (26). Erma Gage pointed out with amusement that her sons had been embarrassed to wear patched blue jeans to school in the 1930s, whereas her grandsons today insist on her putting patches on their jeans even when there are no holes in the fabric. Helen Meret remarked that people's most fervent wish during the Depression was that they would make so much money one day that they would be obliged to pay income taxes. "In those days that meant you'd really arrived" (71). Virginia Payne, who played Ma Perkins from 1933 to 1960 in over 7,000 broadcasts, is not retired, Westin reports, nor is she "the wizened, white-haired lady most fans think she must be" (229). Payne thinks that "if Roosevelt was the father figure of the thirties, then Ma Perkins was the mother figure" (235). In her opinion, American society was far more extroverted in the 1930s than it is today, and her audience was much more interested in character than in plot. Women were "courageous and achieving" during the Depression, she said, and what they could not achieve for themselves they wanted their children to have. "So many of today's accomplishments started from the ambition of those mothers for their children. They made tremendous sacrifices. I'm not sure we'd be willing to do that today with the philosophy of doing your own thing first" (237). Among Westin's vignettes is "Pauline's story," the story of the first black woman to integrate a war plant in Chicago, in 1943. Even at that time, Pauline said, there were stirrings on the part of the blacks. *Making Do* also documents the fact that the feminism of the 1960s and 1970s was not a birth, but a rebirth. Lillian Cantor Dawson told Westin, "My young liberated sisters . . . think they're new in the field. But forty years ago women were fighting for the same things" (182). Dawson maintained that the most positive outcome of the 1934 convention of the Women's International League for Peace and Freedom at The Hague was women's realization that they constituted a power in this world. And Westin's Aunt Kate told her niece that, even though women did not call themselves liberationists at that time, there was a change of consciousness, particularly among union women, in the 1930s. In Mildred Scott Olmsted's view, "Women were beginning to wake up during the 1930s." They found that "the vote wasn't enough—they'd have to be active in politics, putting direct pressure on governments" (289). Olmsted believes that "the WCTU and the Federation of Women's Clubs were the first steps in the emancipation of women" (290).

There is a scattering of comments about aging and about being an older woman in America throughout *Making Do* that show a sensitivity to stereotypes and the ways they affect one's self-concept *and* chances for earning a living. One woman was a little angry at Westin for having asked her age, and said she never tells it and never asks anyone else this question. She stated that when someone tells people how old she is, then people "*see* you that age" (298). Another said, "I'm old enough. It's not how long you've lived, it's what you've done with your time" (300). And Margaret O'Donnell Paladino seemed doubtful that anyone would be interested in the 1930s, except perhaps for "those 'old folks' who live in retirement villages, and are a little bit 'emotionally retarded.'" She said that she finds it difficult to talk with those who are "eternally stuck" on the subject of the times when they were young, and that she thought the only reason the past is interesting is "because it explains how I got here" (210). But she, like the other women with whom Westin spoke, had vivid recollections of her experiences during the Great Depression to contribute to this work of historical reconstruction. One woman Westin interviewed, Jeanne Hutton, had found a gratifying occupation in later life. Hutton talked with Westin in a church basement during an all-day crafts session held for senior citizens. She had turned to painting—something she never had time for when she was young, she said, because she had been too busy with her work as a pianist in a sixteen-piece dance band out of Kansas City. Another woman, Nico Rodriguez, told Westin she does not want to work anymore. She had been a domestic worker for forty years because it was the only alternative she had to becoming a migrant fieldworker, and the only way she could provide for her children's education. "I'm tired, now, I'm old," she said, "but they keep calling me. Not so many young womens want to clean a house today for any lady" (206). And Peggy Gilbert would like to go on working, but finds that her age is a barrier. She "still blows a mean tenor sax, mostly in weekend jam sessions with 'the girls,' but sometimes for pay," and she talked about the all-girl bands that vanished with the end of the big band era after World War II. She still serves on the board of a local of the Los Angeles Musician's Union and is quite busy. Gilbert would like to take a big band out again, but she said they would all be *old* now. She observed that it is all right for Bob Crosby to have white hair, but it is another matter when women have white hair. If old men are good performers, this will be acceptable to audiences, but if old women are the performers, "it's got to be comedy." Gilbert said that she fought this for many years, but she finally gave it up. She said that women have always represented "beauty and romance," and that she supposes this "doesn't go with old" (223).

Westin began *Making Do* by writing about the first woman of the 1930s she knew, her own mother. She spent a year talking with women "in tiny apartments crowded with photos and mementos; in large family homes near-empty and echoing; in senior citizens' centers busy with the postponed hobbies of a lifetime—a year of poking into the places where we keep our elderly—America's 'antique shops'" (319). The women she interviewed were very responsive to the interest she took in their lives. Her purpose was to join the daughters of the women of the Depression with their foremothers, "to build clear, simple, strong bridges of human experience between us" (320). A record of the history of women of the 1930s may, at the very least, make contemporary women proud to be their daughters, and "at most, their insights will form a survival handbook for tomorrow" (x). Thus, it was Westin's intention to write a book about the Depression that would not only be informational, but inspirational for younger women today. *Making Do* succeeds in fulfilling this objective. Furthermore, it provides new source material for historians by recording the recollections of people previously overlooked by scholars. What is more, *Making Do* challenges the stereotyped notion all too frequently espoused today that women who lived through the Depression were, one and all, no more than passive victims of social and economic circumstance. In oral history interviews, older women speak for themselves about their lives. Their voices testify to the absurdity and cruelty of caricatures and stereotypes and to the truth that the past lives for those who inherit it as much as for those who experienced it in their youth.

Portraits of Older Women in the Foxfire Books

The *Foxfire* project began in 1966, when Eliot Wigginton asked his ninth-and tenth-grade students at the Rabun Gap–Nacoochee School in the Appalachians in Georgia, "How would you like to throw away the text and start a magazine?"[10] *Foxfire* is run entirely by high school students, and was named by them after "a tiny organism that glows in the dark and is frequently seen in the shaded coves of these mountains" (11). In the oral history interviews reported in the *Foxfire* books, some of which are accompanied by photographs, older women as well as older men speak to their young interviewers about the past and about their present lives. These women are surrogate aunts and grandmothers and great-grandmothers to many of the students.[11] They have much to tell them, about folklore[12] and superstitions, about burial customs and planting by the signs, and about midwives and granny women and boogers, witches and haints. They tell about basket weaving, soap making and broom making, about quilting and weaving, sometimes giving little moral lessons along the way. What these elders have to say is itself a kind of weaving of past with present, crafts instruction with moral instruction, folklore with religious piety.

Aunt Nora Garland is a faith healer. She believes that she was called to faith healing because she had been spared during the flu epidemic. She can draw out fire; she is called every week to say a verse from the Bible to remove warts and to stop bleeding. But she could not tell the *Foxfire* editors how she did these things. She said that was between herself and God. She does not think she could heal by faith if she charged money for it. Once a doctor offered her money to tell him how to stop bleeding, and she refused the offer.[13]

The other night, Aunt Nora told the young people, she was lying on her bed, thinking about how much she loves life in the country. She described the log house she used to live in, and said she could almost see it in her dreams. She lives in a stone house north of Clayton, Georgia, on the highway. Next door is a block building she and her husband owned for many years, in which they ran a grocery store. They sold out last year, she said, and among the many things that remind her of the store is a cash register they bought secondhand twenty-five years ago.

The *Foxfire* editors thought of Aunt Nora as always being in the kitchen, making something good to eat. She had much to tell them about the past. She recollected how people used to play "town ball" and go serenading on Christmas. They worked every day but Sunday. Then they were free, and if it was spring, they would make leaf dresses and leaf hats, and they would swing from one hill to another on grapevines. She remembered sledding at the graveyard, and corn shuckings and candy drawings and candy pullings, and neighbors helping one another when there was illness. She remembered working in the fields—the children hoed corn while her mother did the cooking—and she said she could almost see her mother now as she used to be, sitting on the porch scraping potatoes. She was always the one, she said, who was chosen to climb their four big cherry trees to pick the fruit because she had always been so little and slender. People made their own cottage cheese, picked wild strawberries and canned them, and put up apples. They did not have stoves, so they made huge cakes out of syrup and sweet bread. In about 1906, when she was five years old, she saw her first cook stove, a Wilson Patent stove. She remembered the poem that was made up about it, and she recited it for the young people.

Christmas was brought to life again for her listeners as Aunt Nora described the stack of apple pies and pumpkin custards and sweet bread baked on the fireplace, the roasting of apples and chestnuts, and the serenaders' voices as they came near her door. On Christmas Eve, her father used to shoot his gun straight up in the air, and as she spoke of this she said she could almost see him as he did this. They had a big dinner on Christmas Day, but there were no exchanges of gifts. There was a string of popcorn on the tree, and Santa Claus put candy and an apple or orange and a piece of sweet bread in their stockings. They knew their mother had made the baked treats. Her mother used to do a lot for her family, Aunt Nora said. She would weave the material, and spin it. Everyone in the family could spin, she said. And everyone could knit, even her brother. "He could knit a pair of socks as fast as Mother could and there wasn't any shame in it: no, not a bit in the world. Everybody was just alike."[14]

Aunt Nora talked about the old courting customs of her day, and of how medicine was practiced, and dentistry—a man with "tooth-pullers" was called to extract teeth without benefit of anaesthesia. She remembered a tornado that struck the area and blew furniture up on the mountain; her aunt had been killed in the disaster. She described the old jail, and the plank streets people used to walk on, and she told a story her mother had told her about the panthers that used to be as thick as rabbits in that area. In her love of her home and of the land, and the keenness of her remembrance of things past, and in her piety, she resembles Aunt Lola Cannon and Beulah Perry and other older women, even very old women, who appear in the *Foxfire* books. Their young interviewers did more than quote these women. They wrote glowing tributes to their gentleness and generosity, and to how much they had learned from these contacts not only about the skill or art or craft they were researching, but about what life was like earlier in this century.

When they were doing research for their article on "Old-Time Burials," the *Foxfire* editors went to one of their favorite contacts in the black community, Beulah Perry. At that time, Mrs. Perry told them that people used to be closer to one another in the old days and that black and white were more like one big family than they are today.[15] In a later issue of *Foxfire,* there is an article about Beulah Perry, and the students write of her with great affection and say that, although she is 80 years old now, she looks and acts much younger than this. Mrs. Perry's maternal grandfather was brought to this country as a slave. She does not remember his age because, she said, back in those days people aged much more quickly than they do now. The lady of the plantation gave her grandfather lessons and she educated him well enough so that he could teach school after he was freed. Mrs. Perry grew up in Anderson County, South Carolina. She was married in 1915, and the Perrys had four sons. Three of them died in infancy. The fourth died when he was 15 years old.

Years before she mothered her own children, Mrs. Perry had to mother her siblings. She was the second daughter, and when her mother died she and her older siblings had to assume responsibility for childcare as well as work in the house and fields. They had no machinery, and worked with hoes and mattocks, shovels and plows. Her family dried and stored their vegetables and canned their fruit. Her father always made their own syrup. The young ones learned how to care for the mules and cows, and the hogs and chickens. They grew wheat and oats and one kind of corn—not sweet corn—for themselves and the animals. And they had big cotton patches, and her grandfather grew tobacco for his own use. Her mother gardened and churned; her father farmed and made baskets and bottomed chairs. When she was a child, people did not buy or sell things, but gave to one another. Since they churned every day, her mother would send the children across the field or up the road to give butter and milk to a neighbor. One family of neighbors, German people, taught her how to mend shoes, a skill Mrs. Perry can still practice.

The children were raised in a "good, old-time Christian home," Beulah Perry said. Their parents were good to them, but very strict. They were not allowed to question what they were told to do. And every night, her parents would read the Bible to them. Her father would have a prayer said around the table every night, and most mornings as well. She does not think that young people are responsible for the fact that they are losing interest in the Bible and in church life. Rather, the older people are responsible because they do not take the time and do not have the patience one needs to have with children. "Back when I was a girl, people's mothers and fathers worked at home—they didn't go out and work. It was on the farm, around the house."[16]

A deeply religious woman, Beulah Perry said there is "a great big space" between the way things were and the way they are today. She spoke of her love for young people. "My time is passed," she said, "and it's the young people's time, and all we can do—anything we can do—we ought to help them and do it with them" (411). She believes that people were happier when she was a child. They had very little; sometimes there was only a half a stick of candy to be divided among nine children. They had no entertainment as it is known today. The way they passed the time in playing was with homemade rag dolls and with the mud pies they made in the yard. There is too much emphasis placed on money now, and "Me and money, we're so far apart." There is something she still wants to do, and that is to go on a foreign mission field in Africa. This has been her wish since she was thirteen years old. At that time, her father's uncle sold his plantation and took his family with him to Africa. They did not know much about the African people then, she said, but it seemed to them that there was a need for mission studies there. She says she has been a missionary all her life. The first thing she wants to do when she rises in the morning is to go to a door or a window, "and look out and I stand there and look, and thank the Lord for being able to see that beauty one more time. It's a wonderful thing to try to live a Christian life and to love the Lord. We have so much to be thankful for" (415).

Older women told the *Foxfire* editors about the "superstitions" some folks still believe in. Aunt Nora Garland explained the beliefs about the "news bees," the yellow bees that brought good news at the time of childbirth, and the black bees that brought bad news. Although they were skeptical about the "old wives' tales," the women talked about the experiences and observations that gave rise to them. Midwifery was an awesome responsibility, and midwives were thought to have extraordinary powers. They were held in such high regard by some families that baby daughters were given the midwife's first name as a middle name. "Over Georgia alone," Jo Brewer said, "we had thousands of granny midwives. They are dying out now, though. In the state today there are about eighty-five granny midwives who are over 65 years of age, and there are only 196 total."[17] One of the best-known midwives of Rabun County, "Aunt Lizzie" Keason, who has since died, was 87 when Billy Dilworth wrote of her in the *Anderson Independent* that she had given her thanks to God because, in over 525 births for which she served as midwife, not one mother or baby died. "The little mountain lady, whose hands showed work, had built a city of more than 525 persons—an average American small town" (283n).

Some older women still plant by the signs. Margaret Norton, famous for the way her gardens prosper, plants strictly by the signs. She says this must have been in the design of things when the world was made, and she reminded her listeners of the passage in Ecclesiastes in which it is said that there is a season for all things. Lizzie Lovin' said that her mother used to say the moon is just like a man, and that it changes every eight days. Many strange and wonderful tales and fragments of lore are passed along through the oral tradition, like the blue-eyed mule Hob Duvall once had that would go blind at a certain time of the month for about two weeks "when the moon got on the dark side,"[18] and Anna Howard's harrowing story of a night when she and her mother were called to deliver a baby for a family named "Jones"—a night when it had been prophesied that a comet would appear, a night of milksick madness and death and birth and a furious storm[19]—and the list of all the properties that ginseng is supposed to have.[20] Maude Shope told the *Foxfire* editors one superstition after another—that if you tell your dream before breakfast, it will come to pass, and that if a man comes to your house first on New Year's morning, you will have good luck, but that if a woman comes first, you should throw the broom in front of her before she enters, or bad luck will come. People used to believe it was inviting bad luck to take the ashes out between Christmas and New Year. And you were not supposed to eat black-eyed peas on New Year's Day. "I seen a piece in th' paper where someone was eatin' cabbage for New Year," she said. "If I had cabbage *any* time through th' year, I'us proud of it."²¹ She said that it's folks' privilege to believe in these things if they so choose, but she herself does not pay any attention to the superstitions.

There are portraits in *Foxfire* of women who are quite old, and yet still very active. Maude Shope, born in North Carolina within seven miles of where she now makes her home, was 76 when she was interviewed, and she was still riding her 32½-year-old mule, Frank. She had raised twelve children, she had been a midwife, she had taken part in numerous corn shuckings and log rollings, she said; she had spun wool and sewn clothing and done countless other things, and does not think she has slowed down much. Ninety-three-year-old Anna Howard has a strong drive to go on working, although she had been hospitalized for over a year, and despite the fact that she was unable to walk, she continued to cook and keep house and tend her garden by getting around in a homemade wheelchair. Anna has compassion for old people who live alone. She visits an old friend, bringing along a glass of jelly or of pickled beans or kraut. "She ought t'see more people than my old ugly face," Anna says. "Her neighbors aren't a'doin' their duty."²² Another old friend who lives alone can't fill her own pipe because she shakes so badly:

> "She'd crumble tobacco up in her lap and put it in her pipe, and ashes and all 'ud pour out. I asked her if she wanted me t'fill it up fer 'er. 'Well,' she said, 'honey, I'd just be glad, for I'll never get t'smoke.' I filled it up fer 'er, and every time we went over, I had t'clean her pipe up. And she was so proud of it, th' poor old thing. I just felt sorry fer 'er." [268–69]

She has not had much of a happy life since she was widowed, Anna says, and after her children left her home she felt as if she were alone in the world. She felt "further and further away" from things after all her kinfolk died. But she always has work in hand to keep her mind occupied when there is no one around to talk with; she says that she loves to knit socks. She speaks of her gratitude to God for the strength she has been given to withstand the infirmities and loneliness of old age.

Aunt Arie was one of the first contacts of the *Foxfire* project. She lives by herself in a log cabin, draws her water from a well and her heating from a fireplace, and raises her own vegetables. She had been widowed several years before the *Foxfire* editors first visited her, and had since suffered a stroke which left one side of her body paralyzed. Even so, she will not leave her home far back in the mountains. "With her husband's clothes still hanging inside, washed and ready to wear, her home has become a sacred place over which she alone must now keep watch."²³ Mike Cook writes that talking with her was like talking with one's grandmother, and that he found it reassuring that Aunt

Aries are still around to teach the truths of an earlier time. Paul Gillespie reports that only after five months of working on *Foxfire* did the void between himself and the old people close. Aunt Arie's "log cabin was a time machine taking me back to the eighteen eighties" (20). During the students' first meeting with Aunt Arie, she was working to remove the eyes from a fresh hog's head that was given to her by a neighbor so that she could prepare souse meat. When she was asked if it bothered her to pull out the eyes like this, she said, "I don't care fer't bit more'n spit'n'th'fire. . . . I've just done anything'n'ever-'thing in my life 'til I don't care fer nothin' 'at way" (21). As the students helped her, she laughed and said she wished she was stout, like she used to be, but then she went on to say that it was useless to "call back" the years and that it is silly to wish you could go back over your life again. She said there was nothing she had done that she was ashamed of, and she advised the young people not to do anything that they would not want their parents to know. "And then, when th' last roll's called, you'll be ready t'go where you're gonna spend eternity out yonder." She said she would be glad to meet every one of them there. "'Cause that's where I'm a'headin' for. Some of these days I'll have a road t'walk on 'stead'a walkin' in th' mud" (22). She asked them if they were ever going to get the hog's eye out, and one of the boys said he got it. She told him to give it to her so that she could throw it away. She threw it out of the back door, and it landed on a tin roof nearby and rolled off and hung bobbing on the clothesline. The students reported that they were laughing so hard they could barely see to get to work on the other eye.

She and her late husband, Ulysses, used to smoke the meat, Aunt Arie said. She recalled how Ulysses used to hold the knives while she turned the grind rock on the crib shed. But Ulysses is gone. She said she hoped none of the boys ever has to live alone. "In one way hit's a joy, and in another way hit's lonesome; uneasy many times—nobody t'he'p y'. Don't make no difference how bad sick y'get—nobody t'hand y'a dose a'medicine, ner t'do a thing in th' world" (22–23). When she went to the door to throw out the second eye, she remarked, "I trot m'self to death. Ulysses used t'holler t'me about trottin' s'much" (26). She invited the young people to come and eat with her any time that winter, saying that she would open a can of souse for them. She taught them how to prepare tongue; she recollected a good chicken dinner she had made and found herself eating alone on Thanksgiving. She said that if she could afford to, she would put in a short sink so that she wouldn't have to trot outside every time she has to pour out the water she drew from the well. And she said that her porch needed fixing. She had been offered a lot of money for her place, but she did not intend to sell it. She said she does not care about money. She told them that she was born and raised on Hickory Knoll until she was eight years old, and that life had been hard. Her mother had never been well in her life. "She was born with somethin' th' matter with her head—one side'a her head run from th' time she was born 'til she died." She said that she took care of her mother day and night and that she rejoices now that she did. She advised the students, "don't never care a cent in this world t'wait on your mother, whether she's sick or not sick. When she's gone, you'll be glad y'did" (27). She told them God would repay them for this.

Life is easier today, Aunt Arie said. She remembers hoeing corn many a day for a quarter, and picking huckleberries and swapping two gallons of them for one gallon of syrup. But in those days there was always plenty to eat. She advised against getting into debt, and said she is terrified of debts. She worries all the time, she said, that she owes for the road. She advised the students to be good neighbors, too. When they asked her if she was bothered at times because she was all alone, she answered that "it's mighty lonesome," and that when there are storms "an'things like that, it's not s'good." But still she said she does not mind it at all. She is only afraid of one thing in this world, and that is a snake. She told them she is not like "this pore old woman" who lives nearby, who is afraid of a bear and carries an axe with her every time she comes Aunt Arie's way. "Tickles me. A little old hand axe." Aunt Arie asked the lady what she intended to do with that, and the answer was that she would kill a bear with it. But Aunt Arie had lived in the area for eighty years, and had never seen a bear in her entire life. She said that there is nothing in the world that bothers her there, except the groundhog and the fox because they will not let her have a chicken. She and her husband had made a good life there, she said, "but we put in lots'a'time." There are many nights when she is still working at two o'clock in the morning, "cardin'n'spin-nin'n'sewin'. They want me t'sell an'move away from here, but I won't do it. It's just home—'at's all. I spent my happiest days here" (30).

Many of the older women in the *Foxfire* books spoke of the way they could become deeply absorbed in their work. After her sons were grown and had left home, Marinda Brown took up weaving to occupy her time, and now she is constantly at work weaving rugs, belts, mats, stoles, ponchos, pocketbooks, and other pieces of work. She had tried knitting and embroidering, but found that her eyes troubled her when she did close work. She continued to look for something useful to do, and happened to take her rags over to Calmia and began weaving rugs there. She said she found it fascinating to blend the various colors. She compared weaving to playing music; once she sees a pattern draft, she wants to try it out. She says weaving is very satisfying, and that "if you're interested in what you're doing, you can just sit down an' ferget everything." She has noticed that feelings affect weaving, and that sometimes she has to go back over her work because of this. She compared this to working a beater: "Sometimes you give it a harder jerk than y'do other times. An' it makes your weaving a little closer together. It'll tell on you all th' way through."[24] Edith Darnell also spoke of how engrossed she can become with weaving. She said she would weave even if she did not sell any of her work, that she would rather weave than eat. Weaving gives her a gratifying sense of achievement, and it dispels loneliness and distress. She said that she can become very happy and very involved with her work when she is weaving or quilting. Gertrude Keener said that weaving teaches the great lesson of patience, and recalled that when she taught children at Camp Dixie, she found that weaving was an excellent cure for homesickness. She saw a metaphor for human development in her work:

"When you watch your pattern grow, t'me it's like life, more like living. It's more like building character than anything else I can describe it with. It's like teachin' a child from th' beginnin' to grow—as your pattern grows'r as your cloth grows, it's just like a child growin' up. You weave your life into somethin' beautiful." [255]

The older women in the *Foxfire* books were often called "aunt" and "grand-mother" by the young people who spoke with them. Here is one place in the United States where the young and old are rediscovering how much the generations have to offer one another. The students were amazed at Annie Perry's remarkable memory at the age of 83. When Aunt Celia Wood, who at the age of 100 was *Foxfire*'s oldest contact, became ill and died, they felt her death as the loss of someone of close kin. Through human contacts and with growing affection, the young learned what it is to be old. As for the old, they had what may be the greatest joy of an old person, interested listeners. They felt comfortable enough with these high school students to tell them they ought to observe the Sabbath, to tell them to be good and to tell the truth ("let 'er pop"), to say they disapproved of fooling with the moon, and of long hair, too—even to say that it seemed that Judgment Day was close at hand. Florence Brooks said that there are times when she wonders if the past was real. But the past lives as long as it is remembered, and remembering is what *Foxfire* is all about. Corn shuckings and log rollings and quiltings were *human* activities, *social* events. They are recreated through oral histories in a way they never can be in the most artful arrangement of artifacts in a museum case. The memories of the old are treasure troves of culture and history and folklore, and when they speak of these things they restore the past. When the elders are gathered together, the memory of one has a way of igniting the memory of another, so that individual recollections become woven into a collective remembrance. In *Foxfire,* there are passages in which excerpts from transcripts of tape-recorded interviews of several different people are pre-sented on the same page. In this way, a chorus of voices is heard, a collective life review is created. Was there as strong a communal spirit in the past as the elders claim? How did we lose the old-timey neighborliness, why did we for-feit self-reliance and resourcefulness? Memory is more than a backward look. There is a fostering of the future in it; Cicero wrote of "the treasury and guardian of all things." At the turn of the century, when today's elderly people were born, 40 percent of the labor force in the United States were engaged in agriculture. Today, that figure is not much more than 4 percent. The entire society has undergone a transformation over the decades. Many old people today have something to say about this transformation. Along the way, they have much to say about what it is like to be old in the United States today. They are still here. They can still be asked.

Oral Histories of Italian, Jewish, and Slavic Grandmothers

In her autobiography, American writer Mary Heaton Vorse wrote that she came to realize why 365,000 men and people of 20 nationalities went on strike in 50 communities and 10 states in 1919 on the day she went with an organizer to Butler, Pennsylvania. Down the road was the suburb of Lyndora. There, before the great shops of the Standard Steel Car, she saw a row of sheds that she said could not be dignified by the name of barracks. Nothing green could be grown there. In every doorway were women and children, and in every window were the "flags of hope" flown by the wives of the steelworkers—their coarse white curtains. Here and there she saw, "like the promise of a garden to be, a geranium blooming in a tin can," and in her memoirs she remembered what she had written about the white window curtains, the women's "flag of defiance against the dirt":

> You cannot go into any foul courtyard without finding white lace curtains stretched on frames to dry. Wherever you go, in Braddock or in Homestead or in filthy Rankin, you will find courageous women hopefully washing their white curtains. There is no woman so driven with work that she will not attempt this decency.
>
> It is the way these women have of reassuring themselves against the drifting soot and the slack sifting in by night and by day. It is their way of saying, "I love cleanliness and beauty." One could write a tragedy about these window curtains. They have become to these women a fixed idea. They wash their sash curtains every week, and this in towns where the water must be carried in buckets from courtyards.[25]

Two days after she had arrived in Pittsburgh, Vorse wrote, her personal life had been obliterated by the great steel strike.

Some of the women who had set their flags of hope asail in the soot-darkened air, who flocked in the doorways with their children around them, are grandmothers and great-grandmothers today. Vorse was a living witness to the conditions of their lives when they were young. Now, in their old age, a woman historian returned to their world to gather the oral histories of ethnic women of three generations. In a paper on the economic roles of the oldest of these Italian, Slavic, and Jewish American women in the Pittsburgh area, Corinne Azen Krause recalled, "The steel industry and the city growing around it had attracted thousands of immigrants bringing diversity to the older English, Scotch, Irish, and German families. By 1910, over 62 percent of the city's population was either foreign born or born to foreign parents." Among those crowding into Pittsburgh in search of work were Poles and Slovaks and Croatians, Serbs and Italians and Jews. According to census data, both foreign-born and native-born women worked outside the home before they were married, but after marriage, very few foreign-born women remained in the work force. But an oral history study of 75 ethnic grandmothers, 25 of whom were Italian, 25 Jewish and 25 Slavic, "presents a totally different picture of these women and documents a great variety of work done by married women that is totally absent from the census data."[26] Krause presents evidence for the vitality of their economic roles.

In this comparative oral history study conducted under the direction of Krause, the vitality of ethnicity in the lives of these women is heavily documented.[27] Women of each of the three generations and three ethnic groups were found to have strong and positive attachments to the past. Krause believes "that ethnic background is a deep and significant fact of life, often ignored, often unconscious, but psychologically important" (5). She points to the role ethnicity plays in the development of women's identity and the fostering of a feeling of belonging in a world that is becoming ever more impersonal. Many cultural values are transmitted through the mother. But the culture of the everyday lives of women of various ethnic backgrounds remains unexplored. What is more, ethnic women do not have a representative literature. "No Puzo or Bellow or Roth has recorded the life cycle and emotions of ethnic women" (7). And Erik Erikson's developmental psychology applies to men, not women. In 1974, the National Institute of Mental Health published a bibliography of multiethnic literature for the nation's high schools. Krause observes of this bibliography that it

> includes only one Italian-American novel with a strong female character and she is a religious fanatic; Jewish-American novels present destructive, neurotic women invented by male authors; the few Slavic-American novels listed present no significant female characters at all. While these novels may tell us something important about the way women are viewed in traditional ethnic cultures, they in no way contribute to the self-esteem of the female student body. The limitations of relying upon fiction as "a tool for mental health" only underscore the need for factual, objective studies as a resource for scholars and a basis for curriculum materials. [3]

At the time of this study, 92 percent of the grandmothers, as compared with about 49 percent of the mothers and 22 percent of the daughters, identified themselves as housewives. None of the grandmothers was currently employed full time; 17 percent were engaged in part-time work. About two-thirds of the grandmothers had been employed when they were single, and the work histories of most of these women had been erratic. When they were still unmarried, about 17 percent had worked in a family business, about 8 percent in stores, and over 34 percent in unskilled or semiskilled jobs in factories, restaurants, laundries, or bakeries, or in domestic service. None of them had been professionals. After they were married, more than one-third of the grandmothers worked in a family-related business or helped their husbands in their occupation. Krause found that the most striking differences between women of the three generations were in the material conditions of their lives:

> Sacrifice for their children was the way of life for the grandmothers. Their goal was a better life for their children, and this goal was largely achieved. The poverty and struggle of the grandmother generation contrasts sharply with the comfort and security enjoyed by the granddaughters. Contrasts

between immigrant grandmothers and their granddaughters are particularly striking. One European-born grandmother labored barefoot in the fields as a child; her granddaughter took music lessons, rode horses, and went to college. Pride in their children's and grandchildren's accomplishments fill the hearts of grandmothers. [158–59]

The emotional support so freely given by grandmothers to their granddaughters, their service as loving confidante to younger family members, is a special kind of mental health support offered by elderly people. But these elderly women, whatever their ethnic background, have certain problems in common with one another. They are dependent almost entirely upon family for emotional support. "Yet their daughters are working in ever growing numbers, their granddaughters have other aims and other values. The changing family structure will leave grandmothers more and more without the vital supports they need," and in Krause's view these needs will have to be met through the community (167).

World War I marks the separation between the traditional world and the modern world. The grandmothers were young women then, when that fateful turn was made. Two of every three in this study had been uprooted from a European home. They came to this country, some of them without family, all of them bewildered and frightened, most of them unable to speak a word of English, many of them in desperate need to find a job. Through their oral histories, these grandmothers spoke of what they remembered of the upheavals in the world when they were children and young women, of how they had fared in and around the city of Pittsburgh when they were raising their families, and of their present lives as elderly Americans.

Grandmother R was born in Bulgaria in 1910.[28] Her mother died when she was very little, and although she said her aunt and grandmother had been very good to her, she felt her orphanhood very keenly. She used to recite her poems at school, and the theme was always the same, the theme of the orphaned daughter. In the early months of her marriage, before she and her husband left their country for the United States, she had not been able to bring herself to address her mother-in-law as "Mom," even though she was very fond of her. Only a few days before her oral history interview, she had been sitting outside thinking about her childhood and her motherlessness. She said that one must experience orphanhood or widowhood to understand fully what they mean.

A young girl growing up in her culture had to learn how to spin wool and use the loom, R said, and how to keep house, make bread, make material, and do embroidery. At a recent folk festival held in Pennsylvania, R had demonstrated how yarn is made from raw wool. A girl learned these skills by watching others work. She spun cotton and made her own material for bedspreads and bed linens and clothing. It was considered disgraceful for a girl to be outside playing in the streets with the boys in her country. There had been a strict division of labor based on sex.

In her oral history interview, R spoke of the customs of her people observed on New Year's Day and the three-day Christmas holiday and St. George's Feast Day, which is now a secular holiday for the shepherds. She explained how silkworms were raised, and described the harvesting of the roses that had been an augury of summertime in her childhood. She talked in some detail about the day when she first met her future husband, and she told her interviewer all the traditions that had been observed on her wedding day.

In 1929, R came to America. She saw her first Christmas tree, and she saw bananas for the first time. And she had been amazed to see green beans served in December in the Greek restaurant where the immigrant couple had dinner. Across the street she saw men operating the giant cranes, digging before the foundation would be laid for the Empire State Building. Laughing, she told her interviewer that the oranges and the gas were the most important incentives she had for staying in America. Even King Boris could not live as well as she could, because there was no gas in Bulgaria.

The newlyweds stopped in Pittsburgh for ten days, and then went on to New Castle, where they lived for three years. From there they went on to Homestead, where they bought a grocery store, which they lost in 1937. During the times when her husband could not find any work at all because of the Depression, he had stayed home and cared for the children while R worked. She had worked in a grocery in Homestead for $10 a week; she had worked as a seamstress for a year. And there had been a time when she did laundry for a family of seven for $1.50 a week. In 1943, she was hired to work at U.S. Steel, and she continued to work there until the end of the war.

With the help of a Bulgarian-English dictionary, R taught herself the language for a while; later, she went to evening school. She and her husband did not have any kin or even any people from their town or the areas near their town in Europe who were living in America when they first came here. They were "two lost birds," R said. When she went to the hospital to have an operation, she pleaded with a close friend who was childless to promise her that she would take care of her children if she did not survive the surgery. When her children were born, R said, she felt that she herself had been reborn. She wanted to give them the mother's love that she felt she had missed. She said she had been very lonely during those years when she first came to this country and did not know the English language. In the 1930s, R began introducing her ethnic heritage to Pittsburgh. She began to organize a club and to raise money, and she saw to it that a program about her national culture was added to the Fourth of July celebration. When her children were very small, they began learning the national dances; at the age of five, her daughter was leading the kolos. R said when she was younger and traveling to different towns, she used to look for a certain combination of letters in a name in telephone books—a combination that suggested the name might be Bulgarian. She would call up the people and pretend that she was lost and ask them for information. She said that she made many new friends that way, and that they would visit one another after that. To this day, R misses her family in Europe. They are growing old, and she wonders if she will ever see them again. When she looks at old photographs and listens to the tapes her daughter plays for her, she feels sadness and a longing to be there. She has visited her country four times since 1960; when she was young, she felt she could go any time, but her age and the state of her health make it very difficult for her to travel now. When she feels very depressed, she writes letters home.

Born in Homestead at the turn of the century, Q is the daughter of parents born in Austria-Hungary. Her strong sense of responsibility to her community was a legacy from them both. They were more than just business people, Q said; they were very community-minded. Her father taught young men the butchering trade, and sometimes they had four or five students living with them while they were apprentices. She knows every area of her town because, when she was very young, she was given the responsibility of delivering meat orders to the boardinghouses. She remembered the panic of 1907 and the circulation of scrip. At that time, her father had a soup kitchen open for anyone in need of food who happened to come by. As a guest lecturer in a class on Ethnic Women in America in a college in the East, Q told the story of the strike of 1919. She described how the Pinkerton men went ahead of the "scabs" and clubbed the strikers down, and she explained how the butchers, grocers, and landlords formed a support system for the strikers. Once, she saw a policman's horse chase a man up a flight of stairs between two homes.

Even as a very young child, Q had been sent on errands to the grocery store, carrying a little basket on her arm. Sometimes her parents "farmed her out" to stay overnight with a young bride whose husband was working the night shift. At the age of fifteen, she became the first president of her church's sodality. She worked at that age as an interpreter for doctors, accompanying them on their rounds and serving as interlocutor. She was fluent in Slovak, Polish, and Russian as well as English, and also knew some Hungarian. During the flu epidemic of 1918, she worked as an interpreter and helped to locate the next of kin of many immigrants who were without family in this country. Hospitals were improvised wherever this was possible, even in hotels. She saw many tragic things, she told the class, and they have remained with her all her life.

In those days, Grandmother Q recalled, young men emigrated from Europe to escape the draft, and few of them had much command of English. Only grocers or hotel people had telephones then, and indoor plumbing was a rarity. Women did their washing in the backyard, and for those whose home was a boardinghouse this was hard and time-consuming labor. She recollected the boardinghouse passbooks, the early days when the steelworkers used to be paid with gold coins, and how the "lady of the house" had to be a "jack of all trades" who sometimes was called upon to scrub the backs of the boarders when they took their baths. From the age of ten, she had run errands for her father's customers; when there was sickness, she was sent to fetch the doctor. She had been exposed to diphtheria and typhoid and scarlet fever, and as a very young girl she witnessed miscarriages and childbirths. On Sundays, she used to tell her girl friends about her experiences. At that time, mothers did not talk about such matters to their daughters. Sometimes when she had delivered an order of meat she was asked to look after the customer's children for a while. Her classmates used to help her on her rounds, and if a wedding was being celebrated in one of the Russian or Hungarian halls, the group would stop in for a dance or two and then go on to delivering orders again. She remembered how young men used to take clothesline props and knock over outhouses as a Halloween prank, and every now and then there was still somebody inside. In those days, both young and old shared in the festivities of the churches and fraternal organizations. People danced the czardas and polkas as well as the Big Apple and the Black Bottom.

Grandmother Q remained actively involved from childhood to old age with family and community as well as business. She had traveled extensively throughout the United States, attending school-board conventions. And she had made trips to South America and Europe with her brother. She began a business career when very young and stayed with it all her life. In her opinion, women who want a career must be dedicated to their work, and those who accept offices in organizations ought to have a higher motive than the wish to receive the prestige such an office would confer. When people comment on her good fortune in having fine relationships with her grown children and their families, she answers that she has built her fortune in this, and that it cannot happen by itself.

Aged 80 at the time of her oral history interview, Grandmother A had been the fourth in line of 14 children. She had been expected to do the housework and to help with the cooking and childcare from the time she was very young. She raised all the siblings born after her except for the youngest, whom she left to her mother's care because she had taken a job. Only two of all those children are now living—she and the sister she had raised from the age of nine when her mother, who had then been in her early fifties, had died. Grandmother A had helped her daughter with the grandchildren when they were babies. She said she had been younger then, but now she could not do all this work. She had raised children all her life, she said, and she is tired of all the washing and ironing, and glad to get away from all the hard work. She had married when she was 25—"up in years"—because she had been needed at home to care for her younger siblings. Italians want their daughters to marry young so they "won't get into trouble," but they also want their daughters to marry someone who has a trade or an education or some capital, so he can provide for them. At first, when she had told her father she wanted to marry, he had asked her who would take care of the four children who were still living at home at the time. She had replied that she thought they were old enough to look after themselves. Later, she said, her father approved of her marriage because he saw that her husband would be a good provider.

Grandmother W, now in her seventies, remembered a song the young people used to sing in Russia: "Where Is My Youth?" In Odessa, there was famine. People died in the streets from hunger and from typhus. When she was very young, W was responsible for her family. Her father had died. Her mother, who was hard of hearing and who communicated with her by reading her lips, was ill. Her brother was in hiding from the army; her sister was ill. She was the only person who could bring food to the house. She and her husband's family and her sister-in-law were the only Lubavitchers in Odessa. She said that she has never lost her faith. When they were living in New Jersey, she and her husband sent their children to Yeshiva school in New York. They were determined that their children would get a strong religious background. She spoke of her joy that her children had all surpassed her, that her daughter is ten heads above her and her grandchildren will go even higher. After fifty-five years, she has not forgotten the Russian language. Nor has she lost the woman that as a child she knew she would become. When she was very young, she would always rise earlier then the others to say her morning prayers before going out. In old age, she never goes to bed without first saying a prayer.

Two of every three of the grandmothers in this study had been born in Europe. Despite differences in ethnicity, women in the oldest generation had certain characteristics in common with one another. More than one-third were wholly unaware of menstruation before their own first experience with it, and even those who knew something about it,"usually picked up from whispered conversations with peers," had little factual information.[29] Forty percent of the grandmothers said they knew nothing at all about sex before their wedding night. These women were private persons to a greater extent than were their daughters or granddaughters, and were less inclined to acknowledge problems in their oral history interviews. "Many of them experienced much hardship," Krause writes, but "there were very few words of complaint or self pity" (103). They were least likely of the three generations of women to talk about mental health problems in the family or to acknowledge that they or their children had used professional mental health facilities or had seen a psychiatrist. As a group, they were strongly family-centered. Their greatest source of pleasure was "love and attention" from family members. The high incidence of these responses, especially among the Italian grandmothers, "coupled with 'loneliness' as a source of feeling bad indicates the importance of being part of a family" to the women of the oldest generation (116).

Of course, ethnic differences were found, as well as differences between women of the three generations. Slavic women reported concern about childbirth, menopause and jobs to a much lower degree than did Jewish and Italian women. A very high percentage of Jewish women expressed concern about problems with children. And Jewish women also expressed concern about jobs and their roles as a woman to a significantly higher degree than did Italian or Slavic women. It was also found that the family is central in the lives of Italian women regardless of their social class. Indeed, the sense of responsibility for family members was very strong among Italian women, and extended beyond parents and children to encompass siblings, nieces and nephews and aunts and uncles. Many ethnic differences were found to persist over the generations, confirming Krause's thesis about the significance of ethnicity in the development of identity. Certain generational differences were striking. Each succeeding generation of women was older at the time she was married, had fewer children, and achieved a higher level of formal education. (The grandmothers had completed 7.5 years of schooling on the average.) Many more women of the oldest generation had married men of the same ethnic background than had their daughters and granddaughters, and many more reported that they still used their native European language, at least occasionally. More of the oldest than the two younger groups thought it important to socialize with those of a similar ethnic background, and important to marry someone of the same religion. Many more grandmothers believed that raising children is a mother's job. Grandmothers did have a much more traditional view of what constitutes women's work than their daughters or granddaughters, who, on the average, had been instructed far more about sexual intercourse, conception, and childbirth, and were much more likely to mention their own achievements as a source of personal satisfaction. Interestingly, grandmothers were also more likely than women of the other generations to place a very high value on intelligence as a quality for a husband.

Among the oldest women in this oral history study were those who had firsthand experiences with the upheavals of the early decades of this century—the migrations from Europe, World War I, the flu epidemic of 1918, the Johnstown flood, the steel strikes, the Great Depression, World War II. There are collective memories in their transcripts of hard times and of expectations so much humbler than those of their daughters and particularly their granddaughters that they exclaim over the difference. For many of them the responsibilities of girlhood and young womanhood were very heavy. There was domestic work in households crowded with many children and with the boarders, who so often were felt to be members of an extended family. There was work outside the household in lampshade factories and chocolate factories, in cigar factories and in the mills. When these women were young, a girl could work a full 40-hour week and only earn $13, half of which she needed for room and board, lunches and carfare, and the other half of which was often turned over to the family or sent back to the needy family in Europe. The more privileged were given music lessons: in those days, piano lessons cost 50 cents. In many of these life stories, the grandmothers remembered the grief of separation, sometimes forever, from home and family they would never see again, the fears and hopes in passage to America, and the economic struggles, the culture shock, the efforts to learn English and yet to keep something of the Old World alive as a legacy for their children.

Grandmothers all, some of them great-grandmothers, these daughters in their own late lives reflected on the character and life of their mothers. The absence of a mother who died young is as powerfully there on the pages of these transcripts as is the maternal presence of those who lived on. One grandmother says she tells her children that her mother was like a sister to her, that she had always felt free to go to her for counsel, and that she missed her very much when she died. Another said she and her mother got along very well, and that they used to sit and sew or crochet together in the evening and sing "like two birds." Her mother had disapproved of a young man who was once a suitor, a cousin and therefore not an acceptable mate according to the Serbian religion. She had promised her mother that she would not run off with him but would stay home and help with her six younger siblings. She had not wanted to go against her mother's wishes. Even after she was married, her mother's influence continued to be very strong in her life. One grandmother said that her mother had died in her arms when she was 17, and that she had felt there was nothing in life for her after that. Grandmother N's mother had the idea that a girl might get in trouble if she went to high school, and therefore did not permit N to go. She had loved learning, and hoped she would be forced to attend school. But N said that her mother had never been well—she had fainting spells and other physical problems—and N had been needed to work at home. Asked by her interviewer to describe what she had been like at age 21, N said she had been disappointed and heartbroken. At that age, she had lost her son, she had lost her mother, and she had had several miscarriages. She said she could not get over her mother's death.

Until the time of her mother's death, Y said, she used to talk with her on the telephone every day after she was married. And even now she wants to dial that number. Her mother used to think for her children and make plans for them; Y said that she was always right. She had taught Y that she was responsible for her younger siblings and that, if they were hurt in any way, it would be Y's fault. Her siblings came first in her life, Y said, and she had been like a second mother to them. She liked to read, but if her mother caught her reading, she would take the book away from her and tell her to work. Once she remarked about all the babies her mother had, and her mother slapped her. Her mother's last baby was her fourteenth; the thirteenth had lived only one day. There was nine months' difference in age between Y's youngest sibling and her own daughter. The two girls graduated from high school together, Y said. She told a story that one day, when her mother did not have enough milk to nurse the baby, Y nursed her sister. She felt she resembled her mother in that she was cautious about her health, but she felt inferior to her. She described her mother as having been very ambitious, capable, and self-confident. She had to be, she said, because her parents had sent her to America when she was 12 years old.

There were mothers remembered in these oral histories for having been very strict, and mothers who had been creative but who had never had the opportunity to cultivate their talents. There were mothers remembered as having been very healthy and "spry" in their old age, and mothers who had died before their time, worn with work and childbearing. One grandmother recalled that her mother used to take her to afternoon concerts at the park and to ballets when she was less than 6 years old and they were living in Philadelphia. But her father died when she was 8, and after that she had to help in their kosher restaurant. It was more like a boardinghouse, she said, than a commercial restaurant; the young immigrants came there for regular meals. This was in Braddock where her parents had moved shortly before her father died. When the concerts came to Braddock, they would attend them. Sometimes they went to Carnegie Music Hall and to the theater when the road companies came through town. This grandmother used to get books from the library for her mother, who had been an avid reader of the classics though she had little time for anything but work. She remembered that when Eugene Debs came to Braddock to speak on the street corner, her mother had been too tired to go to hear him. In these retrospectives, the grandmothers remembered old joys and long-buried grievances and sorrows. One laughed during her oral history interview when she recalled the mischief maker she had once been. She recalled the imp-self that her long-dead mother had known so well. In all this reworking of the past, the grandmothers spoke of what had changed and what had remained steadfast in their long lives. What appeared to be timeless and changeless to them was this ancient bond between mothers and daughters.

Many women of the oldest of the three generations in this study said they could recall the distant past more clearly than what had happened a week before the interview. One grandmother was precise about naming the date when she came to America, and said she could remember people she knew sixty years ago and that her memory is very good. There were those who had a visual memory. One grandmother described people as if she were painting them. She remarked how much an old boy friend of hers whom she had seen thirty-five years after he left their town in Italy had aged. Her friends shock her because she says they age so much more quickly than she does. Another grandmother had a spatial memory. She was specific about the locations of streets and neighborhoods in Pittsburgh throughout her interview.

For some of these women, the very act of remembering appeared to evoke particular scenes and impressions. One grandmother, who was in her eighties when she was interviewed, said she remembered her grandfather's house distinctly. She described it in some detail, and said that across from the porch where they used to sit was a little lake and that she had wished at times in her life that she could go down the hill to see that house and the lake in front of it again. She remembered a train ride she took through Berlin and spoke of the flower boxes she saw in every window. She had been only 6 years old at the time and was on her way to America. She said she remembered the boat quite clearly and all that had happened when she was in passage to this country.

During her oral history interview, V was asked what she had done the day before, and she mused aloud, "Yesterday, what was yesterday?" She reminded herself that yesterday had been Tuesday and that tomorrow would be Thursday. Later on, she remarked that she does not always rely on her past, but that she lives every day anew. "What's gone is gone," she said. Even so, she described her childhood home in Vermont and the big icehouse nearby in some detail. She remembered the little garden she said she had cherished when she was young and the public concerts that were held in the park on Friday nights.

Sometimes the temperatures would fall to 20° below during the Vermont winters, she said, and windows were so frosted over no one could see through them. Children used to put pennies against the frost on the window to make an impression of an Indian head. They had contests to see who could make the most perfect penny. She recalled the sleigh rides and heating bricks in the oven for days and then putting them in the sleighs to warm their feet. She remembered making featherbeds while the phonograph was playing. And she recalled how they used to go to the woods in the spring to collect the sap of the maple trees. They used to pour maple syrup on the snow to make suckers. Once, after she was married, she and her husband went to Vermont from Johnstown to visit her parents. The train was so covered with ice they could not get out, and they had to stay there and ride it back to Johnstown. She remembered sitting there looking at her parents through part of the window. She said it must have been 40° below that winter. Although she could not remember just when her father had died, and although she had to stop and figure dates aloud so she could remember how old her children were when certain events had taken place, she had vivid memories of the 1936 flood and even more vivid recollections of her childhood.

Several grandmothers spoke of the bargains and contracts they had made with God, and the silent pledges and promises that were part of their prayers for their children's safety. One of them said that she "lived in church" during World War II, when two of her sons were in the service. Another prayed that illness would strike her rather than her children. Many spoke of how important it is for a mother to be home with her children when they are small and of how happy those days seemed to them to be in retrospect. When the interviewer asked AG how she had prepared herself for the time when her children would be grown and gone from home, she said, "It hurt. I am sure that every mother can say the same thing. You feel letdown. And the worst is when you go in the closet and see their clothes. Just like when someone dies, you see their clothes. But I usually keep myself busy."

Years ago, it was not taken for granted that all one's children would live. Many of these grandmothers had children who died in infancy or childhood or early youth. One remembered her little girl who had died at the age of one month; everyone had said the infant was too beautiful to live. Her brother had comforted her when the baby died, saying that it was a blessing that "the Lord had taken her" because she had gone blind in her illness. Another grandmother lost her firstborn baby during the flu epidemic. She had lined a basket with pockets and had used hot water bottles to keep the baby warm; she had been born premature, and there were no incubators in those days. After her baby died, she would never go back to the apartment where they had lived. One grandmother lost her second baby, a girl, and when she was pregnant with her third baby she did not allow herself to think it might be a girl. She was afraid to wish even to herself to have the daughter for whom she longed. There were grandmothers who had lost their children in maturity. One showed her interviewer a photograph of her son who had died when he was 35. He was "the finest," she said. "I don't have him anymore." Another said her son was 27 years old when he died and that she still sees him very clearly as he used to look when he came home from work. In one year, her son, her husband, and her brother died, she said, and she always thinks about her son.

She worries more about her grandchildren than her children, V said, "because they have a harder hill to climb." Another said she longs for great-grandchildren. Although she believes her grandchildren are wonderful, she wishes they would ask her now and then if they could drive her somewhere. Even the one to whom she made a gift of a car does not think of offering her a lift. This woman had taken the recovery of one of her grandchildren upon herself after the girl had been hospitalized for depression. She used to stay up until the early hours of the morning, listening to her. "I was her doctor," she said, "because we talked about everything. Eventually I made her well." Another said that after her children had married, she still had her husband for a while, and she had been happy that their children had found mates. Some of the grandmothers said that they had been devastated by widowhood and that women ought to prepare themselves for being alone. "As the years go by, it gets worse," one grandmother told her interviewer. When a neighbor had said she did not realize how hard it would be, she had said, "Well, it is."

Jewish and Slavic grandmothers, Krause reports, were much likelier to have arranged to be alone at the time of the interview than the Italian grand-mothers, whose tapings were often interrupted by visits from grandchildren, nieces, or cousins.[30] But as interviewers know, there are many presences in the room during the taping of an interview. Sometimes a person is only one room away and not really out of earshot. One grandmother called out to her husband now and then to ask him to confirm the truth of what she had just said about him. Sometimes, there are imaginary audiences, hidden censors of whom one becomes conscious in speaking about private matters. There are people who need to be constantly reassured that the interviewer will respect the seal of confession and protect their privacy. One grandmother spoke over and over again of "them" and of how "they" would "shoot" her when they heard what she said. The presences of the dead were felt and mentioned in answering some of the interview questions. There are the earlier selves who are the characters in one's life story and who appear as very real presences before the reflecting mind. The speaker may address them in her oral history as if to appease them or to accuse them or silence them. In the republic of the self there is always at least one censor who decides what will be allowed to remain in the life record. One is never completely alone in telling one's life story, and the emotional tone of the narrator shifts as these presences are admitted to conscious thought. And the interviewer's presence influences the nature and the direction of oral reminiscence. Furthermore, some people are most meticulous in their recollections; other ramble. All these considerations enter into what social scientists call "the ecology of the interview." It is not surprising that even though these women were not interviewed about their thoughts and feelings on the subject of aging, their interviews offer a number of illuminations on growing older in the United States today. These might appear anywhere on the transcripts, some of which are 70 pages long—or longer. The reader of the transcripts needs to remain alert to the possibility that insights into subjective aspects of aging might be given at any point in the oral history, as well as to the complexity of the ecology of the interview.

There were grandmothers who voiced their frustration at being incapacitated or immobilized after having been active all their lives. One 80-year-old woman said she had never looked forward to a time in her life when she would not be able to work, and she spoke of how much she suffers from being physically handicapped. Some said they hoped they would die quickly, without prolonged suffering and without becoming an encumbrance. Some spoke of their compassion for friends who were now confined to nursing homes. One said she could not understand why people's lives are sustained when they are beyond medical treatment. Many had a keen interest in politics. Some spoke at considerable length about the lessons to be learned from history. One grandmother said she saw a parallel between the mistreatment of Jews in Eastern Europe and the mistreatment of blacks in Pittsburgh. Many spoke of their admiration for Eleanor Roosevelt. Though some were more prolix than others, a number of these women appear to care very much about the world and the future.

One grandmother said her children want her to buy new furniture. "I'm old," she remarked, "Why can't the furniture be old?" She does not like change at this time in her life. Another ventured the opinion that people are harder to get along with as they age. She said her retired husband had too much time on his hands, that he sat around in the house too much with nothing in particular to do. Another, who was talking about why she loves good plays, remarked that the Barrymores left something of themselves in the world, "like a dynasty . . . there are dynasties of businessmen, there are dynasties of religion . . . they left something behind . . . then you never die." Many laughed about ethnic differences. One said her associates in business made her an honorary Presbyterian; they called her a "Presbyterian Jew." Another said of her widowed daughter's Slavic husband, "I think he was Italian when he died. . . . We made an Italian out of him." Grandmother K said, "So you go through life so much, some time you wonder." She said everyone can write a book about her or his life. Prejudice is so foolish, she observed, "we all come and we all go. Nobody lives forever. We don't take nothing with us, anyway." Aged 80, she summed up her point of view:

"Listen, life is not all full of roses. We all have our ups and downs. We have snow, we have rain, we have sunshine, we have everything in life. So we can't say, 'I want this, I want. . . .' There is no such thing as you want in life. But the only thing we have to do, what we get, be thankful. And it shouldn't be worse."

When she worries, she asks herself why she should worry. She reminds herself that there is nothing she can do about whatever it is that is troubling her. When she is "down in the dumps," she said, she crochets; she gets up at two or three or even four in the morning, and she crochets. She has hardening of the arteries, and when she feels the symptoms coming on, she forces herself to get dressed and to go downstairs and talk to people, and she says the circulation starts and she feels all right. Sometimes, she says, she writes poems. She does not tell people about her problems. She says she puts on lipstick and powder and earrings and fixes her hair, and then she goes downstairs. People comment on how well she looks and ask her how she feels. And she answers that she feels all right, since she looks good.

The population sample in the study on women, ethnicity, and mental health, Krause reflects, "is skewed toward families in which the women have remained close, since the cooperation of daughter, mother, and grandmother was a necessary precondition for inclusion in the study."[31] Of course, since the United States is a multicultural society, no study of elderly people may be said to be representative of all the elderly in America today. But regardless of the population sample interviewed or the focus of research, oral history studies are of much benefit to the elderly themselves. The three generations of women in this study had all been notified that they would receive a typed transcript of their interviews and that they could correct it and keep it for themselves. Several women called to say that they had felt pleasure and pride from "remembering." One woman wrote a letter in which she said that the interviews "had helped her and her daughter discuss more honestly the problems of an emotionally disturbed grandchild." Several women had asked to be reassured of complete privacy before they consented to participate in this study. But after the study, they had their transcripts bound and they shared them with family members. "Transcripts," Krause writes, "rest on coffee tables in the homes of many of the grandmothers." She suggests that the mental health service provided by the oral history interview may be of particular value for elderly people "who no longer live in ethnic neighborhoods within walking distance of old friends or community centers" (168). One grandmother had said in her interview that she had wanted to write a book about her life. The interviewer replied that this is what she was now doing.

The Uses of Oral History

Anthropologists often have included the gathering of oral histories in their research studies of various cultures and subcultures, and since the elders of a community are the keepers of tradition wherever people live by the oral tradition, it is odd that anthropologists are recent arrivals to the study of aging.[32] Nonetheless, theirs is a radiant advent with the publication of Barbara Myerhoff's book about 300 members of the Jewish Community Center who live near the beaches of Southern California.[33] These women and men had migrated to this country from the ghettoes of Eastern Europe in their youth and from jobs in the garment centers of Chicago and New York to Southern California in their old age. "No natural audience in the form of progeny or a younger generation was recording their existence" and therefore they had to bear witness for themselves (32). They dreaded oblivion more than suffering or death, and looked for ways to make themselves visible. "They narrated themselves perpetually, in the form of keeping notes, journals, writing poems and reflections spontaneously, and also telling their stories to whoever would listen" (33). To recount their early years of shtetl life was to restore those years to life. "Professor Barbara" offered a Living History class, a forum where memories were gathered and sorted. There, dreams and wishes, questions and daily trivial concerns were interwoven into the *bobbemaysehs*, the "grandmothers' tales," the stuff of what Rachel, one of the class members, called Domestic Religion. Aged 88, Rachel said that the pictures of her earlier life came back to her in class, came up "like lava. It just melted away the earth from all those people . . . and they became alive. And then to me it looked like they were never dead" (39). Storytelling, the passion of these people because it was the core of their culture, rescued the past from irrevocable loss and brought it to life again: Rachel could see her mother "engraved in my head" (38). Reminiscing is not escapism, but a means through which old people integrate their lives. This enables them "to age well and die well" (222). It is ironic, but the very isolation of these old people from family and the "outside world" that grieves them so deeply gave them the freedom "to find their own way," to "indulge their passion for things of the past" (9).

Old people are, in a way, survivors, and they are all alike in this, much as they may differ in many other respects. And survivors bear the burden of guilt. Therefore, old people are morally responsible for examining their lives. There is a moral necessity in the life review, which may take the form of storytelling. Exploring her own feeling of guilt for having invaded the privacy of these old people, Myerhoff came to see that guilt has a bright side in this, that it expresses the feeling of responsibility one has for the well-being of others. The members of the center are survivors, not only of youth, but of the Holocaust. Although one can be crippled by the guilt of the survivor, it can also become the agent of transformation of one's life. The guilt these old people at the center felt "made it impossible for them to lead the unexamined life" (24). Because of it, they turned strongly toward the symbolic life. They transformed it into conscience.

In the old women at the center, Myerhoff saw her own future. She was aware that to hold other people in reverence, to be a little in awe of them, or to take a protective attitude toward them is a way of keeping them at a distance. These old people were not saints or heroes to her, and that is why what they achieved is so significant in her eyes. She wanted her work "to be a full-length portrait, light and darkness with more shading than sharp lines" (28). She knew neutrality would be impossible, so she worked for balance. Old people who are invisible to those in the outside world are in danger of becoming invisible to themselves. They need to be *seen*, so they know this life is not a dream and that they are alive. They are in a "double bind." Dreading senility, they need to show self-control and poise and dignity. But dreading the loss of the feeling they are still alive, they need intensity and passion. Through telling their life stories, old people reaffirm that they are not ghosts, and that there was continuity. Oral histories, parables, little stories, grandmothers' tales—through these the old become architects of the meaning of their lives, weavers of designs from experiences, dreams, reflections, and memories.

Myerhoff found that the old women at the center seemed to flourish, as her grandmother had, while the old men, like her grandfather, seemed to shrivel. She asks why biology and culture seem to conspire to favor women in giving them a longer life expectancy. In tracing the culture of the center back to its roots in the shtetl, she builds a powerful case in support of her perception that an "underground female role" was in the making all their lives that endowed these women with flexibility and pragmatism. These are qualities of inestimable value in old age. There were no stereotyped sex roles at the center except during the ceremony of the Sabbath and in the serving of food. Women did the real work of organization and administration. They dominated events that required physical endurance. They could outexercise and outdance the men. They were more outspoken and more assertive in every form of verbal expression. They composed and performed wonderful cycles of song duels. They devised brilliant strategies for fending off loneliness and for making do with very little money. They made aging into a veritable career. What they had experienced of domestic life as children they now transformed into Domestic Religion. It served them faithfully in their old age. Ever connected with others and needed by others, accustomed to having been nurturers, the old women care better for themselves than the old men do. And there is continuity in their humblest tasks. "Perhaps women in general are more prepared for the inevitable infirmities of old age," Myerhoff reflects, "by a lifetime of acceptance of their bodily limits and changes." Many men come to experience these things for the first time in late life. "Old age is a brutal check on omnipotence fantasies" (264). Age is a wound to more than narcissism and vanity. It is a wound to dignity and pride. The old women at the center endured. They "communicated a quiet conviction and satisfaction with themselves, perhaps because they did what had to be done, did it as well as it could be done, and knew that without what they did there would be nothing and no one" (268). Looking back upon the work of one's life, this is more than a little consolation.

Of the living old women, Myerhoff wrote of many who moved her deeply. Among these is Basha, who made a ceremony of her meal of chicken-foot stew cooked on an electric hot plate. Of those no longer living, she wrote of Sofie, her grandmother, who had the gift of transforming the world for those she loved, of standing between the outside world and home, of protecting those she loved against dangers both real and imagined. The stories Sofie told her granddaughter in reward for every bite of food she ate, taught her that no one with imagination and memory need ever be bored. "Sofie knew and taught me that everyone had some story, every house held a life that could be penetrated and known, if one took the trouble." Sofie (whose very name is a symbol of transformative Wisdom) taught her granddaughter the fascinating possibilities that lie just under the surfaces of things. Some of the old people at the center knew this, too. "Stories told to oneself or others could transform the world" (240).

There is an anthropological spirit abroad in the United States today that is manifest in the collecting of oral histories of old people, a task sometimes undertaken, as in the *Foxfire* project, with a sense of urgency. Telling stories of family history, Grace Paley observes, is a way of saving some lives.[34] It is also a way of shattering stereotypes and caricatures. In *Number Our Days* there are "powerful personages thinking, reflecting, loving, arguing and, above all, articulating their long experience of living—in splendidly rich language."[35] In *Jewish Grandmothers,* a book of oral histories of older women who emigrated to this country between 1900 and 1920 and settled in Chicago, New York, Boston, Philadelphia, and other major cities, no one incarnates the stereotypes and caricatures of Jewish women created in many short stories and novels, perhaps most notoriously in *Portnoy's Complaint:*

> Sophie Portnoy is a perpetuation . . . of the convention of the Jewish mother as seen by Americans . . . a querulous, loud, castrating, smothering inflictor of guilt. . . . we see her through the eyes of her son, who admits he does not understand her, or through the eyes of the author, whose forte is caricature. This makes for a funny and often dramatic novel, but not necessarily for real and understandable characters. Roth has seized upon the most obvious elements of Jewish motherhood. While he may feel his satirization is precisely the point of his novel, because of it, his depiction of life is finally shallow. Like a stereotype itself, the novel fails to capture the full reality.[36]

Many grown children do not know much about the lives of their aging mothers. Before this generation of elderly people has vanished forever, oral histories of the old women ought to be gathered, for "American history will never be rounded until the lives of its women, immigrants or not, belong to the public; it will stand unfinished until the experiences of its minority groups complete it; it will flow shallow until the words of its elderly deepen it" (xv–xvi).

Throughout oral histories are scattered illuminations on the subjective experience of aging. Beatrice Pollock, aged 72, does not feel she has been pushed away "into a segregated world of the useless old" (103). Nor does Anuta Sharrow, who attended Chicago Musical College after her children had grown up and married and she had become a grandmother. Nor Katya Govsky, who went to school in her old age to get her teaching certificate, and fooled them all when "they" told her she was too old to learn how to drive a car. Nor Ida Richter, the "entrepreneur/raconteur," who turned from work as a businesswoman to the writing of novels in her old age. To her, "widowhood and old age are a challenge, not an ending" (119). Aged 80, she says that when she was younger she resented the physical changes aging brings, but now she is happy to be old. But Ruth Katz spoke in her oral history of the fear and depression many people feel in old age. The elderly, she said, are more than just "memory banks." She said that it is not growing old that one regrets, but the heartbreaking feeling that everything one has experienced has no meaning, and the pain of loneliness. She said it is not a blessing to live to be old, and that old people are forgotten people. "I didn't know what old age meant," she told her interviewers. "You see, I wasn't home with my parents when they got old, so I didn't know" (139). It is precisely this knowledge that oral histories reveal.

This knowledge of the meaning of old age is probably best sought and given indirectly in oral histories. Otherwise, the elderly memoirist may speak only in "ready-made generalities." This insight was discovered by Kenneth Koch when he introduced the idea in his poetry workshop at the American Nursing Home that his students might write a poem about growing old or being old. Koch wanted to encourage a positive feeling about aging on the part of his elderly students. He had expected they might become mired in "ready-made generalities" about the sadness and loss that comes with aging, but in this he found he had been mistaken. There were actually more ready-made generalities about serenity and acceptance in old age. Koch read some poems aloud to his students. And he spoke to them about his own feelings:

> I said I was fifty, spoke of how strange it was to be the same person in my mind, yet a different one outside, how odd to be the same person I was at twelve and at twenty-five, and yet to be so different. Actually, I said, a person lives in a lot of different times at once and is many different ages at once. I feel a loss from being older but also a richness from it, a sense of time and distance and different identities.[37]

Koch decided that he was trying to cheer up his students and to put a better face on growing old than he honestly thought it could have. And "that's no way to help people to write well" (202). He read Yeats's "Sailing to Byzantium" aloud, with the idea that this poem might seize his students' imagination, and "suggest ideas for similar transformations in themselves" as Yeats's transformation in the poem (203).

Writing about growing older was more difficult for those in the poetry workshop and further away from their feelings than writing about colors or flowers. Indeed, in poems about colors and flowers, the feeling of old age had been evoked in very moving ways. Koch came to see that old age can be too vague to think about, and, what is even more damning, it is "strongly connected to ideas (and fears) about how one is supposed to feel" (203). In his reflections, he arrived at the probable truth

> that the most passionate awareness one has of one's changing age comes only at isolated moments. . . , and it's then that it makes one cry, or gasp, or

have a vision of what life is about. It is something like the end of World War
II. And such moments can't be planned but are come on by surprise, when
. . . listening to music, or writing about something else. They have to be
suggested, if at all, . . . in an indirect way. [204]

The 25 students in this workshop, most of whom were in their seventies or
older, were working-class people who had only a limited formal education.
The most dramatic discovery Koch had made was that he could use great
poetry directly, to inspire his students to write, and "to write wonderfully
well." He also found that elderly people could express feelings from childhood and youth. "In feeling and imagination, there seems to be a way in
which a person is all the ages he has been" (141). This insight is as useful for
the oral historian as it is for the teacher of a poetry workshop. Oral histories
are nonfiction only in part. They are also works of imagination and feeling.
And in these realms, the memoirist is every age that has been lived. The
awareness of this that may come with a sudden flash of perception during a
recording of an oral history leads to a deeper understanding of aging than a
thousand coded ready-made generalities given as responses to direct questions.

In the Pittsburgh study, one grandmother mentioned a diary she had kept
as a young bride, another, the poems she was writing in her old age, and many
others, the letters they exchanged over the years. Some regard these as "lost
literature," and there are efforts currently being undertaken to recover written as well as oral records made by people commonly overlooked by researchers. Elizabeth Meese reflects, "In a very real sense, every time someone dies, a
piece of human, regional, and cultural history dies with them—lost to offspring, neighbors, and scholars. Oral narrative and folklore encourage us to
determine our roots. They validate the significance of life as it is experienced
by most people."[38] Meese writes that what literature by women, blacks, and
poor Americans is available is often labeled as "regional literature," of only
local interest. In her view, feminist critics should define "literature" so broadly
that it could encompass every instance of creative expression, and this would
include oral histories as well as written documents (autobiographies, diaries,
journals, letters) and works of fiction. Once excluded testimonies and documents are admitted to this broad category, the formidable task of developing
sophisticated critical modes for the analysis of intellectual prose forms must
be confronted. Meese includes oral narratives among these prose forms.[39]
Sherna Gluck has pointed out that the oral histories in the special issue on
women's oral history of *Frontiers* have such richness of language that "the
collaboration between interviewer and interviewee results in more than new
'historical' documents. It allows for the creation of a new literature." In this
literature are the experiences and language of people "who do not ordinarily
have access to such public expression except perhaps through the more
anonymous forms of folk culture."[40] Gluck points to the unique potential that
oral history has for moving "beyond the written record—which reflects the
experiences of more privileged women, usually white and educated—to docu-

ment the lives of all kinds of women" (4). Tape-recorded reminiscences of older women who have not led a public life enrich and extend the task of oral history in preserving the cultural heritage and conserving human experiences. If "literature" is defined broadly enough to encompass oral narratives, the tape-recording of these oral histories may also be seen as a creative act.

Many older women remark in the course of telling their life story that they wish they could write a book about their lives. Some say that a dozen books could not exhaust their memories. There are older women who perceive life as a teacher. There are others who say it is a dream. But no one who reads through hundreds of pages of transcripts of oral histories can fail to perceive the longing people have in old age to tell what life was like once, even to *show* another a house, a road, a street, a lake, a person once passionately loved or hated. Old people need to tell their stories as much as, and perhaps in some cases even more than, they need bread. Looking inward and looking backward are "natural and healthful integrative" processes of aging.[41] One may review one's life many times over in passage along the life course. But the life review has special significance for those who have a keen awareness of their mortality:

> Simply summing up one's life can enhance pride and self-esteem; elderly people who are not active in the present often gain pleasure in recalling what they have accomplished in the past. The life review may serve to restore a sense of ethnic identity. . . . Reminiscence can reweave these lost threads of the past. The review process can also function as a gift to society, carrying with it the gratification and sheer pleasure of being a storyteller to a younger audience who wants to listen. Such a review can provide an opportunity for people who have a particularly strong need to justify their lives. . . . Like dreaming, fantasy can serve to ease the conflicts of waking life. [99]

In every oral history there are reconstructions of private or public experiences and events, and therefore every oral history is a form of life review. There is sorrow in looking inward and looking backward, since failings and limitations are bound to surface—there will be pleasures and there will be regrets. The summing-up of the oral memoirist provides both resource material and internship experience for students of social gerontology and builds a bridge for communication between the generations. And because the life review has the possibility of revelation of truths heretofore undisclosed,[42] it provides the narrator with the occasion for reconciliation with the still-living past.

The walls between academic disciplines are makeshift and crumbling. Oral histories are grist for anthropologists, folklorists, gerontologists, historians, philosophers, physicians, psychologists, sociologists, and all those in the world of the literary arts of drama and fiction and poetry as well as nonfiction. They may be seen as a subspecies of documentary because they are a broth of fact and emotion and a celebration of experience. Oral histories intended to provide evidence of sociological plight, that have the flavor of the exposé and are presented to portray the truth of life lived from the inside so that the "facts" of that life speak for themselves, are virtually indistinguishable from documentaries. This is nowhere more apparent than in the photo-essay. But whether they are accompanied by photographs or not, oral histories of older women are arresting in their vividness, concreteness, and immediacy. The stories of older women in the *Foxfire* books appeal to feeling and imagination and the senses as well as to the intellect. An old woman remembers the "blood medicine" her father used to make in language that rings in her listeners' ears and echoes long afterwards. In the recollections of ghost tales about boogers, witches, and haints, there is a conjuring up of the light from a kerosene lamp flickering over a grandmother's face. In remembering the Great Depression, older women restore particles of culture in the 1930s—the "white plague" of tuberculosis, the radio characters who were as real as the people in the neighborhood. Older women of rural America lived by a different rhythm than those in the city, one that might seem so slow in tempo and so adapted to seasonal change, so attuned to nature as to appear dreamlike to some of the grandmothers in the Pittsburgh study. Theirs was a life of tending to the needs of boarders, of striving to balance job and family responsibilities. Theirs was a hurried pace through streets teeming with people of diverse languages, nationalities, and customs. But many of the foreign-born and some of the native-born grandmothers in Pennsylvania remembered a rural childhood and would find much to share with the grandmothers of Rabun Gap, Georgia.

"We must be careful," Fischer writes, "not to think of" the change in the American family structure of the last century and this one "as a shift from 'extended' to 'nuclear' families, or from nuclear families to isolated individuals. The process was much more complex. Throughout American history, most households have tended to consist of nuclear families. But early American *neighborhoods* were made up of extended families." Households that were related to one another were usually close together. Often, they were even on adjacent plots. "A regular pattern of interaction developed between related nuclear families within their neighborhoods." It is this pattern which gradually changed, so that by the middle of this century "it had become unusual for the members of an American household to be related to their neighbors."[43] Many older women speak with nostalgia in their oral histories for a time when people were so much closer together, a time when Americans shared experiences, shared *lives*. Nothing can take the place of a sense of community. The isolation and loneliness of so many older people today is often wrongly attributed to ungrateful grown children. It is more than family that older women miss: it is neighborhood, community. To be old and utterly alone is a crisis. And, "When crises occur, one searches the depths of one's memory to discover some vestige of the past, not the past of the individual, faltering and ephemeral, but rather that of the community, which, though left behind, nonetheless represents that which is permanent and lasting."[44]

Some older women may be reticent and reserved in recording their memoirs, not only because that is their personality, but because of the moral space they feel between themselves and younger women. "To the extent that feminism rewards women for nontraditional activity," Elinor Waters and Betty White observe, "it may bring into question the value of the traditional lives led by most women who are now old."[45] Young women in general, and fervent feminists in particular, need to be more sensitive and self-aware than they sometimes are in collecting older women's oral histories. The rewards are rich for those who can be interested without being patronizing, sympathetic without being falsely sentimental. The portraits of two black women in the South evoke flesh-and-blood human beings possessed of qualities of will and character that women anywhere would do well to emulate. Here is the critical edge that oral histories will always have over statistical studies. Humanitarian motives cannot make loaves of bread from stones. In statistical terms, an older woman is a patchwork of numbers. Jacquelyne Johnson Jackson says she believes "the increasing pulls upon older black women to belong to a multiplicity of organizations devoted to blacks, to women, to the elderly, and so on" is a dangerous trend. Ultimately, this segregates black older women "on the basis of their race, age, sex, health, and poverty statuses."[46] The fragmentation of "older black woman" into endless and abstract parts exceeds the organizational energies any person has, Jackson writes, even as it diverts attention away from critical problems that black people in general face. Fragmentation, the division of a human being into parts or "variables," dismembers and abstracts one whom, however imperfectly, the oral history presents as living and whole. This fragmentation may be done for high humanitarian purposes. But good intentions are not enough, and sometimes they get in the way of seeing the human being who is there. In this way, one stereotype is substituted for another.

Oral histories can restore the past to those who lived it and those who inherit it. They can be powerful instruments of revelation and reconciliation, and a means of reuniting the young with their elders and ancestors. They are also gateways to an understanding of the workings of memory. Spicker has argued persuasively that the model of time as linear and objectified must be abandoned in future studies of the structure of memorial consciousness in old age.[47] He has shown the mistiness of labels often applied to the old— "senility," "intellectual impairment," "dementia," "mental disturbance," "disorientation"—and hence the need for clear distinctions to be made between nonverbal memory, language ability, motor ability, and psychomotor problem-solving. Older people are not all alike, and any one person thinks and feels differently about things from one day—even one hour—to the next. What is more, if it is true that a person has suffered a " 'loss' of mentation in some respects, it is probably not *mere loss* but a restructuring of the patient's entire mentation" (165). It is too airily assumed that the mid-twenties to the mid-forties are the "prime" years of a human life and that aging is the same as diminution. It has by no means been proven that old people are incapable of scientific reasoning, analysis, or comprehension. And all too often these are taken to be the only forms of cognition and the highest modes of achievement and expression. Spicker has called for a Piaget for the old who would set them free from the image of an adult in the condition of ineluctable decline. He believes that the study of mentation in senectitude, encompassing both cognitive and conative functions, "would disclose growth and development as well as decline . . ., knowledge which might well assist us in understanding, preventing, and managing multiple conditions of infirmity and disability in the very aged" (172).[48] Doubtless, this Piaget for the aged would find a key to many mysteries of memorial consciousness in the growing treasury of oral memoirs.

Older women, even more than older men, are apt to be seen as dependent and incompetent. This negative image may educe feelings of protectiveness and caring concern; but, when it does, the mien of the caregiver is unmistakably patronizing. As Carol Giesen and Nancy Datan observe, patronizing the elderly reflects a view of older people "as victims unable to help themselves."[49] The validity of this view is brought into question by a study of transcripts of older people's oral memoirs. In gathering the retrospective first-person stories of older women residents of Morgantown, West Virginia, and the surrounding area, Giesen and Datan rediscovered the truth that "life brings change, change brings growth—and with growth, competence" (58). These women, most of whom were the wives of underground miners, spoke of how they had grown in competence over the years by meeting the challenges and crises they perceived as impelling them to change. They saw Life as a teacher; looking back, they saw that they had learned from their experiences to trust in their capability for meeting and resolving the problems they had to face. And along the way, they had learned how to be patient, how to weigh and consider, how to be reflective. "Their perceptions of themselves as more effective individuals were described as increased self-confidence and as being 'stronger in a lot of ways,' 'more independent,' and as 'better at solving problems' " (63).

Ever since their childhood, these West Virginia women had been expected to do chores around the house and farm. Each member of the family was expected to contribute to the welfare of the group, whether this was by milking the cows or by going inside the mine to get the water dripping underground when spring water was unavailable. Some reared their younger siblings or cared for elderly grandparents. Some had to leave high school to go to work. By the time these women were adults, they were confident they could fulfill the responsibilities of being a spouse, a parent, and—if need be— a wage earner, as well. Many learned home skills that are commonly assumed to be men's work—"shearing sheep, making hay, putting up siding, repairing home appliances, doing plumbing, driving trucks, managing a small business, and . . . becoming politically effective." In their oral narratives they said that other women they knew had worked just as hard as they had and that the variety of skills they had acquired and the competence they had shown in putting them to use were a normal part of the responsibilities of wifehood and motherhood: "in fact, they believed that doing what needed to be done for their families, and doing it well, was their primary role responsibility" (66).

Most of them "felt that becoming a parent was a major source of change in their lives and that they felt they had matured and become more effective . . . as a result" (67).

In their interviews these women said that they expected their personal development would continue as they grew older. They had spent forty or more years "coping with a harsh environment and economy"—a competence that is *not* relinquished in later life. For most of them there will be no retirement—a woman "does not retire from the occupation of homemaker" in her sixties. As the burden of their responsibilities as parents is lifted, many will become more active in other areas of life:

> One older woman, for example, became interested in ceramics in late middle age and as her parental responsibilities decreased over time a hobby became a full-time business, including production, retailing and conducting classes. Another woman pursued her early interest in politics. . . . Still another . . . found full time employment when her husband retired, worked until her own forced retirement, and then replaced this activity with full-time voluntary services. [66]

Competence, effectiveness, instrumentality—these are qualities fostered in those growing up in rural Appalachia in a tradition that extols "independence, endurance, and the acceptance of a difficult and labor-filled life." (68). Some might argue that women growing up in a very different tradition are destined to become passive and dependent as they age and that these West Virginia women are exceptions to the rule of women's incompetence in late life. "This argument fails," Giesen and Datan write, when these women are compared with the older women in *Four Stages of Life*. Despite the fact that the two groups of women live and work in very different social worlds, despite differences between them in the number of years of formal education they received and in their values, the older women interviewed for both studies saw themselves as growing in competence with the passage of the years and as quite capable of assertiveness on those occasions calling for assertiveness. And the research findings of *Four Stages of Life* are in agreement with those of another study in which it was found "that elderly victims, both female and male, of flood disasters were better able to cope with the emotional impact and material losses than were younger victims." Indeed, the competence of both elderly women and elderly men in meeting the challenges that confronted them was so impressive that the researchers "suggested that a support network" of elderly men and women "be organized to cope with future incidences such as floods and other natural disasters" (59–60).

The oral history interviews of these West Virginia women suggest that women have had to acquire as much competence as men throughout the life course. They also suggest that precisely because of the broader range of skills these women had to master, and precisely because of the variety of emotional and material problems they had to resolve, they may have been preparing themselves even better than men have had to do to meet the challenge of old age itself. If women in our society today grow old with a better grace than men do (and Giesen and Datan are not alone in their implication that this may be so[50]), it is possible that the reason for this is that women have had to come to terms with their many-sidedness much earlier in their lives than men have had to do. In his *Senescence,* Hall remarked that specialization makes dwarfs of us, and until very recently, almost all women were denied the privileges of access to this estate. The economic measure of the high price that has been exacted of women for not having a profession, a "career," a niche, a room of their own is well-known, but the spiritual cost—never being taken seriously— is at least as heavy, even though it is borne in silence. At the same time, those who are competent in more than one undertaking do not lose their sense of usefulness upon retirement. For these people, retirement is no more than an occasion that marks the official completion of one task, setting them free to perform others to which they have been committed all along. Looking back on her life, one West Virginia woman saw some of its events as trials that she had to overcome. This acceptance of the nature of experience, this understanding that life is ruled by Chance and Change, is childhood's end. Reached at a very early age by most people who have lived on this earth, it is always hard-won. Yet it is just this—and the versatility that can become a condition of survival— that redounds to a "good age." Chrysee Kline has suggested that women adjust to later life just *because* women have had to accept change over and over again, just *because* women have had to come to terms with impermanence as a fact of daily life. She thinks that it is a myth that modern workers, whether men or women, experience continuity in their work roles and have steady careers from the time that formal education is completed until retirement. She recommends that women's activist groups reconsider the objective of striving for only one goal over the entire life course. In her view, both women and men ought to adopt a pattern of "career flexibility," since impermanence and discontinuity may be a fitting apprenticeship to later life.[51]

Old women have more to share with one another than with younger members of their own families, Mildred Seltzer writes, whether they are blacks from the rural South, or Jewish or Polish or Italian grandmothers. "They had to change, to accommodate to new traditions and beliefs. The strength that made it possible for them to survive until old age in the midst of a hostile environment may be the very characteristic upon which negative stereotypes are based."[52] There is irony in this, that the very oral history interviews that contravene the stereotype of old women as passive, dependent, and incompetent might be cited as the source of the stereotype of the old woman as a meddling materfamilias or neighborhood scold. But that would be an abuse of oral history that more than any social scientific document or literary genre is resistant to stereotypy precisely because of its resistance to form. As technique, source of documentation, or genre, oral histories remind us that of all the needs that older women in America have, the most vital is to be understood neither as saints nor as witches, neither as victims and objects of pity nor as domineering matriarchs, but in full humanity. And that is the gift an oral history offers to the discerning listener.

Notes

1. Sherna Gluck observes that the three types of oral history, the topical, biographical, and autobiographical, shade into one another. Sherna Gluck, "What's So Special About Women? Women's Oral History," *Frontiers* (Summer 1977) 2(2):5.

2. Ibid., p. 6.

3. Diana Hume George, "Community and Creativity, An Approach to Teaching the Subject of Aging," paper presented at the Modern Language Association Special Session, Perspectives on Aging, New York, December 1978.

4. Louis M. Starr, Introduction, *Columbia University: The Oral History Collection of Columbia University*, Elizabeth B. Mason and Louis M. Starr, eds. (New York: Oral History Research Office, 1973), p. vii.

5. This issue of *Southern Exposure* is entitled "Generations: Women in the South," *Southern Exposure* (Winter 1977) 4(4).

6. Margaret Rose Gladney, "If It was Anything for Justice," *Southern Exposure* (Winter 1977) 4(4):19. Hereafter, all references to this article will be cited in text by page number.

7. Wendy Watriss, "It's Something Inside You," *Southern Exposure* (Winter 1977) 4(4):76. Hereafter, all references to this article will be cited in the text by page number.

8. Jeane Westin, *Making Do: How Women Survived the '30s* (Chicago: Follett Publishing Co., 1976), p. 319. Hereafter, all references to this book will be cited in the text by page number.

9. In her paper on "Community and Creativity" cited in note 3 above, Diana Hume George observed that this is the first major generation of elderly people who are living and dying with television in the background, or more commonly in the *fore*ground of their lives. She believes that the youth orientation of television programs viewed by the elderly reinforces their sense of being useless in society.

10. *The Foxfire Book*, ed. with an introduction by Eliot Wigginton (New York: Anchor Press, Doubleday, 1972), p. 10. Hereafter, references to this book will be cited in the text by page number.

11. In *The Foxfire Book*, Wigginton writes that Foxfire projects could be initiated elsewhere, not only in Appalachia, but on many Indian reservations, and among Black cultures near the southern coasts and communities in the Ozarks. He writes that the logical researchers of the cultural heritage that could be passed on from the elderly in America are young people in their communities. Projects such as Foxfire do more than gather materials for historical societies and museums. Because they feature articles about the work of local craftspeople and craft cooperatives in areas that are deprived educationally as well as economically, they may attract "a flow of income from a population grown weary of a plastic world." Ibid., p. 13. See Wigginton's introductions to each *Foxfire* book for a continuing assessment of the development of the project. In *Foxfire* 3, he reports that the students have served as consultants in the initiation of similar projects in many states. In *Foxfire* 4, he reflects that all who worked on the project came to realize "how much our success had depended on that very outside world we feared so greatly," and that as immensely important as it is for the students to know their own roots and heritage, he has learned that "to be truly effective citizens, they must next acquire an equally sophisticated knowledge of their culture's relationship to others. We are a multicultural world, and we are all linked one to another, for better or for worse." *Foxfire* 4, ed. with an introduction by Eliot Wigginton (New York: Anchor Press, Doubleday, 1977), pp. 8, 10.

12. Richard M. Dorson remarks that Wigginton has, though not intending to do this, "ventured deeply into the province of folklore studies" as he developed the concept of *Foxfire*. Richard M. Dorson, "Afterword," *Foxfire* 4, p. 482.

13. *Foxfire* 3, with an introduction by Eliot Wigginton (New York: Anchor Press, Doubleday, 1975), pp. 480–81. In an article on Faith Healing in *The Foxfire Book*, Charley Tyler is quoted as saying he may have taught 500 faith healers—all women—and that the women teach the men. He himself was taught faith healing by a woman. Harley Carpenter told the editors that you lose your power to heal if you tell others how to do it. Nevertheless, shortly after the article on faith healing

220 Chimes of Change and Hours

appeared in the magazine, two women healers came forward and said they would reveal their methods if their names would not be used. *The Foxfire Book,* pp. 365–67. Aunt Nora's story about refusing to accept money from the doctor in exchange for telling him how to stop bleeding is in *The Foxfire Book,* pp. 354–55.

14. *Foxfire* 3, p. 472.

15. *Foxfire* 2, ed. with an introduction by Eliot Wigginton (New York: Anchor Press, Doubleday, 1973), pp. 318–21.

16. *Foxfire* 3, p. 411. Hereafter, all references to this book will be cited in the text by page number.

17. *Foxfire* 2, pp. 282–83. Hereafter, reference to this book will be cited in the text by page number.

18. *Foxfire* 4, p. 241.

19. *Foxfire* 2, pp. 297–98.

20. Colonel Byrd, in his *History of the Dividing Line,* wrote that chewing ginseng as one walks along helps to cure fatigue, "cheers the heart of a man that has a bad wife," and makes "old age amiable by rendering it lively, cheerful, and good humored." *Foxfire* 3, p. 247.

21. *Foxfire* 2, pp. 26–27.

22. Ibid., p. 268. Hereafter, reference to this book will be cited in the text by page number.

23. *The Foxfire Book,* p. 17. Hereafter, reference to this book will be cited in the text by page number.

24. *Foxfire* 2, pp. 251–52. Hereafter, reference to this book will be cited in the text by page number.

25. Mary Heaton Vorse, *A Footnote to Folly: Reminiscences of Mary Heaton Vorse* (New York: Farrar and Rinehart, Inc., 1935), p. 282.

26. Corinne Azen Krause, "Italian, Jewish, and Slavic Grandmothers in Pittsburgh: Their Economic Roles," *Frontiers* (Summer 1977) 2(2):18.

27. Corinne Azen Krause, *Grandmothers, Mothers and Daughters: An Oral History Study of Ethnicity, Mental Health, and Continuity of Three Generations of Jewish, Italian, and Slavic-American Women* (New York: The Institute on Pluralism and Group Identity of The American Jewish Committee, 1978). Hereafter, all references to this publication will be cited in the text by page number.

28. The cassettes and transcripts of the oral history study cited above are deposited with the Historical Society of Western Pennsylvania in Pittsburgh, and the transcripts are also deposited with the Archives of Industrial Society, Hillman Library, University of Pittsburgh. These transcripts, numbering some 14,000 pages, are unpublished. I wish to acknowledge my gratitude to Krause for providing me with photocopies of selected transcripts of the oral histories of those of the oldest generation. Coded designations of individuals quoted have been changed to letters of the alphabet for reference and citation in this chapter.

29. Krause, *Grandmothers, Mothers and Daughters,* p. 56. Hereafter, all references to this publication will be cited in the text by page number.

30. Ibid., p. 162. There was only one occurrence of an interruption of this sort during interviews with Jewish and Slavic women. Krause writes, "Being alone was something that Italian women did not arrange." Ibid. See p. 17 for ethnic differences in responses to the telephoned request for participation in the study.

31. Ibid., p. 146. It was found that 88 percent of the grandmothers see their children at least once a week, and that nearly half the grandmothers see at least one adult child every day. Interesting ethnic differences in living arrangements obtain for this sample. For the Jewish families, the most frequent living pattern is three separate residences for women of the three generations. Ethnic differences in housing and mobility patterns for the three groups of women are reported on pp. 132–40. Jewish grandmothers had the lowest percentage living in houses and the highest average number of moves during their lifetimes. On p. 156, evidence is presented to show that women of the middle generation feel strong responsibilities to their aging parents. On pp. 171–73, there is a listing of some areas in which ethnicity has implications for mental health. Among these are the importance of having their families near them for Italian grandmothers, the importance of having their own home for Slavic grandmothers, and the finding that Jewish

grandmothers value their independence more than they value their houses. Hereafter, reference to this publication is indicated in the text by page number.

32. Margaret Clark, "The Anthropology of Aging: A New Area for Studies of Culture and Personality," in *Middle Age and Aging: A Reader in Social Psychology,* Bernice L. Neugarten, ed. (Chicago: The University of Chicago Press, 1968), p. 433.

33. Barbara Myerhoff, *Number Our Days* (New York: E. P. Dutton, 1978). Myerhoff's methodology, which included participant observation and extensive interviewing, and her collaboration with Lynne Littman in producing the documentary film *Number Our Days,* are discussed on pp. 28–33. Myerhoff met and talked with about half the 300 center members. She knew eighty of them personally, and interviewed and spent most of her time with 36. Ibid., p. 29. Hereafter, all references to this book will be cited in the text by page number.

34. As quoted from Grace Paley, "Debts," *Enormous Changes at the Last Minute* in the epigraph to *Jewish Grandmothers,* Sydelle Kramer and Jenny Masur, eds. (Boston: Beacon Press, 1976).

35. Victor Turner, "Foreword," *Number Our Days,* p. x.

36. *Jewish Grandmothers,* p. xiv. Kramer and Masur, who report that their own stereotypes were shattered in the course of this oral history study, discuss the purpose and methodology of their work in "Afterword: For the Record," pp. 152–55. They decided to work in Chicago not only because they live there, but because they thought that immigrant histories usually emphasize the experiences of people centered in New York (153). Hereafter, all references to this book will be cited in the text by page number.

37. Kenneth Koch, *I Never Told Anybody: Teaching Poetry Writing in a Nursing Home* (New York: Vintage Books, 1978), p. 202. Hereafter, all references to this book will be cited in the text by page number.

38. Elizabeth A. Meese, "Telling It All: Literary Standards and Narratives by Southern Women," *Frontiers* (Summer 1977) 2(2):63.

39. Ibid., p. 64. Meese remarks how the absence of reliable studies on female ontology and female epistemology impede the progress of feminist scholarship (Ibid.). She writes that only when both history and literature are broadened to accommodate oral narrative will it be possible to begin to establish the full truth of our national consciousness and to appreciate the full meaning of the nature of art (66).

40. Sherna Gluck, "What's So Special About Women? Women's Oral History," p. 6. Hereafter, reference to this article will be cited in the text by page number.

41. Harriet Wrye and Jacqueline Churilla, "Looking Inward, Looking Backward: Reminiscence and the Life Review," *Frontiers* (Summer 1977) 2(2):98. Hereafter, reference to this article will be cited in the text by page number.

42. Robert N. Butler, "The Life Review: An Interpretation of Reminiscence in the Aged," in *Middle Age and Aging,* p. 496.

43. David Hackett Fischer, *Growing Old in America* (New York: Oxford University Press, 1977), pp. 146–47.

44. Saul Friedländer, *When Memory Comes* (New York: Farrar, Straus and Giroux, Inc., 1979), p. 69.

45. Elinor Waters and Betty White, "Helping Each Other," in *Looking Ahead: A Woman's Guide to the Problems and Joys of Growing Older,* Lillian E. Troll, Joan Israel, and Kenneth Israel, eds., (Englewood Cliffs, N.J.: Prentice-Hall, Inc., 1977), p. 186.

46. Jacquelyne Johnson Jackson, "Older Black Women," in *Looking Ahead,* p. 154.

47. Stuart F. Spicker, "Gerontogenetic Mentation: Memory, Dementia and Medicine in the Penultimate Years," in *Aging and the Elderly: Humanistic Perspectives in Gerontology,* Stuart F. Spicker, Kathleen M. Woodward, and David D. Van Tassel, eds. (New Jersey: Humanities Press, Inc., 1978), p. 160. Hereafter, all references to this article will be cited in the text by page number.

48. For an inquiry into mentation that encompasses three generations of women, see Lillian E. Troll, Helen Lycaki, and Jean Smith, "Development of the Cognitively Complex Woman over the Generations," in *No Longer Young: The Older Woman in America* (Ann Arbor, Mich.: The Institute of Gerontology, University of Michigan–Wayne State University, 1975), pp. 81–87.

49. Carol Boellhoff Giesen and Nancy Datan, "The Competent Older Woman," in *Transitions*

of Aging, Nancy Datan and Nancy Lohmann, eds. (New York: Academic Press, Inc., 1980), p. 57. Hereafter, all references to this book will be cited in the text by page number.

50. See Myerhoff, *Number Our Days,* pp. 261–68.

51. Chrysee Kline, "The Socialization Process of Women," in *The Older Woman: Lavender Rose or Gray Panther,* Marie Marschall Fuller and Cora Ann Martin, eds. (Springfield, Ill.: Charles C. Thomas, 1980), pp. 59–70.

52. Mildred Seltzer, "Jewish-American Grandmothers," in *Looking Ahead,* p. 161.

Part 2

4

Times Remembered and Time's Passage:
Written Memoirs and Reflections

> One's life-story cannot be told with complete veracity. A true autobiography would have to be written in states of mind, emotions, heartbeats, smiles, and tears, not in months and years, or physical events. Life is marked off on the soul-chart by feelings, not by dates.
>
> —HELEN KELLER,
> *Midstream: My Later Life*

"The last years may matter most."[1] So Florida Scott-Maxwell, a writer who began training in analytical psychology under Jung's direction when she was 50, wrote in a notebook she kept when she was 82. Age puzzled her: "I thought it was a quiet time. My seventies were interesting, and fairly serene, but my eighties are passionate. I grow more intense as I age" (13–14). There is a wild life that flames in the old. But that is their secret. For they are "wreckage to the eye," and this "fierce energy," this passion, is all but incommunicable. Transposed into action, it leaves one spent (32). Old age is a time for sorrowing, for mourning. But it is also a time for discovery, a time for claiming the events of one's life. In this way, you "make yourself yours. When you truly possess all you have been and done, which may take some time, you are fierce with reality" (42). The old want to teach, to advise, and to warn, for when one is old one sees over great expanses of time. One has watched the generations follow one another and seen "the same qualities . . . working the same sad havoc." One sees the same wounding witnessed long ago. But the old know "it is almost useless" to speak of these things (38). Scott-Maxwell would like to tell people who have precise expectations of life that "Life does not accommodate you, it shatters you" (65). For this is what life was meant to do. And she makes the admission "that it takes more courage than I had known to drink the lees of life" (86). The old "know that age is more than a disability. It is an intense and varied experience, . . . something to be carried high. If it is a long defeat it is also a victory" (5).

The chance to explore the interiors of old age is a challenge not every woman meets. The desire to communicate the experience of that inner journey is not always so intense. To write of it in the pages of a notebook and to make of that a public offering is even more rare. *The Measure of My Days* is a work to be prized by gerontologists as a major contribution to literary perspectives on aging. From personal documents such as this, and from essays as well as from works of the literary imagination, the subjective aspects of aging are harvested.

Women's personal papers are a Rosetta stone for the historian's study of "America through women's eyes," and for those in the world of letters who are engaged in the recovery of women's "lost literature." They are a treasure trove for the gerontologist as well. Written remembrances of things past, and reflections on the look of life from those on the other side of it are rich sources of knowledge about the subjective aspects of aging. What women have thought and written about growing older is truly "uncharted territory." This chapter is a report and a commentary of an expedition into that region, and I have had to draw my own contour map to follow in this venture. I wanted to know how older women in twentieth-century America viewed their lives— their frame of mind, their moral attitudes—and what sense and design they perceived in them. I wanted to know what older women wrote about their mothers, and who in their circle of families, friends, and colleagues they thought had strongly influenced their character. I wanted to know how they thought they had come to choose their vocation. And I wanted to know what they thought and felt about growing older, about being old, about the workings of memory. In exploring these questions, I read some forty-odd autobiographies by women writers and women in other walks of life, in the arts and sciences and in the service of social causes. In some of these, I found a wealth of material—more than could be contained here. In others, the material was very limited. And some had no value whatsoever for this research. In addition to these autobiographies, I read a number of essays and full books on aging by and about women, and a few diaries, collections of letters, journals, and notebooks of older women. Here, again, I found that women varied considerably in their interest in aging and old age and in their inclination to write about these subjects. This is to be expected. In his *Senescence: The Last Half of Life*, G. Stanley Hall wrote that perhaps only a genetic psychologist can appreciate how widely different the successive stages of human life are from one another. Indeed, he thought the differences to be so great that, even if we move from one stage to another by barely perceptible gradations, "we all really live not one but a succession of lives."[2] Furthermore, people resist moving from maturity to old age just as they once resisted the passage from adolescence to maturity. To complicate matters still more, insight into the self at any stage of life may be the rarest of gifts. Hall wrote, "There is a sense . . . in which those in each stage of life know least of it" (175). Of all life's stages, old age is least understood: "It is very hard for any but the strongest mentalities to realize the changes that age brings, to adjust to, feel at home in, and come to terms consciously with it." In Hall's opinion, "Self-control, poise, a calm, judicial state of mind even with regard to things that concern us most deeply, are among the chief, if also among the rarest, virtues of senescence" (332–33).

Often it happens in social science, as in art and in life, one finds what one seeks. I was in search of diversity, and that is what I have found. I do not believe there is a Way to age or a Truth about women's aging. I believe there are many ways and many truths—as many as there are lives. I believe that every woman has her own life to live, and that this is the hardest thing to do, to live one's own life and not the life of another or the collective life. I do not believe that it is given to any of us to make a moral judgment about the life of another, only about our own. And this, I think, is the test of life's meaning for the one who lived it. As an older woman studying older women, I do not see myself as a victim—for that is a denial of my humanity—or as an incarnation of wisdom. That, too, is a denial of my humanity, for the Old Wise Woman is an archetype, and I am very human. I am not angry about aging; neither am I inclined to write rhapsodies about it. I do not find the thought of my aging and my mortality amusing. Neither do I find it terrifying. I find it compelling. I want to know more about aging because the subject intrigues me. I have found that every question I ask leads not to an answer, but to another question. And I believe that this is as it should be.

As one grows old, one becomes more free both to make sense of the life that was lived and to be who one essentially is. Scott-Maxwell wrote that it is a great ordeal to be oneself, but that to accept the task of living one's individual destiny leads to self-respect and to respect and courtesy and compassion for others. She wrote in her notebook of the "precious difference" of every person. Reading women's memoirs and reflections on aging in a variety of genres (I have found that an essay can be a memoir, a letter can be a meditation on aging) affirms this "precious difference." Even so, and oddly for this very reason, in reading of the lives of others, there are flashes of recognition of our own. These are recognitions of selves not realized, of lives unlived. Each of us has only one lifetime, and it is not long, even if one lives a century, for those who are striving toward wholeness. Choices must be made, and these lead to others, and so a lifeway is shaped. In reading the lives of others, we live out in imagination the lifetimes we did not choose for ourselves. Some shadow of the many-faceted self walks on every road not taken. Knowing this, we begin to know the possibilities of human life itself.

Sources and Transformations

"A person reaches fifty at least," Catherine Drinker Bowen writes, "before he cares about his ancestors." She began to think about her own when her brother Harry died, and this might have been because "suddenly, I missed them. Somewhere in all of us there is an underground tide that lifts, carries us on. With me it had seemingly ceased to flow; a continuity, a connection was lacking."[3] It is possible that she has been writing this book, "a celebration and a mourning," all her life, for she thinks her brothers were looking over her shoulder, "seldom approving but always challenging" as she wrote her biographies (xiii). In *Family Portrait*, Bowen meets her brothers "not obliquely but head on" and she is "at long last their equal; my eyes are level with theirs and I see them whole" (xiv). She never doubted that ancestors are part of every biography. Indeed, she herself is part of her biographical subjects, although they were all old men. To phrase it in Jungian terms, Bowen is very much in communication with the "wise old man" that is an aspect of every self. She herself writes that she has had to invent answers to the question people ask her as to why she never wrote about a woman. "The real answer, 'But I did, six times,' would be incomprehensibe" (xiii–xiv). When Bowen's parents were in their eighties, she had lived in their house with them, "watched them as the days passed, and set down in a notebook things they said and did." She asks herself why she chose men who had lived to a great age as the subjects of her biographies. And now she is certain "that I chose them largely because of the way their lives were rounded out, the way they met their deaths" (281).

Bowen's family members were avid record keepers. Her mother was only 6 years old when she began writing her journal. Bowen was 11 and her sister 16 when they began writing diaries. And both her father and her brother Harry wrote (unpublished) autobiographies. These, and old letters wrapped in bundles, refreshed her memory (xv). Many American families have a cache where they store papers, and these may be a writer's window on the past. The view is not always clear. Josephine W. Johnson wrote of this:

> Mother's memories were parceled out to us in precise sentences, gentle comparisons or wry descriptions. The little remembrance she wrote for us three years before she died was reticent. Perhaps she recognized in our request, as in all too many things, the condescension and rejection of my generation for the past, for the people of that past and the way of life that was Oakland.[4]

Another writer, Ruth Suckow, commented on her minister father's writing habits in her memoir. "Writing had always been one of his special employments," Suckow recalled, and he wrote prolifically in his later years.[5] He kept a journal of the social, economic, and political changes he observed during the Depression and post-Depression years. He also wrote a book about his ideas on religion, and an autobiography, which he typed and bound. Since he had not been much given to retrospection up to that time, his autobiography surprised the family members. "He was never thoroughly at home in a personal form of writing—his diary, for example, consisted mostly of brief notations regarding the weather!" (253) Suckow believed that her father's perspective broadened as he aged. When she was younger, she had thought that the writing of sermons and the writing of fiction were very different occupations, and even opposed to one another. Only when she wrote her memoir did she recognize her closeness to her father "in purpose in literary composition" (260).

However one comes by written records of family history, whether through the example of an older person who is at heart a scribbler or by natural inclination, personal documents are an irreplaceable, life-giving source for the older self in search of origins and influences and life design. Fewer gifts are so freely given to us, and fewer still so unwisely and recklessly squandered as the gift of literacy. Words written on a page reveal and communicate in a way that is quite distinct from words that are spoken, whether face to face or over a telephone or onto tape. And written communication may keep others alive and real despite their absence. Eleanor Roosevelt recalled the "minute daily life correspondence" of her father's kin of the older generation. Her father's "Aunt Ella" (Mrs. James Bulloch) maintained close ties with those in the United States through this kind of regular correspondence with her sisters. The English "keep in touch with one another though scattered to the four corners of the earth in their far-flung empire, by writing an almost daily diary of little inconsequential happenings to the children sent home to be educated or to the parents living in the old family home." Family members circulate these letters, and in this way "keep up a kind of intimacy which wipes out time and space."[6] Written documents are sometimes assembled preparatory to writing an autobiography. When Rose Pesotta undertook the task of writing a book about her experiences as a labor organizer, she and her friend, John Nicholas Beffel, who edited her work, referred to memorabilia accumulated over the years that included letters, articles written for the labor press, leaflets, pamphlets, diaries, and statistical reports.[7] Some women refer to their own diaries when writing their memoirs, as did Harriet Monroe and Welthy Honsinger Fisher, in this way transforming one genre into another. Some personal documents have been expurgated, either by those who kept them or by others, and there is a story in that as well.[8]

The very nature of a personal document may change over the years as the writer changes her perspective. Anaïs Nin's diary began as "an enticing 'letter,' a Scheherazade, to bring back the lost father." In the 1930s, it was her "kief, hashish, and opium pipe," and by 1955, it was "evolving into an ever more consciously applied artistic instrument"[9] There are other kinds of transformations over time: Ruth Suckow recognized something of her father's sermons in her fiction. Another writer, Jessamyn West, transformed her mother's stories into literature. The life West's mother, Gracie, had given her daughter to write about was not Gracie's own. Nor was it the life of Gracie's parents. Rather, it was the life of her grandparents. The stories Gracie told her daughter about her grandparents were not anecdotes. The life of which she had spoken "was too tenuous, too shimmering, too hearsay" for that.[10] West wrote of the life her mother gave her—a life that was transformed into her book *The Friendly Persuasion*. When Gracie was dying of a disease that affected her memory, West tried to identify herself to her. She said she was the oldest of her four children, "the one who wrote those Quaker stories." And Gracie asked, "Did I get those stories written?" (101) They were both written and published, West replied. She had always wanted to write those stories, Grace said, but she had married early and she had not been well. She thought she had dreamed she had written them. But her daughter told her it was not a dream. "What she thought she remembered was purest fiction," West wrote, "something that never happened. What *had* happened, . . . these, the realities of which she told me, had been *my* dreams. It was a strange exchange. She accepted my fiction as real. Her memories and long-time musings had become my fiction" (102). West reflected that her mother had given birth to her three times, and that the third time was when she gave her that life that was West's writing.

The Self and Others

There may be a portrait of more than one older woman in an older woman's memoirs. The self as subject and creator of the work can be known through representations of the self as object. She is revealed in those passages in which an older woman writes about her inner life, or reflects upon her changing appearance, or takes an attitude toward her older self. These, together with what she may perceive to be the condition of being older, or the situation of older people in her society, are the illuminated portions of her text from the point of view of the gerontologist. These passages provide insights into the subjective aspects of women's aging. And, if the writer is a perceptive observer of the societal landscape, her memoirs provide insights into the objective aspects of aging, as well.

But even the self-portrait is at once a representation of the self and of others who are thought to have entered into its shaping. Therefore, in many memoirs there are studies, sketches, and even full works of portraiture of older women other than the creator of the work. They are part of the memoir because they are part of the self. Very early, our lives become intertwined with the lives of others. The fatefulness of these relationships is disclosed only in the passing of the years, and that is precisely why old age is a time for discovery of the fullness of being. When an older woman looks long and deeply within herself, she finds many selves—all the selves she remembers, and the selves she once imagined she would become, and all the selves of others who have grown fast to the woman she beholds. For many women, the most arduous task in life is the separation from the mother—the separation in the psyche, in the spirit, in the soul, between daughter and mother. Some women never complete this task. They remain their mother's daughter above all else, even at 40, even at 60, even to the end of their lives. The woman who is her mother's daughter first and always may fall into a deep depression when her mother dies. Her mother's death may be the severest crisis in her life, whatever her calendar age may be, since it is a crisis of her very identity. The mother-daughter relationship is only now beginning to be explored in our society. I have found that some of the most poignant passages in women's memoirs are the writings of daughters about their mothers—daughters who are grown, grown older, even grown old.

In *Earth Horizon* (shifting from the third person—and occasionally the second—in books 1–4 to the first person in book 5),[11] Mary Austin wrote that she and her mother, Susie, saw things differently. Mary told stories when she was a child, as many fledgling writers do, and to Susie, saying one had seen things one hadn't seen was "storying"—and "storying was wicked" (42). Susie was widowed when Mary was still very young, and not long afterward, Mary's sister Jennie died of diphtheria. Austin remembered

in the bleak little burying-ground looking up at my mother in her weeds and making toward her for the last time in my life the child's instinctive gesture for comfort, and being thrust off in so wild a renewal of Susie's own sense of loss, her rejection of what life had left for her, as leaves me still with no other comparison for the appalling shock and severance of widowhood. [86]

In the early years of her widowhood, Susie's love for Mary was not always able to overcome the "personal reluctance" she felt toward her, for her attitude toward her daughter "was sharpened by reminders of the dearer loss." This might have warped Mary, had the distance between her and her mother not been bridged later by the "deep concern for the meaning and destiny of womanhood" they shared (92).

Many years later, when Austin was in Bishop, her brother wired her that their mother would have to have an emergency operation in a hospital in Los Angeles. The wire arrived too late for her to make the triweekly connection with the Mojave stage, so Austin made preparations to take the return train by way of Reno. At dusk, her husband sent her out to sit on the high stoop of their house while he gave their daughter, Ruth, her supper and put her to bed. It was then that her mother appeared to her "in the clear obsidian twilight" as Austin remembered her in her youth. There was a rose in her hair; she was dressed in white, and smiling. She told her daughter she did not need to take the train now, since all was well. Austin believed her, but the next morning when she awakened, she knew. She was weeping, and her husband was trying to comfort her, when the telegram came. Austin wrote:

There is an element of incalculable ravening in the loss of your mother; deep under the shock of broken habit and the ache of present grief, there is the psychic wound, the severed root of being; such loss as makes itself felt as the companion of immortality. For how should the branch suffer, torn from the dead tree? It is only when the tree is green that the cut bough bleeds. [273]

When at last she began to write her autobiography, the writer Virgilia Peterson felt "... *driven by an irrepressible need ... to do so in the form of a letter to my mother.*"[12] She wrote of her narrative that it "is my *sursum corda,* my attempt to rise up out of my own limitations and those the fear of you imposed on me, and look for some meaning beyond the experience of being both your daughter and myself" (5). Often, her mother had, even while she was still living, been Peterson's "unwelcome but inescapable *Döppelganger,* casting your shadow now behind and now before." There were times when Peterson thought that a little figure she saw in a crowd was her mother's. Once, at twilight, when the aging figure stopped, Peterson ran toward her, calling, "Mother!" and was "shaken and aghast" when she reached "the unknown woman" and saw her look of surprise (134). Peterson's mother was 88 when she died, and in this book her daughter absolves her *in absentia* from sharing in her guilt. Even as a child, the daughter had been determined not to be like her mother; she had resolved that nothing should show that they were related. "If there is something sharper than a serpent's tooth, it is, I have cause to remember, a mother's fang" (278). Peterson could not remember any other moment when her mother had held out such balm to her as when she had said of Peterson's book *Polish Profile,* "I never knew how hard it must have been for you." But just after the healing words were spoken, the daughter answered, "Not any harder than at home." Even though this was true, she wrote, it "does not excuse me for loosing an arrow I would now give much to have withheld. Thus does the custom of the bow so train the thoughtless fingers that, rather than let one bird go free, it shoots the dove of peace" (115).

Many older daughters, myself included, know well that "custom of the bow." Probably very few are equal to these confrontations with the Terrible Daughter one sometimes was: it takes a high courage that is very rare, for one must confront the Terrible Mother *she* sometimes was when the lines of battle were drawn. Louise Bogan wrote to a friend whose mother had died, "You will have sad days, and a flood of memories will come back to you, and you will feel that a part of your life is over." We must mourn, Bogan wrote, but we must not feel guilt. A physician told Bogan after her own mother died that she "must think of her as a complete person: with all her faults as well as all her virtues." If we think of those who are dead in this way, this "relieves us of our own guilty sense of mortality; and leaves us free to live our own lives—which is our *main task.*"[13] In her journals, Bogan wrote:

> We must not bring back and describe "the bad mother"—"the Dragon mother"—in order to justify ourselves. Only to understand.—To hold the portrait of this evil figure unresolved, into age, is madness. It should be resolved in late youth. (The last Chinese box . . .) The artist must resolve it into art . . . the man of action into action . . . the philosopher into ideas. After a certain age, one should glimpse it most often as a dream—or v. infrequently in *consciously* evoked meaning."[14]

In 1953, Anaïs Nin went to California to stay with her mother, who was then over 80, while Nin's brother, Joaquin, was away. Nin wrote in her diary:

> My mother sits in the house with the shades down shutting out the sun (a Cuban habit), rushes out to scold dogs and children for making noise, works on lacemaking, reads detective stories, observes her swollen legs and feet, and waits. The horror of aging, the deafness, the false teeth, the more and more restricted areas of life. She can no longer enjoy films.[15]

A year later, Nin wrote that every time she visited her mother in Oakland, she felt it might be for the last time. She wanted to be able to sense when she *should* be there, so that she could express her love. But she had had no premonition, and her mother had died after Nin had returned to New York from a visit. In retrospect, Nin suffered guilt and regret."The pain of irrevocable loss . . . greater and deeper . . . because there was no sense of unity. . . . All my life I had struggled to come closer to her, and now she was lost to me" (176). When Nin had sought a life of her own years before,

> My mother closed the door on me . . . , and after that I spent endless effort and time returning to her, being a good daughter.
> What a burden of guilt when a mother serves you, does all the menial tasks, . . . but then does not approve what you become. Do we all withhold our feelings and our thoughts because of this fear of condemnation? . . .
> Caring for their children physically but not approving their final development, is this an epitaph for all mothers? [177]

Nin wanted to remember her mother as she had been at 70, when she had visited her daughter in New York, singing and talking with an Irish carpenter working in the apartment. She asked herself what her mother's life would have been had she not had children, had she followed singing, which was her first passion, had she traveled and performed in concerts and been acclaimed as Nin's father had been. Now she and Joaquin had to dispose of their mother's belongings, her few properties—"A box of holy medals, rosaries, and a prayer book. . . . A box of lace remnants . . . her gold thimble" (179). Her suffering was deepest when she handled her small personal things—her bobby pins, her comb. She and her brother felt as if they were criminals, dispersing parts of their mother. With the final dispersion of objects, Nin felt, the separation was final. She felt deeper pain than when her father had died. She felt that she had not loved her mother well enough. Alive, her mother had been a threat to Nin's "aspiration to escape the servitudes of women" (182). Now that Nin had lost her, her love for her mother was reawakened, and her rebellion had collapsed. She felt that her mother's spirit possessed her. There is a moment "when we cease to struggle against the parent's own image of us and accept our resemblances as part of our being." This is far better than safekeeping of material objects as mementoes of the dead. "Surely our parents give birth to us twice, the second time when they die, and as they die, in rebellion against death, we accept the legacy of their character traits" (184).

The leitmotiv of the mother's sacrifice plays in the memoirs of her grown daughter *in largo tempo*—in the memoirs of women whose lives were as far apart as Isadora Duncan's and Helen Keller's, the one who danced her life and the other who thought of herself as a statue. Duncan's mother filled her children's lives with music and poetry. She did not care at all for material things: she taught them "a fine scorn and contempt" for possessions and belongings. Because of her mother's example, Duncan never wore jewelry: "She taught us that such things were trammels."[16] Her mother never tired of playing for her; she would play the entire score of *Orpheus* over and over while her daughter danced; she "was an angel of self-effacement and abnegation," whose only desire was to help Isadora in her work (77). In Greece, the "clan Duncan" of the mother and four children vowed to remain together forever, and to build a temple, Kopanos, reflecting the spirit of their little community. In later years, her mother's character changed. The Irish, Duncan wrote, cannot "stand prosperity as well as adversity." But there was more to it than that. For many years, Duncan's mother had devoted herself completely to her children, and now that they were absorbed in interests that took them away from her so often, "she realised that she had actually wasted the best years of her life on us, leaving nothing for herself; as I think so many mothers do, especially in America" (187). When Helen Keller's mother died, Keller recalled that she used to tell her "how happy she was when I was born. She dwelt on her memories of the eighteen months when I could see and hear."[17] Her mother had been reticent, sensitive, and shy. Because her hands were afflicted with rheumatism, it was very difficult for her to write in braille. This was a keen disappointment to her because she did not like anyone else to read her letters to her daughter. Keller felt grieved that her radicalism added to the weight of her mother's sadness over her, although she was consoled in remembering the delight they took in talking together, whatever their differences might be. When she and her mother were standing at Twin Peaks, her mother drew her close and said, "This is a reparation for all the sorrow I have ever known" (163). Looking back at her mother's life, Keller wrote that a fateful change came when she was only 23—when her daughter's illness left her deaf and blind: "It was as if a white winter had swept over the June of her youth; I know, although she never said it, that she suffered more through me than through her other children" (217).

In Eleanor Roosevelt's autobiography, there are only brief—though telling—recollections of her parents, both of whom died when she was still a child. The very first sentence in *This Is My Story* reads, "My mother was one of the most beautiful women I have ever seen."[18] The memoirist's father is remembered as "the love of my life for many years after he died." In childhood, she felt "he and I were very close . . . and some day would have a life of our own together" (6, 20). But it was Roosevelt's grandmother whom she felt had strongly influenced the way she responded to her experiences, and once again the theme of maternal sacrifice emerges. She wondered if the family might have benefited if her grandmother's life had been less centered on them all, and what the consequences might have been had she had a life of her own. Perhaps she could have developed the talent for painting she had shown when she was young. Perhaps she would have been happier, and her children would have benefited, if she had remarried. "Her willingness to be subservient to her children isolated her, whether they realized it or not; and it might have been far better, for her boys at least, had she insisted on bringing more discipline into their lives simply by having a life of her own" (300). The effect of her grandmother's life on Roosevelt's own was considerable, "for even when I was young I determined that I would never be dependent on my children by allowing all my interests to center in them. The conviction has grown through the years" (300–301). She believed that her grandmother could not be objective about her children and thought that her gratitude for their affection "was something almost pathetic and showed how little else she had in life" (301).

Actress Ilka Chase remarked her resemblance to her maternal *great-*grandmother. This pleased her, since she thought the lady "something of a glamour girl."[19] She had left Chase's great-grandfather and their children, Chase's Grandma among them, during the Civil War, and married a Southern doctor and raised another family. After the doctor died, she returned to her first husband, who had since been remarried and widowed, and became his wife again. "Great-grandfather eventually passed to eternal rest, but Great-grandmother hung on till the age of ninety-two, when she died from injuries received in an automobile accident while out joyriding with a beau" (4). Chase's Grandma, who had left two husbands herself, was understanding about her mother's love life. But she never forgave her for having deserted her when she was a baby. At 80, she still spoke of herself as "poor little motherless Laura." Chase recalled her Grandma as "a peppery old party with a will of solid granite and a hot, flaring temper" (4). She had a great gift for self-dramatization, and a strong sense of theatre, fancying herself "in the role of a dear little old lady in cap and lavender taffeta." But if she heard an opinion contrary to her own, she responded with a ferocity and lung power all out of proportion to her fragile person. "She became tiny in her old age, like a little gray leaf, but her periodic rages, instead of destroying her, seemed to infuse her with new vitality" (5).

Margaret Sanger remembered her mother as slender and beautiful and sensitive to beauty, a sensitivity that was expressed in the flowers that were always gathered from nearby woods and fields to grace their table. With her mother's early death, Sanger's immediate occasion for reading medical books came to an end, but she had a "deep conviction that perhaps she might have been saved had I had sufficient knowledge of medicine. This was linked up with my latent desire to be of service in the world."[20] Sanger's father was a nonconformist, a freethinker who had studied anatomy, medicine, and phrenology in order to perfect his skill in modeling. His livelihood was "chiseling angels and saints out of huge blocks of white marble or gray granite for tombstones in cemeteries. He was a philosopher, a rebel, and an artist, none of which was calculated to produce wealth" (13). A strong advocate of women's suffrage and of Mrs. Bloomer's bloomers, he was the first socialist in his community, though he "also took single tax in his stride and became the champion and friend of Henry George" (17). His best patrons were Catholics, whom he alienated, first by joining the Knights of Labor, and then by inviting Colonel Robert G. Ingersoll to speak in Corning. He taught his children to leave the world a better place for having lived in it. After Sanger's mother died, her father became cruel and tyrannical. In time, Sanger, who had to take her mother's place, came to understand the reasons for this sudden metamorphosis. He had been devastated by the loss of his wife's love and understanding.

In Sanger's autobiography there are intimations of the shaping influences she felt her parents to have been upon both her character and her calling. Anthropologist Margaret Mead wrote of these influences in some detail in her memoir. It was her judgment that her father, "even more than my mother, whose career was limited by the number of her children and her health, . . . defined for me my place in the world."[21] She wrote of her parents' aging, her mother's death, her father's later years. She felt fortunate because when she was well past middle age she could still look up to her parents' minds. "And I watched my father grow—shed his earlier racial prejudices and come to respect new institutions of the federal government." Mead reflected in this passage, "Watching a parent grow is one of the most reassuring experiences anyone can have, a privilege that comes only to those whose parents live beyond their children's early adulthood" (45).

But it was Mead's judgment that the most decisive influence in her life was not that of either of her parents. It was that of her paternal grandmother, who lived with the family from the time Mead's parents were married until her death in 1927. Her parents had given her the *content* of her conscience. "But the strength of my conscience came from Grandma, who meant what she said. Perhaps nothing is more valuable for a child than living with an adult who is firm and loving" (56). She had learned her ease in being a woman from her grandmother, Mead wrote. And when her own granddaughter was born, Mead saw in the baby's eyes the same flashing glance of her grandmother reappearing for the first time over the generations. All her life, Mead's closest friends were people who had grown up close to a beloved and loving grandparent as she had. Her great love for this woman was reborn in her great love for her granddaughter. "The known and loved particular child," she wrote, "makes it possible for one to understand better and care more about all children" (310). She believed that to love children in the abstract is most difficult, and that to be fully human, every person needs to have access both to grandparents and grandchildren:

> In the presence of grandparent and grandchild, past and future merge in the present. Looking at a loved child, one cannot say, "We must sacrifice this generation for the next. Many must die now so that later others may live." This is the argument that generations of old men, cut off from children, have used in sending young men out to die in war. Nor can one say, "I want this child to live well no matter how we despoil the earth for later generations." For seeing a child as one's grandchild, one can visualize that same child as a grandparent, and with the eyes of another generation one can see other children, just as light-footed and vivid, as eager to learn and know and embrace the world, who must be taken into account—now. [311]

Willa Cather did not write an autobiography; she was so reserved a woman that such an undertaking would have been completely out of character for her. One must look for her memoirs and her reflections on youth and aging in her fictions and in the writings gathered in her book *Not Under Forty*. The title of that book means that it would have little interest for those younger than that age: "The world broke in two in 1922 or thereabouts, and the persons and prejudices recalled in these sketches slid back into yesterday's seven thousand years."[22] In the sketch "Joseph and His Brothers," she reflected that Joseph had been put to the test by life and had proven himself equal to it: "he was one of those whom mischances enlighten and refine. . . . The world is always full of brilliant youth which fades into grey and embittered middle age: the first flowering takes everything." To Cather's mind, greatness is made of slow development or of the capacity for surviving "the glamour of . . . early florescence" and continuing to learn from life (116–17). Older people are fascinated by gifted youth, for only the passage of time reveals which early gifts ripen and flower, and it is this mystery that is so compelling for the fostering elders. "Kindly effort to shelter them from struggle with the hard facts of existence is often to take away the bread (or the lack of it) by which they grow, if the power of growth is in them" (117).

Cather's first sketch in this book is of a woman past 80 with whom she had "A Chance Meeting" at Aix-les-Bains at the Grand Hôtel d'Aix. This was in August 1930, during one of the hottest seasons known in that area. Cather had often noticed this Frenchwoman alone at lunch and dinner, and re-marked the fineness of her head and a rare loveliness about her temples. She was somewhat lame, but disregarded this completely. "One saw that she was contemptuously intolerant of the limitations of old age" (5). Cather had ob-served that she often went early in the morning to the mountains to sketch and, after dinner, to the opera. One evening they spoke, and the lady men-tioned a concert to be played the next day. Cather felt she ought to say that she intended to go. She attended the performance, and rose to leave after the second intermission; she had enjoyed the Ravel, and felt the concert had been long enough for her, and she was not much interested in the last group to be played. Her new friend detained her to suggest that Cather have tea there and return to hear the last group. The writer thanked her, but said she did not intend to hear the entire concert. "Seeing things through was evidently a habit with this old lady," she reflected. That was plain from "the way she was seeing life through, going to concerts and operas in this wilting heat; being concerned that other people should go, moreover, and caring about the way in which Ravel was played" (11). The writer felt she "had escaped from an exacting preceptress" (12). Clearly, the lady believed one ought to do as much as one could, and always a little better than before, in the time one was given.

Cather still did not know the lady's name, though she felt no particular curiosity about this. A few days later, she and a friend happened to be talking with her, and the friend mentioned Turgeniev. The lady said she knew Turgeniev well some time ago, for he had been a good friend of her uncle's.

The name of her uncle, the man who had brought her up and who had been more than a father to her, was one they might know, she said. For he was also a man of letters, Gustave Flaubert. Cather wrote:

> The meaning of her words came through to me slowly; so this must be the "Caro" of the *Lettres à sa Nièce Caroline*. There was nothing to say, certainly. . . . It was like being suddenly brought up against a mountain of memories. One could not see round it; one could only stupidly realize that in this mountain . . . lay most of one's mental past. Some moments went by. . . . I took one of her lovely hands and kissed it, in homage to a great period, to the names that made her voice tremble. [15]

The writer noticed how alive Mme. Franklin-Grout was to any form of pleasure and how much keener she became from it—how, as at the performance of *Boris Goudounov,* artistic excellence brought to life again the period of artistic excellence that was within her. When Cather had to leave for Paris, Mme. Grout invited her to come soon—*soon,* for she was 84—to see the Flaubert collection. She asked the writer if she would like to have a souvenir of their meeting. It wounded Cather that Mme. Grout would think she wanted a material reminder either of herself or of her uncle. Flaubert's name, spoken at parting, seemed a staff his niece carried firmly. "A great memory and a great devotion were the things she lived upon . . . her armour against a world concerned with insignificant matters" (34).

In Paris, Cather read the letters Flaubert had written to this niece again and felt the pages glow with Mme. Grout's personality. She had the startling recognition that Flaubert had been solicitous "about her progress in her English lessons—those lessons by which I was to profit seventy-three years afterward!" (35) She felt gratitude to Fate for having given him a niece of such sensitivity and intelligence. Months later, she received a letter from Mme. Grout. It had been forwarded to Cather through three publishing houses. Mme. Grout had addressed it to a bookseller in Paris where she had bought one of Cather's books, and she wrote that she was enclosing a letter from Flaubert to George Sand. But the envelope had been opened, indeed almost destroyed, and the enclosure had been removed. A few months later, Cather read that Mme. Grout had died.

But Willa Cather already had the things of Flaubert that mattered to her. And "a chance meeting" had brought her face to face with the reaping of what had been sown and fostered in a young person by her elder. I think she knew that fostering is the vital impulse of those in later life who know how to love the young. Toward the end of her life, Cather came around again, from old age to youth, in her literary art. For seven years, when old age and illness and disability were upon her, she worked on a manuscript, entitled *Hard Punishments,* a novel set in medieval Avignon. It was a story about youth, and Cather did not live to complete it. She had ordered that it be destroyed after her death. So in old age, Cather had turned her attention to "the best years" of life once more.[23] I suspect that she knew better than most people do what Time's circularities are. Youth and age are neither strangers nor enemies, but part of one another. *Not Under Forty* contains sketches of older women—of Mme. Grout and of the widow of James T. Fields of the publishing firm of Ticknor and Fields, and of "Miss Jewett," whose eye and ear and sensibility Cather so respected. But it contains "Joseph and His Brothers," too. Time works its transmutations through us, so that what once was seed becomes grain, and then again part of the harvest. Age sees in youth its history, and youth in age its future. The fate of both depends upon what they do after this moment of recognition.

The Sense of a Calling

Jane Addams perceived a resemblance between the dreams the young have of the future and the dreams the old have when they remember the past.[24] Addams made the telling point that, while the reminiscences of the old may soften the past, they are selective, and this may bring about an assault upon the very traditions and conventions thought to be so strongly held by the aged. And the dreams of the future that young people imagine, even though they veil it in a roseate mist, "contain . . . the inchoate substance from which the tough-fibred forces of coming social struggles are composed" (xii). Many a memoirist circles back to an earlier self bearing dreams and ambitions to the place where the roads cross, and then follows the remembered figure on the road taken. Historical reconstruction is a formidable undertaking, and in the reconstruction of personal history, one needs not only imagination and intelligence but distancing—and, therefore, courage. A memoir without these qualities can be no more than a political or sociological treatise or an exercise in self-congratulation or self-pity. A memoir that has these qualities shapes a lifeway. This lifeway is a metaphor of every reader's self.[25]

A young girl may read her fortune in her name. Catholics do this, Mary McCarthy says:

> Christian names are chosen for the spiritual qualities of the saints they are taken from; Protestants used to name their children out of the Old Testament and now they name them out of novels and plays. . . . with Catholics. . . . The saint a child is named for is supposed to serve, literally, as a model or pattern to imitate; your name is your fortune and it tells you what you are or must be. Catholic children ponder their names for a mystic meaning, like birthstones.[26]

McCarthy pondered hers, her first and second and confirmation names, for their meanings for her character rather than for her calling, which she at first thought was the life of the theater. While I did not find that these women whose memoirs I read—whatever their faith—attached much significance to their given names, I did find marked differences between them in their sense of a calling. There are those who began with one vocation in mind who

followed another. Welthy Honsinger Fisher, who went to China as a Methodist missionary in 1906, thought when she was a girl that she would be an opera
singer.[27] Edna Ferber, Edna St. Vincent Millay and Harriet Monroe, as well as
Mary McCarthy all thought they would become actresses (and they all became
writers). And the literary life is not one, but many callings, as the life work of
these and other writers attests.[28] On the other hand, there are women who
seemed destined to become writers when young and who changed their
course. Margaret Mead had strong literary inclinations, and it was not until
she was at Barnard, where she met the highly gifted Léonie Adams, that
writing poetry changed from a vocation into an avocation.[29] "At different
times," Mead wrote of her earlier self, "I wanted to become a lawyer, a nun, a
writer, or a minister's wife with six children" (86).

Mead's account of the way she arrived at the choice of a vocation in anthropology exemplifies the process of self-examination and examination of
alternatives—a process of rational deliberation—that marks the way some
women decide what their work in life is to be. Of course, the story is more
complicated than that: Chance played a part, and coming to know Ruth
Benedict, which may be the same thing, was fateful. But her choice was *a
choice*, rather than a submission to Fate, a yielding to an appointed destiny.
That was Isadora Duncan's sense of a calling—or, rather, that is what Duncan's autobiography conveys—a sense of predestination to the life of dance.

Isadora Duncan. That she was born by the sea, under the star of Aphrodite,
was a sign to Isadora Duncan. Aphrodite, too, was born on the sea, "and when
her star is in the ascendant, events are always propitious to me. At these
epochs life flows lightly and I am able to create. I have also noticed that the
disappearance of this star is usually followed by disaster for me."[30] She believed Love and Art to be inseparable, and the only lover to be the artist. She
believed there to be a spiritual line in every life, "an upward curve," and that
whatever holds to this and makes it strong is life in reality, "the rest . . . but as
chaff falling from us as our souls progress" (239). Art was her spiritual line,
and her life was governed by Art and Love, and these are engaged in endless
strife. In her life, Love was destructive of Art, and Art so imperious that it
often brought Love to a tragic end.

The future is there; it waits for us. So Duncan believed. It lies beyond the
next turn in the long road of past, present, and future, that part of the road
hidden from our sight. She had known that she was pregnant with her firstborn, Deirdre, when she dreamed of Ellen Terry dressed in a shimmering
gown, leading a little girl by the hand who resembled her exactly, and calling
her name and the name of Love. And before the tragic accident that took the
lives of her two small children, Deirdre and Patrick, she experienced premonitions of evil, sinister forebodings that oppressed her. Looking back, she saw
those last days before she lost them as the last days that she was spiritually
alive. In Art, her vision was not the simple one of dancing Solo. She was
possessed by the dream of a school when she danced Beethoven's Ninth, a

dream that led her "from one catastrophe to another . . . like the light of Tantalus" (213). In Love, she saw herself as an "Inspirational," a mediatrix, never a Vampire or a Salomé (218). Her life, even seen from the outside, had the proportions of tragedy. Even as she asked which child it was, Deirdre or Patrick, who was reborn in her third child, the infant died in her arms. This was in August 1914. Outside her window, she heard the cries for mobilization as her body flowed with milk and blood and tears.

Even at the age of five, Duncan wrote, she was already a dancer and a revolutionary. Although she wrote that it seems impossible to believe in a Providence when one reads of sudden disasters, and that the thought that Providence guides one's little life is egotistical, absurdly so, she had such extraordinary experiences that at times she believed in predestination. One of these happened when she was on a train to St. Petersburg on January 6, 1905. Because the train was delayed for twelve hours by snowdrifts, she chanced to witness the ghastly procession of men carrying the coffins of the workers shot in front of the Winter Palace the day before. The dead were buried at dawn to avert revolution. Had she not seen this, she wrote, her entire life would have been different. It was then that she vowed to dedicate her life to the cause of the oppressed. How small and useless her own desires and sufferings seemed to her then, "How useless even my Art, unless it could help this." The compassion and rage she felt in that dawn "was to bear fruit in my life thereafter" (162).

That was before the tragic deaths of her children. Some time after, her brother, Raymond, persuaded her to leave her "selfish" grieving, and go back with him to give comfort and nurturance to the Albanian women and children refugees. Once she had regained her health and strength, she felt she could not continue her work with the refugees. She perceived a great difference between the life of the artist and the life of the saint, and wrote, "My artist life awoke within me" (281). Some time after, as grief worked its slow passage to desolation, she wrote of her envy of "the resignation of those nuns who pray with pale lips, murmuring incessant prayers all through the night before the coffins of strangers. Such temperaments are the envy of the artist who revolts, who cries, 'I will love, love, create joy, joy'" (332). In this passage, Duncan echoes the theme of her autobiography—that she was born of a different goddess than other women and that her life had the proportions of a myth.

When the Clan Duncan ascended the Temple in Athens, Isadora Duncan wrote, she had a sense of epiphany, a feeling of being born anew. Other women's autobiographies do not dramatize the self as Duncan does, yet in many of them there is this same intuition of having been elected to the life course they followed. Welthy Honsinger Fisher wrote that, although her *essential* self had not changed throughout her life, she had been reborn in the far places where she traveled, and that in one lifetime she had experienced reincarnations. Mary Austin wrote that, while her contemporaries were active in the labor movement, *she* chose to defend Indians. Her life among the Indians convinced Austin that she must have had Indian ancestry in the remote past. For "hen-medic" Bertha Van Hoosen, there were intimations of a call to science and to the practice of medicine in childhood.

Bertha Van Hoosen. Van Hoosen wrote that she was given one of her earliest lessons in physics when her father installed a water system for their farm-house and barns. Several years later she was initiated into the science of building as she watched him construct a barn from foundation to cupola. Van Hoosen spent little time indoors when she was young, and did not feel consci-entiously about helping her mother with the housework. "I was the doglike companion of my father and, in consequence, acquired an empirical founda-tion in agronomy and animal husbandry. When Father announced, 'Well, lambing is over and the creek is pretty high so I guess we better shear next week,' I trembled with delight."[31] She began the study of what was to become her favorite subject, anatomy, at hog-killing time: "Without a peep into Grey's anatomy I reveled in seeing what was under the skin" (29). This study that so fascinated Van Hoosen was pursued even earlier than that, when she learned how to dress chickens and turkeys.

To Van Hoosen, life on the farm had dignity, security, and freedom. Only when she entered the town school did she become aware of the gulf between people of the town and countryfolk. She felt favored to be the daughter of a farmer, and it shocked her to hear her father referred to as a "hayseed," a word that encompassed his "clothing, manners, speech, surroundings, and even the beautiful simplicity of his character" (42). Life on a farm is a lesson in resourcefulness. When she needed playthings, she made them of wood or a pumpkin or odds and ends. When she needed companions, there were farm animals and birds and fish. She had a 400-acre farm for running when she needed to run, and a garden, a cellar, bushes and brambles, roots and gums offered a rich and varied food supply to satisfy her hunger and her curiosity. The family farm in Stony Creek was the "solar plexus" of the family to Van Hoosen, where she, her mother, her sister, and her niece were born, where her ancestors were buried, where she was given the rudiments of her educa-tion in the sciences and the foundation of her physical resistance. When she saw the city children going to the playgrounds in the summer, she compared their "silent artificial cement pool" with "the purling spring-fed creek that pulses and curves like a life-giving umbilical cord over the length and breadth of the farm" (17). Of the creek in each season of the year and of all the wild flowers and fruits of the countryside she had intimate knowledge. And al-though botany, horticulture, ornithology, and entomology were not words in her vocabulary in childhood, the foundations in these branches of science were laid for her then through her sister Alice's instruction.

Van Hoosen devoted the first two years of college at the University of Michigan to her "social career" and after that she began considering what she would do with her life—a question she turned her attention to "with positive ferocity." She sat herself on her mother's haircloth sofa and declared she would not move from there until she had made up her mind about the choice of a calling. This took three days, during which this tough-minded and humorous woman put up with her family's amusement at her method of deliberation. She weighed and considered. She wanted marriage to play the same part in her life that it does in a man's, and she wanted to prepare herself to be independent if it should happen that she would need to be. She wanted to be able to continue her work as long as she pleased without being summarily retired because of her age. She wanted, like her father, to be her own boss. And she wanted to deal with people of all ages and attainments and to find use for her every aptitude. She was aware of the dignity and social status, the friendships and colleagueship the practice of medicine offered. Most important for her was the opportunity medicine offered "for growth and advancement in an ever-expanding science." In 1947, this woman who was born in 1863 reflected, "Perhaps, after all, in my choice of a medical career, unconsciously I was responding to a call of the woman in me—woman, preserver of the race—to mitigate suffering and save life" (55). Although Van Hoosen certainly needed money, she was sure that her choice was not influenced by the desire for wealth. And she weighed the disadvantages, chief among them the demanding life of the physician. Once she had made up her mind, she felt twice-born, and dedicated herself completely to her chosen profession.

Van Hoosen had a strong mentor and friend in Dr. Mary McLean, who inspired her and helped her and encouraged her. And in Van Hoosen's own later years, she was called "Mother" by the young women who spent some time in surgical training with her and whom she regarded as her "surgical daughters." It so happened that Van Hoosen never married. But she came to regard herself as the "father" of her sister's child, Sarah, whom she had delivered, and for whose life she had fought for hours, long after the family had given up hope that the infant would live. Of her "surgical daughters," she wrote, "Like all mothers I have carried them so long close to my heart that I can see no flaws in them, but I try never to omit an opportunity to perfect their technique or increase their knowledge" (216). Like many mothers, too, she felt that her daughters had taught her more than she had imparted to them. Of this need of the generations for one another, of this love that flows between them, the bond that unites them is woven. There is great passion in this love, though it is the passion not of Eros but of Agape, the passion that is the purest, most civilizing force in the world, upon which the very continuance of the human race depends.

A young woman may have a sense of her calling even in childhood. Isadora Duncan believed that a baby expresses what it is going to be. But I have read memoirs of women who were still seeking their vocation in midlife and even in very late life. Some women only come into their own when they are old. Age sets them free or endows them with a sense of their calling. Harriet Monroe and Mother Jones are, respectively, outstanding examples of women who found a direction for their lives in middle age and old age.

Harriet Monroe. In midlife, Harriet Monroe was still in search of her vocation. She began to write her autobiography when she was 75, and in it she recalled that when she was quite young, she "felt a deep sense of responsibility, of consecration to a high destiny." Once the idea of a career on the stage faded, she thought she was destined "to be a great poet, a great playwright, and I must set about fulfilling my 'vocation.'" Even as a child, Monroe told herself and God "that I was to be 'great and famous'—I cannot remember the time when to die without leaving some memorable record did not seem to me a calamity too terrible to be borne."[32] This sense of consecration was felt intensely even after she turned 30. She believed she would rather have art than life, and she was prepared to sacrifice the ordinary happiness people have for "immortal fame."

More than any other person in twentieth-century America, Harriet Monroe fostered the writing of poetry in the English language. That was her calling, although she did not find it until she was 52, in 1912, when *Poetry* was launched. After the Columbia Exposition in Chicago in 1893, when she "found her first fame," came "an interval of twenty years of striving and disillusionment that slowly brought her to the greatest purpose of her life and disclosed her real destiny . . . at an age when most . . . consider the moment for action past, she braved public skepticism, personal reputation, and unknown risks by launching *Poetry*."[33]

Looking back, Monroe marveled at the audacity she had when she was very young to sue a great metropolitan newspaper for having published the ode she wrote for the Columbian Exposition without her authorization. Her lawsuit, *Monroe* v. *The Press Publishing Company*, came to trial in December 1894. When Napoleon was asked about his ancestors, Monroe recalled, he had replied, "*Je suis ancêtre!*" So, too, "my little lawsuit, being without precedent, established its own precedence and became a textbook case, defining the rights of authors to control their unpublished works" (139). By the end of "The Middle Years," Monroe was still seeking a direction for her life. She had decided not to marry, and she wrote that she never regretted her decision. She took much pleasure in her family and her friendships. But she felt she had powers that she was wasting. Dividing her time between writing, working as art critic for the *Tribune* once again, as she had done fifteen years before, and teaching English a few hours a week at a girls' school, she became ever more indignant at the clear evidence she saw at every hand that poetry was "the Cinderella of the arts." She noticed that "the minor painter or sculptor or architect was receiving every encouragement . . . to develop his art and become distinguished in it, while the poet, whether minor or major, encountered nothing but indifference and neglect" (241). Poetry "must have listeners," for it "cannot sing into a void" (242). Her credo was that "only when the creative impulse meets an equally strong impulse of sympathy is the highest achievement possible in any department of human effort" (327). Of "A Banquet: Yeats and Lindsay," she wrote that it "was one of my great days, those days which come to most of us as atonement for long periods of drab disappointment or dark despair" (339).

Mother Jones. "I am not a suffragist nor do I believe in 'careers' for women," Mother Jones declared, "especially a 'career' in factory and mill where most working women have their 'careers.'" She believed that women's great responsibility and "most beautiful task" is to train children.[34] She made her position on suffrage clear to a group of 500 women when she was in New York raising funds for the families of miners in Colorado: "You don't need a vote to raise hell!" She told her audience, "I did not believe in women's rights nor in men's rights but in human rights" (203–4).

For all that, Mother Jones made a career—more, a calling—for herself, not so much in later life as *of* it. And she made great, good capital of being a woman, and an old woman, at that. For, as Fred Thompson asks, "who would have expected the coal miners' most noted organizer to be an old woman?"[35] Here was a woman who proclaimed she was about ten years *older* than her actual age. She was probably born not in 1830, as she claimed, but in 1839 (xxii). She may have been a mere 80 in 1919, and not 89; all the same, her vitality in preparing for the steel strike was astounding. And she lived to celebrate what she said was the hundredth anniversary of her birth in 1930 in Hyattsville, Maryland, where she died later that year. Perhaps the Great Depression would have gone differently if Mother Jones had lived on.

Mother Jones's birth date is but one example of the mis-dating in her autobiography. The way the book was prepared—was it dictated? written? edited? were there others who helped her write it?—remains a mystery. All that does not matter much, as Thompson remarks, for the book stands as "a great piece of working class literature" and Mother Jones herself a legend born of the cry, "Mother, come organize us" (xxxvi). For half a century, she was the mother of union struggles. She told her "boys," the miners, "Pray for the dead and fight like hell for the living!" (41) She was quick with the special .38 she kept under her gingham apron, and she had a quick tongue in her head. Arrested for attempting to speak in Homestead, she was brought to appear before the judge in the Pittsburgh court, who asked her if she had a permit to speak on the steets. "'Yes, sir,'" said I. 'I had a permit.' 'Who issued it?' he growled. 'Patrick Henry; Thomas Jefferson; John Adams!' said I" (213).

In 1903, when thousands of textile workers were on strike, she assembled children, many of them maimed, all of them undernourished, in Independence Park, from whence she paraded with them, banners flying, to the court house. In the public square in front of city hall, she had children display hands with missing fingers, hands that had been crushed or crippled by factory machinery. She told the crowd that the mansions of Philadelphia were built on the broken bones and quivering hearts of children. With knapsacks and banners, and an escort of adults with tents and a wagon stacked with provisions, Mother Jones's army of children set off on their march. She had planned to bring the children to President Theodore Roosevelt and to enlist the support of Senator Platt for a bill limiting child labor. Neither of these objectives was realized. Nonetheless, public attention was drawn to the issue, and it was not long after the Children's Crusade that the Pennsylvania legislature passed a child labor law.

When the miners in Greensburg, Pennsylvania, went on strike for higher wages, a group of women who had gathered in front of the mine to jeer the scabs who "were taking the bread from their children's mouths" were arrested for disturbing the peace (145). Mother Jones told the women to take their babies and small children with them to court, and this they did. As the judge was pronouncing their sentence of $30 or 30 days, the babies wailed so loudly he could hardly be heard for the din. On the way to jail, the inter-urban car stopped to take on some scabs, and the women set to work to "trim the fellows" (146). They sang as the car went through Greensburg, and a crowd followed, joining in the singing, and cheering them all when they arrived at the jail. Mother Jones told the women to sing through the night and to sleep by day, and after five days and nights during which everyone in the town had been kept awake all night, the judge ordered their release.

Mother Jones was in Hazelton when the strike call was issued. To win the strike in the district, the Coaldale miners had to be organized. She went to McAdoo, a nearby mining town, and asked the women "to leave their men at home to take care of the family" and "to put on their kitchen clothes and bring mops and brooms with them and a couple of tin pans." Her army marched fifteen miles, "beating on the tin pans as if they were cymbals" (90). After an encounter with the Crack Thirteen of the militia, who at first offered to charge them with bayonets—it was three o'clock in the morning—and then detained them until dawn and let them go, the McAdoo women went on to persuade the Coaldale miners to join the union. Her army was so enthused by their success "that we organized the street car men who promised to haul no scabs for the coal companies. As there were no other groups to organize we marched over the mountains home, beating on our pans and singing patriotic songs" (91).

Mother Jones was married in 1861, in Memphis, to an iron molder who was a loyal member of his union. Six years later, there was a yellow fever epidemic there, and among its victims, who were mainly the poor and the workers, were her husband and all four of her children. She nursed the sick until the epidemic ended, and then went to Chicago and returned to the dressmaking, by which, together with teaching, she had made her living before her marriage. There she contrasted the lives of the poor with those of her employers, "the aristocrats" of the city (12). She saw people jobless and cold and hungry in the winter, people who slept in the parks in the summer to escape the stifling heat of the tenements. After her business was lost in the Chicago fire of 1871, she became ever more dedicated to the cause of the labor movement. As ardently as she took up the cause of the workers and their families, she was even more passionately the defender of working-class children. She saw long lines of gray children file into the factories at dawn, "into the maddening noise, into the lint filled rooms" (120). Of the child labor she witnessed in

Cottondale, she wrote, "Sometimes it seemed to me I could not look at those silent little figures; that I must go north, to the grim coal fields, to the Rocky Mountain camps, where the labor fight is at least fought by grown men" (119). She saw children of six with faces of 60-year-olds working for wages of ten cents a day for an eight-hour shift. Of a rope factory in Tuscaloosa where she worked, she remarked that the little laborers die of consumption and pneumonia and bronchitis. "But the birth rate like the dividends is large and another little hand is ready to tie the snapped threads when a child worker dies" (122). She said she knew the shortcomings of the working people and she knew there were betrayals by their leaders. But this did not outweigh the fact that the working class—*her* class—"is exploited, driven, fought back with the weapon of starvation, with guns and with venal courts whenever they strike for conditions more human, more civilized for their children, and for their children's children" (197).

Mary Heaton Vorse. The realization of what one's life was about, the entelechy of the calling, is the gift of time, time that is much maligned as a thief. As some of these women grew older, care and compassion flowed in ever-widening circles from their work into the life of the world. Of this there are but intimations when the work begins. Writer Mary Heaton Vorse reflected in her autobiography (which was her fourteenth book):

> I could not be an organizer or a labor leader; I was too impatient of results to work for a possibly perfect society. I could do one thing. I could write. I could try to make other people see what I had seen, feel what I had felt. I wanted to make others an angry as I was. I wanted to see wages go up and the babies' death rate go down.[36]

Vorse was a widow with young children when she married Joe O'Brien in 1912. By 1916, O'Brien was dead, and, after a "bitter struggle" with herself over leaving the children with their grandmother, she responded to the urging of Elizabeth Gurley Flynn and Bill Haywood to write about the strike of metal miners on the Mesabi Range in Minnesota. The following winter, she had a sense of panic for the first time; her stories were not selling just after they were written as they had in the past, and she had numerous bills to pay. Heaton wrote fiction as well as nonfiction. Her life had been transformed by her witnessing of the Lawrence strike, and then once more by her attendance at the International Congress of Women in Amsterdam in 1915 and by what she had heard there and later seen for herself of the ravages of war. Of the glory of war, she had seen nothing. "I had seen the boys go off singing. I had seen them come back mutilated and blinded. . . . I had seen the hospital trains bring in the wreckage. I had seen what happens to . . . the simple people who make up a country" (127). When she returned to Provincetown, she felt that she had experienced a revolution more far-reaching than that brought about by the Lawrence strike. "A revaluation of all of life. It was again the difference between knowing academically that war exists and the emotional realization of it, as different as knowing that death exists and seeing one's own dead before one" (128). In 1918 and 1919, she saw more of this ravening from Salonika to Astrakhan, and asked what its purpose could possibly be.

Just after she had come back from the Women's Peace Conference, Vorse believed "that women hate war" and that women's most intense moment was birth, and man's was war. She thought of woman as "lifegiver and conserver and man the destroyer" (125). By the 1930s, she no longer believed these things. Yet she wondered "what would happen if there were a peace movement as resolute and fanatical as that for suffrage" (125). She had a vision of a great, mythical person, collective Woman (she called her "Ma") who after the war would find temperance and religion not to be enough, who would leave the kitchen and organize for the sake of young children (168). Children—that is what Vorse's calling had been all about. She had a vivid memory of the children she had seen in Serbia in 1919, dancing the kola in the yard of a Red Cross orphan asylum. Their parents had been killed in the war. The children themselves had been under bombardment. They had gone through unspeakable terrors. They had endured terrible privations. And there was a boy playing his harmonica, and there were the war orphans dancing the kola "with grave intentness, one intricate step after another" (224). The children she saw in steel towns, in mining camps and tenements were Vorse's most vivid memories of what she had witnessed. In wartime, she wrote about trench children and the blockaded children of Central Europe and the children of famine in Russia. Children are the theme of *Men of Steel.* Her autobiography itself "is the record of a woman who in early life got angry because many children lived miserably and died needlessly." She had thought it was a book about war and imperialism and the labor movement, but she discovered it was a book about children. "For when you come down to it, the labor movement is about children and about homes" (404).

In the memoirs of some women, the passion of motherhood is very intense. I have found this in the autobiographies of women whose lives appear to bear no likeness one to another—Isadora Duncan, Margaret Mead, Virgilia Peterson. In the memoirs of other women there is a great reserve about their feelings for their children or other people's children. And in some memoirs, this great feeling for younger people is a love not so much for children as for youth. This is most clearly expressed in the diaries of Anaïs Nin. But in the memoirs of many women, whatever their calling—the memoirs of Isadora Duncan, Welthy Fisher, Margaret Mead, Mother Jones, Eleanor Roosevelt, Margaret Sanger, Bertha Van Hoosen, Mary Heaton Vorse—a care and compassion for the life of the world, a fostering and furtherance of life itself, is unmistakable. This compassionate, fostering love is the essence not of parenthood, but of grandparenthood. It is *this* which unfolds and is expressed through following a vocation. Let every women find her own path, whether in art or science, in education or social reform. All paths lead to this if service is to that which is greater than the ego. In this sense, every calling is the same: the calling to set the transformative power of love free in the world. In later life, a woman may discover that this was her highest vocation realized through work and service in a field that only now she sees is part of a limitless estate.

Women's Reflections on Aging

"I have never come across one single woman, either in life or in books, who has looked upon her own old age cheerfully. In the same way no one ever speaks of 'a beautiful old woman.'"[37] I have found otherwise, and therefore do not concur with Simone de Beauvoir in this judgment. In part, this is because I have been consulting and comparing different sources than those adduced in *The Coming of Age*. In greater part, this is because my approach to the question of aging is at variance with that taken in Beauvoir's impressive study. "Change is the law of life," she writes, and with this I have no quarrel. But I do not agree that "it is a particular kind of change that distinguishes aging—an irreversible, unfavourable change; a decline" (20). Women's reflections on aging—and even the reflections of a single woman—are too complex and too protean to permit this or any other final judgment to be made. What is true about aging for and of one woman cannot be taken as true of and for another, much less of and for all women.

Mary Austin thought that women have "times."[38] One woman may adopt the metaphor of "seasons" for these times, and another the metaphor of "milestones." For some, the beginning of a new decade of life is a milestone. "O dangerous age of 49!" Bogan wrote in a letter to Rolfe Humphries.[39] To Morton Zabel, she wrote that she could not believe she was 49, but that she looked forward to the next decade with some eagerness. "White hair, a calm philosophy, some extensive dental work, which will give me back my *radiant* smile; soft shawls of gray-blue, and a pliant mask (with a 'living face' behind it)—what fun!" (256–57) In this letter, she wrote of 50 as a "dreadful milestone." The Bogan wit is much in evidence here. One must read *all* her letters to appreciate how multifaceted Bogan's views on aging were. To be old means to fail to grow, she reflected, writing to May Sarton of her meeting in 1955 with Evelyn Scott. When she was in her thirties, Bogan recalled in this letter, she greatly feared the "dark and dank time" into which Scott had fallen (300). It was George Sand, whose love complemented Flaubert's sourness, that Bogan admired tremendously: "she was not an artist, but she was a big woman. . . . She went through a life that would have killed ten men, and at the end, at seventy, she was wonderful" (101). Bogan intended to put herself in training so that, if she were to have an old age, it would be like George Sand's. At the age of 50, Bogan wrote Zabel, "one has stories to tell." She wondered if she were "the girl to tell them" (258). At 51, she wrote him of financial pressures—she *had* to earn more money before she was 60. A year later, she wrote William Maxwell of the good news that Katherine White had accepted a poem, and remarked that this proves "that *women* can carry on to some slight degree, *in* their 50's!" (267n.) In 1950, she wrote Karl Shapiro that now that she was over 50, "I find that stray wisps of *theory* are beginning to form in my mind" (273).

But it would be a mistake to weave any theory about growing older from Bogan's writings, and to look for anything resembling a theory would be to misunderstand her genius completely. It is true that in her collected letters, and in Ruth Limmer's mosaic, *Journey Around My Room*, Bogan returned again and again to the great subject of aging. And it may be fair to say that for Bogan, changes in creative energy were the hinge of aging. (Of her six books of poetry, two—the *Collected Poems* and *The Blue Estuaries*—were published after she was 50, as were her three books of criticism, her four books of translations, and the anthology of poetry for young people.) Certainly, she believed that the wellsprings of poetic creativity are not intellectual but emotional and intuitive. And she believed that literary talent is a gift; inspiration comes when it will come, and not at any summoning by the writer. So it is with illuminations on this complicated business of growing older: they break into feeling and thought when they will, and not at the behest of some calendrical event. Because what she cared about was the experience itself, not any events giving rise to it, her writings on the subject of aging (she wrote about it often when she seemed to be writing of something else) are true to this experience—sometimes playful, sometimes serious, always intensely *aware*. It is enough—more than enough—that she wrote Zabel that in later life one ought to explore life's mystery and the mystery of the Self. (Bogan was well versed in Jungian psychology; there are references to it scattered throughout her letters, journal entries, and other writings.) For publications about milestones—turning 50, 60, 70, 75, 80—one must look elsewhere.

At 50, Dorothy Parker awakened knowing there was something terrible she had to remember. "Not just plain terrible. This was fancy terrible; this was terrible with raisins in it. Ah, yes, I have it. This is my birthday." *This* birthday was "the one that does it. You have said farewell to the thirties for the tenth and last time."[40] It had not done her much good to try to lie about her age. In the first place, she could not shave off more than a couple of years. In the second place, if she had moved away even to Trebizond, she would have met someone there who used to be in her class in school (schoolmates turn up everywhere). Middle Age had arrived, and it was the word "middle" that did it. "Any phrase it touches becomes the label of the frump" (596). If only she could leap ahead to 70, which has chic, or 80, which has elegance. Parker reminded herself that she was the same *inside*. Then, too, "You're the only one who is passionately interested in your age; other people have their own troubles" (596–97). One ought to think about all that is ahead in friendship and work and laughter, and even perhaps "a series of rather stately adventures." All the foolish mistakes, after all, have already been made. She bade Middle Age to enter, and looking straight at it, uttered this (Parkeresque) prayer, "*Oh, God help me . . . help me*" (597).

Dorothy Parker cried, "Promise me . . . I won't get old" when she already *was,* Lavinia Russ commented, and as for herself, she had always known she would be 60, and that her sixties would be "a proving ground" for her seventies and eighties.[41] Ever since the time Russ happened to see a hanging ruffle of flesh on the undersides of her Grammie's upper arm, and vowed no one would ever see her upper arms when *she* was old, Russ has been "an old lady watcher." She had been fascinated by old ladies since childhood— "crotchety or benign, feisty or serene, imperious or comic, they all seemed to be characters. . . . I loved them all" (4). Russ writes that she has enjoyed the seven years she has lived in her sixties because she has accepted the fact that she is an old lady. One may drift along being 40 for years, but eventually the time bubble bursts. It did for her when she was retired and would have no more paychecks after six weeks, and her wealth consisted of $37.50 in the bank and severance pay. Awakening with the panics, she had a clear vision of her mother, "a wild, zestful Irishwoman, . . . always on stage, and always stage center," and she vowed to her Ma that she would find a new part for herself to play (7). Since that time, Russ has been defining and redefining her role for the sixties. She recommends that women her age take a complete inventory of their resources so they can begin to create a new design for living. She cautions against "Boring From Within," by prefacing remarks with references to "*my* day," or by telling anecdotes betokening self-pity, or by making a novel of what ought to be a short narration. Habits can be "insufferable bores." A litany of gastronomical preferences and taboos is boring. And one ought to check the tendency "to make a David Merrick production out of an errand" (21). As women grow older, Russ observes, they "have a way of getting to look like men," a "tendency that can be minimized by feminine clothes and hair-dos" (26). Some women have mustaches and hair on chins and other areas of the face that they ought to attend to "unless they are stand-ins for Macbeth's witches" (31). Together with suggestions for attending to the matters of habit, dress, and finances, Russ's book contains a measure of moral instruction for older women, delivered lightly and humorously. "Motherhood doesn't make me eligible for a seat on Olympus," she remarks. It can turn a girl who was once free and happy-go-lucky "into a walking book of maxims and morals." The canard "that the act of giving birth transforms a girl into an all-wise Earth Mother . . . has turned many a young, exuberant girl into a guilt-ridden old hag" (98).

Writer Elizabeth Gray Vining kept a notebook about her seventieth year.[42] When in their thirties, Vining and a friend classified old ladies into four categories—"the Whiny Old Ladies, the Bossy Old Ladies, the Fussy Old Ladies, and the Batty Old Ladies" (30). Vining did not intend to live to old age, but she decided then that if she did, she would become a Batty Old Lady, and now she declares that is what she is. In re-reading old journals and notebooks, she found the entry in which she classified old ladies. She had written that she was sorry for them: "Failing faculties and failing looks must be a constant irritation to unfailing vanity." Even though "the answer to the riddle of life is so near," she had written years ago, they are only interested in "the satisfying of their own whims, their own comforts, the obtaining of admiring audiences." She had compared them with children because of their demanding ways; but, unlike children, they are still accustomed to being in authority. "One pities them, one loves and cherishes them, one can so rarely like them" (136). In retrospect, Vining found these to be harsh words; all the same, they were salutary for her at 70. She had not understood then the demoralizing effect of physical deterioration. The old ladies she knew then, her mother and an elderly aunt and cousin, had not dwelled on their physical problems. Now she perceived their gallantry. And there was a passage in that journal entry made at 31 that she found now to be wise and true. In it, she had praised the *joie de vivre* of some elderly women: "An old lady who has a genuine joy in living is an old lady who draws people to her. She is sufficient to herself. She has something to give—a gift the more precious and the more endearing because it is quite unconscious" (137).

This "business of growing old" has so many facets (133). Vining overheard one woman telling her friend that she did not want to live so long that someone would have to take care of her. She perceived an element of universal truth in that. "A whole generation of women, weary of caring for . . . parents, aunts, older sisters, looks with bleak eyes at their own prospects." Women whose daughters are very devoted are no longer so certain their children must and should care for them to the end. "The burden has become too heavy. It goes on too long" (12–13). Over the course of the year, Vining weighs the decision she needs to make about her own future: she could remain living where she is, or move to Kendal, the Quaker retirement community. She is alone, and only those with responsible family members "can afford to live dangerously" (29). On the other hand, even the finest retirement communities separate the elderly from the young. In the end, she decides to move to Kendal, but it is a difficult decision to make.

In her meditation on being 70, Vining makes a trip to Japan and observes that two of the week's best-sellers are books about aging. She reflects that the growing interest in aging on the part of younger people is new, and that the foresightedness of those now young may create a future for the aged far surpassing the conditions of life that now prevail. On her forty-fourth wedding anniversary, she reflects that her and her husband's love and the time they had together "were the greatest things in my life" (90). Widowed very young, after only four years of marriage, she feels she is more her husband's wife today than she was when they married in 1929, and that his love released her for further growth. When one is old, one can afford to be an observer. Contrary to popular thought, one still cares passionately about the world when one is old. She cares even more than she had when she was younger. And she does *not* face death every day. As for the darker aspects of aging, there is still shame. She is stricken with shame by her forgetfulness. And it is difficult to accept that one is not interesting to the young. The loneliness of old age is very real: one may be surrounded by people and have no one to talk to who will listen and respond. And when the age of temptation or commission of "the grosser sins" is past, "the hidden spiritual sins come flocking:

pride, envy, jealousy, anger, all forms of concealed unlovingness, and . . . hypocrisy" (85). She concludes that her continued growth will be on a course already set. To Vining, "We each have some earthly task to do, and when it is done, we go home. . . . The task . . . must be some inner act of growth, some hidden contract to be met, some ripening" (125–26). With age, acceptance of who one is has become a necessity. An old person must learn to expect pain and learn how to live one moment at a time. For Vining, there is meaning in the universe, and love is at its center.

"Milestones" was the title Eleanor Roosevelt chose for an account of her seventy-fifth birthday.[43] She looked back upon her life then, so that she might evaluate it and gain a perspective on it. She had never planned a career in life. Her objective was to live life as fully as possible and to use every opportunity to add to her knowledge of people and social conditions. It did not seem human to her to plan life from the beginning without making allowances for change or development in character or circumstances. When young, she wanted to do her duty as this was defined by others, for her greatest need then was for love and approval. In young womanhood, the focus of her strict sense of duty was her family, and she regretted having been "so concerned with bringing up my children properly that I was not wise enough just to love them" (412). In middle age, she found the courage to develop interests of her own. Her objective then was to learn, and she discovered that knowledge and understanding generate further knowledge and understanding, that the capacity grows with the exercise of the faculty. Long before she turned 75, she had known her overall objective in life, one rooted in all she had witnessed of the ravages in Europe after World War I: "I wanted, with all my heart, a peaceful world" (412). She devoted her later years to promoting understanding between peoples, for she believed this to be the only way to lasting world peace. She had always seen life in personal, human terms rather than in the abstract: "my interest or sympathy or indignation is not aroused by an abstract cause but by the plight of a single person whom I have seen with my own eyes." When she saw a child who was dying of hunger, "the tragedy of hunger" became of the greatest importance to her. "Out of my response to an individual develops an awareness of a problem to the community, then to the country, and finally to the world" (413). She had learned that one can only make a contribution to resolving world problems if one cares deeply about them and that this caring comes from the capacity for empathy. Her compassion, which was awakened in her childhood, began with a concern for the fate of individuals and extended to the fate of all humanity. "It is within that larger framework that one must think today if mankind is to survive the threat that hangs, in a mushroom cloud, over it" (414).

In 1938, Charlotte Conover's little book about being 80 was published with accolades from Eleanor Roosevelt, Booth Tarkington, and Bishop Henry Wise Hobson.[44] Conover concedes that one's eightieth birthday *is* "a sort of judgment day." She had always despised the forgetfulness of old people, and now finds that she, too, is forgetful. She, too, "makes other people trouble" and is guilty of slips of judgment. But she has a fervent affirmative answer to the question about whether or not there are compensations for being old. She believes one ought to engage in "armchair participation" in community and world affairs, so as to keep one's mental machinery in order and to keep from falling into "a fatal inferiority complex." A "humble octogenarian" testifies that life becomes more interesting with the years. Since her editor expected her to be didactic in her screed ("It's not much in my line, but I'll do my best"), she counsels younger people to cultivate imagination and appreciation, to begin to prepare for old age when still in youth.

Conover was soon to have a "chair" in a university for the education and enrichment of those over 60. The "entrance lobby" of her curriculum would be a department of Acquiescence or Resignation, and the curriculum would have two major divisions, Learning and Unlearning. The Unlearning would be of habits of mind grown rigid, for these are the great obstacles to world progress and creatures of these habits can be "a public menace." Intensive lectures on Gratitude were planned as supplementary to the Department of Resignation. Another department would be the Department of Bluff. Courses in Elementary Bluff and Advanced Bluff would serve as concomitants to the art of unlearning of old habits, as of locomotion. Most students "will save bones and money in discovering that the proper rate of progression for eighty is a ponderous carriage in rallentando tempo" The course of instruction would include a number of don'ts, prominent among them, "Don't contradict your grandchildren."

Conover was blind, and in "Signposts in the Dark" wrote about blindness at 80. For those for whom blindness is a New World, there are severe problems—being a trouble to others—and ludicrous problems—seeming to be impolite—that must be faced. The fixed, forced smile adopted to meet the latter, which Harvard students referred to then as the "dry grin," is a problem itself. For it is "apt to fall on the just and unjust alike." Conover warns that "an introduction is a pit in which many a blind person has been wrecked." She remembers once having politely excused herself to a side of beef she had inadvertently jostled in a crowded market. She advises the blind to be prepared for the unexpected "by-products" of their condition, among them defective hearing, difficulty in maintaining balance when walking, forced inactivity, and the lack of privacy: "From your underwear to your checkbook, everything is open to the world. Every letter to a dear and intimate friend has to go through the medium of a third person." Conover met her admission to the Kingdom of the Sudden Blind in late life with "the proud defiance of a thwarted human soul." She had been given intensive training, for her mother had been blind. Each thing must be kept in its place, for the only endurable life for the blind is "to do for one's self." The challenge "must be grasped like a nettle." She saw each challenge as "a hope, and hope means growth, and growth brings freedom of the soul." At the end of her book, Conover wrote that a minister—"who has seen many years, is tired, and perhaps has not too good health and is not too successful"—would be the right person to preach a sermon on her favorite text, "The Pools Are Filled With Water."

Retrospectives

In 1911, *Autobiography of an Elderly Woman* was first published. Vorse began writing some chapters for the book a few years before, when she was only in her twenties. Her mother was her model for the book, for she felt she knew exactly how her mother felt about aging.[45] The narrator sees her life divided into four parts: the years before she was married, which now seem to have been dreamed; the years of her marriage until the time when the oldest of her four children was almost grown and she was widowed; the time she lived as her children's comrade—the "middle way" she once thought would go on indefinitely; the time she became of another generation from that of her children: "they now are the strong, I the weak" (9). Everywhere, elderly mothers and their grown children are at war, "the children trying to dominate their parents with the end in view of making them take abnormal care of their health," and the parents "fighting ever more feebly and petulantly for their lost independence" (22–23). The parents chafe at the restrictions imposed by "watchful, devoted children" and fight "for the little glimmer of youth that is yet left them" (23). The narrator resists leading the packed-in-cotton-wool existence grown children and doctors want to impose on the old. Children want "to delay by their care the hour which they know must come, while we try to ignore its approach" (24). The old do not want to be reminded continually that their work in the world is over. Now, too late, she understands her own old mother's relief at being in her own familiar surroundings. Now she knows her mother's "very restlessness and occasional discontent were the signs that life was keen within her" (50). Grown children can be tyrannical. To one of her four alone, she is "the mother of younger years . . . to whom to turn for advice and strength, and I leap out to meet it" (243–44). Custom, too, can be a tyrant, and patronizing younger women sometimes hold opinions about how the elderly should live that are medieval. "I will not, at my time of life, have my individuality pruned and clipped" (68).

Age has its compensations. Old people are free to express their opinions, free from encumbering duties and oughts, free from senseless conventions as they had not been since childhood. At last there is time to do what one always wanted to do, and that is a "priceless gift," though one must contend with "the limitations of the flesh" (111, 120). And age has its deep sadness and its regrets. Awakening to the knowledge that one is on the descent is the epiphany of old age, all else thereafter proof of this. As one grows older, one sees ever more clearly how isolated the generations are from one another: one becomes a spectator of grown children's lives. One learns how useless it is to speak out about the needless suffering every generation endures. A mother

regrets that she did not treasure her children more when they were little. She
is never free of the burden of the feeling of responsibility for what her
children have become, a burden she carries to the end of her life. The narrator reflects that at every moment we are deciding what kind of an old
person we shall be. She sees vacancy or discontent on the faces of some old
people: "all these things bespeak a feebleness of the spirit. . . . There is
something in character that seems to survive even the mind" (248). She believes, "The question of growing old as one should is a very deep one . . . as
deep as life itself" (267).

In their letters and memoirs, women write of their losses. There were losses
by fire sustained with grace and courage by Louise Bogan, Welthy Honsinger
Fisher, Edna St. Vincent Millay, Margaret Sanger. Isadora Duncan and Margaret Sanger suffered the most grievous loss of all, the death of young children. "I believe," Duncan wrote, "that although one may seem to go on living,
there are some sorrows that kill."[46] Sanger had had terrible premonitions
about the date, November 6, when her daughter Peggy died in 1915. She
wrote that "joy in the fullness of life went out of it then and has never quite
returned." Her daughter lived in a "hidden realm" of Sanger's consciousness,
where she grew into womanhood and "leads an ideal existence untouched by
harsh actuality and disillusion."[47]

And some endured the great sorrow of widowhood—Vining and Vorse
when still young, Helene Deutsch and Pearl Buck in later life. Pearl Buck had
gone to Japan to work on the filming of her book, *The Big Wave*. In Tokyo one
morning at 5:00 A.M., she came awake, feeling she "had been summoned in
some way." When the call from her daughter came through some time later,
she knew, "The day I had dreaded had come. The final loneliness was
here."[48] Her husband's illness had brought in its wake a slow and irreversible
decline, a fading of perception, a loss of speech and language, a failure of
eyesight. There came a time when "the brain ceased to live except in sleep."
She had had seven years to prepare for the final loneliness that now was here.
She was grateful that he had not undergone a radical personality change, but
continued to be "what he had always been, lovable, patient, unwilling to cause
trouble" (60). And she was grateful that he "did not know of his own decline,"
for that would have caused him suffering (90).

"Long ago," Buck wrote, "when I knew my child was to be permanently
retarded, I learned that there are two kinds of sorrow, one which can be
assuaged and one which cannot be assuaged" (72). She had learned how to
accept, first by yielding oneself to the situation physically, then spiritually;
then, "to recognize inexorability" (73). And this cannot be done at once. She
addresses the women who may read her book when she writes of the "silent
last moment" when the dead must be left and one must return to the empty
house: "I can only say there is no escape from such moments. . . . They must
be lived through, not once but many times in memory. I have been told that
they grow easier. I do not find it so" (96).

Afterwards, Buck reflected that she had always known that it would be she and not her husband who would be widowed, and after she returned to Japan, she asked herself if she should contemplate the possibility of life after death. Lying on her bed, "I fought off the mighty yearning to go in search of him. . . . For surely he was looking for me, too. We were ill at ease, always, when apart. But what are the pathways?" (181) And there came a moment when she knew that he was dead, that there would not be communication between them, a moment when she knew "he was neither awake nor aware" or he would have found a way to respond to her overwhelming need to share a stunning experience with him (226). She felt the "desperate weariness" of acceptance; she knew now that, "There is an eternity where one walks alone and we do not know its end" (227). In the days thereafter, she experienced "a profound insurge of peace," a healing sense that she was part of all things. Then, when she returned to New York, it happened that she was given a sign that she might be in communication with her father, long dead and buried in China. And she asked herself how she could dare to say that they were *not* in communication. She believed there will come a day when we shall know, and that this will not be through a miracle but through learning how it is done. A scientist might receive the proof. Or "a woman, waiting at a window open to the sky" (256).

"It is because of bereavement that I now have time," Margaret Anderson wrote.[49] She imagines someone arguing that she must come to Paris where "we should all be together as we grow older." The imaginary debater warns that she will become "a melancholy shadow" and talk to herself if she goes on living as a recluse in Le Cannet (215). But Anderson will not become a shadow, but a source. She *wants* to live alone; she does not want to merge her life with others:

> I drink a cinzano with Monique in the garden, eat an omelet. . . . We sit in silence as night comes on. . . . I read, without interruption—no telephone, no television, no neighbours. I take another walk. I contemplate. . . . Why am I "happy?" What are my inner springs that keep rewinding themselves? Why am I so immensely contented living as I do in serenity, seclusion, solitude? . . . Why do I feel like a source of life? [203]

She was born to be 40 years old, Anderson wrote; if only she could have remained 40 years young for a thousand years! It would be unnatural to die; she longs not to die: "I am still looking and feeling and thinking with an endless energy that is like an exercise in delight." She keeps a photograph of her younger self on a table "as a defiance to time and fading" (194). Anderson, who founded the *Little Review,* was an "appreciator," grateful that five of her great friends were born writers. She doubts that she will ever find a great friend again, even if she lived another 20 years, because a great friendship takes so long to build. And if she dies now, she would die knowing there were still three people on earth who would say "the difference to me."

Margaret Anderson lives on in Normandy, Alice B. Toklas wrote in a letter to Annette Rosenshine in 1949, "much quieter than formerly but quite as beautiful," so she had been told by someone who had seen her recently.[50] In 1948, Toklas wrote this same correspondent how shocked she had been to read of Gertrude Atherton's death, "for though she was very very old one thought of her as going on forever." When Toklas and Gertrude Stein had seen Atherton in 1935, "she was then well over seventy and very beautiful in an outrageously pale blue dress." Both Toklas and Stein had felt enthusiasm for Atherton's novels, and Toklas had reread them during the Occupation, "and was surprised and delighted to find how successfully she wrote. Though markedly dated they held one's attention to the end—she had something of the grand manner" (124). Toklas "stayed on alone" for 21 years after Stein's death, and died shortly before her ninetieth birthday. Of her own old age, Gilbert A. Harrison recalled that she would be taken out to lunch by a caller after she could no longer cook. In her eighties, she had an eye operation that enabled her to read with the help of a huge magnifying glass. "A chain smoker, she gave up cigarettes at 87. By then she could no longer walk. The white poodle, Basket II, was dead. The Paris winters had turned colder" (xvi). Toklas, who said she had been baptized as a child, was admitted to the Roman Catholic Church in 1957. She took great comfort in her faith that Gertrude Stein was in "life everlasting . . . there waiting for us" (364).

On women's writing of the physical changes and losses that come with aging, I have found nothing that rivals the calm, unflinching, and wholly objective appraisal of the face and body in the mirror made by Athena Tacha. Tacha, who is a sculptor who has planned large-scale earth and architectural projects, has been watching for the signs of aging since she was a high school student. In her account of the changes she had observed on her face, neck, and body, she wrote of her disbelief when she found the first few white hairs on her head. "Half of my life gone, this is the point of reaching maturity, I guess," she concluded. "The other half will be the way to old age and death."[51] A beautiful woman is a rarity, and for such a woman, aging can be tragic. A woman who was born homely might have an altogether different feeling about her looks as she grows older. "Every girl who lacks beauty knows instinctively that she belongs to an underprivileged group," Catherine Drinker Bowen writes, "and that to climb up and out she will have to be cleverer and stronger and more ruthless perhaps than she would choose to be." A number of notable women had spoken to Bowen about this, among them Agnes de Mille, who had said that "the condition made her fiercely ambitious. . . . Lack of looks was a spur." Bowen remarked, "Oddly enough, women who use their talents to the full become handsome in later life; they grow to a special beauty of their own. Perhaps fury gives them stature . . . rebellion quickens all their movements and their faculties."[52] The reader of Eleanor Roosevelt's autobiography cannot fail to perceive how wounding it was for her that she could never be the belle and beauty her mother had wanted her to be. She referred to herself as an "ugly duckling." Even in maturity, she was haunted by self-consciousness about her looks. "Luckily for them all," she wrote, "the children have inherited their looks from their father's side of the family."[53] But there are those who would say that she became more handsome as she grew older, and there are others who would remark that beauty is more than a matter of appearances. Many women dread growing older because they fear that the physical changes aging brings may cost them physical love. A woman facing middle age, poet Gwendolyn Brooks writes, "is resentful. Love of all kinds, she feels, is gone forever. She shivers. She knows it is fall, and that winter is on the way. She feels done and dusty."[54] Fortunate the older woman who desires and is desired! All too many believe that lovemaking comes to an end in middle age. How wrong they are, Isadora Duncan wrote. She felt pity for

> those poor women whose pallid, narrow creed precludes them from the magnificent and generous gift of the Autumn of Love. Such was my poor Mother, and to this absurd prejudice she owed the aging and illness of her body at the epoch when it should have been most splendid, and the partial collapse of a brain which had been magnificent. I was once the timid prey, then the aggressive Bacchante, but now I close over my lover as the sea over a bold swimmer, . . . encircling him in waves of cloud and fire.[55]

Anaïs Nin, born in 1903, was middle-aged when she wrote the last four volumes of her diaries. In the entries she made in her forties, she does not mention her chronological age, but writes of youth and age instead. She experienced a conflict "between the openness of the young, their curiosity, exploration, receptivity, playfulness, nimbleness, as against the heavy, opaque, solid, immovable mass of maturity I meet at parties."[56] She writes of the passage of time as "deterioration, loss, shriveling" (26). For Nin, the young have a quality of luminosity, even transparency. They are elusive and tender, vulnerable and spontaneous. They are spiritual. And age means denseness, opacity. In the presence of the mature, she feels "their rigidities, their tight crystallizations. They have become, at least in my eyes, like the statues of the famous. Achieved. Final" (64). She was attracted to the young not because she wanted to protect or to guide them, but "because I feel as they do, act and think as they do." All the while, she played "the wise mother" or "the clear-sighted muse" or the "mature and stable woman" (95). The young are fluid, always becoming; they fascinate her because they are still in the process of growing and changing. They are compelling because of the mystery of what they will become.

Creativity is the working of magic, transformative powers: creation of the Now, the present moment, creation of one's own myth, transformation of sorrow and grief into art. Nin wrote of change as continuous:

> Changes occur constantly according to the vision, image, or myth which possesses one. We do not grow absolutely, chronologically. We grow some-times in one dimension, and not in another, unevenly. . . . We are relative. We are mature in one realm, childish in another. The past, present, and future mingle. . . . We never discard our childhood. . . . We relive fragments of it through others. We live buried layers through others. We live through others' projections of the unlived selves. [127]

Nin believed that the task of every person was to work on her or his individual development. She believed each person must continue to grow, influencing history "from within," rather than through systems (9). She thought
that we must learn how to restore wholeness and that the whole person is
dismembered if that person is seen only from the point of view of analytical
rationality. She wrote of the need to find passion and faith, and to rediscover
how to live the life of the senses and the life of feeling. In her view, we must
confront the whole of our nature and face the dark otherness within that she
had heard Esther Harding speak of as the "shadow" (59). She perceived that
those who deny the darkness within are dangerous, since they project what
they deny: "Those who suffer from inner disturbances are contagious" (79).
"The psychologists," she wrote, "are doing the only constructive work in the
world" (120).

Much as Nin loved youth for its clear vision, she recognized when she was in
her early forties that the generations need one another. "The young's attraction for the old is for the protection of their future," she wrote. "The need of
faith and the elder's vision into the future" (127). Soon after she turned 50,
she wrote that "compassion for our parents is the true sign of maturity." And
a few years later, she wrote "Aging can be a concession to the inevitable
withering, but each line can be a line of meaning, like a scroll, like the aging of
wood or statues." Then in her middle fifties, she reflected, "I thought aging
meant the loss of sensibilities, of vibrations, but I feel more intensely alive
than ever." In her seventies, she wrote, "I have spent much of my time seeking
to help women overcome the fear of aging."[57]

Gertrude Stein once said to Welthy Fisher, "There is no such thing as
middle age, old age and youth. We are all contemporaries. We all have to
adjust or we're already dead."[58] Yes and no. Yes, all who are alive on this
earth are contemporaries. But, no, youth is *not* middle age, nor are either the
last phase of the cycle. Each is part of the whole—but a separate part. Later
life has possibilities of its own, and perhaps the most resplendent of these is
valor. Writer and editor Irene Kittle Kamp has valor. Kamp had to have her
nose surgically removed because of cancer. Yet she told her doctor she loves
being old: "I love the relaxed, wry, amused knowledge which comes to the old
that . . . so very much is of no importance whatsoever," she said. "I think and
read and ponder small and large matters in a clearer, less agonizing way than
ever." Kamp believes the things in her head are better ordered than they ever
were before. "But the body—aye, there's the rub. You have all this lovely
acceptance, affection, forgiveness, but you don't always have the strength to
put it to work."[59]

Pretty-Shield, Medicine Woman of the Crows, had valor, too. She spoke in
signs, half to herself, half to Frank Linderman, of her worries for her grandchildren, whom she might have to leave "any day now."[60] Linderman marveled at her will power. He thought, "Old age will have a tussle with *you*." For
she was almost twice as old as their interpreter, Goes-together, who often
complained of her physical problems. Yet she "had nothing to complain of, no

affliction, excepting grandchildren; and this was an affliction of simple-hearted love" (74). As a child, Pretty-Shield heard the women mourning, and she wept. "I knew, even then, that some day I should mourn, and that like them I should feel myself to be alone on the world" (129). But she had always liked to laugh, and often now, she laughs when she is alone. "Our hearts stay young if we let them," she said (86). Linderman had been deeply moved by her moral courage and her love for her grandchildren. At the close of his transcription of the story she had told him in signs, he wrote of Pretty-Shield, "May her moccasins make tracks in many snows that are yet to come" (253).

Women's Reflections on Memory

One summer night in Merriewold in 1914, Agnes de Mille promised herself she would never forget *this* moment. And she kept her promise. In the radiance and rapture of this memoir, all the restorative powers of memory are affirmed. The drinking water was "alive, . . . rocky, delicious as the air which was new and fern-fresh. You took a breath and flew. . . . It cleared the head like snuff, colors deepened, hearing sharpened." At Merriewold, "You heard with your skin; you breathed light and shade. . . . And you were free."[61] There, "Days followed days, summer followed summer in the idyllic, dream-like tranquility, amid the fragmentary glimpses of white dresses and parasols down green and shadowed vistas, the flash of color as a kerchief showed through the hedges, the sound of the swish of twig brooms, high voices calling" (191). The meaning of Merriewold was that "Mother and Father loved absolutely . . . this green secret; this expectancy." There was "the look he bent upon her, and the blue dazzle of her return gaze. The whole forest quickened for me. . . . Everything was beginning and the good, free summer lay ahead" (20). That fall, when they were leaving Merriewold for California, they could all feel how things were changing. De Mille did not want change; she did not want to grow older. They all sensed that autumn of 1914 would be the last. "Silently, all through the windless air, the yellow leaves drifted down, golden, golden, falling forever. They made a sound like a pricking, a sort of tinkling. It was the sound of time." (281)

It may be, de Mille thought, that like sound, like light, events leave their imprints on the atmosphere, and one day we shall find the way to read back through them. I, too, believe this; but until then we have only the old ways of "memorizing," of "learning by heart," of *committing* things to memory. Dorothy Day and her sister kept notebooks when they were young, as much for the sake of present life as for the sake of redeeming time past. "Recording happiness made it last longer, we felt, and recording sorrow dramatized it and took away its bitterness; and often we settled some problem which beset us, even while we wrote about it."[62] Ilka Chase was in awe of those who save letters, and even more awed by those who keep diaries. She did not have much of a collection of papers to use as sources for her autobiography.

"Either my friends don't go away, or if they do they are wretched correspondents." In any case, Chase remarked, there is a dearth of letters since American Tel and Tel arrived and prospered. "I dare say the Messrs. Plutarch, Boswell, and their ilk wouldn't have been so glib with their reminiscences if all they had had to go on were a few remembered phone calls and here and there a telegram"[63] Then, too, Chase had a healthy respect for the mischief that could be wrought by blackmailers. But Margaret Sanger thought that perspective becomes "far-sweeping" as one ages, and details become misty. She thought perhaps there ought to be "a school course to emphasize the importance of keeping diaries, so that you would know the really momentous happenings to put down."[64] When she had to repeat verses of the New Testament in French as a young girl, Eleanor Roosevelt thought this to be "a great waste of time, but later found very useful the well-trained memory which all this learning things by heart gave me."[65] Edna St. Vincent Millay's Conversation at Midnight poems were all destroyed by fire. "Fortunately, I have a very good memory," she wrote in a letter, "and have been able to recall all those that were completed; but with those on which I was still at work I have been having an exhausting and nerve-wracking time."[66]

But memory can be a trickster, a being with a will of its own and its own secret ways of working. "Where in the brain, I wonder, is memory seated?" Virgilia Peterson wrote. "Does anyone understand why it sleeps and why it wakes?" She wondered, too, at "how widely people differ . . . in their ability to consign memory to . . . artificial sleep!" There are those who "appear to have mastered the technique of forgetting, and I say 'appear to have mastered' advisedly," for while a thing may appear to have been lost, "it can only be mislaid, there being no real limbo for memory."[67] To those who approach memory for the purpose of vivisection, it can be unyielding, it can turn itself into stone. Helen Keller thought that "it is impossible to analyze honestly the subtle motives of those who have influenced our lives, because we cannot complete the creative process with the freshness of the situation clinging to it. Analysis is as destructive of emotion as of the flower which the botanist pulls to pieces."[68] Creative memory works in its own way, Mary Austin reflected, "blazing out for itself incidents to serve as perpetual markers for rewarding starts and excursions."[69]

The stuff of dreams even is more tangible than memory, Isadora Duncan reflected. Ilka Chase found it strange to look back over all that happened in one's life, "after the future has become the past," and to foresee from the past, to have the belated gift of clairvoyance. To her, this affirms the simultaneity of past, present, and future. Yet she wrote of a day of peace and pleasure in her life that it was "caught in my memory like a fly in amber."[70] Rose Pesotta began her autobiography by recreating events in the past that were decisive for her. In the first chapter of her book, she shuttles back and forth in time. Of the night her father was shot, she wrote, "Terror comes to my home-town. 'General' Petlura's 'army' of hooligans, both anti-Bolshevik and anti-Semitic, sweeps into Derazhnia in the night like a swarm of rats. There are heavy footsteps on the porch of my family's home."[71] What wand arouses this being from its slumber? Edna St. Vincent Millay looked at photographs of the three houses where she lived in Camden: "And one exciting memory after another fills my mind as I look."[72] Pearl Bailey had only to say she intended to write a book about her life when she began to relive it: "I was standing on the corner in Newport News. . . . I was on the coal circuit playing rummy in the back room. . . . Once again, I could hear the screaming for encores with the USO in Texas. All of it came right back."[73] As she was writing about her beloved friend, Alexander Graham Bell, Helen Keller had this experience: "Little incidents that I have not thought of in years come back to me now as if they had been written on the pages of my mind in secret ink."[74] Pretty-Shield told Linderman she was beginning to like the work of remembering. "It is like looking for things in a bag. I just feel around till I find something."[75] Yet there were other things she willed to forget that would not be forgotten—"it stays in my mind as though I wished to keep it there," she said of a dread time she had "tried to forget" (82). When she told a happier story, Linderman saw how "her eyes brightened by remembrance" (205).

Young people think the past is "a fixed quantity," but it is as insecure as the future is insecure. As time changes, all that is *of* time and *in* time changes, and the meaning and value of events are interwoven with "the personality they visit. . . . Mysterious is the past and strange and fortuitous. It veils its face like the future. We cannot remember what we will; we forget the very things that we have loved and felt and suffered."[76] This is the beast and the god, the demon and the angel with whom the writer must wrestle; this is the Muse the writer implores, "Speak, Memory." And I believe that every person on earth wills to be the author of his or her own life, and that this will has its greatest force in old age. It is then one feels that the key *must* be found. When Edna Ferber was writing of the Mississippi River at floodtime in the early chapters of *Show Boat,* she did not consult books or interview "old-timers." She simply took her childhood memories of both the Mississippi River and the Des Moines River at floodtime "out of the back of my head where they had been neatly stored for so many years and pinned them down on paper." In this passage, Ferber mentioned the odd sensation most writers have of *knowing* what they are writing about, even though they have had no experience of it. The thing is "writing itself." How is this possible? It is because whatever happens to the professional writer goes "into the attic." She called to mind "a shabby old yellow trunk kept in the storeroom of the Ferber household in my childhood. When you lifted the rickety lid there was wafted to you the mingled odor of mothballs, lavender, faint perfumery, dyes, and the ghostly emanation peculiar to castoff garments."[77]

Ferber thought that memory may at times extend far back beyond a person's lifetime experiences. It was of this "almost mystical sense of the life common to all the centuries" that Jane Addams wrote in *The Long Road of Woman's Memory,* of this "and of the unceasing human endeavor to penetrate into the unseen world." Through responses of memory to "racial records," one perceives the growth within of this sense. And these records point the way to "a past so vast that the present generation seems to float upon its surface."[78] Early in this century, old women flocked to Chicago's Hull-House to see the Devil Baby rumored to be there. Many of these impoverished visitors "had been forced to face tragic experiences, the powers of brutality and horror had had full scope in their lives and for years they had had acquaintance with disaster and death" (10). Addams understood that "our chief concern with the past is not what we have done, nor the adventures we have met, but the moral reaction of bygone events within ourselves" (101). Listening to the old women's story about the Devil Baby, she thought that the tale might "condense that mystical wisdom which becomes deposited in the heart of man by unnoticed innumerable experiences." She understood that, for these women, a story such as that of the Devil Baby serves as the most effective means of giving domestic moral instruction (9). The legend was that a man had committed a hideous crime years before marrying an innocent young woman, and had not confessed this crime to her; he had deceived both her and the priest who performed the marriage ceremony. And his sin had become incarnated in his child, a Devil Baby born to the trusting mother. To the old women, "this simple tale, with its direct connection . . . between wrong-doing and punishment, brought soothing and relief, and restored a shaken confidence as to the righteousness of the universe." They used it "to tame restless husbands" and to warn young daughters who might wander off with strangers (32). The story loosed the tongues of the old women. Some, "under the domination of that mysterious autobiographical impulse which makes it more difficult to conceal the truth than to avow it, purged their souls in all sincerity and unconsciously made plain the part borne in their hard lives by monstrous social injustices" (xii–xiii). Memory, Addams reflected, has an inherent power to sift and to reconcile. She realized "that old age has its own expression for the mystic renunciation of the world." The old woman's impatience with all that is not essential brought Tolstoy's last journey to mind again. And she saw in these careworn old women a vast emotional serenity. She saw the appeasing working of Memory in them "with its ultimate power to increase the elements of beauty and significance and to reduce . . . all sense of resentment" (22–24).

Old people who have suffered greatly may idealize the past. This transmutation of what they have experienced may be traced to a power inherent in memory. Memory works to interpret and appease the life of a person, and as a selective agency in social reorganization. Addams discovered that the two functions may support one another (xiii). But sometimes, one may be sacrificed for the other. In war-ravaged Europe, she discovered Memory will insist "upon the great essentials, even to the complete sacrifice of its inherent power to appease." Women who had lost all they had loved "sat shelterless in the devastating glare of Memory. Because by its pitiless light they were forced to look into the black depths of primitive human nature," one of them would from time to time "ignore the strident claims of the present and would insist that the war was cutting at the very taproots of the basic human relations so vitally necessary to the survival of civilization" (xiv). As if by instinct, Addams thought, the haunting memories of women "challenge war as the implacable enemy of their age-long undertaking" (140).

War, Helene Deutsch wrote, "the horrible despot that ignores all biological, social, and psychological problems in pursuit of its own deadly aims, automatically solved for me the problem of women's proper place in society."[79] It so happened that doctors were needed at the time of World War I, and Deutsch was a doctor, and she felt the obligation to serve. In her autobiography, Deutsch "confronts" herself, not only as a professional woman, but as daughter and student and friend and lover, as wife and mother and grandmother—the "Gruhu," the Babayaga:

> Babayaga is *me*, and the legend of this Polish witch leads directly back to my childhood. In Polish folklore, Babayaga is a good witch who is especially kind to children; she is also a rustic witch, usually seen carrying on her back a load of wood, and sometimes children. Thus both my love for my grandchildren and my fantasies about being a country woman have fitted in very well with this figure; she is the prototype of the kind grandmother. [194]

Deutsch looks at her earlier self with the objectivity of an old person and discerns the forces that were at work in a relationship. Some recollections do not flow freely for her, and she comments on this. She writes why she believes herself to be objective about certain matters. She expresses astonishment at the precision of her memory in restoring details that are seemingly not important. Where her memories are fragmentary and anecdotal, she remarks what this may imply about the meaning the experiences had for her. And when she sees a scene clearly over the span of eighty years, and knows that some aspect of the memory must be false, she searches out the reason for this. In this instance, she found that her present loneliness and her "ceaseless mourning" for her husband "are visibly influencing the associative course of my memories," and she perceives a resemblance between the workings of memory and the workings of dreams (53).

As she wrote, Deutsch had the experience that "more and more memories emerge from the amnesia that seemed, during my psychoanalysis, to have buried deeply the first five years of my life" (48). She believed there are certain distinctive psychobiological conditions that obtain when old people write their memoirs. "The process of sublimation active in the writing of autobiography and the weakening of sexual impulses create an atmosphere for the free welling-up of memories." Furthermore, the punitive force of the superego is on the wane, and the sense that death is nearing opens the way even more widely for the past to return (13). While a long life ought to confer objectivity on the memoirist, there is a possibility that psychic distortions may be at work because of the weakening of the sense of identity. Deutsch provides the example of the old person's tendency toward paranoia. Then, too, an old person wants to defend and protect against losses. "It is a great psychic achievement," she writes, "to accept the disillusioning present just as it is, yet at the same time preserve the values that still remain" (14).

In her aloneness and loneliness, Deutsch felt a great need to set her past life and her past self down in writing. She wanted to relive the achievements and disappointments of her life and set them down *sine ira et studio* in autobiographical form. She draws a contrast between psychoanalysis and the writing of memoirs: free association is the essence of the former, whereas there is much firmer self-control in the writing of autobiography. Therefore, she was amazed when memories she recognized as "long buried beyond the reach of consciousness" returned so readily as she was writing (15). In the course of her writing, she had recollections from which she sometimes learned more about herself than she had learned from psychoanalysis. She concluded that "memories loaded with guilt feelings offer less resistance if they are called up in the course of autobiography as an objective historical report on oneself" (16). Deutsch's life was enhanced immensely through the writing of her memoirs, and she attributes this to "the memory process itself: the intense emotions that arise when we meet or confront once more the loved and hated figures of the past" (15). She has identified certain patterns in her life from childhood to old age in this work. She believes that the biological destiny of old age, as that for all the developmental phases of the life cycle, is strongly influenced by the events of adolescence. She writes that her own *Sturm und Drang* period, which went on far into her mature years, "is still alive within me and refuses to come to an end" (216). She found it easier to write about the past than about her present life, for she felt there had been a mellowing of her experiences by "the patina of time," and that owing to this she was less inclined to blame others and more tolerant of her own flaws (213). She still loves, and she feels loved, even though "old people are seldom loved; they bear too much of *memento mori.*" In bringing many "ghosts of the past" to life again through writing her autobiography, she found they had never really left her, that "they have become part of me" (215). There is a fortune for gerontologists in this memoir, for it is a meditation on the very process of writing autobiography and, through that, on Memory itself.

Forms and Transformations, Truths and Fictions

History is the other side of the fabric of these memoirs and reflections, and in reading them I have unearthed a lodestone for a dissertation on twentieth-century America as seen through women's eyes. The works by Jane Addams, Dorothy Day, Mother Jones, Rose Pesotta, Eleanor Roosevelt, Margaret Sanger, and Mary Vorse are rich with lore for the labor historian and the social historian. Ilka Chase's autobiography and the letters of Edna St. Vincent Millay are excellent references for those interested in the age of radio in America. Mary Austin's *Earth Horizon* is a treasury of fact and commentaries

on American family history, on widowhood in America, on Chautauqua, Prohibition—and even the Whatnot: "I am sure if I had a proper Whatnot at
hand, I could lead you by it through the whole aesthetic history of the Mid-
dlewest."[80] Indeed, there were more discoveries in my research than could be
contained here. Mary Anderson's autobiography provides a history of the
Women's Bureau, and presents a cogent argument opposing the theory that
women work for "pin money."[81] And Helen Bevington's memoir vividly
evokes the post–World War II years and the period of the McCarthy witch
hunt.[82] Those interested in the history of medicine in the United States would
not want to miss Bertha Van Hoosen's discussion of "twilight sleep"
(scopolamine-morphine anaesthetic) in her *Petticoat Surgeon*. Then, too, the
names of some of the most distinguished figures of nineteenth- and twentieth-
century America appear in the pages of these books and personal papers, not
only as friends (Mark Twain was one of Helen Keller's cherished friends), but
as kin (Agnes de Mille's grandfather was Henry George of the "Single Tax"
theory). And the paths of many of these women crossed: Mary Austin knew
Vorse; Vorse worked with Sanger and Mother Jones; Bogan corresponded
with Harriet Monroe and, through correspondence with her friend Ruth
Benedict, kept abreast of the news of Margaret Mead's activities. Van Hoosen
did not know Isadora Duncan, but in her autobiography, she writes the story
of how she decided to go early and fight with the mob to get a seat in the
gallery of Orchestra Hall when Duncan performed there in Chicago. Van
Hoosen saw a few patients, rushed to the hall, stood in line for nearly half an
hour, ran up five flights of steps and then down the steps of the gallery and
left her bag and coat on a seat. Then she ran back to her office and saw the
patients who were waiting for her. At 2:30, she dashed back to Orchestra Hall,
ran the five blocks, climbed five flights of steps two at a time, and found her
seat to be the only one not occupied. "Time never passed more quickly—all
eyes riveted on her every movement. . . . Her audience held her like a passionate lover who refuses to say good-by."[83]

Autobiographies, diaries, essays, journals, letters, notebooks, memoirs, and
meditations on aging: these are all forms of literature, all "sources." Yet, one
genre may contain fragments of another, or one form may flow into another.
Autobiographies may contain fragments of diaries. I have found letters in
diaries, recipes in (Toklas's) letters, references to lists of poems entered in old
diaries in (Monroe's) autobiography. Who can say what the odyssey of a paper
will be? Dorothy Day recalls a letter received from a reader of *The Catholic
Worker* in the state of Sonora in Mexico, who said he

> had tossed in an uncomfortable bed on a hot night until he got up to turn
> over the mattress and under it found a copy of *The Catholic Worker*. A miner
> found a copy five miles underground in an old mine that stretched out
> under the Atlantic Ocean off Nova Scotia. A seminarian said that he had
> sent out his shoes to be half-soled in Rome and they came back to him
> wrapped in a copy of *The Catholic Worker*.[84]

And the form in which the story is told, the moral lesson taught, makes all the difference in how it is received. Eleanor Roosevelt wrote that she had the instincts of a novelist; when hearing a story told to her in outline, she built up in her mind all that was unsaid.[85] Gwendolyn Brooks believes that "An auto-biographical novel . . . is a better testament . . . than a memoir."[86] Then, too, there are all the blank spaces in the record of a human life, whether kept by that person or by another. Ruth Limmer notes that Bogan's collected letters are but a sampling of a much more extensive correspondence, and that, although Bogan "used postcards with delight and abandon," almost none of these has been included in the collection.[87] As for Edna St. Vincent Millay, her husband, Eugen Boissevain, assumed much of her correspondence after her marriage, to leave her free for her work.[88] And, anyway, Millay said she had a severe case of *epistolaphobia;* there was almost nothing on earth she would rather not do than write a letter: "I would rather lay a pipe-line; I would rather dig a grave" (332). There are other reasons that autobiographical sources are altered. Nancy Oestreich Lurie reports that there were special difficulties in translating the tape-recorded accounts made of her life by Mountain Wolf Woman because of initial uncertainty with the microphone. "Thus, my translation is primarily an effort to make her meaning clear rather than a close translation of her every word."[89] Finally, there is the intention of the writer to be considered. Ferber commented on an inundation of the United States by autobiographies. This was in the 1930s, and fifty years later, the country is still being flooded with first-person life stories. The wheat, of course, must be sorted from the chaff. One indication of a memoirist's intentions is the choice of a title for the book. Perhaps another is the number of photographs included in its pages.

"What a word is truth," Lillian Hellman writes. "Slippery, tricky, unreli-able."[90] Many of the women whose memoirs I have read expressed much the same thought. Even a diary, Käthe Kollwitz wrote, presents a half-truth.[91] And an old person may find it was another person who wrote his or her early diaries: "I am not who I was and there's no mistake about it, because the young man I was is plain to see in my diaries."[92] So did an elderly man speak of his former self to Ronald Blythe. As for the "loss" of memory, Vida Scud-der wrote at the age of 70 that she did not think it necessarily portends the loss of one's very being. Scudder thought there is reason to believe that memory that seems to be gone is *suspended,* and she wrote that she knew of two cases in which a mind was radiantly restored. In both cases, as death approached, every detail of past and present life shone forth clearly. To Scudder this was convincing proof of immortality.[93]

In his classic work *Senescence,* Hall wrote that "resistances to anything like confessionalism increase with age."[94] For some, this resistance may be due to a strong feeling of moral responsibilities for other people whose privacy ought to be respected. Scott-Maxwell wrote, "One cannot be honest even at the end of one's life, for no one is wholly alone."[95] And Margaret Mead wrote a thoughtful epilogue to her autobiography on the moral responsibilities of the memoirist.[96] On the other hand, as Deutsch's memoir suggests, there is much conjuring up in the writing of an autobiography. There is a quality of unexpectedness about the activity. Who can say what—or who—may be resurrected when the ashes are stirred? Linderman once had the impression that Pretty-Shield was addressing the shade of her husband as she talked with him. Mary McCarthy felt "a distinct uneasiness," as she began writing about her deceased grandmother, "as though her shade were interposing to forbid me."[97]

For many, the symbiotic bond between mother and daughter that is the subject of Nancy Friday's *My Mother/My Self*[98] holds fast even until the end of life. I have found the most profound exploration of this subject to be Stephanie Demetrakopoulos's essay on the realm of the matriarchate in women's autobiography.[99] "Women," she writes, "derive a sense of feminine godhead from their biological connections with one another" (180). Throughout a child's life in the home, the influence of the mother is much stronger for a daughter than for a son. And only woman *directly* experiences matrilineal consciousness, that is, "the mother/daughter patterning of generations" perceived by Jung and Kerenyi in their writings on the Eleusinian mysteries. Demetrakopoulos finds that autobiographies by women, especially those by American women, "recount this Demeter/Kore matrix of being" (181). A son can achieve a sense of separate selfhood without bringing the influence of the mother into consciousness; indeed, he must reject her and the entire realm of the matriarchate if he is to individuate. Although some psychohistorians believe that the influence of the mother in shaping the personality of the male autobiographer is much greater than has been appreciated (even by himself), "the struggle to extricate and separate the self from the mother is not a struggle for a man in the way it usually is for a woman" (182). Demetrakopoulos suggests that the emphasis on their mothers that is found in women's autobiographies may be attributed to aspects of the woman's psyche that are innate and archetypal and that were given expression in the Eleusinian rites. She suggests that there is a vacuum in our collective sense of identity, whether we are women or men, and that it is being filled by those autobiographies by women in which the realm of the matriarchate is "the bedrock out of which a woman forges her identity." She writes that coming to terms with the forces of this realm is much more important to women than to men, that women "are signing up in droves for courses on women's autobiography," and that "woman's mythos is taking shape as women present their lives and persons for public scrutiny" (183).

Demetrakopoulos perceives that the archetype of a matriarchate encompassing four generations is the bedrock of Margaret Mead's *Blackberry Winter*. Mead's "sense of transcendence, yet loving understanding of process, is consolidated by her experience of the last transformations of the Demeter/Persephone myth, in which finally the daughter (Kore or Persephone) gives birth to a child" (190). This archetype, which is evoked in da Vinci's St. Anne, is "of the endless chain of mothers/daughters" and it "underlies a woman's sense of kinship." By her trust and her adherence to this force throughout her life, Mead has shown "how it helps the personality 'unfold.'" In Demetrakopoulos's view, the life Margaret Mead lived shows "that one need not separate from the matriarchate in order to develop, to self-actualize fully; her life proves that a woman can individuate without rejection of the matriarchate. Indeed, rich and full development can come by remaining always rooted into it" (190).

In her essay, Demetrakopoulos perceives the resemblance between Maxine Hong Kingston's "vision of interconnected, acausal transcendent reality," Margaret Mead's experience when her granddaughter was born, and Anaïs Nin's experience of the archetype of the Sophia, and she writes that Jung's insights into the Eleusinian mysteries may be among his most brilliant analyses. She recalls that Kerenyi wrote that participation in these mysteries offered men as well as women "a guarantee of life without fear of death, of confidence in the face of death," and interprets this to mean that

> the symbol of matrilineal ongoingness symbolizes hope for immortality, the continuity of the individual life. Men obviously stand apart in this mother /daughter duality although they clearly respond to the image. It is the privilege of women to present the image and to embody the consciousness toward which the image strives. The energy with which women autobiographers are analyzing and establishing their matrilineal roots seems the clearest and perhaps most publicly accessible demonstration of this force, now emerging, becoming articulate once more in a period of human history thirsting for spirit and meaning. [205]

Under the gaze that is the contemplation of the self in the written retrospective, other representations may emerge into the light. These are representations of psychic forces rather than of individuals who had a powerful influence on our lives. Bogan, who was very knowledgeable about these matters, wrote with that wit which is emblematic of her that she was waiting "to meet my *personus,* and the Wise Old Man, and other Jungian archetypes." (She added that this was "to little purpose. For one thing, I can't *stand* Wise Old Men."[100]) Catherine Drinker Bowen, on the other hand, recalled a remark that may have been made by Walter Bagehot, to the effect that "a Cavalier is always young." Bowen wrote of herself:

> I could not write about a Cavalier because I love old men, with their magnificence and their ferocity; to write about Justice Holmes, at eighty and at ninety, was a joy and an inspiration. Even if, for lack of space, I am obliged to end the story fifty years before my hero's death, as in *John Adams and the American Revolution*—even then I have the sense of my subject's eventual old age, of a fruitfulness and ripening before the hero is cut down. I am possessed by the belief that a man's youth and early character are influenced by what his old age will be.[101]

If Jung was right about this—and I think that he was—the second half of life is a striving toward wholeness. On the way to individuation, a woman will meet manifestations of many archetypal forces of the psyche—the Wise Old Man (whom Bogan could not abide, but whom Bowen loved), and the Old Wise Woman, too . . . and the Baba Yaga, and the Sophia . . . and the Terrible Mother, and the Terrible Daughter, as well. All these are aspects of each of us and all of us. In the examination of the self that is the driving force of true autobiography, all confrontations are possible. That is what makes the undertaking so harrowing and that is what makes it redemptive.

Many gerontologists have observed how much old people like to read autobiographies. Reading the lives of others may be an expression of the striving toward wholeness.[102] This is because autobiographies of others are stories of selves unrealized, of lives unlived by the reader. Through the very act of reading them, the self is magnified, the lifetime is extended. Written memoirs and reflections from the other side of life are works interweaving imagination with memory. At this loom, each weaver creates a pattern of her own. But every pattern discloses the daedal fashioning of a human life and of all thought.

Notes

1. Florida Scott-Maxwell, *The Measure of My Days* (New York: Alfred A. Knopf, Inc., 1969), p. 112. Hereafter, all references to this book will be cited in the text by page number.

2. G. Stanley Hall, *Senescence: The Last Half of Life* (New York: D. Appleton and Co., 1922), p. 319. Hereafter, all references to this book will be cited in the text by page number.

3. Catherine Drinker Bowen, *Family Portrait* (Boston: Little, Brown and Co., 1970), p. 285. Hereafter, all references to this book will be cited in the text by page number.

4. Josephine W. Johnson, *Seven Houses: A Memoir of Time and Places* (New York: Simon and Schuster, 1973), p. 9.

5. Ruth Suckow, "A Memoir," in *Some Others and Myself: Seven Stories and a Memoir* (New York: Rinehart and Co., Inc., 1952), p. 253. Hereafter, all references to this book will be cited in the text by page number.

6. Eleanor Roosevelt, *This Is My Story* (New York: Harper and Bros., 1937), pp. 71–72.

7. Rose Pesotta, *Bread Upon the Waters,* ed. John Nicholas Beffel (New York: Dodd, Mead and Co., 1944), p. v.

8. George Eliot's journal was expurgated either by herself or, what is more probable, by William Cross. Mary Jane Moffat and Charlotte Painter, eds., *Revelations: Diaries of Women* (New York: Random House, 1974), pp. 181–82. Margaret Sanger wrote that, after papers and books, among them forty copies of *Family Limitation,* were confiscated by Customs, she left spaces in her diaries rather than writing out names, "because I never knew who was going to see them." Margaret Sanger, *Margaret Sanger: An Autobiography* (New York: W. W. Norton and Co., 1938), p. 321.

9. Gunther Stuhlmann, Preface, in Gunther Stuhlmann, ed., *The Diary of Anaïs Nin, 1947–1955,* volume 5 (New York: Harcourt Brace Jovanovich, 1974), p. viii.

10. Jessamyn West, *The Woman Said Yes: Encounters with Life and Death (Memoirs)* (Greenwich, Conn.: Fawcett Publications, Inc., 1976), p. 96. Hereafter, all references to this book will be cited in the text by page number.

11. Mary Austin, *Earth Horizon* (Boston: Houghton Mifflin Co., 1932). For an interpretation of the changing uses of first, second, and third persons in *Earth Horizon,* see Elizabeth Winston, "The Autobiographer and Her Readers: From Apology to Affirmation," in Estelle C. Jelinek, ed.,

Women's Autobiography: Essays in Criticism (Bloomington, Ind.: Indiana University Press, 1980), pp. 107–8. Hereafter, all references to *Earth Horizon* will be cited in the text by page number.

12. Virgilia Peterson, *A Matter of Life and Death* (New York: Atheneum, 1961), Foreword. Hereafter, all references to this book will be cited in the text by page number.

13. Ruth Limmer, ed., *What the Woman Lived: Selected Letters of Louise Bogan 1920–1970* (New York: Harcourt Brace Jovanovich, Inc., 1973), pp. 277–78.

14. Ruth Limmer, ed., "From the Journals of a Poet," *The New Yorker* (January 30, 1978) 53 (50):60.

15. *The Diary of Anaïs Nin*, 5:130. Hereafter, all references to this book will be cited in the text by page number.

16. Isadora Duncan, *My Life* (New York: Boni and Liveright, Inc., 1927, 1955), p. 22. Hereafter, all references to this book will be cited in the text by page number.

17. Helen Keller, *Midstream: My Later Life* (Garden City, N.Y.: Doubleday, Doran and Co., Inc., 1929), p. 216. Hereafter, all references to this book will be cited in the text by page number.

18. Eleanor Roosevelt, *This Is My Story*, p. 1. Hereafter, all references to this book will be cited in the text by page number.

19. Ilka Chase, *Past Imperfect* (Garden City, N.Y.: Blue Ribbon Books, 1945), p. 3. Hereafter, all references to this book will be cited in the text by page number.

20. Margaret Sanger, *Margaret Sanger: An Autobiography*, p. 45. Hereafter, all references to this book will be cited in the text by page number.

21. Margaret Mead, *Blackberry Winter: My Earlier Years* (New York: William Morrow, Pocket Books, 1975), p. 45. Hereafter, all references to this book will be cited in the text by page number.

22. Willa Cather, Prefatory Note, *Not Under Forty* (New York: Alfred A. Knopf, 1936), p. v. Hereafter, all references to this book will be cited in the text by page number.

23. George N. Kates, "Willa Cather's Unfinished Avignon Story," in Willa Cather, *Five Stories* (New York: Vintage Books, 1956), pp. 175–214.

24. Jane Addams, *The Long Road of Woman's Memory* (New York: The Macmillan Co., 1916), pp. ix, xi–xii. Hereafter, reference to this book will be cited in the text by page number.

25. See James Olney, *Metaphors of Self: The Meaning of Autobiography* (Princeton, N.J.: Princeton University Press, 1972).

26. Mary McCarthy, "Names," in Mary McCarthy, *Memories of a Catholic Girlhood* (New York: Harcourt, Brace and Company, 1957), p. 129.

27. Welthy Honsinger Fisher, *To Light a Candle* (New York: McGraw-Hill Book Co., Inc., 1962). At the age of 98, despite a broken knee and subzero temperatures, Fisher made a trip to China to visit old friends who share her interest in women's education. Sharon Johnson, "Welthy Fisher: Woman with a Mission," *New York Times*, April 2, 1978, p. 54.

28. Bogan, who was a critic as well as a poet, wrote short stories until the mid-thirties, a fact that is not well known. Ruth Limmer, *What the Woman Lived*, p. 28, n. 1.

29. Margaret Mead, *Blackberry Winter*, p. 116. Hereafter, reference to this book will be cited in the text by page number.

30. Isadora Duncan, *My Life*, p. 10. Hereafter, all references to this book will be cited in the text by page number.

31. Bertha Van Hoosen, *Petticoat Surgeon* (Chicago: Pellegrini and Cudahy, 1947), p. 20. Hereafter, all references to this book will be cited in the text by page number.

32. Harriet Monroe, *A Poet's Life: Seventy Years in a Changing World* (New York: The Macmillan Co., 1938), p. 55. Hereafter, all references to this book will be cited in the text by page number.

33. Morton Dauwen Zabel, Epilogue, *A Poet's Life*, p. 473. All references to this book continue to be cited in the text by page number.

34. Mary Field Parton, ed., *The Autobiography of Mother Jones* (Chicago: Charles H. Kerr Publishing Co., 1977), pp. 237–38. Hereafter, all references to this book will be cited in the text by page number.

35. Fred Thompson, Introduction, *The Autobiography of Mother Jones*, pp. vi–vii. Hereafter, all references to this book continue to be cited in the text by page number.

36. Mary Heaton Vorse, *A Footnote to Folly* (New York: Farrar and Rinehart, Inc., 1935), p. 21. Hereafter, all references to this book will be cited in the text by page number.

37. Simone de Beauvoir, *The Coming of Age,* Patrick O'Brian, trans. (New York: Warner Paperback Library, 1973), p. 440. Hereafter, reference to this book will be cited in the text by page number. In her eighties, Olga Knopf observed that it appears that none of the people in Beauvoir's book, "including the author herself, has progressed to the state of self-acceptance that alone can help master the misery and liberate the old person for new fields of interest, that can make him welcome new challenges." Knopf expressed the hope "that Madame de Beauvoir will reach this stage before long and give us an equally fine study of 'Old Age Defeated.'" Olga Knopf, M.D., *Successful Aging* (New York: The Viking Press, 1975), p. 38.

38. Mary Austin, *Earth Horizon,* p. 285.

39. Ruth Limmer, ed., *What the Woman Lived: Selected Letters of Louise Bogan 1920–1970,* p. 255. Hereafter, all references to this book will be cited in the text by page number.

40. Dorothy Parker, "The Middle or Blue Period," in *The Portable Dorothy Parker* (Harmondsworth, Middlesex, England: Penguin Books Ltd., 1976), p. 594. Hereafter, references to this book will be cited in the text by page number.

41. Lavinia Russ, *A High Old Time or How to Enjoy Being a Woman Over Sixty* (New York: Saturday Review Press, 1972), p. 4. Hereafter, all references to this book will be cited in the text by page number.

42. Elizabeth Gray Vining, *Being Seventy: The Measure of a Year* (New York: The Viking Press, 1978). Hereafter, all references to this book will be cited in the text by page number.

43. Eleanor Roosevelt, *The Autobiography of Eleanor Roosevelt* (New York: Harper and Brothers, 1961), pp. 410–20. Hereafter, all references to this book will be cited in the text by page number.

44. Charlotte (Reeve) Conover, *On Being Eighty and Other Digressions* (Yellow Springs, Ohio: Antioch Bookplate Co., 1938), n.p. "On Being Eighty" and "Grow Old and Like It" were originally written for the Dayton *News.* There is no pagination for these articles or for "Signposts in the Dark" and "The Pools Are Filled With Water," which are the other two articles gathered in this book.

45. Mary Marvin Heaton Vorse, *Autobiography of an Elderly Woman* (Boston: Houghton Mifflin Co., 1911, Reprint Edition 1974 by Arno Press, Inc.) Vorse mentions this undertaking in her own autobiography, *A Footnote to Folly,* p. 33. Hereafter, all references to *Autobiography of an Elderly Woman* will be cited in the text by page number.

46. Isadora Duncan, *My Life,* p. 267.

47. Margaret Sanger, *Margaret Sanger: An Autobiography,* p. 182.

48. Pearl S. Buck, *A Bridge for Passing* (New York: The John Day Co., 1962), p. 60. Hereafter, all references to this book will be cited in the text by page number.

49. Margaret Anderson, *The Strange Necessity* (New York: Horizon Press, 1969), p. 198. Hereafter, all references to this book will be cited in the text by page number.

50. Edward Burns, Ed., *Staying on Alone, Letters of Alice B. Toklas* (New York: Liveright, 1973), p. 158. Hereafter, all references to this book will be cited in the text by page number.

51. Athena Tacha, "The Process of Aging," *The Village Voice* (February 26, 1979) 24(9):57.

52. Catherine Drinker Bowen, *Family Portrait,* p. 128.

53. Eleanor Roosevelt, *This Is My Story,* p. 172.

54. Gwendolyn Books, *Report from Part One* (Detroit, Mich.: Broadside Press, 1972), p. 184.

55. Isadora Duncan, *My Life,* p. 357.

56. Gunther Stuhlmann, ed., *The Diary of Anaïs Nin, 1944–1947,* volume 4 (New York: Harcourt Brace Jovanovich, 1971), p. 75. Hereafter, all references to this book will be cited in the text by page number.

57. These quotations are, in order of their citation, from Gunther Stuhlmann, ed., *The Diary of Anaïs Nin,* volume 5, p. 188; Gunther Stuhlmann, ed., *The Diary of Anaïs Nin, 1955–1966,* volume 6 (New York: Harcourt Brace Jovanovich, 1976), pp. 90 and 118 (in this volume, Nin also wrote about the double standard of aging—see p. 61), and Anaïs Nin, Letter, *Ms.* (July 1974) 3:7. In the letter, Nin said she had made herself an example of how a woman could work. live, act, and look at the age of 70.

58. Welthy Honsinger Fisher, *To Light a Candle*, p. 211.

59. Irene Kittle Kamp, "Facing a New Face," *New York Times Magazine*, September 9, 1979, p. 130.

60. Frank B. Linderman, *Pretty-Shield, Medicine Woman of the Crows* (Lincoln, Neb.: University of Nebraska Press, 1932, 1972), p. 23. Hereafter, all references to this book will be cited in the text by page number.

61. Agnes de Mille, *Where the Wings Grow (A Memoir of Childhood)* (New York: Doubleday and Co., Inc., 1978), p. 31. Hereafter, all references to this book will be cited in the text by page number.

62. Dorothy Day, *The Long Loneliness, The Autobiography of Dorothy Day* (New York: Harper and Brothers, 1952), p. 115.

63. Ilka Chase, *Past Imperfect*, p. 1.

64. Margaret Sanger, *Margaret Sanger: An Autobiography*, p. 493.

65. Eleanor Roosevelt, *This Is My Story*, p. 29.

66. Allan Ross Macdougall, ed., *Letters of Edna St. Vincent Millay* (New York: Harper and Brothers, 1952), p. 284.

67. Virgilia Peterson, *A Matter of Life and Death*, p. 29.

68. Helen Keller, *Midstream: My Later Life*, p. 148.

69. Mary Austin, *Earth Horizon*, p. 216.

70. Ilka Chase, *Past Imperfect*, pp. 203, 211.

71. Rosa Pesotta, *Bread Upon the Waters*, p. 15.

72. Allan Ross Macdougall, ed., *Letters of Edna St. Vincent Millay*, p. 350.

73. Pearl Bailey, *The Raw Pearl* (New York: Harcourt Brace and World, Inc., 1968), p. 205.

74. Helen Keller, *Midstream: My Later Life*, p. 125.

75. Frank B. Linderman, *Pretty-Shield, Medicine Woman of the Crows*, p. 75. Hereafter, references to this book will be cited in the text by page number.

76. Mary Vorse, *Autobiography of an Elderly Woman*, pp. 32–33.

77. Edna Ferber, *A Peculiar Treasure* (New York: Literary Guild, 1939), pp. 46–47.

78. Jane Addams, *The Long Road of Woman's Memory* (New York: The Macmillan Co., 1916), p. 168. Hereafter, all references to this book will be cited in the text by page number.

79. Helene Deutsch, M.D., *Confrontations with Myself—An Epilogue* (New York: W. W. Norton and Co., Inc., 1973), p. 124. Hereafter, all references to this book will be cited in the text by page number.

80. Mary Austin, *Earth Horizon*, p. 111.

81. Mary Anderson, *Woman at Work, The Autobiography of Mary Anderson as told to Mary N. Winslow* (Westport, Conn.: Greenwood Press, Publishers, 1951).

82. Helen Bevington, *The House Was Quiet and the World Was Calm* (New York: Harcourt Brace Jovanovich, Inc., 1971).

83. Bertha Van Hoosen, *Petticoat Surgeon*, p. 168.

84. Dorothy Day, *The Long Loneliness*, p. 182.

85. Eleanor Roosevelt, *This Is My Story*, p. 183.

86. Gwendolyn Brooks, *Report from Part One*, p. 190.

87. Ruth Limmer, "Notes on Editing," *What the Woman Lived*, p. xiv.

88. Allan Ross Macdougall, Foreword, *Letters of Edna St. Vincent Millay*, p. x. Hereafter, reference to this book will be cited in the text by page number.

89. Nancy Oestreich Lurie, ed., *Mountain Wolf Woman: Sister of Crashing Thunder, The Autobiography of a Winnebago Indian* (Ann Arbor, Mich.: The University of Michigan Press, 1966), p. 141, n. 1.

90. Lillian Hellman, "Lillian Hellman on Reading Her Own Work," *The New York Times Book Review*, March 25, 1979, p. 45.

91. As quoted in Moffat and Painter, *Revelations: Diaries of Women*, p. 206. See the Afterword to this book, "Psychic Bisexuality" by Charlotte Painter, for an original and illuminating discussion of the diary and inner life.

92. As quoted in Ronald Blythe, *The View in Winter: Reflections on Old Age* (New York and London: Harcourt Brace Jovanovich, 1979), p. 217.

93. Vida Scudder, "The Privileges of Age," *Atlantic Monthly* (February 1933) 151(2):205–11.

94. G. Stanley Hall, *Senescence: The Last Half of Life*, pp. 330–31.

95. Florida Scott-Maxwell, *The Measure of My Days*, p. 142.

96. Margaret Mead, *Blackberry Winter*, pp. 311–25.

97. Mary McCarthy, *Memories of a Catholic Girlhood*, p. 198. McCarthy wrote a sequel to each of the memoirs gathered in this book, in which she discusses the ways memory and the literary imagination entered into their composition. In the note "To the Reader," she writes that, often, *"in the course of doing these memoirs, I have wished that I were writing fiction. The temptation to invent has been very strong. . . . Sometimes I have yielded. . . . Then there are cases where I am not sure myself whether I am making something up." Memories of a Catholic Girlhood*, pp. 3–4.

98. Nancy Friday, *My Mother/My Self: The Daughter's Search for Identity* (New York: Delacorte Press, 1977).

99. Stephanie A. Demetrakopoulos, "The Metaphysics of Matrilinearism in Women's Auto-biography: Studies of Mead's *Blackberry Winter*, Hellman's *Pentimento*, Angelou's *I Know Why the Caged Bird Sings*, and Kingston's *The Woman Warrior*," in Estelle C. Jelinek, ed., *Women's Autobiography: Essays in Criticism* (Bloomington, Ind.: Indiana University Press, 1980), pp. 180–205. Hereafter, all references to this essay will be cited in the text by page number.

100. Ruth Limmer, ed., *What the Woman Lived*, p. 309n.

101. Catherine Drinker Bowen, *Adventures of a Biographer* (Boston: Atlantic Monthly Press, 1959), p. 155.

102. In a note in Grace Elliott's *Women after Forty*, she quotes from Mary Austin's *Earth Horizon* to illustrate the experience of wholeness. Grace Loucks Elliott, *Women After Forty* (New York: Henry Holt and Co., 1936), p. 19n.

5

Aspects of Aging: Selections from the Works of Five Women Writers

Time changes folks . . . as they go along the road.
—ZORA NEALE HURSTON,
Seraph on the Suwanee

In all ages there have been seekers of the secret of immortality, of the keys to that kingdom beyond Boreas where the chosen dwell forever young and fair, of the buried map pointing the way to the fountain of eternal youth, of the formula for the elixir that restores life's "glad season." Many chronicles of these dream-journeys have been lost. The few that remain have taken myriad forms, for in every generation there are alchemists at work transmuting the great mythic truths into modes of art and science that might speak to their contemporaries. Measured in terms of the time humanity has been on this earth, the study of gerontology is very young. But its most profound concerns are as ancient as human consciousness, as the presence of the "thinking reed" among the creatures of this planet.

From this perspective, Gertrude Atherton's *Black Oxen* may be seen as a work that carries the task of transmutation forward to our time. Her novel is a variation on the theme of rejuvenation—and a quite recent one, at that. It was published in a decade when the pursuit of youth was unusually heated in the United States, and this no doubt accounts for the enormous popular appeal of the novel at that time. It was not the idea of restoring youth and beauty and vitality that was new, but Atherton's choice of the protagonist: *Black Oxen* is about the rejuvenation of a woman.

Women's experience of aging, the many meanings of growing older from women's perspectives . . . these are "secrets" almost as well kept as the path to that fountain that flows with restorative waters. The *King Lear* of women's aging, the older woman's *Don Quixote,* her *Death in Venice,* is yet to be written. Even so, it is not true, as it is all too commonly supposed, that women of letters have been silent about the great questions of aging and mortality. What is astonishing is not how little has been written by women about these questions, but how little is known of the literary treasures that are there. In this chapter, there can be only intimations of all that has been thought and said about growing older by these five women writers. Their illuminations are as lamps lighted by a woman as she walks from room to room and ascends the staircases of a many-storied house.

These five worlds—of the "fool's paradise" of early twentieth-century California, of Tidewater Virginia and Scotch Presbyterianism, of Eatonville and the Harlem Renaissance, of the life of the solitary in New England, of "old New York" and expatriation in Europe—are separated by vast moral distances. What five women writers of such different gifts, fortunes, and temperaments could possibly have to share with one another beyond the fact that they inhabit the same century and country—this could hardly be imagined, perhaps even by themselves. Yet, whoever reads their works will recognize that each and all of them return again and again to the essential questions, in correspondence or personal essays or memoirs as well as in fiction. The changing weathers of inner life as one grows older, the radiant insights and the quiet discoveries of later life, the sorrows and dreams of aging—these are revealed in their personal documents as well as in their short stories or novels.

Each of these women of letters has her own point of view, her own moral attitude toward aging. Each has a distinctive voice, and not one of them is unrelievedly elegiac. What all five have in common is a keen awareness of the passing of time and the ephemerality of all things, and the curiosity and courage to look long and closely at the other side of life. These pages are a weaving of selections from their fictions and nonfictions that reveal aspects of aging as seen and experienced by five extraordinarily perceptive women.

One day soon, the masterpiece on women's aging will be written. The origins of the composer and the form her work of art will take—these, too, are secrets. But this much is certain, that the great truths of that composition will be woven of the motifs appearing in the works of these five writers—the waiting and the wandering that is later life, and the transformations of Eros and Agape, and the redeeming of time and loss through reconciliations.

Gertrude Atherton (1857–1948)

In the spring of 1922, Gertrude Atherton was visited by the presentiment that a book awaited her in New York.[1] She had not written anything that satisfied her since *Perch of the Devil,* and she had grown restless from "playing about" in San Francisco while waiting out the writer's dry season. Intuitions such as this had seldom proven themselves wrong before, so she obeyed the inner prompting. She took a room at the hotel in New York then known as 37 Madison Avenue, overlooking Madison Square. Once established there, she idled for several weeks, wondering if her mind had grown sterile as she had so often feared. Years before, a German psychotherapeutist who had treated Atherton for insomnia had assured her that she would never lose her creativity so long as she kept in perfect physical condition and so long as her brain remained "free of unpoisoned blood" and her body of microbous disease. But she had fallen ill since then, more than once, and seriously. She had had pneumonia, and that was "microbous," to be sure. That might have poisoned her brain, indeed.

One morning, reading the newspaper in bed, she came upon two items. One was an interview with Dr. Lorenz, a famous orthopedic surgeon from Vienna who had lost his wealth and practice during the war and who had, as a consequence, suffered a premature senescence. Persuaded by his friends to enter one of the clinics offering the Steinach "re-energizing" treatment, Lorenz submitted himself to the "slight operation," and it was a success. Then in his late sixties, he felt he had the energy and endurance of a much younger man. Following this item was an interview with Dr. Harry Benjamin, a former associate of Steinach's who was now practicing medicine in New York. Benjamin explained the Steinach procedure in plain language as the newspapermen had requested, and went on to remark that women were descending upon the Steinach clinic from all over Europe. Among them were Russian princesses who paid for their treatments with the currency for which they exchanged their jewelry. Once their energies were restored, they could make a living without their jewels. It was this that gave Atherton's mind "a violent jolt":

> Five years before I had been lying awake one night when a sudden vivid picture rose in my mind. It was in a theatre on the opening night of a new play. At the fall of the first curtain a woman, very beautiful, very unusual in appearance, rose, turned her back to the stage, lifted her opera glass and surveyed the house. This is a common occurrence in Europe—I had done it myself—but unheard of in America.
>
> Of course there was an immediate buzz in the audience. Who was this woman? No one had ever seen her before. She looked "European," yet subtly American. . . . She looked about thirty. [556–57]

Atherton knew there was a story in back of that figure who was so graceful and arresting and mysterious, but it eluded her for five years, during which this woman remained "planted in that theatre, her back to the curtain, surveying the house, and I couldn't get her out. . . . Theme I had none. Now, in a flash, I knew I had found one" (557). She made an appointment immediately with Dr. Benjamin. Intrigued by the unwritten novel that haunted Atherton, he answered her questions about the Steinach treatment. And when she confided that she had been mentally sterile for over a year and was dissatisfied with the books she had published before that, Benjamin wanted to know why she herself did not consider taking the course of treatments, which, for women, consisted of a series of X rays. This Atherton decided to do.

The effect of this series of X rays varies from one woman to another. Atherton found the eight treatments to be painless and "rather boring." They left her brain torpid for a month, during which she slept sixteen hours of every twenty-four and was so stupid that she could not carry on a conversation with anyone. Had she been ruined for the rest of her life? Dr. Benjamin laughed at the suggestion, and she did not have the energy to worry about it anyway. Then, about one week after the treatments had been completed, she had the sudden feeling that a black cloud was lifting from her brain, "hovering for a moment, rolling away." The torpor disappeared; her brain "seemed sparkling with light. . . . I almost flung myself at my desk. I . . . marched that woman triumphantly out of the theatre." Months later, dining with Avery Hopwood, Atherton had a lightning flash of memory, and knew what the title of her novel would be.[2] Even as she was telling Carl Van Vechten she had not yet found a title for it, Yeats's last lines in "The Countess Cathleen" returned to her:

> The years like great black oxen tread the world,
> And God the herdsman goads them on behind,
> And I am broken by their passing feet.[3]

In *Black Oxen*, Madame Zattiany, the onetime Mary Ogden of America, was 58, and Lee Clavering 34, when the two first met in New York. That was her age in years; in appearance, she was about thirty. She liked to wear shades of green: "In the subdued light she looked like a girl playing at Undine."[4] Clavering tells her of the craze for youth that has overtaken this country. Madame says she has discerned this from reading the novels of the time. In almost all the American novels, the heroines are too young. The European novelists are ahead of their American contemporaries, since they find women to be interesting at any age. Young women, she remarks, are too fluid to have much psychology. Clavering agrees, but he believes that this country is too young to countenance heroines who are middle-aged. Americans are very conventional, he tells her, although our faddism might lead one to think otherwise, and we hold to certain formulae. We believe that love ought to be associated only with youth; perhaps we think of autumnal love as somewhat "indecent." Madame asks him if he believes this. Still innocent of her secret, still under the impression that her "cousin," Mary Ogden, was a brilliant and attractive woman who had liaisons even when she was older, Clavering says he does not suffer from age prejudice. He tells her that he never had, and that when he was 17 he had been in love with a woman of 40. In Europe, Madame Zattiany observes, women "learn the technique of gallantry" when they are still quite young, and women and men make a cult of one another. The reason European men do not understand American girls is that they find sincerity to be more mystifying than subtlety and guile. In Europe, naturalness is thought to be gauche, and it is art that "commands homage." In Europe, "the game is everything" (55). How sad for older women, who have made a cult of men, for then their liaisons are merely a matter of technique. And the supreme achievement of European women is the cult of men.

Years before, Madame Zattiany had given up the hope and even the desire for feeling anything more than "a keen mental response to the most provocative of men." She was utterly without illusion about the ancient dream of human happiness; indeed, she was scornful of it. She thought that at heart it was nothing more than the blind instinct of the human race to perpetuate itself, and that its original purpose had been covered over by the fictions of civilization. How could there be mental, spiritual, and physical unity between a man and a woman, when man was by nature polygamous and woman in essence the "vehicle" of the human race? And when the "embittered gods" had decreed that the individual soul must dwell alone forever? "Life itself was futile enough," but this dream of perfect love seemed to her the most futile and the most ravaging of all the dreams of civilization. Love is ephemeral and functional, but only "savages" and the "ignorant masses" know this (56–57). No woman had given herself to the illusion more completely than she; no woman had searched with more fervor for the soul that would complete her own. "And what had she found? Men. Merely men. Satiety or disaster. Weariness and disgust." Well, she was done with all that. When it had come to her that, given her gifts of intellect and fortune, she had much to do in this world "that would resign her to the supreme boredom of living," she had felt deeply grateful for her liberation from "the thrall of sex" (57).

Young love, Madame once says to Clavering, is no more than "the urge of the race. A blaze that ends in babies or ashes" (92). Although Clavering knows that many men feel a deeper need for offspring than some women, that the desire to perpetuate oneself is more insistent for men, and that a man has a stronger sense of duty to the human race, he doubts if a man would choose having children over the chance to mate with a woman such as Mary Zattiany; certainly, he himself would not. Clavering's former girl friend, Anne Goodrich, calls Madame's rejuvenation a farce, because even though her youth and possibly her youthful feelings have been restored, the fact remains that she is unable to bear children, and to Anne, the ability to have children is what youth in women is all about. However, the prospect of childlessness does not deter Clavering; he wants Mary for his wife. His friend, the novelist Gora Dwight, advises him to give Mary up before it is too late—that is, before he loses his literary creativity. This does not dissuade him either. From the beginning he had feared Mary, not because he sensed he was falling in love with her and would suffer because of this, but because of the power he sensed in her. He liked strength in women, but not too much of it. A man had no chance at all with a woman who was stronger, "man's strength as a rule being all on the outside. Women grew up and men didn't. That was the infernal truth" (61).

Clavering's friend old Mrs. Oglethorpe confesses to him that she would pay with the price of her immortal soul if she could be 30 years old again—or if she could just *look* that age. She had made the appalling discovery that her heart was still as young as Mary Ogden's. Nature plays women an appalling dirty trick, she says. There had been a time after her husband died when she "hated growing old with the best of them," although she had not admitted this even to herself for a good while. She had been 50 then, and free for the first time in her life, with her older children married and the younger ones in school in Europe. She had already begun to think of herself as an old woman, when she "made the terrible discovery that the heart never grows old." She fell in love four times with men many years younger than herself. But she would never have permitted them to find this out. "Even then I had as little use for old men as old men have for old women. Whatever it may be in men, it's the young heart in women." She did not try to deceive herself about the fact that she was 50: "My complexion was gone, my stomach high, and I had the face of an old war horse." But there was the damnable trick that nature plays, and she had the romantic fantasy, as ardent as those of her youth, that these clever and intelligent men would see through the "old husk" she had become and recognize the youthfulness of her heart and the wisdom she had attained, for she knew she had more to give them than many younger women had. But she discovered that, although beauty may be only skin deep, "the skin is all any man wants, the best of 'em." These younger men treated her with the greatest respect, and she came to hate the word *respect* for the first time in her life. They enjoyed her company "because I was an amusing caustic old woman" (195–96). She was born too soon, Clavering says—born into an epoch when women are still "submerged."

Mary discloses her secret to her old friends. The biologists expect her rejuvenation to last ten years. The renewal of power is manifest not only "in mental activity, in concentration, in memory," but in the disappearance of "that distaste for new ideas. . . . People growing old are condemned for prejudice, smugness, hostility to progress, to the purposes and enthusiasms of youth." All this is due only to aging glands. It is an instinct of self-preservation that makes older people pretend to a calm and mocking superiority and to a righteous conservatism (140). She tells Clavering she believes the human life span is too short. If one has lived "sanely," one withers and dies just at an age when one begins to see life whole, "with that detachment that comes when his personal hold on life and affairs is relaxing, when he has realized his mistakes, and has attained a mental and moral orientation which could be of inestimable service to his fellow men, and to civilization." Old people are irritable not because of a "natural hatefulness of disposition and a released congenital selfishness," but because of the atrophy of their glands. And perhaps they are rebelling because Nature consigns them to ineptitude just when they ought to be entering upon their best period of usefulness and enjoyment of life. She reminds Clavering of how often science has defeated Nature, of its marvels, its spectacular triumphs. It is not a wonder that science can arrest senescence, but only that it has not yet done so (175–76).

Mary's dream was to accomplish great things in Europe. But nothing in human life is rarer or more precious than love, and now that she loves Clavering, she asks herself why she should risk losing this for the sake of a dream that may be chimerical. She reflects that it is in our very nature to love and to desire, that nine-tenths of the dream of accomplishing great things in this life is personal vanity, that if she follows that dream, she might be throwing the rest of her life away. She believes "that when we leave this planet we go to a higher star," where we will be made complete. Perhaps the more completeness one achieves on this earth, the less waiting there will be on that higher star. But it is only very rarely that it is given to two human beings to realize this completeness together in this world (299–300).

When Hohenhauer commands her, as Marie Zattiany, to renounce her dream of young love, a dream that is commonplace, a dream that is unworthy, to take her place at his side, he reminds her that nothing can change the march of the years and that she is only two years younger than he. She is indebted to Austria for her rejuvenation, he says, and she must work with him "to make Vienna the capital of a great and powerful Republic." If she would but look inward, she would find cause to feel ashamed and foolish. He asks her how she could fail to see that it is indecent for a woman of her mental age to allow herself to imagine that she truly feels "the authentic passions of youth." He asks her if she is able to bear children or to "love with unsullied memory." He asks her if she has youth's ideals or flexibility, or its hopes or illusions. He asks her if she still has "even that power of desperate mental passion . . . of the mature woman who seeks for the last time to find in love what love has not? The final delusion." He tells her that her rejuvenated glands gave her back youth's appearance and its strength, but that she has no more illusions now "than when you were a withered old woman in Vienna" (321).

"No man," Hohenhauer tells Marie, "is interested in an old woman's psychology." Although their love has long been dead, he tells her she must marry him if she is to use her intellectual gifts, her political genius, her restored beauty, and her wealth to their full advantage, that as his consort she could wield great power. This miracle of science may restore youth to the body, but it cannot make the mind youthful again. Of what use is it to be young again, if one is to use those years to make the same mistakes all over again? Elka Zsaky is older than Marie, and in her time she was a *dame galante*. She took the Steinach treatment, and now she looks much more youthful "than when she was a painted old hag with a red wig." Although she must still use artifice, at least she has lovers once more, and this is why she took the treatment. "Vienna is highly amused." Women such as Elka will want rejuvenation just so that they can have lovers again. But many European women of intellect will want the treatment for the sake of renewing their mental faculties and the energy and endurance they would need to continue their work. She must seize the day. She must return with him to Vienna now, while she still has the chance for this career. She must give up her vain dream of young love, for it is out of season. Soon it will be too late. Soon rejuvenation will be within the reach of women everywhere (323–26).

Black Oxen became the best-seller of 1923; it even obscured Sinclair Lewis's *Babbitt,* which had been published the year before.[5] Atherton might have had a premonition of its success while writing the work: The rejuvenation of Madame Zattiany "as a subject for the press . . . rivalled strikes, prohibition, German reparations, Lenin, prize-fights, censorship and scandalous divorces in high life."[6] Atherton would have preferred that her own favorite, *Tower of Ivory,* had enjoyed the reception the public gave *Black Oxen,* but she accepted the gifts the gods had provided her.[7] She was deluged with mail from women all over the English-speaking world who wanted to know if her story was fact or fiction. And the book all but ruined Dr. Benjamin. Women descended upon him, pleading for the Steinach treatment "free of charge or at a minimum price." And he could not find it in himself to turn the "most appealing cases" away. There was disapproval, too, and Atherton had expected this "in a country which dismisses professors for teaching the doctrine of evolution." In her view, the world in general, "and the great and free United States in particular, is full of narrow-minded, ignorant, moronic, bigoted, cowardly, self-righteous, anemic, pig-headed, stupid, puritanical, hypocritical, prejudiced, fanatical, cocoa-blooded atavists, who soothe their inferiority complex by barking their hatred of anything new." If these people had their way, progress would come to an end; they find the very word *science* to be abhorrent (560–61). Steinach had suffered from the likes of these people in Europe: thanks to the jealousy of his confreres in medicine and the thundering denunciations of clergymen of his "interference" with Nature, he was not awarded the Nobel Prize. If Steinach had deigned to reply to the charges leveled against him, he might have inquired about the "interference" with Nature and the insult to Almighty God perpetrated by his adversaries when they themselves sought remedies for failing powers and for illnesses. Clergymen denounced Atherton, too. And "certain club women, who regarded anything beyond their limited comprehension as immoral," joined forces in an effort to stop the sale of her book. Once when Atherton was asked if she could suggest anything that might improve the morals of the American people, she answered that it was not want of morals from which Americans suffered so much as want of brains. The wrath with which *Black Oxen* was greeted by some people reminded her of this observation she had made and confirmed the validity of this opinion to her. She wrote five novels in quick succession after *Black Oxen*. Writing in her seventies, she reported that she continued to enjoy renewed vitality and recommended ways that writers fallen in a dry season might renew themselves: rest, the high-frequency treatment of the pituitary she described in *The Sophisticates*, "and a visit to a chiropractor, who cracks one up and releases the flow of energy to the brain." Of course, there is the Steinach treatment, too. "We live in an age of scientific marvels," she wrote in 1932, "and those who do not take advantage of them are fools and deserve the worst that malignant Nature can inflict upon them" (562).

In a feisty essay, "Defeating Old Age," Atherton remarked how much could be written about the difference in attitudes to "Life" between the young, who dream, and those who no longer have the illusions of youth, who plan. The most clear-sighted planners are aware that they may fail, and yet they persevere. These are the makers of history; it is to them that we owe whatever progress has been achieved. Even those of a less aggressive nature, the artistically gifted, must summon up great courage if they are to survive the inexorable disappointments and the "calculated assaults of the envious, and neuronic strain." Unless they fall prey to an incurable illness or are victims of an accident, they, too, will survive and develop an attitude toward life that is an expression of personality, rather than circumstance. "It is this attitude, beginning definitely in middle life . . . which is the most interesting single expression of human personality."[8]

A generation or two ago, Atherton observed, middle-aged and older people did not question "the Biblical decree that man's normal life-span was three score and ten" nor the notion that the last third or quarter of life "was given over to a slow disintegration of the organs. The psychological effect of this belief was lamentable." Thanks to laboratory research, the life span has been prolonged. Most people have been apprised of the importance of observing the laws of hygiene and of the practice of moderation in dietary habits, respect for the need for sufficient sleep and an annual physical examination, and for the need to pay "close attention to the glandular constitution." Only those who have unavoidable heart strain or severe economic hardships or "vicious addictions" need suffer a loss in vitality. What is more, psychologists have admonished everyone not to "get into a rut." Those who do "might just as well take an overdose of chloral hydrate and have done with it. The final result of too much routine is death in life" (59–60).

Mens sana in corpore sano, Atherton adjures here: the chances for fruition and adjustment are far better for this generation than for those which have gone before. Good physical health confers buoyancy and hope and the aspiration to achieve, and a continuing interest in one's own life and the life of the world. Therefore this generation must take a new attitude toward life during the later years. "Only the beaten . . . sink into their empty selves and watch the collapse of the mind into the ruin of the body" (60). As for mature women, they would be fools to dress like the flappers, but wise to dress fashionably and to take pains with their appearance. Those "old relics of the Victorian Age, who pride themselves upon never having even powdered their noses, disdain the changing fashions for their shapeless bodies, stoop more from laziness than age, and wear flat-heeled buttoned boots . . . feel superior and look like hell." There are cosmetic surgeons, there are cosmetics in the drugstores, there are beauty parlors, there is the Steinach treatment. Madame de Staël might have given much for a beauty parlor, for though she was very plain, she was certainly not wanting in feminine vanity, and at the age of 45 she married a man twenty-three years her junior (61–63).

In this essay, Atherton remarks the sadness Edith Wharton expressed in *A Backward Glance* in writing of the loss of friends sustained by all who survive into old age. The death of friends arouses a fighting instinct in her, Atherton confesses, and even a measure of resentment toward those who died because they did not take better care of themselves. There is nothing for it but to

tighten your belt, make new friends, make Life yield as many interests as possible. Thrice blessed are those that have a daily and congenial task, more particularly in one of the arts. And clubwomen . . . have an almost cruel advantage over middle-aged and elderly widows whose children are married, whose income is too limited to permit travelling and social diversions, and who exist, not live, in the gray fog of monotony and trivial routine. Well, even they may wake up in time. . . . Anyone with spirit fights his enemies instead of lying down and shuddering under the soles of their feet. And Life is the most persistent and pitiless of man's enemies. To fight and confound her is the antidote for all ills. [64–65]

In another essay, Atherton recommends "A Course in Life and Human Nature."[9] She would teach girls the wisdom of the proverb *Tout lasse, tout casse, tout passe.* And she would have Stepmother Nature shown for the creature she is. Who knows what girls might do once they understood "that all She is after is the continuance of the race, that youthful passion . . . is merely a poison brewed by that old harridan . . . to victimize the young and fruitful"? (88) Screen, radio, light fiction all ought to be reformed, "for girls, too, become middle-aged with time" and need to know that love and sex are only two of the major interests of life. In middle age, a woman may be given the chance to begin life all over again, a chance for freedom for individual development, a chance to have a future. The very word beckons, speaks of "unknown possibilities, new and multiple interests, adventure; above all, independence, freedom." The very word evokes a rejuvenation of the spirit. No one is ever too old to begin life again (89–91).

In "Superwomen," Atherton says she is living in "the most interesting period in the world's history" and one that is "a Godsend to women."[10] Once she has passed her first youth, a woman need not concern herself about her age, since no one else does. And her position in life has little to do with her marital status. Careers in a number of fields are open to women. For the first time in modern history, women are comparatively independent of men. "It is not so long ago that some man was the arbiter of every woman's destiny, and if no man at all dawned upon her horizon that was sheer tragedy." While a woman "whose hormones are properly balanced" would rather have a mate and children than travel "life's long journey alone," and while the more intelligent women are, "the more satisfaction they get out of the companionship of men . . . if they cannot find husbands life is full of other resources" (113). Millions of women in the modern world know that keeping their "looks" has a psychological as well as a business value. "When past middle age they have outgrown the folly of wanting to look 'young,' but they are determined to look *well;* in other words to laugh in the face of the years." Attention to outer appearance is not enough, however; the intelligent older woman "watches the behavior of her organs and glands," particularly the thyroid. A woman may live to be a centenarian and still "look well" and remain as active as she was at 40. "They will have an accumulated wisdom and experience that no young woman can hope to rival; the only fly in the ointment will be that they are likely to outlive their male contemporaries" (114–15). Women have greater physical resistance than men and a tougher moral fiber. Atherton remarks that she often pities men and that this would have sounded quaint, indeed, only a generation or two ago.

Women were once the ruling sex in many parts of the ancient world, and now, after a long era of male dominance, they "are striding, millions strong,

along the road to complete equality."[11] Jung commented that there ought to
be societies for the protection of young men from girls, and Atherton quotes
this observation with hearty approval. She detects many signs of a movement
toward equality of the sexes on the social horizons of the late 1930s, and it
amuses her to note the gathering forces of this revolution "while men grow
excited over the menaces of fascism, communism, the proletariat." Nature
had this equality in mind "when she planted male hormones in women and
female hormones in men" (23–24). Once the mating season is over, American
women have little choice but to take refuge in one another's company.[12] Most
of the more intelligent would like to be the companions of men, but this has
been made almost impossible to achieve. The consequence of this will be "a
solidarity of women, too experienced to quarrel and hate one another, that
will increasingly threaten the supremacy of the male" (46).

In her autobiography, Atherton wrote that the domestic virtues seemed to
have been left out of her, as well as any maternal instinct.[13] She had always
loved freedom, and felt domestic life contrary to her nature. Her hatred of
routine was passionate. Mother of a son who died in early childhood and of a
daughter, she was widowed when she was young, and never married again. "I
doubt if any artist should marry," she remarked, "if only because there are
martyrs enough in the world" (174). She believed one must fight for what one
wants in life. She could not abide her mother's "supineness" in the face of her
disastrous marriages. But years later, she came to accept that character is fate,
that "no one can be made over" (44). Her mother had been "very beautiful,
vivacious, flirtatious, fascinating, with a naturally brilliant mind and not an
atom of common sense" (6). She had always made a fetish of her beauty;
despite the harsh winds of San Francisco, she managed to keep her soft, fine
skin. And she kept her figure for many years. Though she rarely left the
house or saw anyone in her later years, it was a consolation to her to "look
well" to the last. "But she resented bitterly the passing of youth." That she
could not be reconciled to the loss of the first freshness of her beauty had a
salutary effect on her daughter: "I took a great interest in my own looks as I
grew older, but made up my mind to have something to fall back on when
they departed" (34).

Atherton's "itch to write" was apparent very early: this "little fiend" with the
golden curls and eyes of seraphic blue used to stand in front of a long mirror
in the hall of her grandmother's ranch house, where she once lived, and tell
herself wild tales of adventure. Her father was in his cups and her mother in
hysterics during much of the time she was "on the way," and it may have been
that her parents' incessant quarreling "caused that dislocation of particles, or
rotten spot in the brain . . . that produces fiction" (8). Though she despised
religion in every one of its forms, she "rather liked" the notion of reincarnation, and even more the idea "of being born into other worlds where human
intelligence may be more highly developed than it is on this planet." In any
case, she said she was "far too much of an egoist to believe that physical death
will be the last of me" (328). She was often visited by a sense of unreality, a

sense that life is a dream and that nothing is "really" happening. This feeling came to her when nothing was out of the ordinary otherwise, and not during "life quakes." She thought it might have the same source as her sense that she was "a spectator of life, never a part of it" (128). When she wrote her historical novels, she breathed the very air of the past. She felt she had lived in the Athens of Aspasia and Pericles that she recreated in *The Immortal Marriage* and *The Jealous Gods* (575–76). She wrote an early novel whose heroine was all she would have liked to be,"the most fascinating and beautiful of women, widowed at an early age that she might go abroad and play a great role in European politics. A mélange of Madame de Staël, Madame Récamier, and Lady Blessington" (101). Marie Zattiany seems a broth of these.

In *Black Oxen,* Clavering reflects that, "Towering individualities often go down to defeat in old age."[14] Not so Gertrude Atherton, who lived to be 91, and who wrote 34 novels, 4 short-story collections, and 3 histories in a career that spanned sixty years. She believed fervently that women ought to remain free, independent and productive to the end of their lives. Perhaps she, like Gora Dwight, had found "that power, after sex has ceased from troubling, is the dominant passion in human nature" (336). Perhaps she spoke through Mary Zattiany's parting words to Clavering: "The gods in a sportive mood made us for each other—and then sent me into the world too soon. . . . I must go on. It is not in me to go back nor to remain becalmed. Hohenhauer told me many cruel truths" (344).

Ellen Glasgow (1873/4?–1945)

When Dorinda Oakley of *Barren Ground* was 33 years old, she "was already beginning to break." Her youth was leaving her, and she had never realized the completeness she had expected of life. She had not missed love, for there had been Jason, even though he had betrayed her. It was not motherhood she missed, but something deeper that she could not name. Before too long, she would be wrinkled and gray like her mother, and she would never have known happiness. Nathan wanted her to marry him. Though she knew sex emotion was dead for her, she could still feel respect, "and a marriage founded upon respect and expediency might offer an available refuge from loneliness." In growing older, Dorinda did not fear death or poverty so much as "the lonely fireside."[15]

Again, at 50, Dorinda reflected upon aging. Now she felt that, although she had been less happy than other women at age 20, at 50 she was far happier. At 20, her happiness had been dependent upon love. At 50 it was dependent only upon herself and the land. "To the land, she had given her mind and heart with the abandonment that she had found disastrous in any human relation" (470). Because youth had given her so little, there was little to regret about its passing. With aging, her hair had changed, and her complexion, "but her eyes were still bright and clear," although they had lost their "caged look." In growing older, what she felt more keenly than anything else "was the failure of elasticity. The tyranny of detail was more exacting, and she rebounded less quickly from disappointment" (461).

When she saw how Jason's life was ending, in old age, illness, and poverty, she knew that, if she had done nothing, "time would still have revenged her; for time . . . always revenges one" (506). There was a fleeting moment when she remembered Jason as she had first known him. But then "the gleam faded" and Dorinda "felt that he was passing with it into some unearthly medium where she could not follow." She felt this was no more than "the endless riddle of mortality" that is renewed in every person, "the old baffling sense of a secret meaning in the universe," the intimation of a reality under the appearances of things. "The reserve of . . . every human being was impenetrable." She could never know what it was he was thinking then, or if he had ever really loved her in their youth, or if he would have been faithful to her had things gone differently long ago. She would never know whether it was his love or his faithlessness that was the real accident. "She felt that the mystery was killing her," but she recognized that she would never be able to solve it (512).

In her last illness, Dorinda's mother returned in her mind to her girlhood, her youth, and to the young missionary to whom she had once been engaged to marry. The years she had lived as a wife and mother "vanished from her memory." After a night of heavy dreams, she exclaimed to Dorinda how odd it was that dreams could be so much more real than present reality (343). Later, when Dorinda had her own "visitations of the past," she thought it was the same for her as for her mother with her missionary dream, that it was not so much mood that brought them on as "some fugitive quality in time or place which evoked them from the shadows of memory." Just as she was hanging the lantern on the nail above her head, "she felt that the meadow-scented breath of the cows was woven into an impalpable vision of summer. . . . a window in her mind opened suddenly, and she saw Jason coming toward her through the yellow-green of August evenings" (420–21).

It was when Dorinda was standing at Jason's grave that her thoughts and these visitations "stirred and scattered" like the dead autumn leaves. "Memories that had outlived emotions, as empty as withered husks, were released from their hidden graves, and tossed wildly to and fro in her mind. Little things that she had forgotten . . . that mean nothing when they happen and break the heart when they are remembered." It was not Jason she mourned then, but the love "she had never had." From the "whirling chaos in her mind, Jason's face emerged like the face of a marionette." Then it dissolved, and the face of every man she had ever known emerged and dissolved, each in quick succession of the other. "Faces. Ghosts. Dreams. Regrets." Like the dead leaves in the autumn wind, all that might have been whirled and danced in her mind. Then Dorinda "saw life crumble like a mountain of cinders and roll over her" and felt herself to be "buried alive beneath an emptiness, a negation of effort, beside which the vital tragedy of her youth appeared almost happiness." She felt crushed by the futility of everything. "She knew now the passive despair of maturity which made her past suffering seem enviable to her when she looked back on it. . . . Youth can never know the worst, . . . because the worst that one can know is the end of expectancy" (519–21).

In the rain falling on the shingled roof, on the box-bush and the white turkeys, and on the sandy road and "the crushed leaves smelling of autumn," Dorinda was at the place where everything still lay before her. "There is no finality when one is young." The years of her youth had been unendurable to her while she lived them. Now they "were edged . . . with a flame of regret." She would give the future for the chance to live her life again in a different way; it seemed so small to her as she cast this backward look "through the narrow vista of time." It was too late. Her youth was gone. But because of this, "she felt that the only thing that made life worth living was the love that she had never known and the happiness that she had missed" (521–22). All that she might have known and had, returned to torment and mock her now. "It was as if the sardonic powers of life assumed, before they vanished for ever, all the enchanting shapes of her dreams." Her memory was of a past she had imagined, not of the life she had actually lived. And Jason appeared to her as he had been at the time "when she had first loved him." In spite of her efforts to think of him as broken and ruined and repugnant, Jason came back to her "in the radiance of that old summer," young and ardent, with his eyes glowing with happiness and his lips smiling "that smile of mystery and pathos. . . . In that hour of memory the work of thirty years was nothing." Time and reality, success and achievement and victory over fate were all "nothing beside that imperishable illusion." The only thing that made life desirable was love, "and love was irrevocably lost to her" (523–24).

After the storm was over, and those "hag-ridden dreams of the night" had ended, Dorinda felt her spirit refreshed and given new strength by the spirit of the land as it flowed into her; she felt "her own spirit . . . flowing out again toward life." Endurance and fortitude: these were what she had. So long as the spirit has vitality, so long as the mind has eagerness, the future would always hold the chance for discovery and adventure. She had been defeated by destiny in a way, for her hopes had not been realized. But there was a victory in her defeat. She could face the future with "integrity of vision" now, at middle age. She told herself "with clear-eyed wisdom" that the best of life lay ahead (524–25).

In *The Sheltered Life,* Ellen Glasgow illuminates the vision of life of the very old through the inner reflections of General Archbald. Part one of her novel is entitled "The Age of Make-Believe," part two, "The Deep Past," and part three, "The Illusion." In part three, when he is 83 years old, the General awakened with a feeling of euphoria from an hour's nap in his library. He had just learned that Eva Birdsong was over the worst and that she would survive the "maiming" operation. Yet it was more than simple relief he felt just at that moment. "It was as if the April wind had blown through his thoughts and scattered living seeds over the bare places." He had often felt this sensation in sleep before, especially at Stillwater in his youth, this "sudden breaking off of a dream so blissful that the ecstasy had brimmed over into his life." Drowsing, he thought that the world is good, after all, and that he would not be surprised if the best years might be ahead for him. Wanting nothing, no longer subject to Chance, his last years might be tranquil. It was only in old age, he saw—and he worked to hold on to this before it vanished—that one can know "that final peace without victory which turns a conflict of desires into an impersonal spectacle."[16] Free of longing, he might make the most of the spring, and after that, of the summer splendor. And beyond these lay the years that would be happiest of all, because nothing would be necessary to him, not even life. He had found it "a relief to drift alone into old age and beyond. Life ceased to be complex as soon as one escaped from the tangle of personalities" (252). Eva, too, had longed to escape this entanglement. Before her operation, she had looked at the General, and he had realized then that she did not want to live through it; she did not want to continue. "What she feared most was not death, but life with its endless fatigue, its exacting pretense" (245). Afterwards, Eva told him that "no fame on earth is so exacting as a reputation for beauty." She said that a beautiful woman is always afraid she will lose love and the power it so easily won for her, that nothing can be so terrible for a woman as to be loved because she is beautiful.

The General thought of how different love is for men. In his youth, he had had the impression any young man has when he is young, that every woman appears to be moving toward him. But when a man is old, he comes to the realization that women are all moving away. And the General supposed that is the reason they seem, just as all else in life does, "to diminish with time" (184). But Eva tells him that last love matters far more to a woman than first love, and that when first and last are the same love, like hers for George, the virtue that stays by one, the virtue that makes last love matter more, is even stronger. She says that only you and your lover are in first love, and that this changes as it must, as all that only lives through two human beings must change. Yet she says that last love has courage and finality in it, also—the confrontation with the ending of life, and all its emptiness. She asks him if it is not true that finality is all that really survives, while all else, even love, ceases to be.

The more distant a scene was in time, the more clearly the General could see it. Events do not diminish with time; on the contrary, they are magnified by it. And the faces of those who died long ago become more vivid and more "lifelike than life itself." He could not, no matter how much effort he made to do this, stay his thoughts from their backward rambling. And he could not "trace a connection between the past and present" (143–44). Even as he was deep in meditation, he felt that the shape of the outer world dispersed and faded away into thought. Up until then, remembering had been the work of "the skin of his mind, not . . . the arteries," but at this moment when the concrete world vanished, he "plunged downward through a dim vista of time, where scattered scenes from the past flickered and died and flickered again"

(147–48). This was always how the past returned to one at the age of 83, never complete, but always in fragments followed by fragments. Not even an episode returned whole. And he thought that life had seemed to be important to him every hour that he had experienced it, but now he was aware that it was made up of things, each of which was so little in itself, of "mere fractions of time, of activities so insignificant" that all of them "passed away with the moment in which they had quivered and vanished." He wondered how anyone could find a meaning, a pattern in all of it (148). He was borne by memory to the forest trail at Stillwater, to the place his body had left half a century ago, where he had decided to help a runaway slave. It was November. "There was the tang of woodsmoke far off in a clearing. Frost was spun over the ground. The trees were brilliant with the yellow of hickory, the scarlet of sweet gum, the wine-red of oaks." No matter that there were two of him, for one life held both the old man and the young boy who had wanted to be a poet. "Time was stranger than memory." Time is "the bloom, the sheath enfolding experience" (148–49). In time only, there was a connection between the two lives of the old man and that young boy.

He knew that rambling is a sign of old age, but the General could not hold on to the present moment, nor to the faces most familiar to him—not even to his dead wife's, Erminie's, face. But even as he thought this, there was a clearing, and the features of all the faces of the women he had slept with melted and were assembled again in one face he had not forgotten. And his beloved, whom he had lost nearly sixty years ago, returned to him. He asked why the dead could not remain dead. It had been half a century ago. Even so, she returned to him, and time had not spoiled her. Her advent was "out of the drifting haze of the present" (153). He did not know why he had loved her. Yet here she was "when he turned back, clear, soft, vivid, with some secret in her look that thrilled, beckoned, and for ever eluded him. Her eyes were still eloquent with light; the promised joy was still infinite; the merest glimmer of a smile had outlasted the monuments of experience" (154). It was April then, it was in England, when and where they had met and fallen in love. That moment when they had first spoken had the clarity and coldness in his vision now of something embedded in crystal. That moment then had brought the whole world to life and had made everything vibrate with light. A voice "on the surface of thought" asked, "What is memory . . . that it should outlast emotion?" For although the General remembered, he could not feel anything of that rapture, or of its "wildness, the illusion of love's immortality" (156).

Of that "burning ecstasy of desire" nothing remained but "emptiness, and the gradual chill of decay." He demanded to know why it had happened and what it all meant, now that he was "caught within the twisting vision of age." He demanded to know why a passion that had the strength to ruin his life had forsaken him while he still lived, leaving no more than "two diminished shapes, performing conventional gestures" in a milieu that was neither time nor eternity. He demanded to know if these diminished shapes still existed somewhere, in a reality where there was no time. And if they did, was he a

survivor there as well as here? Which David Archbald was real, the lover he
had been and now remembered, or the old man drawing in the warmth of the
sun? Or were the lover and the old man both no more than "spirals of cosmic
dust, used and discarded in some experimental design?" It came to him that
"Life was not worth the trouble . . . if only that faint outline remained" (156–
57).

In the long afterward since he had lost his beloved, the General could
recover the past only in his dreams. At first, only the anguish had remained
with him. When that went, it took the poet in him with it, and his compassion.
Nothing, not even death, not even dying mattered much; once the dream of
happiness was over, there was so much pleasure to be had! "Little things
began to matter supremely." Where there had been desire, now there was
appetite. And that was all to the good. He thought that if one took care not to
search too deeply into living, there was much to be said for it. He had grown
accustomed to the sense that a part of life was missing. He had even been
"prepared . . . for those mocking resemblances that beckoned him in the
street, for those arrowy glimpses of her in the faces of strange women." He
had not been so mocked by life as this for nearly forty years (163).

When he was 75 years old, General Archbald had still not given up his hope
for an Indian summer of happiness, "that patient hope of the old" that does
not have the elasticity of the hope of young people, but that is more lasting
than theirs. Yet even this hope "was slowly strangled by life . . . and by the
suffocating grasp of appearances" (35). Now in his eighties, the very sight of
his granddaughter, Jenny Blair, walking toward him shattered his tranquility
and acceptance of disappointment, and made him keenly, regretfully aware
of the signatures of old age on his flesh and in his bones. Visiting Eva in the
hospital, he felt for a fleeting instant that the greatest misfortune was to be
old, to be infirm, to fumble for things, to forget the most familiar things. He
longed to be needed; he longed for a listener; he longed to speak of his
sufferings, his experiences, his reflections. He wished that just once, he might
release the past that was sealed in his soul. But no one cared to take the time to
listen. He knew now "what it felt to be old, to be finished, with life still
unappeased in his heart" (222). "He was easily nettled nowadays, sometimes
by trifles, sometimes by nothing at all." And when someone ruffled his temper, there was a hollow drumming in his ears (244).

When he was waiting out Eva's operation, the General thought what a relief
it was to drift alone into old age and then beyond it. He went to the window. A
rain was falling still. A lifetime ago, he had walked in the rain asking himself
"why he submitted to life. . . . Yet that English rain was still falling, slow, silent,
eternal, somewhere within a lost hollow of memory." It had been years—a
generation—since he had remembered enough. "Then yesterday, without
warning, he had stumbled again into that lost hollow" (253). How strange it
was, he thought in one of his meditations, "how trifling impressions, the
merest snatches of sensation, flickered to life again" (306). He had lived his
time on this earth, and there was no fear in him of any form, nor of formless-

ness, the Absolute. His age was coming to an end; like him, it was drifting to an end. But there was a calmness in this thought, and "the calm of being old was strangely like happiness." He experienced moments when the present blended with the past. Now, as death was approaching, he felt a presence near him. This presence, this indistinct outline, brought him happiness, serenity, the courage to die, and the acceptance of life. He found himself saying aloud that after all, "character may survive failure. Fortitude may be the last thing to go" (378–79).

In 1944, Ellen Glasgow wrote to Signe Toksvig that, next to *Barren Ground*, she liked *The Sheltered Life* best of all her novels. General Archbald was profoundly real to Glasgow: "I seemed to discover in him level after level of downward seeking and upward springing, which I thought of as the inner poetry (or rhythm) of life." The reflective vision in the middle section of the novel "pierces more deeply, I have always felt, than most visions" and this is the writing Glasgow hoped to be remembered by in the years to come. "Even when I was very young," she wrote in this letter, "I liked to write of old people, because the old had attained a kind of finality."[17] Twelve years earlier, in a letter to Daniel Longwell, Glasgow wrote that in reading *Barren Ground* again, she felt as she had when writing it, "that it is the truest novel ever written. Not true to a locality only . . . but to life and to the inevitable change and fall of the years" (118). In *The Sheltered Life*, which she had just completed at that time, and in *Barren Ground*, it was her intention to "give the scene an added dimension, a universal rhythm, deeper than any material surface. Beneath the lights and the shadows, there is the spirit of place; beneath the region, there is the whole movement of life" (116). In his Introduction to her letters, Blair Rouse reflects that she was interested in historical time, and "even more interested in time as an active force in life, in time enriching and fulfilling lives, or in time as an eroding and corroding force, wearing away the spirit and destroying the soul" (16).

In her early thirties, Glasgow experienced a spiritual awakening. "For a year," she wrote Mary Johnston, "I was so dead that I couldn't feel even when I was hurt because of some curious emotional anaesthesia, and, like you, I had to fight . . . not for my reason but for my very soul." When she "came out triumphant," walking as if on light for three entire months, "I was like one who had come out of a dark prison into the presence of God and saw and knew him, and cared for nothing in the way of pain that had gone before the vision" (56). Although the rapture of recovery cannot last,

the strength of the victory and the memory of it . . . are built into the eternal forces of one's spirit. . . . The old sorrows, the old temptations, the old fights are like so many steps by which we go on and upward. . . . I was born with a terrible burden of melancholy—of too much introspection—but for a whole year, for the first time in my life, I have not known a single instant of the old depression. I am perfectly willing to die, but I can say now, as I never could before, that I am equally willing to live until I come to where my road turns again. The sense of eternity—of immortality that is not a personal immortality has brought me not only reconciliation, but the kind of joy that is like the rush down from the battle of the senses. [56]

Even before she had turned 30, she was keenly aware of the passage of time. Even then, she felt that "the few intense joys of childhood are the best that life has to give." Even then, she sensed "that the past is quite as strong as the present and much more sacred" (34). Her work was her life. She existed on the surface, and lived "deep down in some world of inward creation" (159). And, nearing 60, she wrote Stark Young that she felt her best work was still ahead of her, that in spite of "the long tragedy" she felt her life had been, she did not think her creativity was exhausted. What she had saved "out of the wreck" was "the gift of work" (112).

She did not like this world, she wrote in that same letter, nor could she remember when she ever had. The desperately poor are all around us. Not even the dignity of literature, she remarked in a letter to Lewis Gannett, matters very much in a world where there is starvation, where people are being "burned up in prisons" (111). Except, perhaps, for one hour and one day, she wrote Bessie Zaban Jones, she had not liked her life. In 1935, a year after she wrote her this, she said in another letter to her,

> The agony of the world has always pressed in upon me, even when I was a child, and the curious part is that my power of suffering, both personal and vicarious, has not diminished as I have grown older. I still blaze with rage at the injustice and cruelty of life. Only I realize now that it is all wasted. [171–72]

In childhood, she saw a dog being chased, being stoned, and she herself became the hunted, beaten with clubs, caught in a net, dragged away to a dreadful fate. Something deep within her came awake then, "something with a passionate, tormented hatred of merciless strength, with a heartbreaking pity for the abused and inarticulate, for all the helpless victims of life, everywhere"[18] In childhood, she saw old Uncle Henry being taken from his cellar and put into the wagon that would carry him to the poor house. He was "penniless and half-witted and old" and he cried out that he did not want to go (11). Growing older had disappointed her in this one respect: "I had hoped—and this expectation was founded on literature and philosophy—that time would act as a sedative on my nerves, and my imagination would become less sensitive to the horrors of a world I would not have created" (272).

A critic had advised her apropos of her first book "to stop writing, and go back to the South and have some babies." She suspected then, "and later I discovered, that the maternal instinct, sacred or profane, was left out of me by nature when I was designed. I sometimes think that a hollow where it might have been was filled by the sense of compassion; but even of this, I am not entirely sure" (108). She thought that it would be wrong to bring another human being into the world in which she had suffered greatly, and the "secret wolf" of her deafness confirmed this attitude. When she fell in love for the first time with her whole being, this was a miracle to her, for until then she had felt herself unsuited for marriage. "Loneliness had exercised a strange fascination; and I felt that I could not surrender myself to constant companionship, that I could not ever be completely possessed." Then, too, she lacked the maternal instinct, and, apart from this, believed that her growing deafness might be passed on to a child, and that this would be "a sin against life" (153). Of her love, whom she never married—indeed, Glasgow remained single all her life—she reflected, "it is a law of our nature that the memory of longing should survive the more fugitive memory of fulfillment" (163). She learned from dark years of suffering that her finest work would come afterward. When those years had passed, they had left her with "a deeper source of creation, a more penetrating insight into experience, a truer knowledge of what the human heart can endure without breaking. Beneath dead and dying illusions, *Barren Ground* was taking form and substance in my imagination" (241).

As time brought a form of fulfillment to Dorinda Oakley, so it did to Ellen Glasgow. At 60, she was "hopelessly frail," and yet in some strange way she had more vitality than ever before in her life. She could not say whether it is a blessing or a curse that inner life could have more vigor and endurance than the body. She felt her life expanding in her later years, and thought she lived her fullest and richest years between the ages of 50 and 60. She was 70 when she wrote this, and in her Epilogue, she revealed the "thrilling discovery" she had made over the past few years, "that until one is over sixty one can never really learn the secret of living" (282). Of youth and age she wrote:

> Youth is the season of tragedy and despair. Youth is the time when one's whole life is entangled in a web of identity, in a perpetual maze of seeking and of finding, of passion and of disillusion, of vague longings and of nameless griefs, of pity that is a blade in the heart, and of "all the little emptiness of love." Then the soul drifts on the shallow stream of personality, within narrow borders. Not until life has passed through that retarded channel out upon the wide open sea of impersonality, can one really begin to live, not simply with the intenser part of oneself, but with one's entire being. For sixty years, I was learning this elemental truth; and in the very moment of my discovery, I found also that the shadow I had imagined my own was the shadow of death. [283]

In her fictions, she brought her characters out to that wide open sea. When Victoria Littlepage was 55 and knew that she was dying, she felt a "luminous veil" fall between herself and life.[19] She withdrew from reality then: "Time flowed round her and beyond her into an unconquerable vastness, and she knew that whatever happened or did not happen would not deeply concern her" (170). She felt a "senseless irritation" when she talked with her beloved daughter, and the effort to keep this out of her voice exhausted her (184). Her very soul "had become merely a rustling vacancy" wherein "all moral problems . . . were blown like straws in the sultry wind of oblivion" (190). She had visitations of "that poignant sense of the hallucination of all mortal experience" (192). Her meditations on her husband's life and her children's, on war and the League of Nations, and on established beliefs "were merely the formal patterns of inherited opinions. Like faded petals that enclose the living heart of a flower, they were folded round a radiant centre below the shifting surface of consciousness." Though they would wither and fall, "she knew that her deeper self, her hidden centre, would remain inviolable" (201). She remembered the dream she had had as a girl, but only once as a young wife, where on an immense and level plain she heard the thunder of galloping horses. A "liquid fire ran in her veins" and she wondered if the young Lochinvar were coming at last. "Then, in her sleep, she was lifted by an arm like the wind, and borne away, with the wild horses, over the rustling broomsedge, into a sunset that was like the fire at the heart of an opal" (151). But she had found that "Life, even at its best, was never what you had dreamed, was seldom what you had expected" (151). So Dorinda had thought to herself, and in these very words, at the end of *Barren Ground*.[20]

In *Vein of Iron*, Ada confides to Ralph during their interlude of happiness that she likes to hear the rushing noise of Cockspur Run at night: "It sounds as if time were going by and leaving us alone on an island of happiness."[21] Her grandmother had known the past was alive; she had felt the secret life of the generations beating in the pulse of the manse at Ironside. There, time had carried Ada from childhood to girlhood, and through love into young womanhood when, at Ralph's sudden smile, "she felt that her heart was a wheel turning" (79). In its passage, she sensed there were two selves, perhaps two lives, and once she stood in *this* point of time, "still waiting for the lost gleam to flash out of life" as she watched her own vanishing image "a shadow among shadows, within the hyacinth-colored circle of mountains" (314). Ada had intimations that "the actual world, not the inner vision . . . was wanting in substance. The core of life was within her heart" (227). There had been a moment when, "Suddenly, without reason, the meaning that sometimes starts out of life and seems to make everything clear and simple flashed back at her from the valley, the stream, the mountains, the sky. An instant only, and then it was gone" (249). Grandmother, who lived to be 87, had taught Ada that no one, not even the old or those in despair, wanted to come to an end in time or in eternity. Ada knew that the will was toward life. Her father, John Fincastle, taught her, too, that, "Love is a terrible power, and it's more deeply rooted in the old than in the young. When it's torn up in age there's nothing left but decay" (251). Young and passionately in love, she found "that changeless tranquility of the old which came from not wanting things" to be unbearable (150). Older, she recognized Ralph's meaning when he spoke of the "queer stillness" in her old father's face; she had seen it come over him "like twilight on a pond" (379). She saw his heart was elsewhere.

The aged John Fincastle stood in front of the breadline. Since the doctor had told him of a "general breaking-up," he had eaten only enough to keep alive. And once the pangs of hunger were over, he felt a strange exaltation that "flooded his mind with light" (415). At the end of life, he knew he had been renounced by time. There were moments when he had the sensation of swiftness, the feeling that he was flying out of himself. Now that he was failing, he longed to return to the places where he had been happy. The day he began his journey from Queenborough back to Ironside where it was always spring in his memory, he felt as eager for his adventure as when he had been a boy coming awake at the manse. Only there would he be free from "this terrible will." Only there would he be free "to sink back into changeless beatitude, into nothing and everything" (452). Though the manse was in ruins when he arrived there at last, he saw it unchanged and felt "a peace too deep for happiness, too still for ecstasy" (456). Though he remembered everything with perfect clarity, he knew that "between his childhood and the present moment when he was old and dying there was nothing but loneliness" (457).

In childhood, Ellen Glasgow lived in a world of nature spirits. Trees were living creatures with distinct personalities, and she gave each one of them a human name. Perhaps in a former life in the age of fable, she had been a dryad.[22] She imagined other lives for herself, though perhaps in all of them she would have been an exile and a stranger; she had "never, like Margaret Fuller, made the great acceptance."[23] She believed that the novel owed a debt to Freud, and more truly to Jung, that was incalculable (269). As a child, she had worshipped trees, the symbols of individuation. As a woman and an artist, she transformed indestructible memories—the hunted dog, the hunted Uncle Henry—into unforgettable fictions. In life and letters, she transformed maternal love into compassion,[24] afflictions into creativity. As an initiate at the Villa of the Mysteries comes to terms with relatedness, so Glasgow came in later life to "the wide open sea of impersonality." Like General Archbald, she sought to integrate the self in time and the self in timelessness. In her art, she worked through the conflict between her father's and her mother's worldview, a conflict waged in her very soul. Her mother had been the center of her childhood, the sun in her universe who "made everything luminous."[25] At the end of her life, the red and white oleanders that bloomed at the foot of their front steps were still visible to her in all their vivid clarity, and above them was her mother's face still smiling at her. In time's passage, that beloved face became clearer, younger. The passage of Dorinda's life had moved from Broomsedge to Pine and then to Life-everlasting, and watching Jason now revenged by Time, it came to her that it is sensation that dies last.[26] Sensation was Ellen Glasgow's earliest impression.[27] This may have been the wellspring of her gift, deepened by the wound inflicted by her "secret wolf." This may be the wellspring of memory where the old return as pilgrims to have their lives restored to them. For years, Glasgow had forgotten the love of her youth. Then, when she was almost 60, she went out to a foreign restaurant in New York one evening. The street was strange, "yet vaguely familiar. I smelt the scents of crushed apples and crowded places; and, suddenly, I remembered. I saw him again, clearly; I heard again, from very far off, that little nameless Hungarian song. For one moment alone . . . not ever again" (281).

Zora Neale Hurston (1901?–1960)

There is a moment in Zora Neale Hurston's *Their Eyes Were Watching God* when Janie is confronted with the possibility she dreaded most, that she has been made Time's fool. After two unhappy marriages, she met Tea Cake, a man much younger than herself. Tea Cake persuaded her that the difference in age between them did not matter, and she went away with him. But it was while she was waiting in a hotel room in Jacksonville for him to come back with some fish for their breakfast that she discovered her $200 was missing. In late morning, she remembered what had happened to Annie Tyler. When Annie was 52, she was widowed. Her husband left her "a good home and insurance money." The young men came calling, and Annie bought them what they wanted, and they left her. Then Who Flung came, and he wanted her to sell her house and go to Tampa with him, and he talked her into it. Janie remembered how the town had witnessed Annie's departure. She was wearing high-heeled slippers that were too small for her feet, and she had squeezed her body into a corset, but she was laughing and she was sure, just as Janie herself had been. Only two weeks later, Annie had been helped off the train at Maitland by the porter and the conductor. The cheap dye she had put in her hair had streaked it gray and black and blue and red; her slippers were bent; her corset was gone. She was a "shaking old woman," who was "broken," who had lost her pride. She had followed Who Flung to "a shabby room in a shabby house in a shabby street" and he had promised her that he would marry her the next day. Janie remembered that they stayed in that room for two days, and then Annie woke up and found that Who Flung and her money were gone. "The thing made itself into pictures and hung around Janie's bedside all night long."[28] But Tea Cake came back, and when he did, he told Janie that her being older didn't make any difference to him. He said that if he ever messed around another woman, it would not be because of Janie's age, but because that woman got him just as Janie had, so that he would not be able to help himself.

Another time, Tea Cake told Janie that, if two people think alike, they'll make it, that it's thought that makes the difference in ages. She had had her doubts for a good while. When she first saw him, she was about 40 and he looked to her to be about 25. She also noticed that he didn't look like he had much money. She told herself that Tea Cake might be just hanging around her to get in with her, and then he would take away everything she owned. Yet he could talk to her so that—for a moment, anyway—she "was lit up like a transfiguration" (159). Then in the next moment, she had the thought that he was using the fact that he was younger and that he would soon make fun of her for being old and foolish. Even so, she wished she could be twelve years younger than she was so that she could believe all that he told her. When she told him that she was nearly twelve years older, Tea Cake said he had thought about this and that he had tried to fight against it, but that it did no good. He told her the thought of his youth did not satisfy him the way her presence did. She answered that most folks think a difference in age like that is very important. But Tea Cake said that things like a difference in age have a lot to do with convenience, but that they have nothing to do with love.

When she was little, Janie had been twisted by her Nanny in the name of love. She felt she hated the old woman for having done this to her. Nanny had wanted Janie to marry Logan Killicks. She had wanted her granddaughter to have a different fate than to grow up and become a mule of the world. So Janie married Logan. But she hadn't been married a year before she noticed that he didn't talk in rhymes to her anymore, or "wonder at her long black hair and finger it" (45). Janie thought that Nanny belonged to the kind "that loved to deal in scraps." She "had taken the biggest thing God ever made, the horizon . . . and pinched it in to such a little bit of a thing" that she could tie it around Janie's neck "tight enough to choke her" (138). Janie had observed that most people did not love one another.

After a time, Joe Starks came along. Janie held back from him for a good while "because he did not represent sun-up and pollen and blooming trees." But Jody "spoke for far horizon. He spoke for change and chance" (50). The memory of Nanny held her back, too, for a while. But there came the time when she decided to go with Jody, and after that the years went by, and they "took all the fight out of Janie's face" (118). In the beginning, Janie did not have cause to think too much about the inside state of their marriage. She liked Jody's store, except that she had to sell things, and she would much rather listen to the men sitting around on the porch passing their thought pictures to one another, thought pictures that "were always crayon enlargements of life" (81). But Jody found occasion time and again to tell her that women could not think any more than children or chickens and cows could, and that gave her cause to think about the relationship. She fought him back, but that only made him fight harder; he wanted her to submit to his will. So there came a time when "the spirit of the marriage left the bedroom and took to living in the parlor" (111). When she was 24 and Jody's wife of seven years, he slapped her face in anger over a failed dinner that happens to every woman now and then. She was a good cook, but this once the fish was not quite done and she had scorched the rice. He slapped her again and again until her ears were ringing, and he "told her about her brains" before stalking back to his store (112). It was then that Janie found that her thoughts and feelings would never be for him again. She was saving them now for a man she had never seen. Now she knew she had an inner person, and she would keep her separate from the outside Janie.

During the years she was married to Jody, there were times when Janie thought about her future and imagined living a different kind of life. She thought about running away, but where would she go, now that she was in her thirties and everything in life had changed for her? She did not read books, so she did not know that she herself "was the world and the heavens boiled down to a drop." Then it happened that she sat and watched the shadow Janie taking care of the store and bowing before Jody while the real Janie sat in the shade of a tree feeling the wind in her hair and her dress—"Somebody near about making summertime out of lonesomeness." It took her by surprise, but after a while she became used to doing this, and it lulled her, and in a way it reconciled her to the way things were. And then one day she saw "Joe wasn't so young as he used to be. There was already something dead about him" (119). Maybe Jody had seen this even before she had and was afraid that she would see it, too. He started to talk about her age all the time, now. It was as though he did not want Janie to stay young while he was growing old. He would tell her to throw something over her shoulders before going outside. He'd remark, "You ain't no young pullet no mo'. You'se uh ole hen now" (120). She could see right through his skull into his thoughts when he told her she was too old to play croquet, and so she let it pass. She knew that he was hurting.

But when Jody told her, "You ain't no young girl to be gettin' all insulted 'bout yo' looks. You ain't no young courtin' gal. You'se uh ole woman, nearly forty," she told him right back that he was already 50. She asked him why he didn't ever talk about *that*. He said it wasn't any use for her to get mad at him for mentioning that she wasn't young anymore, because old as she was, no one was looking for her for a wife. It was then that Janie "robbed him of his illusion of irresistible maleness that all men cherish." And what was worse than that, she did it in public, and made him a laughingstock. She was all woman, she told him, even if she did look her age, and that was more than *he* could claim. "You big-bellies round here and put out a lot of brag," she said, "but 'tain't nothin' to it but yo' big voice. Humph! Talkin' 'bout *me* lookin' old! When you pull down yo' britches, you look lak de change uh life" (122–23). Joe hit her then, and drove her out of the store, and after that night he moved out of their bedroom and slept downstairs. He wanted her to think he hated her, but she knew he was licking his wounds. The silence between them from that time on was "the sleep of swords." She asked herself why he was so mad that she had made him look small. He'd been doing that to *her* for years. She thought he might get over it. And she noticed how baggy he was getting "all over. . . . A little sack hung from the corners of his eyes and rested on his cheek-bones; a loose-filled bag of feathers hung from his ears and rested on his neck. . . . A sack of flabby something hung from his loins and rested on his thighs when he sat down" (125–26). But these things, too, ran down in time.

Jody used to scorn root-doctors, but now he got one to help him. Janie did not know that what drove him was that he hoped desperately "to appear the old-time body in her sight" (126). She felt sorry for Jody because she thought that what he needed was a real doctor. There was a rumor in the town that she had had Jody "fixed." Janie's friend Pheoby told her it was too late for a divorce. "Just g'wan back home," she advised her, "and set down on yo' royal diasticutis and say nothin'" (127). Janie had been married to Joe for twenty years, and now she had to carry around that accusation.

When Jody died, Janie studied herself in the mirror long and carefully. She remembered then that many years before, "she had told her girl self to wait for her in the looking glass." What she found from a close examination of her features and her skin was that, "The young girl was gone, but a handsome woman had taken her place." And she saw, after she removed her kerchief, that her hair was still heavy and long, that "the glory was there." She checked herself before combing her hair and tying it up in the kerchief again. "Then she starched and ironed her face, forming it into just what people wanted to see." And she opened the window and called the people to come, telling them that her husband Jody had died, that he was gone from her (134–35).

A month had not gone by after Joe's funeral before the men started coming around—men who had never been close to him—to tell her about their concern for her welfare and to offer advice. But Janie knew what the well-wishers were after. And, anyway, "This freedom feeling was fine" (139). It was after this that Janie met Tea Cake, who told her many times that he did not care that she was older. And when he was dying, and Janie told him there was no use in his being jealous, that she couldn't love anyone but him, and, besides, she was just an old woman that no one else wanted, he said again that her age was not what mattered. He told her that she only sounded old when she told folks what year she was born, and that there were plenty of men who would gladly take her and work hard for the privilege of it. He told her she should not call herself old, that she was a little girl baby. "God made it so you spent yo' ole age first wid somebody else," he said, "and saved up yo' young girl days to spend wid me" (268).

Tea Cake had taught Janie that love is like the sea—that although it is a moving thing, "it takes its shape from de shore it meets, and it's different with every shore" (284). Toward the end of another novel, in which Hurston explores the changing relationship between a wife and husband (a white couple) as they grow older, she writes that water longs for the sea—all water is on a journeying home to the sea, Jim Meserve tells Arvay in *Seraph on the Suwanee*.[29] It changes places and forms thousands of time beyond imagining, but it always comes back home. "Maybe it's like that with everything and everybody," Arvay says. "If it's in there, it will return to its real self at last" (294). And Jim finds that well-spoken. Arvay is finding the way to win him back. When that huge diamond-back was tightening its coils around Jim's body and its head was freeing itself, he had asked for her help. And she had failed him; she'd just stood there, frozen. That was when he had decided to leave her. They might have the right papers, but their bonds had never really been consecrated. "Two people ain't never married until they come to the same point of view," Jim told her. And since they never had, he would be moving to the coast. If ever Arvay would show a sign of coming to be the woman he had married, he would try again. Until then, they were parting ways (234).

There were times after Jim left her that Arvay "felt herself lost in the edges of the wastes." The hours hung around her doorway like homeless dogs, waiting for her in the morning when she got up, "and still whimpering and whining of their emptiness when she went to bed at night" (235). Earl, their firstborn was dead, and the other two, Angie and Kenny, were grown and gone from home. Now Jim had left her, too, Jim who had once loved her for more than her good looks, for that power she had to change for him "when she was stirred for him," when that mysterious green light would come into her blue eyes, and they would change "to a misty greenish-blue like the waters of the sea at times and at places. It warmed him, it burned him and bound him" (94).

That thing that she had feared but would not confront had happened to Arvay—her family circle had been broken. She knew that when she held her daughter in her arms, when Angie sobbed of her love for Hatton. "It was as if a crack had opened in the wall of her home and a cold damp draft was blowing through" (153). During the year after Angie's marriage, Arvay felt "the old familiar things in her life . . . fading away" (169). Even though Kenny wrote often from Gainesville, it wasn't the same as having him around the house. As for Angie, Hatton came first for her. No one needed Arvay much now. She had that feeling of emptiness and uselessness. There was a silence in the house. And Jim had been so taken up with the Howland Development that this threatened her more now than the swamp used to, with its dark foreboding.

When Arvay found out that Jim had given his consent to Angie marrying without telling her about it, she wept in her bed and made resolutions against him. But what was the use? They "were just like the lightning-bugs holding a convention." At night, those resolutions would meet and make "scorning speeches against the sun" and swear they'd do away with it and give *their* light to the world. But next morning, they'd crawl under the leaves, owning "that the sun was boss-man in the world" (175). Then Jim gave Kenny permission over the phone to leave school and join a band in New York. Arvay told him he'd never know how she felt, that all the little family she had went and left her in some way or another. If only she hadn't been in the bathroom with her stomach troubles when Kenny called. If only she'd been sitting quietly on the porch when that phone rang, so she could have handled her feelings. She felt that her old power had been broken. Jim said that Arvay still had *him*. But she left him standing there, looking at her as she went into her old bedroom and closed the door. And there "she went forth to face the demon of waste and desert places and take him for her company" (210). With Earl dead, with Angie married and Kenny doing so well, and with Jim so taken up with his boats, Arvay "felt empty-handed and sluggish." She "had no arrangements for spending idle time. She did not read things, and was not even given to fancy-work. Her life had been patterned to serve and now there was nobody for her to wait on and do for" (213).

To travel alongside Jim had been a struggle and a journey, and Arvay had paid a high price for it. She meant to find the courage and strength to hold to life. She meant to begin again with Jim. It came to her on that boat that everything that had happened to her in life was a part of her, that "what was in you was bound to come out and stand." Earl's birth "had purged her flesh," and that was meant to be. "Somebody had to pay off the debt so that the rest of the pages could be clean." She'd been made by God to be a mother, "to give peace and comfort around." Earl had fulfilled his purpose, and his sufferings were over. And Angie, "female beauty, had come out of her." And Kenny, "bringing the music part inside her that she had never had a chance to show herself." With Jim these wonders had been made. It was natural that children "would grow up and seek for partners just as she had done." It was meant to be. Now she hoped that Angie and Kenny would find the fulfillment she had found. She'd been meant to mother, to serve. Her parents, her sister, her children, Jim had all wanted her to mother them. "Her job was mothering. What more could any woman want and need?" Once she had thought this was her cross. Now she saw it "as her glory" (309–10).

In a letter to her editor at Scribner's, Hurston wrote of *Seraph on the Suwanee*, "Millions of women do not want their husbands to succeed for fear of losing him. It is a very common ailment. That is why I decided to write about it."[30] For whatever reason, Hurston's literary biographer Robert Hemenway observes, she "could not grant Arvay the attainment of a truly independent selfhood" of the kind she had idealized for herself, and that she had realized in her own life (313). In both these novels, *Their Eyes Were Watching God* and *Seraph on the Suwanee*, Hurston explored questions she found compelling in her own life, about the many meanings of love and freedom for an older woman.

Hurston had been married and divorced twice, and she was so secretive about her private life that the fact of her second marriage was virtually unknown to many people who knew her well. The year of her birth, too, is unknown: on her second marriage license, she claimed to have been born in 1910. Her brother, who prepared a family genealogy, cites 1891 as the year of her birth. She herself sometimes said she was 9 years old, and sometimes that she was 13 years old when her mother died, and the date of her mother's death is given by most family members as 1904. Once, Hurston asked her brother "to list an erroneous birth date on his application for a . . . driver's license so that he would appear older than she." Although 1901 is the year Hurston most often gave as her birth date, Hemenway says that he does not have much confidence in it, and he comments that it is possible that, if Hurston were born in 1891, she could have been married for ten years, as Janie and Logan Killicks were, and then have decided to banish those years from the record. (32, n. 8). In her fiction, the difference between Janie's and Tea Cake's ages did not matter to him. In her life, it might have been otherwise.

When Hurston married Albert Price III in 1939, he was 23 and she was at least 38. But he claimed he was older, and she claimed she was born in 1910 (273–74, 316, n. 2).

The passage of time was deeply haunting for Hurston. When she was a child of no more than 7, she had visions of what her life was to be. She fell strangely asleep, and, "Like clearcut stereopticon slides, I saw twelve scenes flash before me, each one held until I had seen it well in every detail, and then . . . replaced by another."[31] She knew that these scenes, which did not have the continuity of dream-scenes, were telling her the truth of her destiny, "and my soul writhed in agony and shrunk away. . . . I was weighed down with a power I did not want" (65). These scenes foretold her fate of orphanhood and homelessness. In time, each vision came true, and she passed each as a station. Her childhood ended with the coming of these pronouncements. Of her second vision picture, she wrote that when it came to pass, she found "that all that geography was within me. It only needed time to reveal it."[32]

Once Hurston learned how to walk, she always had that inside urge to wander. Her mother used to say that a woman who was an enemy of hers must have sprinkled "travel dust" around the doorstep the day her daughter was born. As a child, she used to climb to the top of the chinaberry trees at their front gate and look out over the world, and the most interesting thing she saw was the horizon. She wanted to walk out to it and see what it was like at the end of the world. Trees were alive—the loving pine that "had a mighty fine bass voice when it really took a notion to let it out," and another tree "that used to creep up close to the house around sundown and threaten me. It used to put on a skull-head with a crown on it every day at sundown and make motions at me when I had to go out on the back porch."[33] Spirits kept her company all her childhood. Then they vanished in a shining meadow. The Norse tales struck her soul deeply; the Old Testament exhilarated her. This early reading caused her anguish when she was young, in a way: "My soul was with the gods and my body in the village" (64).

Hurston could not say just when she began making up stories. "People seldom see themselves changing" (78–79). One day she came into the house to tell her mother how a bird talked to her, a bird who somehow knew her name, a bird with a long, soft beautiful tail that she climbed so she could sit up in the tree and have a long talk with her. Another time, she told her the lake had let her walk all over it without even wetting her feet. It was her grandmother, not her mother, who glared at her. Her Mama had told all her children to "jump at de sun." Her Mama always stood between the children and her Papa. She granted that her daughter talked back a lot, "but she didn't want to 'squinch my spirit' too much for fear that I would turn out to be a mealy-mouthed rag doll by the time I got grown." That made her Papa furious. "He predicted dire things for me. . . . Mama was going to suck sorrow for not beating my temper out of me before it was too late" (29). But she was her mother's child. And then,

That day, September 18th, she had called me and given me certain instructions. I was not to let them take the pillow from under her head until she was dead. The clock was not to be covered, nor the looking-glass. She trusted me to see to it that these things were not done. I promised her as solemnly as nine years could do, that I would see to it.

What years of agony that promise gave me! In the first place, I had no idea that it would be soon. But that same day near sundown I was called upon to set my will against my father, the village dames and village custom. I know now that I could not have succeeded. [94]

She knew now, Hurston wrote, that her father, who had physically restrained her from fulfilling her deathbed promise to her mother, was with the mores. She knew now she could not possibly have kept her word to her mother. A part of her life came to an end at that moment when she failed her mother: "I was old before my time with grief of loss, of failure, and of remorse. . . . That hour began my wanderings. Not so much in geography, but in time. Then not so much in time as in spirit" (97).

In *Jonah's Gourd Vine,* the second baby born since Lucy and John came to Florida was their second daughter. The baby has John's gray eyes, but he sees a look in them that tells she knows something. Lucy carried the rest of her babies in her belly, she says, "but dat one wuz bred in mah heart. She bound tuh be diffunt."[34] Her name is *Isis.* When Lucy lies dying, she speaks to the 9-year-old Isie, her child above all the others, and tells her to get all the education she can: "Dat's de onliest way you kin keep out from under people's feet. You always strain tuh be de bell cow, never be de tail uh nothin'." Lucy pities her "po' li'l' sandy-haired chile" who will "suffer uh lot 'fo' she git tuh de place she kin 'fend fuh herself." She says Isie must never love anyone more than herself. "Do, you'll be dying befo' yo' time is out." And she says, though she knows the child will not understand this for years to come, that a person can be killed without being struck a blow. And then, she asks of her, "Isie, when Ahm dyin' don't you let 'em take de pillow from under mah head" (206–7). Lucy tells Mrs. Mattie Clarke not to worry about her: "Ah done been in sorrow's kitchen and Ah done licked out all de pots. . . . Nothin' kin touch mah soul no mo'. It wuz hard tuh loose de string-holt on mah li'l' chillun" (209). But she had done that, too.

On the gravestone placed by Alice Walker in the segregated cemetery in Fort Pierce, Florida, in the Garden of the Heavenly Rest, the words "A Genius of the South" are engraved under Hurston's name, and under the dates of her birth and death, "Novelist, Folklorist, Anthropologist." Daughter of a preacher who was elected mayor of Eatonville for three terms, and who wrote the local laws, Hurston came to know the truth of what Brother Harris told Hattie in *Jonah's Gourd Vine,* that the Bible is the best conjure book in the world.[35] The child who sensed the aliveness of Nature grew into a woman who saw how the sun "laid a red sword westward across the swaying water" and, in a little time, how it "had become a light yolk yellow and was walking with red legs across the sky."[36] She rejoiced when she was sent to collect Negro folklore, because she "couldn't see it for wearing it." Only when she was away in college, away from that "pure Negro Town" of Eatonville, could she "see myself like somebody else and stand off and look at my garment. Then I had to have the spy-glass of Anthropology to look through at that."[37] As a social scientist, she was well aware of the reluctance of people to disclose "that which the soul lives by. . . . The Indian resists curiosity by a stony silence. The Negro offers a feather-bed resistance. . . . we let the probe enter, but it never comes out. It gets smothered under a lot of laughter and pleasantries" (18). A richly creative oral tradition was received by an infallible ear. When Hurston was a "play-pretty" for a theater company, the thespians were enchanted by her idioms. She wrote that they were not aware of how Southern children, whether they are black or white, are brought up

> on simile and invective. They know how to call names. It is an everyday affair to hear somebody called a mullet-headed, mule-eared, wall-eyed, hog-nosed, 'gator-faced, shad-mouthed, screw-necked, goat-bellied, puzzle-gutted, camel-backed, butt-sprung, battle-hammed, knock-kneed, razor-legged, box-ankled, shovel-footed, unmated so-and-so! Eyes looking like skint-ginny nuts, and mouth looking like a dish-pan full of broke-up crockery! They can tell you in simile exactly how you walk and smell. They can furnish a picture gallery of your ancestors, and a notion of what your children will be like.[38]

In the South, Hurtson wrote, that particular stratum of the population is not given to reading books, and therefore the similes they use are taken straight from "the barnyard and the woods. When they get through with you, you and your whole family look like an acre of totem-poles" (144).

The thought-pictures that were passed around that store porch in Eatonville, those crayon enlargements of life, were transformed into anthropological lore and folklore and hoodoo (voodoo), into fiction and song and drama and dance. They were as inexhaustible and exuberant as her spiritual energies. She had known firsthand the smell like death that is in poverty, she had known how "people can be slave-ships in shoes" (124). "They said she couldn't become a writer recognized by the world," the minister C. E. Bolen said at her funeral. "But she did it. The Miami paper said she died poor. But she died rich. She did something."[39] Hurston had written of the incomparable agony of carrying an untold story inside oneself, and in this passage she recalled the tale of the Spartan youth who carried a fox under his cloak.[40] She was writing of the creative force that drove her. She wrote *Their Eyes Were Watching God* in seven weeks, in Haiti.

"The hours went past on their rusty ankles and midnight stood looking both ways for day."[41] So did time grind by the night of Lucy's watch, when the men came to get John Pearson. Time's passing could be that long agony of the night watch. It could move calmly, too, as if it had carried away wrongs and the wronged forever. "You think it's dead," John says to Zeke and his wife, "but de past ain't stopped breathin' yet" (223). When he tells Hattie that he never hit Lucy, he has a thought-picture, 7 years old: "Lucy's bright eyes in the sunken face. Helpless and defensive. The look. Above all, the look!" He stares at it, fascinated, horrified. "The sea of the soul, heaving after a calm, giving up its dead" (228). He has dreams that are so real, so true . . . but then they fade. Time came when John looked at the street from the deep porch, and "it seemed changed in a dream way." He thought then that maybe nothing is real, maybe there is no world, there are no elements; maybe we all exist "'jus' somewhere in God's mind,' but when he wiggled his tired toes the world thudded and throbbed before him" (291).

That world with its thuds and throbs was real enough, Hurston well knew. And time told by calendars and clocks was real enough to divide lovers and to break the circle of the family. "Time changes folks," Arvay had told Hatton, "as they go along the road." This, too, Hurston knew. Her love, like Arvay's, "had mounted her to the tops of peaky mountains. It had dragged her in the dust." Like Arvay, Hurston "had been in Hell's kitchen and licked out all the pots."[42] Perhaps like Arvay, too, she had had a tree that was her "memory thing." Hurston's mother's death had sent her on her wandering way. And Time revealed the geography of her inner life as she jumped at the sun, as she reached for the far horizon.

May Sarton (1912–)

In one of her copybooks, found after the fire that destroyed the Twin Elms Nursing Home, Caroline Spencer asked herself if she was senile. "The trouble is that old age is not interesting until one gets there," she wrote, "a foreign country with an unknown language to the young, and even to the middle-aged."[43] She wished she'd learned more about it. It is a disguise only the old see through. Although she felt 21 inside, "the outward shell conceals the real me—sometimes even from itself—and betrays that person deep down inside, under wrinkles and liver spots and all the horrors of decay" (80). It had taken her two weeks to obtain her first notebook and a pen—that is the courage needed in old age—and her first entry reads, "I am not mad, only old" (9). She cautioned herself in her journal that she must not dwell on why she was brought *here*, that she must not fall into the paranoiac trap awaiting the old.

Twin Elms is "a concentration camp for the old, a place where people dump their parents or relatives exactly as though it were an ash can" (9). Caro is 76 when her 80-year-old brother John brings her here. She'd had to close her home after suffering a heart attack, and she was not getting on with John and his younger wife, Ginny. Why doesn't John visit her? Was he told not to come? But when John and Ginny finally do visit her, Caro makes two mistakes. She weeps when she sees them, and begs to be taken away from the place.

Caro can't blame John entirely for putting her here. In his own way, he is fighting to keep whole, too. She names her journal *The Book of the Dead,* and she keeps it to keep her sanity in the face of the threat of a failing memory. In the Hell that is Twin Elms, she intends to make herself whole. She prepares for death as for "a great final journey. . . . this path inward and back into the past is like a map, the map of my world" (10). If it is drawn accurately, it will tell her where she is. "Old age, they say, is a gradual giving up. But it is strange when it all happens at once. That is a real test of character" (14). Even after a few days there, one begins to feel like a caged animal, the sense of having been completely abandoned, "so at first one goes way down deep into oneself and stays there just as a frightened animal does" (22).

At Twin Elms, Caro learns "that any true cry from the heart of an old person creates too much havoc in a listener, is too disturbing, because nothing can really be done to help us on the downward path" (79–80). There are those who respond to the cry with the cliché that the situation will improve or that the old person exaggerates. Cruellest of all is the refusal to believe it. And there are those who respond by treating the old person as if one were speaking to an infant. John's voice had been unnaturally cheerful when they arrived at Twin Elms, as if she were a child. Or feeble-minded.

Feeble-minded? The kin of the old men at Twin Elms are probably told by social workers, and even by the doctors who so rarely come around, that old people become "mental." That word always amused Caro, "as it seems to suggest the opposite of what it means" (51). Childlike? She thinks about childhood often, "not because I am in my second childhood (What a myth that is—children have hope!) but because the humiliations are the same . . . like being treated as if they knew nothing or were incapable of adult emotions" (60–61). Many times as a child, Caro had been sent to bed without supper as punishment for her tantrums. Why in her whole long life had she never come to terms with that inner anger? But anger "is the wicked side of fire." It was fire that made her "a good teacher and a brave fighter sometimes. Fire can be purifying" (44). It was anger that kept Standish Flint alive, though he was bedridden and so deaf she had to communicate with him through shouts and signs and smiles. Her fellow in abandonment, Standish held fiercely to his dignity. The other old men were tranquilized. It is cruel to interpret anger in the old as a sign of madness or senility. "I feel things *more* intensely than I used to, not less," Caro writes. Inside, she is as young as when she was 21. But she is afraid to appear ridiculous. "People expect serenity of the old. That is the stereotype, the mask we are expected to put on." Just writing her dissent renews her vitality. "Among all the other deprivations here we are deprived of *expression*. The old men slowly atrophy because no one asks them what they feel or why. Could they speak if someone did?" (81)

This onetime math teacher now wants to "make a final perfect equation before I am through" (24). She needs to think of Twin Elms as the House of Gathering, where she could make herself whole and, through this, find her redemption. Only after hope left her could she begin "the road back . . . into the central self that no environment can change or poison" (35). When she came to Twin Elms, she brought three treasures with her, a Japanese bronze turtle, a small Swedish glass vase, and the *Oxford Book of English Verse*. She had longed to see the Piero della Francesca Nativity and to hear sacred music. When Reverend Thornhill brought her a transistor radio, she could hear the Fauré Requiem again at last. When his daughter, Lisa, brought her flowers, she moved them to the bed table "so I could smell the two deep red roses and also the faint bitter smell of chrysanthemums. How starved I am! I realized in the presence of these flowers that every sense except my eyes is starved here" (66). Though the food is fair, the dishes, the glass, even the tray cloth are plastic, and Caro has become

> very sick of mashed potatoes and colorless meat covered with thick brown gravy out of a can. I cannot even imagine what it would be like to feel a tender caress. . . . in a place like this where we are deprived of so much already, the small things that delight the senses—food, a soft blanket, a percale sheet and pillow case, a bottle of lavender cologne, a linen handkerchief seem necessities if one is to survive. We are slowly being turned into passive, maltreated animals. I wonder whether memory itself might not be kept alive partly through the *senses*. [66]

Caro is dying for want of love. The tide of love "goes out, little by little . . . and whatever is left of us lies like a beached ship" (121). Even Anna is taken away with the receding tide. Caro's final resolution is to end everything in a purifying fire. "Absolute nakedness may be madness," but "It is what is *required*" (126).

Did not one expect to feel less naked in old age, or at least less desperate? This is what Hilary Stevens's old friend asked her in a letter.[44] But when young Hilary admonishes old Hilary to *think* about her mother and not to feel so much or to weep over what is irrevocable and finished, old Hilary answers that it may be irrevocable, but it is not finished: "We may come into the world naked, but we go out of it clothed in anguish" (61). At 70, Hilary had found that age confers certain privileges on one. You can be utterly honest, for instance. But everything is harder when you're older, even buttoning your slipper. You have to stoop, as if you were a donkey. And she had found that age did not diminish her power to attract others and to be attracted to them. "Old, young, male, female—her capacity to be touched, to be involved, to *care* was . . . that still of a young girl. How did one keep growing otherwise?" (55) When young Mar cried that he was tired inside, tired of feeling so much, Hilary shouted that he had only just begun to feel. She "had always imagined that one of the blessings of old age would be that one might live by and for these essentials . . . the light on a wall. Instead one dragged around this great complex hive of sensation and feeling" (57).

Hilary's solitude was so inhabited by the past that the only time she was alone in it was when she was wholly absorbed in her work. And she could not come near one part of the past without bringing the whole of it to life, "without being assailed by ghostly presences. On the surface she could be quite consciously brisk and analytic, even detached. But under the surface, she was filled with echoes and rumors, with startling images" (97). Yet at 70, she had found that there were things she could not remember, that whole lives could fall into oblivion, that memory could be cruel. That she could still recite a poem she had loved filled her with an intense joy.

There were two selves of Hilary, twins warring with one another. One was "a hortatory and impatient person . . . irritated by her lethargic twin, that one who had to be prodded awake and commanded like a doddering servant" (12). It was this lethargic other who was growing old, who wanted to be left in bed, left in peace. Returning from dreams where she had flown over immense distances and had so often been reconciled with her ghosts, swimming up from the deep waters swarming with dreams, Hilary had to force herself "cold-awake" and out of bed. "Old crone," she said to the self who was her life companion in the mirror, "with hardly a wisp of hair left, and those dewlaps, and those wrinkles" (13). But she could not expect to review the life she had lived in twelve hours without feeling—and showing on her face—the weight of it.

When Hilary looked in the Venetian mirror, she saw herself at 25 in the drawing of her that Sargent had made, and she thought that Age was standing there with Youth, like a ghost. But all along, young Hilary is inside of Old Hilary, talking with her, reminding her of things, giving her advice. She had had a bad night, and in those suspenseful and tense hours before the interviewers came she felt her old emotions toward her parents coming perilously near the surface again. She called out to them; she asked herself if the mourning for parents ever ends. In one of her conversations with herself, Hilary remembered how she had shouted at her mother that she was nobody's child. An old scene when she had hugged her mother returned to her together with the feeling of it. Over and over, she asked herself the same questions about her parents. There was still something she had "to track down, lost somewhere at the bottom of all her musing like a shining pebble of truth" (67). And it came to her in a vision rising upward, a vision of her mother pruning roses, her mother burying her face in a dark red rose "with a look of . . . sensuous delight" (67). Hilary tells the young interviewers at the end of their talk together that she had sometimes imagined her last book might be about her mother, that "it is time to die when one has come to terms with everything" (192–93). Her mother's death had left her desolate, yet it had liberated her. But what was the freedom for, after that? Her mother remains her "great devouring enigma" (193). Hilary had been devastated by her mother's power even as a child. Either that, or it had marked her to become a poet. She could never forget her mother's voice reading Arnold's *Forsaken Merman*, "and the anguish of that cry 'Margaret, Margaret!' I still wake sometimes to that lament, to what I heard . . . of longing and starvation, wake in tears" (193–94).

It came to Hilary sometimes that life's natural inclination was toward chaos, that just to empty the ashtrays and wastebaskets and make the bed was all that could be asked of one, "as if one never got to the real things because of the constant exhausting battle to keep ordinary life from falling apart" (14). There was always the impulse to entangle herself with new obligations. There was always the battle to keep her temper in the face of constant interruptions. And *that* was woman's work. "Each single day she fought a war to get to her desk before her . . . energy had been dissipated, to . . . cut through an intricate web of slight threads pulling her in a thousand directions" (18). Her passion for flowers took so much time from her work. What man would trouble himself about flowers? But her house felt empty without them. The demands of housekeeping kept her caged. During the years of her marriage to Adrian, she had never awakened with the psychic energy the writer must have. She had felt called to perfectionism in the domestic tasks, and this had left her no time to create.

When Adrian's mother had remarked that Hilary's writing must mean to her what Adrian's horses meant to him, she had felt like a person who had been starving and just been given bread. She had told her mother-in-law then that nothing seemed real to her unless she could say it. Now, lying down from an attack of vertigo, young Hilary tells old Hilary that she has too much to do, that she can't die yet. And Hilary feels expectancy and hope again. "All the living, all the caring, all the anxiety had only been a prelude to that not impossible poem, the thing that would justify it all, and stop forever the whirling of the past with all its images, make the whole world stand still!" (53) Balancing art and life is harrowing, she tells her interviewers. And life comes before art. Only a monster would put art first. But art and life ask for different kinds of fidelity. Art is served at the expense of every human being. For the writer, though, love—the life of life itself—is "the waker of the dead, love as conflict, . . . the mirage. Not love as peace or fulfillment, or lasting, faithful giving" (156).

Striving toward wholeness—that, too, is woman's work: "Never to categorize, never to separate one thing from another—intellect, the senses, the imagination, . . . some total gathering together where the most realistic and the most mystical can be joined in a celebration of life itself" (172). Hilary had come into touch again with what she saw as the masculine side of her talent, when Mar criticized her poetry. She had lost the boy in herself in her love for Dorothea, when the woman deep within her had begun to take possession. For Dorothea, the long-buried anarchic Aphrodite had been brought to life through that same love. Both had turned the face of the Medusa around, had seen their *selves*. To Mar, an older Hilary spoke of the boy she had once wanted to be, the boy whom she kept alive in herself, the boy who had written the poems. It was in the light of that boy's eyes that she justified her way of life. To reconcile the warring twin selves within her, to reconcile the young Hilary and the old Hilary, and the masculine and feminine sides of her talent, and the boy-self and the woman-self—at 70, this was Hilary Stevens's task. There were times, she told her interviewers, when she thought of life itself "as merely a long preparation and waiting, a long darkness of growth toward these adventures of the spirit, a picaresque novel, so to speak, in which the episodes are all inward" (174).

In *Plant Dreaming Deep*, a book Sarton wrote in praise of Nelson, she explored the passages of this long waiting. Her friend Perley was changing. In five years' time, he had moved from what he still felt was the prime of life at age 70, into old age. In those same five years, Sarton had learned that there was a difference between youth and middle age, and that she, too, had been changing. She could not work so many hours in the day as she had before.[45] Sarton had experienced a midlife crisis. After her parents' deaths, their house was sold, and all they had shared together was dismantled. She "went through those months like a person in a dream, hardly conscious, making decisions because they had to be made" (22). The old pieces of Flemish furniture that had been stored away began to haunt her "as if they were animals kept underground and dying of neglect. How long would they stay alive? And how long would the life in me stay alive if it did not find new roots?" (23) She made the decision, then, to buy the house in Nelson, though she knew nothing of either houses or life in the country, and though she knew that, because she was in her forties, this change would have as radical consequences for her life as would marriage at that age.

Sarton had moved to the country not to exorcise her demons, for perhaps that would be asking too much of her new life, but to try to come to terms with them. She had consciously chosen to cut life to the marrow. But in the first year of her new life, the old demon of impatience assailed her with great force. The midlife crisis "has to do as much as anything with a catastrophic anxiety about time itself. How has one managed to come to the meridian and still be so far from the real achievement one had dreamed possible at twenty? And I mean achievement as a human being as well as within a career" (87). Her father's dedication to his work had taught her by example that, "Routine is not a prison, but the way into freedom from time. The apparently measured time has immeasurable space within it, and in this it resembles music" (56–57). So she lived through her depression by going on with her work. That first winter in Nelson, she suffered from anxiety in knowing that the time ahead was limited. She had begun a new life in middle age, yet at the same time she was continuing a pattern of devoting herself to two arts. She had always thought that in time she would grow, both as a poet and as a novelist. Now she felt time shrinking, perhaps running out. And at 50, she feared that the life it had taken her twenty years to build, a life of balancing writing and teaching, was falling apart; she thought she would have to begin all over again. It came to her then that middle age is not youth, that at 50 one cannot face uncertainty and insecurity about the future with the arrogance of the youthful spirit. At middle age, the resilience is no longer there. It is only when one is young that one feels that nothing is final. In midlife, Sarton learned she must become the "old nurse" to the life in Europe that this life had once been to her: the roles were reversed now. In midlife, she experienced the interior earthquake that betokens a major shift in consciousness, the interior earthquake that accompanies passage to a new life-stage.

At Nelson, Sarton knew what La Rochefoucauld meant when he said, "*Nous arrivons tout nouveaux aux divers âges de la vie"* (179). Why would one want to stay young

> when adventure lies in change and growth?
>   It is only past the meridian of fifty that one can believe that the universal sentence of death applies to oneself. At twenty we are immortal; at fifty we are too caught up in life to think much about the end, but from about fifty-five on the inmost quality of life changes because of this knowledge. Time is suddenly telescoped. Life in and for itself becomes more precious than it ever could have been earlier. . . . it is imperative to taste it, to savor it, every day and every hour, and that means to cut out waste, to be acutely aware of the relevant and of the irrelevant. There are late joys just as there are early joys. . . . in middle age, afternoon light marbling a white wall may take on the quality of revelation. [180]

Past the meridian, there is the delight of communicating as an equal with those who were once elders and who are now contemporaries. There is the richness of becoming more accessible to young people and more needed by them. There is the joy of having the chance to encourage the talent of young people. There is "the inward-turning of the life adventure" (181). Friends are loved for what they *are* more than for what they can give us. At the age of 55, she was, as a long-distance runner, setting her course for a distant goal. She found that the adventure of life opens out in every direction and at the same time has greater depths. She felt she had the power now to sustain longer periods of work than she had when she was younger. She remembered how her father had found renewed energies in cutting back to what is essential. "Old writers do not fade away," she found, "they ripen" (183). At Nelson, Sarton learned not so much how to mourn her dead as how to build what was into the living present. She did not so much think about her parents as find herself "in a hundred ways doing things as they would do." Her mother "tasted color as if it were food" and when Sarton delighted "at a band of sun on the yellow floor in the big room, . . . I am not so much thinking of her as being as she was" (184).

   In *Plant Dreaming Deep*, Sarton wrote that the only way to live without despair is "to make myths of our lives" (151). One reason she kept *Journal of a Solitude* for a year was that she had felt that *Plant Dreaming Deep* created the myth of a false Paradise, a myth she now wanted to destroy.[46] If she continued to wear the mask of that mythical person her earlier book had created in the minds of her readers, she would cease to grow. And she felt that it was time for a change, a radical change, in her life again. Still, there is a continuity between these books beyond that myth of that wise woman on the hill who is above all impassioned engagement, for both are notebooks that explore the inner life of the solitary.

   In *Plant Dreaming Deep*, Sarton came to know the bright and shadowy sides of solitude—solitude that is not at all the same as loneliness, although at times it may wear its face. She learned that solitude makes one as alert as an animal to a change in the light and to changing sounds. Her house had come to inhabit her, just as she inhabited the house. The life of solitude is the inner life. It is a way of waiting for that which is unseen to show itself, for that which is silent to be heard. And it is a place alive with the presences of every friend who ever visited there. At Nelson, Sarton moved into a new phase of life: now her attention is subtly drawn to the changing light on the hills around the village at dusk, where once it had been drawn to "the changing light on a human face."[47] In *Journal of a Solitude,* she wrote of how difficult it is to keep one's balance in this, the great challenge, but that if solitude is sacrificed for the sake of being with others for any extended period of time, even with someone who is beloved, "I lose my center. I feel dispersed, scattered, in pieces."[48] She is still open to experience, still engaged, and much more vulnerable and unfinished than *Plant Dreaming Deep* led some to believe. And it is through a love that takes of the whole person that one grows. But *time* is needed, time to distill meaning from all that has happened:

> The problem is to keep a balance, not to fall to pieces. In keeping her balance in her last years Louise Bogan stopped writing poems, or nearly. It was partly . . . that the detachment demanded of the critic (and especially his absorption in analyzing the work of others) is diametrically opposed to the kind of detachment demanded of the poet in relation to his own work. We are permitted to become detached only after the *shock* of an experience has been taken in, allowed to "happen" in the deepest sense. [143]

In the earlier work, Sarton wrote of her discovery of the magic in the hourly changing light; she wrote of silence as food. Solitude is the bread of inner life. The solitary is not calm, not tranquil; in solitude, one waits. All of life is a long waiting. And perhaps patience is the last lesson we must learn, the lesson saved for the last of life. "On attend toujours." In *Journal of a Solitude,* Sarton recalls these words of Jean Dominique, who was old and blind then, and over 60 years of age. At the time Dominique said this to her, Sarton was not even 30, "and I was amazed to think that someone so old could still wait for someone so intensely. But now I know that one does so all one's life" (170).

Old age is a time to set forth on the journey to completeness, a time to put away all that is not essential. Old age is the time to become a wanderer, in search of wholeness. Once one arrives there, one must be prepared to struggle "not to sink into apathy" (117). When she was 66, Sarton wrote that her sixty-fifth year had been the happiest and most fruitful year in her life. She had looked forward to being old since she was 17: "Far from a liability I saw it as possibly the most interesting of adventures to come," and time had proven her right. All that had diminished was sustained energy, but this was compensated for because she knew better now "how to handle myself. I have more fun because I am less compulsive, less driven by time curiously enough." Old age is seen as a problem, perhaps, because some of us cannot perceive or even imagine "a state of growth that might have to do with contemplation, pure joy, and above all the elimination of the nonessential." Old people are privileged in that they do not feel so guilty about what was left undone as they had when they were younger. In old age, material things do not matter so much; only the little comforts really count, as they do at any age. Old people have the right to explore the self. They "have earned the right to make our souls in peace." For this, one needs time, "time for reflection, time that may look empty from the outside." Old people sitting in the sun doing nothing are not to be pitied, for they are busy *being*. It is the young who have created the myth that old age is a sad ending of all that is most desirable. It is not easy to be old, Sarton acknowledges. But, then, growth is never easy:

> If the whole of life is a journey toward old age, then I believe it is also a journey toward love. And love may be as intense in old age as it was in youth, only it is different, set in a wider arc, and the more precious because the time we have to enjoy it in is bound to be brief.
> Old age is not a fixed point. . . . Old age is not an illness, it is a timeless ascent. As power diminishes, we grow toward more light.[49]

Sarton wrote these words with the sense of being then on the edge of old age. Old age, like dying, is a time to reckon up one's life, and for either task one needs space, one needs to be left alone.[50] In *A Reckoning,* dying sets Laura free of all that is nonessential. But she must suffer the pain of disentangling herself from all her relationships. As Laura takes her leave of life, she asks Mary to turn her son's painting to the wall, because now it is too alive for her. Still, she tells her sister that the one who is dying is really very young, that only the body knows that one is aging, and that what is most real to her now are things that happened in the past. When she lay down to listen to music, the images that floated up to her were scenes from childhood and youth. "Perhaps that was because all the deepest questions were asked then. Whatever she was to become had made its irreversible imprint then" (89). And this was why her mother, Sybille, had come to haunt her now.

It took Laura time before she could achieve the sensation of floating, "but finally as the dawn came and she could distinguish the objects in the room, she rested her eyes on her blue wrapper flung over a chair. The way it lay in folds to the floor . . . reminded her of paintings of Piero della Francesca" (186). It was always this way, that a precise image opened the door to this floating. When she closed her eyes, processions of people passed before her, "her mother in a blue dress with a square lace collar, bending to kiss her good night in the hospital in Switzerland . . . her mother walking across a field in Maine with a bunch of wildflowers in her hands" (230). Women haunted her now, as if there were something unfinished here. "Perhaps indeed it had to do with herself as woman, woman in relation to herself" (186). Her journey is taking her "deeper and deeper into what it is to be a woman" (190). It is a way of joining herself to all women. To achieve this, she must go beyond Sybille, her earthly mother. "No one had ever loomed so large, no one so to be reckoned with, beautiful and terrible. Terrible as Medusa, she had frozen her children into people somehow diminished themselves by her extraordinary power"

(239). She must go beyond Sybille's possession of her to reach "Communion. Something women are only beginning to . . . understand, a kind of tenderness towards each other as women" (252).

Sarton had rejoiced to hear from another person that her mother's presence could be felt everywhere in her house in Nelson.[51] Her mother's "light ghost" hovered in her garden. She was never with her more than when she went out to do some furious weeding—to cast away all that stifles the plants, all that stifles the person, to cast out the demons: "How often I have seen my mother come in from such a battle flushed with joy" (127). She felt that her mother's dying was an expression of her very essence, and she likened it to the closing of a flower. At the last, "she seemed . . . to have become nothing but light, an impersonal light, as if there were nothing left for death to take but the soul itself" (134). Growing old is a journeying toward this, an ascension toward more light. It is a time for restorations and reconciliations. The old cannot harvest their years in a place like the Twin Elms where the senses are starved, for memory comes through the gateways of the senses. And old age cannot be harvested unless one finds how to live like Anne Thorp on Greening Island, who is in her seventies now and stooped, but whose "profile is still that of Nefertiti and her long stride that of a goddess." She, who is still accessible to everyone, whose capacity for experience seems unlimited, "lives each moment of the day as if it were the first and the last, with the whole of herself."[52]

Edith Wharton (1862–1937)

Evalina Jaspar had been expecting Anson Warley that evening.[53] Her big Fifth Avenue house had once been a machine of entertainment, even after her sons and daughters, for whose amusement and prospects she had reigned as "leading hostess" of New York, had all been married off. A niece of Evalina's had confided to Warley

> that the poor old lady, who was gently dying of softening of the brain, still imagined herself to be New York's leading hostess, still sent out invitations (which of course were never delivered), still ordered terrapin, champagne and orchids, and still came down every evening to her great shrouded drawing-rooms, with her tiara askew on her purple wig, to receive a stream of imaginary guests. [70]

Warley had been pleased to "decline the boredom" of Evalina's luncheon invitations on many occasions. This evening, walking briskly on Fifth Avenue to dine at the home of an old friend, his memory fails him. He goes on walking, amusing himself with the joke of declining that boredom to clear his head, and then—since he disliked hurting anyone—resolving to call on Evalina soon. And he finds himself standing in front of her brightly illumined house. It comes to him then that it was with Evalina that he was to dine this evening.

Mrs. Jaspar had been expecting Warley. Earlier that evening, she had told her nurse that she had made her invitation to him at a dance at the home of people who had been a prominent part of the social circle long ago. So it comes about that Miss Cress and Lavinia watch, through cracks in the Coromandel screen in the dining-room, as the couple dine on mashed potatoes and spinach, served by George in blue crockery dishes from the servants' hall. They see the bunched-up newspaper in the dishes of priceless Rose Dubarry porcelain. They watch George pour from a bottle of Apollinario wrapped in a napkin.

As for Mrs. Jaspar and Warley, after George has served the other guests they take their elegant repast on gold plate. Orchids have been placed in the Rose Dubarry dishes. And George announces "Perrier-Jouet, '95" and "Château Lafite '74" and "the old Newbold Madeira," as he pours successive glasses for their toasts to "old times." After dinner, Mrs. Jaspar invites Warley to join the ladies after cigars. "Slowly, majestically, the purple velvet train disappeared down the long enfilade of illuminated rooms, and the last door closed behind her" (100). Warley dons his fur-lined overcoat. He must slip off at an early hour, for he has another engagement. On his way, "he took a step forward, to where a moment before the pavement had been—and where now there was nothing" (101).

From the day nurse's point of view, Mrs. Jaspar had been particularly difficult. She demanded that her diamonds be brought to her. She could not receive her guests without them. But the night nurse is certain that the old maid Lavinia will know how to manage her mistress. When Mrs. Jaspar comes in to say that she heard carriages driving up to the house, Lavinia assures her that the skirts of her low-necked purple velvet dress are full enough that, with the measured steps she is taking, she would manage "entirely to conceal the broad round tips of her black orthopaedic shoes" (77). The woman Lavinia sees this evening is "not the old petrified Mrs. Jaspar with porphyry face and wig awry . . . , but a young proud creature, commanding and splendid in her Paris gown of amber *moiré*." (80). Lavinia sees the other Mrs. Jaspar.

There are two Anson Warleys, too. But he had always known this, although he had refused to acknowledge it even to himself. There was "a small poor creature, chattering with cold inside, in spite of his agreeable and even distinguished exterior" (63). For years, these fellows had remained separate, but now he had found that they had fused into one, the lesser self sent forth by the other on his "social escapades" among the highbrows. Aging brought its afflictions to Warley—the stiffness in the joints, the growing fastidiousness about people and food and comfort, and the vertigo. But it brought its sudden insights, also. Warley realizes "that he had reached the time of life when Alps and cathedrals become as transient as flowers." It was his awareness "that all was fleeting" that gave him vertigo, that "dizzy plunge of the sands in the hour-glass." He had turned pale from the fatigue this revelation had caused him when it came. But when his hostess had remarked his pallor, he replied in a jocular way, and joined in the talk at the table "with a feverish loquacity." For how could he tell them that they, too, would one day arrive where he had arrived only that morning, "at the turn in the path from which mountains look as transient as flowers"? (73).

Once that fatal turn is taken, it may be that it is the lesser self who is sent forth into the world by the other; it may be that truth becomes the plaything of memory. Those who have not arrived at that turn, who peer at the old through cracks in the Coromandel screen, do not guess at the life of the other—unless, like Lavinia, they can remember an earlier self who inhabited the aging body. Without memory we are nothing, our lives have never been, we are ghosts. Yet, in the very name of mercy, even in the name of love, old people's truths are challenged when they hurt no one, when nothing is at stake. Only those who have not yet arrived at that turn in the path imagine they know the nature of illusion.

This story of age and memory was published when Edith Wharton was in her late sixties. In her autobiography, published a few years later, she wrote that the story of her own growth would have to be the story of the two or three greatest friendships of her life that had so stimulated and enlightened her. After the intellectual isolation of her childhood and youth, she came, in her early thirties, into the company of these rich and varied intelligences. Her chance to extend herself through this comradeship was "of a quality so rare that it ought to illuminate all my pages." Yet, she lamented, she herself was not a Boswell, for had she been, she would have committed all that radiant talk to the written page. Nor had she a Boswell of her own to record it. High company so exhilarated her that note-taking was unthinkable: "I enjoy the commerce with great minds as a painter enchanted by the glories of an Alpine meadow rather than as a botanist cataloguing its specimens."[54]

Some time before, when Wharton found herself sitting next to Bergson at a dinner table, she told him how these "odd holes" in her memory distressed and perplexed her. She asked him how it could be that her recollection of trivial things could be so unerring, whereas, "when it came to poetry, my chiefest passion and my greatest joy, my verbal memory failed me completely, and I heard only the inner cadences, and could hardly ever fill it out with the right words?" Bergson did not appear particularly interested in this question. "*Mais c'est précisément parce que vous êtes éblouie*" was his quiet reply—"It's just because you are dazzled." He did not make any effort to pursue the subject. At the time, Wharton had hoped for much more from Bergson than this. Now, she wrote, she knew there was no more to be said on the subject; "the gift of precision in ecstasy . . . is probably almost as rare in the appreciator as in the creator." She had been intellectually isolated for so long, that good talk brought her a joy that precluded the possibility of setting it down on paper. But that did not mean that it was utterly lost or forgotten. Rather, it entered her mind "with a gradual nutritive force sometimes felt only long afterward."

Good talk "encloses my universe in a dome of many-coloured glass from which I can detach but few fragments while it builds itself up about me" (170–71). It returned to her, often in other than verbal form.

The very act of recollection was for Wharton an occasion for the return of the "long days at the Mount, in the deep summer glow or the crisp glitter of autumn, the walks in the woods, motor-flights over hill and dale, evening talks on the moonlit terrace and readings around the library fire." These and the figures of that "inner circle" returned to her as she was writing her autobiography "with a mocking radiance" (192). The glimpses of London that had so delighted her had become "no more than a golden blur," so far in the past and so much of a world "convulsed and shattered," that even as she looked back upon them in the effort to recapture the details of certain scenes and talks, "they dissolve into the distance" (224). Even as she was writing, "I yearn back to those lost hours, all the while aware that those who read of them must take their gaiety, their jokes and laughter, on faith, yet unable to detach my memory from them" (256). If one has lived a long life with few personal ties, those ties are all the more precious. The loss of a dear friend is deeply grievous. These losses are all the more poignant in the brave new world foreseen by Aldous Huxley, "and already here in its main elements—a world in which so many sources of peace and joy are already dried up that the few remaining have a more piercing sweetness" (375). But it seemed to Wharton that what was saddest of all was to witness the untimely deaths of those young people whose lives held great promise.

The world of Wharton's old New York had vanished, too—the world that had seemed so intolerably ugly to her as a child returning from Paris, Seville, Rome, or London, a child who never could have guessed that half a century later it would be "as much a vanished city as Atlantis or the lowest layer of Schliemann's Troy," even its social organization fallen into oblivion (55). It was the disappearance of her old New York that made her childhood worth the remembering. Her own life, she said, had not been eventful enough to warrant an autobiography. It was that vanished city and its moral treasures whose "pathetic picturesqueness" was apparent to her only after World War I that justified the writing of these reminiscences. This task was made all the more difficult, she wrote, because she "never kept even the briefest of diaries" until 1918 (6).

Wharton was 70 when she worked on her autobiography, and Lewis writes that, although she could remember clearly the events of her childhood and adolescence, as is true of many older people, "her memory grew progressively less dependable as she approached the later periods." There were times when she was forgetful of events that had taken place just a few days before, and she wrote to Lapsley that she was afraid of repeating everything she had said the week before, adding that she resembled "the pathetic case of the old lady confessing over and over again her one adultery."[55] In *A Backward Glance*, Wharton wrote of the "rush of juvenile memories" that came to her in Spain just before World War I, and of how she had exclaimed at every step she took that she had been there before, that she had already seen this: "A child of four stores up by anticipation so much of what the mature self is later to enjoy that the adventures of a little girl may incalculably enrich the inner life of an old woman."[56]

Edith Wharton was, like all of us, a republic of selves. In *A Feast of Words*, Cynthia Griffin Wolff writes that Wharton "would not manage to become a genuinely coherent person until much later in her life."[57] As autobiographer, she is "the elderly woman ('The Author' who gazes from the first photograph in *A Backward Glance*, serene in pearls and fur)." But there had been a child first, small, desolate and lonely, and after that a little girl, whose successor was "a timid debutante." She had been followed by the young matron, who was succeeded by "a passionate lover, a lover for the first time unexpectedly, miraculously, in middle age" (10). When she was 45, Wharton had her love affair with Fullerton, an affair that began with a drive through the Berkshires on the second day of Fullerton's visit to Lenox. Snow had fallen early that year of 1907: it was only late October. The road was slippery, and the chauffeur stopped to put chains on the car. The couple took a stroll through the woods, and then stopped to sit on a hill and smoke a cigarette and talk:

> Near them . . . they noticed a shrub known as witch hazel, its delicate yellow flowers just coming into bloom. Each took a sprig, and Edith felt, suddenly, a personal symbolism in the juxtaposition of autumnal snow and the blossoming witch hazel: in botanical lore the shrub, which only begins to flower when other plant life is dying, is sometimes called "the old woman's bloom."[58]

Fullerton enclosed his sprig in a courtesy note that had an unusually intimate tone for a note of gratitude from a weekend guest at the Mount. "Three days later," Wharton began the Love Diary, "a private journal addressed directly to Fullerton, though not at this time destined for his eyes" (184).

In 1908, Wharton kept two diaries, this private journal and a standard page-a-day diary. Yet, in *A Backward Glance*, she wrote that she had never kept even the briefest of diaries until 1918. Perhaps she meant "diary" in the sense of a record of her earlier life in New York. Or perhaps this was "The Author" speaking her. It does not matter, since the writer's recollections and revelations are there in the fictions as well as in the personal documents—and sometimes even more so. Wharton's rejecting mother, the cold and disapproving Lucretia, has been seen as an obvious model for Mrs. Welland in *The Age of Innocence*, and her Aunt Mary Mason, "a magnificent wreck of a survival in Edith's youth," presiding over much of this same novel "in the guise of the redoubtable Mrs. Manson Mingott."[59] In her autobiography, there is a loving portrait of her maternal grandmother, who visited them during one of their Paris winters. Here, a woman in her seventies remembers her grandmother as she had seen her as a child, always "in lace cap and lappets, a bunch of gold charms dangling from her massive watch-chain, among the folds of a rich black silk dress, and a black japanned ear-trumpet at her ear," and always in an armchair, smiling, bent over her needlework. Her only gesture had been to put her stitching aside upon hearing her granddaughter's approach, and to reach for the ear-trumpet, into which the child Edith Wharton would shout Tennyson for hours, reading aloud to her "long-suffering ancestress."[60] Wharton herself appears, in the guise of one or another of her many selves, at least as much in her fictions as in *A Backward Glance*.[61] In her later years, the lives lived and the lives imagined came together. Lewis writes, "James, Simmons, Teddy, Walter Berry: they had all become characters, now, in the long novel of her life. She spoke of them as she did of figures in a story by Balzac or one of her own tales." In his judgment, Wharton had reserved her most intense feelings for her writings, and these made up "the life she had most truly and deeply lived." More and more, all those she had loved, and all that she had experienced came to be seen by her as characters and portions of a fiction she was still to write: "In one of her last remarks to Elisina, Edith recalled acquiring the habit of 'making up' in her childhood, even before she was able to read. In the reminiscences of the closing hours, she was still making up."[62] It is clear to him that Wharton expected that one day she would be the subject of a biography. "In this regard she differed markedly from, say, Emily Dickinson, Henry James, or Willa Cather, writers who carefully destroyed a great many personal documents and who left strict instructions about the eventual burning or long inaccessibility of other papers" (xi). Among the documents Wharton left behind were autobiographical fragments and diaries, unpublished poems, and fragments of stories. It was from all these scattered papers, together with her fictional works and *A Backward Glance,* that the composite representation of Edith Wharton would be drawn.

It is the same with the work of reconstructing her attitude toward aging. On her birthday in 1902, she wrote Sara Norton, "I excessively hate to be forty. Not that I think it a bad thing to be—only I'm not ready yet!"[63] When she turned 48, she said that she passed that birthday "sadly and soberly."[64] At 60, she would say at times that when she was dressing, she found herself "wondering who is the ugly old woman using my glass."[65] But in 1930, she wrote to John Hugh-Smith, "It's really more and more fun to be old, and to see all the theories come full circle" (396). And in 1933, nearly 70 years old and alone at St. Claire, she wrote in a summary statement about age that she had been given so much love and beauty in her life that she would go away from it grateful—not satisfied, but grateful.[66] In her biographer's judgment, there were moments when she yearned for motherhood, and other moments when she felt it was just as well that she and her husband had never had a child.[67] Her growing fascination with those half a century or more younger than herself was reflected in *The Children,* a fictional work written in her later life. In old age, she "was developing an almost sociological interest in the phenomenon of children" (485). Her curiosity, Wolff writes, was "ravenous" when she questioned Lady Aberconway so closely about them.[68] In her late sixties, "she began to take a genuine interest in . . . the life, the teachings, and the practices of the Church of Rome." It was in her sixties that she reached a "rather rare kind of full human maturity . . . , something expressed elsewhere in her novels on the parental theme. Maturity and the religious sensibility were becoming related in her mind."[69]

After the death of Walter Berry, Wharton wrote in a letter to Berenson of how keeping "this long vigil alone with all my past, wears the nerves thin." But she also wrote him of how, with growing age and solitude, there was a growing feeling of "the pregnant, piercing, beauty of mere being-aliveness" such that "I find it difficult to enter into the other state of mind." And three years after this, she wrote that she did not know, although she wished she could, "what people meant when they say they find 'emptiness' in this wonderful adventure of living, which seems to me to pile up its glories like an horizon-wide sunset as the light declines. I'm afraid I'm an incorrigible life-lover, life-wonderer and adventurer" (514). It was in her early seventies, Lewis writes, that she "entered into a new mood of sensuality, as women of that age are said not uncommonly to do" (520). And he suggests that in her last years, she "moved gradually into a new state of being" (524). With the help, no doubt, of having written her autobiography, "she had entered into almost total possession of her *personal* past" and "had arrived at a deep harmony with her own life history and was able, unperturbed, to confront the whole truth about herself."[70]

In her fifties and sixties, when Wharton's deepest feelings flowed into her work, "she took to drawing upon her writings *for* her writings" (xiv). In her later works of the literary imagination, there are echoes of intuitions received in youth, now apprehended in full maturity; there are these circularities that are Time's gift. Only the old can have this; how mean in spirit to be ungrateful for it! No single fragment, no paragraph in a letter or diary or novel encapsulates the Truth about growing older, for its Truth is apprehended in little truths, as brilliances flashing from the faces of a turning prism. The subject of aging in the works of a mature artist, as in the inner life of an older person, is many-faceted and it has its contradictions.

Wolff perceives a striking shift in the focus of Edith Wharton's fictions after *The Age of Innocence*. In later life, one must learn to accept loss, and one must overcome envy of the young so that the future may be entrusted to them. Trust, the first value, is also the last. *The Mother's Recompense, Twilight Sleep, The Children*—these are novels about families and about the relationship between the generations.[71] Wharton's personal tragedy was that she had "discovered and accepted her time only after it had passed her by" (342). Her time "had passed, and she had never truly lived in it; now, too late for reconciliations, it was gone forever" (344). Her fictions were her children—so she wrote of them in her letters to friends. In *The Age of Innocence*, she had affirmed the value of family. But she herself had no family. The sorrows of aging began for Wharton in the mid-1920s, and these "gave rise to the theme of the would-be parent in these later fictions" (373). What is "remarkable . . . about her vitality as an artist is that she brought herself to focus on the problems of old age as subjects for her fictions." She herself felt resentment, yet she was able "to identify resentment and envy as enemies of life; she recognized the problems of age *as* problems, and she developed a fictional mode in which to render them" (380).

In *The Mother's Recompense,* Kate Clephane receives a telegram from her daughter Anne, asking her to come home from the long years she spent in exile. Once Kate read the telegram, the very pavement of the streets where she walked had lost its familiarity; all that was in her mind "hot and cold, and beating and blowing about, like the weather on that dancing draughty day."[72] At the milliner's, and later at the dressmaker's, she reflected, "with a retrospective shiver, that her way of dressing and her demeanour must have thoroughly fixed in all these people's minds the idea that she was one of the silly vain fools who imagine they look like their own daughters" (20–21).

The death of old Mrs. Clephane, her arch-enemy, had summoned Kate from her limbo, and had released her into Time and Change and Chance. It had brought her face to face with the old world she had forsaken in her youth, with Anne in whom she saw "her whole youth, her whole married past, in that small pale oval . . . and John Clephane's straight rather heavy nose, beneath old Mrs. Clephane's awful brows" . . . with Fred Landers, "the heavy grizzled man with a red-and-yellow complexion and screwed-up blue eyes whom Time had substituted for the thin loose-jointed friend of her youth" (36).

Anne was now so complete a being as to be awesome. As the days went by, Kate marveled how it could happen

> that one could cast away one's best treasure, and come back after nearly twenty years to find it there, not only as rare as one had remembered it, but ripened, enriched, as only beautiful things are enriched and ripened by time . . . as if one had set out some delicate plant under one's window, so that it might be an object of constant vigilance, and then gone away, leaving it unwatched, unpruned, unwatered—how could one hope to find more than a dead stick in the dust when one returned? But Anne was real; she was not a mirage or a mockery. [75]

In time, Kate came to feel that she and Anne were as perfectly fitted as two halves of a life, that Anne was "the half she had dreamed of and never lived" (76). She had left Anne to the care of all the "scrupulous self-controlled people" of the world she had fled in her own youth. She "had somehow run the mad course allotted to her," and had survived it "sane and sound, to find them all waiting there to give her back her daughter" (83).

When the full meaning of this recompense came to Kate—that Anne was in love with Chris Fenno, Kate's former lover, that Anne intended to marry Chris—she felt, for a time, that grief, far from aging her, had restored her youth. On her way to Baltimore, to tell Chris he must not marry Anne, Kate "had never been more quiveringly, comprehensively alive" (160). But once she understood that Anne would not let him go in spite of Kate's disapproval—a disapproval she could not bring herself to explain to her daughter—and once she had resolved to play the part of "the acquiescent, approving mother," Kate acknowledged to herself that "she was old enough to be, if not his mother, at least his mother-in-law" (275). From the very beginning, she had defined her relationship to Chris in terms of the difference in their ages, of her awareness that it could not last. "Anything rather than to be the old woman clutching at an impossible prolongation of bliss—anything rather than be remembered as a burden instead of being regretted as a delight!" She had told him many times she had wanted him to remember her as "something vanishing and sweet" (275–76). Then, when she came upon Anne and Chris embracing, when she stood there unseen, unheard—a ghost—she felt "a furious flame of life" rush through her. And she came face to face with the possibility she felt a physical jealousy of her own daughter, with the root of the feeling that she had suffered from the very beginning, that "some incestuous horror hung between them" (278). It was unimaginable that she could keep her daughter near her after the couple married: "She must put the world between them. . . . The very grave . . . would be hardly black enough to blot out that scene" (279).

In the end, Kate Clephane came to hate, at least for a burning, bitter moment, all "that mocked her with the barren illusion of youth" (300). In *Twilight Sleep,* it is the mother who keeps her illusions after the denouement, and the daughter who carries the burden of awareness, who feels apprehensions she has not lived long enough to meet and yet

> could not shake off. . . . It was as if, in the beaming determination of the middle-aged . . . to ignore sorrow and evil, "think them away" as superannuated bogies, survivals of some obsolete European superstition unworthy of enlightened Americans, to whom plumbing and dentistry had given higher standards, and bi-focal glasses a clearer view of the universe—as if the demons the elder generation ignored, baulked of their natural prey, had cast their hungry shadow over the young. After all, somebody in every family had to remember now and then that such things as wickedness, suffering and death had not yet been banished from the earth; and with all those bright-complexioned white-haired mothers mailed in massage and optimism, and behaving as if they had never heard of anything but the Good and the Beautiful, perhaps their children had to serve as vicarious sacrifices.[73]

The mother, Pauline Manford, meets the anxieties and vexations of life with rest cures and mental uplift, with silent meditation and eurythmic exercises. She will not permit herself to worry, since worrying leaves traces in fine wrinkles around the lids and lips. For Pauline, there is a healer, an evangel or guru, a treatment or a right frame of mind for every form of suffering. For Pauline, suffering is the same as sin. It is her daughter Nona who knows there is no such thing as looking one's age because we all have a hundred ages. It is Nona who knows that there has been a denouement, whereas the only difference in Pauline that she could detect, "physically, at least, . . . was that a skilful make-up had filled in the lines which, in spite of all the arts of the face-restorers, were weaving their permanent web about her mother's lips and eyes. Under this delicate mask Pauline's face looked younger and fresher than ever, and as smooth and empty as if she had been born again." Nona reflects that Pauline *has* been born again (363–64). Even so, once and then again, "Nona seemed to see the flicker of anxiety pass back and forward, like a light moving from window to window in a long-uninhabited house" (371–72).

To be born again . . . for Kate Clephane, the price of this would have been the price of her soul. And so she returned to her limbo to live out her later years. Foolish Pauline still quickened at the thought of rejuvenation, still sought an anodyne, a twilight sleep, for aging. In *The Children,* Boyne, too, imagines rejuvenation may be possible.[74] Judith Wheater is more child than woman when they meet. But her fierce determination to keep the flock of Wheater children and "steps" together arouses his fatherly protectiveness . . . and then that deeper disturbance. Widowhood had set Rose Sellars free to marry Boyne, but it was with reluctance that he left Judith and the flock to meet Rose. Freedom had rejuvenated her; he found her more attractive and youthful than when they had parted five years before. But now, Boyne asked himself, "Was it a sign of middle-age . . . to take beatitude so quietly?" (91) What with his idling and her "old-fashioned scruples," they lingered too long in the Dolomites. "It probably wasn't safe for middle-aged people to have too much leisure in which to weigh each other's faults and merits" (222). It was too late for him and Rose Sellars. In a little time, he discovered it was too late for him and Judith, too.

For a full quarter of a century, Edith Wharton "carried the fictional world that is finally realized" in *The Mother's Recompense* in her imagination.[75] But there was this change, that twenty-five years earlier, she had focused on the predicament and fate of the daughter. In its final form, this work of fiction is Kate Clephane's story. There had been a change in *The Children* also—more radical and more sudden. Wharton's original outline was followed in the novel "with one crucial exception." It was "to have ended with Boyne's marrying Judith . . . 'but as if he were taking a little sister home'" (381). The novel was "to end 'on a note of quiet emotion, sad yet hopeful.'" But the tone of the resolution of *The Children,* Wolff remarks, "is one of renunciation and bleak resignation, a finality of loneliness." Why Wharton decided to change the ending can never be known for certain. But between the time she began writing it and the time she completed it, there had been "one catastrophic event . . . that inexorably brought home the devastations of old age and the inescapable erosions of time. The death of Walter Berry" (382).

"Every artist works," Wharton wrote in her autobiography, "like the Gobelins weavers, on the wrong side of the tapestry, and if now and then he comes around to the right side, and catches what seems . . . a firm sweep of design, he must instantly retreat again."[76] So, perhaps, each of us works in weaving the design of our lives. The truths of all we have done and been are strewn in a thousand places, and every gathering up creates a different design. So it is that in her Donné Books and Commonplace Books, in the way Mrs. Manson Mingott spoke to Newland Archer "with the cold-blooded complacency of the aged throwing earth into the grave of young hopes,"[77] in the "orchids" of bunched-up newspaper in the dishes at the table where Mrs. Jaspar and Warley dine, in the stratum of *The Mother's Recompense* where it is Edith Wharton who is returning to her old world after a long expatriation, seeking contact with a younger literary generation,[78] in all these places in life and in art are the many and changing truths of Edith Wharton's point of view toward aging. There is no last word on the subject; rather, there is a first word in her autobiography. Here Wharton recalls that she had told herself years before, "There's no such thing as old age; there is only sorrow." But she wrote that with the passing of time she had learned that this is true, but that it is not "the whole truth." Sorrow is not the only producer of old age; there is another, and this "is habit: the deathly process of doing the same thing in the same way at the same hour day after day, first from carelessness, then from inclination, at last from cowardice or inertia." Fortunately, Wharton wrote, "the inconsequent life is not the only alternative; for caprice is as ruinous as routine." She believed that habit itself is necessary, but that if one is to remain alive, one must fight incessantly against "the habit of having habits." Her first word on old age was this, that, "In spite of illness, in spite even of the arch-enemy sorrow, one *can* remain alive long past the usual date of disintegration if one is unafraid of change, insatiable in intellectual curiosity, interested in big things, and happy in small ways."[79]

Notes

1. Gertrude Atherton, *Adventures of a Novelist* (New York: Liveright, Inc., 1932), p. 554. Hereafter, reference to this book will be cited in the text by page number.

2. In chapter 6 of his *Senescence*, G. Stanley Hall describes the Steinach procedures in some detail. G. Stanley Hall, *Senescence: The Last Half of Life* (New York: D. Appleton and Co., 1922).

3. William Butler Yeats, *The Countess Cathleen* in *The Variorum Edition of the Plays of William Butler Yeats*, Russell K. Alspach, ed., assisted by Catharine C. Alspach (New York: The Macmillan Co., 1966), p. 169, lines 946–48.

4. Gertrude Atherton, *Black Oxen* (New York: Boni and Liveright, 1923), p. 35. Hereafter, reference to this book will be cited in the text by page number.

5. Charlotte S. McClure, *Gertrude Atherton*, Boise State University Western Writers Series, Number 23 (Boise, Id.: Boise State University, 1976), p. 12.

6. Gertrude Atherton, *Black Oxen*, p. 215.

7. Gertrude Atherton, *Adventures of a Novelist*, p. 560. Hereafter, reference to this book will be cited in the text by page number.

8. Gertrude Atherton, "Defeating Old Age," in Gertrude Atherton, *Can Womem Be Gentlemen?* (Boston: Houghton Mifflin Co., 1938), p. 59. Hereafter, reference to this essay will be cited in the text by page number.

9. Gertrude Atherton, "A Course in Life and Human Nature," in *Can Women Be Gentlemen?* Hereafter, reference to this essay will be cited in the text by page number.

10. Gertrude Atherton, "Superwomen," in *Can Women Be Gentlemen?*, p. 113. Hereafter, reference to this essay will be cited in the text by page number.

11. Gertrude Atherton, "Are Women Born Liars?," in *Can Women Be Gentlemen?*, p. 19. Hereafter, reference to this essay will be cited in the text by page number.

12. Gertrude Atherton, "Why Do Women Hate One Another?," in *Can Women Be Gentlemen?*, pp. 45–46. Hereafter, reference to this essay will be cited in the text by page number.

13. Gertrude Atherton, *Adventures of a Novelist*, p. 79. Hereafter, reference to this book will be cited in the text by page number.

14. Gertrude Atherton, *Black Oxen*, p. 179. Hereafter, reference to this book will be cited in the text by page number.

15. Ellen Glasgow, *Barren Ground* (New York: The Modern Library, 1936), pp. 355, 373. Hereafter, reference to this book will be cited in the text by page number.

16. Ellen Glasgow, *The Sheltered Life* (Garden City, N.Y.: Doubleday, Doran and Co., Inc., 1932), pp. 264–65. Hereafter, reference to this book will be cited in the text by page number.

17. Blair Rouse, ed., *Letters of Ellen Glasgow* (New York: Harcourt, Brace and Co., 1958), p. 354. Hereafter, reference to this book will be cited in the text by page number.

18. Ellen Glasgow, *The Woman Within* (New York: Harcourt, Brace and Co., 1954), pp. 9–10. Hereafter, reference to this book will be cited in the text by page number.

19. Ellen Glasgow, *They Stooped to Folly* (New York: Doubleday, Doran and Co., Inc., 1929), p. 164. Hereafter, reference to this book will be cited in the text by page number.

20. Ellen Glasgow, *Barren Ground*, p. 525.

21. Ellen Glasgow, *Vein of Iron* (New York: Harcourt, Brace and Company, 1935), p. 213. Hereafter, reference to this book will be cited in the text by page number.

22. Blair Rouse, ed., *Letters of Ellen Glasgow*, pp. 356, 108.

23. Ellen Glasgow, *The Woman Within*, p. 279. Hereafter, reference to this book will be cited in the text by page number.

24. Mrs. Littlepage knew that "this benevolent impulse, . . . this expanding and flowering of the maternal instinct into a vital sense of compassion, . . . made persons who did not understand her . . . imagine that she was sometimes without tact, that she was too interfering, that she was never happy except when she was improving something or somebody." Ellen Glasgow, *They Stooped to Folly*, p. 226.

25. Ellen Glasgow, *The Woman Within*, p. 13.

26. Ellen Glasgow, *Barren Ground*, pp. 503-4.

27. Ellen Glasgow, *The Woman Within*, pp. 3–4. Hereafter, reference to this book will be cited in the text by page number.

28. Zora Neale Hurston, *Their Eyes Were Watching God* (New York: Negro Universities Press, 1969), pp. 177–79. Hereafter, reference to this book will be cited in the text by page number.

29. Zora Neale Hurston, *Seraph on the Suwanee* (New York: Charles Scribner's Sons, 1948), p. 294. Hereafter, reference to this book will be cited in the text by page number.

30. As quoted in Robert E. Hemenway, *Zora Neale Hurston: A Literary Biography* (Urbana, Ill.: University of Illinois Press, 1977), p. 313. Hereafter, reference to this book will be cited in the text by page number.

31. Zora Neale Hurston, *Dust Tracks on a Road* (New York: Arno Press and the New York Times, 1969), p. 65. Hereafter, reference to this book will be cited in the text by page number.

32. Ibid., p. 123. "Although meant to explain Hurston's life," Hemenway comments, "the visions do not successfully structure the autobiography." Robert E. Hemenway, *Zora Neale Hurston: A Literary Biography*, p. 282.

33. Zora Neale Hurston, *Dust Tracks on a Road*, p. 78. Hereafter, reference to this book will be cited in the text by page number.

34. Zora Neale Hurston, *Jonah's Gourd Vine* (Philadelphia: J. B. Lippincott, 1934), p. 187. Hereafter, reference to this book will be cited in the text by page number.

35. Ibid., p. 231.

36. Zora Neale Hurston, *Seraph on the Suwanee*, pp. 291, 293.

37. Zora Neale Hurston, *Mules and Men* (Philadelphia: J. B. Lippincott Co., 1935), p. 17. Hereafter, reference to this book will be cited in the text by page number.

38. Zora Neale Hurston, *Dust Tracks on a Road*, pp. 143–44. Hereafter, reference to this book will be cited in the text by page number.

39. As quoted in Robert E. Hemenway, *Zora Neale Hurston: A Literary Biography*, p. 348.

40. Zora Neale Hurston, *Dust Tracks on a Road*, p. 221.

41. Zora Neale Hurston, *Jonah's Gourd Vine*, p. 164. Hereafter, reference to this book will be cited in the text by page number.

42. These quotations appear, respectively, in Zora Neale Hurston, *Seraph on the Suwanee*, pp. 165, 153.

43. May Sarton, *As We Are Now* (New York: W. W. Norton and Co., Inc., 1973), p. 23. Hereafter, reference to this book will be cited in the text by page number.

44. May Sarton, *Mrs. Stevens Hears the Mermaids Singing* (New York: W. W. Norton and Co., Inc., 1975), p. 59. Hereafter, reference to this book will be cited in the text by page number.

45. May Sarton, *Plant Dreaming Deep* (New York: W. W. Norton and Co., Inc., 1968), p. 117. Hereafter, reference to this book will be cited in the text by page number.

46. May Sarton, *Journal of a Solitude* (New York: W. W. Norton and Co., Inc., 1977), p. 176. Kathleen Woodward suggests that the titles of *Journal of a Solitude* and *As We Are Now* are "virtually interchangeable. Curiously so, in fact." In her view, "The novel is the shadow, to use the Jungian term, of the journal." Kathleen Woodward, "Aging and Disengagement: May Sarton's *As We Are Now* and *Journal of a Solitude*," paper presented at the Modern Language Association, Chicago, 1977, pp. 10, 12. See also Kathleen Woodward, "May Sarton and Fictions of Old Age," in Janet Todd, ed., *Gender and Literary Voice* (New York: Holmes and Meier Publishers, Inc., 1980), pp. 108–27, in which Woodward observes that Sarton's theory of aging is primarily Jungian, and that the writer belives that old age offers the possibility of special growth, that the threshold of old age is marked by the passage from Eros to Agape, and that the last phase of life is ideally devoted to the composing of the self. Woodward discusses the ideal of graceful aging as it appears in Sarton's work prior to 1973, relates this ideal to Sarton's theory of art, which is feminist, and shows how in the *Journal* and in *As We Are Now*, the writer's depiction of aging and the single woman becomes more complex and her ideal of graceful aging "yields to guerilla warfare." Hereafter, reference to *Journal of a Solitude* by Sarton will be cited in the text by page number.

47. May Sarton, *Plant Dreaming Deep*, p. 94.

48. May Sarton, *Journal of a Solitude*, p. 195. Hereafter, reference to this book will be cited in the text by page number.

49. May Sarton, "More Light," *New York Times*, January 30, 1978, p. A21.

50. May Sarton, *A Reckoning* (New York: W. W. Norton and Co., 1978), p. 86. Hereafter, reference to this book will be cited in the text by page number.

51. May Sarton, *Plant Dreaming Deep*, p. 64. Hereafter, reference to this book will be cited in the text by page number.

52. May Sarton, *Journal of a Solitude*, pp. 172–74.

53. Edith Wharton, "After Holbein," in Edith Wharton, *Certain People* (New York: D. Appleton and Co., 1930), pp. 63–101. Hereafter, reference to this short story will be cited in the text by page number.

54. Edith Wharton, *A Backward Glance* (New York: D. Appleton-Century Co., 1934), pp. 169–70. Hereafter, reference to this book will be cited in the text by page number.

55. R. W. B. Lewis, *Edith Wharton: A Biography* (New York: Harper and Row, 1975), p. 503.

56. Edith Wharton, *A Backward Glance*, p. 330.

57. Cynthia Griffin Wolff, *A Feast of Words: The Triumph of Edith Wharton* (New York: Oxford University Press, Inc., 1977), p. 48. Hereafter, reference to this book will be cited in the text by page number.

58. R. W. B. Lewis, *Edith Wharton: A Biography*, pp. 183–84.

59. Ibid., pp. 24–25, 13. See also Cynthia Griffin Wolff, *A Feast of Words*, p. 435, n. 104.

60. Edith Wharton, *A Backward Glance*, pp. 37–38.

61. R. W. B. Lewis, Introduction to Edith Wharton, *The Age of Innocence* (New York: Charles Scribner's Sons, 1968), pp. viii–ix. See also Cynthia Griffin Wolff, *A Feast of Words*, p. 435, n. 104.

62. R. W. B. Lewis, *Edith Wharton: A Biography*, p. 531. Hereafter, reference to this book will be cited in the text by page number.

63. As quoted in Cynthia Griffin Wolff, *A Feast of Words,* p. 144.

64. As quoted in R. W. B. Lewis, *Edith Wharton: A Biography,* p. 279.

65. As quoted in Cynthia Griffin Wolff, *A Feast of Words,* p. 345. Hereafter, reference to this book will be cited in the text by page number.

66. Edith Wharton, *Quaderno dello Studente,* n.p., entry May 12, 1933.

67. R. W. B. Lewis, *Edith Wharton: A Biography,* p. 134. Hereafter, reference to this book will be cited in the text by page number.

68. Cynthia Griffin Wolff, *A Feast of Words,* p. 378.

69. R. W. B. Lewis, *Edith Wharton: A Biography,* p. 510. Hereafter, reference to this book will be cited in the text by page number.

70. Ibid., p. 524. This was manifest to him in two very different documents, the fragment of the fictional work entitled "Beatrice Palmato," and the account of an afternoon visit in autumn to Edith Wharton at the Pavillon Colombe in 1935 or 1936, given by Philomème de la Forest-Divonne. Ibid., pp. 524–26. Hereafter, reference to Lewis's book is cited in the text by page number.

71. Cynthia Griffin Wolff, *A Feast of Words,* pp. 342–43. Wolff interprets Wharton's development with reference to Erik Erikson's theory of ego development. She writes that *The Mother's Recompense* and *The Children* "both focus with exact precision on the crises of generativity and ego-integrity." Ibid., p. 381. Hereafter, reference to this book will be cited in the text by page number.

72. Edith Wharton, *The Mother's Recompense* (New York: D. Appleton and Co., 1925), p. 13. Hereafter, reference to this book will be cited in the text by page number.

73. Edith Wharton, *Twilight Sleep* (New York: D. Appleton and Co., 1927), pp. 47–48. Hereafter, reference to this book will be cited in the text by page number.

74. Edith Wharton, *The Children* (New York: D. Appleton and Co., 1928.) Hereafter, reference to this book will be cited in the text by page number.

75. Cynthia Griffin Wolff, *A Feast of Words,* p. 357. Hereafter, reference to this book will be cited in the text by page number.

76. Edith Wharton, *A Backward Glance,* p. 197.

77. Edith Wharton, *The Age of Innocence,* p. 154.

78. R. W. B. Lewis, *Edith Wharton: A Biography,* p. 465.

79. Edith Wharton, *A Backward Glance* ("A First Word"), p. vii.

6
Older Women in Selected
Twentieth-Century American Fictions

What I hoped would come clear was that in the whole sur-
round of this story, the world it threads through, the only
certain thing at all is the worn path.
—Eudora Welty,
"Is Phoenix Jackson's Grandson Really Dead?"
The Eye of the Story

In short stories and novels, American women of letters in the twentieth century have brought a variety of sensibilities and literary styles to bear on the
aspects of aging considered throughout this book. Selections of the fictional
works discussed in this chapter were made with an appreciation of the conso-
nances between the motifs in these short stories and longer works and the
concerns of social scientific works about women in the second half of life in
twentieth-century America. Here are older women seen as companions,
friends, neighbors, kin—aunts, grandmothers, great-grandmothers, wives,
mothers, grown daughters. And here are solitaries, widows, survivors, inmates in nursing homes. Here are recognitions by children, adolescents,
young women, and older women looking back at older women in their lives.
Here are older women journeying, older women attending to last things; here
are some of our contemporaries. There are older women here from the
country, the small town, the city. There is a Midwestern farm wife transplanted in California. There are Southern women. And there are Jewett's
New Englanders. There are older women of the early decades of this century,
older women of the 1950s, older women of today. There are rich and poor
and all the strata between, black and white, Christian and Jew, middle-aged
and the very old in these stories. All are told by women writers of this century
who speak in very individual voices of aging in America. All are literary
perspectives on creativity, freedom, responsibility in the second half of
women's lives, literary illuminations of change, of the workings of time's passage in the lives of older women.

The truths about women's aging are many; the subject itself is as many-
faceted as it is inexhaustible. Literary perspectives on aging illumine the
wholeness of particular lives, the wholeness of experience and of remember-

ing. Imaginative writing is different from scientific writing, creative thought from analytical thought, in so radical a way that the apprehending of a work of fiction is quite distinctive from that of a work of social science. In literature, thought and feeling are interwoven rather than separated for the purpose of ratiocination. The fiction writer creates *characters;* the social scientist abstracts *characteristics.* Every work of fiction has its own rhythms, takes its own shape, *tells* in its own voice, whereas all works in social science are developed according to a master plan of scholarship that guides method, structure, and language. Therefore, the crafting of a short story or a novel calls for the uses of different faculties from those put to work in the making of a study or a treatise in social science. Characters in fiction "are not labels but are made from the inside out," Eudora Welty writes, and they "grow into their own life."

In the same way, a plot has "a living principle on which it hangs together and gradually earns its shape. A plot is a thousand times more unsettling than an argument, which may be answered. It is not a pattern imposed; it is inward emotion acted out."[1] Fictions are not arguments or programs for social reform, although they are often used as "documentations" of what is the case. I have suggested elsewhere how works fashioned in the world of letters *and* in the world of social science may be seen as interlacings of fiction and social fact.[2] But there are different standards adopted for judging the fitness or rightness or workability of an idea. Surely the reader can hear the echoes, perceive the interests held in common, the truths that overarch the disciplines of philosophy, history, anthropology, psychology, social gerontology, and sociology without making of literature what it is not. Humanists in all disciplines are alive to the ways that works of fiction spear open the conceptual so the reader can hear the pulse and feel the breath of life within, how they can give flesh to social fact, substance to the aery psyche. Myriad characters, myriad fates can spring from the stone of circumstance or sociological condition: in the hands of the sculptor, these are organic materials.

Most of the fictions discussed in this chapter are short stories. Mary Sohngen, Fellow of the Scripps Foundation Gerontology Center at Miami University, has prepared an annotated bibliography of novels published between 1950 and 1977 in the United States in which the protagonist is a woman over 60 years of age. In these novels, the narrative point of view is essentially that of the protagonist.[3] Sohngen has also prepared a list of 87 titles of commercial novels published between 1950 and 1975 in which the protagonist is aged 60 or more, and in which the narrative point of view is substantially that of the protagonist.[4] She suggests three uses for this list of novels. Reading and discussing novels broadens the personal vision of students of gerontology whose field experience might be limited to nursing homes or senior citizen centers, and enhances awareness of the complexity of the aging experience: Students "can learn to look sensitively at their youthful enthusiasm for intervention." What is more, mature students enrolled in courses on the "Philosophy of Aging" or participants in discussion groups focusing on retirement may be hesitant to discuss their fears and guilts openly. Talking about characters in a novel "can open the way toward sensitized consciousness and mutual support." If fictional protagonists are found to be bewildered or obstinate or fallible, then readers of these works may come to accept their own fallibility and become more tolerant of themselves and of old people they know. Finally, mature students enrolled in *either* a course on the contemporary novel *or* a course in social problems ought to read novels about the elderly as "a valuable supplement to those about adolescence or early maturity" (72). Sohngen's recommendations for the uses of the bibliographies of novels she has compiled are perfectly fitting for the uses of the short stories and the few longer works discussed in this chapter. The fictions selected for commentaries in these pages are rich materials for literary perspectives on aging in an interdisciplinary inquiry into older women in twentieth-century America. That many of these fictions could appear under other rubrics chosen as subheadings for this chapter—"The Flight of Betsey Lane" is *about* companions in old age as much as it is *about* journeys in late life; "The Scream on Fifty-seventh Street" is a work of interiors as much as it is a story about widowhood—attests to the nature of literary art, that it is always "about" so many things, that it overflows the boundaries of "topics."

Sarah Orne Jewett (1849–1909), the oldest of the women writers whose stories are discussed here, is of the last century far more than this; yet, no consideration of literary perspectives on older women would be complete without her work. "She once laughingly told me," Willa Cather recalled, "that her head was full of dear old houses and dear old women, and that when an old house and an old woman came together in her brain with a click, she knew that a story was under way."[5] Cather herself wrote about older people, women and men, in many of her fictions, as did Ruth Suckow, who through all her works "sought the means of meeting the immense problems of loneliness, old age, and the frustration of cherished dreams."[6] Older women—and *old* women—appear in Eudora Welty's novels as well as stories, among them *The Optimist's Daughter* and *Losing Battles.* And, years ago, Edna Ferber wrote that even when she was still in her twenties, old people engaged her interest as short-story material. *"Theirs is the final, the inescapable, tragedy,"* Ferber commented. In her view, life had *"managed this matter rather badly,"* and if we were born aged 80, we might begin to enjoy the flavor of life by the time we were about 70, becoming ever more vigorous as we grew young, and ending between the age of 10 and infancy *"with no regrets and no gnarled and baffled old age to contemplate. Old age, the philosophers say, has its compensations. Name two."*[7] (Of course, this was Ferber's attitude. It was certainly not Jewett's, or Welty's or Cather's, or, indeed, anyone else's. And for all we know, Ferber might have had second or third thoughts about the matter.)

"Older women in twentieth-century America" is a subject of such immensity that it is doubtful that literary perspectives could be discussed in a single volume, let alone a chapter of a book. Some topics have not been included here. One of these is the fading of physical beauty, a topic that deserves a book of its own. Whoever writes it would not want to miss Willa Cather's "The Old Beauty" and *A Lost Lady,* and Jean Stafford's "The End of a Career." And the study of literary perspectives on aging could be approached in other ways. One or a few women writers might be selected for an intensive study of aspects of aging in their entire *oeuvre.* Or, since "a novel provides time and space for an author to develop a fuller portrait of what it feels like to be old,"[8] a few novels might be explored in depth for what they reveal of the changing sense of self with the passage of time. The choice of short stories and a few longer works for this chapter was guided by the intention of representing the varieties of women's experience of aging in this century and in this country, and by an appreciation of the convergences in these fictions and the concerns of works appearing throughout this book. Women in midlife and later life have not been neglected by women writers of the past any more than they are neglected by contemporary women of letters. Rather, it is our *literature* that is neglected, and that is another, most melancholy story. Rich treasures are gathering dust in our libraries; very fine works being written today will never be read by those outside the small circle of subscribers to a literary journal; some works of the literary imagination are "lost" entirely. If this chapter leads readers to the fictions themselves, it will have achieved its essential purpose. For, thanks to fiction, aging may be seen from the inside out. Sohngen has observed that most of us have a chance to know very few old women in our lives, and these few women are likely to be either members of our own families or our social circles. She has reminded us that fictional representations are ways whereby we can know different old women and "can gain insight into many different life experiences and responses to life." When we look imaginatively "at those who have gone before us," whether this is in our lives or through fictional representations of them, "we see that they carry with them the weaknesses and the strengths that come from their past." And each of us carries burdens and weapons like these into our own old age (6). These are the gifts the creators of short stories as well as of novels have to offer us.

Companions in Old Age

In Sarah Orne Jewett's "Aunt Cynthy Dallett," Aunt Cynthy's niece, Abby Pendexter, is visiting with her friend, Mrs. Hand. Abby confided that the other night she awakened with a start, wondering what her aunt would do if there were a fire. She could not rest until she went to her north garret window to look up at the mountains. She had often wished her aunt's house were closer so that the old woman, confined by her lameness, could signal her niece if she needed help. "I used to plead with her to come down and spend the winters with me, but she told me one day I might as well try to fetch down one o' the old hemlocks."[9] Aunt Cynthy had laughed and said she expected there would come a time when her niece would have to move up there and take care of her, Abby recalled. She and Mrs. Hand agreed that this was quite a concession for such a self-contained woman to have made. Mrs. Hand said she understood both Aunt Cynthy and Abby very well, for she, too, liked to have her own home and to do things in her own way. It was during that visit that Abby revealed something of the financial straits she was in. When she was leaving, Mrs. Hand proposed that they go up the mountain together to keep New Year's Day with Aunt Cynthy.

When the two women set out for their visit, each pretended not to see the suspicious-looking swelling under the other's shawl. Mrs. Hand was bringing along her best mince pies, and Abby a hen roasted for their New Year's Feast. On their way up the hill, Abby confided—with an effort at gaiety—that she had a worry on her mind. She had to sell all but one of her hens to pay the last quarter's rent, and it was that remaining hen that she was carrying now under her arm. Mrs. Hand said that Aunt Cynthy ought to know Abby's situation. Her old aunt was all the near kin she had, Abby replied, and she had always felt there would come a time when she needed her, "but it's been her great pleasure to live alone an' feel free" (287). She would have it hard that winter, but she would get along somehow. Perhaps someone would want help for a spell. But she was afraid she would have to give up her house.

Aunt Cynthy beamed at the sight of her surprise guests. "She was the tiniest little bent old creature, her handkerchiefed head was quick and alert, and her eyes were bright with excitement and feeling, but the rest of her was much the worse for age; she could hardly move, poor soul" (298). As they talked about their walk up the hill, Aunt Cynthy confessed that although she would not want to live anywhere else, for she had been brought up on a high hill farm, she *did* feel the loneliness more now than she had when she was younger. The age-worn look and the careful darns of her niece's dress did not escape Aunt Cynthy's sharp eyes. She was getting older. And they both needed company. The question is raised delicately, with Abby inviting her aunt to come down and spend the winter with her, and her aunt wondering if her niece would be willing to come up there and stay until spring, instead. For she was too old to move at 85, she said, and she would be homesick in the village. When Abby accepted, with "a hard tug at her heart" at the thought of her own little home, "the great question was settled, and suddenly . . . it became a thing of the past" (304–5). Mrs. Hand felt she and Abby had "gained the battle of Waterloo" (306).

In Ruth Suckow's "Sunset Camp," Mrs. Grobaty's companion in old age is her husband, "Mister," who she knows is very ill—"far gone"—though she does not allow herself to think about this very often. They had made the trip from Iowa to California, and some things had not changed. Mister still slept on the outside. Her internal clock still ran by Iowa time. She missed having her own place, but found it pleasant to see all the cabins around her and exciting to live where there was so much going on. She missed her big kitchen, but she has learned how to make good use of the small one-burner oven in the kitchenette of their cabin. She could even make cornmeal gems here, and since Mister was still sleeping, she decided to bring some over to her young neighbors in the next cabin. Back home, folks brought some of their baking to the neighbors. But the embarrassed look of the young people when someone finally answered her rapping, and the noise and laughter inside, and the disorder she glimpsed, and the sight of the young girl running into the other room with a man's coat over her flimsy nightgown—all that left her feeling fluttered and upset. She felt like waking up her husband and telling him that they would have to leave this place. Now the cabins all around her looked "hostile and mysterious. She wanted to get home where she knew folks and knew just what was what. . . . And off there were the strange blue mountains, the stretches of desert land . . ., and on the other side the unknown wilderness of the sea."[10]

Later that morning, Mrs. Grobaty found that her husband had wandered off. Once she satisfied herself that he was all right, just sitting on one of the benches talking to a new friend, she decided to stay in the cabin and rock awhile. Long ago, she had thought she would never be reconciled to living in Ioway, and now Ioway, not Pennsylvania, where they had come from, was "home" for them. Once, Ioway had seemed as strange to her as this outlandish place did now. "Folks could get used to more than they thought." She did not have to approve of her neighbors to accept them. She could imagine what the folks back home would think about some of the goings-on at Sunset Camp, but she was not back home, after all, and the world had many different kinds of folks living in it. "She didn't know as she was called upon to make up her mind about everybody" (230). Their children had been telling them to take a trip, saying it was only in their minds that there was anything to keep them in Iowa. There was something in that, Mrs. Grobaty admitted to herself. In Sunset Camp, the Grobatys "didn't have to think of the weather, the children, anything but just themselves. . . . They might as well enjoy whatever they could" (231).

Alone together after so many years of family life, the Grobatys were calling one another Nellie and Henry again, every so often. As long as she had lived with her husband, Mrs. Grobaty did not know there was this side of his nature that she saw out here in the way he became attached to a cat that befriended him. It was good to have the store nearby, good that he was letting her decide more about how the money ought to be spent, good that they both were learning not to be so particular. There was the satisfaction of getting away from all that cooking. The Millers were from the next county to theirs back home. When they left Sunset Camp, she almost had the feeling she and her husband were being deserted. She rebelled against the transitoriness of their life. But when she returned to her cabin and found him just waking up, going through his struggle of coughing and wheezing, it came to her that nothing mattered much next to this, that he was seriously ill. "All the vigor her healthy old body had left in it went out to support him" (226). That feeling overwhelmed the other feeling of being lost out here. Things looked somewhat brighter after he'd had some breakfast. They'd moved to a strange place before when they went to Iowa from the old home in Pennsylvania. "Then she had depended upon Henry as the only sure thing in a wilderness of the unknown. He used to come into the house, sometimes, from his plowing, just to see how she was getting along and let her know he wasn't far away" (227).

Given the choice, many older women prefer not to live as solitaries. With all their troubles, most aging couples stay together. Although "Sunset Camp" is one of a collection of Suckow's stories published in 1931, it is closer in time to us than "Aunt Cynthy Dallett." The move from the Midwest to California, the uprootedness, the way the look and feel of the landscape change with the changing weathers of Mrs. Grobaty's inner life—all this has a most contemporary ring. Many older people find themselves in a strange new world at the last of life, in need of summoning up resources—flexibility, openness to change, buoyancy in the face of an uncertain future—that flow more easily for the young. But there are many older women, friends as well as kin, who weigh the freedom and privacy of keeping a place of their own against growing isolation and dwindling resources—many for whom sharing a home is an alternative answer to "the great question." Many women find that old age is not a settling down into an established pattern, but a wandering, a moving on, a challenge that comes at a time in life when one least expects to be challenged.

In "The Journey," one of Katherine Anne Porter's sequence of stories, "The Old Order," Grandmother and Aunt Nannie are companions in old age. They would sit together over their sewing during certain hours every day during the summer in the side garden under the trees, a post that commanded a fine view, and during the winter in the city, in Grandmother's room, an excellent listening post for the various sounds of the household. They had in common this passion for cutting scraps and stitching them into a patchwork—this and a past they had shared since childhood, a past they had loved despite its bitterness. The origins of their friendship seemed to both old women to have the proportions of myth. Both had questioned that "burdensome rule" under which they had lived; neither expected an answer to the question. Nannie had been sold with her parents, who went on working in the fields after she went to live in the big house as a playmate for 5-year-old Miss Sophia Jane. Missy gave her 1827 as her birth year, the same as her own, picked June 11 at random as her birthday, and entered the date in the family Bible. When she was married at 17, Miss Sophia Jane was given Nannie and the young man with whom she was married off, who later became known as "Uncle Jimbilly," as a wedding present. After that, the two women entered "their grim and terrible race of procreation," each giving birth about every sixteen months.[11] Nannie nursed Missy's first four babies; when she became seriously ill with puerperal fever, Sophia Jane nursed both Nannie's and her own newborn. From then on, Miss Sophia Jane decreed each would nurse her own infants. Emancipation was a sweet word to Nannie. It had not changed the way she lived at all, but it made her proud to be able to tell her mistress that she intended to stay with her so long as she was wanted. So they shared their long lives, and it came to be that neither of them could imagine how she could possibly get on without the other. Far on the other side of life, the two old women looked back with a common moral attitude upon a past they had shared intimately. They had observed, they had experienced, they had endured. The bond between them had outlasted all others. They talked about religion, about rearing children, each in turn criticizing her own and defending the other's; they talked about gardening and preserving and their hope of spending eternity together. They talked about the laxness of moral standards; they remarked "how strangely things come out in this life" (332). A scrap of material in their hands evoked lengthy reminiscences of family life. Over and over, they delighted in observing "how the working of their memories differed in such important ways" (328).

Nannie and Grandmother were life companions to one another in a way that neither of them had been to her husband. Under the aegis of "the old order" of slavery, patriarchy, and a feudal economy, they were divided by race but united by sex and age. Over the years, their lives had grown together as they managed a large and complex household and watched over an extended family unto the third generation. Nannie's marriage had been one of convenience. When the reasons for it dissolved, so did the union, and after that she and Uncle Jimbilly did not pay attention to one another. She spoke of the children as hers; he spoke of them as his; they had no common memories to share. Sophia Jane had learned to despise men; her husband had squandered her dowry and property in wild investments in Louisiana and Texas. After his death, she accepted the heavy responsibility of providing for the future of the family. After the children were grown, her son Harry's young wife died, and then she began life all over again as mother to her three orphaned grandchildren. Although Miss Sophia Jane had long ago become Grandmother, Nannie remained Nannie (Aunt Nannie to Maria, Paul and Miranda) until Grandmother died.

There are certain resemblances between the bond these two old women forged and the tie between co-wives in a system of sororal polygyny. Though they may sleep and take their meals under separate roofs, women living under these social arrangements are surrogate mothers for one another's children—and children's children, if they live to old age. In their close sharing of the tasks of the daily round, they build a life in common. In old age, they drink their memories from the same well. Co-wives are ranked formally by age or date of marriage in many polygynous systems, and informally by favoritism on the part of the spouse they hold in common. Therefore, the sororal bond can be weakened or torn by rivalry: in any family system, siblings are united and at the same time divided by the filial tie. But the distance between these ranks could never be so great as that between the castes in the system under which Nannie and Grandmother lived. They were as sisters under the skin, but they lived and loved in a world in which the skin was destiny. All their devotion to one another, all the maternal care they lavished upon one another's children, all the domestic responsibilities they shared and their hope of heaven could not alter the fateful fact that their relationship had its origins in that evil institution. Nannie did not move out from its shadows into the sun of her own person and selfhood until late old age. It was after Grandmother died that she retired. Grandmother's death was the occasion for her declaration of independence from "the old order."

Harry and the children had been surprised and a bit hurt when Nannie asked for a little cabin across the creek. They had the place fixed up for her, and let her take this and that from the house, amazed to find that she, who had not seemed to have wants, had wished to have certain things for herself. After she moved away, trying for the sake of the family not to seem too pleased about leaving, she was not the servant Nannie anymore, but had become "an aged Bantu woman of independent means, sitting on the steps, breathing the free air. She began wearing a blue bandanna wrapped around her head, and at the age of eighty-five she took to smoking a corncob pipe" (349). The children, who had taken her presence and her labor for granted, missed her sorely as they grew up. Their need for her was all the greater as their fortunes declined, for they had few servants. Things fell apart: work did not do itself, and they had not learned to do it. As for Uncle Jimbilly, he had not seemed to notice Aunt Nannie had moved into her own cabin up the hill; she had left without a look or word for him. One day he went by and saw her sitting on the doorstep with her pipe. He sat down, too, to sun himself and he asked her what she was doing with that big house all to herself. "Tain't no more than just enough fo' me," was her reply. "I don' aim to pass my las' days waitin on no man. . . . I've served my time, I've done my do, and dat's all." Uncle Jimbilly went back to the little attic over the smokehouse where he slept and did not go near her again. So Nannie passed her retirement, sitting by herself long after dark on summer evenings, smoking to keep the mosquitoes at bay and not going in until she was ready to go to sleep. "So she would sit in the luxury of having at her disposal all of God's good time there was in this world" (351).

An old woman who has given her time, energy, and devotion to others all through her life has earned rest and peace in her old age. The time that is left to her is time to bask in, time not as currency for spending, but as a space for indwelling. Children forget, if indeed they ever knew, that the woman who mothered them has other selves. So often they bring their needs and dependency to an aging mother as if they were bringing her gifts. It may happen that those who need another come to imagine that she will always be in need of *them* and everlastingly grateful for the chance to serve them. Then only with distancing—or death—is there enlightenment. In her late hour of old age, Nannie claimed freedom, claimed her selfhood. The death of someone very close is always a setting free, a liberation. Grandmother's death was soon followed by the laying to rest of the faithful old servant and the birth of the aged Bantu woman of independent means.

Sophia Jane turned into Grandmother and never came back again; it was as Grandmother that she died, on a visit with her third son and his family. But a spark of the girl she had once been flared and glowed for a moment when she made her yearly sojourn in the early summer to the country. Within an hour after her arrival and her survey of house and yards and garden, barns and hayfields and huts, the frenzy of restoration began. After it was all over and it was time for her to leave, she called Fiddler, her old saddle horse, to take her on her annual gallop. "The two old creatures would greet each other fondly" (324). Grandmother would mount him with Uncle Jimbilly's assistance. "Fiddler would remember his youth" and would go galloping off, although stiff-leggedly, and off Grandmother would go "with her crepe bands and her old-fashioned riding skirt flying. They always returned at a walk, the Grandmother sitting straight as a sword, smiling, triumphant." It was important to her to go on this annual gallop; "it proved her strength, her unabated energy." Although Fiddler "might drop in his tracks" at any time now, Grandmother would not. "She would say, 'He's getting stiff in the knees,' . . . but she herself walked lightly . . ., or so she chose to believe" (325).

Grandmother had made herself indispensable or had become so; perhaps this is the same thing. But an old woman knows she cannot live forever. That there is a little time left is the best she can hope for, and the gallop with Fiddler reassures her. This skirmish with mortality is one more little victory in the long siege none of us will win, and all the more glorious for that. A bit of the girl she once was glows through the character-dress of Grandmother, as shining raiment through a tear in a drab cloak worn to conceal it. That girl blazes to life again when she has an exchange with her sister, Great-Aunt Eliza, about how one ought to conduct oneself at her time of life. Both Grandmother and Eliza—who dips snuff and examines every particle of the material world that intrigues her through her microscope and burning glass, when she is not up on the henhouse roof studying the skies through her telescope—behave like two bickering schoolgirls, two young sisters nagging one another as only sisters know how to do. The girl inside the old woman may be visible only to one who has been her life companion. We can believe still that we were young once so long as our Fiddlers, whether human or animal, remember. And those who were young then, too, keep *their* faith by *our* memories. In the new order, many of us are soon separated from those with whom we shared our childhood. We grow away from them; we move away, and move away again. Physical distance has a way of becoming translated into social distance and moral distance. With marriage, there is more loosening of old bonds with siblings, playmates, schoolmates, friends as well as parents, and later with grown children. Even under a common roof, many of us build a separate life. In old age, we have more in common in *present* life than in the past. Indeed, talking about the past divides many old people from one another in the new order, whereas it bound Nannie and Grandmother ever more closely to one another. It affirmed that the past was real, that it all happened; it was their grand passion in a way it cannot be for most of us today. A sense of the past, of how it is all around us, is the root of memory. If we meet older people as strangers, or meet as strangers in old age, we will need to use our imagination. It is a great gift, and one on which our spiritual life depends. Old age is one of many masks we wear as creatures of a particular time and place. Youth is another. Whoever studies either mask closely will perceive signs and reflections of the other, and recognize what lives beneath them both.

Interiors

In Willa Cather's *My Mortal Enemy,* Nellie Birdseye used to walk by herself around the Driscoll place when she was older. It was the finest property in Parthia, Illinois. It was here that Myra's uncle, John Driscoll, had raised his niece after the girl had been orphaned. As good as his word, he had bequeathed the property to the Sisters of the Sacred Heart, cutting Myra off without a penny when she ran off to marry Oswald Henshawe. When Nellie was a little girl, her Aunt Lydia used to take her for a walk on the flagstones that surrounded the fenced grounds and tell the child about that exciting night when Myra Driscoll walked out of the big iron gates for the last time, turning her back on her uncle's fortune to marry the son of a man Driscoll detested. Years later, Nellie would go there after school when it was spring and the nuns could be seen strolling among the blossoming trees. In the girl's mind, the place was "under a spell, . . . ever since that winter night when Love went out of the gates and gave the dare to Fate."[12] But she knew it had not happened in quite that way. Driscoll had lived there alone for many years after Myra's elopement. Indeed, though only 6 years old at the time, Nellie remembered his funeral—its blazing candles, and the masses of flowers, and the bishop and priests in their bright vestments going to meet his coffin.

Myra Driscoll Henshawe returned to Parthia once when her husband came West on business, and it was then, when Nellie was 15, that she met her for the first time. Myra was about 45 then, "a short, plump woman in a black velvet dress, seated upon the sofa and softly playing on Cousin Bert's guitar" (5). She had deep-set flashing grey eyes and a haughty carriage to her head—perhaps because she was sensitive about beginning to have a double chin. Nellie was abashed by Myra, and to avoid looking at her directly, she looked instead at her necklace of carved amethysts. Though ill at ease all evening, the young girl observed much that passed between Myra and her husband. She came away disappointed by her first glimpse of Myra, who was twenty-five years older in the flesh than she had been in her imagination. In Nellie's mind, John Driscoll had suddenly changed places with his niece. She remembered his funeral—the procession, the swinging, smoking censers—and thought that Driscoll "had got, after all, the more romantic part" (19).

Aunt Lydia and Nellie were invited to spend the Christmas holidays at an old hotel on Fifth Avenue near the Henshawes's apartment. There, Myra confided to her that Oswald did not really belong in business, but had gone into an office because they had been so much in love and wanted to be married. She had two sets of friends, the "moneyed," whom she cultivated for Oswald's sake, and the "artistic," whom she loved passionately and upon whom she lavished affection, care, and compassion. Nellie saw how fiercely loyal Myra was to her husband, how recklessly grand Myra was in her sense of what life ought to be for herself and for those she loved, how impatient she was at any sign of pettiness. Myra magnified those she loved, and entangled herself in their affairs. Her ambition seemed insane to the young girl, her gestures and attitudes extravagant. On New Year's Eve, Helena Modjeska brought a young Polish opera singer with her to Henshawe's party, and this Emelia sang the Casta Diva aria for them after the other guests had departed. The music seemed mysteriously akin to something in Myra's nature, "a compelling, passionate, overmastering something" (48). Nellie came upon a bitter quarrel between the Henshawes and, after that, was relieved to return to Parthia with her Aunt Lydia.

Things went badly for Nellie and her family, and she took a position in an experimental college in the West. Now quite poor, she took lodging in an apartment hotel. It was there that she saw the Henshawes for the first time in ten years. They, too, had come down in the world and were living in that same hotel. Oswald had aged physically far beyond his 60 years. Myra, though she was now in a wheelchair, had been far less changed. Although crippled, "she looked strong and broken, generous and tyrannical, a witty and rather wicked old woman, who hated life for its defeats, and loved it for its absurdities" (65). She made tea nicely with her own silver tea things every afternoon. Nellie would keep her company, and it pleased her to bring Myra flowers during the late winter months. These were her consolations in her fallen and shabby state. For Myra, the cruellest suffering inflicted by poverty was that she was at the mercy of the tramping and banging noises of the people upstairs. She spoke of them as animals, as pigs.

Early in the spring, Nellie went for a drive with Myra along the shore. The road led to a bare headland with a solitary twisted tree. Below them was the sea. Myra recognized its likeness to Gloucester's cliff in *Lear*, and asked to be wrapped in the rug so she might lean against the trunk of the old cedar and look off to the sea. She passed a beautiful hour of the silence she now found to be healing, and she told Nellie she would love to see the place at dawn: "That is always such a forgiving time" (73). When the two women returned to Myra's apartment, they heard the noise overhead again, and Myra cried, out, "*if youth only knew.*" She said she and Oswald have destroyed one another, that they have thrown their lives away, that she should have stayed with her uncle. It had been so like him to have left a clause in his will that the home for aged and destitute women in Chicago to be established with the money he left for this purpose was to take her in, if things came to that. "She'd roll herself into the river first, the brach!" he must have thought. But she would ask his pardon now, if John Driscoll were still alive,

because I know what it is to be old and lonely and disappointed. Yes, and because as we grow old we become more and more the stuff our forebears put into us. I can feel his savagery strengthen in me. We think we are so individual and so misunderstood when we are young; but the nature our strain of blood carries is inside there, waiting, like our skeleton. [82]

On the anniversary of Madame Modjeska's death, Myra showed Nellie where she had hidden away some gold pieces. It was her wish that her young friend give them to Father Fay to celebrate a mass for the repose of the soul of Helena Modjeska. It was then that Myra confessed that she knew it was hard of her to spoil the past for Oswald. But that was her nature. "People can be lovers and enemies at the same time," she said. "A man and woman draw apart from that long embrace, and see what they have done to each other." She said that the feeling "goes through natural changes" if a couple has children. Otherwise it remains very personal, and then "something gives way in one. In age we lose everything; even the power to love" (88–89). Myra had herself taken to Gloucester's cliff to die alone. Not long before that, Nellie heard her ask softly in the night, "Why must I die like this, alone with my mortal enemy?" (95)

It is only when one is young that one may imagine that our fate is wholly determined by forces outside ourselves. When the old look inward, they can see the workings of inheritance. In life, we carry our ancestors within us; in death, as the prayer has it, we are gathered to them. Only in taking the full measure of oneself can one hope to wrest something that endures from all that has shown itself to be perishable. This is the critical turning point—the full awareness of mortality—that one may reach at 50, and another at 70. Chronological age is not a measure of readiness to look within, to recognize our own "heart of darkness," to accept responsibility for the part each of us plays in making our life.

Many critics have remarked that Myra is not a character one could love or even like much. She rebuked Oswald for not having redeemed her from subjection to the noise of "coarse creatures." She said that if the situation had been reversed, she would never have allowed this to happen to him. She told him how bitter it was for her to have to be cared for by him—bitter just because she once loved him so much. But other women would have found this sweet for the same reason. And if they had not come down in the world? Then she would have ended her days in luxurious surroundings, being waited upon by servants. Then she could have lived and died in the grand manner. She would not have objected to being served by those she saw as of a lower station, only by Oswald. There is nothing noble in this ambition, nothing admirable about wanting to have the world at one's feet. She was too proud to want Oswald to carry her about. But she would not have minded having his money or her uncle's fortune purchase these services for her. This is an independence as false as it is fierce.

Childless, Myra spoke of how the marriage relationship was adversely affected by childlessness. But she was at least 55 then; if they had had children, she and Oswald would be living as a couple again by then. Besides, Myra devoted herself to her friends as passionately as or more than many mothers devote themselves to their children. And the lives of mothers often continue to be intertwined with those of their children even after they are grown, even after—*long* after—there is the wish on both sides to find a way to loosen this powerful bond. In her last illness, if she were the mother of children, Myra would still long for a cloistered place of solitude and silence where she might pray for forgiveness and absolution. Indeed, an anxious, devoted, protective grown daughter or son would make it as difficult for her to disentangle herself from the web of human relationships as any beloved friend would. And if her friends had remained close to her over the years, she would have sought release from them in the same way. As it happened, only the sheltering Oswald remained. And Myra had to resolve what the Jungians call "relatedness" for the last time.[13] All relationships pull us back from that final encounter.

When her hour had come, Myra found a way to return to the bare headland with the twisted tree. There the prodigal daughter asked forgiveness of the fostering parent-figure. And *there* was a death to match her vision of how life ought to be lived! But a woman whose love begins in this splendor of passion and intensity is destined to meet her mortal enemy one day. If she has not come to know its name and nature, she will not understand that it wears the mask of her aging lover.

My Mortal Enemy is a story told by a young woman haunted by an older woman, even after her death, haunted by that question she had asked during the night watch. That question returned to Nellie whenever she saw love's bright beginnings. The story of Myra Driscoll Henshawe had changed her life. Oswald had given her the necklace of amethysts to remember Myra by, and Nellie found that it was unlucky. What had gone before cast a shadow over what was to come.

In Josephine Herbst's novella "Hunter of Doves," it is the other way around: youth, in the person of Timothy Comfort, draws the older woman backward in time. And at first Mrs. Heath was unwilling to follow him there. She did not even trust his motives. Nor did she want to play any part in what she saw as a betrayal of her dead friend, Noel Bartram. Timothy Comfort wanted to know all that she could tell him about Bartram and his works, those three short novels "that were the sum of his art." Bartram had died, but now might become twice-dead because his work could be the very means by which his image would be obscured forever. And this Timothy Comfort "must have been a mere brat in the 'thirties'" when Bartram was writing. "Youth was well and good, but did it not seek first of all to serve itself? The eyes—were they actually truthful or only self-consciously determined to look trusting?"[14] He had been industrious; he had gathered a huge sheaf of notes. But what would those notes become, and what relationship would all this have to the Bartram she had known?

Mrs. Heath's medium was painting, not writing—literature had been Bartram's medium and her husband's. There is no need for "literal documentation" in painting. When she thought of painting, she felt calm, released from the obligation of "going back, step by step, bruising her feet over each separate stone." The years were to be recalled not in a series of days but "enclosed in a memory of a single, sun-parched afternoon. . . . In the smell of a spring hyacinth" (319). Now that she had been summoned to return to the past, Bartram's image was shattered into a hundred fragments, and she saw an image of herself among them. Returning, she found, "there had been many Bartrams and she was conscious of them as she was aware of her many selves" (332).

She had wanted to be a mediatrix for both her husband and Bartram. Telling Bartram he *must* finish his work had been, she knew, intended to reach Heath, to "fan the flame" for his own work, so neglected then. Heath would draw designs of sloops and ketches and barges; she had asked herself where they were meant to carry him. That fall, when the three of them were together so much, "she was aware . . . of the burden that their individual talents laid upon them," and she felt they had reached a critical point in their lives (323). It was not Bartram she had loved and desired, but the Heath who had once been so confident and who had reached an impasse in his work. But no one had really been himself then. "The world was dazed for it was the time of droughts, foreclosures and despairs. Time for divorce, too, for among their friends, this was the season" (327). Bartram had become a dandy; he had got himself a fine dog and a fine gun, and the persona of an English squire. It might have been because of his mother's continual harping that his work would not sell, that there was no future in it. It might have been the "state of the nation, deep in a depression," that awakened in him "the desperate struggle of one trying to escape the common fate." For whatever reason, he began looking at things from his mother's perspective after his second book was finished. "There was no hope for slow growth in this country of quick returns" (334–35). A real writer had to be a pariah, and Bartram did not want to be that. The hunter of doves had died in a head-on collision. And Heath had sailed away with another woman.

For some, the past is alive. For the rest, it lies sleeping. In her later life, Mrs. Heath met with this young intruder. Talking with him, she thought of the image of honeycomb. She felt "a terrible nostalgia for all the richness that living could impart" and she wanted to shake him "out of his self-satisfied preoccupation" (312). She longed to find a way to make him see through the appearances of things into the complication of it all. The young, she thought, were in such a hurry, rushing into the legend of the 1920s. The reality had been so different. At first, Timothy Comfort had seemed hateful to her. Here was this young man "who so lightheartedly and for his own selfish purposes came stirring and digging, roiling up the soil on the grassy mounds." What could she tell of all of it, and what could he know? "How little seeped through of the real agonies." He had seemed brash to her, a stripling. He had asked her to "call back the actual dead and the living dead"—for there was no way to disentangle one memory from the other. "She was no filing cabinet, neatly documented, but a living soul, who had been abandoned in Arcadia by the two of them" (324).

In the end, Timothy Comfort told Mrs. Heath that no one ought to keep Bartram's work down, and for the first time she respected him. In the end, she too said the work should not be kept down. Had she been another sort of person, this story would have ended quite differently. It could happen that many years from now, some of us may be asked to pass judgment on the life and work of someone we once knew. How we meet this awesome responsibility will take the measure of our moral character, of what we once were and of what we have become. In "The Old Beauty," Willa Cather has Henry Seabury reflect, "Nobody ever recognizes a period until it has gone by . . . : until it lies behind one it is merely everyday life."[15]

Journeys in Late Life

"After my tryin' hard for risin' forty-five year to provide for bein' past work, here I be, dear," 76-year-old Mrs. Peet said to her fellow traveler on the train ride in Jewett's "Going to Shrewsbury."[16] Her farm had fallen into the hands of her perfidious nephew, a prosperous moneylender. She could have stayed on the place only as a dependent, but that would have hurt her pride. The old widow confessed that now she regretted she had never had children. It was her intention to "airn" her own living; she did not mean to sag on to anyone. "I've got more work in me now than folks expects at my age" (103). Who knows, but she might be of use to one of her nieces in town? She had written them that she was moving there. But her prospects were uncertain. It was hard to move twenty-two miles away from where her home and friends had always been: "an uprooteder creatur' never stood on the airth" (102).

Mrs. Peet had always wanted to see something of the world, but now that she had the chance she didn't value it so greatly. Even so, along the way she did declare over having the experience of riding in the cars. "Ain't it jest like flyin' through the air?" (95) Her fellow passenger was happy to see her forget her troubles after a while and look about herself, and even make astute observations about some of the travelers seated near them. "But when the conductor came to take her ticket she relapsed into her first state of mind, and was at a loss" (100). In the search for her ticket, the cat nearly escaped from the cat-basket, and Mrs. Peet's bundle-handkerchief came untied. Its scattered contents made "a touching collection of the last odds and ends" of her housekeeping. There were "some battered books, and singed holders for flatirons, and . . . a faded little shoulder shawl . . . and a goose-wing for brushing up ashes, and her much-thumbed Leavitt's Almanac" (101). But the good soul brightened again to say she might like living in Shrewsbury first-rate, for she had always wanted to go off and see how other folks lived. Still, when they came near the junction where Mrs. Peet was to transfer to the branch line to Shrewsbury, the cat was clawing at the basket and her mistress was beginning to look very old and quite pale. She got up much too soon, and looked as if she were ready to cry as she stood at the car door. Her fellow passenger assured her there would be someone waiting for her at the station in Shrewsbury. But even so, "The sight of that worn, thin figure adventuring alone across the platform gave my heart a sharp pang as the train carried me away" (105).

Left homeless in her old age, Mrs. Peet had gone journeying. What had become of her? In the spring, her fellow passenger on that train to Shrewsbury happened to be driving by on the "sheep-lands road." The sight of Mrs. Peet's former home recalled the train ride, and she asked her companion if she knew how Mrs. Peet had fared. The reply was that the good soul had been going to concerts and lectures all winter, and had taken the view that her nephew had done her a good turn, after all. Then, a little way further, the two travelers met Isaiah Peet, who told them Aunt Peet had passed away the day before. She had been very happy living with her relatives in Shrewsbury and enjoying all her activities in town, he went on to say. "The place here never was good for nothin'" (107). The narrator did not linger to hear much more. She felt she had known Mrs. Peet better than anyone else had; she had hoped to meet her again. For she had "wondered what had become of the cat and the contents of the faded bundle-handkerchief" (108).

In "The Flight of Betsey Lane," passage for the journey in late life came to the adventurer in an entirely different way. Betsey sat picking over a bushel of beans with Aunt Lavina Dow and Miss Peggy Bond in the shed chamber of Byfleet Poor-house when she was summoned to meet a caller. Miss Peggy had been somewhat aggrieved that Betsey closed the door behind her at the foot of the stairs as she went out. It wasn't as if anyone intended to listen, or as if she and Aunt Lavina did not once have folks who came to call. But Aunt Lavina expected "'t was only the wind shoved it to," and she hoped the visitor would be taking dear Betsey off to show her a good time.[17]

Betsey's caller was the granddaughter of General Thornton's household where she had served as aid-in-general for most of her life. And after she left, Betsey tucked the roll of money she had been given into the bosom of her gown: it was time to blow the horn to call the men-folks to dinner. The "company of waifs and strays" were hungry, and too absorbed in partaking of the meal to ask questions Betsey was eager to answer. Then, when they were filled and ready to hear the morning news, a "wrong note" was struck. The young widow with seven children who stood out from the other town charges because of her cheerless attitude remarked that Betsey must feel she was too fine to be setting with common folks. Betsey, who took pride in having good manners, replied that she thought she was behaving as she always had. She had nothing to add to that. Later, when she and her friends were planting corn, she had a moment alone at the end of her row in a corner of the field. It was then that she took out the money for the first time, and saw with astonishment that she had fresh bank bills for a hundred dollars. She tucked it away quickly and began to drop her five kernels to a hill as, first, the top of Peggy's head over the knoll, and then, all of Peggy Bond herself came into view.

Miss Peggy was well on in her seventies, "a very small, belligerent-looking person, who wore a huge pair of steel-bowed spectacles" (23). She was blind by more than half, and had "suffered much personal damage" now and again because she never looked where she was going. For all the falls she had taken down hatchways and cellarways, for all her wandering into deep ditches and brooks in the pasture, she took pride in being "upsighted" as was her father before her. "At the poorhouse, where an unusual malady was considered a distinction, upsightedness was looked upon as a most honorable infirmity" (24).

Miss Lavina Dow was at least well on in her eighties. "She made a great secret of her years; and as she sometimes spoke of events prior to the Revolution with the assertion of having been an eyewitness, she naturally wore an air of vast antiquity" (26). Compared with Peggy's upsightedness, Aunt Lavina's rheumatism was plain and everyday. Nonetheless, she presided as hostess and social lawgiver at the Poor-farm. Many inmates took residence there only during the winter. Most of them had been impoverished by old age in that it had limited their powers of endurance, but they did not lament the fact that they were town charges: far from it. "They rather liked the change and excitement" of residing there during the season (23). Mrs. Dow lived on the town-farm the year round. She had once been an energetic worker, but her rheumatism had crippled her badly, so she had not left the place to work for many years. She had the advantage that she could remember every inmate and everything interesting that had happened for almost forty years. In addition to that, she had an impressive command of town history and biography that reached back three or four generations. She and her dear friend Betsey "led thought and opinion—chiefly opinion—and held sway, not only over Byfleet Poor-farm, but also the selectmen and all others in authority" (25).

Betsey was the youngest of the trio at 69, although she looked much older. She had been left in good circumstances when the Thornton household disbanded. But her legacies and savings had been diminished both through misfortunes and her own generosity. And illness had left her with a stiffened arm and more uncertainty. So, "the good soul had sensibly decided that it was easier for the whole town to support her than for a part of it" (26). She had not given up the hope of seeing something of the world before she left it. She was descended from adventurous, seafaring people, but she had never gone further than Danby and Northville, towns no more than thirty miles away. It was her dream to go to the Centennial in "Pheladelphy."

When later that summer Betsey Lane's bed was found empty and her person gone, Peggy Bond said she might have gone to spend the day with the Deckers. But Mrs. Dow thought her disappearance was ominous. She had heard Betsey groaning in her sleep. What is more, Betsey's aunt on her mother's side had drowned herself. And as time went by, the curiosity and speculations of Betsey's friends changed to fear. She was not visiting the

Deckers. She could not have taken the train from South Byfleet, because it did not start until after eight o'clock. At that hour, Betsey, who was in her best clothes at that, surely would have been seen. Either she had left early in the morning to put an end to her life, or she had gone to the Centennial. But why had she been wearing her best clothes? And if someone had given her money, surely she would have told Mrs. Dow about it.

Nine days after Betsey's disappearance, "two pathetic figures might have been seen crossing the slopes of the poor-farm field, toward the low shores of Byfield pond" (58). Peggy, who was having one of those days when she was all but blind, blundered along; Aunt Lavina was so stiff in the joints, she made her way wheezing and leaning on a stick and grasping the arm of her up-sighted companion. It was Peggy's hope that they would not find Betsey, as Mrs. Dow was dread certain they would, floating atop the pond. It was while they were standing over the water, on which nothing was floating except pond-lilies, that Betsey Lane greeted them. She had taken the short way home from the railroad. What stories she had to tell of her great adventure! Early in the morning of the day of her flight, she had been given a ride in a boxcar on a freight, thus making her way to the South Byfleet station all unseen. She had been to the Centennial in Pheladelphy, where she beheld "the wonders of the West and the splendors of the East with equal calmness and satisfaction; she had always known that there was an amazing world outside the boundaries of Byfleet" (53). She had made friends all around; she had bought little presents for all the folks at home. And she had happened to speak with a doctor who would be coming to the Poor-farm in August to see what he might do for her upsighted friend. She had enough to think about, enough to tell for the rest of her days to these two friends who had set out on such a "doleful expedi-tion." She had seen how spool cotton is made; she had seen diamonds as big as pigeon's eggs, and hogs "that weighed risin' thirteen hunderd" (62). Someone from the neighborhood ought to be to the Centennial, even if just for the good of all, and Betsey had thought she had better be that person. And she had had no intention of asking the selectmen about her decision. Now, dusty and all but beat out, Betsey thought Peggy might take her bundle-handkerchief and her basket, and let Mis' Dow sag on herself, for she could "git her along twice as easy." That done, "the small elderly company set forth triumphant toward the poor-house, across the wide green field" (63).

Old women can show one another how to be, as Hochschild remarked of the old women at Merrill Court.[18] The Poor-farms have vanished; the *Bicen-*tennial has come and gone. Today, this goodly company might find them-selves in a public housing development, making yarn dolls in the recreation room, rather than picking beans in the shed chamber, or bringing their goodies and their five-piece band to entertain the poor dears at a nearby nursing home rather than planting corn on a strip of land alongside a great field. All the same, at Merrill Court *or* at Byfleet Poor-house, elderly widows have much to talk about, and in the silences between conversations might join in the same hymns with voices like "autumnal crickets," as Jewett perfectly put it. The sororal bond at Merrill Court was fashioned by women who could do for themselves and for one another. So it was at Byfleet Poor-farm. Mis' Dow could do the seeing for Peggy, and could sag on to her upsighted friend to make her wheezing way along. Betsey's flight was a spreading of three pairs of wings, at least. Three were as one in adventure and in triumph. That is the way with friends—and, sometimes, with sisters.

In Eudora Welty's "A Worn Path" Phoenix Jackson traveled from Old Natchez Trace to Natchez in her long, dark-striped dress made of bleached sugar sacks, tapping her way along the frozen ground with the cane that had been made from an umbrella. The eyes of this old Negro woman "were blue with age. Her skin had a pattern all its own of numberless branching wrinkles and as though a whole little tree stood in the middle of her forehead, but a golden color ran underneath."[19] She told them all out loud—foxes and owls and beetles, jack rabbits and coons and wild animals, bob-whites and big wild hogs—to keep out of her way, for she had a long way to go. She spoke out "in the voice of argument old people keep to use with themselves" about how something always took hold of her on the path that ran up the hill—"pleads I should stay" (274). She told herself she had come up through pines and now must go down through oaks. She had to free her dress that was caught in the thorns of a bush at the bottom of the hill. Then she had to cross the creek by walking on a log. And then go through a barbed-wire fence. She came upon a buzzard and asked it what it was watching. She asked who the tall, black, skinny moving figure in the field of dead corn was the ghost of. She went on "through the whispering field" and followed a wagon track through the fields, through trees "silver in their dead leaves, past cabins silver from weather, with the doors and windows boarded shut, all like old women under a spell sitting there" (277). On the road, a black dog came up to her. When she hit at him with her cane a little, she fell in a ditch, and a white man came along and lifted her out. She saw a "flashing nickel" fall out of his pocket, and distracted him and his dog long enough to pick it up unseen and put it in the pocket of her apron. "God watching me the whole time. I come to stealing" (280).

In Natchez, she made her way to a big building. In that building, she walked up and around a tower of steps until she came to a door that had inside a document on the wall that "matched the dream that was hung up in her head" (281). Was her grandson's throat any better, the nurse wanted to know. Phoenix Jackson's memory left her for a while after her long trip. When she recovered it, she explained, "I never did go to school, I was too old at the Surrender" (283). But she knew now she'd come for the soothing medicine for her grandson's throat that closes up every once in a while ever since the time he swallowed lye. He was waiting for her to bring it back. "He got a sweet look. He going to last" (284). It being Christmastime, the attendant offered to make Phoenix Jackson a present of a few pennies. Five pennies make a nickel, the old woman said, and she accepted that and matched it with the one in her apron pocket. Then she tapped her cane on the floor and spoke of her intention: "I going to the store and buy my child a little windmill they sells, made out of paper. He going to find it hard to believe there such a thing in the world. I'll march myself back where he waiting, holding it straight up in this hand" (284–85).

Every old woman making her way alone, whether to Shrewsbury with a cat basket and a bundle-handkerchief, or to Natchez with a dream in her head, has a story to tell about the things that can happen in this life. Mrs. Peet was going on 76 when she found herself on the road seeking her fortune. Phoenix Jackson might have been older than that when she went on her "errand of love." Who can guess all that the sight of an old woman wandering might be saying to us? "One day I saw a solitary old woman like Phoenix," Eudora Welty recalled.[20] She made up an errand for her, and she brought her up close so she could be seen, but the indelible figure was the one "moving across the winter fields." The subject of "A Worn Path" is "the deep-grained habit of love" (161). The worn path is the only thing that is certain; that is what the story means. "The habit of love cuts through confusion and stumbles or contrives its way out of difficulty, it remembers the way even when it forgets, for a dumbfounded moment, its reason for being. The path is the thing that matters" (161–62).

Her Place in the Family

Ferber's Ma Mandle had a relationship with "*my son Hugo*" that "was more than that of mother and son." It had in it "something conjugal."[21] At four o'clock of a summer afternoon, she and Mrs. Lamb, Mrs. Brunswick and Mrs. Wormser presented "a decent black silk row, on a shady bench in Washington Park (near the refectory and afternoon coffee)" (145). While Ma Mandle, queen of a six-room flat on South Park Avenue, Chicago, boasted about how her crown jewel "my son Hugo" spoiled her, the other three complained about their daughters-in-law. For the other three lived with their married sons, "tolerated and dependent." These deposed queens were as ladies-in-waiting who flattered Ma Mandle, yet were jealous of her. They admired her, yet they were resentful. Hugo, at 40, had no intention of marrying. For fifteen years, he had been paying all the bills, but in such a way that his mother never felt herself to be his beneficiary. He always brought her two species of gifts when he came back from his business trips—a practical gift and a silly. He and his mother took evening walks together; he gave her matinee tickets for herself and a friend; he praised her cooking. He bought her candy, and lavished her with playful compliments about her hats and clothes. The three friends predicted that "my son Hugo" would marry yet. Mrs. Wormser thought he was the kind who marries late. "And they get it the worst" (148). She had told Hugo a million times that he ought to marry some nice girl and settle down, Ma Mandle said, but he would say that no one could cook dumplings like the ones she made.

Then "my son Hugo" did marry, "suddenly, breathlessly, as a man of forty does" (152). Then Ma Mandle became as her friends "a drinker of the hemlock cup, an eater of ashes" (154). At 70, she had to come to terms with "the law of life" that decreed that where once there had been just the two of them, now there had to be Hugo and Hugo's wife, and the grandchild that was soon to be born. "They were the ones that counted, now. . . . Selfishness. . . . They called it love, but it was selfishness" (160–61). She would have to tell the others what she had discovered. Now there would be four deposed queens, where at the beginning of the story there had been three, three who would sit on a park bench "filling their lives with emptiness. They had married, and brought children into the world; sacrificed for them, managed a household, been widowed." Although they were not aware of this, their achievement was magnificent. "They had come up the long hill, reached its apex, and come down. Their journey was over and yet they sat by the roadside. They knew that which could have helped younger travelers over the next hill, but those fleet-footed ones pressed on, wanting none of their wisdom" (147).

In "The Sudden Sixties," Hannah Winter was enslaved by her daughter. Hannah's Marcia, and her son-in-law Ed, would reward her for her enslavement by taking her out from time to time. But she enjoyed going off on a spree with her own cronies much more. To her and her friends, a double ice-cream soda or an interesting book was a fine treat. "Why, at sixty the world walked before them, these elderly women, its mind unclothed, all-revealing. This was painful, sometimes, but interesting always. It was one of the penalties—and one of the rewards—of living."[22]

Hannah lived in a hotel on the lake front where many elderly widows resided. They did a little cooking in their rooms—coffee and toast on an electric grill for breakfast was the extent of it, they said. Sometimes they brought back lunch things in a muff or handbag. And there were miniature iceboxes in the closets of some of the rooms. The hotel management chose not to notice. The women exchanged references of names of a "little" dressmaker or a "little" manicurist, the "little" referring to the prices for these services. Hannah was free there as she had never been before in her life. Yet she was a slave. And she was far from alone in this. "Hyde Park was full of . . . young mothers who were leaning hard upon the Hannah Winters of their own families. You saw any number of gray-haired . . . grandmothers trundling gocarts." The mothers were quite busy, going to class, playing bridge, marketing. "Some of them had gone in for careers" (209). What else were grandmothers for, what else had they to do but take the children for a few hours? If they really cared about the grandchildren, how could they say they felt nervous around them? After half an hour with hers, Hannah began feeling restless and irritable, but she did not try to put the feeling into words.

It was not her birthday that marked Hannah's sudden passage to 60, but an accident she had while hurrying along to meet Marcia; they were to shop for clothes for the children. Hannah saw someone oddly familiar walking toward her, *into* her, in fact. She swerved to avoid a collision with the figure, and there was a crash: she had walked into her own image in the full-length mirror in the marble wall at the north end of Peacock Alley. People came to help her, but she had only bumped her forehead. Now she stared at "this murderess who had just slain, ruthlessly and forever, a . . . high-spirited girl of twenty" (199). She had arrived at the sixties that suddenly. Strangely, the years, heavy as they had been, had rushed by. She admitted to herself that she was tired by things that never used to tire her. "She was older, of course. But she never thought of herself as old . . . never said, 'My work is done. My life is over.' About the future she was still as eager as a girl" (206).

That evening of the accident, Hannah and Marcia found little Joan ill with a sore throat when they returned to Marcia's apartment. Hannah wondered at her own indifference; she had felt panic about the children's throats before now. At supper, she heard an inner voice shouting, "Threescore, and ten to go." Little Joan complained about the plans she had made for the next day. Marcia complained about how Joan's throat ruined *her* plans for tomorrow. Hannah thought that she had done nothing she had wanted to do, that she, like so many, was afraid to do what she wanted because of grown daughters or sons. She thought that she did not want to spend her "ten years to go" taking care of her grandchildren, unnatural as that might make her sound to Marcia. She had raised her own without help. Now she wanted to enjoy herself, "to reap." She wanted leisure: to do all she'd wanted to do for forty years and could not do. "I want, if I feel like it, to start to learn French and read Jane Austen and stay in bed till noon." She wanted to play, not "to bring up a second crop of children." She was too old for that now. "It's terrible to realize that you don't learn how to live until you're ready to die; and then it's too late" (214). When Marcia was suddenly 60, she, too, would understand and not care if she sounded like a selfish old woman. All these thoughts were in Hannah's mind, but there they remained. She told Marcia and Ed to have a good time the next day as they had planned, that she would stay with Joan and take care of her.

Cather's "Old Mrs. Harris" was the mother of eight children. Some had died, and the others, except for Victoria, had "scattered." With neither questions nor regrets, she had left her home in Tennessee to follow Victoria's fortunes. For she believed that old women "were tied to the chariot of young life, and had to go where it went, because they were needed."[23] That chariot had been driven westward, first to a mountain town in southern Colorado, then further north to Skyline. There she shared the Templetons' small rented house with Victoria and her husband Hillary, the "bound girl," Mandy, they had brought with them from the South, and the grandchildren—15-year-old Vickie, the 10-year-old twins, Bert and Del, and Ronald, who was 6, and the baby, Hughie. Kindly Mrs. Rosen, the neighbor who took more interest in old Mrs. Harris than in the younger folks in that household, had observed how much finer the feelings of these people were than the way they lived. She knew that Victoria would not like it if anyone brought sweets into her house that were intended for anyone but herself. She knew that old Mrs. Harris was not supposed to receive visitors alone, and that if she showed pity for the old woman or indignation over her lot, Victoria would freeze her out. Even so, she took the risk, waiting until they were all out so she could bring freshly baked coffeecake over for "de old lady Harris." But, as always, she found the grandmother on her guard. For much as she appreciated Mrs. Rosen's kindnesses, Mrs. Harris would not have her ever think that she was "put upon" by Victoria.

Grandmother Harris slept on a wooden lounge with a thin mattress and a spread of red calico in a cluttered room, a kind of passageway, between the kitchen and the dining room. Once, Mrs. Rosen's young nephew had left a wool sweater behind after a visit, and Mrs. Rosen had given this to Mrs. Harris. When the grandmother felt a coldness and loneliness around her chest on winter nights, she would take this "little comforter" out from under her pillow, where she hid the secret gift from Victoria's eyes, and wrap it around her middle. At these times, she would think that the sweater was more kind to her than her children had been. As it warmed her, she would think about her old house in Tennessee, and her neighbors, and her yard and garden. "Especially she missed her lemon tree, in a tub on the front porch" (82–83). But she would never admit this to her neighbor. Mrs. Rosen, whose bitterest sorrow was her childlessness, had noticed how happy the old woman seemed to be when her grandchildren tumbled about her, asking to be read to, or begging for cookies. The children all have good instincts, she remarked to her husband, even though no one had taught them a thing. Mrs. Rosen commented on the ingratitude and coldness grown children sometimes show to self-sacrificing mothers. Mr. Rosen replied that perhaps, "The way to make your children unselfish is to be comfortably selfish yourself" (86).

Although this feeling vexed her, Mrs. Rosen sensed that in some way she was responsible for Vickie, who often came over to borrow books from their fine library. When Vickie won a memorial scholarship to the University of Michigan, she came to the Rosens first to tell them the great news. And Mr. Rosen wrote on a sheet of purple paper for her Michelet's words, *Le but n'est rien; le chemin, c'est tout.* But the scholarship paid only $200 toward Vickie's expenses; she would need $300 more. The girl was devastated, and when old Mrs. Harris asked her what was the matter, at first she "shrank away. Young misery is like that, sometimes" (136). But finally she told her grandmother of her need. Old Mrs. Harris went to her son-in-law to ask if he could get the money from what was owed for the sale of her house. But he said this could not be managed. Then she asked Mandy to fetch Mrs. Rosen, and she prevailed upon her good neighbor to ask her husband to borrow the money for Vickie. And this Mrs. Rosen was happy to do. When she came to bid Mrs. Harris good-bye, for she was going to Chicago to a wedding, Victoria was in the room. She could do no more than wink and nod to the grandmother, to let her know Mr. Rosen would take care of Vickie's problem.

Old Mrs. Harris knew she was failing. She was happy that she could conceal this from her neighbor as she had from everyone in the household—everyone but Mandy. For compassionate Mandy cared about old Mrs. Harris and sensed what was happening, and wanted to send for the doctor. But old Mrs. Harris said, "Doctors can't do no more than linger you out, an' I've always prayed I wouldn't last to be a burden" (143). Victoria had just discovered she was pregnant again, and bemoaned the fate she could only accept with "stupid animal patience," tired of all these babies and this small house, longing to be back in Tennessee, where she had been free and happy and young. Vickie was bitter at both her mother and grandmother for getting sick just when she had only two weeks to prepare for college. Yet, old Mrs. Harris was happy as little Bertie read to her from "Joe's Luck." She was not listening, but thinking of the passage from *Pilgrim's Progress* she had read to the children many times, where Christiana and her band come to the arbor on the Hill of Difficulty: *Then said Mercy, how sweet is rest to them that labour.* She rejoiced that Mrs. Rosen was in Chicago, and Hillary was away. She felt she would have peace, and she was grateful. She told the Lord it was true that she had always spoiled Victoria, but she had been the prettiest of her children. And Hillary would always humor her, and the children would love her more than most children love their mothers. Mrs. Harris felt certain she would die that night without being a trouble to anyone. She felt herself sinking. Although she did not die until the next day, she believed she had died that night, and she felt blessed.

The townspeople's implicit criticism of old Mrs. Harris's place in the family was not acceptable either to Victoria or to her mother. Mrs. Harris's place among the Templetons was "perfectly regular," and not the exception at all, back home in Tennessee (109). There it was believed that young girls ought to be carefree and foolish, and that when they married and had children, they ought to be given the best of everything. It was hard on a woman to have children, and nothing was more important. "In Tennessee every young married woman in good circumstances had an older woman in the house . . ., who managed the household economies and directed the help"(110). And there were always helpers. "The hills were full of solitary old women, or women but slightly attached to some household, who were glad to come to Miz' Harris's for good food and a warm bed," and the parting gift they were given. Older women who managed their daughter's households might keep in the background, but that background was their domain. And the house was hers. Among the aristocracy, an old woman might still live as if she were young. "But among the middle-class people and the country-folk, when a woman was a widow and had married daughters, she considered herself an old woman . . . and became a housekeeper. She accepted this estate unprotestingly, almost gratefully" (111–12).

It meant everything to Mrs. Harris to keep Victoria from living the life of an "ordinary" woman, a wife and mother and domestic, for that would have meant they had truly come down in the world. And the recompense for her hard life was the love of her grandchildren. They did not recoil from her because she was old. And Victoria was not jealous because they wanted to be with their grandmother so much of the time. In those days, "the common endurance test of old age was to keep going after every step cost something" because broken arches were not attended to (115). And if old Mrs. Harris felt low because her feet throbbed more than usual, she forgot this when she heard her grandchildren running down the stairs to her. She was not an old woman with aching feet anymore; she was part of a family.

Fully half a century has passed since "Old Mrs. Harris" was published. And "Old Lady Mandle" was written in 1920 and "The Sudden Sixties" in 1922. Today, the households of married children are not the sturdy vessels they once might have seemed to be: old women are ill-advised to tie themselves to the chariot of young life. A Victoria who found herself pregnant again when her firstborn came of college age would be unlikely to resign herself to her fate with "stupid animal patience." Most Victorias are far more preoccupied with the challenge of entry or re-entry into the labor force long before their Vickies turn 15. And most old Mrs. Harrises live on in their own homes. Among their numbers are many who would join the labor force along with their middle-aged daughters if they could find employment, since their Social Security checks are a woefully inadequate source of income and their purchasing "power" is steadily diminished by soaring inflation. Today, if an old Mrs. Harris could find her way through the bureaucratic mazes and, what is at least as difficult, access to simple and inexpensive means of transportation, she might have her broken arches attended to by a physician. Today there is Medicare, there are the Meals on Wheels and Dial a Visit programs; there are—in *some* communities—visiting homemaker's and health-care services.

Ma Mandle and "my son Hugo" are a couple caricatured or at least frowned upon today. And Hannah Winter would find strong social support for saying out loud what she was thinking that evening at the dinner table. It is thought to be most unwise for a woman to make a profession (or a religion) of being a mother or a grandmother. It is widely recognized today that grandmothers are entitled to lives of their own. The moral attitude of most of the townspeople in Skyline toward Mrs. Harris's place in the Templeton family—that she was used by her married daughter—doubtless would be taken by most contemporary readers. But the moral issue itself seems out of date. The Methodist church suppers are a thing of the past in many communities. Neighbors do not take such a lively and gossipy interest in one another's lives as they used to do. Many a Mrs. Rosen would not be home baking coffee cakes to bring over to "de old lady Harris," or offering Vickie the use of her library. Vickie and the twins would be busy with friends, with jobs, with activities after school. Even the little ones would be "busy" at nursery school or in kindergarten. Americans today, in fact, are chronically "busy." It is almost a reflex for some of us to look at our watches when we see someone coming along who might want to "pass the time." Why this avoidance? Too much community living is suffocating. But too little means we may regress to a feral state.

Ferber's Hannah Winter was enslaved by her daughter. Sometimes it happens that the daughter is enslaved by her mother, that with the passage of time the aging mother becomes her daughter's daughter. So it was with Suckow's "Mrs. Vogel and Ollie."[24] Mother, Ollie used to say to young Susan, was, after all, a child. Susan's Aunt Grace was shocked at the wild state into which the Vogel place had fallen. The back yard there "was like an outdoor attic, full of horticultural relics" and, in Aunt Grace's opinion, the orchard was a "witch's orchard" (36–37). Mrs. Vogel might be sitting in an old rocker making a doll out of a seed potato on one morning, and on another she might get up at four to dig in the garden. She loved to go fishing, and "the fish bit for her just as the animals ate for her and the plants grew for her" (46–47). She had her cronies in nearly every day, gathering around her kitchen table. Ollie had to keep the tin box full of fresh baking, and the coffee pot bubbling on the stove for those of the neighborhood of "the odd, the solitary, and the left-behind" Mrs. Vogel invited over at all hours—to eat, to visit, to use the telephone (43). In vain, Ollie protested, scolded, implored. Her child-mother, now past 70 years of age, invited the neighborhood bachelors to bring Ollie their laundry. Everyone was welcome to come in and have a cup of coffee and a bite of Ollie's freshly baked rolls or cake or cookies. The phone was there for all to use. "*Mother.* Are we running a free telephone exchange, as well as free lunch and laundry?" The answer was, "Well, we got the phone. We want it used" (45). In vain, Ollie would tell her mother they would have to get after the garden. She confided to Susie, "This dump gets on my nerves. But I can't get rid of a thing, or Mother sets up a wail" (38).

Years later, Susie went back to Woodside to help her Aunt Grace dispose of her property, and while she was there she went to call on Ollie. Mrs. Vogel had died three years before, and Ollie had let all her cronies come over during those last days because she knew that "the one thing that would take Mother off faster than anything else was to be unhappy" (55). Long ago, her Papa had put Mother in her charge, Ollie said; he had told her, "Keep her happy." And she had. Her Mother's last birthday party had been a great success. She had loved the dinner, and the poem Otis Witherspoon had written in her honor, and the toys each of them gave her. After Mrs. Vogel died, folks did not come over. They must have thought Ollie was just an attachment to the stove. And she had been *tired* of having to keep up all that baking. She knew all along Mother had been the attraction. She was always so much fun to be around. But it was work to keep her happy. "Papa and me . . . never shared troubles with Mother—we took them ourselves. All the time Papa was sick, he had to pretend it was indigestion. . . . There was no living with Mother if she was unhappy" (58).

LeRoy Vernon, Ollie's farmer friend, had visited her for years every week; he kept away from Mrs. Vogel's crowd. And he, too, had a mother. Now both old women were dead. Ollie remarked to Susie that she might surprise everyone one of these days, and go out on the farm with LeRoy. Indeed, why not? But it would be

> awful hard to tear myself away from this old place. If LeRoy would come here—! But he feels the same, attached to *his* place. Both of us are like two old animals, I guess, each hanging round his own spot, even when the folks

are gone. LeRoy and I are the grownups, we both spoiled our two old children. Now it don't seem as if two grownups can get together. [64]

There were things Ollie had kept silent about during all those years that she spoke of for the first time that day with Susie. She wept; she said there were so many memories of Mother around the place that there were times when she felt she could not stay there any longer. The light was gone from it, Otis Witherspoon had said. "But I did a lot to keep that light shining!" Somebody had to be standing at the stove to make those good times possible. But, then, "I know I'm ordinary. Maybe the cooking was my part" (64). There were family matters kept secret all those years that she would have to tell LeRoy about if she married him. She did not know how he might take it. Her Papa had not known what he was asking of her, Ollie told Susie. When it was time to leave, Susie thought once more of Mrs. Vogel. "But she was remote, a memory of childhood. The tense, hard, deeply affectionate, little ordinary figure of Ollie rose larger—the fiber of her character upholding all" (65).

Perhaps there will always be parents who imagine their children are their possessions. Perhaps there will always be children who resign themselves to a lifetime of servitude to a parent. Sometimes the lot falls to a son. More often, it falls to a daughter. So it fell to Ollie to nurture and shelter her child-mother, to hold up her little world so she could hold court with her merrie company. The deathbed promise her father exacted, the one she kept, was the exchange of a life for a life. In the sacrifice of self for another, two lives are lost. Neither Mrs. Vogel nor Ollie could find who they might have been or could have become if they had set one another free.

If she lives long enough, an old woman's place in the family is transformed from mother to grandmother to great-grandmother. In the passage of time, she ascends the winding staircase of the generations. The last station in life is that of survivor. A survivor outlives descendants as well as peers. An old woman sometimes outlives her children. And that may be the greatest sorrow of all. In Hortense Calisher's "A Box of Ginger,"[25] Kinny's grandmother admits to being 93 years old; the members of the family think she may be a few years older than that. In 1852, when she had married, she had been in her twenties still, but her bridegroom had been well over 50. Kinny's father was her youngest son, and he, too, had not married until he was nearly 50,

> so if you figured back, here was he, Kinny Elkin, in 1924, with a grandfather, sunken in the ciphers of time, who had been born in the eighteenth century. In his mind, he saw the generations as single people walking a catwalk, each with a hand clutching a long supporting rope that passed from one to another but disappeared into mist at either end. [207]

Kinny's father and his paternal aunts attended the funeral of their brother Aaron that day. Another brother, Nat, had died the winter before, and it was thought that the old woman would not be able to withstand the shock of Aaron's death. When his father and aunts returned from the funeral, Kinny

offered to read a letter "from Aaron" to her. His father had been writing
these letters and having them mailed to her, but that day of all days, he did
not feel up to reading one of them to her, and this either he or Kinny had
been doing. When the boy came to her in her sitting room and asked if he
might read her a letter that had come for her, "It seemed to him that she
hunched into herself like an old bird, listening" (212). She asked him to read
the letter a second time, and he did so, thinking how the phrases in it were like
those his father wrote in letters he sent home when he was traveling. His
grandmother asked for the letter after the second reading, and examined the
paper and envelope closely through her magnifying glass. "She sat for a long
time with the letter in her lap." Then she "sent the magnifying glass across the
room." When she went to get the box of ginger, for it was a little ceremony
they performed every afternoon that she would give her grandson a few slices
of the confection it pleased her to think he liked, she whispered her thanks to
him. "You were good to try" (213).

No place in the family is less enviable than this. On that morning of the
funeral, Kinny's mother had warned him not to let his grandmother suspect
anything. She had said, "It's a terrible thing to grow to a great age and see
your children go before you" (204–5).

Widowhood

Edna Ferber had a sharp eye for the old men filling the benches in Washington Park in Chicago. She wrote of them in her short story, "Old Man
Minick," dated 1922—of the *"spruce and cocky"* ones, the free ones, who lived at
the Old Men's Home, and those who were *"spotty of coat lapel"* and *"unassertive"*
who went "home" to married sons or daughters at dusk.[26] But widowhood
had taken old man Minick by surprise. Like most older couples, he and his
wife had an understanding that it was he who would go first. Everyone sees
"the world is full of widows. . . . But how many widowers? Few. Widows there
are by the thousands; living alone, living in hotels, living with married daughters . . . or married sons. . . . But of widowers in a like situation there are
bewilderingly few. And why this should be no one knows" (111–12). Much has
changed in twentieth-century America, but this has not changed.

Against her better judgment and the entreaties of relatives and friends,
Abby Reynolds in Jean Stafford's "The Children's Game," rented her apartment in New York and went to live in Europe after she was widowed.[27] She
moved from "a Florentine *pensione* for bereft or virginal gentlewomen" to the
same sort of place in Rome; she roomed in the flats of elderly couples in
Vienna and Munich; she lived in a borrowed apartment in Paris. "Although
she was only in her early forties, she had begun to feel quaint and wan" (21).
She felt she was like countless lonely American ladies who lived abroad because they needed the cachet only a European address could have, and that
was needed so they would not be pitied. In this way, she "had come to belong
to that group who have spent their lives leaning on someone—or being leaned

on by" someone, whether spouse or parent, "and who, when the casket is closed or the divorce decree is final, find that they are waifs. They hide their humiliating condition . . . by playing bridge . . . and writing . . . letters . . . and going to lectures" (22). When she and her husband had traveled abroad, they had grieved for these waifs, and she knew that John would find it appalling that she had become one herself. How this had happened, she did not know. John's death had so stricken her that, resilient and gregarious and sanguine as she was, "she had moved like a sleepwalker and had taken the easiest course" (22).

One evening in Paris, when Abby was playing Canfield, "that old-lady game, that game for septuagenarians to whom dusk is the sympathetic time of day," she resolved that she would book passage to return home (23). She found that she would have to wait two weeks. And it happened that she heard from an old friend, Hugh Nicholson, who invited her to join him at a house party in Sussex. Abby fell in love with Hugh just as she saw that it was plainly impossible for them to have a future together. When she saw Hugh betting at the roulette table, she knew that this remoteness "was, though sporadic, constitutional" (28). When she played roulette herself, as he asked her to—"as a clinician," just so she might understand him—she understood him fully. And that was why she could give him up so easily. In that interlude, Hugh was "the agent that reminded her that she must seek a husband" (26). Once, when they were reminiscing about the good times they had had together when John was alive, it came to Abby

> that it was the removal from her life of John's energy that had enervated her, and energy was what she admired and, moreover, required as dearly as food and drink and air. She could burn, that is, with her own flame, but she must be rekindled; she must be complemented so that she could maintain her poise and pride. She was not the sort of woman who could live alone satisfactorily. [25]

In Hortense Calisher's "The Scream on Fifty-seventh Street," Mrs. Hazlitt returned to New York City after she was widowed.[28] Although she had been away for twenty years, she had grown up there: she knew the city "down to the ground," and through the years "she had kept up with it like a scholar" (480). She had subleased an apartment, through an agent, that belonged to Mrs. Helena Berry, who, widowed almost as recently as she, had gone to London. Perhaps Mrs. Berry was living "in the rooms of yet a third woman in search of recommended change" (480).

Sam, her companion of twenty years, had died eight months ago, and until then Mrs. Hazlitt had been able to fall asleep easily, and to stay asleep. But, although her ability to sleep had deteriorated since Sam's death, she had never awakened to what sounded like a scream before. The scream had been without emotion, without soul. Hallucinatory, perhaps: "A harsh word, but she must be stern with herself at the very beginnings . . . of what could presage the sort of disintegrated widowhood, full of the mouse-fears and softening self-indulgences of the manless, that she could not, would not abide" (480). It was after she got up, to "meet the horrors" sensibly and on her feet, that she heard the scream again. She ran into the adjoining room, opened the French window leading to the fire escape, and saw first one, and then a second cab slow up, veer toward her, wait, then go back to the middle of the avenue and speed away. The scream, then, had been real.

Mrs. Hazlitt decided upon which tenants she would approach about the scream, taking care that she would not seem "either eccentric or too friendly, both of which made city people uneasy" (484). Between two carefully contrived "accidental" encounters with tenants (who had not heard the scream), she took a walk to the bakery to buy her breakfast brioches, and when she returned to her apartment, she made phone calls to the laundry and the bank. Later on, she was notified by telephone that an afternoon meeting she was to attend had been canceled. She saw from a glance at her calendar that there would be only two occasions during the next two weeks when she would be in personal communication with people who knew her, knew "who" Mrs. Hazlitt was.

Mrs. Hazlitt had a growing sense of the owner of her apartment, with whom she felt she was compatible. That night she had a conversation with Helena. Why should a grown person be denied the imaginary companion approved of for children? For "this was the century of talk, of the long talk, in which all were healthily urged to confide" (498). When it was over, the silence was soundful. She must get a dog tomorrow. And until tomorrow? She spoke Sam's name at last; she told him she was lonely. In the answering silence, "she thought how wise her resolve had been" that she would never do this. "Too late, now she had tested his loss to the full, knew him for the void he was" (500). She said aloud that she was not lonely, but alone. Now that she could identify the accent of the scream, she went to the French window to hear it again. It was thinking about the dog that had given her the key. There were dog whistles only a dog could hear. The scream she had heard the night before was "audible only to those tuned in by necessity." Its shape would have been, "Alone-oh. Alone-oh. . . . No dog would have heard it. No animal but one was ever that alone" (501).

To Gladys Hasty Carroll, Shakespeare's depiction of the "last scene of all" is obviously that "of a young man at the height of his full physical vigor" who remembered only the helplessness and vulnerability and innocence of childhood, and "knew of age only what he observed."[29] This fate could not but be horrifying to one whose senses "are the channels through which life flows," yet it is inescapable *unless you die young.* But this is a misapprehension of late life:

> Youth is a part of our mortal experience which is never lost and cannot be. The spirit resides in and is dependent upon the body only while what we most need to learn comes through the body. Then—unless it has been seriously damaged during that confinement—it emerges under its own power, tries its wings, and eventually soars. [10]

Of youth, 70-year-old Alice remembers that one of the worst aspects is that something of awful importance may be about to happen, or may have just happened. Either way, the young person cannot know what it may be, or how far its consequences may reach. "You are forever on the brink but unable to see over the edge" (76). And youth and middle age are so demanding that one often feels "the stress will continue until it crushes us. But the truth is it lasts only a minute" (137). There comes a time in life when one recognizes this.

Children forget much of what they have learned while they are growing up; middle-aged people are unconscious of much that they know. In old age, this may return. One who has lived seventy years has the gift of reliving the ecstatic moments "with all their original intensity . . . when one reaches the age when no moments of ecstasy occur to cut off earlier ones from consciousness" (35). These moments return unbidden, when they are least expected. Alice has discovered that reliving is different from remembering. "You remember some of the times you were frightened, despairing, grieved, but those are only memories. By some miracle you are saved from . . . reliving them, and return only to moments of such delight that no words can ever fully describe or account for them" (35). In reliving, Now becomes Then, and Then becomes Now. Once, Alice snapped the switch to turn off the light, and then looked back to be certain she had done this. One who has lived for so many years does so much automatically, and later cannot remember if this or that was actually done. "Comes of one's being transferred so often without warning to another place and time altogether, even to a quite different body and mind and heart" (75).

The awareness of solitude is always emotional, but the range of emotions experienced is very broad: what is felt is a matter of situation and character and mood. For Alice, it is a relief to be alone after being in the company of others. Solitude is vital for those who have much to be done and thought and appreciated; it is spiritual nourishment. She is grateful for the senses, too easily taken for granted, that keep so much inviolate; she is grateful for the time and peace of later life when she can put it all together. Widowed ten years before, after having been married for almost fifty years, she gradually came to understand that Harley was with her—not the memory of Harley, or an occasional reliving of some experience they had shared, but Harley himself. They are inseparable now, she tells a grieving widower. Although, in retrospect, it seems to her that she was suddenly aware of Harley's presence, suddenly aware that she was not alone, "probably it wasn't sudden." Perhaps, she says to the widower, her longing and thinking and remembering seeded her faith "that such a bond as we had forged could not be broken" (209).

Recognitions

Old women may go unremarked, even unseen. They may be hidden away in one of society's nooks or crevices, or taught to take up as little space as possible; they may somehow seem to have grown into the landscape, to have become part of the scenery. Then there is a recognition of their existence.

Sometimes this happens in a flash of illumination. Sometimes it happens long after they are gone.

Eudora Welty's fourteen-year-old Marian is a Campfire Girl making "A Visit of Charity."[30] She has a potted plant for "some old lady" at the Old Ladies' Home: the visit counts an extra point if she brings flowers. There are two old women to each room. In the one where the nurse brought Marian, one of the two old women is bedridden. Her name is Addie. She "had a bunchy white forehead and red eyes like a sheep" (222). Addie remarked that her roommate's head was empty, and so were her heart and her hands and her old black purse. She asked no one in particular if she was supposed to endure the talking and rocking of this stranger forever. What was wrong with Addie, her roommate said, was that it was her birthday. Addie screamed a denial of this. And Marian asked Addie how old she was. And now Marian was able to see Addie "very closely and plainly, and very abruptly, from all sides, as in dreams. She wondered about her . . . as though there was nothing else in the world to wonder about. It was the first time such a thing had happened to Marian" (226).

When a young girl sees an old woman, she may see her fate. Or she may see what she swears to herself she will never become. She may feel compassion; she may feel loathing or dread. "Life Is No Abyss" is one of Jean Stafford's stories of "The Bostonians, and Other Manifestations of the American Scene."[31] Twenty-two-year-old Lily, who is Cousin Will's ward and secretary, does his penance for him by visiting Cousin Isobel Carpenter in the poorhouse. It was Lily's first visit, and she made it for her Uncle Will's sake, for she loved him and was grateful to him. Will was sick in bed with bronchitis, a fact that Lily's beau, Tucky Havemeyer, refused to believe when she broke her skating date with him to visit a cousin who was old and sick, and who had to remain nameless. For no one outside the family knew that Cousin Isobel was in the poorhouse; part of her game was to have Cousin Will pay someone to send mail from her that was posted in Vevey. What had happened was that she had turned her entire fortune over to Cousin Will, who was famous for his ineptitude as an investment broker, and of course she had been ruined. "In the pride of the absolute destitution" to which this had brought her, she had refused the invitations not only from Cousin Will but from all the other cousins in the family who continued to come on visiting days to ask her to live with them. Eighteen months ago, she had taken herself to the poorhouse in her wheelchair, and there she remained, "a fixed and furious reproach to the whole family, loving every moment of her hardship" (93). She gloated over her misery and the ever more cunningly contrived tortures of guilt she caused Uncle Will to suffer.

Cousin Augusta arrived in the three-bed ward during Lily's visit. Now, both women were made audience to a recital of all Cousin Isobel had to endure. With spiteful glee, she spoke of the lack of creature comforts, which were, she said, more tolerable than the company she had to keep, of the screams from the next bed, where three in a row had died screaming only the week before

("Mad at the end, you know") and of the blind and "mental" occupant of the third bed, Viola, who listened perpetually to her radio (95). The radio was Chinese torture. Was it fair "to be imprisoned with an incontinent cretin and her radio, playing that confounded rubbish from matins until vespers?" (106) In vain, Cousin Augusta cheered and cajoled, nagged and wheedled and scolded Cousin Isobel. Lily watched and waited and listened. She saw into the blind Viola's rhapsody at the words from "Bluebird of Happiness" and she was "stricken and sickened and stunned" (104). She saw into the large ward beyond this one, where in every one of the beds that stood in four long rows was "an ancient, twisted woman. . . . among them it would have been impossible to determine which was primarily bleak or mean or brave or imbecile, for age and humiliation had blurred the predominant humor and had all but erased the countenance" (101). She saw into Cousin Isobel: "What a show-off she was! How wicked was her squalor!" (102) When Viola screamed, "Life is no abyss!" Cousin Isobel told both Lily and Cousin Augusta to go away, and, to Augusta's fury, she added, "Poor little Lily will be here to stay soon enough" (110). Lily felt a great passion rise "like a second person inside her" and accused Cousin Isobel of being a vulture, of being utterly without love (110). To Lily, there was only one person in the lot who had love, and that person was Viola, "who can't take anything and can't give anything. The rest of them are flirts" (112).

Miss Totten had been in the school system for forty years at the time of her death. In P.S. 146, between class periods, "when the upper grades were shunted through the halls," most of the teachers stood about talking to one another "in couples," but Miss Totten always stood alone at the door of her "home room."[32] It may have been the same with the teachers as it was with the students, that "she was neither admired nor loathed but simply ignored" (152). Although most of the students in her room that term had been together since the first grade, there was a girl named Lilly Davis they had not seen since second grade, who now reappeared in Miss Totten's class. Lilly Davis had been nicknamed "Mooley" in celebration of her disastrous performance in spelling "mule" and had been transferred to the "ungraded" class after "it became clear that her cringing, mucoused talk was getting worse" (155). This term, all the ungraded classes in the city's schools had been disbanded. Calisher's "A Wreath for Miss Totten" is the story of the teacher's dedicated work with Mooley, who, thanks to that, could call out answers to drills with the best of them on Visiting Day, before the principal and the assembly of mothers and dignitaries. Lilly Davis had found her voice, her speech. Later that term, when Miss Totten died, the students were told at Assembly that they might pay their respects at the chapel if they cared to. No one went, probably not even Mooley, and after a day or two when they spoke her name ("it was really death that we honored, clicking our tongues like our elders"), Miss Totten was forgotten. "But memory, after a time, dispenses its own emphasis, making a *feuilleton* of what we once thought most ponderable, laying its wreath on what we never thought to recall" (162).

In "Almera Hawley Canfield," Dorothy Canfield writes that of course she never saw her great-grandmother, who had died in 1874, years before she herself was born.[33] Even so, she was more human than any living figure Canfield knew because of the portrait she left of herself in this world. This is not "the portrait over the dining room mantelpiece, showing her as a withered old woman in a frilled cap," for that might have been any old woman (61). Rather, it is the portrait various people had painted for her great-granddaughter in stories they told about her over the years. Lemuel Hager, who came to the house to mow in the orchard once a year, saw a look around Dorothy's mouth that put him in mind of Almera, although the child was only 8 years old then, and Almera must have been 60—and Lemuel 18—when she made up her mind she was going to teach him how to read. Mrs. Pratt remembered how "Aunt Almera" had insisted that one keep at a task until it is done right. The janitor recollected how Aunt Almera had taken it upon herself to clean the community sitting room in the Town Hall, where all the social gatherings were held. Times had been hard, then, and "the Selectmen said *they* couldn't do anything. And nobody else would, because it wasn't anybody's business in particular, and nobody wanted to be put upon and made to do more than his share" (64). Old as she was, Aunt Almera put on an apron, and brought her mop and pail and broom, greeting the townspeople pleasantly as her industry put them all to shame. Another stroke of the portrait was painted when Dorothy's aunt told her niece of an amusing incident in church. And when Dorothy met an old minister who came to visit during the centenary celebration of their parish, he told her why he remembered her great-grandmother as a "detestable incubus" (69). An old Irishwoman remembered an act of great charity; a Civil War veteran had a vivid recollection to tell; a doctor could not forget how she had died—as if she had a newborn baby with her: "even in her sleep her face had that shining new-mother look" (75).

Reading one's fortune in the lives of ancestors may have become a lost art in a society so little given to commemorative ceremony as our own. Yet for citizens of "the global village," the tracing of bloodlines is only the beginning of the search for roots. And the recognition of ourselves in the lives of others and the exchange of recollections, which are the source of communal life, are in themselves acts of commemoration.

Last Things

In Canfield's "The Bedquilt," Aunt Mehetabel was an old-maid dependent in the Elwell family, and its "most unimportant member." In those "old-time New England days, . . . an unmarried woman was an old maid at twenty, at forty was everyone's servant, and at sixty had gone through so much discipline that she could need no more in the next world."[34] Aged 68, it was taken for granted both by Aunt Mehetabel and by every member of the busy household that she would perform the lowliest, least interesting, and most tedious tasks. The Elwells were vaguely fond of her, but she mattered so little in their lives that she was all but unseen by them, and she accepted this as unconsciously as it was given. "She gathered what crumbs of comfort she could from their occasional careless kindnesses and tried to hide the hurt which even yet pierced her at her brother's rough joking" (53).

The one mark of distinction of this old woman, who had been too shy even at 20 to imagine that she might have a life of her own, was her cleverness at patching bedquilts. Now, a "great idea" visited her. She did not know if she had dreamed the inspiration, or if it had been "sent" to her, but she felt she could not have conceived of the pattern of the bedquilt that was to become her masterpiece without help from the outside. She created a matchless design for a quilt, and after she had finished drawing it, she could not believe it to be her own handiwork. For a long time, she did not think of transforming the pattern into material reality, but the urge to create was too powerful to resist. After five years of dedicated work, the bedquilt was completed. During this time, the Elwells came to recognize that this was a work of art. They set aside a work area in the sitting room for Aunt Mehetabel. First, the minister and his wife came to see her handiwork, and then neighbors, and, later, even strangers. The family saw to it that the children did not bother Aunt Mehetabel so much as they had before. She would sit straighter in her chair when she heard the children being admonished about this; she held her head up higher. "She was part of the world at last" (57).

When the bedquilt was finished, Aunt Mehetabel's brother said that it must go to the county fair, something she had hoped but would never have requested. There it was taken, and there it was displayed in a glass case in "Agricultural Hall." And Aunt Mehetabel, who had never traveled further than six miles from home in all her life, and had never attended an event more exciting than a church supper, was given a ride to the fair by a neighbor. She saw her quilt displayed; she heard the praise of the visitors; she chanced to be there just when a first-prize blue ribbon was pinned in it. In the third year of her work, Aunt Mehetabel had fallen ill with pneumonia, and had been "horrified by the idea that she might die before her work was completed" (57). But she had endured, she had triumphed. After she returned from the fair, there was "on her tired old face the supreme content of an artist who has realized his ideal" (60).

Sometimes, a settling of accounts is part of last things. Unlike the televised production shown on March 3, 1980, Katherine Anne Porter's story "The Jilting of Granny Weatherall" is told from the point of view and inside the mind of Granny.[35] Doctor Harry was a brat who belonged in knee breeches. He did not speak to her as he ought; he did not respect his elders. He had not even been born when she pulled through milk-leg and double pneumonia. As for Cornelia, she behaved as if her mother had no ears, no eyes, no voice. "Wait, wait, Cornelia, till your own children whisper behind your back!" (82) And Father Connolly was murmuring Latin in a very solemn voice, and tickling her feet. "My God, will you stop that nonsense? I'm a married woman"

(88). It was Hapsy she wanted to see again. "She had to go a long way back through a great many rooms to find Hapsy standing with a baby on her arm" (85).

Granny felt the pillow rise and float under her, "pleasant as a hammock in a light wind." She thought of tomorrow, but then she gave thanks to God "there was always a little margin over for peace: then a person could spread out the plan of life and tuck in the edges orderly" (81). She did not feel the need to bring death up again, for at 60 she had felt old and finished and had made trips to see her children and bid them farewell. After that, she had made her will and come down with a long fever, and when she got up from that, she had got over the idea of dying, once for all. The children kept reminding her she was old, yet they still came to her for advice. "They had been so sweet when they were little." She "wished the old days were back again with the children young and everything to be done over" (83). Hard as they had been, nothing—not all the food she had cooked, all the clothes she had made and the gardens she had planted, and not digging post holes for the fencing in of a hundred acres that she had done herself once, or riding country roads in the winter—had been too much for her. She asked herself what it was she had set out to do, but she could not remember.

Tomorrow's business was to go through the box in the attic with the letters from George and John and her letters to them. There were times when she had wanted to show the children to John, to show him that she had not done too badly in raising them after he was gone. But that was for tomorrow, too. It was strange to think that all the children were older than their father now, and that he would be a child beside her and could not possibly recognize her. Fencing in a hundred acres "changed a woman" (83).

She was remembering George now, and the day she had put on the white veil and put out the white cake and he had not come. "For sixty years she had prayed against remembering him and against losing her soul in the deep pit of hell" (84). Cornelia whispered was there anything she wanted to be done, and Granny said she wanted to see him, she wanted them to find him "and be sure to tell him I forgot him. I want him to know I had my husband just the same and my children and my house like any other woman" (86). But there had been something else, not given back.

Granny felt a storm was coming. The children's faces drifted around her. "She was so amazed her thoughts ran round and round. So, my dear Lord, this is my death" (88). But it was not time to die, and she had always hated surprises, and there were some things still to be done, and what if she were not to find Hapsy? "Her heart sank down and down, there was no bottom to death. . . . For the second time there was no sign. Again no bridegroom and the priest in the house" (88–89). There was nothing more cruel than this. She would never forgive it. Granny took a deep breath "and blew out the light" (89).

To her children, Eva in Tillie Olsen's "Tell Me A Riddle" was Ma, and they felt she and Dad ought to be past quarreling, for they had lived together for forty-seven years.[36] To their children's children, she was Grandma. They wanted her to tell them a riddle, but she did not have any riddles. To her, before either of them knew this would be her last sickness, David was Mr. Importantbusy, who had a card game or a meeting he should go to instead of trying to talk her into moving to the Haven. And at the end, he was a coward, a runner, a weakling, who would leave her in the hospital and run. He was a betrayer who had run all his life. Years ago, he had left her alone with the children and the housework and the humiliation of begging credit from the grocer, never once staying home so she could go to talk about Chekhov, Peretz.

To him, she was so many people. She was Mrs. Word Miser, who could give no reason for not wanting to sell the house and go live with him in his lodge's Haven, who could only say she was used to their five rooms. She was Mrs. Enlightened, Mrs. Cultured, because she saw nothing on television but shadows when a whole world was coming into their house through the screen. She was Mrs. Unpleasant, who could be rid of him—and he, of her—when the house was sold. She was Mrs. Take It Easy when she lay down the third Sunday in a row at their son Paul's house, instead of being busy in the kitchen after dinner as she had always been before. When she asked for his company one night the summer she took to her bed more and more, letting the house go untended, letting the birds pick at her pears in the garden, she was Mrs. Live Alone And Like It. Mrs. Free As A Bird had a new song: "Do not go. Stay with me" (83).

After Doctor Phil had had her examined and operated on, and they had found malignancy everywhere they looked, he took her to visit the children one by one. Then she was Mrs. Telepathy, reading minds, saying Phil "is sick of sickness by the time he comes home" and that Hannah had no time for herself and the grandboys did not know what to say to either of them (88). She was Mrs. Excited Over Nothing because she was upset when Hannah asked her to light the Sabbath candles. When she wanted to leave Vivi's after only a week and go home, she was Mrs. Inahurry, and he shouted this name "for the fear of the future raced in him" (94). In Vivi's house, she was Mrs. Bodybusy, trying to do too much when she was supposed to rest. When she accused him of having sold the house, when she said that was why they were not going home, she was Mrs. Suspicious. When he brought her to California, where their granddaughter Jeannie came to see them still wearing her Visiting Nurse uniform, she was Mrs. Invalid. They visited her old friend Mrs. Mays, who had been their next-door neighbor in Denver when the children were little. She was Mrs. Orator-without-Breath, then, when she said of Mrs. Mays's "slab of room," with photographs "foaming" everywhere, "After a lifetime of room. . . . You remember how she lived. Eight children. And now one room like a coffin" (107). At the last, she was Mrs. Miserable, who had worked hard all her life, and now worked hard dying. She was Mrs. Philosopher, who sang and spoke as if she had been hiding a tape recorder for seventy years, "and that maliciously she was playing back only what said nothing of him, of the children, of their intimate life together" (118). She was Mrs. Babbler, who had cunningly saved her words while calling others babblers. She was Mrs. Live Alone, but he remembered she had not always wanted solitude. He listened to her singing as he played solitaire. With her dying would go "their youth of belief out of which her bright, betrayed words foamed" (121–22). He asked her if she had to awaken everything. When she began to sing a school song she had learned from the children when they were small, "instantly he left the mute old woman poring over the Book of the Martyrs; went past the mother treading at the sewing machine, . . . past the girl in her wrinkled prison dress, . . . and took her in his arms, dear, personal, fleshed" (124).

For her last journey, she had to take her leave of the five rooms she would not give up for his Haven, for she had finally come to the place where she did not have to move to the rhythms of others. She had to take her leave of her children to go unto the region of her self. At Vivi's, she had not been able to embrace her new grandchild. Was she an unnatural grandmother? But she had loved her children:

> The love—the passion of tending—had risen with the need like a torrent; and like a torrent drowned and immolated all else. But when the need was done—oh the power that was lost in the painful damming back and drying up of what still surged, but had nowhere to go. Only the thin pulsing left that could not quiet, suffering over lives one felt, but could no longer hold nor help.
>   On that torrent she had borne them to their own lives, and the riverbed was desert long years now. Not there would she dwell, a memoried wraith. Surely that was not all, surely there was more. . . . Somewhere an older power that beat for life. . . . If they would but leave her . . . to journey to her self. [92–93]

On that last day, Jeannie came to comfort her Grandaddy in his grieving; Grandma "said she would go back to when she first heard music, a little girl on the road of the village where she was born" (125). She was not here, Jeannie told him; she had promised her granddaughter that she would not be here, but would return to that time and that place, where there would be a wedding, and dancing, and the joyous playing of flutes.

In Alice Walker's "The Welcome Table," an old woman walked alone the half mile from her house to the white church. She was dressed in her best clothes and wearing an old corsage. The old woman "was angular and lean and the color of poor gray Georgia earth, beaten by king cotton and the extreme weather." There were "centuries . . . folded into the circles around one eye, while around the other, . . . ages more threatened again to live."[37] There were those at the church who saw age and poverty, and there were those who saw servants, "children denied or smothered." Many at the church "saw jungle orgies in an evil place, while others were reminded of riotous anarchists looting and raping in the streets." The ones who felt the law hesitantly crawling toward them "saw the desecration of Holy Church, and . . . an invasion of privacy" they worked at believing they still kept (82).

Some thought the reverend said, "Auntie, you know this is not your church," but none remembered, none spoke of this afterwards, and she brushed past him, hurrying inside, where she took the first bench from the back (83). She told the young usher to go away, in a "*bothered*" voice, when he whispered to her—calling her "Grandma?"—that she ought to leave. The ladies told their "burly indecisive husbands" to "throw the old colored woman out" (84). And throw her out they did, and after that, the church was warmer inside. Outside, the old woman stood bewildered. The singing in her head had been interrupted, and now she began singing again; her song was sad. Suddenly, she saw Jesus coming joyfully down the highway. He looked just like the picture she had taken out of a white lady employer's Bible and put up over her bed at home, except that he was not carrying a little sheep in one of his arms. When he came close to her, he told her to follow him. They walked along together. He smiled beautifully as she told him of this, that after all her years of cooking and cleaning for them and nursing them, they had thrown her out of his church. And again, when she told him how glad she was that he had come, for she had often looked at his picture, but never expected he would come in person. She began to sing some of the old spirituals she loved, but then fell silent, and they went on walking. Although the people in the white church did not speak of the old woman afterwards, "Most of them heard sometime later than an old colored woman fell dead along the highway. Silly as it seemed, it appeared she had walked herself to death." It was said that she had been alone. "Some . . . wondered aloud where the old woman had been going so stoutly that it had worn her heart out. They guessed maybe she had relatives across the river, . . . but none of them really knew" (87).

Last things for an old woman might be a flowering of creative expression after a lifetime of insignificance. Or the reckoning, when her whole life passes in review before the inner eye of a strong character, with roads taken and not taken crossing, and final judgment made. In the long seeking of the self, last things might be the drawing of the circle, joining ending to beginning. Or the beatitude of finding at the end of that long journey what she had been seeking all her life.

Contemporaries

Mama's children, Joe Lee Peoples and Task and Elo, objected to the way she was danced with Bovanne.[38] It was at the benefit for her niece's cousin, who was running for office in a Black party. Toni Cade Bambara's "My Man Bovanne" wasn't her man, but "just a nice ole gent from the block that we all know cause he fixes things and the kids like him. Or used to fore Black Power got hold their minds and mess em around till they can't be civil to ole folks" (382). He is blind, and the blind have a "hummin jones," they make a *thizzin* kind of hum. He was invited because he is grassroots. Grassroots is the reason that Mama and Sister Taylor were invited, too, and the women who work at the beauty parlor and the men who work at the barber shop, even though they'd never been further south than Brooklyn Battery. Only yesterday, Mama's kids were telling her to take the rags off her head and to be cool. "And now can't get Black enough to suit em" (383).

Out in the kitchen, where the three of them hauled her, Mama felt the police were giving her the third degree. Elo told Task she thinks Mama has had too much to drink; she doesn't talk directly to Mama since an ugly argument they had about wigs. Task said Mama was making a spectacle of herself dancing like that; she was acting like an old lady who was sex-starved. Elo said Bovanne is a tom. Mama asked if this was the generation gap. Elo said "generation gap" is "a white concept for a white phenomenon" (384). Joe Lee said it was a matter of pride, that she was embarrassing herself and them by dancing that way. Task said Mama's dress was too short and too low cut for a woman of her age. And Tamu, the new name Nisi had taken, would be introducing her that night, because she was expected to organize the council of elders. Joe Lee reminded Mama that her drinking would lead to loudness and carrying on, and he said for a woman of her age, she should not be dancing like that. Mama asked them how old she was. When Joe Lee started to say she might be 61, she said that was a damn lie. And when she got up to leave, Elo put a hand on her shoulder

> like she hasn't done since she left home and the hand landin light and not sure it supposed to be there. Which hurt me to my heart. Cause this was the child in our happiness fore Mr. Peoples die. And I carried that child strapped to my chest till she was nearly two. We was close. . . . Cause it was more me in the child than the others. And even after Task it was the girlchild I covered in the night and wept over for no reason at all. . . . And how did things get to this, that she can't put a sure hand on me and say Mama we love you and care about you and you entitled to enjoy yourself cause you a good woman? [386]

Mama's children went through the swinging door and left her in that messy kitchen. Then the door swung the other way, and Bovanne came in. And Mama took him out of there, past Nisi and all the others getting ready to talk, past Joe Lee and his wife looking at her accusingly, and they left the place. She took this man who was blind and too old for anybody to care about since they grew up and didn't need his help to fix their skates anymore. She told him they were going to buy him some sunglasses, and then go to the supermarket. After that, she was taking him to her house, and she was thinking of the nice warm bath and the good rubdown and the glass of tea and the massage she would give him, and the grand dinner tomorrow. "Cause you gots to take care of the older folks. And let them know they still needed to run the mimeo machine . . . and fix the mailboxes for folks who might help us get the breakfast program goin. . . . Cause old folks is the nation" (387–88). Nisi was saying all this, and Mama wanted to do her part.

Images of aging from life in Bette Howland's partly autobiographical sketches, *Blue In Chicago*, and in Elizabeth Hardwick's novel of memory, *Sleep-less Nights*, complement those in short stories about our urban contem-poraries. At Chicago's public library[39] the old are among the regulars. And there was a crank, dressed all in gray, "with feet laced up in combat boots," who came in to use the bathroom. She "had been sighted all over the city; a familiar figure at downtown hotels during conventions" (79).

In spring or Indian summer, when the weather is warm, old people sit by the underpass on the park benches. "They come from the Shoreland, Sherry-Netherland, Del Prado, Windermere—hotels . . . now providing package care for the elderly."[40] There is a line-up of folding chairs in front of the Wood-lawn Nursing Home. The place "is in the thick of a desolate black slum. Burned out, bombed out, boarded up. Charred timbers, rubble, shattered windows" (125). Inside, people check the time. It is almost 4:30. The patients, mostly women, primp for dinner. Old people move down the corridors, tap-ping their canes, or holding on to the handrails, or "propping their shiny chrome walkers before them" or rolling along in their wheelchairs (125).

There are more than fifty places in Chicago where "hot, nourishing, low-cost lunches" are served to the elderly. This is not charity, but many think of it this way, especially those "who have not much left but their pride" (127). Jews who came over on the boat are only one group of the Golden Diners. But Golden Diners and Golden Agers all "must be in the same boat; they are not entirely of America either" (134). Bette's mother, "dashing about, radiantly white-haired in her light blue pants suit," is a new employee of the Golden Diners Club (131). And her Auntie Hodl came to the lunch. She walks lurch-ing from side to side. Her husband has vertigo; he walks backward. They make their way together, "him toppling backward and her from side to side" (129–30). Bette's great-aunt Yetta, who unfastened many locks and chains from her door when Bette came to bring her to the lunch—the family was meeting there, and would be going to a funeral afterwards—said she could not go. But her sister, Auntie Hodl, might. Auntie Yetta's distorted legs were the mark of the ethnic disease, the "very exclusive Jewish disease," from which many women of the East European diaspora suffered, and which her daugh-ters had inherited (128).

Bette's grandmother lives in a large old elevator building Uptown, where the "internal immigrants" are: "Uptown is the home of the displaced, the disinherited, the uprooted. . . . Appalachians, American Indians—aching with homesickness; the poor, the elderly, the halfway houses." The secret of Up-town is that it "is a D.P. camp." The old there are "more than old; they are outcast. They have escaped the net; they are outside every sort of social institution" (143). Her grandmother has journeyed from Transylvania to Kentucky to Chicago to this building in her lifetime, and this is a far better building than the one she moved out of a few years before. The lobby is too dark and off to one side to give a good view. So, sometimes she sits, as other old ladies do, in the large plate-glass window of the A & P, shopping bags at her side. She likes to live here, because it is not just for the elderly. She furnishes her apartment mostly with junk. She carries very little along with her from the past.

After her grandmother fell and broke her hip, and Bette was witness to a show of anger between her mother and her mother's brother's wife, she began to understand why her grandmother resisted the idea of going to live with any of her children. "Maybe it wasn't just pride—shame for her own condition. Maybe she was more ashamed for theirs."[41] Bette came to feel that her mother was trying to use *her* mother to get Bette in her power once again. And her mother felt, as all the grandmother's children felt, that time was running out for *them* as well as for her. "How did they know how much they had left? . . . It was her life against theirs" (165). Both women sensed that they had failed the old woman in their feelings for one another. After the grandmother died, the family gathered at Sylvia's. In the room where the women were, where it so happened that the Mothers were sitting on one side and the Daughters on the other, Bette suddenly realized her own children were grown, and that she was in the middle now. And she saw that the story she was telling was "a love story." Her grandmother may have died with dignity, after all: "even to the end she would rather have had us believe that she didn't know us, she was losing her memory, than let on how truly defenseless she was. And she didn't ask for anything. . . . She was always so afraid of taking. You'd think someone was giving" (182).

New York is "a woman's city," Elizabeth Hardwick writes.[42] "The bag ladies sit in their rags, hugging their load of rubbish so closely it forms a part of their own bodies. . . . They and their rubbish a parasitic growth heavy with suffering." She prays: "Have mercy on them, someone" (52–53). She prays for mercy for her old neighbor, Miss Cramer, too, who has moved around the corner to a smaller place, "down near the abandoned police station, among the damnation of emptying red-brick buildings waiting for the executioner" (53). She greets Miss Cramer, who walks toward "an appalling wreck of great individuality, a black woman who wanders in and out of the neighborhood," who carries three large bags of rubbish effortlessly, although they are larger than herself. Miss Cramer and this woman "meet suddenly at the corner. . . . They are both fearless. . . . These are not cases, they do not fill out forms or wait for the mails. They are gladiators, creatures of the trenches" (55). These two are not aware of what they look like. They "do not see their lives, and so they wander about in their dreadful freedom like old oxen left behind, totally unprovided for" (56).

Judith is only in her early forties. She has a Ph.D.; she has bad news, and therefore says "of course" and "naturally" often. She has a 21-year-old son, a "mess," who lives with a couple who are both psychiatrists. Judith calls him often, but he will not talk to her. When he was a little boy, he was beautiful. "This thing with him is never going to be over, never" (51). There is a young man whose father died, whose mother has collapsed. His mother had hated nursing his father; she had planned how she would live after widowhood. But now, "she announced herself as the broken partner of a splendid alliance"

(62). And her young son "ground his teeth as he heard the hearse of love coming his way" (63). There is a woman who, at 87, "found an adorable friend." This young man adored her, and "most gratifying of all . . . believed her to be a *character* . . . an old Boston pedigreed specimen" as she saw herself (124). He was a character, as well; she, who "was nearing senility" and he who "was a wound-up toy . . . had a good time together." She left him a good sum of money when she died. "She paid her bill" (125).

Ida survived a disastrous liaison with Herman, who took everything of use that he could find in her house. When Hardwick came to see her, Ida embraced her. The laundry was done, the baskets ready to be picked up. Ida had "the ambiguous smile of an old hearth goddess, an icon to which no offering was ever made without a grumble" (140). Miss Lavore is remembered, "passing in the halls of the rooming houses near Columbia" (142). She was in her late fifties. She "had a life." After work most week nights, she would cook dinner and then shower and dress up for Arthur Murray's dancing classes. She had a special ten-year Arthur Murray Club membership. Many dancing partners held Miss Lavore in their arms. Lavore was probably not her name. In her dreams, she is part of a famous European dancing team "and when she whirls and dips she is caught by a slim man in a black tail coat, a man with a Balkan name like people in the circus" (146). Young women might pack and leave tomorrow, leave forever. When the older women move on to another arrangement like this one, it is "defiantly, as if to say: You cannot destroy a ruin" (147).

"Society tries to write" the lives of older unmarried women "before they are lived. It does not always succeed" (24). Hardwick has known from home women who have tricked fate. *Sleepless Nights.* "If only one knew what to remember or pretend to remember" (3). Her mother was completely indifferent to the past. For over thirty years, she had lived very close to her mother, but it could happen on some morning that she would be very remote. And it could happen that in the dark of Hardwick's nights, her mother's life would come back to her.

In her discussion of Muriel Spark's *Memento Mori,* Saul Bellow's *Mr. Sammler's Planet,* Kingsley Amis's *Ending Up,* and Tanizaki's *Diary of a Mad Old Man,* Celeste Loughman writes that since *Memento Mori,* many novels on old age focus on degeneration and decay.[43] Mr. Sammler, the wise old man figure, is the most *engaged* of the characters in these novels. "But he learns at the end his sense of potency is an illusion" (83). Sexuality is a recurring form of self-assertiveness in these novels, but the impulse is expressed in aberrant ways. None of the authors offers much "to mitigate their naturalistic treatment of old age—the isolation, the impotence, and the decay which are intrinsic to the aging process." The bleakness is unrelieved. One would want to resist it. But "the dramatic force of these novels makes the vision ring frighteningly true" (84).

It is possible that a careful examination of novels of senescence with *women* protagonists might reveal this "new naturalism" of which Loughman writes.

Here is a timely and fascinating subject for research. What might be discovered, however, can be no more than conjectured now, since most of the novels of senescence discussed by critics and social scientists are novels about the aging of men, not women. Literary works by women about aging and older women have received very little attention from any quarter. Therefore, our literary perspectives on aging are one-sided, biased, warped.

Novels of senescence by and about women in any one country and time period could include a dazzling array of sensibilities and points of view; certainly this would be the case for twentieth-century American novels of senescence by women with women protagonists. Ultimately, selection would be imperative. However, no novelist may fairly be said to "represent" women's attitudes toward aging. There are truths, not Truth, and a rather wide net must be cast to catch them. That is why almost all the fictions selected for discussion in this chapter are short fictions. Wide reading of that priceless, yet much-neglected genre, the American short story by American women of letters, attests to the variety of illuminations about "older women in twentieth-century America." Perhaps for gerontologists there is no more effective antidote to what Mary Beard called "specialisms" than to read what a number of women have written about women in the second half of life in this genre. In short fiction by women about older women there is something for each of us and something for us all. That is the gift of a good work of the literary imagination: the characters are always in some way our contemporaries.

It is a long way from the bean-pickers in the shed chamber of the Byfleet Poor-house to the Golden Diners in Chicago and the bag ladies in New York City. It is only human, perhaps, to imagine that the past was better. But it is wrongheaded, all the same. Not every Abby Pendexter had an Aunt Cynthy she might go to live with when the rent-money ran out. And brave Mrs. Peet, with her cat basket and bundle-handkerchief and poor prospects, would have found a Social Security check very useful, either at home on the farm *or* in Shrewsbury. Sunset Camp is not new; it was there fifty years ago: it is only that there are more of them now. Then as now, there was poverty, there was loneliness. Then as now, grown children sometimes enslaved their parents, or parents, their grown children. And some very old women outlived their children. To make a romance of the past is to abdicate our responsibilities for our lives in the present world. To know where we are, we need to know where we have been.

In American literature in the mid-twentieth century, Fischer writes, we find the same "broad spectrum of belief on the subject of old age" as was found in nineteenth-century American literature. "But that spectrum has again shifted to the left. And the last traces of veneration have disappeared."[44] Fischer has found that old age is rarely a central theme in major works of twentieth-century American literature, and that when it does appear, "it has usually been cast in one of four major motifs" (123–24). Of these, the most favorable to age is the theme of Hemingway's *Old Man and the Sea,* with its message of Emersonian romance and its ending on a note of "Emersonian triumph." In

Hemingway's attitudes toward age relations, "he occupied the right wing." The other three themes were more common—the pathos of age, its weakness and dependence (as in Steinbeck's *Grapes of Wrath* and Frost's "Death of the Hired Man," among other works); the emptiness of old age (as in T. S. Eliot's "Gerontion"); and an even more complete ugliness: for Beckett, in *Krapp's Last Tape,* "the emptiness and misery of old age become a revelation of the absurdity of life itself" (126). As each broad spectrum of opinion about old age succeeded another, from the early nineteenth century to the mid-twentieth, it shifted "toward the left, toward an increasing antipathy for old age" (127). These themes, perhaps especially that of the pathos of age, appear in some of the fictions discussed in this chapter. But there are others in these works and in the works of Atherton, Glasgow, Hurston, Sarton, and Wharton that give breadth and depth to literary perspectives on aging precisely because they are written about *women's* aging by American women of letters. Love and friendship, the journeying of the old both in the world and in inner life, creativity, friendship, responsibility to self and others in later life—women have written of these, and write of them today. We need to know much more about what women have said, are saying, about the workings of time and memory. And why, finally, should we read these fictions at all, if they quicken our sense of our mortality? "In the sense of our own transience," Eudora Welty writes, "may lie the one irreducible urgency telling us to do, to understand, to love."[45]

Notes

1. Eudora Welty, "Must the Novelist Crusade?," in *The Eye of the Story: Selected Essays and Reviews* (New York: Random House, 1978), p. 150.

2. Audrey Borenstein, *Redeeming the Sin: Social Science and Literature* (New York: Columbia University Press, 1978).

3. A copy of this bibliography, entitled "A Gallery of Old Women," was graciously provided me by Professor Sohngen.

4. Mary Sohngen, "The Experience of Old Age as Depicted in Contemporary Novels," *The Gerontologist* (February 1977) 17(1):70–78. Hereafter, reference to this article will be cited in the text by page number.

5. Willa Cather, Preface, *The Best Stories of Sarah Orne Jewett*, The Mayflower Edition (Gloucester, Mass.: Peter Smith, 1965), p. xvi.

6. Abigail Ann Hamblen, *Ruth Suckow,* Boise State University Western Writers Series, Number 34 (Boise, Id.: Boise State University, 1978), p. 42.

7. Edna Ferber, Introduction to "Old Lady Mandle" in *One Basket: Thirty-one Short Stories by Edna Ferber* (New York: Simon and Schuster, 1947), p. 145.

8. Mary Sohngen, "The Selfhood of Aging Women in the Contemporary Novel," paper presented at the Modern Language Association Session on Women: Aging and Death in Literature, Chicago, December 1977, p. 2. Hereafter, reference to this paper will be cited in the text by page number.

9. Sarah Orne Jewett, "Aunt Cynthy Dallett," *The Best Stories of Sarah Orne Jewett*, p. 281. Hereafter, all references to this story will be cited in the text by page number.

10. Ruth Suckow, "Sunset Camp," in *Children and Older People* (New York: Alfred A. Knopf, 1931), p. 225. Hereafter, all references to this story will be cited in the text by page number.

11. Katherine Anne Porter, "The Journey," *The Collected Stories of Katherine Anne Porter* (New York: New American Library, 1970), p. 334. The sequence of stories entitled "The Old Order"—"The Source," "The Journey," and "The Last Leaf"—appears on pp. 321–68 of this edition. Hereafter, all references to these stories will be cited in the text by page number.

12. Willa Cather, *My Mortal Enemy* (New York: Vintage Books, 1926, 1954), p. 17. Hereafter, all references to this short novel will be cited in the text by page number.

13. Cather's mode was elegy, Marcus Klein writes, "and as it must be for all elegists, the enemy was time, mortality, itself." Klein recalls that Cather wrote in her essay on Katherine Mansfield's fiction that "human relationships are the tragic necessity of human life; that they can never be wholly satisfactory, that every ego is half the time greedily seeking them, and half the time pulling away from them." In his view, "the struggle to get beyond the necessity of human relationships . . . is the secret history of all Willa Cather's novels, only as time went on, as the struggle turned, one supposes, more desperate, its nature became more apparent." The enemy in *My Mortal Enemy* "is friendship and love, human relationship itself." Marcus Klein, Introduction, *My Mortal Enemy*, pp. xv, xvi.

14. Josephine Herbst, "Hunter of Doves," *Botteghe Oscure* (1954) 13:310. Hereafter, all references to this novella will be cited in the text by page number. I am grateful to Elinor Langer, who is writing a biography of Herbst, for leading me to this work. Langer wrote me that the character of Mrs. Heath is based upon Herbst.

15. Willa Cather, *The Old Beauty and Others* (New York: Alfred A. Knopf, 1948), p. 36.

16. Sarah Orne Jewett, "Going to Shrewsbury," *The Best Stories of Sarah Orne Jewett*, p. 92. Hereafter, all references to this story will be cited in the text by page number.

17. Sarah Orne Jewett, "The Flight of Betsey Lane," *The Best Stories of Sarah Orne Jewett*, p. 33. Hereafter, all references to this story will be cited in the text by page number.

18. Arlie Russell Hochschild, *The Unexpected Community: Portrait of an Old Age Subculture* (Berkeley, Calif.: University of California Press, 1973), p. 140.

19. Eudora Welty, "A Worn Path," in *A Curtain of Green* (New York: Doubleday, Doran and Co., Inc., 1943), p. 274. Hereafter, all references to this story will be cited in the text by page number.

20. Eudora Welty, "Is Phoenix Jackson's Grandson Really Dead?," in *The Eye of the Story: Selected Essays and Reviews*, p. 161. Hereafter, reference to this essay will be cited in the text by page number.

21. Edna Ferber, "Old Lady Mandle," in *One Basket: Thirty-one Short Stories by Edna Ferber*, p. 151. Hereafter, all references to this story will be cited in the text by page number.

22. Edna Ferber, "The Sudden Sixties," in *One Basket*, p. 211. Hereafter, all references to this story will be cited in the text by page number.

23. Willa Cather, "Old Mrs. Harris," in *Obscure Destinies and Literary Encounters* (Boston: Houghton Mifflin Co., 1938), p. 83. Hereafter, all references to this story will be cited in the text by page number.

24. Ruth Suckow, "Mrs. Vogel and Ollie," in *Some Others and Myself: Seven Stories and a Memoir by Ruth Suckow* (New York: Rinehart and Co., Inc., 1952), pp. 35–65. Hereafter, all references to this story will be cited in the text by page number.

25. Hortense Calisher, "A Box of Ginger," in *The Collected Stories of Hortense Calisher* (New York: Arbor House Publishing Co., Inc., 1975), pp. 204–13. Hereafter, all references to this story will be cited in the text by page number.

26. Edna Ferber, "Old Man Minick," in *One Basket*, p. 110. Hereafter, reference to this story will be cited in the text by page number.

27. Jean Stafford, "The Children's Game," in *The Collected Stories of Jean Stafford* (New York: Farrar, Straus and Giroux, 1969), pp. 19–33. "The Children's Game" is one of the sequence of stories entitled "The Innocents Abroad." Hereafter, all references to this story will be cited in the text by page number.

28. Hortense Calisher, "The Scream on Fifty-seventh Street," in *The Collected Stories of Hortense Calisher*, pp. 479–502. Hereafter, all references to this story will be cited in the text by page number.

29. Gladys Hasty Carroll, *Unless You Die Young* (New York: W. W. Norton and Co., Inc., 1977), p. 9. Hereafter, all references to this novel will be cited in the text by page number.

30. Eudora Welty, "A Visit of Charity," in *A Curtain of Green,* pp. 219–27. Hereafter, references to this story will be cited in the text by page number.

31. Jean Stafford, "Life Is No Abyss," in *The Collected Stories of Jean Stafford,* pp. 93–112. Hereafter, references to this story will be cited in the text by page number.

32. Hortense Calisher, "A Wreath for Miss Totten," in *The Collected Stories of Hortense Calisher,* p. 152. Hereafter, all references to this story will be cited in the text by page number.

33. Dorothy Canfield, "Almera Hawley Canfield," in *A Harvest of Stories: From a Half Century of Writing by Dorothy Canfield* (New York: Harcourt, Brace and Co., Inc., 1956), pp. 61–75. Hereafter, references to this story will be cited in the text by page number.

34. Dorothy Canfield, "The Bedquilt," in *A Harvest of Stories,* p. 52. Hereafter, references to this story will be cited in the text by page number.

35. Katherine Anne Porter, "The Jilting of Granny Weatherall," in *The Collected Stories of Katherine Anne Porter,* pp. 80–89. Hereafter, references to this story will be cited in the text by page number.

36. Tillie Olsen, *Tell Me a Riddle* (New York: Dell Publishing Co., Inc., Laurel ed., 1976), pp. 72–125. Hereafter, references to this story will be cited in the text by page number.

37. Alice Walker, "The Welcome Table," in *In Love and Trouble: Stories of Black Women* (New York: Harcourt Brace Jovanovich, A Harvest Book, 1973), p. 82. Hereafter, references to this story will be cited in the text by page number.

38. Toni Cade Bambara, "My Man Bovanne," in *Bitches and Sad Ladies: An Anthology of Fiction By and About Women,* Pat Rotter, ed. (New York: Dell Publishing Co., Inc., 1975), pp. 382–88. Hereafter, references to this story will be cited in the text by page number.

39. Bette Howland, "Public Facilities," in *Blue in Chicago* (New York: Harper and Row, Inc., 1978), p. 72. Hereafter, reference to this story will be cited in the text by page number.

40. Bette Howland, "Golden Age," in *Blue in Chicago,* p. 123. Hereafter, all references to this story will be cited in the text by page number.

41. Bette Howland, "How We Got the Old Woman To Go," in *Blue in Chicago,* p. 154. Hereafter, reference to this story will be cited in the text by page number.

42. Elizabeth Hardwick, *Sleepless Nights* (New York: Random House, Inc., 1979), p. 52. Hereafter, all references to this novel will be cited in the text by page number.

43. Celeste Loughman, "Novels of Senescence," *The Gerontologist* (February 1977), 17(1):79. Hereafter, reference to this article will be cited in the text by page number.

44. David Hackett Fischer, *Growing Old in America* (New York: Oxford University Press, 1977), pp. 122–23. Hereafter, references to this book will be cited in the text by page number.

45. Eudora Welty, "Some Notes on Time in Fiction," in *The Eye of the Story: Selected Essays and Reviews,* p. 168.

Part 3

7

The Chance for Further Flight: Creativity in Older Women's Lives[1]

> The chance for further flight prolongs forever
> The flight itself.
> —Lucretius,
> *Of the Nature of Things,*
> Book I, The Infinity of the Universe

Creativity, freedom, and responsibility in the lives of older women are not three separate values, but three aspects of a central value, the value of transcendence in the second half of life. The creative older woman, chosen as the focus of this chapter, exemplifies the unity of creativity, freedom, and responsibility in midlife and later life. To create, there must be freedom. To be free, a woman must take responsibility for her own gifts. She must accept responsibility for using the special gift with which every person is endowed if she would live her own and only life creatively. And if her work is to flower, she must find a way to do this without severing her relatedness to others and to the life of the world.

Women who loosen their hold on the vital center of their creativity during the first half of life—and their name is legion—undertake the main task of life when their youth is gone. This main task is the search for the meaning of that life. The search may begin for one woman in her thirties and for another not until her sixties. It begins when a fateful turn is taken along the life course, or with a crisis that points the way to "critical" change. To accept the gift of freedom is to take up an awesome responsibility. Women who continue to sacrifice their creativity refuse the freedom that is the bequest of extended life. Women who sacrifice their relatedness to others for the sake of serving the narrow needs of the ego—the need for admiration or comfort or security—sever their connection to the very life-source of their creativity. This is a refusal of responsibility to contribute to the life of the world. In the second half of life, the challenge is to find the meaning of that life. Its very source is seared for those who refuse to meet it. The older woman who would live consciously, creatively, and responsibly guides a small and fragile craft between the rock and the whirlpool. This is a fitting subject—perhaps the central one—for humanistic gerontology.

Women's Creativity at the "Turn of Life"

G. Stanley Hall's *Senescence: The Last Half of Life* is a rich book to read even today, nearly sixty years after its publication, although his prejudices will take some overlooking. His long, convoluted sentences will also put the tolerance of today's reader to the test. On the other hand, this is no arid textbook report on the subject of old age afflicted with that labored writing and that jargon that make the content of so many works in social science inaccessible to the lay reader. Hall took a point of view toward old age, and a very positive one at that. His personal account of his experience of retirement, and his report on the returns to the questionnaires he sent to old people, most of whom were eminent in their chosen professions,[2] are especially engaging and informative. Hall had a broad and luminous vision of the vital contributions old people can make to the life of the society and the world. In this, and in his conviction that people ought to begin to plan for their old age at least by midlife, he was a true precursor of humanistic gerontology. As much can be said also of his profound respect for individual differences in aging, of his warning about the negative psychological effects of an over-emphasis on heredity as a determinant of longevity (he thought this to be worse than depressing: he wrote that it is lethal to old people), his conviction that the world is much indebted to the impulse for writing autobiography, which he thought is natural in later life, and his encyclopaedic range. He also argued forcefully against the rule of mandatory retirement. His work is a twentieth-century classic, and yet it is listed in the bibliographies of very few studies of old age that have been published over the past five decades in the United States.

Hall believed that "senescence" begins in the early forties, and in many cases even in the thirties, for women, so he would have approved of the definition of older women as women from about age 40 on. He wrote that for men, the infancy of old age is age 40, its boyhood extends through the fifties and its youth the sixties, and that it reaches its "majority" at the age of 70. In contrast to this, women—who pass through the same stages as men—experience the infancy of old age earlier, and the majority of old age later. He described life as a binomial curve that rises from a base line at birth and falls back into it at death, and he wrote that at midpoint, which is the highest point that has the longest ordinate, people "come in sight of the descent while the ascent behind is still visible" (1). The onset of these "meridional perturbations" is earlier in women than in men, and he supposed that they mark the advent of the "dangerous age." He reported that for men, the forties, and for women, the thirties are the decade "of the triangle, of the paramour, and of divorces," but conceded that the only available evidence that could confirm this are divorce statistics (2).

In 1912, Karin Michaëlis's *The Dangerous Age* was published, and Hall was much impressed with this book, which he said caused a sensation in Western Europe when it appeared. Michaëlis, whom he thought had emancipated herself more completely than any other woman writer from the male viewpoint, had been called a traitor to her sex because of her revelations about women's psychology. Hall quoted a passage from her book at length, although he thought that no excerpt could do justice to her style, her acute self-observation, the breadth of her experience, and the depth of her insight into the inner life of women at the threshold of senescence. In this excerpt, Michaëlis wrote that a sisterhood for women between the ages of 40 and 50 ought to be founded, which would be a haven for them during the years of transition. Women, who are all somewhat mad at this time, although they try to conceal this, would be happier if they could live in freely chosen exile during these years, or at least wholly separated from men. Michaëlis felt alone and shut out from all living creatures who have "the right to pair," and she was envious of every young woman who went off with her lover while she sat waiting for old age. Women's doctors can never know the confidences women exchange only with one another, and there is not only a deep and lasting hostility between the sexes, but an "abyss": men and women simply do not understand one another. The pain a woman would suffer if she walked barefoot across burning ploughshares would be very slight in comparison with that she endures when she takes leave of her youth "and enters the region of despair we call growing old" (28).

Hall was inclined to the view that women are many-faceted by nature—a view that was not widely held by feminists of the 1920s and 1930s, and which is certainly not espoused by very many feminists today. He thought that because of woman's many-sidedness she is especially well equipped to work toward creating the synthesis so sorely needed in an age of "distracting specializations" (405). And in his judgment, the creation of this synthesis is the most important task old people have to perform in modern society. He wrote that the climacteric is followed by an Indian summer of greater clarity and efficiency in intellectual endeavors, and that perhaps in women more than in men, the loss of procreative power is accompanied by an increase in benevolence. In their Indian summer, mature people become more judicial, and their perspective on the world broadens. There may even come "a genuine psychic erethism or second-breath, half-ecstatic" (406). And after that? Hall thought the old have a mandate to *make* old age more venerable, and that only the old can be prophets with vision. He wrote that the world is in need of "a kind of higher criticism" of life and of all the institutions of life, and that only the very old have the "sapience" for this because only a very long life can grant this sapience (411).

Hall predicted that the first advent of the Superman will be in the form of a "glorified old age" (428). He might very well have used the word *Superwoman* here. Michaëlis's book had offered him insights into the unique psychology of women on the threshold of senescence. When the chance for the "supreme felicities" of wifehood and motherhood fade, he wrote (for the world "knows," he thought, that the very heart of women's existence is love, wifehood, and motherhood), it may not be extravagant to say that a woman feels despair. And the woman who has not mated has come to terms somewhat "with the death of the phyletic instinct within her" by the third decade of life, and has experienced intimations of the meaning of old age. For Hall, however, women have certain advantages over men. The older woman has rich gifts to offer humanity that she confined herself to expressing within the narrower circle of domestic life when she was younger. Now the world was waiting to see, he wrote, if she can find the courage to meet the "vital problems" of her sex and the wisdom to resolve them, or if she will content herself with doing "man's work in man's ways" (389).

Woman is older than man, Hall thought, in the same sense that it can be said that the child is older than the adult. That is, her qualities are more generic than man's, and she is nearer to the human race and a better representative of it. Furthermore, "she sublimates sex earlier and more completely. . . . But she is also younger than he in that she is . . . less specialized"(389). In his view, woman's physiological change is more abrupt, but her psychological changes are more gradual than man's, and her instincts, the moral instinct among them, are keener and surer than those of the male.

Received in today's climate of opinion, Hall's assumption that love, wifehood, and motherhood are the heart of women's existence would be found facile at best and outrageously sexist at worst. Certainly, his implication that all women's work outside the domestic sphere is sublimation of the "phyletic instinct" would be attacked on a number of fronts. *Senescence* would also be found wanting in any appreciation of our androgynous nature and of the desirability of remaining sexually active to the last of life. For all that, there is rich cargo here that should not be jettisoned. Whatever its flaws, Hall's book is informed by a Renaissance vision of the possibilities of old age. This vision may have been even brighter for women than for men because of his impression that women are less prone to "dwarfing specialization."[3] Humanistic gerontology is inspirited by this vision. (Of course, it is entirely possible that men, as much as women, are many-faceted in their interests and capabilities. Men, too, have an "Indian summer" when procreative power may be transformed into creative power. This is the "turn of life" that is the turn toward true maturity. Here is a worthy subject for study, one that is beyond the scope of this one, but that would be guided by the same vision of ripening and continuing personal development after midlife.)

In Michaëlis's time, the "years of transition" or "the dangerous age" may have been clearly demarcated as the years between the ages of 40 and 50. In our own time, it is thought that major life-events or "life quakes" and not particular birthdays are the catalysts for critical change in women's lives. For one woman, it is widowhood, for another, the death of her mother, for still another, the departure of a grown daughter, for a fourth, retirement, for a fifth, divorce. The span of the "years of transition" may be at least a quarter of a century if measured by individual differences rather than by biological changes. The despair, the "madness" of which Michaëlis wrote is the experience of a profoundly sensitive woman when she becomes fully conscious that her youth is over, that is, fully conscious of her aging and her mortality.

Withdrawal from human company, depression, an acute sense of the chasm between the sexes, the desire for renewal of the ancient sororal bond—all this is familiar to some women who fear that the loss of youth means the loss of love, the very source of life and its vital center. For some, the "turn of life" is a turning inward. In coming face to face with "the beginnings of old age," some women come face to face with the question of the meaning of their lives. This is the inner journey, the search undertaken during the years of transition from youth to age. It is a search for the relationship between love and creativity. There are women artists for whom love and creativity are the very root of life. When that is severed, there is death-in-life, the "life" of a ghost or a shadow. No ghost, no shadow can create a life of its own. No ghost, no shadow can create a work of enduring art.

Throughout human history, very few women have been able to live from earliest childhood on as artists above all else. From the very beginning, other selves claim a woman—daughter and sister, then wife and mother. In some tomorrow, women may be able to bear children throughout the life course, and like all gifts, this will bring new responsibilities in its wake. But in the past and for the present, a woman knows she must come to a decision about the great question of childbearing before a certain age. For the dancer, even a very great dancer, there are "morbid spells" in her late twenties or early thirties:

> The needs of the heart cannot be cheated forever. The dancer grows frightened. The dancer realizes suddenly she is a spinster and aging, no matter how fast she gets around the room. The life of merciless effort, the dimming chances of permanent fame, exhaustion and the growing comprehension of what old age means to a fading athlete without family or home suddenly terrify even the staunchest. The conviction grows that the sacrifice has been too much and perhaps not necessary. There is many a *volte-face* at this point and a marriage with at least one child in a frantic effort to put life back on balance.[4]

But our theater does not accommodate family life. If the dancer chooses Life over Art, the decision—for women more than for men—is irrevocable.

In this case, unless she is unusually favored by circumstance, a woman artist feels forced to choose between love and creativity. De Mille remarks that five million young girls in the United States alone are studying to be professional dancers (and this was over twenty years ago) and this may mean dancers believe they can find a way to have both. "Marriage," she reflects, "is difficult with any artist." It may be most difficult of all for artists in the theater because they cannot completely control their work. The partners to the marriage must meet the challenges of conflicting loyalties. The essential question here, as in *every* field of endeavor, is whether or not men can learn to accept their wives' interests and achievements as proudly as women have always accepted their husbands'. The question must be faced: "Pandora's box is opened. The girls are earning money." What is at issue is not whether men or women work better, but the recognition that they work in different ways, and that both men and women should be given the chance to make the effort without being penalized for it.

De Mille's grandmother George, who had no career beyond that of caring for her family, said, "Never destroy any aspect of personality, for what you think is the wild branch may be the heart of the tree." De Mille believes that the desire for "a double life" both as a devoted wife and mother and as an outstanding artist, a desire not every woman has, ought not be denied a woman simply because she is a woman. It is just as difficult "to be an artist with no root experience in life" as to live that double life. And,

> It is impossible to be a good wife or a wise mother, embittered, balked and devoured by inner energies. Creative exercise can be disciplined to a house-hold schedule . . . women everywhere prove it can be done. . . . And the children will reflect the zest and energy of the parent's life—and as to the work, how it flourishes! . . .
> I think this is what Isadora Duncan meant when she spoke of founding a new religion: the total release of women's hearts, the total use of their gifts. [230]

In the past, "Women have bent to the yoke and the scars of their durance are upon their children." But as social and religious restrictions against the free and full expression of a woman's creative gifts are removed, there is still one barrier that must be surmounted. This is "her husband's good will. Failing this, she fails all. She must have his blessing, his pride in her achievement. Let him dower her with this and there will come the great works for which we have waited so long" (231).

Isadora Duncan wrote that throughout her life, Art and Love were engaged in constant strife. Was this Chance or Necessity? Those with a tragic sense of life would say Necessity. They would say that Love must be sacrificed on the altar of Art or Art on the altar of Love, that it is impossible to live two lives fully. Those who believe with Hall that mankind "as he exists to-day is only the beginning of what he is to be and do . . . only the pigmoid or embryo of his true and fully entelechized self,"[5] would say we think it is Necessity only because we are wanting in imagination and will and generosity. The question is still open. And it is far from idle. Of the generations of older women encompassed in this study, most of those who *had* a choice chose motherhood. Of these it can never be known how many—again, given the choice—would still so live that their children came before all else in life, if they were given their lives to live over again. Every woman who has borne children can only ask this question of herself, and it is a question a woman will never have done answering. But this much is known, that numbers of women artists beyond reckoning have lived the first season of their lives as artists underground. It is only in the second half of life, if even then, that most women are free to explore the possibilities of full expression of their creativity. Furthermore, this freedom is enjoyed only by those living in favored circumstances in favored countries in the world, and then only very recently in human history. The chance for further flight for these favored few is the chance to live the "second season" creatively. Not the first season—at least, not yet. This is why the question of the relationship between creativity and aging is a crucial one in humanistic gerontology and for older women today who are seeking ways to express their gifts in later life:

> *All our mothers' lives are cautionary tales. We can learn from them and from each other. On the alert at last, I watch my own progress with great care. And I look to my friends who have been on much the same route as I, who now live lives enriched by work they love—work they either postponed or discovered after the pressure of their child-rearing years was over—women who know from experience that you seldom, if ever, can have it all—and certainly not all at once.*[6]

Until now, most creative women who became mothers were mothers first before they were artists. During those years of raising a family, years never so long in retrospect as they seem to be at the moments of conflict between the artist-self and the mother-self, there is a continual striving toward balance. During those years, there are "silences." Tillie Olsen recalls that Balzac wrote of creation in terms of motherhood, and she finds resemblances between the two, when motherhood is intelligent and passionate, beyond "the toil and patience. The calling upon total capacities; the reliving and new using of the past; the comprehensions; the fascination, absorption, intensity. All almost certain death to creation—(so far)."[7] What is lost is not the demiurge but the possibility for *sustained* creation: "More than in any other human relationship, overwhelmingly more, motherhood means being instantly interruptable, responsive, responsible. Children need one *now.* . . . *there is no one else responsible for these needs.*" (18). There are interruptions, there are distractions, and therefore there is "blockage—at best, lesser accomplishment. Unused capacities atrophy, cease to be. . . . Almost no mothers—as almost no part-time, part-self persons—have created enduring literature . . . so far" (19).

Even in this passage, in which Olsen writes specifically of the silences of the mother, she makes the point that where the gifted of either sex "have remained mute, or have never attained full capacity, it is because of circumstances, inner or outer, which oppose the needs of creation."[8] But throughout human history, the circumstances working in opposition to the expression of creativity have been overwhelming for most of the human race. If this were not so, the earth would be filled with artists. In every age, the human drama may be seen as a conflict between the forces of creativity and the forces of destruction. Every person—for every person has gifts—is a participant in this drama.

It is only in this century that so many have been granted extended life, and of these there are more women than there are men. The central question of humanistic gerontology is how the gift of longevity will be received. When women have the possibility for sustained creation, will they work to realize their gifts? Millions of women today expect to live a full third of their lives after the childbearing years, the years of being part-self and part-time, are over. Whether an artistic gift has atrophied, whether a silence can never be broken again because it has gone on too long—these are still open questions. The creative spirit may be broken by the passing feet of Yeats's "great black oxen." Or, driven underground, it may lie in wait, wakeful for its hour.

The silences of the writer *can* be broken after the long passage of the years. It is very difficult, but it is not impossible. An instrument that was put down at 25 can be taken up again at 50. And there are artists who never put it down, yet who do not come into their own until the childbearing years are over. Edith Wharton, whom Olsen includes in a list of women writers who, although they married, never had children, "was forty-nine when she finished *Ethan Frome* in early 1911. Already well into middle age, she had finally hit her stride as a novelist."[9] Willa Cather, whom Olsen lists among women writers who never married at all, did not "hit her stride" until she was middle-aged.[10] Among our contemporaries, Barbara Tuchman describes herself as "a late developer." She was 50 years old before *The Guns of August* "put her on a great tidal wave of fame and popularity that has continued to swell with her other books."[11] A woman can take up the pen, the brush, the chisel, the needle, a musical instrument again after many years of silence. She will never achieve all that she might have had she never put down the instrument. But if she thinks of that, she will be silenced forever. There are instruments time wears upon ineluctably, irreversibly—the human voice, the body of the dancer:

> Painters and sculptors and architects and poets can stay in their métiers for a hundred years, if they live to that age, but nature tells a singer when to halt. Yet, very few of them ever heed the warning. They prefer to have others say it for them that it's time to quit. I chose to leave when I knew I could still continue if I wanted to. The public is a marvelous inspiration to anybody before it, but it is very cruel if you go beyond the moment you should stop.[12]

Stop—or transform creativity in performance into creativity in directing, choreography, teaching. The time for transformation is determined by the woman and her art. Each life is different. One woman artist may begin having a family in her late thirties, and work part-time at her art for many years after that. Another may begin creative work at the age of 60. Jean Barlow Hudson, who moved thirty-five times in as many years of marriage, and who gave birth to four children, the last one at the age of 50, began to write novels at the age of 60. Writing of her struggles for focus and concision, she says that trying to retrain herself "is difficult, perhaps impossible, in one's 60s."[13]

It is not the "impossible" that matters, but the "perhaps." Of course, it *is* impossible, it is a miracle whenever a work of art is created, a victory over forces of incalculable power. "The creative person," May Sarton writes, "the person who moves from an irrational source of power, has to face the fact that this power antagonizes. Under all the superficial praise of the 'creative' is the desire to kill. It is the old war between the mystic and the nonmystic, a war to the death."[14] Older women artists ought to light flares for one another, to inspirit and encourage one another. "Il n'est pas nécessaire d'espérer pour entreprendre," William of Orange counseled, "ni de réussir pour persévrer." Older women artists need to serve as the *femme inspiratrice* for one another. We underestimate—grossly underestimate—the force of the creative spirit in our time and culture. We are too ready to see ourselves and one another not as creators but as creatures—victims—of circumstance. But that is to succumb to them, to surrender, to put out the light. So long as we dwell on its limitations we can never see the possibilities of life.

The creativity of women who did not even own their own *lives* is a call to release our own. Alice Walker writes powerfully of the demiurge and the myriad forms of its expression in the lives of the great-grandmothers, grand-mothers, and mothers of today's black women. Jean Toomer called the women he saw in the Post-Reconstruction South "Saints." In truth, they were Artists who were driven mad by their own creativity, for there was no way to release it. These Creators were rich in spirituality, and spirituality is the basis of Art. Yet it was this very richness that accounted for the spiritual waste of their lives, because they were driven mad by the strain of having to endure artistic talents that were not used and were not wanted. Walker asks what it meant for a black woman to be an artist three or four generations ago, and she writes, "It is a question with an answer cruel enough to stop the blood."[15] Black people were forbidden by law to read or write for most of the years they have been in America. How, then, was the black woman's creativity kept alive? Phillis Wheatley, a slave in the eighteenth century, not only did not have a room of her own and enough money to be independent; she "owned not even herself" (62). Yet she was an artist.

Walker summons black women to identify with their lives the living creativ-ity that some of their great-grandmothers "were not allowed to know," and she writes *some* because most did know their spirituality and had no intention of surrendering it. In search of the secret of what has nourished the "vibrant, creative spirit that the Black woman has inherited," Walker went to her own mother (63). Although no song or poem will carry her mother's name, many of the stories Walker writes are her mother's stories. Nor is this all. Walker's mother "adorned with flowers whatever shabby house we were forced to live in." So creative was she with flowers, "even my memories of poverty are seen through a screen of blooms." The artist's daughter has noticed "that it is only when my mother is working in her flowers that she is radiant, almost to the point of being invisible—except as Creator: hand and eye. She is involved in work her soul must have" (64).

Every work of art is a living force awakening the indwelling artist in all who experience it, releasing the creative spirit in the beholder who responds with her or his own creative fire. "Wherever we find the creative principle, in the Great Individual and in the child, . . . we venerate it as the hidden treasure that in humble form conceals a fragment of the godhead."[16] Throughout the Western world, Leonardo da Vinci is recognized as an incarnation of this creative principle. The essential quality of Leonardo's vision was not its aston-ishing range of interests and curiosity so much as his integration "of all this multiplicity into a symbolic human existence." For this man of the Renais-sance, art was not all. For him, science was a secret kept to and for himself. Although he did not know it, his entire life was impelled by the urge to integrate all the aspects of his personality. He, like Goethe, sought "a life of wholeness, which seems to be in keeping with the intimate intention of West-ern humanity."[17] All people resemble Leonardo in this psychic tendency toward wholeness. Every person, in the conception of humanity in the Old Testament, is not only a creature made in the image of the godhead, but "also a creative force demanding fulfillment."[18]

The founders (*vattikim*) of the kibbutzim in Israel were feminists. They wanted to do away with not only the traditional dependence of the wife on her husband but the consequences of *ha tragedia ha-biologit shel ha-isha*, "the biolog-ical tragedy of woman." Since "woman must bear and rear children, she has had little opportunity for cultural, political, or artistic expressions. If she could only be freed from this time-consuming responsibility, as well as from . . . other domestic duties . . . she would have the time to devote to these other interests." Then she would become man's equal.[19]

It may happen that our daughters or our daughters' daughters may so transform the social arrangements that the full creativity of women will be released all along the life course. The great questions of the past are asked by those of every generation, and whether biology defines Necessity or Necessity defines tragedy will surely be counted among them. There is another ques-tion, or perhaps another way of phrasing this one. It is asked by today's generations of older women artists who have come to that place where they are confronted, as artists of all historical epochs and of both sexes are con-fronted, with that other Challenger to the creative spirit. It waits in the wings, and it will have its hour. There comes a time in the life of every creative woman when she can no longer bear children, when full-time motherhood is no longer an issue in her life. Now it is not her sex that is the Challenger so much as her aging and her mortality. Can the "turn of life" mark her passage to a full creative life?

Margaret Mead, who once thought she might become a poet and who became another sort of poet, an anthropologist, wrote in her autobiography that babies kept her alive in contexts in which she could rarely exercise her sense of touch. She found Bateson's perception about solitary fieldwork to be true, that it was frustrated *gentleness* and not frustrated sex that is very hard to bear. And she much preferred babies to pets that she could hold in her arms and have as playmates.[20]

Mead never doubted that she would have children one day. Throughout her childhood, she had enjoyed caring for the younger ones, and in many ways she thought of her two younger sisters as her own children. In 1926, she was told that she could never have any children. Later, when she was doing fieldwork in Mundugumor, she witnessed for the first time in her life how adversely a society is affected by an active dislike and refusal of children. It was her strong conviction that "a culture that rejected children was a bad culture" (268). She began to hope again that she might be able to have a child. After she was married to Bateson, she had several early miscarriages. And in 1938, when it seemed that she might be have a premature menopause, she felt a regretful sadness:

> Something very special sometimes happens to women when they know that they will not have a child—or any more children. It can happen to women who have never married, when they reach the menopause. It can happen to widows with children who feel that no new person can ever take the place of a loved husband. It can happen to young wives who discover that they can never bear a child. Suddenly, their whole creativity is released. [269]

Mead, who did have a child after all, had a "flash of insight" in 1940 when she was talking with a small delegation of people who had come to request that she address a women's congress. She was holding her baby on her lap, and as they talked she remembered what her psychology professor had said about why women are not so productive as men. He had spoken of Harriet Beecher Stowe's comment in a letter that she had been thinking about writing a novel about slavery, "but the baby cried so much." It came to Mead that if she had said rather that "the baby smiles so much," this would have been far more plausible. "It is not that women have less impulse than men to be creative and productive," Mead reflected. "But through the ages having children, for women who wanted children, has been so satisfying that it has taken some special circumstance—spinsterhood, barrenness, or widowhood—to let women give their whole minds to other work."[21]

Transcendence: Women's Creativity in Later Life

Gerontology has been said to have arrived at the threshold of a third stage of development. In the first stage, the focus was on medicine and biology, and in the second on psychology, sociology, economics, and demography. In the third stage, it will turn more and more to the humanities for insights into aging. Drawing upon the "humanistic psychology" of Abraham Maslow, who believed that the fullest realization of the possibilities of the self can only come with aging, Walter G. Moss suggests that a humanistic gerontology might begin with the question of how older people could develop their potential most fully, and the question of how society might be made into a better place for older people. The humanities appear to be ideally suited to helping older people achieve transcendence over declining physical powers and diminishing life expectancy. They are also "ideally suited to those who wish to emphasize the potential positive aspects of aging: the growth of the spirit, of wisdom, of experience, rather than the negative aspects of physical decline."[22]

It has been reported that "Americans spent $5 billion in 1970 for beauty aids, while the government spent $1.86 billion for old-age assistance in the same year." Olga Knopf asks, "Would everyone not wish the figures were reversed?" and she observes, "Tragically, much of the expenditure for cosmetics can be attributed to the enormous efforts people in a youth-oriented society make to improve their appearance and to hide the signs of aging."[23] So long as we remain fixated upon appearances, we shall continue to dread old age. The fear of growing older, which may be cause as much as consequence of the idolatry of youth, is a denial of the fullness of human experience. Like all fears, it is a form of enslavement: it condemns us to immaturity. Humanistic gerontology offers passage to freedom from this fear. These appearances may be taken as symbols or keys that open the door to possible meanings that never can be revealed if we see them as things in themselves. This is the approach taken by Geri Berg and Sally Gadow, who explore meanings of aging beyond the "physiological-psychosociocultural-economic experience."[24] In search of alternatives to the negative valuation of aging offered by the sciences, Berg and Gadow seek to discover or develop positive meanings of aging. They suggest that both the negative view of aging as deterioration, decline, and partial or total dependency, and the falsely positive view that aging is made more human the more it is made to resemble youth or middle age, are instructive for those looking for a positive view. The negative view places too low a value on the realities of aging, and the falsely positive view *over*values them:

> the realities of aging: that the body moves slowly, that the senses alter, that some structures grow rigid while others become flaccid, that the skin folds back upon itself, that the memory winds around and restructures itself, that some capacities disappear, and that somewhere dying begins. For the negative view, these spell the doom of aging. . . . for the stay-young view, they are excluded from aging. [85]

These realities may be taken as symbols or keys to possible meanings. Slowing makes it possible to explore experiences "not in their linear pattern of succeeding one another, but in their possibility of opening for us entire worlds in each situation and each person encountered. We slow ourselves to be more gentle with these experiences, to take care to let their . . . rich density emerge." In old age, we move *into* time as well as *through* time. The "alteration of smooth surfaces and straight lines" in body and mind—wrinkling of the skin, curving of posture, the winding ways of memory—all these may "express the greater intricacies, the finer articulations that are possible in the person for whom reality has become many-layered, folded upon itself, woven and richly textured" (86). That the skeleton grows rigid and the soft tissue becomes flaccid may express the clarifying of the completed character and a shedding of the inessential. There is growth to the last, a growing clarity and decisiveness about the form that one's existence is to take. And that there is a growing recognition of the finitude of life may mean that there is a growing exercise of freedom in personal determination of the meaning that approaching death will have for the life yet to be lived. It is precisely this freedom "which is the essence of aging as a human value" (87).

Berg and Gadow explore images of aging in art and in the personal statements made by artists in the works of their later years. They find that a study of a series of early and late works documents the aging of the artists selected, and that aging was an enriching and deepening experience for most of them. The artists' views on aging were decidedly not either negative or falsely positive. The art historian and philosopher conclude that the meanings of aging in art and philosophy are a many-textured fabric, and that to encompass the richness and complexity of aging, there must be a dialectic between ideals in their fragile abstractness and images in their concrete immediacy. Age is a time for slowing, for turning inward, for distilling the essences of experience, for determining the final form of the self and the world, and for finding the personal meaning of death. The "freedom to decide about one's ultimate character and to slow oneself to a temporality more intricate than serial time, is the basis for creating any images of the ideality of aging" (92).

Very little is known about the relationship between creativity and aging.[25] It is assumed by many that productivity and creativity decline with age, a notion that was given considerable support by the materials presented in Harvey C. Lehman's *Age and Achievement*.[26] In his study, Lehman presents age-curves to illustrate the range of ages of *outstanding* achievement in diverse fields of endeavor and the years during which the greatest volume of work was accomplished. For a variety of artistic and intellectual fields, his age-curves show a consistent favoring of the third decade of life as the time of the greatest likelihood of creative and productive work. A number of objections may be (and have been) raised to Lehman's method, and therefore to the conclusions reached in his study. In all fairness, it must be noted that Lehman himself acknowledges that certain qualifications should accompany his "findings." He is careful to say that his age-curves do not depict the growth and decline of *individual* creative ability. And he states that they may not be taken as representations of ability in the abstract and that they may not be applied to single individuals. The curves depict *group* rather than *individual* performance, and "Prediction in an individual case is quite different from the analysis of general trends."[27] In this passage, Lehman wonders aloud how the researcher might construct age-curves depicting individual creative ability at successive age levels. Elsewhere he argues against applying the general rule to the individual case. The substantial and numerous individual variations at every age level ought to dissuade a person from thinking that his or her own life and work are ruled by some iron law about the human being's "most creative years" (220). However, despite these and other disclaimers, Lehman has justifiably been named an intellectual heir of Quetelet, whose interest in probability led him to formulate the concept of the "average man." This fellow—more accurately, this phantom—has actions and characteristics that appear as the smooth peak of central tendency on the bell-shaped (Gaussian) curve.[28]

Genius, however, is not enough. This is why John McLeish does not accept

the idea that a review of "a cavalcade of famous Ulyssean people" need dis-
courage the older person from undertaking creative work. It is not
Michelangelo's genius alone that accounts for his spectacular achievements in
later life, but "his strength of will and his summoning-up of what Kipling calls,
'heart and bone and sinew' for herculean tasks in spite of all kinds of fears and
sorrows," and these qualities are accessible to every older person.[29] It is
McLeish's conviction that again and again in their later lives, invitations to
creative thought and activity are extended to people, and that what older
"Ulysseans" have in common is that they have never lost the sense of wonder
and the quest for meaning. Their common desire to "drink life to the lees," to
continue to explore and to grow, unites "Ulysseans otherwise so different as
an existential philosopher (Gabriel Marcel), a small craft circumnavigator of
the globe (Ben Carlin), and a blind teacher of the blind (Susan Miller)."[30]
McLeish does not confine "creativity" to a few forms of artistic or scientific
endeavor, and his book contains as many examples of women "Ulysseans" as
of men. He does not believe that "masterpieces" are the measure of achievement. Lehman, whose book he has read with appreciation, although with a
critical eye, is, McLeish remarks, "impaled time after time on the criteria of
the masterpiece" (149). In brief, McLeish does not limit the chance for further
flight to a favored few. Those who put courage and resourcefulness to use in
later life, he maintains—and he provides plentiful examples to substantiate
this claim—can be found "in every stratum and ethnic group in our world of
the late twentieth century."[31]

   Quoting Jouhandeau's praise of transcendence, Simone de Beauvoir writes
the sharp rejoinder, "This mystical twaddle is indecent when we look at the
real condition of the immense majority of old people: hunger, cold and disease certainly bring with them no kind of moral gain." In her view, all this is
baseless "nonsense."[32] She writes that old people face a "limited future and a
frozen past" (562). Many are paralyzed by this. A few race against time. If old
age "is not to be an absurd parody of our former life," there is only one
solution, "and that is to go on pursuing ends that give our existence a meaning" (802). In this as in many other passages in her impassioned book,
Beauvoir insists that "these possibilities are granted only to a handful of
privileged people" (803). In "Old age and everyday life," she writes that the
case of Grandma Moses is an exception: "it is often impossible to open new
paths even within our own praxis. How much vainer, therefore, is the claim to
make an arbitrary discovery of new interests and pleasures" (672).

   But *every* person is an exception. We underestimate human beings, as
Louise Nevelson remarks. Nevelson detests the phrase "the common man."
She thinks *no* one is common, that "in every human being there is
greatness."[33] A stunning example of the truth of this was the re-awakening of
the indwelling poet of the inmates of the American Nursing Home through
Kenneth Koch's poetry workshop. They came, these unlikely students, old
and ill. They were about twenty-five in number, and some were in wheelchairs, others with walkers. And in the face of memory loss, of physical pain

and depression, of blindness and serious impairments of hearing and speech
. . . in spite of their confinement, their doubts about their worth . . . in spite of
being quite out of the habit of learning in a classroom . . . each of them
rediscovered the artist within. "Almost none of our students were able to use
their hands to write—either because of muscular difficulties or blindness."[34]
So they told their poems to Koch and his assistants, who sat with each person
individually, to take down the lines.

I Never Told Anybody challenges many stereotypes about the elderly. Koch
discovered that it is wrong to think that what old people really want and need
is peace and quiet, and that it is wrong to think that subjects that have to do
with power and energy and passion should be avoided because they may cause
old people pain or alienation. "Passion and energy are what life is all about"
(30). A teacher is not there to protect students from experiencing strong
emotions, but to look for ways to help them express what they feel. It is not
unusual for a writer to weep while working, he reassured those who cried
during the act of creating a line of poetry: "Tears were something on the way
to the poem" (37).

The purpose of teaching poetry in a nursing home is not therapy, not
helping people adjust to the immediate conditions of their lives—for who
would want to adjust to a life without imagination or achievement? The purpose is to change in some way the conditions of that life. It is not to distract or
console old people, or to give them busy work, but to help them become more
fully alive. Writing poems must have made a difference to these workshop
students, "because the thoughts, memories, and feelings poetry is about are
just the things some of them feared they had lost touch with or lost the power
to use and to communicate to others" (45). Poetry gave them freedom from
conventional ideas about themselves. Writing poetry restored to them that
which had always been theirs, but had been in some way lost. They came from
worlds where almost no one wrote poetry. They had not thought of themselves as poets. "They had fifty or more years behind them of not being poets,
a rare thing for a poet to have. Many had spent most of their adult lives at jobs
like housework, steam-pressing, being a short-order cook" (56). Looking at
their lives as poets, now, what did they see?

> I thought the poems would be about the past, be full of nostalgia and
> regrets. . . . I was unprepared for the devastating directness of some of my
> students' poems, for the sensuousness, for the imaginative and . . . literary
> power. I was surprised, and moved, at discovering feelings and perceptions
> in strange perspectives, in lives and situations where I wasn't in the habit of
> thinking they were. [53]

Welthy Honsinger Fisher was sent a scroll from China "just before her ports
were closed again to the West. 'In the autumn of your life,' the lettering reads
in Chinese, 'you are still announcing dawns!' "[35] Now in late winter, Fisher
announces them still. So, too, did Grandma Moses, called a "primitive"
painter,[36] who wrote when she was 87, "Why did I start to paint in my old age?

well to tell the truth, I had neuritis and artheritus so bad that I could do but little work, but had to keep busy to pass the time away." Her first attempts were at worsted pictures, and after that she tried oil. "It is a very pleasant Hobby if one does not have to hurry, I love to take my time and finish things up right."[37]

Grandma Moses began to make pictures intended to be framed and hung on the wall when she was in her late seventies and could no longer do housework. Kallir says that her artistic progress in just two years' time was "astonishing." In the beginning, he had seen her work as "interesting and appealing folk art," and then it came to him "that here was an outstanding painter" (50). Although the artist began to paint seriously only in old age, she had done painting and decorating in her home since her early childhood.[38] Her early attempts, paintings on a fireboard and a tip-up table, "already show a painterly technique rarely found in works of self-taught artists" (28). When she was 89, she said that she thought she had made her last picture with each one she completed, and yet she would go right on working. To the very end of her life as an artist, she earnestly endeavored to "improve." What is remarkable about this is that "some people did everything they could to make her repeat what had led her to fame" (249).

In her eighties, Grandma Moses worked in her bedroom. Since it was much too small to accommodate an easel or a large enough table, she would lay the canvases on her bed to work on them. It was not until she was almost 90 that she went back to painting smaller pictures, acknowledging that the strain of working on larger ones was becoming too much for her. Her hand remained steady into extreme old age. "Supporting her right hand with the left, she would fill in with absolute accuracy the finest details." By her ninety-ninth year, some pictures "show a changed way of painting whereby the subject matter is almost dissolved into color" (255). After her hundredth birthday, she completed more than twenty-five paintings. But when she was taken to a nursing home in 1961, she was not permitted to paint. Her doctor stated that she "would not rest if she had her paints" (189). During one of his visits, she hid his stethoscope, promising to return it if he would take her back to Eagle Bridge. She died in December of 1961, and when Kallir visited her before her one hundred first birthday, he found her in good spirits and mentally alert. She told him she planned to paint again when she returned home.

How strange Memory is, and Hope, she wrote when she was 88, "one looks backward, the other forward. The one is of today, the other is the tomorrow, memory is History recorded in our brain, memory is a painter it paints pictures of the past and of the day" (120). She was her own character, an original. She chose to write down her recollections rather than tape-record them, because she did not like microphones. After most of her memoirs had been written, she dictated the connecting passages, insisting upon corrections in spelling although the editor much preferred to retain her originality in self-expression. She attached very little importance to her success as a painter in comparison with the vividness of her remembrance of a full life as a "farm wife and head of a large family" (169). She said that she wrote of her life "in small sketches, a little today, a little yesterday, as I thought of it, as I remembered all the things from childhood on through the years, good ones, and unpleasant ones, that is how they come, and that is how we have to take them." She looked back upon her life "as a good day's work, it was done and I feel satisfied with it" (122). She, like Shaw, Brancusi, Churchill, and Schweitzer, became an example of those old people who "pay the world the great compliment of being reluctant to leave it, and their reluctance becomes a benediction" (193).

Although Louise Nevelson had written and spoken bitterly of the anti-Semitism and narrow-mindedness of Rockland, Maine, the "WASP Yankee town" where she grew up, her return there after almost sixty years was a "happy homecoming." The internationally renowned sculptor, who worked obsessively at her art throughout her entire life despite years of "almost total lack of remuneration and public recognition," was welcomed by the town "with a major exhibition of her works at the local museum, with a key to the city, with standing ovations."[39] She remembered "they laughed here" in the town where she grew up. "But I've lived long enough that I have the best laugh." At the age of 80, she says that it is miraculous that she survived and rose above all the years of poverty and obscurity. "But nature endows you." No sacrifice was too great for her to continue working.

An artist, Nevelson says, is born with the gift. She knew in childhood that she was going to be an artist. She demanded much from life. To persevere and grow as an artist took courage and despair. "And the hardship gave me total freedom."[40] When she was only 9, she had decided she "would never—in principle—work for anyone as long as I lived. I was gifted and I knew it, and I wasn't going to permit anyone on earth to take my true heritage" (2). She believes that every person "is entitled to recognize their full being." She believes that a person is born with a pattern not of her or his conscious choosing, and she would like to say that in the future there will be freedom from "superiors," from all the restrictions of the environment, that one day "you will claim your true heritage and you will have a choice of taking a name . . . not having yourself stamped" (18). But she does not accept "luck" or "break," and she would not permit "breaks." She thinks "we create our lives" (76). She calls herself "a work horse." To work is to breathe, to live. She prefers to work at a certain speed. She likes excitement; she does not care for a meditative life. "I think that there is such a thing as energy, creation overflowing. And I always felt that I have this great energy" (115).

People have different kinds of memories, Nevelson says, and hers is a memory for form, and basically for wood. She had always wanted to show people that "art is everywhere, except it has to pass through a creative mind." What others call *scavenger* "is really a resurrection" (81). When objects of black wood, her raw materials, pass through her creative mind, they are "retranslated." The magic is that they are both translated and transformed. For Louise Nevelson, death itself—and she has never feared it—is transformation.

Nothing is ever forgotten. Everything that happens is a source of new revelations. Nothing is ever lost. There are "people . . . that are misplaced and all of a sudden they become geniuses. Why weren't they geniuses the year before? They weren't in the right atmosphere and the right combination. That doesn't mean they didn't have it. They just had to wait for their own time" (83). She believes that a creative person ought not to be disturbed by lack of recognition. "You belong to yourself. . . . *nobody* . . . on earth is *your* center. *Your center* is *your center*" (3). All of us fail, "but some of us have something that we pick ourselves up and go on, to greater things. . . . Life isn't one straight line. *Never*. Most of us have to be transplanted, like a tree, before we blossom" (4). There is a strong desire for art in our times. "The soul is in search," perhaps more so than ever before. America has accomplished so much in art so quickly: in just the past few decades, "this whole land has blossomed" (182). But the great danger for the artist is that of being intimidated by the powers-that-be and permitting "a monster to intrude" rather than working from her or his own center (183).

A creative mind, Nevelson says, is many-faceted. To see the world as made of concrete and stone is to be blocked; to see the world in transparency is to have freedom to move. She speaks of character as structure, as "the architecture of the being. And once you go into the inner being, you will find that everything you encompass, in any direction you choose, is your own" (153). She knows that all materials in nature must crumble in time. Although there is the promise in the beginning, she says, just as the body strengthens and is prepared to function, and does function, it is "destroyed and destroyed and destroyed. The human spirit—creation works in the opposite direction" (188).

There is no formula for creative work. The clock ticks, the heart beats, the hoof of time pounds louder and louder. "Death plucks my ears and says, Live! I am coming," Oliver Wendell Holmes said when he was 90. There must be watchfulness, discipline, a terrible patience, faith during the dry seasons. There will be "imaginative days" when the mind "is like a stained-glass window through which . . . marvellous forms and richest colours" are visible. There will be days when the windows are "dull, grey-glass," and beyond them there is only the "rubbish heap called Life."[41] There are no "creative years." Any year can be everything—or nothing.

Ninety-two-year-old Imogen Cunningham seemed youthful to the last of her life because, like Emily Dickinson, "she 'dwelt in possibility.'" She "always claimed that her best photograph would be the one she would make tomorrow."[42] Her final project, the photographing of people at the far side of life, was humble and therefore entirely

in keeping with the direction of her lifelong creative interest in the particular, in the human core of a person, and it reflects her acceptance of her own aging. There are no more prizes and awards. There is just courage, courage to look through the lens and see herself mirrored in others, always looking with a childlike curiosity, learning from another's reality ways to be strong, active, interesting, and useful. [18]

Of her own aging face, Cunningham felt no shame. She wanted to free herself of vanity, and to endow those she photographed with this liberation. Neither idealizing nor denigrating people, she invited her subjects and viewers to come to the same acceptance that she had realized for herself. Her photographs "are a kind of visual research, straightforward studies of the way people are at the end of life, revealed in a face, an expression, a gesture, a posture" (11).

Imogen Cunningham is remembered as having been magnetic in manner. Her wit was "peppery" and "irreverent" and her curiosity about people insatiable. She had "a look that was straight, that measured and weighed you inside and out" (10). Her very presence was an affirmation "that life could be lived fully, savored even into late old age" (23). What was her secret? one may ask. Cunningham, whose friends see her still "striding around San Francisco," unmistakable for "the beaded cap atop a fringe of white bangs and the black cape winging behind her intent little figure," did not believe in secrets (10). She believed in work. She called answers "bunk." She lived her conviction that the goal in life is that a great deal of work ought to be done every day.

A full quarter of a century after the age regarded by so many as the age for the ending of activity and creativity, Cunningham took up her camera to learn from it once more. For her, the camera was a teaching instrument, and learning was a natural part of living, of experiencing. Consummately human, her life inseparable from her work, Cunningham was a broth of contradictions, a complex person who never ceased growing to the day of her death, at the age of 93, in 1976. The person who emerges from *After Ninety* is one who achieved a full openness to life, a capacity for transformation, for continuous "refocusing of the self" (22).

In her vivid portrait of Georgia O'Keeffe at 90, Mary Lynn Kotz writes of a woman who is "anything but old." Kotz compares O'Keeffe's conversation with that of a 40-year-old woman, "with one exception: she can flash her phenomenal memory back and forth from last week to last century, with clarity, wit and breadth of description. She is both sturdy and vibrant, joyful as ever in her desert environment."[43] O'Keeffe is up before daylight every morning, to watch the sun come up over her mesa. She says that after exercising and breakfast, "I go on about my day. When I have an idea, I paint. When I don't, I do all the other things that need to be done." She speaks for the first time about her eyesight when she tells Kotz she no longer sees well enough to prepare her own breakfast. Kotz observes:

> She is surefooted along narrow paths and precarious bridges, pointing with her cane to all sorts of details in her garden. She looks carefully at her new paintings and watercolors, telling me about them. She also chides me when I am not looking at her. She points out every mountain on the horizon. Her distance vision appears to be perfect. It is the small, closeup thing that she cannot see. And yet, she says, sometimes she can see the tiniest piece of lint on the floor. [40]

Her trouble with her eyesight does not bother her now, O'Keeffe says, although when it first began she found it very frustrating because it had always been exceptional. Instead of despairing when her eyes began to change, she turned to a medium that was new to her, and her assistant, Juan Hamilton, says that her work in clay led her back to painting. She did not allow her handicap to overwhelm her, but adapted to it as best she could, finding a way to work with the eyesight she still has. Hamilton attributes this to O'Keeffe's strong sense of survival and to her keen interest in the events of the world as well as of her own life.

"The people whose old age is most favoured are those whose interests are many-sided," Beauvoir writes. And the "greatest good fortune, even greater than health, for the old person is to have his world still inhabited by projects: then, busy and useful, he escapes both from boredom and from decay."[44] O'Keeffe is an exemplar of the truth of this. Her assistant attests that she needs always to be involved in projects. She lives as though she has several lifetimes. She always wanted, she says, "to be five or six of me."[45] When she speaks about her next lifetime, Kotz asks her what she would be then, "and she answers, without a beat, 'A blonde. And I would like to have a very high soprano voice. I would sing very high, very clear notes, without fear'" (43). O'Keeffe says that she has been able to create so much in part because of "the ability to guard her privacy, to close doors, to say 'no.'" Concentration matters most in her work, she says. "Making a decision to do something and then doing it requires *not* doing a dozen other things" (44). O'Keeffe says that she does not think she has a great gift, that it is not simply talent that accounts for her art. One needs something else, she says—"a kind of nerve . . . a lot of nerve, and a lot of very, very hard work" (45).

Creativity, Freedom, Responsibility

Creativity can be expressed in response "to a religious calling, . . . to art, . . . to a scientific or an ethical vocation."[46] It can be expressed in holding a family together, keeping a family spirit alive.[47] It can be expressed in service to a cause; there is something in the spirit of many older women working for a cause that "keeps them forever young."[48] It can inspirit a blind woman to learn braille at the age of 81 and then "to embark upon a new career helping other elderly blind people overcome their handicap."[49] It has always been expressed in the domestic arts. In their oral history of quilters in Texas and New Mexico and of the domestic art of quiltmaking, Patricia Cooper and Norma Bradley Buferd came to see the quilt "as art coming directly out of the home, out of familial interactions" and the home where quilts were made as "studio, art school, and gallery."[50] One quilter said, "I pieced this one after I was nearly blind and you can just turn it over and look at my stitches. They are little, let me tell you. I can thread a needle still" (142). When she was very young, another quilter watched her father build a wooden windmill. He was working with the same problem she contended with when she "made a Dresden Plate that like to never circled" (51). Mrs. Mary White, who had made forty-five quilts for her family, and written a note for each that was a message of love, said:

> You can't always change things. Sometimes you don't have no control over the way things go. Hail ruins the crops, or fire burns you out. And then you're just given so much to work with in a life and you have to do the best you can with what you got. That's what piecing is. The materials is passed on to you or is all you can afford to buy . . . that's just what's given to you. Your fate. But. . . . You can put them in any order you like.[20]

In *Occupation: Housewife,* sociologist Helena Znaniecki Lopata writes that according to the negative stereotype of housewife, which pervades American society, creativity on the part of persons "limited" to the housewife role is impossible. Women who are housewives are seen as passive, unimaginative, and parochial in their interests, shackled to routine and unable to understand the work other family members perform outside the home:

> Simultaneously they are not trusted in major decisions because of "masculine protest" or their emotionality. This combined stereotype is present not only in Betty Friedan's *The Feminine Mystique,* which evaluates work for money as the only worthy effort, but in the pronouncements of most feminists and anti-feminists, men and women. They even label other-than-in-the-home activities of women, such as community participation, artistic effort, educational or child-oriented actions, not challenging to anyone with intelligence. The only source worthy of intellectual identity is the "job" or "career."[51]

Lopata remarks that this ideology flies in the face of the heterogeneity of American society, and she has shown that it is utterly false. Her studies of 568 Chicago-area women indicated a growing competence and creativity in the lives and activities of housewives all along the life course. She also found that women who were employed did not perceive their work as a means of self-expression.

Older married women who are employed—and less than one of every two aged 45 to 55, less than one of every three aged 55 to 65, and a much lower ratio after 65 are counted among the "employed"—have two "jobs," and are paid for one. Somehow, they must live two lives. If an older woman is dedicated to community work or to an artistic endeavor, and if she is employed and responsible for a family, she must live not two lives, but three. Juanita Kreps does not find the lip service given to the worth of these activities to be convincing:

> Despite our protests that growth in income is not to be equated with improvements in welfare; that society places a high value on the services of wives in the home and in the community; that the absence of a price tag on a particular service does not render it valueless—despite these caveats, the

tendency to identify one's worth with the salary he earns is a persistent one. This tendency is not peculiar to men who earn salaries; it pervades as well the thinking of women who work at unpaid jobs.[52]

Labor in childrearing, in volunteer community services, labor at the loom or quilting frame or in the garden, or at the easel or typewriter or piano—all these have in common that they are "labors of love." In our society, they are thought to be play. But without them, any society would be a necropolis.

It has been remarked that most programs and services for the elderly are designed to meet the needs of the body, and few are responsive to the needs of the human spirit. Phyllis Lehmann reports that, perhaps because of the idea that older people can neither participate in nor appreciate artistic activity, the elderly may be more isolated from cultural institutions "than even the poorest, most disadvantaged of younger Americans."[53] Older people, Lani Lattin maintains, are "important contributors to our cultural heritage" and "irreplaceable cultural treasures." Jacqueline Sunderland says that most people in their thirties and forties today have an eight out of ten probability of being tomorrow's elderly—"younger, healthier, more educated, more articulate, with higher expectations more easily expressed" than today's older adults, and she asks, "Will Craft Kit Kitsch, painting by numbers, kitchen bands, and popsicle art satisfy our desires for creative experience?" (4)

Such was G. Stanley Hall's vision that he believed, with H. G. Wells, that humanity in Europe, and perhaps everywhere in the world, "has reached the 'dangerous age' that marks the dawn of senescence" and that if we do not develop what Renan called "a new enthusiasm for humanity," that is, "a new social consciousness, and a new instinct for service and for posterity," our complex civilization and all its institutions "will become a Frankenstein monster escaping the control of the being that devised and constructed it and will bring ruin to both him and to itself."[54] Early in this century, Hall wrote that national and individual egoism are degenerative and must be arrested. He wrote that life is too short for us to master it, and that unless we enter upon a longer apprenticeship to it without fear, "we shall drift into far more disastrous wars that will leave even the victors exhausted, and mankind will either sink into an impotent senility or into a Tarzan bestialism" (31).

These words ring clearly over sixty years of history, and Hall's faith in eugenics and in the re-education of all mankind can be put aside more easily than his contemplation of the darkness of the future that is now our past, the future that followed upon the fading of Wilson's fleeting dream of a "federated world" (31). In the 1980s, it may be amusing to read Hall's citation of a Professor Raymond Pearl's prediction that the population of the United States would reach an upper limit of 197,274,000, with 66 persons per square mile, about the year 2100 (167). It could happen that the predictions of the age-sex composition of the twenty-first century North American population will invoke a like amusement half a century from now, however. But the challenges of realizing the possibilities of later life will have to be met by the survivors of those who are young today. In Hall's view, there are personal questions and more difficult and complicated problems that affect all humanity with which "we rarely come to anything like a masterly grip till the shadows begin to slant eastward, and for a season, which varies greatly with individuals, our powers increase as the shadows lengthen" (30).

"Everybody now is talking about the impossibility of life," Katharine Hepburn said of Emlyn Williams's *The Corn Is Green*, "and this play is all about the possibility." Each of us has "55 to 90 years, and it isn't long, and yet we spend so much time moaning." What Williams shows so brilliantly in this play, she said, is that "you have to study and you have to work, because the biggest thrill in life is to realize your potential. I don't think we accomplish one-quarter of what we could."[55] This conviction, that life is far more rich in possibilities for "self-actualization" than we imagine, is one of the central themes of Abraham Maslow's work, as is his suggestion that full self-actualization is possible only for those in the second half of life.[56]

The confirmation—indeed, the celebration—of these beliefs is one of the many offerings made by poet Marc Kaminsky in his book about doing poetry groups (not workshops, not poetry therapy, but poetry *groups,* for in these groups the participants found the poem in the person and the person in the poem). In 1972, Kaminsky became a group-worker with the Jewish Association for the Services for the Aged and began doing poetry groups. In *What's Inside You It Shines Out of You,* which begins with a remembrance of each of his four grandparents as his teacher, Kaminsky recounts his work with the Thursday Poetry Group and with other groups. He tells of the beginnings of autonomous creativity by group members, of writing and healing (the poetry *workshop* is centered on the making of the poem, and poetry *therapy* is centered on the person), of his work with memory poems, of the poetry group process itself, and of Songs of Healing. Kaminsky was as much concerned with the people he was working with as he was with the poems—the "growing and suffering creatures" who made up the group and who were the creators of the poems they spoke. The Thursday Poetry Group began with three old women and Kaminsky, "a somewhat rabbinical-looking poet," sitting in a small circle at the district office of the Jewish Association for the Services for the Aged in Brooklyn; beyond the picture window of the office, on the sign of the health spa across the street, a huge male was flexing "mountainous biceps." In his work with this group, Kaminsky learned the proper uses of storytelling and of silence. He shows in his chapter about their Thursday sessions how the group developed by the making of their poems, and how the poems developed by the making of the group. One of the women especially reminded him of his grandmothers, and that was a challenge for him to meet. He deeply respected that each woman had her own vocabulary and her own experience to work with, and that each of them could be left to put all these things together in a way that would have meaning and value for her. Kaminsky found that the assignments that poets use in poetry workshops can call forth the full creativity of the persons the poet works with, but that even when they do not, they represent a form of "practice," preparing the whole mind for the creative act. Part 3 of his book, which is comprised of "The Poems," attests to the creativity of these older people. In this book, which is both a classic and a poem in itself, Kaminsky tells us that one of the things he learned was how the poetry group could help someone change her life. Another was that old women's mourning-dreams are true acts of creation.[57]

Our collective responsibility to those who come after us is to create conditions of life worthy of humanity at every age. Our responsibility as older people is to "develop positive and realistic attitudes about old age."[58] Life is a gift; we forget this so easily, and all too often. Our responsibility to ourselves is to receive it as such. Once, Martha Graham said to Agnes de Mille:

> There is a vitality, a life-force, an energy, a quickening that is translated through you into action and because there is only one of you in all of time, this expression is unique. And if you block it, it will never exist through any other medium and be lost. The world will not have it. It is not your business to determine how good it is nor how valuable nor how it compares with other expressions. It is your business to keep it yours clearly and directly, to keep the channel open. You do not even have to believe in yourself or your work. You have to keep open and aware directly to the urges that motivate you.[59]

And because there is only one of you in all of time, this expression is unique. And if you block it, it will . . . be lost. The world will not have it.

Notes

1. Some of the thoughts in this chapter were presented as part of my Maurice Falk Memorial Lecture, "The Chance for Further Flight: Creativity in the Later Years," at Marist College in Poughkeepsie, New York, on March 22, 1979.

2. G. Stanley Hall, *Senescence: The Last Half of Life* (New York: D. Appleton and Co., 1922), p. 321. Hall had gathered reports on old age from inmates in homes for the aged, and concluded from these he would not find "true old age" as he thought of it in these institutions. Hereafter, all references to *Senescence* will be cited in the text by page number.

3. Ibid., p. 350.

4. Agnes de Mille, *And Promenade Home* (Boston: Little, Brown and Co., 1958), p. 227. Hereafter, all references to this book will be cited in the text by page number.

5. Hall, *Senescence*, p. 515. Hall wrote here that he believed that the desire for and belief in immortality is the best augur and pledge of this.

6. Luree Miller, *Late Bloom: New Lives for Women* (New York: Paddington Press Ltd., 1979), p. 56.

7. Tillie Olsen, *Silences* (New York: Delacorte Press, 1978), p. 18. Hereafter, reference to this book will be cited in the text by page number.

8. Ibid., p. 17. See also p. 21.

9. Cynthia Griffin Wolff, *A Feast of Words: The Triumph of Edith Wharton* (New York: Oxford University Press, Inc., 1977), pp. 191–92.

10. George N. Kates, "Willa Cather's Unfinished Avignon Story," in Willa Cather, *Five Stories* (New York: Vintage Books, 1956), pp. 175–214. See especially p. 184.

11. Nan Robertson, "Barbara Tuchman: A Loner at the Top of Her Field," *New York Times*, February 27, 1979, p. C10.

12. Mary Garden and Louis Biancalli, *Mary Garden's Story* (New York: Simon and Schuster, Inc., 1951), pp. 247–48.

13. Jean Barlow Hudson, "The Double Enemy," *Broomstick* (March 1980) 2(4):5.

14. May Sarton, *Mrs. Stevens Hears the Mermaids Singing* (New York: W. W. Norton and Co., Inc., 1975), p. 169.

15. Alice Walker, "In Search of Our Mothers' Gardens," *Southern Exposure* (Winter 1977) 4(4):60. Hereafter, all references to this article will be cited in the text by page number.

16. Erich Neumann, "Creative Man and Transformation," in Erich Neumann, *Art and the Creative Unconscious (Four Essays)*, tr. Ralph Manheim (New York: Pantheon, Bollingen Series LXI, 1959), p. 168.

17. Erich Neumann, "Leonardo Da Vinci and the Mother Archetype," in Erich Neumann, *Art and the Creative Unconscious*, p. 4.

18. Erich Neumann, "Creative Man and Transformation," p. 168.

19. Melford E. Spiro, *Kibbutz: Venture in Utopia* (New York: Schocken Books, 1963), p. 122.

20. Margaret Mead, *Blackberry Winter: My Earlier Years* (New York: William Morrow, Pocket Books, 1975), p. 167. Hereafter, all references to this book will be cited in the text by page number.

21. Ibid., pp. 269–70. Anaïs Nin wrote in her first diary of the birth of her first and only baby, a daughter, who was born prematurely and who had died *in utero*. When she was pregnant, Nin remembered that Lawrence had said to her, "Do not bring any more children into the world, bring hope into the world." When she saw her dead daughter, Nin thought that Lawrence's symbolic motherhood was the only one left to her: "This child . . . denied me as if to point up my destiny in other realms." Gunther Stuhlmann, ed., *The Diary of Anaïs Nin*, 1931–1934, volume 1 (New York: Harcourt Brace Jovanovich, 1966), pp. 338, 346.

22. Walter G. Moss, "Aging in Humanistic Perspective," in *Humanistic Perspectives on Aging*, Walter G. Moss, ed. (Ann Arbor, Mich.: The Institute of Gerontology, University of Michigan–Wayne State University, 1976), p. 6.

23. Olga Knopf, M.D., *Successful Aging* (New York: The Viking Press, 1975), p. 31.

24. Geri Berg and Sally Gadow, "Toward More Human Meanings of Aging: Ideals and Images from Philosophy and Art," in *Aging and the Elderly: Humanistic Perspectives in Gerontology*, Stuart F. Spicker, Kathleen M. Woodward, and David D. Van Tassel, eds. (New Jersey: Humanities Press, Inc., 1978), pp. 84–85. Hereafter, all references to this article will be cited in the text by page number.

25. This subject has been named as a central concern of a new national Academy of Independent Scholars, for which a planning conference was held in 1979. See "Senior Scholars Unite," *Science*, May 11, 1979, 204(4393):596.

26. Harvey C. Lehman, *Age and Achievement* (Princeton, N.J.: Princeton University Press, 1953). Alex Comfort defines creativity as "an attribute officially scheduled, if we may use the expression, to decline with age since the work of writers such as the psychologist H. C. Lehman." Alex Comfort, *A Good Age* (New York: Crown Publishers, Inc., 1976), p. 55.

27. Lehman, *Age and Achievement*, p. 36. Hereafter, reference to this book will be cited in the text by page number.

28. See James E. Birren and Vivian Clayton, "History of Gerontology," in *Aging: Scientific Perspectives and Social Issues*, Diana S. Woodruff and James E. Birren, eds. (New York: D. Van Nostrand Co., 1975), p. 18. Beauvoir writes, "Lehman's statistical method is utterly erroneous when it is applied to art and literature. In science it is easier to evaluate the number and value of the discoveries." Simone de Beauvoir, *The Coming of Age*, trans. Patrick O'Brian (New York: Warner Paperback Library, 1973), p. 575n.

29. John A. B. McLeish, *The Ulyssean Adult: Creativity in the Middle and Later Years* (Toronto: McGraw-Hill Ryerson Ltd., 1976), pp. 27–28.

30. Ibid., p. 179. It is interesting that Lehman himself, in marshaling "evidence" in support of his thesis, acknowledges that the nature of creativity resists precise definition. See Lehman, *Age and Achievement*, pp. 119–20. Hereafter, reference to McLeish's *The Ulyssean Adult* will be cited in the text by page number.

31. Ibid., p. 13. McLeish writes of "three envoys" from "the country of the aging," those who have lived lives of Total Expectedness, those who are aware of chances missed, and a third group, which includes many successful adults in search of new worlds to conquer, who are pessimistic about what older people can hope to achieve. The fourth protagonist, the "Ulyssean Adult," may be a man or woman who embarks upon new creative enterprises in later life (Ulyssean One) or the older person who continues to be creative or productive into late life, Ulyssean Two. Ibid., pp. 8–31.

32. Beauvoir, *The Coming of Age*, p. 469. Hereafter, reference to this book will be cited in the text by page number.

33. Louise Nevelson, *Dawns + Dusks—taped conversations with Diana MacKown* (New York: Charles Scribner's Sons, 1976), p. 3.

34. Kenneth Koch, *I Never Told Anybody: Teaching Poetry Writing in a Nursing Home* (New York: Vintage Books, 1978), p. 6. Hereafter, all references to this book will be cited in the text by page number.

35. Welthy Honsinger Fisher, *To Light a Candle* (New York: McGraw-Hill Book Co., Inc., 1962), p. 4.

36. A "primitive" painter is an artist who has not had professional training. Because Grandma Moses's technical ability progressed as she worked, and because her gifts as a painter continued to develop, her artistic achievement has been said to far outrank that of the "primitive." Otto Kallir, *Grandma Moses* (New York: Harry N. Abrams, Inc., 1973), p. 225.

37. Grandma Moses, quoted in ibid., p. 269. From conversations with the artist, and even more from her letters, Kallir "found, to my delight, that her ability to express herself was not limited to painting. She had a most vivid and personal style, as well as a spelling all her own" (101). Hereafter, all references to *Grandma Moses* will be cited in the text by page number.

38. The artist's father, who painted also, would get white paper for her and for her brothers for a penny a sheet. Once, he told his daughter he had a dream foreshadowing her fame (270).

39. Leslie Bennetts, "Louise Nevelson: Homecoming in Triumph," *New York Times*, July 16, 1979, p. D8. In keeping with her creative transformation of "found objects," the townspeople donated a growing pile of pieces of wood in every shape that the sculptor will transform into art.

40. Louise Nevelson, *Dawns + Dusks*, p. 1. Hereafter, all references to this book will be cited in the text by page number.

41. Isadora Duncan, *My Life* (New York: Boni and Liveright, Inc., 1927, 1955), p. 344.

42. Margaretta Mitchell, Introduction, Imogen Cunningham, *After Ninety* (Seattle, Wash.: University of Washington Press, 1977), p. 15. Hereafter, all references to this book will be cited in the text by page number.

43. Mary Lynn Kotz, "Georgia O'Keeffe at 90: A Day With Georgia O'Keeffe," *Art News* (December 1977) 76(10):37. Hereafter, all references to this article will be cited in the text by page number.

44. Simone de Beauvoir, *The Coming of Age*, pp. 674, 733.

45. Mary Lynn Kotz, "Georgia O'Keeffe at 90," p. 40. Hereafter, all references to this article will be cited in the text by page number.

46. Erich Neumann, "Art and Time," *Art and the Creative Unconscious*, p. 128.

47. Luree Miller, *Late Bloom*, p. 114.

48. Margaret Sanger, *Margaret Sanger: An Autobiography* (New York: W. W. Norton and Co., 1938), p. 129.

49. Carey Winfrey, "At 81, a Blind Teacher Gives a Lesson in Determination," *New York Times*, December 15, 1979, p. 20.

50. Patricia Cooper and Norma Bradley Buferd, *The Quilters: Women and Domestic Art, An Oral History* (Garden City, N.Y.: Anchor Press/Doubleday, 1978), p. 17. Hereafter, all references to this book will be cited in the text by page number.

51. Helena Znaniecki Lopata, *Occupation: Housewife* (New York: Oxford University Press, 1971), p. 362.

52. Juanita Kreps, *Sex in the Marketplace: American Women at Work* (Baltimore: The Johns Hopkins University Press, 1971), p. 74.

53. Phyllis Lehmann, "The Aging and the Arts," *The Cultural Post* (July/August 1977) 12: 1. Obstacles to participation in arts programs on the part of older people include difficulties in obtaining transportation, fear of going out at night, the "hidden elevator syndrome"—an absence of signs indicating that those with physical impairments can be accommodated in the building— and the notion that older people are unable to understand or take part in arts programs. Jacqueline Sunderland challenges this: "Who has the right to say when human potential ends?" she asks. "I don't know if a 60-year-old can become a great painter at 80, but who is to say he can't?" Ibid., p. 4. Hereafter, reference to this article will be cited in the text by page number.

54. Hall, *Senescence*, p. 30. Hereafter, reference to this book will be cited in the text by page number.

55. As quoted in Benedict Nightingale, "After Making Nine Films Together, Hepburn Can Practically Direct Cukor," *New York Times,* January 28, 1979, Section 2, p. 29.

56. Abraham Maslow, *Motivation and Personality* (New York: Harper and Row, 1970).

57. Marc Kaminsky, *What's Inside You It Shines Out of You* (New York: Horizon Press, 1974).

58. Florence E. Vickery, Preface, *Old and Growing: Conversations, Letters, Observations, and Reflections on Growing Old* (Springfield, Ill.: Charles C. Thomas, 1978), p. xii.

59. Agnes de Mille, *Dance to the Piper* (Boston: Little, Brown and Co., 1952), p. 335.

8

Self-Portraits of the Artist as an Older Woman

> Now, who is to know when somebody has a breakthrough? Or who is to know who is great? There are some people that maybe we are not recognizing, working quietly somewhere, who don't really want, subconsciously, the responsibility of a public life.
>
> —LOUISE NEVELSON,
> *Dawns + Dusks—taped conversations with Diana MacKown*

During the spring and early summer of 1979, each of these nine artists talked with me individually about the meaning of creativity in the life of an older woman artist. The self-portraits in this chapter are drawn from the transcripts of these tape-recorded sessions. It was not difficult for me to find older women artists to interview about aging and creativity. I have been a lover of the arts all my life, a creative writer since childhood, and a silent observer of the interworkings of creativity and aging for many years. I was familiar with the work of each of these artists through their exhibits or performances or publications. I knew six of the nine personally, and it was they who introduced me to the other three when I wanted to know the artist who created the works I saw or heard or read, works that moved me very deeply.

I was searching for very particular artists, for women past 40 (and the older the better) who had been dedicated since they were very young to the dance or to music or to painting or photography or literature. I wanted to talk with women who continue to struggle, to create, to learn, and to grow in the face of whatever challenges life throws down before them, in the face of whatever suffering or losses. At the same time, I wanted to talk with women artists who care very much about what is happening in their communities, in society, and in the world. Nor was even this enough. I wanted to interview older women who would speak frankly about their age and about what growing older means to them. All these women gave of themselves willingly in this adventure, the six I knew and the three I came to know, the three I had known before only through their art.

We had little to guide us in our colloquies. Excellent works have been published on feminism, on women's work histories, on the meaning of race or ethnicity or religion in women's lives, on women's loves, on mothering. But the subjects of women in the arts and women's aging have not been taken up together and gathered into a single work on creativity or in gerontology. Yet they are one subject, a vital subject. For in what way do we human beings resemble the divine more than in our creativity? And what more fateful difference is there between the human and the divine than our mortality? We had only one small beacon to light our way. We knew that a creative woman is not fulfilled either by giving birth to human beings or by creating art. She is not fulfilled because there *is* no such thing as fulfillment. There is only the struggle. Only and always the struggle. And the struggle to gain a perspective on one's life, that, too, is unceasing. None of us comes into possession of it for once and always, so that it can be put in a cache for safekeeping, like the philosopher's stone. We gain this perspective only to lose it again.

I asked each of these women to give herself a make-believe name by which I might address her during the interview. The point of this little game was that they might in this way achieve some distance from themselves, so they could see their lives as they had lived them thus far. Whether or not they would keep this name on the final transcript was their decision to make.

Over the course of a year of reading, I had composed an interview question guide. I did not follow it strictly. Each woman had her own way of seeing, and each had something of her own to say about creativity and about growing older, and this I respect above all else. We talked about freedom, and about caring about the lives of others. We talked about our mortality, our little vanities, what it was we want to leave the world—and I asked each of them what she would take away from this earth, if she could. We talked about Castillejo's "autumnal ripening," Hall's "Indian summer," Bogan's "dreadful milestone," Glasgow's "visitations." Some of my questions were probably outrageous. I am a Celt by half, and there is a strong mystical streak in my nature. They put up with this, and I am grateful. We talked about death, but more often, by far, about life and love and art. Sometimes we laughed helplessly. Sometimes we were very grave. Sometimes we even felt we were coming close to Wisdom.

These are very private women. While that is what I wanted in subjects for these interviews (famous women artists have more opportunities than these women here may ever be given to talk about these matters for publication), I want to thank them here for their generosity in giving of themselves in this way. And I want to thank them, too, for refraining from rewriting their transcripts. If interviews are an art form—and I am coming to think the best of them may be—then these are forms of oral literature. In every person's talk there are irruptions of moral character and insight, intimations of a most individual magic. The voice of each woman comes through, expressing her own demiurge and her own moral attitude in a way that is uniquely her own.

Each of these is intended as a gift to young people everywhere. I salute each giver in respect, admiration, gratitude—and affection.

Gail *(Gloria Greenberg/Gloria Greenberg Bressler)(Forties)*

I don't think I've ever gone through a period in my life when I didn't know that I was a painter. Even when I'm not painting, the feeling of myself as being a painter, *having been* a painter, tides me over very rough times so that I can know I will eventually be in my studio and be painting. Meanwhile, I make images in my mind. Those images are so much a habit with me that at times I lose track of the reality of my life, and go into fantasies and *tremendous* reveries. This is happening more so now as I mature.

My painting began very early. I must have been 6 or 7 when I knew that this was what I was going to do. My mother used to give me paper bags to draw on. We didn't have very much money. As a child right after the Depression, this is what I had to draw on. I was *delighted* by the brown paper bags and by being able to paint or draw on them with any materials that I could find. My writing definitely developed later. I didn't feel myself as a poet until I was 12 or 13. I want the writing to happen naturally. It has given me much enjoyment to be able to take a blank piece of paper and just write a poem . . . however it forms itself. This kind of freedom is so necessary in my life. Since I was trained in art school and developing in a gradual but very structured way in the painting aspect, I would like to keep the writing free. Sometimes I wonder about that— whether I should have any additional formal training in writing, or let it go.

The materials I use and the experiences I have had will make the picture come true or the poem come out. There's a way that I work which is very hard to define—I let it happen. When I let myself go, the beauties that happen on the canvas or the piece of paper are what I'm truly interested in. People who are too concerned about not making mistakes can miss a lot of the joy in art. Those very mistakes can be used—in life as well as in art. I don't believe in freedom. I believe in a *feeling* of freedom. There's a great difference. I don't think human beings are free. But I think that one can *capture* that feeling of freedom and *do* something with it. You can *share* that with someone. Another person can feel free because of your work.

I feel there is a kind of pregnancy situation in each painting I make. There's a conception and there's a birth. And with each piece of art I do, I get that pregnant feeling. And there's a marvelous kind of release also. In making the art, there was a magic that released me and made me feel much more whole.

Many years ago, I dreamed a painting that I actually was able to put forward the next day. And the transformation there—it's very difficult to be *positive* about this—but I knew *exactly* the colors to use; I knew what materials to gather together. And I knew how it would turn out. I was so *sure* of myself in my dream. I'll never forget the painting. It meant so much to me to know that there is a part of me, possibly the unconscious, which had *invested* itself in painting. So there was less of a division there. Because I knew I was all together then, at that point, in my dreams and in waking. Yes, I felt compelled to express that dream. I do feel driven sometimes by ideas I have in my head. I know now from experience to give them a chance to grow without wanting them to be a certain way. I have made such good use of the accidents that happen along the way. I revel in that. I *love* the accidents along the way. And to be able to use those, to make it more beautiful.

Suffering is part of life. I don't think any of us can get away without it. And if it's part of life, it's going to be part of my creation. It's how you cope with it, and how you take it. I think art is *all* transformation. You transform your suffering and your pleasure into something else. And that's the joy of it, that's the beauty of it. I used to pity people because they couldn't make art and transform themselves and get that lovely, joyous feeling. But I think they transform in different ways. Just in getting from one day to the next, one has to transform oneself. And most people just to get to work have to go through a transformation from sleep to getting up to go to work. This is a daily thing. I think it's inherent in a human being, artist or nonartist. I don't like to put the artist into a separate class. We have been put into a class by ourselves by society. And I think the artist in people has to come *out*. In most people there may *be* an artist. I think if people were sensitive to it in their young children, that more of us would be artists.

The alone time I need for the painting or writing is such a necessary part of my life. Being alone is what gives me the direction in my work. However, I do have a need for the work to be shown, and more for it to be seen. I get just as much feedback by people coming into my studio and seeing my work and recognizing something in it as I do by exhibiting it. My feeling for publishing and exhibiting has been there since I was a child. Even in public school, without the knowledge that someone was going to look at it—and I still feel that way today—I would find my art barren. It's *not* enough for me to paint and to look at it and keep looking at it. It's enough for me to write poems and just read them myself. However, there's something marvelous about publishing. I've had several things published, and there's a *thrill* that I find in the poem being seen on paper, and being printed. I think that exhibitionist part of me exists in both areas. I *do* want people to understand what I'm saying. I *do* want the message to come across to someone else. I feel like sharing it. I feel that the work is *transformed* by someone looking at it or reading it. There's a transformation in art through the other person observing it. When I read, I feel that I have transformed the poem or the painting I've seen. I must respond in my own personal way. I think that this happens to be true of everyone. I don't believe in closeting my art.

I do have a fear sometimes that my art, my actual presentations on this earth, won't be taken care of. And I become very gratified if any piece of mine is protected in somebody's home. That it will live after me. I get great enjoyment from having one of my pieces at Kennedy Airport for all to see, from knowing it's there for the time being. I know that nothing is forever. Even so, the artist strives to make her work last for a longer time than *she* can last. There's only so much space that we human beings can *take* on this earth, and there's only so much space that my studio *has*, to hold my works.

I began having recognition very young. I think this kept me going as an artist. I know people who haven't had recognition or who haven't allowed themselves to recognize the recognition. And they gave up. I know recognition has goaded me on and I know it will in the future. But it's not enough for me. I need to define myself, as well. My mother recognizing my talent was very important. My mother was someone I could hold up my work to and show it to. My teachers were that way also. The artistic part of my life was always accepted. And acceptance has always been inherent in my strivings. Because as a middle child, I didn't know whether to look up or to look down, whether to look back or to look forward. What happens is, you have to know yourself. Otherwise you can very easily attach yourself to, or identify yourself with, your older sibling or your younger sibling. And it can make you very upset and very crazy. I did have to know myself very early on, in order just to survive in that kind of relationship.

It's important to me to sign all my art works now as Gloria Greenberg. Yes, you *do* have to lay yourself open to the accusation of being selfish and self-centered. But you have to come to the understanding that selfishness and self-centeredness are not bad things to have. For women who might be reading this, I want to say that I think you can just try to get a natural attitude about that and realize that this is a *marvelous* thing to have, and you will be much freer to make art.

What interferes most with my being as creative as much as I would like is the need to make money. It's a human necessity; I'm not against it. But it interferes with my work and my work time. The *pleasure* of time involved in making art . . . I feel it's not recognized in our society that the artist *needs* that composure. To keep on having a full-time job, as I'm doing now, does definitely interfere with my work time in art. However, I think if you are *desperately* in need of making art, you will do it anyway. What's so delightful is that I can now make a painting in less time than I *used* to. Maybe it's more experience. Or maybe it's because I let it *go* much more easily than I did before.

I'm in publishing, and I design children's books. It's a field that I enjoy. But the time I have to put into it is not enjoyable. I feel I need more time to express my *fine* art. But the children's books give me a certain amount of gratification, and I know at least that I have an object in my hands after all this work. And that this object is being transformed by other people's eyes—little children's eyes. That gives me great pleasure.

At the age of 38, I was in a terrible accident and I was in a coma for six days. This has to have been the greatest crisis of my life. I faced death for the first time. Before that, I felt I was immortal; after that, I knew I wasn't. Whether I fully recovered from that I don't know. But I know that I've been enlightened by it. I feel *great* gratitude just to be able to live in this world. Because when you know your physical vulnerability, when you can face that, the joyful moments are better than ever.

I'm beginning now to feel my age. I feel my body is not as spry as it used to be. I can't do what I used to do, physically. But mentally I feel more adept, so there's a kind of compensation there. There's just no question but that physically I can't manage the amount of work I used to do. There's something so beautiful about actually knowing it, and not trying too hard to do that.

I am moving in new directions now. I have gotten to the point now, I think, because I have faced death. The realization that I faced death, came so close to it, has given me more of a knowledge of my own physical boundaries. I find there are people who are giving me lots of advice on how the rest of my life should be. This is what I'm fighting against. This is my battle now. Because I know the limits of time now. I know that people live and people die. I know that my life isn't going to be forever. And I would like to start making the best of it right now.

I married very young. And I married within the bounds of how a "regular" girl should do things. And I lived that way for part of my life. At this point, I can be more *free* about that. And I don't think that's a *bad* way of doing that, I'm not saying it is. But I'm just positive that my daughter isn't going along in that direction. And I don't think it's necessary for all people to follow a pattern. At this point, I'm trying to get myself out of any patterns that other people make for me. It's a very difficult way of being. When you're a responsible wife and mother for so many years, to kind of break out and . . . it's not that you're not responsible anymore, but that you are responsible mostly to yourself and to the people who are near you.

Being able to raise two children in a crowded situation, economically not very secure, I have at times had to work under tremendous difficulty. And because I *had* to, I've used the people in my life. Even people who have interfered, or who are interfering now in my life—I feel that I use them for my art. And I have to say that anger is a very great part of all my work. Certainly, as a painter, as a poet, and as a woman, I share this anger with a lot of my sisters. And I know that if I'm going to leave the anger out, I'm going to leave out a very great part of myself.

My children were so much a part of my life. In turn, I was so much a part of *theirs,* that the separation between my two children and me as they're growing away from me is a very, very hard part of my life. I want so much for it to happen. Yet I still want to be their mother, I want to claim myself as their mother. Yet I want them to be full people without me. I think this struggle goes on forever. I don't know if one really separates from one's children. I'm learning this.

I think I married younger than I needed to. I would have liked to have found myself in other areas earlier on, and then given myself a chance. But I *never* would have been content without a marriage and children. That was a part of me ever since I started developing. I'm very happy I had this great adventure of having a husband and children. I don't regret that at all. I do sense now that I'm giving myself a chance to be a young person *now*, a chance to do some things I didn't do during that period that I thought were lost to me.

I don't think the nurturing part of my life is over. But seeing my children grow has given me a feeling that I've already done that. And at this point—it's hard to describe, but I am nurturing myself. I feel that I have to be my own mother now, in a sense. It's a very experimental point in my life. I'm frightened a lot of the time. I know that I am going through a crisis by being experimental in *many,* many aspects of my life. I think I'm experimental with my own children. I'm just at the point now where I've started to let *them* go. It *really* means letting myself go, as well.

I feel that socially conscious people in reality may not be living their own lives. I believe in a balance. I *need* time to myself in the studio; that's when I make art. But in order to make art, I need the experience of being with people, and not necessarily artists. I'm now regaining freedom to experience people in fields that I know I wouldn't be good in. Because they give me a little bit of balance in *my* life. This is a new attitude.

I'm very fortunate to have my mother and father still living. And I'm very fortunate to have *had* a mother who was supportive of my art. I know that a lot of us can't *say* that. My father, without realizing it, helped in a way also, by encouraging me to be fearful of talent alone—I awoke to the necessity of earning a living. What happened in my family was that my mother at the age of 60 started painting. All those years, she hadn't known that she was capable of it. She had been holding back all those years. When I saw the little paintings she was making, it confirmed *myself.* I felt more assured as a painter myself because, even though on the one hand I thought, "Maybe I'm doing what she wanted to do herself," on the other hand I knew that it was such an old thing with me. And I was just so happy to see my mother start doing it at her age that at that point I felt free. Because I knew that we can break through any crises at any point in our lives, even in old age.

I think my mother had the right idea. She wanted to separate from the children. But she gave us the idea that the children were her whole life. And it makes a child extremely vulnerable to separate from the parent if she thinks that she's her whole life. Because there's a fear that the parent will fall apart. And this does happen very often. I overcame that, to a degree. I compensated for that by giving my own children the sense that I had my own work. Of course, they might have suffered from that knowledge to a degree. But the full realization of it now for them—they have both revealed to me that they appreciate very much that I have my own field. And this is a great comfort to me. It took a certain amount of growth on their part to be able to tell me that. And at times I feel much stronger because of it. I think it's very difficult for us mothers to get this across to the children. But when they see us busily at work, especially at work in art, where we need to be alone, where we need them not to be with us . . . but it's a very, very hard thing for a child to bear. Yet later on, I think they realize that it's one of those things they have had—the *ability* to be alone at times.

Some people I have known ever since early adolescence are now becoming my friends in a special way. Especially women. And I love to be with younger people. I feel like I'm a more experienced person when I'm with them, especially if I can help them in some way or if I can reveal to them how I kept on doing my art work. The young women I see now are looking to me and wondering how in *hell* they're raising their children and making art at the same time. The younger people now coming in, taking over the cooperative gallery that I started along with my former husband and some other people . . . they seem amazing to me, that they have the strength to *do* it. So I do feel like a mentor to them.

I am in a sense becoming more impersonal as I grow older. I think that kind of generosity was lost to me for a while. You become so self-absorbed in bringing up a family and just trying to feed that family and have them live. Now I'm getting out of it a bit and I'm very much involved in how *other* people are experiencing life. The only step beyond destruction is generosity of the human race. We *must* be generous to one another.

Peacefulness, or my feeling for Nature and for the ocean comes before anything. My feeling for Nature makes me feel more integrated. And it gives me ideas for my work. What would I take from the earth with me? I'd like to take all the flowers that grow. I'd love to take the ocean. I would like to know how my children are going to be. I feel very concerned about them. I want them to live and experience the pleasures that are their very own, not *my* pleasures, but their own.

The capacity to know how to keep a sense of wonder is the most important thing for an artist. It's a paradox. One has to have a child's eyes to *have* that sense of wonder. And to be able to keep that through adulthood—this is our task, to keep it with equilibrium, because we're put down at all ages for not growing up. If you can keep that sense of wonder, knowing that you're still an adult, then you're still growing. That's the trick. It takes courage. One has to keep open to what one gets. The truly gifted seem to have enormous patience. Expect what you see before you to be a pleasure each day, each minute, if possible. So that you can take that and transform it into art.

Dusty Sklar (Fifties)

You need a free head in order to be creative. If I'm anxious about family or health, if I've had a lot to drink or eat, or my physical energy is not as strong as at other times, I find that I'm not as productive. I need both a free head and a healthy body in order to be most creative, although that in itself is no guarantee of creativity.

Desire to communicate with somebody else begins with emotion. You have to feel charged up about something in order to want to look into it. Something has to arouse your passion. As to inspiration, it comes when you've *done* a lot of hard work, you have made a commitment to look into a subject. You may be bogged down. But all that energy that you've poured into the subject, not seeming to get anywhere, is a preparation for the inspiration. Yes, anger is a spur to me. If it's all-consuming, it clouds your thinking. But, for example, when the nuclear reactor developed this trouble at Three Mile Island, I felt this *rage*—absolute *rage*—and it did spur me on to want to do something, to want to talk to people. And it was the kind of anger that *could* result in an article or a book. And I think that's true of every anger that I've ever felt, that it *has* resulted in something. That's the great thing about *being* a writer—that you can take your anger and your joy and give them form.

I want to be in control, to be powerful. I don't want to manipulate people. But I want to figure out, for example, how to keep my old parents from dying any sooner than they have to. That's the kind of power I want—the power of the shaman.

I do believe the universe is governed by a force or forces, that nothing is haphazard, and I want to know. Not only *want* to know, but I *have* to know. In order to be able to say to you what the central myth of my life is, I'd have to know more. I don't know enough about what I'm doing here. My myth is the search for meaning. No, no regrets. I have a certain view of things that precludes my feeling sorry about anything. Whatever happens is the only thing that *can* happen at the moment.

From the time that I can first remember, I've always had trouble with so-called reality. I've always been attentive. I'm attending to you *now*, and there's something *unreal*—you know, isn't this odd, what we're doing? There's always that sense of the oddness of life, the awesomeness of it. Not knowing quite what to make of life. So, when you say "present reality," I feel, "Isn't it strange?"

There certainly *is* a relationship between my concern about matters in the community and society, and my writing. Very early in my life, I came under the influence of Henry George, who is not widely known now but who was an important force in American thinking in the late nineteenth century. He was a beautiful human being, and a very important writer who has made important contributions to philosophy and political economy. And that influence has shaped my life. It early put me at odds not with my community, but with the most respected citizens of our country. I've always been an iconoclast—I've sort of enjoyed that role—and as I grow older, I do want more and more to be useful. I'm not an organization person; I detest organizations. But I do have a sense of our being interlocked with one another as a community, bound together.

If being a writer is being an acute observer and being curious about everything, yes, I've been a writer since I was a child. You ask about my separate selves as a fiction and nonfiction writer. They're well coordinated, yes, in the sense that some years back, I decided not to try to harmonize the separate parts. They were there, and there was no reason for them not to be there. The struggle to make everything fit was ridiculous, and a loss of energy. The divided selves—or at least what I *saw* as the divided selves—were a desire to be playful and a desire to be scholarly. That kind of thing. At one time, this gave me a lot of trouble. I thought, Who the hell am I? Am I this impish person or am I a serious thinker? It was an embarrassment to worry about how the world would consider me if I were both—if they found me to be impish, then they wouldn't take me seriously as a thinker, you see. But I stopped worrying about that and began to enjoy that, too.

My husband has always been my patron, so I haven't had the financial struggle. Nor have I ever made any money. Money is not an issue. My husband is an ideal patron, and he asks nothing in return. There are no strings attached. I don't have to write what he wants me to write. There's actually no tension, no rivalry. Nothing but sheer support and delight. I feel very lucky. At the same time, he wasn't very great about taking on the housework when the kids were little, so that I could spend more time writing. He's not perfect.

Recognition? I have learned a lot about it since my book came out. I relived an adolescent crisis—the feeling that I was an outsider, that I was not allowed into some exclusive club. I thought I had found a way, and then a door would close. It was *maddening.* I had always seen ambition as partly a bad thing. But I wanted it anyway. Yes, it was a spur. But I bloodied my head on the desire for recognition. It brought me nothing but unhappiness. There's another spur. Part of the reason I wrote *Gods and Beasts* was that I saw something that I wanted to communicate with other people. That brought me nothing but happiness, I would say. Everything rotten in connection with the book has to do with lack of control over publishing. I had lost interest in fiction years ago, both reading it and writing it. And yet when I read great stuff today, or hear it discussed, I get that quickening of the pulse that tells me, This is the stuff of life. This is really what matters. I'm very confused on that subject. But they're not at war with each other. I feel very lucky to be able to write anything at all. And I also feel very lucky to get the little recognition that I've gotten.

Feeling free to me means not having any emotional hangups or feeling obsessive about some area of your life. It's the ability to put all of yourself into whatever it is that you want to concentrate on without getting leaks from something that's troubling you. That's grown stronger as I've grown older. I was quite neurotic until age 35. Then there was a sudden change, and I became much calmer, more able to concentrate my energies. Observing the people around me who are aging, I wouldn't say that you necessarily grow wiser or calmer as you grow older. But if it comes, calm does bring the ability to reflect on things.

Yes, I've grown more impersonal as I have grown older. My relationships are actually better, because I'm less neurotic. But I am less intensely involved with people on a personal level than I was when I was younger. I have been better able to do my *own* work as I grow older, yes. But I also feel that as I've grown older, I've become a better mother, wife, friend—for the reason that there are fewer emotional hangups. I think that solitude has a lot to do with it. Because, after all, when you're alone and enjoying that solitude, you're able to look into things in a tranquil way. The moment you stop and look into things objectively, you're going to be somewhat less personal. You can't get as caught up in a relationship or an idea if you're an observer impartially weighing all the facets of what you're looking at, in the same way that you can when you're responding passionately.

I have friends of all ages. My criterion for being drawn to people is always a certain alertness—a lively mind or some colorful personality. Yes, younger people do come to me as a guide, and I do take that role very seriously—both friend and guide.

To judge from my own life and from what I know about younger women through my daughter and her friends, and friends of mine, I think you're trying to make major decisions at *every* age of your life. I'm trying to make major decisions today. I was less conscious when I was younger. I observe this about my young friends, that they are so caught up in desires, often contradictory desires, desires that have not been made conscious, that they're not in a good *position* to make important decisions. You really do need a clear head in order to decide anything.

If our conditioning is such that we're made to feel that we're decaying at age 50, that's very much going to affect what we feel. I was determined to fight that feeling at 50, though because of certain bodily symptoms I could easily have given in to the feeling of decaying. My book came out around that time, and it was in many ways a very trying time. I've never done this sort of thing in my life—I gave myself a fiftieth birthday celebration. I invited about seventy-five friends. Everybody was shocked that I was announcing to the world that I was 50. I'm in my menopause, feeling all kinds of bodily symptoms. I can't say that I feel a *physical* ripening, but I do feel a mental and emotional ripening.

One thing I felt very strongly when I began to get hot flashes was a loathing for my body. And that really had me worried. I began to research everything that I could find on what causes hot flashes, what they really were. I talked to people. I made up my own theories. And one way or another, I got rid of them successfully. So I felt very triumphant. I felt powerful. And that's been my feeling all through my life, that there are things that are obstacles in my way. And I use my intelligence to overcome them, and then feel triumphant.

I began to collect aging models, maybe in my mid-thirties. I always prepare well in advance for a stage. And I began to see what I liked in older women. And what I liked was not vanity or preening or excess of concern about appearance—I've never liked that. At the same time, I think that we're repulsive to other people if we don't try to look as well as we can. If anything, I've spent more time on my appearance. I never cared at *all* about my appearance until menopause. Never gave it any thought at all. I certainly give it more thought now. I select clothing more carefully; I do tend to take more time, but I don't think of it *entirely* as vanity. I think of it as lifting the spirits of those around me by not looking too bad. We are all models for each other, and if we're our best selves as much of the time as we can remember to be, that's good for everybody else as well as for ourselves. Looking good is part of that, you see. But not looking excessively good; I don't want to become a clothes horse, or become so vain that it's obvious to people that I spend a lot of time preening. That's not worth the price.

Yes, I do think that women are more sensitive about a great many things for reasons that have to do with conditioning. Conditioning has made them much more responsive to what other people think and feel. If somebody in the room is in pain, I just pick it up like a radio receiver. Most men don't do this.

When I was writing fiction about that period in my life when I was young, yes, then the times when I was a young girl or in my teens seemed near to me. But the teens and childhood were very unhappy times. I think of them when I am involved with young people. Or when I see their suffering, my own remembrance of suffering as a teenager and a child becomes stronger. You ask if there is a relationship between suffering and creativity. If you can transcend suffering, yes. I've known and loved people who just suffer and are not able to make anything of that suffering. And for them it has not been good. And these may be artistic temperaments who have no outlet for their suffering.

Social class has been terribly important for my writing. I was lower class. It's given me insight and motivation. I have no *organized* religion. My family is Jewish, but I've never felt strong ties to the Jewish religion at all. I feel drawn toward many fellow Jews; I feel repelled by some fellow Jews. I don't think of this as self-hatred, no. I have an antipathy to nationalism of any kind. So that makes it hard for me to think in terms of identifying with a particular group of people, though, because of common experiences and ways of looking at things, and other people's view of us, I do have a strong feeling of identification with many Jews—those who are sensitive and intelligent or decent people, but not those who aren't. Yes, the Holocaust does bind us together, because it happened; it meant that an outside force was persecuting us and took a certain attitude toward us. I feel very strongly that the Jews have been made scapegoats for political and economic reasons as well as for psychological reasons. But whenever any people is manipulated because of a catastrophe, it irritates me. I guess the people I most admire are not parochial. I understand why many Jews do feel parochial, I *do* understand that. And it's not an area I've entirely resolved. But I think on the whole my sympathies are most with people who feel that we're all related.

I kept my ambition to be a writer private. My family is not, like many other Jewish families are, oriented toward learning or education. I didn't tell them that I wanted to write, but I was an obsessive reader when I was a kid. And this seemed unnatural to them. My father calls me "Einstein" derisively, yet proudly.

What would I like to leave the world? I want everybody to know the ideas of Henry George. Here's a *much* overlooked philosopher who's telling us why poverty, war, and other social problems exist, and what we can *do* about them. At 18, I worked with a man who taught his philosophy. That's the office where I met both him and my husband, and we both got turned on to Henry George. Yes, I do care, *very* much, about what happens to the world after we're gone. Many of our terrible problems can be solved very simply, if we only thought about them in the right way. What gets in the way is the power elite, which wants what *it* wants, to increase its domain. And it will kill us *off* if it *has* to in order to get that. We stupidly believe that we're in the hands of benevolent rulers who are looking after everything. That disturbs me most—that people are as docile as they are. I would like people to become independent thinkers. No, I don't see people as basically selfish. But I don't understand the mentality of the people who run the institutions, who build the nuclear reactors which are so dangerous to the rest of us. The only thing that tempers my pessimism is Henry George, who feels that there is another way, a way that could *work*.

You ask about character. I like what William Gass said in an interview I had with him, where we were talking about what makes some writers write for money, and others not. And he said the desire to be a good writer is the desire to be good. And I thought that was true. The desire to do anything well is the desire to be good.

Claudine (Natalie Minewski) (Fifties)

You need two lives to be an artist. Ideally, you should have a life as a person and a life as an artist. If you're a woman, that makes it even more difficult. It's a matter of upbringing. I wonder what's going to happen with the next generation. I was trained as a woman to think of myself as being of service to a man. I've been married twice, and both of my husbands have been creative. My first husband was a writer and my second husband is an artist. So I think that it's been *extremely* difficult for me to put my own art first. Because to me, art in general is so important. I felt that my first husband was a very good writer, and I wanted to do everything to further his career, both for him as my husband and for the art of literature. The marriage didn't work, and I think part of the problem was that I was too involved in his work. With that experience behind me, I try in my second marriage to involve myself more with my own creative efforts and to allow my husband as much time and freedom to do as he pleases without pressure. Being the mother of a creative child probably amounts to the same thing.

I had my first and only child when I was 39. For me, it was wonderful. It is wonderful to know yourself first, to begin on your career, to use your strength when you're young. And then you have more to give to your children. I can't advocate this for everybody, but for me it was a whole new rebirth. It made me young again. When he was very little, I was involved in *that* creative act—the creation of a child, and caring for a child, and watching this. The development of a child was such a creative experience for me that at the *time* I don't think I felt the urge to paint. But I think that experience later *on* really played a part in my creative development. Especially since I had a good start as an artist when I was younger.

Yes, I am going through a crisis right now, because everything that happens in your personal life is a part of what you have to deal with. My husband is very, very ill, and it's an experience that possibly will be a turning point in my life. He's got cancer, and he's a creative individual. Right now, I'm using my experience to help him with what may be his last big exhibit—planning his catalogue. I'm excited about his upcoming exhibit, as well as about being involved in an exhibit of my own, and about my own work. I don't know what's going to happen next. Life is a big question mark. I have no idea how this experience is going to reflect on my future or what's going to be the next thing. To me, life is nothing but continual change. The only thing you can do with life is to *live* it. You've got to cope with the changes, *work* with the changes and realize that life is change. From the very beginning of life, for everybody, there is this constant flow that changes from exaltation and happiness to despair, and back and forth again. I can't conceive of life being one way for very long. I've gone through a crisis and felt utter despair, and I've said to myself, "Look, this is life. I can commit suicide, because things are just too difficult and I can't stand it. I can commit suicide, or I can *commit life.*" Either one is a commitment. If you commit yourself to life, it's not just living it, it's committing yourself to whatever is happening and working with it.

You ask me if there's any change I would make if I lived my life over again up to now. As an artist, I would change. As a woman, a lot of times I really gave up what I wanted to do to promote the art of my husbands, particularly my first husband. I think that was a very bad mistake. I did a lot of sacrificing. I think there could have been more of my art. And I think that women who do that are not helping. They're living through the other person's art. And the sacrifice has to come out some way or another.

Definitely, older women *have* served as models for me. But older women who have really been very *strong*. And strength is probably the key to the whole thing in preserving their own work, which means preserving against odds and fighting for their own work against any interference.

I think in a way it's easier to create as I grow older. I have become much more free. When you're younger you're concerned with so many other things—the beginnings of your career, the striving, the whole sex thing is *so* involving. At least for me, it's taken its place in my life so that I don't have to be so concerned with it. The search for relationships when you're younger is *so* important—friendships, love, all of that. And it detracts from your work. I feel much more free. I care much less about competitiveness, much more about what I feel I want to do. Being older *is* more free. Problems? Oh, yes. Always. Everything can interfere. There's always a sense of guilt over what you should be doing. I think that's true of every creative artist, male or female. You need a ruthlessness, and a strength, and a *will*, if you're going to be able to focus on what you want to do.

Yes, I feel angry and upset and hurt, and *very* frustrated when others interfere with my desire to create. Because sometimes when I *do* feel like working and I can't do it because I've got other obligations, I feel terribly frustrated. And this is very destructive to the creative act, because even if I do put it off, when I do it, it will be different than if I did it when I really felt like it. I think that you always do in your life what is a priority for you at the moment. And if the priority happens to be to do your own thing, then you will have to sacrifice other things. Those are the choices that you have to make; and, really, they are your own choices. When I was younger, I didn't realize how much the choice was up to me. I made excuses that I had to do this or that. It's still hard for me to say No. And it's always more of a woman's problem. I don't know whether it's innate with women or whether it's a matter of upbringing. I think that men are much more ruthless and selfish, and that is why they've been saying all these years that men are more creative than women. Because I think that *forever* men have been more selfish about these things and put their own priorities first.

I was always drawing on paper bags or whatever material I was able to get. We didn't have much. Or I'd paint on rocks. We used to go up to the country during the summer, and since I was too shy to participate much in the social life, or not much interested in the other kids, I would spend a lot of time drawing on rocks, with flowers or things like that. I'd find materials. I think now that it was my mother who encouraged me. She never drew, never painted; she never did anything creative. But she always encouraged it in her children. I think that's what she wanted to do. She didn't have time. Now she's doing it. Now she's over 70, and since she was 65 or so she's just beginning to do her own work. My mother and I separated, physically. She's in California, I'm on the East Coast. And now that she can't *lean* on her children, and she *can't* share in our everyday life, she is *doing her own work*. And it has released her creativity, and she's enjoying doing her own thing. It's just absolutely wonderful. And, yes, I think I've felt more free to create because I haven't had the burden, really, of everyday commitment to my parents. Which doesn't mean that the love isn't there or the concern. It's the *time*. If you're concerning yourself with other people, it takes up so much time. On an everyday basis.

What I've observed of my mother has shaped my perspective *very* strongly. Because my mother is a *very* creative woman. She sacrificed *everything*. She didn't even know that she *couldn't* sacrifice. So that she *never* did any creative work. Therefore, she put it all on her children and encouraged both me and my sister to be artists. And she's always been a martyr. And it infuriates me. It's had a tremendous influence on my life. Because when I find myself being that way, I get so angry with her and so angry with myself that I react against her. It helps me to be ruthless—to a degree. I see a lot of my mother in me, and more and more as I get older. And I try very hard to avoid what I think were the mistakes that she made. Because it *hurts* me so much that she gave up so much of herself for her children. And it makes me feel *terribly* guilty. And so I try hard not to do that with my child. I think the awareness is there more in me than it was in my mother.

When I was a little girl? I do know that I was a very *good* little girl. I was very, *very* timid. As a teenager, too, I was terribly shy and terribly repressed. I *admire* the teenagers of today, how *open* they can be. Because I went back to college to get my teaching degree when I was 45, and I was with the young college students. I've changed physically very much. When I was young, my whole physical problem was that I was so skinny and so self-conscious about being thin and flat-chested. And that was such a big important thing at the time, in the 1940s and 1950s. It was devastating. Now I'm overweight! All that adolescent suffering—you realize that it was so unnecesary. As an adolescent, if you're going to be a social person, you're not going to be a creative person. So in a way, it helps. I think you have to have some kind of introversion and introspection to be creative.

What would I tell younger women artists? I would tell them all that I don't think I made a mistake in not having children young. Now, this isn't true for everybody. It's amazing the differences in people's needs and priorities. When I give advice to young people who sometimes come to me, I say, "Don't rush. There's time, time for a lot of things." When you're young, you need time to know yourself and to develop, particularly to develop as an artist. For a visual artist, it is *very* important to *travel*, and to see some of the art work of the past, in Europe and other places. You need to know the *history* of visual arts. You *cannot* get that from a book or slides. It's not only seeing the cathedrals, the museums and art work, but seeing different ways of life that's so important. You can only *know* yourself as an individual if you are in a different environment. You just are *forced* to know yourself. You're not just a part of your upbringing. It never leaves you. But I think traveling is an experience everyone should have.

I don't think I ever was afraid of growing older. I certainly would not want to go through being an adolescent again. With maturity, I have hopes that I can use my past experiences fruitfully. I like people of different ages. Some young people I know are so *old* and set in their habits and some older people I know are so *young* in their approach to life. The attitude toward life is what's important. Life is so unpredictable and so different for each person. There are all kinds of crises. Unfortunately, as you grow older there's the tendency to get ill. That can stop everything. That is tragic. Maybe the key to the whole thing is health—at any age, but especially when you're older. If you're older and you're healthy, so many of the problems are over. You can concentrate on new things. You can have a kind of rebirth and concentrate on your creativity.

Yes, I think definitely life is an ascent, not a decline for some people as they grow older. Many people in the creative field, just as probably in other fields, are so concerned with competition and comparison with others that I think it interferes with their work. I know recognition matters to a lot of creative people. But it doesn't matter to me if my work is recognized on any big level. I like it to be recognized for what it is among people who *can* recognize it. To be recognized in the art world means that you've got to be involved in business, in selling yourself and your work. *If you're going to deal in trying to achieve recognition, the whole business aspect, you have to be very hard and very insensitive.*

And how can you be a sensitive artist and create, and still deal in this whole world of business, which is what is involved in recognition? I don't see the solution to the artist's problem of needing to make money. You just have to be two different people. You really need two lives. You have to have a whole life as an artist and a whole life as a wage-earner and a mother and everything else. You really have to live two lives in one. And it's frustrating.

Needing to earn a living is extremely destructive to creativity. It's a tremendous war. I have had to be so concerned with having to earn a living. And it makes me angry and frustrated and furious and sad. That's the insoluble problem for an artist. I've been trying all my life to see some kind of solution. The only solution is if you have a patron. Like Von Gogh's brother or Cézanne's father, who gave him a stipend all his life. But there will always be problems. If you have a patron, then you have to please the patron. If the government is to take over and give artists a stipend, it will create other kinds of problems.

What would I like to leave to the world? My son is very important to me. I would say that I would leave him to the world. Art is not only a personal thing. It's the whole world of art or creativity that concerns me. You know that we named our son Titus—his middle name—for Rembrandt, because we couldn't think of a name that would be as important. So we named him after Rembrandt's son. Which is a kind of continuum I think we felt even then, both of us. And I don't know what I'm going to produce in the future. No, I can't say I regret that I haven't produced more art. There's so much junk around. Why more art? The world doesn't need more pieces of canvas that have paint on them. It needs commitment to art itself—and quality, not quantity.

To a limited degree, I do believe in wisdom. There's always more to learn. You don't achieve final wisdom. There are constant decisions that have to be made. In life, you get perspective—the place of each thing and how it relates to the other parts. It's all there, it's all a part of you, even if you don't consciously think of it or remember it. Memory cells are there, whether they're being activated or not. It just needs pinpointing, you know, pricking, getting that cell activated. How can it not be there? Your experience has got to be enriching in some way, and it comes out in your art.

I think all people—men *and* women—need to feel complete. We all need recognition and affection and love. Perhaps women are more vulnerable to any lack of love and affection, and feel incomplete if they do not succeed in the role of woman, wife-mother-mistress. Men are perhaps more vulnerable if their "work" is not recognized. But this is a generalization. Each person, man or woman, has certain needs. And they differ as much as people differ physically from each other. People's needs change as they grow older. But what everyone needs in order to create is *freedom*—freedom from emotional and physical pain—and *time* to use that freedom. Life is a complicated process of growth and change and chance. Art uses those elements to give the complicated process a form. A woman has the tendency to become so involved in the *process* of living that art can become secondary. One must make the choices every day. I don't feel I've missed very much, but there is much, much more I'd like to do in the next thirty years or so.

Norah (Darcy Gottlieb) (Fifties)

My work habits were dependent in the beginning on when I could find time for myself after teaching, raising my daughter, doing housework, shopping, cooking and so on. I was a product of the 1950s—one of the invisible women—and everything else took precedence over writing my poetry. I was not a closet writer so much as that I was writing out of the need at a given time and I had a certain sense of urgency. The creative pulsation was *extremely* strong at that time, especially. It almost seems that the busier I was, the more I was creating. So I would stay with a poem, or a poem would pester me until I could get to it. I began to create a world inside myself. There was a period of time in my life when I was *really* productive in the disciplined sense, after I stopped teaching and decided that I couldn't split myself anymore, that if I was ever going to get a book out and do the writing I wanted to do, I'd have to stop teaching because it was siphoning off my creative and physical energies. So I stopped at the age of 50 to take time for myself. Every day I would get dressed as if I were going out to work, and I would go down to a studio in a place that we rented in our apartment building, and I would work. And it was then that I not only got my book out, but I produced about fifteen short stories, several articles, did reading and research, correspondence—in a room of my own, in other words.

I love solitude, and some of the commitments that the world demands of you have to be *denied* in order to have that solitude. Of course, this means conflict. But it also means creativity. I like the quiet inside my mind when I am thinking creatively, concentrating on any kind of writing, but poetry especially, where time literally does not exist. Now that I'm older, I find that time simply does not exist when I'm writing. I go down like a scuba diver, way down deep, and that's where there's no sense of time.

Freedom is, of course, relative. This is something that means a kind of psychic space around one. I learned to work under tension or adverse conditions, however, because freedom is internalized. That's where I found my freedom—inside myself, the way Dylan Thomas speaks about "singing in one's chains"—that's part of achieving freedom. By being aware of those chains and learning to ignore them. Freedom is something that has to be worked at, and that comes like an unexpected gift out of nowhere, sometimes. It can't always be sustained. I do believe freedom comes with age. I feel freer to be quirky and say what I mean. I'm bolder in my poetry, especially in my second collection. I don't feel the restrictions that I used to feel, the restrictions which were imposed by parents, society, and even myself. I've always been a kind of rebel, breaking from the church early, marrying out of my ethnic group. I suppose there's a kind of freedom for the rebel and the isolate. I look at myself as one who's been self-isolated by choice quite a lot throughout my life. And this isolation, although it can be a painful thing, socially—gives a kind of freedom that I needed in order to be myself and do my own *thinking*. It becomes a joyful contract with life.

Whatever I did, I put everything else before myself, including my creative impulse, in my busiest years. However, I always got *to* it—I mean I just squeezed it in. In the early days of mothering, my daughter and my husband took precedence over my days and my nights. Now, of course, my daughter is married and I've learned how to say No to social commitments. It's only hard to say No to those who are close to me. I value my time so much that I have created a kind of space around me as a protective device. I'm sure my neighbors consider me a hermit. I have a very cooperative husband in this second marriage—he shares chores, understands my needs. We give each other privacy—space. But as a poet primarily, I'm not writing twenty-four hours a day. If I were working on a novel, it might be different. Poetry is capricious and comes when least expected. It comes from the inside, urges itself; it demands to be written. And when that demand comes, I listen to it and stay with it until we're both satisfied.

Knowing yourself more as you grow older comes without being sought. It's a process—a knowing and unknowing, learning and unlearning—a rhythmic pattern in the flow of life you hold to as long as you can. It links you with the rest of the world. I can see my growth in my journal writing over the past thirty years—a kind of spiritual odyssey of widening horizons, perceptions, and so on. Am I nurturing myself in my journals? It's very possible. Because my mother died when I was in college, and that's the time I began to keep a journal. I was 22, and my major role model was gone. My journals reflect a self-education in a way.

I view life as a series of stages, of moving on—like the nautilus, you know—moving out from one room to the next. And my philosophy is not to look back. All along my life, I have detached myself from something or someone when I felt ready to—like the chrysalis in nature. Naturally, you carry the repository of everything that you've accumulated along the way. All we do is add to what we already are. My feeling is that we become more of what we already are. So therefore, the child, the girl, the unmarried woman, the divorced woman, the mother—all these have been like accretions in nature, the way coral shapes itself under the sea. They're all part of me as stages. If I should stop growing, I think I would die. So I always look for growth *forward*.

I'm not driven by great passions as I once was. I feel that I've developed a sense of humor over the years. I even have a few poems that have a light touch, which pleases me. And I'm attracted to satire. There's not very much play in me. I'm afraid that I've been one of those solemn creatures all my life, taking everything very seriously. The closest I get to playfulness is in a satirical sense. I recently did a poem called "Defrocking Prufrock."

I've always been close to Nature, even in imagination. My kinship with

Nature began when I was a child in California and had firsthand knowledge of the mountains, desert, and the ocean. It has shaped my philosophy, which in turn shapes my poetry. My sense of kinship was never very highly developed in the sense of family, so maybe that's why it has gone outward more toward the natural world, to humanity at large. I have a dual kinship with humanity and with Nature. My poetry now has become more personal, and occasionally more political. I think this happens when I feel a need to comment on the world around me—the cruelty and injustices. I try to write about that. Sometimes I see the political in terms of the natural world. I'm not an activist. I have concern and anger about cruelty and injustice, but I've never been a joiner of anything. As a poet I feel a need to speak out at times. And the women's movement gave me a sense of kinship. The idea of sisterhood was something I've longed for for a long time. I wanted to be involved and *was* involved through teaching writing workshops. The movement made me aware that there was some supportiveness out there somewhere, that other women were struggling the way I was, and might even care about what I was doing.

Milestones—I like to call them "rites of passage." One milestone for me was when I won the Dylan Thomas Award, simply because somebody out there suddenly told me I was a poet. Until then, I didn't think anybody else knew but me, and then I wasn't always sure. And that was a milestone because it affected my self-image. And the inner milestones are marked off in the ripening process which comes slowly over a period of time, slowly enough for us to get used to it—the way a leaf begins to loosen from the tree.

There are any number of physical things that come just as inevitably as clockwork—like the menopause, for example, the kinds of things I used to hear my mother or grandmother or anybody older talk about. Naturally, I thought, "That will never happen to me." Suddenly the mirror, mirror on the wall does *not* say, "You are the fairest of them all." And if you've gotten to that point and are living close to your natural self—I mean, you have discovered your own personal rhythms—then it becomes a process, a kind of rhythmic pattern under the surface of things that continues until you make a kind of pact or peace with yourself. You *do* fight it at first. I was pulling out all my gray hairs when they first showed, and then I saw how futile it was. You fight it and then give in to it, fight it and give in. Until you begin to take pride in your inner development and the fact that if you've come this far, you can go farther. I feel very strongly about this. But aging is a learning to trust the mind and body as one, to read their symbiotic messages. And that signaling is just as sure as Nature in any other way signals changes. You sense them coming when you *know* your body and your mind.

I would say that the fear of death takes precedence over vanity, although they are related, aren't they? But one makes a certain peace with the idea of death, also *in advance*. The only thing I feel strongly about is, I have so much in my mind, so much I still want to write. In my files, I have so much I want to get at . . . the only terror I would have would be if I couldn't read or write.

You mention people who have destroyed some of their work in midlife. As a matter of fact, I did a whole novel and put it away in a box at least twenty years ago and was considering destroying it recently. But I was urged not to. I do believe certain early things that I did were thrown away because they were part of the learning process. Now, however, I find that I'm keeping *all* drafts of poems—dating them, too—something I hadn't been doing. And that's beginning to take up a lot of space. I almost did put something down an incinerator once, but I pulled it back. Because it was too much a part of me. And I didn't want to destroy that self. I wanted to keep it intact.

I've had young women, when I was a high-school teacher, look up to me—very much so. Sometimes as a mother substitute, I'm afraid. But at other times, I did inspire them to go into writing and literature. More recently, both younger and older women in my women's classes have, I feel, been inspired by me. They've written me letters of praise. So in that sense, I guess I've been a kind of role model. I enjoy being around people of all ages, but I must say I do feel very comfortable with women ten to fifteen years younger. I've heard that the older you get, the more you are aware of that young self inside. You're *you* inside the body, the case, the violin case that encloses the music, even if it is getting gnarled like a tree. Inside, you feel in control more than you ever have. But you can also have these moments where you feel as if you're being booted aside by the younger generation coming right behind you, breathing down your neck, in your field especially. At times I feel magnanimous about this. I mean, that it's their turn now, and they should have their turn in the sun, and that I can help them by being there if they need me. At other times, I resent this because I know that I still have much to offer because of the *very* fact that I *am* older and I'm not ready to be kicked upstairs.

My memory? I have enough material stored in my *head,* as well as outside in files, for years of work. When you're an isolate, you have more opportunity to observe and record the world around you. And a way of seeing is a way of intuiting. My eyes take in more than a camera; I am sensitive to peripheral vision. At the same time, there's often a feeling that goes along with this way of seeing. I wrote a poem about my mother's death thirty-two years after she died. And that's proof of storage, if anything is. Nothing is ever lost. And there is the ripening. One has to be ready for it before it surfaces. I never go *fishing* for a poem or for an idea for a poem. It comes of its own accord. I'm beginning to pay more attention to my dreams now. They even have healing qualities which I never recognized before.

Some of the themes of my life are the search for the lost mother—a sense of abandonment; a search for a sense of wholeness; a sense of wonder. And loving life for itself alone, which has been arrived at after much pain. Does suffering make me creative? It stops the flow. Eventually, something creative *does* come out of it. But when I'm suffering in any way, I'm absolutely immobilized. It paralyzes the creative force. I think it's an overblown romantic concept to think that one has to suffer to write. One *does* get down to the lower depths that way, but I don't think that helps you to write at the *time*. You ask if joy does. That's an interesting question. *Both* ends have to be cooled off for me—the recollection-in-tranquility bit. I think that anything that puts one in touch with the deeper self is partner to the creative process. Now obviously, anything that puts you in touch with the deeper self is hardly going to be in the middle area. A poem might emerge years later out of the original raw *stuff*. But it's chaotic in the beginning. I have a partner. It's myself, The Self. I don't have a Muse as such.

Any regrets? Yes. I wish I had started sooner. Recognition? It has mattered *more* to me as I've grown older. I suppose this is natural when recognition comes late. Once you have published, it sets in motion a whole new attitude about yourself. It confirms what you've always known about yourself. And with *that*, it gives a new impetus to go forward and do even *more*. And it's that *giving* of the self—and giving to the *craft*—the *commitment* that has opened up. And you can't turn back. Once you've known an audience, you can't back away from it. So that it's traumatic if you lose ground. But you tell yourself just to go on anyway. There *is* a season for all things, and that has to do with the *work* you do. Sometimes you're either too far ahead of the times, or you're too far behind them. The ones always in step are the ones able to match the fashion, the changing fashion of the times. They can ride waves. Hustle.

What I'd like to leave the world, from a personal point of view, is what used to be called a "good reputation." I would like to linger in the minds of those I've known for myself alone. To be loved for oneself alone, regardless of what one has achieved—that's important. What I'd like to take with me when I leave? The song of birds. I think when the birds leave this place it will be a dead planet. Actually, not just the music of birds. I think music is the highest art of all. It is a universal language. Poetry should be on the verge of music.

Wisdom means learning to know yourself, first of all, and your connection to the rest of all living things. I felt *very* different when I was young. Now I've stabilized and feel more aligned with humanity. I have a sense of wholeness, of having found my place in life. I've learned to conserve my energies a lot more; I think that's wisdom. And seeing that I get more space around me—that's self-preservation wisdom. And cutting through the superfluous things and refining choices—that's wisdom. I'm more in control of my life. You're not when you're younger. You care too much about what the world thinks and says and what it makes you do, really. I'm competing with *myself* more now, dispensing with secondary sources on all sides. I'm trying to travel light. And to cultivate my own garden.

Anne Van Yorx Wentworth (Elizabeth Helfman)(Sixties)

I wanted to write ever since I was 11 years old, at which time I did a lot of writing. I wrote stories, I wrote poems. It was entirely for myself, except that I had a story published in a little magazine put out by our local department store. When I was in my teens, I had poems in the local newspaper, and I was published in the St. Nicholas League, which was a wonderful thing for young people at that time. I thought I was going to be a poet; I had no other ambition at that time. But I knew I wasn't going to be able to earn my living that way, so I was also going to be a teacher. I became a teacher; I found that being a teacher was a very creative business, and that there was very little time for writing. For twelve years I taught and really did very little writing, and had simply given up the idea until I had a chance to stop teaching and live off my husband. And when I had a child, I did not feel I could be a good teacher and bring up a child. So I decided I wanted to write for young people. This grew out of my work at the Bank Street College of Education [in New York City], where I studied writing for children under Lucy Sprague Mitchell, who was terrific. She taught me a great deal also about how to look at the natural world and how it connects with people. And so I began writing for young people. By that time, I was about 36 or 37 years old. It's very hard getting started. I was very fortunate in having good connections, which helps. Being a children's writer is a struggle, as being any kind of a writer is. I have never made much money. But I was fortunate in being able to do the kind of writing I really wanted to do. I've had eighteen books published. Not all of them are in print, as happens.

Oh, there is a very direct connection between Nature and my writing. Because I never felt I could sit down and write what is *wanted* by somebody else. I had to write what interested me, in a way that would interest young people, I hope. I would write about the way I felt about the natural world, and then the way people had felt about it in early times and all through history up until now.

On the one hand, being a nurturing kind of person contributes to writing in the sense of understanding the feeling of wanting to nurture the earth and all things that grow, including people. On the other hand, in practical everyday life, there's also a great deal of conflict. Because so much time is taken up by the necessity for being nurturing to one's family and friends. I think because of this conflict, I perhaps have fewer friends than some people, but the few have been very important to me. I always felt there *should* be more solitude as one grows older. I always looked forward to getting older, when I would have more time for solitude. And one of my great conflicts is that it has not happened so far, to any great extent. I get a lot of solitude when I go off by myself. But otherwise, it hasn't been too easy to get it.

I think my horizons have broadened lately. I was a very naïve child, and very unsophisticated until I was about 25, when I began to get some understanding of social problems and became very concerned about them. I always felt I had to resist the pleas of various people to spend a lot of time working on social problems because if I did that, I would have no time for my creative life at all. So the things I have done have been mostly simply writing letters to congressmen and that sort of thing, which some of my friends sneer at as being quite insufficient. But it's all I can do, and I think it helps.

I feel that much of my writing is very religious. I was brought up in my mother's church, which was Congregational, but with my father's ideas, and he was a Unitarian. I was always a very religious person. But I stopped being actively involved with religion in my twenties, when I was moving from place to place on different jobs. I would go to the Episcopal Church sometimes, because I liked the ritual. But then I married my husband, who was Jewish. Religion was never a problem with us. We both felt pretty much the same about it. We joined the Ethical Culture Society, which was kind of a compromise, and felt very happy with it. But I always felt something lacking there; it's a very intellectual religion. So when I moved here, I joined the Quakers, whom I had been interested in for many years, primarily because they believe in a direct relationship with God, which I feel is very important.

My girlhood and adolescence have been getting nearer as I grow older. That surprises me a little. I have the impression that some people really do pretty much forget what it's like to be a child. And I have not forgotten that. I feel this should be helpful in my writing for children, especially if I do fiction, which I now want to do. I feel very intimately involved with myself as I was when I was a child. It's partly because I suffered a great deal. I was a peculiar, very shy child who suffered a great deal in human contacts and from being pestered by other children, who, of course, could be very cruel.

Even if a person's mind is confused, the character remains? Oh, I think this is true. You know, when I think of my mother, who lived to be 87, she got so her mind was very confused. But she was definitely herself. She went on complaining about the same things and worrying about the same things. When she was actually dying, she certainly remembered me and was glad that I was there.

As I look in the mirror, I feel a great blow to my vanity. I wasn't beautiful, but I was a nice-looking young person. And I certainly don't think I am now. I hate to have my picture taken. I suppose I identify more with my mother, and in that sense I think of myself in terms of what happened to her. I do feel that I understand certain things about her better because I am now getting old as she did. My mother had many hard things to cope with. I don't think one can *blame* her. She was mentally ill some of the time, and that wasn't her fault. How did she feel about my writing? Oh, she was very pleased. I don't think she ever *read* it very carefully, but she was pleased. Oh, yes, she did have literary ambitions. She was a very frustrated woman. She would have made a very good writer. She didn't become one because, in the first place, her family thwarted her desires for education. They didn't think she needed to go beyond the young ladies' school in town. She would have liked to be a teacher. And then she had a lot of physical problems, many of them psychosomatic, and some mental problems. She had a family to bring up, and she just didn't ever get to writing. But she would *say* poems to me—very poetic things. And the diary she left after my brother died was very touching. So I felt she *could* have been a writer. There are a lot of people around who could have been writers and for some reason weren't. Who do I feel very strongly in my life who is no longer there? Several people, I suppose. My brother, especially, who died when he was 29, was very close to me and very understanding, and helped me a great deal.

I feel it's important to have friends my own age, and we have certain things in common, especially where I live now, where we feel we're all in the same boat and we *help* each other. But it's very important to me to have friends who are younger, too. Very seldom do I feel younger women looking to me for guidance, and I would welcome that. This *did* happen in the class I took, a journal-writing class, where one of the young women became very attached to me and really looked up to me. I *liked* this very much. Yes, perhaps she was a surrogate daughter. I would have liked to have a daughter. And she was just the age that she might have been my daughter. Also, she had a problem that interested me particularly, in that she had a retarded child. I was interested in handicapped children through my work with Blissymbols, which are used for communication with children who can't talk.

Oh, yes, when I was young, I did look up to older women for guidance. I had a high-school history teacher who was a very close friend of mine and a tremendous influence on my life. The main thing was that she *cared* so much about young people. She loved to *do* things with young people, and I was one of them. I wrote to her just a couple of years ago to tell her how much I still appreciated this. And she was still alive. I got a note from her.

There is a ripening that is *possible* for an older person, but I don't think it always *happens*. Oh, I would say it would happen around the age of 65 to 70, and even sometimes older. I feel that the creative person has a greater opportunity to experience this because creative work can be done at home on your own time. If you've had a job and you're retired, you can still be creative, so there is a real opportunity for a ripening. I think if you don't have the desire and courage to know yourself, you will not *have* this. And some people also don't have enough imagination to experience this at all.

I think my mind is just fine. I have no worries about it at all. It's as keen as it *ever* was. And it's doing very good things for me. My body isn't that good, but my mind is. My mind is working better in some ways as I grow older. And my understanding is better, my feeling for people is much better because I feel more at home with myself. I feel more in touch with, so help me, the universe or God or whatever you want to call it. And this makes me much more able to relate to other people. My mind is not as keen in the sense of being able to cope with detailed material. I can still do it; it takes longer, that's all. But as a result, I think I am going to stop doing the informational books anyhow, because it's a lot of work and very little pay. I just want to do the kind of writing that *I* want to do because I want to do it. While I hope it will be published, I'm going to do it primarily for myself. No, economic worries don't trouble me. Except for the fact that if I had more money, I would have domestic help, and perhaps I could have had more baby-sitters when I had a young child. I have not had to depend on my writing for a living, though I would live better if I made more money.

I think my dreams have had a lot to do, at least indirectly, with the writing I have done that has to do with mythology and also anthropology. I try to interpret them. I've been doing this only since I was about 25, when I had a Jungian analysis. Besides dreams, though, I have a very active life in what is called "active imagination," which is, I suppose, a form of waking dreaming. Although it's guided somewhat by consciousness, it's not the same as fantasy. And *this* I write down. I have a continuous tale of my own mythology, you might call it, which is ongoing.

In some ways, I would like to write my own autobiography. But I guess I don't feel quite ready to put it into patterns. I do feel that as you grow older it is possible to see the whole of life as a growing pattern all the way through. You can't do that at age 40 in as real a way. Also, I feel as I grow older a much more real feeling for eternity. I don't know how else to put it. Eternity and the universe—I feel that I'm a part of it. I don't believe in immortality, of course, in terms of one's body. But I feel there is something. And that's an outgrowth of this belief in myself and everyone as a part of the universe. Reincarnation? Well, I think this is a possibility. I have a friend who believes in it *firmly* and feels much better about her physical infirmities because in her next reincarnation she probably won't have them. I don't feel that strongly about it; maybe it's true. What would I take away with me from this earth if I could? First of all, the *people* who mean most to me. Then perhaps one piece of earth in the woods, a particular rock in a particular woods where I like to sit. What would I like to leave this world? I have written things that I *hoped* would stay around, and that people would read. Whether this will happen, I don't know.

I had always thought that people who were older remember a lot of things because they have a lot of time to sit and remember, and I don't have time to sit and do any such thing. Yet I find that I *am* remembering a great many things from my past that I hadn't thought of. One reason, of course, is that I had gotten out my diaries from my college years and gone over them and given them to the college historian. I think what I remember the most are the relationships with people. I enjoy remembering these things; they're all a part of what became me. That's true in a way, that the past is variable. You can't plan what you will remember and what you will forget. You *may* remember things that you *wish* you would forget. Lately, I find myself remembering some terrible mistakes that I have made that I have no reason whatsoever to think of again because the results were not disastrous. Yet these things keep coming up and I feel badly about them. I was brought up with a lot of guilt. I don't think it's fair when you're a grown-up to blame what you do on your *parents* anymore. But I *was* brought up in a very strict *way*. You know, I was made to feel a lot of guilt about small misdoings, and I don't think I ever got over that. Yes, I'm beginning to have a life review. I haven't done much of it yet. Perhaps I'm not quite ready. I'm getting there, but not yet.

Absolutely, I *do* have something to say that I didn't when I was younger. And I'm sure it's to a large extent my own fault that I don't sit down and do it, except that I have to finish the book I'm on now first, anyhow. I'm not lazy, no. I've got to arrange my life better so I'll get these things done. That means arranging things with my family.

I have been writing poetry again recently. I think many things are, as Lucy Mitchell used to say, *more so* as you grow older. And Scott-Maxwell said that she found she felt many things much more strongly when she was older. I find that true, too. And some things that it seemed I could tolerate when I was younger—instead of growing *more* easy to tolerate, become less easy to stand.

I really have a great ambition to do more writing and different kinds of writing, and even writing for adults about what it feels like to be a woman growing older who has no great axe to grind with society. No, I'm not running out of things to write. What I'm running out of is *time*. Oh, I'm not amused by all my unpublished work, either. I have a novel I wrote, and I got it out the other day and I thought some of it was awfully *good*. But few people have ever read it. And so I thought maybe I'd take some of it and make short stories. I think recognition matters *less* as one grows older. Recognition by the few people who *matter* means perhaps more. But recognition by the world as a whole matters less. Publication constitutes a kind of recognition. But, as you say, it can be very limited. I think publication matters just as much as *ever*. Recognition for the publication matters *less*.

You ask about wisdom. I feel I'm becoming very much wiser. I do want to share this. I've written up some of my "active imagination," and I want to share this. Some people I know feel that this is very personal and not to be shared. However, some of my "active imagination" is going to be published in a Quaker publication called *Inward Light,* and I'm pleased about this. I *want* to share my inner life in a way that I seldom get a chance to. This to me is wisdom. In a way, you do what you're destined to do *if* you allow yourself to. Of course, you can cut it off and *not* do that. But if you allow yourself to, then that's the most important thing you can do. Even if it remains unshared. But it's better if it can be shared.

Stella (Eda Fagon) (Seventies)

My musical interest began, I think, when I was born. I had a father who was very musical, and when I was an infant he was first beginning to study and practice the piano. And I just naturally went to the piano and played after him. I didn't believe members of my family when they told me how talented I was, because I thought they were being prejudiced. But other friends of the family said that when I was a tot, when I could just reach the keyboard, I played harmonies. And played whatever I could hear. My father sang with me and played piano with me, and I began to study formally when I was about 9 years old. My father and mother took me to the opera when I was very little, aged 3 or 4, and to concerts. My parents bought a Victrola and I heard great music performed by great musicians. I guess I was most influenced by my father, because he shared with me all of his love of music. And in my whole lifetime, it seems that all of my musical experiences were really the fulfillment of my father's dreams and wishes.

I was very much interested in songs. When I was 11 years old, I was very sick and in the hospital for almost a year. When I had my highest temperatures, my father would come to the hospital and sing the Mendelssohn duets with me. It took me several years to recuperate from this terrible thing. But I practiced, and was a very successful contestant at the musical conservatory where I studied. I won scholarships, and all the medals, despite the fact that every time I practiced I had such severe pains in my back. I would die of pain. They were adhesions from back surgery. But I would practice and perform.

When I was in high school I got to taste the joys of complex choral singing. I had a fantastic glee-club teacher in high school who taught the kind of *a cappella* music that I loved. It was there that I was inspired to think of how I wished I could write such music myself. When I was in college I began writing very fiercely—solo songs and choral things. I never was inspired to write solely for the piano, even though I was a good pianist. I wrote songs and choral music because I loved poetry. It was the poetry that inspired me. Ever since I was a little girl, I went to the library and took home armfuls of vocal literature and opera scores. I read every piece of music in the library. And it filled me. I was not a "normal" teenager. I was fat after I had recuperated from my illness. And very insecure. And the music played a very, very necessary part in my life.

I don't know how this can be, but I think that I inherited my love for music from my father's genes. He was Russian-born, son of a very poor sexton of a synagogue. He used to run away to listen to the great choral music in the Russian churches. How I got that love I don't know. I *loved* choral music—particularly Russian choral music. And when I sang more of it in college, I was inspired to write some choral things that might have had that flavor. One of my compositions was sung by my university choir. It was a renowned choir. And I was very pleased to think that I had that chance to hear my work performed.

I think that the big overall thing in my life was the terrible part where I could not cut my umbilical cord. And the big grand thing in my life was meeting my husband. In between there were so many different kinds of music that I needed to write. Music in my life is not just composing. I am very much interested in vocal music, well-composed accompaniments and choral music, and conducting choral music. And in vocal music, I love to be an accompanist to a fine musicianly singer or instrumentalist, because I am a good accompanist and enjoy a musicianly partnership. I lived a lifetime of different kinds of music before I went into teaching. I had the experience of playing piano solos for Frank Lloyd Wright. I was an accompanist and coach for singers at the Chicago Opera Company. I accompanied two well-known opera singers; I would go to their homes every day—this was during the Depression, when I didn't have a salaried job. And I would go there every morning to work with them. And they had me around whenever they had parties. So that I accompanied any number of singers, and met any number of well-known people.

My involvement with music just continues as I grow older. I have had a variety of musical experiences that just roll and roll and roll on, like a snowball, even now in my seventies. It doesn't begin anywhere and it doesn't end anywhere. It's just something that I breathe, like air. That's the way I need to have music. Now that I am retired from teaching and have more leisure time, I can do more other activities in music than I had time to do before, because I had to earn a living. I didn't always have the time and the energy to pursue the composition end. I taught music in the high school and wrote some other choral music for the high-school chorus. But I wasn't too successful with it. My music may have been too sophisticated. Maybe if I had persevered more I'd have done a better job. My energy was too spent, after having taught all day.

I have no vanity about looking older. Maybe one reason is that people never believe that I'm as old as I am. Not that I'm a beauty—I never did have a figure, and I don't have it now. I have physical problems all the time. I've had arthritis all my life, but I suffer more now. Maybe there is a relationship between suffering and creativity. If I have terrible bursitis in my shoulder when I am conducting, I change the baton to the other arm. If I have to do some accompanying and it is difficult for me to turn the page or something, I wince and continue doing what I am doing. Maybe it's a release from pain, physical or emotional, to be able to conduct, to compose, to perform. If one has problems and one can lose oneself in doing this thing that's so necessary for one to do, it doesn't take the problem away. But it helps.

I like this idea you mention of the autumnal ripening. I think that my autumnal feeling is the happiest part of my life. I *did* have milestones in my life, dreadful milestones—the age of 30—but nothing from the vanity point of view at all. It was because I hadn't found myself or the kind of happiness that I felt I should have found by that age. When I was 50, I was a little uneasy. When I was 70, I felt, "Gee, I'm not going to get it all in, I'm not going to do everything I want to do." I sometimes have the feeling, "Gee, Time, don't run away from me yet, because I have too much that I want to do!" I was so miserable as a teenager and a young woman, that this idea of time running away from me didn't dominate me. But it bothered me when I was 30. My fear of growing older is that I won't have enough time to do all that I want to do. I get breathless sometimes with the thought of what I want to do and *must* do, and that nothing should stop me from doing.

I was a very unhappy person when I was young. I had a very neurotic mother who tried to possess me. My family and I sort of tiptoed through life a little bit as a result. I had other very unhappy experiences, although my work did not reflect these miseries. I married late in life, but very happily. I was 39 and a half. That's late. My marriage changed my life very, very much, but not my style of writing. My husband has been most encouraging, sympathetic, and cooperative. The thing that I would like most to do is to tell young people of my experiences and what I've successfully learned, and to give them encouragement and hope to carry their good ideas into the future. I taught high-school music for nearly thirty years, and I came into contact with many, many teenagers. I have been very fortunate to have this feedback. Many of my students, who came from every ethnic background, and who live around the world right now, still write to me and tell me what they remember of what they learned from me in glee club.

Yes, I did look up to some older women, teachers and concert artists, when I was young. And I know that some younger women look up to me. I think one of the reasons I feel this way about teaching, one of the many reasons, is that I have no children of my own, and have very strong maternal instincts. I felt that many of these students in my classes in high school and college were my kids. They referred to me sometimes as "Mama." I was also fortunate to have a one-to-one relationship with many high-school students, as I was an advisor in high school. I told them of my own experiences, my unhappiness in my youth, thinking that I was the only one who had to suffer through my special problems. I told many of them that they were not alone, that this, too, would pass, and that they should go on to do whatever they wanted to do even though they were suffering at the moment from various problems.

I like *all* ages. And I like my peers only if they are alive and interesting. I have a young friend who is 85. And I have an old friend who is 32. It depends on their attitudes toward life and their interests. And there are people I've met in this senior citizenship village where we live winter months, that are so alive and so alert, one never questions how old they are.

Nature? I've been a city person most of my life. And only since I retired from teaching in a big metropolis and moved to the country has it affected me personally. I have written some of my best stuff in the noisiest of environments. I don't know that the peace and quiet help me in my *writing*. But I do know I cannot live where I can't see trees or flowers, or hear bird calls.

My family brought me up to feel and appreciate my ethnic background. But when my playmates would go home to study their catechism or whatever it was, and I was puzzled because I didn't know why I wasn't doing something like that, I asked my parents what was God. And they told me God was Nature. So I was brought up with this idea to feel that all the world around me, and the people in it, were a kind of religion. I was never taught any racial prejudice or any kind of prejudice at all. I was brought up in a liberal home and taught to be aware of what was going on around me. I'm a giver. I can't analyze it. But I have donated my musical services to every kind of organization, if I felt at one with that organization. My horizons are extending themselves as I grow older. I'm as active as I can possibly be. I've worked with the community; I have been involved with everything from schools to church, in community musical endeavors. I was the musical director of the community theatre and worked with some of the college's faculty. I've worked with students with never a thought for recompense.

This idea of Ellen Glasgow's "visitations" that you mention is interesting. I haven't thought about it for a long time. I can't pin down when this started.

But I know that when I'm playing the piano, I am *suddenly* aware that I'm someplace else. I don't know *why*, when I'm in the middle of playing a Chopin étude or nocturne or whatever, and I hit a certain chord or passage and all of a sudden a very vivid scene will flash to my mind: a corner of two streets and some houses. I stop, and I say, Why? Not emotions, just scenes and places. Yes, it's visual, not auditory. Why, when I'm playing Chopin and thinking of how I'm going to interpret it, I get these flashes, I don't know. Not so much technically, because my fingers go there. But what am I playing next? And then all of a sudden—I can't account for it. It's like déjà vu.

Yes, I am constantly unhappy about my memory. I've always had a poor memory, except for music. I can't remember lists, I can't remember names or situations. I go totally blank. And I die, I'm so unhappy about it. It happens more and more. But I had this lack of memory when I was a child. And I am constantly embarrassed. But it doesn't happen with music.

No, I have never tried to publish any of my music. I think there were probably psychological reasons for my not trying to get my music published. I won a composition contest. Many people entered this contest—maybe one hundred competed. We were all doing the same lyric. And my setting of that lyric won the prize. And all the critics of the local newspapers—music critics— gave me many commendations. I was about 26. Evidently, I was so insecure that, despite the fact that I *won* the contest and got the commendations of all these music critics, and it was sung in concert by a very fine singer, I still didn't push it. For one reason—I never was aggressive. I was very insecure and I held back in a lot of things. I think if people can be aggressive, good for them. I had stupid insecurities and I didn't do more with that. For some strange reason or other, I don't care. I wanted to write what I did. I enjoyed doing it. I enjoy hearing my work performed in concert. I enjoyed singers telling me they enjoyed singing my songs, and people telling me that they enjoyed hearing them. And I just didn't care to go any further than that. I have gone to music stores and spent hours of my life going through printed material. I see stuff that's way below good musical standards. And I say to myself, My goodness, *I* can write better than that. I know—I have confidence—that one particular song is good. As a matter of fact, I didn't realize it at the time, but a noted composer made a setting for the same poem that I did. And all the people who have been singing my song say that they like it much better than his version of it. But I didn't try to get it published. I live with this.

What would I like to leave the world? I really would like—since I was a teacher, am essentially still a teacher—that whatever I sifted through from all these various unusual musical experiences that I had, would be translated into something that young people could understand and retain, appreciate and pass on. What would I like to take with me from this world? If I could, I would take my husband with one hand, and the feeling of the spiritual and physical comfort that I have in taking a warm bath in music. Wisdom? The first thing that pops into my mind right now—quick, without even thinking about it—the word *stable* comes to my mind. Someone who is stable, who has a lot of sense and who can look upon something objectively. Wisdom is thinking about something objectively, with good common sense and stability, and not too much emotion.

Jane (Jane Sherman) (Seventies)

"Artist" is too big a name for what I am. I started out as a dancer—a Denishawn dancer from 1925 to 1928, then a member of the Doris Humphrey and Charles Weidman Company from 1928 to 1929. I appeared in some Broadway shows from 1929 to 1931, and I ended up as a Rockette at Radio City [Music Hall] from 1931 to 1935. It was only after I married that I began to try to write. And I wrote and had published several children's books, stories, articles, and poems. Strangely enough, in my sixties I went back to dancing through writing. In 1976, after three years of work and many rejections by commercial publishers, I finally had my book about my tour of the Orient with the Denishawn dancers published by Wesleyan University Press. It's called *Soaring*. In 1978, I received a grant from the National Endowment for the Humanities to complete a work entitled *The Drama of Denishawn Dance*, which Wesleyan will bring out this month of May 1979. For the coming years, I'm working on the biography of Barton Mumaw. He was a distinguished American dancer who participated with Ted Shawn in the building of Jacob's Pillow and in the seven-countrywide tours of the famous Ted Shawn Men Dancers.

Purely physically, I have come to resemble my mother—since my hair has turned white. This is strange because she was a brunette, I was a blonde, and as a child, I looked like my father. My mother certainly did encourage me as a dancer. She was not part of my life when I began seriously to write. When I was a child, she sacrificed a great deal to give me dancing lessons. And she did an exceptional and courageous thing in 1925: right after I graduated from high school at age 17, she allowed me to go to the Orient with Ruth St. Denis and Ted Shawn for a year and a half tour. This was my first job and my first time such a distance away from home, although my sister and I had spent three years in boarding school as children when Mother went on the road as an opera singer. My mother was a gifted soprano. My father was an advertising man. He was not at all interested in things cultural or literary or musical. This created quite a schism between the two. I think I would have followed the conventional pattern for girls of those days—high school, marriage, children—if I had not had a mother who, perhaps out of her own frustration in her career, encouraged me. I don't mean that she was the cliché stage mother. But she gave me almost from infancy a background of constant *exposure* to music (concerts, records, her singing, my piano lessons)—to the theatre (matinees of every good play, but always at cut-rate ticket prices because we never had much money)—to dance (seeing all the great ones of the day as well as taking lessons)—to books (I began to read at 5 and have never stopped!).

If I had not had the misfortune to be a dancer when the Depression hit, and if I'd had enough guts to fight it through as some of the other young women dancers did—they took jobs running elevators, they took jobs as secretaries, in order to study dancing at night with Martha Graham or Doris Humphrey—I would have remained a dancer. I didn't have those guts. Also, I had some obligation to my family. I had to help them. So I went into Broadway choruses, and eventually joined the Rockettes—which was a dreadful, dreadful job. But it paid me $45 a week for four shows a day, seven days a week, regularly. And that was a goldmine at the time. If I would change anything now, I wish I had stayed with dance at any cost—with Martha or with Doris. And I think I would have become maybe not a great dancer, but a respectable one. And as I grew older, I would like to have taught dance to young people.

What would I like you to know as my biographer? Everything I've been telling you! My purpose in writing the dance books is mainly to leave behind a piece of accurate dance history for future generations, because the very important Denishawn era has been distorted. I hope to accomplish this, and if I do, it will make me very happy and proud. One of the things that I certainly want a biographer to include are the two or three years when I worked very, very hard for the Loyalists in Spain. That was a tremendous turning point in my thinking and in my whole attitude toward the world and toward society. Young people today don't know any more about this than they know about the Great Depression. They don't realize—and I suspect their schools do not teach them—that those three years were the Vietnam and the Watergate of our generation. The war in Spain provided for many of us our first exposure to the perfidy of the world, including, especially, the perfidy of the so-called democracies. I saw this clearly because I worked for an organization called the Exiled Writers Committee, which helped bring to this country—or any other country that would accept them—the noted antifascist writers of all nationalities who were trapped in the south of France after the defeat of the Loyalists and at the beginning of Hitler's blitzkrieg. You know, I'm becoming emotional for the first time since we've been talking.

My work is mostly nonfiction. I have been writing fiction and poetry, too, all my life, but with less success in being published. I still write poetry, but I don't write fiction anymore. The nonfiction I'm now writing is more or less a recapitulation of facts and an organization of facts. I don't see a place for the emotions in such work. In stories or poems, I certainly see that they're very important. My verse just seems to come, usually when I'm out walking. Of course, I do *work* over a poem once I have the idea.

These questions about impersonality are questions that I have never really considered. All my six children's books were assignments from publishers. And any time I have an obligation like that, I work on it until it is fulfilled. That part of me hasn't changed. I feel I'm introverted about myself but not in my work, if that's a distinction. I think there are personal and impersonal women artists, personal and impersonal male artists. As for applying the question to myself, I suppose it goes back again to the fact that I don't feel what I am producing now is *art*. It is reportage, as against fiction or poetry. I don't know quite how I could be personally involved in reportage along those lines. I don't think it's possible for anyone to be *im*personal as a dancer. The art itself is unavoidably intensely personal; after all, it's your whole physical *body* as well as your creative *mind*, as both performer and choreographer.

Of course, getting my work published does matter. Mainly for one reason— not out of vanity, not even for the money. But because the only damn reason you want to put anything down on paper is to *communicate* with other *people*. And if it isn't published, you don't communicate. Every once in a while, out of frustration, I'll stick a poem into a letter to a friend, simply to *communicate* something that I can't otherwise write or say. I care about this because I'm back into writing. For a long time, I was just doing community things, living on Cape Cod, socializing a lot. But since I had *Soaring* published, and there's been interest in other works, I've become a fire horse. I want to keep going to the fires! Yes, I think you're right, this business of communicating *is* more important to you as you grow older. I do an awful lot of letter writing, and I think that is a substitute for the nonpublication of my fiction and poetry. And I find that I write very intimate things to people that I would not speak of face to face. I've even developed some very close friendships with, believe it or not, people I have yet to meet. When I was younger, even long after I was married, I was absolutely tonguetied and shy. I never voiced my opinion anywhere. I could do good, hard work, but never verbalize, never relate to people this way. So *that* is one benefit of growing older, with considerable help from my husband. And I think this has also come from having had some success in my work. That has given me the confidence to speak out.

I think I am disciplined. But I think my being a woman affects it. For example, from morning to lunch is the best time for me to work. But I don't get *to* that until after I have planned the dinner, made the beds, done the laundry, and all the rest. Nobody has set these priorities for me, but I feel that's the way women of my generation are conditioned—although I'm far from being a good housekeeper. Fortunately, I'm blessed with a husband who does the marketing and helps with other chores.

I have no feeling about dreams at all. I do have one thing about sleep, or the verge of sleep: sometimes I find that I solve writing and other problems just before sleep, or maybe just when awakening. You ask about the importance of solitude for a dancer and a writer. I think we'd better forget dancing, because at 70 I'm not dancing anymore. When I danced, I was always a member of a group. I never graduated to becoming a creative choreographer or soloist; I always worked with others—in class, in rehearsal, on stage. I have to have solitude for writing. I enjoy it and I enjoy long walks alone with the dog for thinking. I'm not afraid of loneliness except when my husband isn't around, if you can understand that contradiction. I become irritated when I am interrupted while I am working. I hate to be interrupted by the telephone. (I hate the telephone anyway, as an intrusion on one's private moments, and for that reason I seldom call anybody unless absolutely essential.) Since I have had definite writing contracts, with definite deadlines to meet over the past years, I have become even more antisocial than my natural temperament—in the sense of giving parties, dinners, and so on.

I don't really feel as old as my years in any way except for some physical limitations. I don't *feel* this seasonal thing at all. It's all one wonderful going on and going on. The milestones are not, to my mind, in years; they are in seminal events in your life. I don't care whether I've reached year 20 or 50 or 90. But I *do* care when I first began to dance professionally; I care when I had my first book published; I care when I married. *These* are the milestones, not the years. I think one reason my husband and I don't think of years so much is because we have no growing children to measure our aging against.

I think perhaps ideally one *should* have a greater desire for self-knowledge as one grows older, but I'm not that introspective. For me, aging has become an anxiety about my own health and my husband's. It's become a nuisance in waning *physical* activity, because I like *very* much to keep active. It's become a sorrow in losing close friends. And, maybe because of my theatrical background with its emphasis on looks, it's become some hurt *vanity*—in the wrinkles and the fat and the white hair. Otherwise, as far as clothes, and trying to look young and going to the hairdresser, and all the rest of that nonsense, I really don't give a darn about how I look. I think it becomes a bad habit, as we grow older, to dwell too much in the past and to talk too much of the past. You ask about a life review. I always thought I was an introspective person, but I just don't do this. I'm too involved in what's going on today, and in what I hope will go on tomorrow.

We do have a preference for living where there are young people. For example, we have to go to Florida every winter because we can't take the winters here anymore. But we refuse to live in a ghetto of old people even down there. And we like to live in a college town up north because we want that contact with young people. We are at ease with them and they are at ease with us. There is no generation gap because we *know* they are the future and we are the past. You asked if I ever had an older woman who was a model for me. My mother, I suppose, first of all, because she was such a tremendous influence on my life. (To too great an extent, if truth be told. But that's another story.) When I was dancing, Ruth St. Denis was my idol. I admired her more as a creative dancer than as a *person*, frankly. But Doris Humphrey I admired tremendously both as a person and as a dancer.

I should say that my husband and I are not so interested in community involvement as we are in *society* involvement. All our lives we've both tried to act for what we've considered good for the most people—pro-trade union, anti-Franco, pro-FDR, pro-women's lib, against any religious or racial prejudice, against nuclear war. Caring about the world? I don't know how I could care about it more than I *did*, and *have done*. There are times when I don't have much hope for the human race, but that doesn't mean that I no longer care. I would like to see a world where there is no racial antagonism, no prejudice, no war, certainly no nuclear energy and no nuclear war, and I would like to see a world where women are truly themselves, where everybody is free to be himself or herself. I *do* care. But this caring has to be channeled. It can't be spread over every area. What would I like to take with me from this earth? My husband. If I'm permitted to take two things, I'd like to take my dog as well, silly as that may sound.

Wisdom? It's not making the same mistake twice. It's learning from experience. I'm sure somewhere in this book you will emphasize the special conditions under which *women* have to create. And how much more difficult it is to be a woman and to create. I don't mean this in any way to belittle men. I simply mean the way women have been brought up, the way we have been conditioned. And I don't see how women who have children do it. I was reading about Toni Morrison the other day—her career as editor, writer, and mother—and I think such women are the giants of the world.

You ask about moral character unfolding throughout life. Actually, this character could have more of an emotional than an intellectual basis. I don't think it's predetermined in the genes. When one grows older, one could become more intense or one could become more apathetic and resigned and cynical. But I think you have to consider waning physical energy, too. Man does not live by mind alone, alas.

We have found that the cliché about the difficulty of making new friends when you grow older is true. It is almost impossible to establish with people we now meet that rapport which only comes from shared experiences over many years, shared beliefs, a common sense of humor, a background of the same professions. And there is a problem with old tried and true friends arising, I believe, from American rootlessness: distance defeats relationships. One cannot maintain a former intimacy with friends who live miles away. I try to keep it up through letters, but this is not rewarding unless the friends, too, like to write long letters.

A wise person has said that the secret of not growing old is "to continue to solve puzzles." Since "solving puzzles" is really what creative work is all about—once one is faced with the logistics of capturing and expressing inspiration—I am grateful in these later years to have my writing puzzle to work on. And I could wish nothing better for men and women alike as they begin to age than that they each discover an intriguing puzzle that will keep their brains and hearts young.

Willow (Ruth Lewis Hall) (Seventies)

I was first a writer. In my twenties, I wrote short stories. Then I went on to write novels. They are not published, although some of the short stories have been published. I wrote poetry in my teens, short stories in my twenties and thirties, and then novels. I came to photography later—I'd say in my forties or fifties. But it has always been a separate art. Photography is more closely allied to nature, and writing is more closely connected with people. I would say that they are still, in a way, separate in my life. I enjoy both of them and they complement one another.

I would say I'm most creative in the morning. I have to set aside the same time every morning and have the same number of hours for work, if possible. If I am interrupted, or if other subjects take precedence at that time, I am distracted. I also need to be in a quiet place by myself. I have always been that way. It has always been a problem, to have a corner of my own. Even when I was a child, they had to curtain off a corner of the room, and that was my corner. I could retreat there—daydream, read or write, or think about anything I wanted to do or not do. For me, solitude is a necessary precondition of freedom to create. If the people around you understand your need for quiet, they will help. They will not interrupt you or interfere with you.

Creativity and Nature are closely interrelated. I was a city child, and I went to school in New York City. One year, I was sent to the country to a boarding school, and I fell in love with the natural world. That's why I live in the country now that I am retired. I find it a great help to be able to see the birds, the trees, and all growing things. I look upon Nature as a reservoir of strength. The other source of strength is meditation. The inner spirit is the essence of my work. I think painting, photography, writing, and all the arts are interrelated. They all feed the artist. The fields I am in, photography and writing, lean very heavily on Nature and on people. I find them equally important to me.

I think dreams are important for the artist. I wish I could remember more of mine. I think you have to be very aware of the importance of your dreams and record them immediately—instantly on awakening—or they will escape. I did find them turning up in my writing in my early years. I don't find as much of this today. Perhaps it's because I have a greater fund of experience now that I draw on.

I care quite a bit about the world and its people. It is always the people that I am concerned about. I respond to the tragedies and the inequities of the world. Since my twenties, I have been that way. I was oriented in John Haynes Holmes's Community Church in New York City, where we heard all the great thinkers of the world in the Sunday night forums—people like Nehru, Clarence Darrow, Margaret Sanger, and Bertrand Russell. In my twenties, I went to these forums and my social consciousness was awakened. It has always been alive and active.

As I understand the individual person better, I begin to see their likeness to me, to other people, and to the world. It's not just what *I* think. There is recognition of the "You" in me. I am not alone in my thinking or writing. I understand myself better in relation to other people. As I reach out to other people and they respond, I feel *I* grow. I grow all the time.

There are people who need mothering, who look to you *for* it. Other people are supportive of you. You are going to have both kinds of people around you. I cope with this by giving up the creative work and doing the mothering for the time being, because I've always felt that people trying to solve problems were so important. And this is why my creativity and productivity have been so long delayed—because I am a woman and responsive to the needs of others. Friends are sometimes a drain, but that in *itself* is a life experience. Mostly, they are supportive and helpful. When you get to a very low point, subconsciously you choose the friend you can lean on. Then you reach out to that person because you desperately need to lean on someone. When you are on your feet again, then you can help others.

I think there are rises and falls in the life course of a creative person. I don't think they are connected with years. They are connected with circumstances—like a person walking. You walk uphill at a different rhythm than when you walk downhill. There is always a new hill to climb.

The first love affair is always the most tragic. It's the hardest one to get over. I was thinking back in my own life, that when the first love affair ended, I was ready to commit suicide. But what has happened to me in life—the high peaks since—have been *so* much more wonderful. Love has been *so* much more interesting and complete and rich. And that is true of my second marriage. I had one marriage, one extended love affair, and now the second marriage began when I was 67. I think the cycle always renews itself, if you are open to it.

I've never had children. It was my choice not to have children. I didn't want to bring children into a world where there seemed to be no peace and no possibility for peace. That was before World War II. Years later, when I met a friend of my socially conscious twenties who also, with his wife, did not have children, we said to each other, "We made a mistake. *We* are the ones who should have had the children, to help bring about a peaceful world."

I particularly like young people in their twenties. It links up with my philosophy of not having children, because I felt that young people—the teenagers and those in their twenties—were really neglected by their parents, were not understood. *They* were the ones who needed attention, not the infant in the cradle. There were too many infants in the cradle getting all the attention. I wanted to give my attention to young people growing up. I don't know if they are drawn to me, but I am drawn to them. Wherever we are, both my husband and I, we seek out young people. We like people of all ages, but we enjoy young people and the young in heart most.

My father was a very loving man, a dreamer and a philosopher. My mother was a busy career woman. My childhood was good, as childhoods go. I was the baby, and probably at times intractable, impossible. I had two older sisters. My mother was able to manage her household and her husband's business, but she had little time for her children. I was in my twenties when she died. She died before I was married. It was very traumatic for me, because my mother and I never agreed. We were people who argued with each other and fought with each other. One of the things that I've come to understand as I've grown older is that my mother was a person just like me, and that we were very much alike. I've come to think of her as a companion and a pal of mine.

I can't say that I looked up to any older women as models. I looked up to them as friends. The woman I think of particularly was a psychic. And in a way, she became my surrogate mother. When she died, I was devastated. My own mother had been dead for many years.

I guess I don't spend much time looking in the mirror. But if you asked me which side of the family I'm more like, I would say I'm more like my mother. And that's probably why we fought so much. I am a combination of my mother *and* my father. In character, I am both philosopher and realist. But in *looks,* I am like my mother.

I've been interested in social movements, and I still am. Even in photography, when it isn't nature photography, it's photography of people. And not portraits—I don't do commercial work in portraits—but I do character. People whose faces mean something to me, I delight to photograph. I notice physical beauty in others. I notice it in nature. I don't dwell on the physical changes in myself. I accept them. I think it doesn't matter. People will get an impression of you, not only of the way you look, but who you are and what you project and whether you care about them, if you are interested in them or if they are interested in you. I don't think it matters what you look like. I look at the *expression* in faces. I think the eyes say a great deal. But I look at the whole face—more than the face, at what glows in the face. I admire beautiful people as I do beautiful painting or sculpture. I also have a great deal of compassion for them, because I think that a beautiful man or a beautiful woman has a handicap. People judge them for their beauty, which is only a mask, and forget the real person hidden inside, who is often a very sad and misunderstood person.

My memory is more visual—that's why I am in photography. But my ears are also working, because I listen to everything. I'm interested in what people are saying, particularly in the undertones. I've never dwelled too much on my earliest memories. I don't know why. I was always interested in and able to recall things that happened to me since I came into my teens and twenties. Things from then on are much more vivid to me than what happened before. I read articles that say you can lose your memory, but I really don't think that is true. Really, a *child* forgets, a *teenager* forgets, a person in her thirties forgets. And nobody emphasizes that. I don't think older people forget any more than younger people.

I would say to young people, Don't worry about physical change. It will take its place in the circle of life. It is just part of living. And it's not going to be any worse than growing from the cradle to the stage where you totter across the floor to take your first step. It's no more different and no more dangerous than climbing up on a stool and pulling things off the top of the bookcase when you are just learning to walk. Each stage in life has its hazards. And it really doesn't matter, if you know who you are. You hold to that. I think looks are overemphasized in our culture, in all advertising. I think I was more particular about my looks when I was being courted. Through the courting period you are always more aware of this.

I think that every emotion that you feel deeply is part of your work. It may not be *consciously*, but it sure is there. In writing, you sometimes write about people who have been out of your life for *years*. Suddenly the essential part of their character will emerge, and there they are. And not exactly the way you knew them then, but the essential part of them will come forward and you can write about it. I think you can forgive other people, but you can't forget. And I think that's a writer's stock in trade. One of the plays I never wrote would show that no matter which road you took, you would always come to the same place. There's a pattern which you have to complete. Just as a daffodil growing from a bulb has to be a daffodil and not a rose.

I think who you are is not simple. We have to remember this. Who you are is a very complicated person with many facets. You have to be willing to recognize that *all* of them may not come forward at one time. You have to have patience and endurance. You have to recognize that one of your characteristics may come forward today and something completely different may come forward tomorrow. All of it enriches and explains who you are—to yourself as well as to other people. There are people in you that others haven't met yet—and that *you* haven't met yet either, possibly. I didn't know that when I was 20. You have to be open to share yourself with others. If you are fortunate enough to have friends and people around you who recognize that these are all facets of you, they will help you and they will encourage you. You will be able to express and share your selves. And I think that's the meaning of life. You may have many friends, but you will relate to one in one way, and you will make a conversation completely different with another. And then, when you bring those two people together, they have absolutely nothing in common!

No, I don't wish I'd been anything else. I'd have liked to have written plays. But at that stage in my life, I wasn't encouraged, and I dropped it. I think I might have written some good plays. I sometimes feel that, creatively, my life was wasted during those years of my first marriage. And I regret *that*. But I wasn't wise enough to foresee what would happen.

I don't know what wisdom is; it's so complicated. I don't really think women are wiser than men. Maybe men in business have a tradition of being ruthless, but women in organizations can be equally ruthless. It depends on the person and the struggle for power. I don't believe in reincarnation. I believe that the spirit endures in another form. I don't think you can take anything with you. I think what you are intrinsically, and what you discover about yourself—this is what lives, what goes on, in the spirit world. And I look upon death as the great experience. I look upon it as a reward for living my life fully. Death to me is a reward. It will come in its own good time when I've completed the work I'm supposed to be doing right here. In *its* time, not in my time. I don't really know what I want to leave the world, except that I feel that in a way you live on in your friends, as well as in your work. If my work doesn't get a larger audience, I feel that it's not going to matter. My friends will remember. And as long as they remember me, I will be a living spirit.

I don't think I have cared passionately enough about recognition, or else I would have pursued getting things published and printed more than I have. But I think what matters to me is sharing. I really want to share my experiences and my thoughts and my philosophy as widely as I possibly can. From *that* standpoint, I would like to be published and out in the world. But if I'm not, I still feel that my friends will remember. I will live on in that, as well.

You ask what I think about the idea that women strive for completeness and men for perfection. I don't really believe that men and women are different so far as these two things are concerned. I think today the trend is toward wholeness in both men and women. There is a difference between wholeness and perfection. I really think that perfectionism is a block. When I see it in somebody, I am concerned about that person. If you don't have a flaw somewhere, you're not human. But I think wholeness is what men and women need to struggle for. That's what older people find to be such a challenge. As you grow older, you're freer. There's so much to be discovered. Age is a whole new adventure.

Helen Lovejoy (Helen G. Elliott)(Eighties)

Well, in childhood I was always interested in music. My father was musically inclined. He had a very good voice. He was a very kind person and he was very much in sympathy with what I was doing. My mother was not; she was opposed to what I was doing. I would practice at the piano. This was what I wanted to do. I learned about the Music School Settlement on Third Street in Manhattan, where I went to study. I became a scholarship student and I was there for several years. And when I was 15 or 16, having taken a year's course in teacher training there, I was permitted to teach at this settlement. Angela Diller, who was a music educator and one of the heads of the music school, was very interested in young children's attitudes and work toward music and in developing an interest in music. And I became one of her guinea pigs. She developed an understanding of how to handle young children—early childhood in music—using ear training and rhythm. I became so interested in this that this is what I wanted to do, even though later on I received a scholarship to go to the Juilliard Institute, which was then the Institute of Musical Art.

But I did not want to concertize. I became interested only in teaching. And I went out to do some teaching at the Settlement, and then mostly private teaching. I did a little teaching at the Juilliard in the ear-training class. When the ear-training teacher had to be away, she would ask me to take over. I love this work. This is what I wanted. I was able to buy a good piano; I was very fortunate in getting pupils; and it was a joy to teach. I loved doing ensemble work, and down at the Music Settlement we were able to play with string people—cello or violin—and it was something that I enjoyed doing. And my whole life at that time was music and music and music.

As I grew older, I sensed that my mother objected because she felt that maybe I might not want to get married. And *I* felt that I never wanted to marry a musician, that the two of us never could make a good life together. Which was a mistake, because I have since met many friends who are married to musicians and they are very happy. I married a businessman, and my life was practically severed in a very few years. I was left with two young children not even old enough to start school. I lived out on Long Island at the time, and the boy went to the kindergarten and I was able to start teaching. And I had my young daughter with me there. Things were very prosperous for me, fortunately. I was able to organize groups for ear training and rhythm and to do a great deal of piano music. Some of my pupils today are doing very well in the music field all over the country. As for leaving a mark on the world—this is the only way I can look at it. And I'm happy about it.

I moved out to Great Neck, Long Island, where I lived alone for many years. When my daughter settled here, I came to visit them every weekend. And then there was one child, and then a second and then a third and then a fourth. This was joy for me, not only because I could visit my family, but because as the children grew into ages 4 and 5, I was able to organize a group. I had a ten-children group here every weekend that I came up. I had to leave Great Neck because the lady I lived with sold her house and moved away. I couldn't find anything to my liking, so I came to live up here. This was just a few years ago. This is a beautiful place to live. And I love living with my daughter and the four children. My son also married, and lives only about twelve miles away, which makes it very, very delightful.

My daughter began teaching school; she was interested in the nursery and kindergarten. I was able to help and be a kind of a mother to the young children. I continued teaching. My teaching then was mostly in this area. It's been a very happy existence. I want to go on doing what I'm fortunate in being able to. My health has been very good. And fortunately, I have a decent, sensible outlook on things.

I was always ready to go to the piano and do some work at any time of the day. Before I married, I *was* able to spend three or four hours at a time at the piano. Today, I can sit down for two hours. Unfortunately, in the last few years I've had three or four serious accidents to my left arm, and my fingers have shown the result of this. Practicing, working at the piano is very important. That therapy is very good. And now today, I have improved a great deal. In addition to some teaching, I can play. I'm able to play with a violinist, and it's very joyful.

I am never alone. Even when I am physically alone, I never feel that I need somebody to fill in my life. My life is *very* full. I have so much because I think I've developed an inner, beautiful feeling toward everything. And I'm very happy because of that. Even though I'm not a lonely person and do not just start out seeking to be with people, knowing people and wanting to be with people is an important part of everybody's life. It's not paramount, though. I'm never sad when I'm just alone. But my interest in people is not only in adults. I love being with children. And since I'm not doing as much teaching now, I have more time to do some volunteer work. When I was asked to give some time to the gift shop where we raise money for our public library, I was glad to give time to that—selling clothes and supervising. And then when it became a question of giving time for a story hour on every Wednesday morning, I was very glad to do *that*. For there, too, I'm dealing with preschool children. Then, too, I have been a member of the Women's International League for Peace and Freedom for many years, but not an active member— just a dues-paying member. I then realized the need in this community—I felt that it would be very important to awaken people to the need for understanding and feeling for peace and freedom. And I was able to organize just such a branch here. And we've been very successful. I have a beautiful, full life. I have plenty of time for everything.

I've always had a love of trees and flowers. And I have always been interested in animals—how they live, how they die, what is happening to them. On TV, I can see some of the things I was never able to before. When the National Geographic or any such organization has a program on animals, I'm interested in watching. I get great joy out of that. I love animals; we have dogs and cats in our own home. And my grandchildren would love to have little animals around.

Oh, yes, my horizons *have* broadened as I've grown older. Definitely. Recently, an elderly person was visiting our home for a few days. He wasn't a very healthy person, unfortunately. And he welcomed the TV. And he looked at me and he said, "TV is wonderful; it gives old people something to *do*." So I looked at him, and said, "What do you mean—to *do*?" I said, "Don't you think it would be a much greater thing and a much happier thing if people could prepare for these things and not rely on TV? There was a time when we *didn't* have TV. That doesn't give you something to do. You're inactive. You just sit there and something is being thrown *at* you. Well, what are *you* doing?" And he was nonplussed. He said it was important to sit and watch TV.

If I would take time to look back, which doesn't happen very often, I think of my father, who had a beautiful disposition. He was very much sought by everyone. If I could possess part of his beautiful nature, I'd be very, very happy. That's about the extent of my looking back. People have always said that I *look* like my father physically, but I always secretly hoped that I had some of his spiritual feelings.

Growing older? I and a small group of girl friends I had—we were ahead of our times. We tried to look older and to act older than we were. No, I never feared old age. Memory? Yes, I would naturally recall things in a different way now, because I think that as we grow older most of us would benefit by the experiences that we've had. And I feel that I have benefited. And I look at things probably more kindly or with better understanding as I grow older. But not because I'm 50 or 60 or 70—I don't think of age in that sense at all. I think it's important that we *live*. We say that we learn by our errors, we learn by our mistakes. And I think we go on learning for the rest of our lives. I feel today, too, I'm learning. Very often I learn the hard way. I make errors and therefore I learn. Just yesterday I learned something by having to do it two or three times the hard way.

My childhood and my girlhood were divided. One half was miserable and very unhappy and the other was beautiful and lovely. Because I had that division in my parents. From then on, my music was the thing that gave me all my joy and love. My mother did not appreciate music. And she was not a very good-looking woman, and I was a beautiful child, and as a psychiatrist in later life told me, she was very envious of me because both my father and I were good-looking and she was not. And I had a talent, and she did not. And therefore she was trying to thwart me.

I guess I was about 8 when I began to study music. That was the strange thing—my mother was able to show off with me. I was *her* child. I had a beautiful singing voice. And if there was any opportunity to show off with me, whether it was at a performance or someplace else, she was able to say I was her child. And I could sing. In fact, I had such a beautiful voice that even when I was a little older, about 14, a friend of mine who was a very fine musician—we lived in the same house together—her uncle, who was an impresario from Europe, came here to visit them. And when he heard me sing, he wanted to take me back to Europe with him to give me my full education. Which, of course, my mother objected to. So I never went. I never could take advantage of that.

What was I like? I was always interested in children. Even as a youngster, I would take care of other people's babies. I used to lean over the carriages and pet the babies, even when I was too young to handle them. All my life, as far back as I can recall, I was interested in animals. As a little child I would go out on the street and pick up the dirtiest, the sickest-looking cat and put it in my lap and pet it, and want to bring it into the house. Of course, I wasn't permitted to. When I was about 7, we lived in Brooklyn for a couple of years. We were surrounded by farms. And my greatest joy would be—as children, we wore little aprons—my joy would be to go out to the farm and pick up frogs and bring back an apron full of frogs. And, of course, my mother wouldn't permit me to come into the house with them. So I had to come down and empty my apron and let all the frogs out.

There was one unfortunate period. For a number of years, I lived with this lady and I couldn't bring a piano in to do my work. I had no piano there. I had to work either at somebody else's home, or when I came up here for the weekend. So I was really away from work for a good many years. As for practicing, I did nil. It upset me terribly. And just as soon as I was able to come and live here permanently, I was able to start work again. And age never entered into it. I didn't think of it. It hadn't dulled me. It increased my desire to want to do more work. The only thing that stopped me for a while was the injury to my arm.

For a number of years, people have been telling me there are such things as senior-citizen organizations. They have asked me, "Why don't you join the senior-citizen groups?" I never heard anything very attractive about joining these organizations, so I wouldn't. But since I became interested in organizing a branch of the Women's International League for Peace and Freedom, and I wanted to further it here, I joined several groups. And one of them was a senior-citizens group. I went to one or two of their meetings and I was so discouraged. Because these people were just interested in gabbing and having a social time, and they weren't interested in doing anything worthwhile. And I felt that these lives were, to me, lost. If this is doing something, then I'm out completely. I like people of all ages, but I *think* I'm more attracted—mostly because of my disappointment in senior citizens—I'm more attracted to younger people. Any young people who are active, who are doing something, accomplishing something. In any field. It doesn't matter to me.

Recognition is not important to me as an individual. It's very important if people have accepted it and have gained something by it, if their lives are a little fuller and richer because of music. This is the main reason why I feel that it's so important to start with the young child. I think it's very important for the educational departments of all colleges to stress the early childhood more. From what I see and what I hear, and what I've known about it thus far, *very* little attention is being given to music in early childhood in the educational field.

When I go to hear a very fine artist such as Artur Rubinstein or Rudolf Serkin, I have a great desire to go home and work; I feel I want to do something more. That is inspiration, yes. As a student, I always went to concerts with my music; I had my score before me. And as the artist would perform, I would follow and I would record certain things that *I* did that were not as good as what the artist was doing. And I went home and I *worked*. This was an inspiration for me.

Wisdom? I don't think *age* makes a person wiser. It's the experiences people have in life that matter. As you grow older, you see things more kindly. We all grow old, we all die. . . . If you've been an active person, age doesn't matter. It's the kind of life you've lived that matters. But I feel the same as I did forty or fifty years ago. I seem to love the same things. My attitude hasn't changed.

No, aging does not stop me from going ahead with my music. Not one bit. This summer, I'm on my way to a session in Amherst with Dorothy Taubman to study a new and different approach to music that I'm very excited about. What might I say of benefit to young girls today? Develop an interest in some activity, which you will continue to benefit from and share with others.

9
Older Women as Seen Through Social Science and Literature: Views from a Bridge

> So it would seem, if there is in all history any primordial force, that force is woman—continuer, protector, preserver of life, instinctive, active, thoughtful, ever bringing thought back from sterile speculation to the center of life and work. She is primordial in the making of culture and the destruction of civilization, if there is any primordial force in the world, anything but the ever-flowing stream of events, causeless and timeless.
>
> —MARY BEARD,
> Introduction, *America Through Women's Eyes*

Aging, like all great subjects, is many-faceted: it over-arches all the departments of study in the humanities and sciences. An appreciation of the catholicity of interests it embraces is much in evidence in the contents of books of readings in gerontology and in the classic works on aging published in the Western world in the twentieth century—G. Stanley Hall's *Senescence: The Last Half of Life*[1] and Simone de Beauvoir's *The Coming of Age.*[2] Both Hall, a psychologist, and Beauvoir, a writer, made imaginative use of a variety of source materials from a number of broad fields of study—biology, demography, economics, ethnology, history, literature, medicine, psychology, and sociology—in the composition of their works. In the 1930s, that intellectual revolution augured by Mary Beard, that was to bring about a creative synthesis of all aspects of thought and culture, was only beginning to gather its forces. At that time, scholars who were engaged in "collaborative research" were pioneers, for "the phrase 'interdisciplinary research' had not yet been invented."[3] Since Hall's book was published in 1922, he was a precursor of the movement to unify all the "specialisms" of intellectual endeavor.

Half a century has passed since Mary Beard wrote that this movement would have more far-reaching consequences than the Renaissance, and during those fifty years there seems to have been a turnabout. Interdisciplinary studies departments have been opened on many campuses across the country, and there are scholars at work building bridges between the "specialisms."

Even so, few features of contemporary life have been so often remarked as the "fragmentation" of knowledge, the "information explosion" ignited by the prodigious activities of specialists laboring in ever more narrowly defined areas of interest, and the frenetic "busyness" of the media in casting abroad whatever fragments of these fragments their owners hope will attract the attention of the public.

Failure of nerve and eclipse of vision are occupational hazards for today's social thinkers and observers. One must be a bold swimmer to brave the swelling tide of "print culture" on all subjects outside one's narrow specialty. Those who take the risk must be prepared to face charges of eclecticism, intellectual dilettantism, or slovenliness, and of the crimes of heresy against doctrine and high treason against ideology, wanton disregard of "the facts" (which are shaped and even invented to suit any argument) and appalling ignorance. That few take the dare can be inferred from the observation that the level of knowledge most professional people command outside their specialty is that of the college sophomore.[4] (The generosity of this estimate depends upon which sophomore one has in mind.) Thanks to this sorry state of affairs, thinkers and observers, when they communicate at all, continue to talk past one another, specialisms breed subspecialisms, and superficial, fragmentary, and even outrageously false "social facts" are cheerfully and continuously dispensed for the "consumption" of a distracted public. It is in tribute to Mary Beard's vision of the vital role of women in culture and civilization, and to her faith in the possibility—the imminence, even—of a creative synthesis of thought and culture that the risk of writing this book was taken, that this bridge was built.

From time immemorial, and in all societies around the world, social organization has been founded upon what all people have thought to be the essential purpose of human life, "its continuance, care, and protection."[5] And this, in Mary Beard's view, is women's sphere. In the half century that has passed since her words were written, two generations of women have come to maturity. They may be seen as statistical composites of the mothers and grown daughters of two birth cohorts. In 1975, International Women's Year, there were more than 13 million survivors of the birth cohort of the mothers. In that same year, the statistical composite of daughters, born between 1911 and 1930, numbered 22,715,000 women. The statistical mother is or soon will be one of the "old-old," and the statistical grown daughter one of the "young-old." Of these two birth cohorts, that of the mother has been studied more extensively than that of the daughter. Even so, few of the studies of the earlier birth cohort, officially designated as "the elderly," are focused on women. Despite the increase in the numbers and proportion of older women in the population of this country, and despite the fact that the sex differential in life expectancy is ever more evident as people ascend the age-sex pyramid of the demographers, the lives and thought of these two generations of women are truly "uncharted territory." That knowledge about older women in twentieth-century America is slight and scattered is but one reason, although a compelling one, for choosing this as a subject of study in response to the challenge that inspirited *America Through Women's Eyes.* Since nearly one of every three women in the United States today is an "older woman," it is folly to remain oblivious to this "most faint neglect" of the subject of women's aging.

Mary Beard was keenly aware that she was writing at a time of crisis, a turning point in national life. And in the life of a country, as in the life of every person, it is when a critical change is seen to be imminent that the most profound questions of human life are asked. These questions have to do with the direction, meaning, and purpose of that life. In the 1930s, complacency and confidence in the workings of the economy and the direction of the society had been shattered. It was a time for re-examination of the foundations and purpose of the life of the family, of the community, of the economy, and of the nation. It was a time for what Mary Beard called "social thought." And since social thought encompasses all culture and civilization, it was a time for re-examination of women's place in society. She thought that place to be at the very center of life. She knew that every angle of vision irradiates some sector of this vital center. She knew that when the perspectives are combined, it can be seen steadily and seen whole.

The burden of interdisciplinary inquiry is heavier than that borne by multidisciplinary study. To search for common themes and to translate the concerns of social science into humanistic values—creativity, freedom, responsibility—is far more intricate and risky than to examine a subject from a variety of angles of vision. A bridge is meant to join, to connect, to unite. In this work, the question of how older women live in America today is joined to the question of how older women ought to live. The question of how older women are seen by social scientists is joined to the question of how older women are seen in literature. The question of how older women are seen by others is joined to the question of how older women see themselves. To explore these questions, a number of works were selected from seven ways of seeing older women in this country and in this century—perspectives from social gerontology, sociology, anthropology, psychology, history, oral history, and American literature. A variety of studies, documents, and works of literature were chosen from each of these departments of thought, among them demographic studies, studies of older people in "natural settings," publications about the elderly in America, published proceedings of conferences addressing the concerns of older women, cross-cultural studies, works on American social history, works in social psychology and analytical (Jungian) psychology, and fiction and essays, autobiographies, diaries, journals, letters, literary studies, notebooks and memoirs by and about older women in twentieth-century America. To these, I added studies of transcripts of women's oral histories, transcripts of my own interviews with older women artists, and a number of works on creativity in later life. Of all these materials the same essential question was asked: How do older women make sense of their lives, their past lives and their lives as they are now, and what are the possibilities of later life for women? In humanistic study there is no separation between these questions, of what is the case and what ought to be. Humanistic study points the way to the cross-currents of thought among these seven ways of seeing. It shows how they flow together, how vision is the work of connecting angles of vision—perspectives—to one another.

A Call for Transformations

The age composition of a society is always in the process of change. Statistics about the percentages of younger and older people in the population are statements about what is the case at a fixed point in time, as a census year. They are cross-sectional statements about what is seen on the surfaces of the ever-shifting socioscape. The underlying processes and direction of social change are not visible at the surface. A knowledge of history and of the fundamental principles of sociology form a kind of diving bell for this deeper exploration.

Demographic studies document the growing presence of older women in the national population and the fact that women constitute "a majority within the minority" of the elderly citizens of this country. Economic data document the fact that the elderly in general are a low-income group, and that unmarried elderly women, most of whom are widows and live alone, comprise the majority of all elderly persons living in poverty. Social Security entitlements are all the income that these women have. The Social Security system is more than their "safety net." It is their lifeline. Older women are well advised to "choose their strategies carefully" and to "build strong alliances." Current proposals for change of the system represent a challenge—the first challenge in our history—to the principle of adequacy of income. The most compelling issue to be addressed by social-action groups is the issue of economic security in later life, for this is imperative if the promise of humanistic gerontology is to be fulfilled. Meeting this challenge calls for a transformation of the consciousness of feminists—an awareness not only of our common sisterhood, but of our common daughterhood as well.

The future, Robert L. Heilbroner has said, is "the growing edge of the present."[6] We are creating our future at the present moment. If certain issues are not addressed at this very hour, millions of older women aged 45 to 64 in the 1980s will inherit the collective sociological fate of millions of their mothers by the turn of the next century. Many will live in poverty with all its attendant sorrows. Demographers have shown that the "fastest-growing" segments of the elderly population are women, non-whites, and the very old. These are all "populations at risk" of living out their old age in poverty. For some, longevity may seem no more than a sentence of death-in-life. Among women who are middle-aged today, there are those who are especially vulnerable. These are the displaced homemakers. Many are only a marriage certificate away from this status, for divorce and widowhood in middle age admit great numbers of women to the ranks of those living at or below the poverty threshold. Unless they are provided with job training and retraining, with continuing education as well as education about the protections against sex and age discrimination to which they are entitled, the cost to society will be a growing tide of older women on the welfare rolls. The *human* cost is incalculable.

Social observers write of the increase in the labor force participation rate of women in twentieth-century America as "dramatic" and "unprecedented." It is clear that issues related to employment are as germane to the lives of women as to the lives of men. But the consequences of the change in women's worklife pattern have been neither "fully recognized in the literature nor integrated into public policy."[7] Unless these consequences are addressed from a life course perspective, the difficulties encountered by older women workers will be passed on as a legacy to their young daughters. The situation of middle-aged women about to enter or re-enter the labor force after years of unemployment, when they have outmoded skills, no recent work experience, and little access to information about job opportunities, exemplifies the importance of education and training in influencing one's life chances in the marketplace. This could serve as counsel for the young, and it is a lesson responsible mothers teach their daughters.

But economics is far from an exact science, and the workings of the marketplace are far from predictable. At the present time, there is no clear correlation between education and training on the one hand and income or "earning power" on the other. More than that, human life is a risk and an adventure, not a set of strategies followed in accordance with a hedonistic calculus. And the awareness of its limits, its finitude comes, if it comes at all, after youth is gone. There are today, as there were in the past, many young women who do not have the luxury of choice between college and the labor force. There will always be women, at every stage of life, who would choose "home work" over "market work" if they were given the choice. Women who feel their presence is required in the home because they have small children, or a handicapped child, or a disabled husband or dependent sibling or aging parent, ought to have that choice open to them. Women who are in poor health ought to be given that choice. Women who want to dedicate their lives to community service or artistic creativity ought to be given that choice. Home work ought to be considered as covered employment under the Social Security system. Because it is not, many women are now hard at work at two full-time jobs for which they receive one wage—and a low one, at that. However fervently it is preached, the gospel of work will not inspire women who have been working or who are hard-pressed to work now at low-paying, dull, and exhausting jobs.

If home work were considered as covered employment under the Social Security system, the financial situation of many elderly women today would be better than it is, although still far from what it ought to be.[8] Even though Social Security was not intended as such, it has become the "economic mainstay" of most elderly Americans. When an elderly woman is widowed—and the older she is, the more likely it is that she is widowed—her Social Security income is reduced sharply. This is all the income many old women in our society receive. And it is not adequate for meeting expenses that are the very necessities of life for them.

Thus are old women in the United States today recompensed for a lifetime of labor, whether this was low-paid market work or work never recorded in official statistics, work that contributed so much to the well-being of their families and their communities. If from the beginning they had been given the choice between home work and market work, they would be receiving Social Security benefits today in their own name regardless of work history or marital status. They would not be penalized for having been poor all their lives and for having an erratic work history because of this. They would not be penalized for having remained at home to care for family members dependent upon them for their very survival. They would not be penalized for having worked full-time *both* at a low-paying job and at keeping their family together. They would not be penalized for having been widowed or divorced. When will we learn to see that the situation of the middle-aged woman at a turning point in her life and the situation of the young woman weighing work and education and marriage, and the situation of the old woman fighting to maintain her independence, are all interrelated? When will we learn to see that we are looking at the same woman at three different stations along the life course? If social policies continue to be formulated without imagination or intelligence or heart, in a way that is far more respectful of political considerations and profit margins and cost efficiency than of how life ought to be lived and what it is all for, the future will be no more than a mindless repetition of the present. This is an open call for transformations.

The stigma of old age and the negative stereotype of older people are the natural consequence of fear and greed, unimaginativeness and ignorance—of our failure to live responsibly. If old people today are not to be consigned to the status of dependents and the role of invalids, they must marshal every means of preserving their freedom and independence, and young and middle-aged people must support them in this. Housekeeping services, Meals on Wheels, "talking visits," telephone visits, nutrition programs, visiting nurses, day-care services, senior centers, congregate housing, experiments in intergenerational living—to old people living on very low incomes, haunted by memories of the Great Depression, for whom dignity is worth more than bread, these make the difference between life and death-in-life. Employment opportunities are as vital as these services. Many older people are desperate for work. Many would prefer to continue working beyond retirement age, if they could find work they were able to do. The 8:30–5:00 job is a *deus ex machina* of industrial society that we ought to have outgrown. Government, business, and industry are organized around models of work that are antithetical to the human spirit. Life is an organic unity. It cannot be artificially divided into separate phases of learning and labor and leisure without doing violence to its very nature.[9] Mary Beard wrote that the vast superstructure of economics and politics ought to be made responsive to the essential purposes of life, and that a sound and creative community life ought to be maintained at the very foundation of society. Whether or not one agrees that this is women's sphere, it is clear that at every stage of life, women are in a position to see the benefits of a diversified employment market that offers opportunities for part-time positions with equitable earnings and retirement benefits, for flexible working hours, for job sharing, and for continuing education and training programs. The transformation of the labor market will *follow*, not *lead*, a transformation of consciousness about the continuity and the possibilities of human life.

Human society is not the labor market. It is incomparably broader and richer and deeper. A woman is more and other than a daughter, sister, wife, mother, grandmother. She is also more and other than a wage earner, a labor market statistic. Because of the over-specialization of fields of study, human life has been dismembered and quantified, taken apart and hollowed out, often in the very name of justice and mercy. Economists tend to see women as statistics in labor force participation rates. Political scientists tend to perceive women in terms of voting blocs or decision-making power. Sociologists tend to see women in terms of the social history of the family, or in terms of sex roles, or as integers in the economy and society. Gerontologists tend to see women only after they have celebrated their sixty-fifth birthday. These are but four instances of the busywork in the hives of specialism in American society today. No one can live without bread. Women ought to have equal pay for equal work. Women ought to have equal opportunity to be educated so they can earn an income commensurate with their abilities and performance. Women are entitled to retirement pension benefits just as men are. But no one ought to live by bread alone. That, too, is death-in-life.

Women know this, women have always known this, that the life of any person and the life of the whole society are expressions of some vision of our relatedness. Women have always known that youth and middle age and old age are intertwined, that the generations have a covenant with one another. To dissect human life into roles and categories, to make of human life an abstraction, is to do violence to it. To measure and define the worth of human life in currency, in stocks or savings or salaries or pensions, is to do violence to it. To lose the sense of the continuity and wholeness of life is to lose all hope of ever knowing how to live.

In *Late Bloom*, Luree Miller writes, "*Those who are not locked into nine-to-five jobs . . . are on call for the endless emergencies of life. If they were not there to respond, who would? A social worker?*"[10] Miller was writing of "the strengthening tie of trust," of how women support women. Women who are not locked into nine-to-five jobs are also on call for service to their communities. What is miraculous is that there are women who manage *both* a nine-to-five job *and* support of friends and community service. More often than not, these women are *older* women. Ellen Stein writes of how it seems to the older women in the Asheboro Council of Garden Clubs that there is something amiss with the June brides of the Bicentennial year. It is possible that these young women, who seemed so promising to those in Randolph County, North Carolina, did not lay claim to "the civilized essence" that is their heritage.[11] For three generations, the women of the garden clubs of neighborhoods that are black as well as white, rich as well as poor, old as well as new have seen to it that Asheboro is a model of both cleanliness and beauty. Their work has given the Asheboro community indications of the potential for creativity that inheres in its civilization. But the fourth generation of women is not carrying this work forward. Stein observes that the women in these garden clubs are in their fifties or older, and that less than a dozen are 30 years old. She writes of a garden club as "a fellowship," and of its purpose as the achievement of grace in the affairs of the community and the expression of community life that is on a higher plane than "the accomplishments of commerce." But now the leadership, concerned that younger women are not carrying on the work, are asking if the civilizing spirit is waning. The achievements of the challenging Bicentennial year were considerable; the plans for the post-Bicentennial were imaginative and ambitious. However, there are no young people to teach. No one remains to attend to the lessons.

The last census in Randolph County enumerated only 900 women of 40,000 who had attended college. Yet Randolph has an excellent library system, one that generations of women built. Even today, Friends of the Library—unpaid volunteers—continue to carry on that work. As they grow older, it may happen that much of their work will be shifted to the larger body of taxpayers, as public servants are hired to do what was formerly assumed by private volunteers. Stein finds this pattern to be a familiar one for rural areas such as Randolph County.

The task of civilizing society has been the province of the Extension Homemakers in the small mill villages by the side of Deep River and in the farming communities that lie between the ridges of the Uwharries. Stein remarks that when 200 Homemakers gathered for a Bicentennial festival, more than a dozen of them were honored because of their perfect meeting attendance records that dated back to the years before World War II. There were dozens more who had perfect attendance records dating back to the 1950s. Today, there are few members who are young enough to begin to build records to compare with these.

Stein perceives Homemakers to be "mystics." This is because she says that they have a vision of the great forces in the depths of family life itself that can be marshaled and put to use in the service of the social order. She reports that the Homemakers' Bicentennial project was to be responsible for partial funding of Girls' Haven, which is a private corporation that organizes homes for the homeless teen-aged girls of the state. The clubwomen made a quilt, and raised $1,500 by selling chances on it to all donors. They have observed that if every mother were an Extension Homemaker, a place such as Girls' Haven would not need to exist. Stein writes that there are hundred of homemakers firmly enmeshed in extension clubs and that many of them are grandmothers.

When the state commissioned a study of women's needs in 1963, it was predicted on the basis of its findings that "home extension agents could lead the way toward the family of the future." In myriad ways, they could connect the millions of rural families in North Carolina "to the expanding resources and services of an industrializing world." By way of 4-H clubs and teen service organizations, they could lead the way of children and young girls to the world that lies beyond the local mill that they might otherwise never come to know. But young women who are the brightest and the most dedicated trainees in the 4-H home extension system will probably not become a community resource in the way the older agents have. They "are being won for the future by the nation's industry and lost to the personalized, women-centered system which raised them" (68). Stein quotes human development specialist Lynn Qualls, who says that most young women do not do not have the time to become deeply committed to the service projects in which the agents are engaged. The parents of young children, the heads of families at the beginning of the life cycle, Mrs. Qualls observes, are both employed, and either they work in shifts or they send the children to all-day nursery school. The young wives and mothers simply do not have the time to become involved in the ongoing extension programs. The "personal touch" is on the wane in these communities. The June brides and all the other young women in school and already in the labor market "are pulling for themselves," Stein concludes. They are working long hours on the job, at domestic chores, at school, and in child-care responsibilities. Stein believes these young women are coming to be a little more like men in that they are "too busy to trim shrubbery around the entrance to the library." She observes that they would prefer to pay their taxes and to "be left alone and let someone else take care of the city's beauty" (69). For now, that "someone else" is an older woman. But she will not always be there. Unless the labor market is transformed so that it is more responsive to the essential purposes of human life, there will be no one to take her place. The fate of "that civilizing spirit" of which Stein writes is contingent upon the adoption of a life course perspective by the citizens of a community—and, ultimately, of a *national* community. Only when life is seen whole, when learning and labor and leisure are part of every phase of it from childhood to old age, will it be possible to experience it fully.

Transformations begin with individuals working in neighborhoods and communities—and churches and synagogues and mosques. Dieter T. Hessel observes that about one of every four members of "mainline denominations" are over the age of 65.[12] In Maggie Kuhn's dialogue with a group of twelve ministers and a layperson enrolled in the Advanced Pastoral Studies Program of the San Francisco Theological Seminary, she phrased her social criticism and dedication to change in terms of a broad vision of what life could be for people of all ages. She spoke of the maldistribution of medical personnel, resources, and equipment in a society in which nearly four of every ten people live in small towns and scattered rural villages, and of the health-care needs of those trapped in the inner cities. She discussed the vital roles of the patient advocate and the health care advocate, the needs of the elderly and physically disabled for public transportation, and how these needs could be addressed. That broader vision guided her views on every subject: "We need to organize our neighborhoods in a way that encourages extended family life, neighborly interaction and support, and alternative living communities" (46).

Kuhn envisions alternatives to institutionalization of the elderly. She sees the educational and socializing possibilities of the nutrition site, "a real missionary territory, if there ever was one" (88). She believes that the churches ought to be challenged, not discouraged, by statistics about older Americans. She foresees "creative new ministries by pastors and people" (21). She recommends that churches provide counseling services for the adult children of aging parents, that they extend continuing education to provide opportunities for retired people to become involved in the life of the community, and that they provide education and counseling about human sexuality in later life. Old age, she says, is "a time of great fulfillment—personal fulfillment, when all the loose ends of life can be gathered together" (15). It is a time for social involvement, as well, for the elders have social responsibilities to fulfill. Those in the church ought to help people to take responsibility for their own lives. And old people should be encouraged to review their lives. For the life review "stimulates social action, social analysis and protest—all essential for constructive social change" (40). For Maggie Kuhn, learning and growing are continuous throughout life. Old people ought to be encouraged to return to school. For some, "Learning evokes unhappy memories. . . . You could help them see that their own life experience equips them to learn extraordinarily well, if they would just believe in themselves" (78). She told a story of how the social pressure in a town in the Midwest and the social pressure of peers prevented some elderly people from taking advantage of the opportunity to enroll in a nearby college. Variations of this story could be told of older people across the country who suffer a failure of nerve at the very time in life when they have greater freedom for personal development. This refusal of freedom, this failure of nerve afflicts those who do not see the possibilities of later life for growth, for the creative uses of freedom.

Aging is both an inward- and an outward-facing journey. Growing older is a journey through time as well as through ever-changing cultural and social worlds. Most works on retirement are silent about that inner journey. Many people find it to be "toilsome." They are afflicted with "the anxiety and boredom of unending leisure and rest that does not renew or revitalize."[13] The second half of life calls for an inner transformation. A vision of the possibilities of later life is the genesis of the will to transform social institutions so that these possibilities may become realities. So, too, the will to transform the self originates in a vision of later life as a "chance for further flight."

Change and crisis and action are women's estate. Even before she could read, Luree Miller recalls, she was aware "*that women lived through many complicated changes in their lives; by comparison, men's lives seemed linear and one-dimensional.*"[14] The times of critical change, the "milestones" of a woman's life are a matter of major life-events, not of calendar age. The major life-events that predicate the direction that aging takes occur during the fourth decade of a woman's life,[15] and this is one reason "older women" are seen in this study as women over the age of 40. If the study of older women begins with women aged 65 and over, a full quarter of a century of life during which major events—"lifequakes"—are very likely to take place is missed. Much that happens during the fourth and fifth decades of life may be decisive for how life is lived in the sixth decade and after.

There is another, even more compelling reason that two generations of women are encompassed in this study. When women are seen in the last decades of life, they are seen all too easily as—as Beauvoir perfectly phrases it—the Other. When the "elderly" are seen as a collectivity, they are seen as separate from the young and the middle-aged. And their condition is seen as foreign to the observer. But the generations are part of one another. They follow upon one another; as Lucretius wrote,

> In a brief space the generations pass,
> And like to runners hand the lamp of life
> One unto other.[16]

Until we know this, we cannot be free to live responsibly and creatively. It is strange, but Americans, who are said by so many to worship Change, live in denial and dread of the most natural and fundamental change in life, aging and mortality. Until we come to terms with Time and Change, we cannot make sense of our lives.

A cross-cultural perspective on women's aging reveals the cultural relativity of interpretations of the changes in women's lives. Anatomy is destiny only if destiny is defined in purely physical or biological terms. But human beings are social and cultural beings, not creatures of instinct. Myriad lifeways are designed within the limitations of biological possibility. This is evident in the wide fluctuations in the fertility rates of American women during the past quarter-century.[17] If the fertility span has changed at all in recent decades, it has been extended, not abbreviated. It is generally agreed that the onset of the menarche is earlier for young women today than it was for women of past generations. Whether the average age of menopause is later than it was for our grandmothers and great-grandmothers is still being debated, but this much is known, that it is not earlier. If reproduction were a matter of biology only, the birth rate would not fluctuate as it has done, falling from "near-record highs for the 20th century in the last half of the 1950's" to the present point, which is today the lowest in our national history. Indeed, if the fertility span has lengthened, the birth rate would have increased uniformly over the decades of this century if biology alone governed reproduction. But, except for women who live in communities in which high fertility is a moral value, as Amishwomen and Hutterites, childbearing ends years before the menopause. And at the other end of the age spectrum, the trend in the direction of higher average age at first marriage is associated with relatively low fertility. Clearly, we are creatures of Culture, not Nature. "Recent trends toward higher levels of education, increased labor force activity, and the postponement of marriage have been accompanied by decreases in the average number of children ever born to ever-married women" (18).

If a woman's value is measured in terms of her procreative power, menopause will be a stigmatizing event, one that is dreaded and even denied. Doubtless, there are women in the United States today whose worth is measured by members of kin groups, and perhaps by themselves, in terms of the ability to bear children. These women may experience depression at the onset of menopause. A woman's social and cultural world must always be taken into account in understanding the reasons for anxiety or dread of the "change of life."[18] In a society in which youth is made into a cult, as it is in our own, women are seen as desirable only when they are young. Here, the "change of life" marks a woman as a castaway, as one who can no longer love or be loved. This is a great loss for those of every age. Where youth and physical attractiveness are celebrated, young people are not loved but preyed upon, used, exploited. Where aging is defined only in negative terms of decline and loss, aging and mortality induce terror, and older people think and behave in ways they ought to have long since outgrown. Millions of older women will live one-third of their lives after the childbearing period is over. Estelle Fuchs writes of the contemporary older woman as a pioneer, because this is the first time in history that so many older women will be living out their lives without the guidance of traditional roles.[19] Fuchs believes that this generation of middle-aged women must consider how to live, because their experience will light the way for their daughters.

The deep undertow of life pulls us forward. Even the very old are restless, feeling the beat of life, its forward thrust. So do those in the fullness of maturity feel that quickening. In the first half of life, one is preoccupied with finding a mate and a vocation. At midlife, there is a sense that the direction of life is changing. There is a summons from the psyche to find the meaning of one's life, and it is imperious. If it is not heeded, it will come up again and again with ever greater force. This is the approach of Jung's analytical psychology, which is unique for its explorations of life after youth, and for its Renaissance-like vision of the possibilities of later life. In Jung's view, the afternoon of life cannot be lived according to the laws that govern life's morning.[20] If a mature woman projects the meaning of her life outside herself, whether upon a vocation or a lover, upon grown children or an aging mother, she will never find it, for it exists within herself. If she refuses to heed the challenge of the psyche, she is denying herself the possibilities for further growth and for leaving a legacy to the world. She is refusing to accept responsibility for her own life.

Anxieties are attendant upon every critical turning point in life. But in itself, Virgilia Peterson reflects, anxiety is not "a corrosive. On the contrary, I would call it the leaven of life. . . . No great poem has ever been written, no revolution has ever been undertaken, no faith has ever survived the continual encroachment of doubt upon it, except through anxiety."[21] In *Four Stages of Life,* women at the third stage were the most anxiety-ridden and the most desperate of the eight groups encompassed by this study.[22] Whatever their chronological age, these were women who were at the point of completing the childrearing phase of the family life cycle. The "empty nest" was not the cause so much as it was the occasion for examining their lives. For many, it was the first time in their lives that they felt their destinies were in their own hands. They questioned themselves, their marriages; they saw the long years ahead as shadowed, bleak. If the lives of the women at the fourth stage are an indication of what the lives of these women will become, their recovered energies and their rediscovered talents and ambitions will be dissipated. The lives of women at the fourth stage were narrowly circumscribed. They had a keen sense of humanitarian and moral purpose, as did the men at that stage of life, but this was not translated into concrete objectives. The loss to self and society is grievous. The conclusion of this study was that the simplest people were the happiest and that complexity of personality appears to be maladaptive for older people.

The failure to meet the challenges of the second half of life is a failure to fulfill the moral responsibilities older people owe to the young. From time immemorial, there has been a covenant between the generations, that the older would so live as to be an example to the young and that the young would heed this example, that the older would protect and deliver the cultural heritage to the young and that the young would prove themselves worthy to receive it. This sacred trust is the cornerstone of every culture, of all civilization. If the generations are divided against one another, it will be broken. If people refuse to mature, refuse to grow old, it will be broken.

Women's work in the second half of life is the transformation of procreative into creative power. At midlife, a woman becomes keenly aware of the aspects of her personality that she has thus far neglected to develop. At this critical turning point, there are signs that a significant change in the psyche is in preparation. These signs may be missed or delayed if parents are still living.[23] Many middle-aged women who are mothers cannot break free of mothering. They mother children after they are grown, or, as women at the "fourth stage of life" were inclined to do, a woman mothers her husband. Or women become mothers of their own aging mothers. A woman who is closely identified with her mother, as so many women seem to be, may fall into a deep depression when her mother dies. If a woman has projected her self on her mother, she must find her own identity when her mother is gone.

The journey to the self is the way to individuation. It is a striving toward wholeness. In contemporary society there are no rites of passage to guide the initiate as there may have been at the Villa of the Mysteries for the Roman woman. There is no community of believers, no world-view or religion or mythology held in common. For many, the gods have fled, and where they once may have been there is nothing and there is no one. For others, the scientists have taken the place of the gods. But the main task of every human life must still be undertaken, that is, to find the meaning of that life.

In growing older, integration has more and more to do with recovering an inner value than with forming some adaptation to the exterior world.[24] To become whole is to realize one's uniqueness, one's identity as distinctive from collective identity in a family or work group or community. For women, the way to individuation is followed by exploring the Feminine. Jung has shown that in exploring the hidden depths of the psyche, one comes upon "primordial images, pictures of racial experience, archetypes, ancient powerful forces," which influence action and character.[25] He has perceived that one must meet it on its own grounds, that the language of the psyche is a language of symbols and images, expressed through art and dreams. In poetry, painting and sculpture there are personifications of the archetypal Feminine. In these, a woman finds all her selves, those she has realized in her life, and those which represent her unlived lives. The discovery that she is Everywoman is the discovery of all the possibilities of her life in its "second season." The discovery of her identity is the discovery of what is exceptional about herself. In this way, a woman is released from making a religion of only one aspect of herself, whether this is daughterhood or sisterhood, or wifehood or motherhood, or some professional or occupational or racial or ethnic or religious affiliation. Self-examination is an ordeal, a rite of passage to freedom and a life of one's own. The more fully a woman knows herself, the more she will enrich her own life and the lives of all those with whom hers is interrelated. The more she knows herself, the more she will be able to separate that which is personal from that which is transpersonal. Then she will be free to release her gifts into the life of the world. This is the working of transformative power, personified by the Sophia figure who distills Wisdom from experience. This is a call for inner transformations. "Where is the wisdom of our old people—where are their precious secrets and their visions?" Jung has asked. He observed that old people try to compete with young people, and that in the United States, the father who is a brother to his sons and the mother who is her daughter's sister are all but idealized as the right relationships between parents and their grown children. He confessed that he did not know to what extent this confusion may be attributed to false ideals and to what extent it may be attributed to "a reaction to an earlier exaggeration of the dignity of age." He asked if the expansion of life, or usefulness or efficiency, or distinguishing oneself in social life, or finding suitable mates and good positions for grown children are not enough to give meaning and purpose to life, and he observed that for many they do not suffice—the many "who see in the approach of old age a mere diminution of life," and who regard the ideals they had earlier in life as faded. We must remember that it can be said of a very few people that they are artists in life, he wrote. And we must remember "that the art of life is the most distinguished and rarest of all the arts."[26]

Older Women: The Search for Truths and Realities

Research in social gerontology and sociology reveals that many taken-for-granted "facts" are fictions. Among these are the notion that the American family pattern (as if there were such) "evolved" from an extended kinship system to a nuclear unit, that grown children neglect or abandon their aging parents, that people "age" in a certain way regardless of the particular social world in which they live, that "the past" was always better than "today's world," that people in "other societies" (as if there were a "they" any more than there is a "we") are more benevolent toward the elderly than "Americans" are, that people who say they prefer "intimacy at a distance" or that they are retiring "for health reasons" are speaking the truth of their lives, that in America retirement brings massive migrations of "the elderly" in its wake. That people continue to insist upon these as truths in the face of clear evidence that they are fictions or not very glittering generalities would make a fascinating research project in itself.

The truth, it has been promised, will make us free. But the truth is many-faceted, and social scientific truth has a way of creating fictions of its own. One fiction is that social scientific research findings disclose all that is essential about a human life. But collectivities—"widows," "mature women workers," "low-income elderly"—are appearances floating on the surface of society. No matter how ingenious or sophisticated the methods of study of these appearances may be, research confined to surfaces can never penetrate their origins or open the vein of inner life. There *is* a collective aspect to every character, and from this truth all truths in social science flow. But to claim that this collective aspect is the essential truth is to deny the humanity of another, and therefore one's own. What is appalling is that this is done so often in the very name of humanity. The seeds are thrown away, the better to see the husk. In "Generations: Women of the South," portraits of two older women are drawn.[27] Whereas a collective portrait would exhibit the travail and deprivation of these two lives, the individual portraits are radiantly alive with courage and endurance and dedication to the highest ideals of community life. What sense could be made of one portrait without seeing the other?

Every human life is a weaving of character with circumstance. The oral memoirist is a weaver at work recovering the past and making a design of her life. The way a woman sees her life is threaded through the way she tells of it. Remembering does more than re-create: it is a creative act in itself. It is as much a work of imagination and longing as of restoration, as much a work of feeling as of thought. To pull a thread anywhere in the fabric is to unravel it and to lose the design. It has been well said that we need a Piaget for the aged,[28] for to know old age from within we need to know much more about the workings of Memory.

Who is to say which is the greater reality, the fact "established" in oral testimony or the feelings that inspirit the way it is told? By what authority are the memories of the old sorted into what is significant and what is not, into what is Truth and what is Illusion? A grandmother in Pittsburgh marveled at the beauty of her memories of the celebrations of the Italian holidays, of the fireworks on summer evenings, of her father as a man loved by everyone. A Jewish grandmother in Chicago promised that one day she would write a story about the street she lived on when she was growing up, where Germans and Swedes, Italians and Norwegians and Jews created a neighborhood in the true sense of the word. An old woman told the *Foxfire* editors that sometimes she wondered if the old times had been real, for when they went over to the old home place it looked so different, with everything gone. Next summer, she said, she would go back over there to see if she could find just one little rock from the old chimney. Perhaps that rock would be assurance that she had not dreamed her life.

Through oral histories of older women, America is seen through women's eyes, and without these records American history could never be more than half-told. In *Making Do,* women remember the Great Depression. In the *Foxfire* project, women tell of the old-timey ways, of planting by the signs, of midwives and granny women, of the basket-weaving, soap-making, broom-making, quilting and weaving, of corn shuckings and candy pullings and log rollings. Through their oral histories, grandmothers in Pittsburgh tell of how it was to leave the old country for America. They tell of the 1918 flu epidemic, the steel strike, the Johnstown flood, the Depression, World War II, and all throughout, of life in one of America's great cities during the first half of this century. Women's oral memoirs are a gleaming quarry for the folklorist and the archivist.

They beckon to the gerontologist, too. Here are revelations about the subjective aspects of aging, and here are proofs of the continuity of human life. Oral memoirs are an archway wherethrough the generations may see themselves in one another. Jeane Westin intended that *Making Do* would be much more than an informational book about women's experiences of the Great Depression. She meant her book to serve as inspirational, as a way of joining the daughters of the Depression with their foremothers. This vital connection is what the *Foxfire* project is all about, as well. Young editors come face to face with their past and their future, and they learn what it is to be old. In the persons of Beulah Perry and Aunt Arie and the others, they find energy and valor at the last of life. They find humor in the face of loneliness, and the fierce love of life and of the place that is one's home, and the great love of the old for young people. They come to understand the longing of old people to light the way of the young. And they give the old the priceless gift of the eager and attentive listener.

As the sculptor releases the form of a being from stone, so oral histories release these old women from categories—"black, elderly widow," "rural," "low-income aged." They release their love, their laughter, and their speech— " . . . and men wearing moustaches. Now I don't like that either. It'd be like kissing a stinging worm."[29] When oral histories are translated into social scientific facts, much is lost in the translation. There is a loss when they are translated into literary art as well. Data compress and even suffocate the vividness and concreteness and immediacy of what is said in an oral history interview. Short stories, dramas, novels commit another kind of sin against them. An oral history may be enlivened by a vital force that beckons the fiction writer or the dramatist like a dancing light a little further ahead on the path. But that light is the light of Tantalus. The writer may follow it forever; it can never be overtaken. Elusive, alluring, it is the light of the reality of a human life that is a thousand narratives, a thousand thousand plots, that goes on living because every ending is another beginning. There is a hugeness and vibrancy and boldness about a human life no science or art can tame or hold fast. The reach of both analyst and artist ever exceeds the grasp. All of us belong to ourselves in a way we can never belong to anyone else. Every work of the literary imagination, like every work of social science, is an approximation of reality. To see older women in twentieth-century America "in the round," they must be seen in self-portraits of oral memoirs as well as from the angles of vision of social science and literary art. And where a representational literature does not exist, oral histories reveal truths that cannot otherwise be known. Corinne Krause has remarked that the lives of ethnic women have been little explored, and in the few fictions in which Slavic, Italian, and Jewish women appear, they are not so much characters as caricatures.[30] They are not so much women as witches or saints who are mocked or canonized. Works of the literary imagination and social scientific studies both are approximations of realities. Both are relative truths.

Old people need to redeem the past from oblivion as urgently as they need bread. The old people in Myerhoff's *Number Our Days* had no younger people to bear witness for them. They had to bear witness for themselves.[31] This was a moral imperative, for the old feel morally responsible for examining their lives. When older people speak for themselves about aging, about their past and present lives, they create realities and reveal truths that cannot be known by any other means. These realities, too, are approximations. These truths, too, are relative. Sherna Gluck addresses the issue of cultural resemblances and differences between the oral history interviewer and the memoirist. In some cases, there are not enough women of a given cultural tradition who have access to the skills and equipment needed to record oral memoirs. Until these are made accessible to all women—and Gluck believes every woman ought to do all she can to share these skills—"the role of the 'outsider' will remain crucial. Otherwise, the history of Black, Hispanic, Asian, and Native American women will be lost, not only to them, but also to us."[32]

It can happen that an outsider is given the freedom to explore topics that are taboo to those who live by a cultural tradition. Yvonne Tixier y Vigil and Nan Elsasser found in their interviews with Hispanic women that they were more willing to talk about sex with the Anglo interviewer than with the Chicana interviewer, but that in contrast to this, "topics associated with discrimination were more likely to be discussed openly with the Chicana than with the Anglo" (13, n. 8). It would be interesting to know to what extent cultural traditions make a difference in interviews about the subject of aging. Pauline Bart reports that reference to the menopause appears to be related to the gender of the investigator.[33] Gender is probably more crucial than culture, but cultural differences should never be lightly dismissed. Taking careful note of Tixier y Vigil and Elsasser's experience, and well aware that "outsiders" to a cultural tradition do not have the temptation that insiders do to take too much for granted, Gluck writes that, nonetheless, her experience has persuaded her that cultural similarities encourage trust and cultural differences may reinforce feelings of social distance. She reports that she has light hair and a light complexion, and that for this reason, the Jewish immigrant women she interviewed assumed that she was not Jewish. "As soon as I dropped a clue for them, both the content of the interview . . . and the nature of our relationship changed." At the same time, she says that she has "passed" when she interviewed Anglo-Saxon women, both because of the way she looks and because of her socialization into Anglo culture. And she reports that a very light-skinned black student of hers from Texas was treated with politeness by a black 92-year-old woman and her 70-year-old daughter, and that the interview with them "progressed uneventfully," until the third session, when the interviewees "realized that she was 'one of us.'" After that, there was a dramatic change in the nature of the interview. Also, Gluck writes, those few students in her oral history classes who are male were never able to overcome the barriers of differences in gender, in spite of all their efforts to do so. It is more than trust that is involved, she observes. Cultural resemblances, subtly conveyed through expressions of attitude and vocabulary and body language, may be decisive for determining the quality of the oral history interview.[34]

But if cultural traditions cannot be ignored, neither can they be made an absolute measure of truth and reality. If they were, writers of fiction and psychologists have nothing to work with but the leavings of anthropology and sociology. Character makes all the difference in oral memoirs as in life itself. If any two people imagine that they look at the world from the same point of view, they are laboring under one of the grandest illusions of all human experience. What is more, few older women in America today live by a coherent system of cultural beliefs. Few could speak with unshakable confidence, as Mountain Wolf Woman spoke to Nancy Lurie, of what age means, of how long the proper life span is, of what women are like as they grow older.[35] *Study your own kind,* people of ethnic groups other than her own told Barbara Myerhoff in the early 1970s when she was looking for subjects for her studies in ethnicity and aging.[36] But who in America is of one "kind?," one might ask in reply to this most unkind suggestion. There was at that time a celebration of ethnic identity, and it lasted about as long as most fashions of the cultural mentality last these days. All the same, for very few foreign-born grandmothers and great-grandmothers in America today has the clock stopped, the world stood still. Very few can manage to insulate their lives from other lifeways. The impression that one has done so is an appearance, and keen social observers look under appearances. The very ferocity and stubbornness with which a person clings uncritically to some idea from "tradition" betrays a consciousness of change that threatens to engulf all one has lived for. It is a natural response to the cultural shocks that have reverberated throughout this fascinating and tormented century.

The condition and fate of old people cannot be understood unless the old are seen in the living context of society, culture, and human history. Beauvoir rightly insists upon this, and that is why she read the ethnological records in preparing for her encyclopaedic study of old age.[37] Each of us lives inside the cave of a particular time and place and system of social arrangements, and only a cross-cultural perspective can redeem us from the confusion of our individual experience with Necessity. Beauvoir consulted the Human Relations Area Files to find what is "inescapable" or universal about old age. But the Human Relations Area Files are a source of approximations of realities, of relative truths. Initiated by Murdock as the Yale Cross Cultural Studies in 1937, they are a repository of records drawn up by very human observers with very human predilections and prejudices. And since every culture is ever in the process of change, ethnological materials gathered at one point in time should not be taken as true for all historical time. Whether a culture is believed to be in the ascendancy or in decline or at a plateau will certainly affect what is seen and heard about it by outsiders and insiders alike. Moreover, there is always an hiatus between the ideal culture—what people think is supposed to be the case—and the real culture—what *is* the case. And people are always more articulate about the ideal culture, for it is infinitely more difficult to know what is actually going on than it is to know what is supposed to be going on.

Beauvoir remarks that ethnological materials must be used with reservations because few observers see a culture from the inside, and because few of the records are an organized synthesis of observations. She is right on both counts, as she is right in saying that statistics are at least as arbitrary as ethnological reports (66–67). But there is more to the matter than this. Those who see a culture from the inside do not necessarily see it steadily and see it whole. Quite the contrary, in fact—for the inside view is a mote in the eye by definition. Furthermore, syntheses of observations are frequently organized in the service of a particular point of view about human life, which does not exactly make them objective, though they are usually claimed to be so. Although one may begin with the best of intentions to refrain from making very large leaps in the dark in drawing inferences from ethnological materials, good intentions are not enough. One example should suffice to sharpen this point. Hall, who wrote that Boas knew of no compendious work on old age in any language, concluded from this that there was up to his time no gerontologist in anthropology. But he wanted, all the same, to explore "the history of old age." He was more modest than most about his researches. Nonetheless, he succumbed to the temptation to make the general statement that "the unfavorable far outweigh the favorable mentions."[38] One of these "mentions" is this:

> In Tierra del Fuego, Darwin tells how Jimmy Buttons, a native, described the slaughter of the aged in winter and famine. Dogs, he said, catch otters; old women, not. He then proceeded to detail just how they were killed, imitated and ridiculed their cries and shrieks, told the parts of their bodies that were best to eat, and said they must generally be killed by friends and relatives. [39]

Godfrey Lienhardt observes that the picture of "primitive man" emerging around the middle of the nineteenth century was less accurate than that accepted earlier in that century by humane ethnologists, and was the complete reverse of "the noble savage," the romantic picture of an even earlier period. There was a selective use of sources by Herbert Spencer, Sir John Lubbock, and others, to show "lower" characteristics exhibited by living "primitives." Darwin's account of the Fuegians was first published in 1871, and it presents a very different picture of them than that provided by W. P. Snow, who had published a description of them in 1861 in the ("easily accessible") *Journal of the Ethnological Society of London*, based upon his visit to Tierra del Fuego. Later, E. Lucas Bridges, who lived for a long time with these people, wrote in *Uttermost Part of the Earth* (1948) about how the Fuegians were at first puzzled by the kinds of questions put to them in Darwin's time. They began by answering them as they thought they were expected to, for example, as if they were cannibals because it was believed they were. Finally, they "made up fantastic stories for the amusement of seeing them taken seriously." Lienhardt quotes Bridges:

> We are told that they described, with much detail, how the Fuegians ate their enemies killed in battle, and when there were no such victims, devoured their old women. When asked if they ate dogs when hungry, they said they did not, as dogs were useful for catching otter, where as old women were of no use at all.[39]

Just as social and cultural worlds are ever changing and made visible to us through the eyes of others who so often find what they are seeking, so, too, the self is a republic of selves ever in the process of becoming, whose qualities are in the eye of the beholder. The Bali visited by Margaret Mead is another world from the Bali seen by Anaïs Nin. Edna Ferber's Iowa, where in Ottumwa she endured the cruelties of anti-Semitism, is another Iowa than that experienced by Ruth Suckow. Sara Orne Jewett's Maine is a world away from the Maine of Louise Nevelson's childhood.

In the search for the inner experience of women's aging, there is no fixed point of departure and no final destination. Written memoirs and autobiographies may be more revelatory of inner views on aging than other literary forms because the memoirist is inclined to look backward from a life course perspective and to be conscious of the continuity of selfhood through time.

Autobiographies, Eleanor Roosevelt observed, are "only useful as the lives you read about and analyze may suggest to you something that you may find useful in your own journey through life."[40] This is a literary form that has possibilities for moral instruction about the aging process as a continuum and about how to age with grace and intelligence.[41] But these possibilities are not always realized. Confession is not always good for the soul of either the memoirist or the reader. Indeed, autobiographies and memoirs are selective by definition, for there are very reserved people—Willa Cather and Edna St. Vincent Millay, among others—who would not want to make their life stories public. Then, too, there are those who believe it is as threatening to tell your life story as to have your photograph taken.[42] Some "silences" are kept by personal choice.

Who looks through autobiographies and memoirs for the truth about women's aging looks in vain. Every woman takes her own attitude toward her life, toward life itself. Margaret Sanger wrote that she would not want to live her childhood over again. She spoke for Margaret Sanger, not for all women. Ilka Chase wrote that nothing gave her greater happiness than the realization that she could not possibly live her youth over again; she remembered her girlhood as "awful." Not all of us do. There is this "precious difference" between any two people, and this means that old age, like every other phase of the life cycle, is different in some way for every person. At the same time, there are moments of revelation in every person's life that, if they were told, would speak to everyone. In *Seven Houses,* Josephine Johnson remembers, "Growing up is a terrible time. A person lives with such intensity you wonder there is anything left to go on with when it's over."[43] Looking back even further, she reflects that, "Children are serious little old people inside all the time" (135).

Welthy Honsinger Fisher believed that time moves more swiftly as we grow older. Studies in social psychology show that most older people who are asked about this say the same thing. Hall wrote in *Senescence* that the seventieth birthday is the saddest. In *Growing Old,* Cumming and Henry report from the findings of the Kansas City Study of Adult Life that people experience a crisis that is marked by anxiety between the ages of 60 and 65, and after this become more contented, but that again in the seventies, they become restless and irritable. Those who live on after this become tranquil and are satisfied with their lives. Intriguing as these observations are, we cannot take them for more than very general ones. Florida Scott-Maxwell wrote that her seventies were rather serene, but that her eighties were passionate. And there are old people who may experience the passage of time as quite slow-moving. So many of the "truths" about growing older are relative to the person speaking them (and that person's mood). What is a "milestone" for one is as nothing to another. Dorothy Parker's personal essay on turning 50 tells us much more about Dorothy Parker than it does about arriving at the half-century mark.

"Age takes us by surprise," Beauvoir remarks.[44] Now and then, yes, but not at *every* moment that we become aware of how old we actually are. She recalls that Chateaubriand said age is a shipwreck. So it probably seemed to him to be—*some* of the time. (Even Chateaubriand must have had his lighter moments.) Beauvoir states that age is an "unrealizable." Again, this is probably not true for everyone, but even if it were, it is not true for anyone *all* of the time. When Ilka Chase wrote that sometimes she was amazed to find that she was a grown-up,[45] she was writing about age as an unrealizable. It is a very human experience, feeling this amazement—sometimes at being a certain age, and at other times at being alive at all. But no one *always* thinks about aging and mortality with amazement. An insight need not be made into a system to keep its light. Louise Bogan wrote in her journals that the reason older women are inhibited about passionate love is because there are so many ways older women can make fools of themselves.[46] There is much truth in this. Not one whit of that truth is compromised by the fact that there are older women who would gladly pay the price of making fools of themselves for the chance to love like that again. Literary truths are of a different order than the truths of social science. They are arrived at by different means, and they should not be tested or judged by the same canons of criticism.

After a million years, Lillian Smith writes, women are beginning to break the silence about themselves. Smith believes that women write memoirs and diaries and journals exceptionally well, that women's writing in these forms has a down-to-earth, vivid, and sometimes poetic quality that has an enchantment of its own. Women *can* think abstractly, but "*they are, like artists, closer to things, to the human flesh, and human feelings; and they tend to remember that the concrete is always different while the abstract has a deadly sameness.*"[47] Although women writers are vastly different from one another, in their letters and diaries they can all give us "*a superb, unforgettable awareness of fragments of the human experience.*" But in Smith's view, women have not written *great* autobiographies. To do this, the writer must accept the manifold selves and bring them all together. Have men written them? Smith says Yes and No. To write the story of one's life "*is a spiritual and intellectual ordeal,*" and a creative ordeal as well. It is a work in creation of the Self and of one's life. She finds it no wonder that women more often write in diaries, journals, and notebooks. She sees the writing of an autobiography, the search for the meaning of one's life, to be more than a courageous undertaking. She sees it to be a demiurgic task. Yet she believes that it is important for every person living in our times "*to bring our split selves into some kind of unity*" (49).

Striving toward wholeness is much in evidence in women's autobiographies. Isadora Duncan wrote of her many selves—the Chaste Madonna, the Messalina, the Magdalen, and the Blue Stocking were but four among hundreds—and of her soul as somewhere aloft, apart from them all.[48] To look through these autobiographies for a master work wherein all the selves are unified is to look in vain. To look through them for a master work on women's aging (which is the same thing) is to look in vain. For the building of the Self is a task that is never completed, a task worthy of work through the last hour of life. There are fragments of insights, instead. But they are luminous fragments, nonetheless. When Isadora Duncan looked back at the four figures walking down the streets of London, the Clan Duncan of an earlier life, she saw them—her own younger self among them—as creatures who might exist in Dickens's imagination. In another passage, she reflected that life is a dream. Helen Keller looked back on the earlier years at Wrentham as a kind of pre-existence. These passages are a window to the look of life to women who have passed its meridian. There are moral lessons in autobiographies, too. Margaret Sanger believed there are three major tests to character, "sudden power, sudden wealth, and sudden publicity. Few can stand the latter; nothing goes to the head with more violence."[49] Harriet Monroe wrote, "The mystery is not the greatness of life, but its littleness. That we, so grandly born, so mightily endowed, should grope with blind eyes and bound limbs in the dust and mire of petty desires and grievances."[50] Helen Keller compared the writing of her autobiography with the picture her friend Colonel Roebling labored over in the last years of his life, a picture of a river spanned by a bridge, assembled with thousands of fragments of paper. "Into the tray of one's consciousness are tumbled thousands of scraps of experience," she wrote. "That tray holds you dismembered, so to speak. Your problem is to synthesize yourself and the world you live in." This is made all the more difficult "when you find that the pieces never look the same to you two minutes in succession. . . . With each new experience . . . , they undergo strange transmutations." Even when she made a picture that was fairly complete, she found countless fragments in the tray and did not know what to do with them. "The longer I work, the more important these fragments seem; so I pull the picture apart and start it all over again."[51] Keller's autobiography is a miracle of its own. She worked with fragments of notes made in braille. Many of the dots had been worn down with the passage of time. Much of the material she had to use had never been put into braille. Sometimes she composed on the typewriter, pricking notes on the tops of the pages with a hairpin so she could keep track of them. Thousands of papers were stacked on the floor, marked with thousands of directions. Rewriting was done with scissors and paste. The work was spelled to her three times over while she continued to revise it.

In part, ignorance and dread of aging is a consequence of bowing to received opinion—"everyone knows" that older women are unlovely, unloved, uncreative, unhappy, hypochondriacal. Until one sees into the lives of particular older women, one cannot claim to know otherwise. Knowledge of social facts is not enough. To look only at life's surface is to miss its meanings for those who experience it. Those who report social facts and those who write fiction have much to share. But the vocation of social science is very different from that followed by those who take the literary veil. There is a fine and fateful distinction between the two. If it is not respected, the loss to social science, to literature, and through that to us all, will be one day soon beyond redeeming:

It is the lot of the imaginative creative writer always to look on, never to participate. . . . one must be either a spectator or a participant. One can't march in a parade and see it too. . . . A theme . . . may become a glowing moving thing under the magic of genius. For genius is capable of creating flesh and blood out of star dust; and the dimensional men and women thus born live long, long after the cause through which they were conceived is dead or forgotten. That is why imaginative writers should think in terms of human beings first and Cause afterward.[52]

These words, written in the 1930s, are a clarion call for our times. So many roads followed in this book about older women in the United States lead back to that time. It was a time, Ferber reported, when the book lists were all but filled with biography and autobiography, with sociology and science and politics, essays and philosophy—in a word, with "nonfiction." As it was during the Great Depression, so it is today. But there is something else to be considered. Today, non-books are crowding out not only works of fiction but works of serious scholarship. I do not doubt that works of great value in every genre may never come to light. Nonfiction "outsells" fiction by a wide margin, and this is what happens in a society in which artistic endeavor is assessed in terms of what is good for business. But works of nonfiction also are measured in terms of market value. And it is a non-book that is made for consumers. A book is made for readers. Where there is no challenge to thought about the nature and purpose and direction of human life, which is what growing older is all about, we cannot address the central questions of humanistic gerontology. So we are given the gift of extended life, and we make of it a problem for the economists to resolve, and we fall asleep in front of the television set.

When aging is seen from within, truths may be told and revelations made that could not be conveyed by any other means. This is why both Hall and Beauvoir made extensive use of personal documents and literature in their sections on old age in history. This is why both writers included sections on literary perspectives on aging in their wide-ranging studies (although in both books the writings by men far outnumber the writings by women on the subject). American women of letters most certainly have not been silent about aging and mortality. Twentieth-century American literature is rich with their reflections and imaginative literature on these subjects, so much so that the task of selection is as formidable as it is imperative.

In the works of Gertrude Atherton, Ellen Glasgow, Zora Neale Hurston, May Sarton, and Edith Wharton, illuminations on women's aging may be found both in their autobiographies, essays, journals, or letters on the one hand, and in their short stories or novels on the other. Atherton, who believed that one is never too old to begin life anew, wrote of women's rejuvenation in *Black Oxen*. In the "many cruel truths" Hohenhauer tells Marie Zattiany in this novel, Atherton challenges us to say how an older woman, to whom the appearance and strength of youth has been restored, ought to live. In her essays, she would have us see Stepmother Nature for the old harridan Atherton thought her to be, Life as our most pitiless enemy, one to be fought and confounded, and old age to be defeated by the spirited among us. Ellen

Glasgow, in her letters, her autobiography, and her novels, explored the workings of memory (the "visitations of the past") and the freedom from personal entanglements that is only possible in the second half of life. She wrote that only when life moves out upon the "wide open sea of impersonality, can one really begin to live." In the old, it is sensation that dies last. The tang of woodsmoke, the brilliance of the hickory and sweet gum and oak trees in autumn, the rain falling, as that English rain was falling "in a lost hollow of memory," the scent of crushed apples, the sound of someone playing a nameless Hungarian song—these are the wellsprings of memory. These are where the restorative waters flow as from the fountains of eternal youth.

Zora Neale Hurston saw her life unfold in twelve scenes foretelling her orphanhood and homelessness when she was a child of 7. In her wanderings toward the "far horizon," she transformed the thought-pictures passed around the store porch in Eatonville, the "crayon enlargements of life," into fictions and music, drama and dance, folklore and ethnological studies. In her novels, she searched out the many meanings of love and freedom in the life of an older woman. The hour of her mother's death began her wanderings, in time more than in geography—but then again, "not so much in time as in spirit."

May Sarton, like Ellen Glasgow, wrote that it is only youth that has no finality. Once the meridian of life is passed, the meaning of mortality is revealed. Then the innermost quality of life changes, and it becomes more precious than it ever was in youth. Old age can be a "timeless ascent." Then love may be as intense as it was in youth, but it is cast in a wider arc. In late life, a woman may be haunted by her mother's "light ghost" hovering near. A woman's old age may be a time for reconciliation with her earthly mother, and through this with all womanhood.

In a short story, Edith Wharton brings us to that fatal turn in the path "from which mountains look as transient as flowers." Perhaps only after that turn is taken can the traveler know the nature of Illusion. Wharton, who confided to Bergson that she had "odd holes" in her memory, came to understand that "the gift of precision in ecstasy" may be "almost as rare in the appreciator as in the creator." She was, like all of us, a republic of selves. The "timid debutante" was transformed into "a passionate lover" in autumn, in October, when witch hazel, "the old woman's bloom," begins to flower. In her later fictions, Wharton, too, explored the theme of rejuvenation. In one, she created a character as familiar to us today, in the 1980s, as she was to her contemporaries in the 1920s, one who sought an anodyne—a twilight sleep—for aging.

To read twentieth-century American fiction by women writers is to plunge into an ocean of diversity, to meet characters who have grown, as Eudora Welty puts it, "from the inside out." In American short stories, the reader meets old women who are companions in old age, who have discovered that old age can be a time for wandering. To see into the interiors of the second half of life is to glimpse the workings of inheritance whose force is hidden from the young. To see into these interiors is to perceive the image of the honeycomb, the complexity of earlier life. In American fictions, there are old women journeying, with "touching collections" in their bundle-handkerchiefs. In fiction the reader meets old women who created a sorority a century ago at a Poor-farm very like that in the making at the Merrill Courts in today's society. The reader who follows Phoenix Jackson traveling the "worn path" sees how "the deep-grained habit of love" can remember the way.

American short stories can remind us of truths we are always in danger of forgetting. There is the truth that so long as Ma Mandle and "my son Hugo" remain a couple, she cannot grow old. There is the truth that an old woman can be enslaved by her daughter. There is the truth that an old woman tied to the chariot of young life, who carries the burden of the lives of others, prays that she will never become a burden to them. A short story can remind us that there are child-mothers who become their grown daughter's daughter. And that it can happen that to be a survivor means to outlive grown children. In "Old Man Minick," we are reminded of the unspoken agreement between aging couples that the wife will outlive her husband. In "The Children's Game," we are reminded that, when the casket is closed, some women become as waifs in the world.

It is only in fiction that we can hear "The Scream on Fifty-seventh Street," only in fiction that we can understand the last things an old woman must attend to, only in fiction that we can see the centuries folded into the circles around the eye of an old woman coming to "The Welcome Table." In fiction, we meet a woman who knows that "old folks is the nation." Literary art discloses old women "resting" their shopping bags in the plate-glass window of the A & P in Uptown, Chicago, the regulars at the public library, the sorrowfulness of bus stations. In literary art we meet Ida, the "old hearth goddess," and Miss Lavore, who "had a life."

Works of the literary imagination have truths of their own to tell, a life of their own to live. "You kill life by analysing it too rationally," a character in a novel by May Sarton reflects.[53] In another novel by Sarton, a poet rebukes a sociologist: "The trouble with you scientists is that you really begin to imagine you can reach all the answers by a method, some sort of trick, without . . . being willing to be changed. How can you approach a work of art in that arrogant a spirit?"[54] The quarrel between the poet and the scientist is an ancient one, and often it is, as in this novel by Sarton, a lovers' quarrel. Katherine Anne Porter wrote powerfully of the creative artist's attitude:

> There exist documents of political and social theory which belong, if not to poetry, certainly to the department of humane letters. They are reassuring statements of the great hopes and dearest faiths of mankind and they are acts of high imagination. But all working, practical political systems, even those professing to originate in moral grandeur, are based upon and operate by contempt of human life and the individual fate; in accepting any one of them and shaping his mind and work to that mold, the artist dehumanizes himself, unfits himself for the practise of any art.[55]

Good fences, it has been said, make good neighbors. Our fences need mending. Those at work in all the "specialisms" have much to teach and much to learn from one another. But so long as diaries or letters or short stories are dismissed as "impressionistic" on the one hand, and demographic or participant observation studies as "antihumanistic" on the other, there can be no creative interchange.

In the gathering of sources for the symposium that is the spirit of this book, the subject of women's aging seemed at times to have a will of its own—a will to bring this creative dialogue about. Arlie Russell Hochschild's book about Merrill Court, so like a literary work of social realism, and Joyce Stephens's book about the old people living at the Guinevere, so like a work of naturalism, are invitations in themselves to an interdisciplinary seminar on aging. Many works in social science and literature could serve as occasions for a sharing of perspectives. Bahr and Garrett's *Women Alone* includes an entire appendix on Reactions to Disaffiliation among Aged Women: The Novelists' View, which presents an annotated bibliography of novels about the lives of elderly women. Also, I found striking parallels between the case histories presented in books on social gerontology and the themes in American short stories. For example, Edna Ferber's short story "Old Lady Mandle" and a case cited by Minna Field in *The Aged, The Community and Society* both told the same story of an aging mother and her grown son who decides in midlife to marry and have a family of his own. Comparison of the story with the actual case history—of fiction with social fact—could lead to a reconsideration of how certain changes in twentieth-century America have affected the relationships between elderly parents and their grown children. Minna Field's "Mrs. Young,"[56] who did not want to give up her room and bed to her infant grandchild and sleep on the living-room couch, preferring to find a room with a private family to preserve her own privacy, said she did not know what she would have done without her Social Security checks, which supplemented an inadequate income. Ferber's Old Lady Mandle, apparently, *had* an adequate income—fortunately for her, in the days before Social Security. How many millions of elderly before that legislation was passed—as Jewett's ladies of the Byfleet Poorhouse or on Poor-farms of their own—had to depend completely on the largesse of kin and community? One has only to read the searing novel *Years Are So Long* by Josephine Lawrence,[57] published not quite fifty years ago, to be reminded of the conflict between the generations, the rejection of the elderly by the middle-aged and the young, and the dereliction that was the fate of so many old people in the United States even at that time, just before Social Security was signed into law.

We can never be reminded enough that the very life source of social science is the humanistic tradition.[58] The urban *Women Alone*, the survivors in *Communities of the Alone* and in the tough world of *Loners, Losers, and Lovers* have literary counterparts in Hardwick's *Sleepless Nights,* in Howland's *Blue in Chicago.* There are other convergences. There are fictional counterparts to the older women patients, the "aging tomboys," the "perpetual daughters" and others, at the Older Adult Program of Northwestern University Medical School.[59] Psychologist David Gutmann suggests that once children are grown and independent, the chronic sense of parental emergency is eased. At this time in life, both men and women are free to live out the potentialities and pleasures they relinquished earlier in order to fulfill their parental tasks, and each sex becomes somewhat like what the other once was.[60] The consonance between this idea and the strong attraction between an older woman and a young man portrayed in fiction—in Francine du Plessix Gray's *Lovers and Tyrants,* for example, and in May Sarton's *Mrs. Stevens Hears the Mermaids Singing,* and also in Doris Lessing's *The Summer Before the Dark*—is a subject worthy of further study. Certainly it would be a refreshing counterpoint to the overworked theme of the attraction between the older man and the young woman.

Anthropologist Margaret Mead did not find it necessary to conceal her literary ambitions or the fact that she wrote poetry for years. In her autobiography, *Blackberry Winter,* she quotes her last poem, a poem written to her daughter. In the 1930s, at a time when Mary Beard thought that the intellectual revolution uniting all the various departments of life and thought was already underway, poets and anthropologists recognized their common interests. Today their worlds seem very far apart. If a creative symposium were to take place between those in the social sciences and those in the humanities, there are themes in the works listed in the bibliography of this book that could lead to a shared vision of the objectives of humanistic gerontology. The sense of living two lives in later life is expressed by Eleanor Roosevelt, Margaret Sanger, Ellen Glasgow, May Sarton, and Edith Wharton. The fostering love of older women for the young is expressed in the *Foxfire* books, in Willa Cather's essays and fiction, in Luree Miller's *Late Bloom,* and in letters and articles in *Broomstick.* Old women's feeling that they still have lives to be lived appears in myriad forms, among them the oral histories of the grandmothers in Pittsburgh. The vision of old women's transformative power, the older woman's desire for reconciliation with her mother, the creative fire that flames inside the body to the last of life, the wonder-working of memory and wisdom—these, too, are part of every story, every source. Perhaps when all the perspectives of the "specialisms" are combined, all the fragments brought together, they may reveal an age-old story, the story of endless renewal through the reunion of Demeter with Persephone.

It is certainly true that the words *human, humane, humanist,* and *humanities* have been badly confused when used in thinking and writing about aging, and that in helping us find attitudes toward the old we would least like to think about, literature can free us "of complacently euphemistic cant" and of "gratuitous, paralyzing guilt." In this way, literature can enable us "to address the genuine problems of the aging with free intelligences and clear consciences."[61] The point is well taken that sentimentality, guilt, and wishful thinking can only lead to hebetude. And, from the other side, the well-schooled social scientist knows that anger, however righteous, leaves one purblind, and that to study a subject with the closed mind of an uncritical advocate is to study a subject with impaired vision. Writing of this subject from many perspectives, I have worked to see it clearly, worked to set myself free of sentimentality, of guilt, of wishful thinking, of anger. Nevertheless, from the very beginning, I have taken a point of view, a "special lighting,"[62] carrying forward Mary Beard's vision of bridge-building and of woman as a major force in shaping history.[63] Because of this, my point of view has much more kinship with Hall's than with Beauvoir's. From the very beginning, I sensed the truth of what he stated so unabashedly. "Old women," he wrote, in the chapter in which he reported on his questionnaire returns,

> perhaps even more than old men, seem to enjoy an "Indian summer" of life. The best of them grow serene, tolerant, liberal, often devote themselves with great assiduity to charity, to causes, . . . and really guide all about them without their knowledge and without realizing themselves that they are doing so. . . . they illustrate at every stage of life what is true of all its stages, that woman lives nearer to the life of the race, is a better representative of it, and so a more generic being than man, and is thus less prone to dwarfing specialization.[64]

How ought one to live so as to grow old with wisdom and with grace? "*Meublez votre tête*, child!" an old gentleman told Margot Benary-Isbert when she was still a schoolgirl. "The older you become the more you will realize how important that is."[65] To "stock your head" may be the soundest advice of all to give the young. As for advice to give those already old, perhaps only those who have reached that shore may hope that it would be accepted in the same spirit in which it is offered. When Faith Baldwin's daughter presented her with a lightweight cane, the writer took this as an occasion for meditating on her "crabbèd age." In this essay, Baldwin acknowledged that she took exception to Browning's invitation to grow old along with him, since he had written this when he was only 29 years old. Baldwin confessed to a weariness with books advising their readers how to grow old gracefully, with articles extolling old age, and with the admonitions of physicians to the elders. She had not been serene since her days as a toddler, she wrote, and she was not grateful to have all her buttons still, since she had never had a "buttoned down mind." She kept up with the times as best she could, and she had not lost her hopes for the world and for the young. She did not mind being old so much as the insistence that all is sweetness and light for the aged, and the disabilities and prohibitions afflicting late life. Baldwin wrote of her admiration for old people who are still adventurous, and she remarked that she had an inner self who stubbornly refused to grow up.[66]

What are the truths of the experience of old age? The truth is that there are as many truths as there are lives, and that in every life there are truths that contradict one another. It may be true that the personality remains fundamentally the same throughout life.[67] But it may also be true that every day is a birth and a death.[68] There is a confluence of all these truths a little way ahead.

"Whatever form the writer chooses," Catherine Drinker Bowen has observed, whether this be fiction or poetry or scholarship, books are written because the writer "has something to discharge, some ghost within that struggles for release."[69] More than one ghost has been released in these pages. But of all those in the ghost warren that is my portion, the most restless is my sorrow over our hubris in the twilight of the twentieth century. It is only the love for youth that is Agape and our care for the world that belongs to them and to our children's children that can redeem us. This earth and the life of each of us upon it are not for anyone to plunder or possess. We have almost forgotten that we are *all* caretakers. Our responsibilities are awesome and our time is brief.

What is the good society, what is a good age, how shall the gift of extended life be received, what is it that the generations owe one another? The search for the reconciliation of the desire to know and the desire to create and the oldest moral passion is never-ending. Perhaps that is what every human life was meant to do, to make this search. In these pages it was made as a rite of passage. That, too, may be the meaning of every human life.

Notes

1. G. Stanley Hall, *Senescence: The Last Half of Life* (New York: D. Appleton and Co., 1922).

2. Simone de Beauvoir, *The Coming of Age*, trans. Patrick O'Brian (New York: Warner Paperback Library, 1973).

3. Margaret Mead, *Blackberry Winter: My Earlier Years* (New York: William Morrow, Pocket Book ed., 1975), p. 243.

4. The remark was made by Warren Reich, professor of bioethics at the Georgetown University Medical School, according to Constance Holden, "Briefing: Bioethical Reference," *Science* (February 23, 1979) 203(4382):729.

5. Mary R. Beard, "Introduction," *America Through Women's Eyes*, Mary R. Beard, ed. (New York: Greenwood Press, Inc., 1976), p. 6.

6. As quoted in David Hackett Fischer, *Growing Old in America* (New York: Oxford University Press, 1977), p. 196, n. 1.

7. Juanita Kreps and Robert Clark, *Sex, Age, and Work: The Changing Composition of the Labor Force* (Baltimore, The Johns Hopkins University Press, 1975), pp. 1–2.

8. "The Social Security system was deliberately designed to make no major change in the distribution of wealth," Fischer writes, but "the most astonishing fact" about the system "was not that it was passed in so conservative a form, but rather that it was passed at all in so conservative a nation." Fischer, *Growing Old in America*, p. 184.

9. See chapter 13, "Loosening Up Life," in Robert N. Butler, M.D., *Why Survive? Being Old in America* (New York: Harper and Row, Publishers, Inc., 1975), pp. 384–401, and Kreps and Clark, *Sex, Age, and Work*, pp. 79–82.

10. Luree Miller, *Late Bloom: New Lives for Women* (New York: Paddington Press, Ltd., 1979), p. 229.

11. Ellen Stein, "That Civilizing Spirit," *Southern Exposure* (Winter 1977) 4(4):65. Hereafter, all references to this article will be cited in the text by page number.

12. Dieter T. Hessel, Preface, *Maggie Kuhn on Aging: A Dialogue Edited by Dieter Hessel* (Philadelphia: The Westminster Press, 1977), p. 10. Hereafter, all references to this book will be cited in the text by page number.

13. Ibid., p. 76.

14. Luree Miller, *Late Bloom*, p. 184.

15. Marilyn R. Block, Janice L. Davidson, Jean D. Grambs, and Kathryn E. Serock, *Uncharted Territory: Issues and Concerns of Women over 40* (College Park, Md.: University of Maryland Center on Aging, 1978), p. 3. It is interesting that Hall believed there are five major stages in human life, childhood, adolescence, middle life or the "prime," senescence and "old age proper" or senectitude, and that he thought that senescence begins in the early forties, if not before, in women. Hall, *Senescence*, p. vii.

16. Lucretius, *Of the Nature of Things*, Book 2, "Atomic Motions." William Ellery Leonard, trans. (New York: E. P. Dutton and Co., Inc., 1950), p. 48.

17. U.S Department of Commerce, Bureau of the Census, Current Population Reports Special Studies, *A Statistical Portrait of Women in the U.S.*, Special Studies Series P 23, No. 58 (Washington, D.C.: U.S. Government Printing Office, 1976), p. 18. Hereafter, reference to this publication will be cited in the text by page number.

18. See Catherine Ravenscroft, Recorder, "Biological Realities and Myths," in *No Longer Young: Work Group Reports* (Ann Arbor, Mich.: The Institute of Gerontology, University of Michigan–Wayne State University, 1974), p. 17.

19. Estelle Fuchs, *The Second Season: Life, Love and Sex—Women in the Middle Years* (Garden City, N.Y.: Doubleday Anchor Press, 1977), p. 64.

20. C. G. Jung, *Modern Man in Search Of a Soul* (New York: Harcourt, Brace and World, Inc., 1933), p. 109.

21. Virgilia Peterson, *A Matter of Life and Death* (New York: Atheneum, 1961), pp. 190–91.

22. Marjorie Fiske Lowenthal, Majda Thurnher, David Chiriboga, et al., *Four Stages of Life: A Comparative Study of Women and Men Facing Transitions* (San Francisco: Jossey-Bass, Inc., 1975).

23. Jung, *Modern Man in Search of a Soul*, pp. 104–5.

24. Ann Belford Ulanov, *The Feminine in Jungian Psychology and in Christian Theology* (Evanston, Ill.: Northwestern University Press, 1971), p. 71.

25. M. Esther Harding, *The Way of All Women* (New York: G. P. Putnam's Sons for the C. G. Jung Foundation for Analytical Psychology, 1970), p. 23.

26. Jung, *Modern Man in Search of a Soul*, p. 110.

27. Margaret Rose Gladney, "If It was Anything for Justice," *Southern Exposure* (Winter 1977) 4(4):19–23; Wendy Watriss, "It's Something Inside You," *Southern Exposure* (Winter 1977) 4(4):76–81.

28. Stuart F. Spicker, "Gerontogenetic Mentation: Memory, Dementia and Medicine in the Penultimate Years," in *Aging and the Elderly: Humanistic Perspectives in Gerontology*, Stuart F. Spicker, Kathleen M. Woodward, and David D. Van Tassel, eds. (New Jersey: Humanities Press, Inc., 1978), pp. 153–80.

29. "Annie Perry," *Foxfire* 4, ed. with an introduction by Eliot Wigginton (New York: Anchor Press, Doubleday, 1977), p. 214.

30. Corinne Azen Krause, *Grandmothers, Mothers and Daughters: An Oral History Study of Ethnicity, Mental Health, and Continuity of Three Generations of Jewish, Italian, and Slavic-American Women* (New York: The Institute on Pluralism and Group Identity of The American Jewish Committee, 1978), p. 3.

31. Barbara Myerhoff, *Number Our Days* (New York: E. P. Dutton, 1978), p. 32.

32. Sherna Gluck, "What's So Special About Women? Women's Oral History," *Frontiers* (Summer 1977) 2(2):7. Hereafter, reference to this article will be cited in the text by page number.

33. Pauline B. Bart, "Why Women's Status Changes in Middle Age: The Turns of the Social Ferris Wheel," *Sociological Symposium* (Fall 1969) 3:6.

34. Gluck, "What's So Special About Women? Women's Oral History," p. 7.

35. Nancy Oestreich Lurie, ed., *Mountain Wolf Woman: Sister of Crashing Thunder, The Autobiography of a Winnebago Indian* (Ann Arbor, Mich.: The University of Michigan Press, 1966), pp. xvi, 112, n. 4, 114–15, n. 15, and 127.

36. Myerhoff, *Number Our Days*, pp. 11–12.

37. Beauvoir, *The Coming of Age*, p. 57. Hereafter, references to this book are cited in the text by page number.

38. Hall, *Senescence*, p. 38. Hereafter, reference to this book will be cited in the text by page number.

39. Godfrey Lienhardt, *Social Anthropology* (London: Oxford University Press, 1966), p. 11. Snow, incidentally, reported that the Fuegians "accepted the authority of several of the oldest women." Ibid.

40. Eleanor Roosevelt, *This Is My Story* (New York: Harper and Brothers, 1937), p. 363.

41. Walter G. Moss, "Aging in Humanistic Perspective," in *Humanistic Perspectives on Aging*, Walter G. Moss, ed. (Ann Arbor, Mich.: The Institute of Gerontology, University of Michigan–Wayne State University, 1976), pp. 2–3.

42. Myerhoff, *Number Our Days*, p. 42.

43. Josephine W. Johnson, *Seven Houses: A Memoir of Time and Places* (New York: Simon and Schuster, 1973), p. 86. Hereafter, reference to this book will be cited in the text by page number.

44. Beauvoir, *The Coming of Age*, p. 709. (On p. 419, she attributes this remark to Goethe.)

45. Ilka Chase, *Past Imperfect* (Garden City, N.Y.: Blue Ribbon Books, 1945), pp. 265–66.

46. Ruth Limmer, ed., "From the Journals of a Poet," *The New Yorker* (January 30, 1978) 53(50):60.

47. Lillian Smith, "On Women's Autobiography," *Southern Exposure* (Winter 1977) 4(4):49. For a discussion of "Women's Autobiography and the Male Tradition," see Estelle C. Jelinek, Introduction, in Estelle C. Jelinek, ed., *Women's Autobiography: Essays in Criticism* (Bloomington, Ind.: Indiana University Press, 1980), pp. 1–20. For a discussion of autobiographies and diaries, see Lynn Z. Bloom and Orlee Holder, "Anaïs Nin's *Diary* in Context," in Jelinek, *Women's Autobiography* pp. 206–20. Hereafter, reference to Lillian Smith's article will be cited in the text by page number.

48. Isadora Duncan, *My Life* (New York: Boni and Liveright, Inc., 1927), p. 2.

49. Margaret Sanger, *Margaret Sanger: An Autobiography* (New York: W. W. Norton and Co., 1938), p. 255.

50. Harriet Monroe, *A Poet's Life: Seventy Years in a Changing World* (New York: The Macmillan Co., 1938), p. 458.

51. Helen Keller, *Midstream: My Later Life* (Garden City, N.Y.: Doubleday, Doran and Co., Inc., 1929), p. 3.

52. Edna Ferber, *A Peculiar Treasure* (New York: Literary Guild, 1939), p. 245.

53. May Sarton, *The Small Room* (New York: W. W. Norton and Co., Inc., 1961), p. 161.

54. May Sarton, *Mrs. Stevens Hears the Mermaids Singing* (New York: W. W. Norton and Co., Inc., 1975), p. 164.

55. Katherine Anne Porter, Introduction, in Eudora Welty, *A Curtain of Green* (Garden City, N.Y.: Doubleday, Doran and Co., Inc., 1943), pp. xiii–xiv.

56. Minna Field, *The Aged, The Family, and the Community* (New York: Columbia University Press, 1972), pp. 76–77.

57. Josephine Lawrence, *Years Are So Long* (New York: Frederick A. Stokes Co., 1934). The film *Make Way for Tomorrow* was based on this novel.

58. Helene Deutsch, who based a paper she wrote on Balzac's novel *Deux Femmes*, perceives an analogy between some of Freud's observations in his paper "Mourning and Melancholia" and Flaubert's description of Charles Bovary's grief after the death of his wife. Deutsch writes, "Freud had arrived at these insights by scientific observation; Flaubert through his poetic intuition." Helene Deutsch, M.D., *Confrontations with Myself—An Epilogue* (New York: W. W. Norton and Co., Inc., 1973), p. 154. Erminie Lantero writes that Vladimir Soloviev, whom she names as "the first ecumenist of the nineteenth century," believed that Comte's "religion of humanity," together with the dogma of the Immaculate Conception, "pointed to a rediscovery of Sophia." Erminie Huntress Lantero, *Feminine Aspects of Divinity* (Wallingford, Pa.: Pendle Hill Publications, 1973), p. 17.

59. See David Gutmann, Jerome Grunes, and Brian Griffin, "The Clinical Psychology of Later Life: Developmental Paradigms," in Nancy Datan and Nancy Lohmann, eds., *Transitions of Aging*, (New York: Academic Press, Inc., 1980), pp. 119–31.

60. David Gutmann, "Parenthood: A Key to the Comparative Study of the Life Cycle," in

Nancy Datan and Leon H. Ginsberg, eds., *Life-Span Developmental Psychology: Normative Life Crises* (New York: Academic Press, Inc., 1975), pp. 167–84.

61. Richard Freedman, "Sufficiently Decayed: Gerontophobia in English Literature," in *Aging and the Elderly: Humanistic Perspectives in Gerontology*, Stuart F. Spicker, Kathleen M. Woodward, and David D. Van Tassel, eds. (New Jersey: Humanities Press, Inc., 1978), p. 60.

62. "'A point of view and a special lighting are not distortions,' says Santayana. 'They are conditions of vision, and spirit can see nothing not focused in some living eye.'" As quoted in Catherine Drinker Bowen, *Adventures of a Biographer* (Boston: Atlantic Monthly Press, 1959), p. 94.

63. Although "feminists respected Beard's scholarship," they "did not, for the most part, support her thesis that women had been a major force in shaping history." Barbara Kivel Turoff, "Mary Beard: Feminist Educator," *The Antioch Review* (Summer 1979) 37(3):279.

64. Hall, *Senescence*, p. 350.

65. Margot Benary-Isbert, *These Vintage Years* (New York: Abingdon Press, 1968), p. 49.

66. Faith Baldwin, "My Crabbèd Age," in *The Older Woman: Lavender Rose or Gray Panther*, Marie Marschall Fuller and Cora Ann Martin, eds. (Springfield, Ill.: Charles C. Thomas, 1980), pp. 75–78.

67. Olga Knopf, M.D., *Successful Aging* (New York: The Viking Press, 1975), p. 24.

68. Ronald Blythe, *The View in Winter: Reflections on Old Age* (New York: Harcourt Brace Jovanovich, 1979), p. 82.

69. Catherine Drinker Bowen, *Adventures of a Biographer*, p. 156.

Bibliography

Achenbaum, W. Andrew. *Old Age in the New Land: The American Experience Since 1790*. Baltimore: The Johns Hopkins University Press, 1978.

———— and Peggy Ann Kusnerz. *Images of Old Age in America: 1790 to the Present*. Ann Arbor, Mich.: The Institute of Gerontology, University of Michigan–Wayne State University, 1978.

Addams, Jane. *The Long Road of Woman's Memory*. New York: The Macmillan Co., 1916.

Allan, Virginia R. "Economic and Legal Status of the Older Woman." In *No Longer Young: The Older Woman in America*, pp. 23–30. Ann Arbor, Mich.: The Institute of Gerontology, University of Michigan–Wayne State University, 1975.

Anderson, Margaret. *The Strange Necessity (The Autobiography—Resolutions and Reminiscence to 1969)*. New York: Horizon Press, 1969.

Anderson, Mary. *Woman at Work, The Autobiography of Mary Anderson as Told to Mary N. Winslow*. Westport, Conn.: Greenwood Press, Publishers, 1951.

"Ask Them Yourself." *Family Weekly*, November 29, 1981, p. 3.

Atchley, Robert. *The Social Forces in Later Life: An Introduction to Social Gerontology*. 3rd ed. Belmont, Calif.: Wadsworth Publishing Co., Inc., 1980.

Atherton, Gertrude Franklin Horn. *Adventures of a Novelist*. New York: Liveright, Inc., 1932.

————. "Are Women Born Liars?" in *Can Women Be Gentlemen?* Boston: Houghton Mifflin Co., 1938, pp. 3–24.

————. *Black Oxen*. New York: Boni and Liveright, 1923.

————. "A Course in Life and Human Nature." In *Can Women Be Gentlemen?*, pp. 86–91.

————. "Defeating Old Age." In *Can Women Be Gentlemen?*, pp. 58–65.

————. "Superwomen." In *Can Women Be Gentlemen?*, pp. 112–15.

————. "Why Do Women Hate One Another?" In *Can Women Be Gentlemen?*, pp. 38–49.

Austin, Mary. *Earth Horizon*. Boston: Houghton Mifflin Co., 1932.

Bahr, Howard M., and Gerald R. Garrett. *Women Alone: The Disaffiliation of Urban Females*. Lexington, Mass.: D. C. Heath and Co., 1976.

Bailey, Pearl. *The Raw Pearl*. New York: Harcourt, Brace and World, Inc., 1968.

Baldwin, Faith. "My Crabbèd Age." In *The Older Woman: Lavender Rose or Gray Panther*, edited by Marie Marschall Fuller and Cora Ann Martin. Springfield, Ill.: Charles C. Thomas, 1980, pp. 75–78.

Bambara, Toni Cade. "My Man Bovanne." In *Bitches and Sad Ladies: An Anthology of Fiction By and About Women*, edited by Pat Rotter. New York: Dell Publishing Co., Inc., 1975, pp. 382–88.

Bart, Pauline B. "Why Women's Status Changes in Middle Age: The Turns of the Social Ferris Wheel." *Sociological Symposium* (Fall 1969) 3:1–18.

Beard, Mary R. "Introduction." In *America Through Women's Eyes*, edited by Mary R. Beard. New York: Greenwood Press, Inc., 1976, pp. 1–9.

Beauvoir, Simone de. *The Coming of Age.* Translated by Patrick O'Brian. New York: Warner Paperback Library, 1973.

Beeson, Diane. "Women in Studies of Aging: A Critique and Suggestion." *Social Problems* (October 1975) 23(1):52–9.

Benary-Isbert, Margot. *These Vintage Years.* New York: Abingdon Press, 1968.

Benedek, Theresa. *Psychosexual Functions in Women.* New York: The Ronald Press Co., 1952.

Bennetts, Leslie. "Displaced Homemakers: Struggling with Insecurity." *New York Times,* June 15, 1979, p. A16.

———. "Louise Nevelson: Homecoming in Triumph." *New York Times,* July 16, 1979, p. D8.

Berg, Geri, and Sally Gadow. "Toward More Human Meanings of Aging: Ideals and Images from Philosophy and Art." In *Aging and the Elderly: Humanistic Perspectives in Gerontology,* edited by Stuart F. Spicker, Kathleen M. Woodward and David D. Van Tassel. New Jersey: Humanities Press, Inc., 1978, pp. 83–92.

Bernstein, Merton C. "Forecast of Women's Retirement Income: Cloudy and Colder; 25 Percent Chance of Poverty." *Industrial Gerontology* (Spring 1974) 1(2):1–13.

———. Letter, *New York Times,* May 17, 1981, p. 22E.

Bevington, Helen. *The House Was Quiet and the World Was Calm.* New York: Harcourt Brace Jovanovich, Inc., 1971.

Birren, James E., and Vivian Clayton. "History of Gerontology." In *Aging: Scientific Perspectives and Social Issues,* edited by Diana S. Woodruff and James E. Birren. New York: D. Van Nostrand Co., 1975, pp. 15–27.

Blau, Zena Smith. *Old Age in a Changing Society.* New York: New Viewpoints, a Division of Franklin Watts, Inc., 1973.

Block, Marilyn R., Janice L. Davidson, Jean D. Grambs, and Kathryn E. Serock. *Uncharted Territory: Issues and Concerns of Women over 40.* College Park, Md.: University of Maryland Center on Aging, 1978.

Blythe, Ronald. *The View in Winter: Reflections on Old Age.* New York: Harcourt Brace Jovanovich, 1979.

"Boarding House Concept Proposed to Provide Homes for Elderly." *New York Times,* April 17, 1980, p. C14.

Bogan, Louise. "From the Journals of a Poet." Edited by Ruth Limmer. *The New Yorker* (January 30, 1978) 53(50):39–70.

Borenstein, Audrey. *Redeeming the Sin: Social Science and Literature.* New York: Columbia University Press, 1978.

Bouvier, Leon, Elinore Atlee, and Frank McVeigh. "The Elderly in America." *Population Bulletin* (1975) 30(3).

Bowen, Catherine Drinker. *Adventures of a Biographer.* Boston: Atlantic Monthly Press, 1959.

———. *Family Portrait.* Boston: Little, Brown and Co., 1970.

Bradway, Katherine. "Hestia and Athena in the Analysis of Women." *Inward Light* (Spring 1978) 41(91):28–42.

Breslin, James E. "Gertrude Stein and the Problems of Autobiography." In *Women's Autobiography: Essays in Criticism,* edited by Estelle C. Jelinek. Bloomington, Ind.: Indiana University Press, 1980, pp. 149–62.

Brooks, Gwendolyn. *Report from Part One.* Detroit, Mich.: Broadside Press, 1972.

Brozan, Nadine. "Elderly Women: Conference Throws Spotlight on Their Economic Woes." *New York Times,* May 26, 1978, p. A15.

Buck, Pearl S. *A Bridge for Passing.* New York: The John Day Co., 1962.

Burns, Edward, ed. *Staying on Alone: Letters of Alice B. Toklas.* New York: Liveright, 1973.

Butler, Robert N., M.D. "The Life Review: An Interpretation of Reminiscence in the Aged." In *Middle Age and Aging: A Reader in Social Psychology,* edited by Bernice L. Neugarten. Chicago: The University of Chicago Press, 1968, pp. 486–96.

———. *Why Survive? Being Old in America.* New York: Harper and Row, 1975.

Calisher, Hortense. "A Box of Ginger." In *The Collected Stories of Hortense Calisher.* New York: Arbor House Publishing Co., Inc., 1975, pp. 204–13.

———. *Herself.* New York: Arbor House, 1972.

———. "The Scream on Fifty-seventh Street." In *The Collected Stories of Hortense Calisher,* pp. 479–502.

———. "A Wreath for Miss Totten." In *The Collected Stories of Hortense Calisher,* pp. 152–62.

Canfield, Dorothy. See: Fisher, Dorothy Canfield.

Caplow, Theodore. Foreword. In *Women Alone: The Disaffiliation of Urban Females,* by Howard M. Bahr and Gerald R. Garrett. Lexington, Mass.: D. C. Heath and Co., 1976, pp. xv–xvii.

Carp, Frances. M. "Housing and Living Environments of Older People." In *Handbook of Aging and the Social Sciences,* edited by Robert H. Binstock and Ethel Shanas, with the assistance of Associate Editors Vern L. Bengston, George L. Maddox and Dorothy Wedderburn. New York: Van Nostrand Reinhold Co., 1976, pp. 244–71.

Carroll, Gladys Hasty. *Unless You Die Young.* New York: W. W. Norton and Co., Inc., 1977.

Castillejo, Irene Claremont de. *Knowing Woman: A Feminine Psychology.* New York: Harper and Row, 1973.

Cather, Willa. "A Chance Meeting." In *Not under Forty.* New York: Alfred A. Knopf, 1936, pp. 3–42.

———. "Joseph and His Brothers." In *Not under Forty,* pp. 96–122.

———. *My Mortal Enemy.* New York: Vintage Books, 1926, 1954.

———. "The Old Beauty." In *The Old Beauty and Others.* New York: Alfred A. Knopf, 1948, pp. 3–72.

———. "Old Mrs. Harris." In *Obscure Destinies and Literary Encounters.* Boston: Houghton Mifflin Co., 1938, pp. 65–158.

———. "Preface." In *The Best Stories of Sarah Orne Jewett,* by Sarah Orne Jewett. The Mayflower Edition. Gloucester, Mass.: Peter Smith, 1965, pp. ix–xix.

Chase, Ilka. *Past Imperfect.* Garden City, N.Y.: Blue Ribbon Books, 1945.

Chesler, Phyllis. *Women and Madness.* New York: Avon Books, 1972.

Clark, Margaret. "The Anthropology of Aging: A New Area for Studies of Culture and Personality." In *Middle Age and Aging: A Reader in Social Psychology,* edited by Bernice L. Neugarten. Chicago: The University of Chicago Press, 1968, pp. 433–43.

Clay, Vidal S. *Women: Menopause and Middle Age.* Pittsburgh, Pa.: Know, Inc., 1977.

Cohen, Wilbur J. "Social Security: Next Steps." In *No Longer Young: The Older Woman in America.* Ann Arbor, Michigan: The Institute of Gerontology, University of Michigan–Wayne State University, 1975, pp. 95–102.

Collins, Glenn. "Paternity Leave: A New Role for Fathers." *New York Times,* December 7, 1981, p. B18.

Comfort, Alex, M.D. "Aging: Real and Imaginary." In *The New Old: Struggling for Decent Aging,* edited by Ronald Gross, Beatrice Gross and Sylvia Seidman. Garden City, New York: Anchor Press/Doubleday, 1978, pp. 77–88.

————. *A Good Age.* New York: Crown Publishers, Inc., 1976.

Connell, Christopher. "Quietly, Congress cuts $2 billion in SS benefits," *Poughkeepsie Journal,* August 23, 1981, p. 7A.

Conover, Charlotte Reeve. *On Being Eighty and Other Digressions.* Yellow Springs, Ohio: Antioch Bookplate Co., 1938.

Cooper, Patricia, and Norma Bradley Buferd. *The Quilters: Women and Domestic Art, An Oral History.* Garden City, N.Y.: Anchor Press/Doubleday, 1978.

Cowgill, Donald O. "The Aging of Populations and Societies." *The Annals of the American Academy of Political and Social Science* (September 1974) 415 : 1–18.

Crewdson, John M. "New Administration and Congress Face Major Immigration Decisions." *New York Times,* December 28, 1980, p. 1.

Cumming, Elaine. "Further Thoughts on the Theory of Disengagement." In *Aging in America: Readings in Social Gerontology,* edited by Cary S. Kart and Barbara B. Manard. New York: Alfred Publishing Co., Inc., 1976, pp. 19–41.

————. and William H. Henry. *Growing Old: The Process of Disengagement.* New York: Basic Books, Inc., 1961.

Cunningham, Imogen. *After Ninety.* Seattle, Wash.: University of Washington Press, 1977.

Curtin, Sharon R. *Nobody Ever Died of Old Age.* Boston: Little, Brown and Co., 1972.

Cutler, Neal E., and Robert A. Harootyan. "Demography of the Aged." In *Aging: Scientific Perspectives and Social Issues,* edited by Diana S. Woodruff and James E. Birren. New York: D. Van Nostrand Co., 1975, pp. 31–69.

Datan, Nancy, Aaron Antonovsky, and Benjamin Maoz. *A Time to Reap: The Middle Age of Women in Five Israeli Subcultures.* Baltimore: The Johns Hopkins University Press, 1981.

———— and Nancy Lohmann, eds. *Transitions of Aging.* New York: Academic Press, Inc., 1980.

Day, Dorothy. *The Long Loneliness, The Autobiography of Dorothy Day.* New York: Harper and Brothers, 1952.

Demetrakopoulos, Stephanie A. "The Metaphysics of Matrilinearism in Women's Autobiography: Studies of Mead's *Blackberry Winter,* Hellman's *Pentimento,* Angelou's *I Know Why the Caged Bird Sings,* and Kingston's *The Woman Warrior.*" In *Women's Autobiography: Essays in Criticism,* edited by Estelle C. Jelinek. Bloomington, Ind.: Indiana University Press, 1980, pp. 180–205.

de Mille, Agnes. *And Promenade Home.* Boston: Little, Brown and Co., 1958.

————. *Dance to the Piper.* Boston: Little, Brown and Co., 1952.

————. *Where the Wings Grow (A Memoir of Childhood.)* New York: Doubleday and Co., Inc., 1978.

Deutsch, Helene, M.D. "The Climacterium," Epilogue. In *The Psychology of Women, A Psychoanalytic Interpretation,* vol. 2: *Motherhood,* by Helene Deutsch. New York: Grune and Stratton, 1945, pp. 456–87.

———. *Confrontations with Myself—An Epilogue.* New York: W. W. Norton and Co., Inc., 1973.

Dorson, Richard M. "Afterword." In *Foxfire* 4, edited by Eliot Wigginton. New York: Anchor Press/Doubleday, 1977, pp. 482–85.

Dullea, Georgia. "Workers Find 'Flextime' Makes for Flexible Living," *New York Times,* October 16, 1979, p. B14.

Duncan, Isadora. *My Life.* New York: Boni and Liveright, Inc., 1927, 1955.

Edinger, Edward F. "The Outline of Analytical Psychology." *Quadrant* (Summer 1968) 1:1–12.

"Elderly with Proud Tradition Find It Hard to Say, 'Help.'" *New York Times,* September 29, 1979, p. 23.

Elliott, Grace Loucks. *Women After Forty.* New York: Henry Holt and Co., 1936.

Erikson, Erik H. *Insight and Responsibility.* New York: W. W. Norton and Co., Inc., 1964.

Evans, Olive. "For the Elderly, Exploring Some Alternatives to the Nursing Home." *New York Times,* June 5, 1979, p. C12.

Fact Book on Aging: A Profile of America's Older Population, Charles S. Harris, Research Coordinator. Washington, D.C.: The National Council on the Aging, Inc., 1978.

Farnsworth, Clyde H. "Reliability of U.S. Data," Washington Watch. *New York Times,* November 30, 1981, p. D2.

Ferber, Edna. "Old Lady Mandle." In *One Basket: Thirty-one Short Stories by Edna Ferber.* New York: Simon and Schuster, Inc., 1947, pp. 145–61.

———. "Old Man Minick." In *One Basket: Thirty-one Short Stories by Edna Ferber,* pp. 110–27.

———. *A Peculiar Treasure.* New York: Literary Guild, 1939.

———. "The Sudden Sixties." In *One Basket: Thirty-one Short Stories by Edna Ferber,* pp. 198–214.

Field, Minna. *The Aged, the Family, and the Community.* New York: Columbia University Press, 1972.

Fierz, Heinrich Karl. "Preface." In *Psychological Reflections on the Fresco Series of the Villa of the Mysteries in Pompeii,* by Linda Fierz-David, translated by Gladys Phelan, Zurich, 1957, Kristine Mann Library, C. G. Jung Foundation for Analytical Psychology, Inc., New York, N.Y., n.p.

Fierz-David, Linda. *Psychological Reflections on the Fresco Series of the Villa of the Mysteries in Pompeii,* translated by Gladys Phelan. Zurich, 1957, Kristine Mann Library, C. G. Jung Foundation for Analytical Psychology, Inc., New York, N.Y.

Fischer, David Hackett. "Books Considered." *The New Republic.* (December 2, 1978), 179(23):31–36.

———. *Growing Old in America.* New York: Oxford University Press, 1977.

Fisher, Dorothy Canfield. "Almera Hawley Canfield." In *A Harvest of Stories: From a Half Century of Writing by Dorothy Canfield.* New York: Harcourt, Brace and Co., Inc., 1956, pp. 61–75.

———. "The Bedquilt." In *A Harvest of Stories: From a Half Century of Writing by Dorothy Canfield,* pp. 52–60.

Fisher, Welthy Honsinger. *To Light a Candle.* New York: McGraw-Hill Book Co., Inc., 1962.

Flint, Jerry. "Early Retirement Trend Holding." *New York Times,* November 22, 1978, p. A7.

Foner, Anne. "Age Stratification and the Changing Family." In *Turning Points: Historical and Sociological Essays on the Family,* edited by John Demos and Sarane Spence Boocock. Chicago: The University of Chicago Press, 1978, pp. S340–S365.

Fowler, Elizabeth M. "Women without Pensions," Consumer Saturday. *New York Times,* November 21, 1981, p. 12.

Frank, Lawrence K. "Problems and Opportunities in the Maturation of Women: The Interpersonal and Social Aspects." In *Potentialities of Women in the Middle Years,* edited by Irma H. Gross. East Lansing, Mich.: Michigan State University Press, 1956, pp. 105–26.

Franz, Marie-Louise von. *The Feminine in Fairytales.* New York: Spring Publications, The Analytical Psychology Club of New York, Inc., 1972.

Freedman, Richard. "Sufficiently Decayed: Gerontophobia in English Literature." In *Aging and the Elderly: Humanistic Perspectives in Gerontology,* edited by Stuart F. Spicker, Kathleen M. Woodward, and David D. Van Tassel. Atlantic Highlands, N.J.: Humanities Press, Inc., 1978, pp. 49–61.

Frenkel-Brunswik, Else. "Adjustments and Reorientation in the Course of the Life Span." In *Middle Age and Aging: A Reader in Social Psychology,* edited by Bernice L. Neugarten. Chicago: The University of Chicago Press, 1968, pp. 77–84.

Friday, Nancy. *My Mother/My Self: The Daughther's Search for Identity.* New York: Delacorte Press, 1977.

Friedländer, Saul. *When Memory Comes.* New York: Farrar, Straus and Giroux, Inc., 1979.

Fuchs, Estelle. *The Second Season: Life, Love and Sex—Women in the Middle Years.* Garden City, N.Y.: Doubleday Anchor Press, 1977.

Fuller, Marie Marschall, and Cora Ann Martin. Preface and Introduction. In *The Older Woman: Lavender Rose or Gray Panther,* edited by Marie Marschall Fuller and Cora Ann Martin. Springfield, Ill.: Charles C. Thomas, 1980, pp. vii–xv.

Gage, Joan. "Hers." *New York Times,* September 13, 1979, p. C2.

Garden, Mary, and Louis Biancalli. *Mary Garden's Story.* New York: Simon and Schuster, Inc., 1951.

Gargan, Edward A. "As 'Psychiatric Ghettoes,' Boarding Homes Get More Dangerous." *New York Times,* February 8, 1981, p. 6E.

George, Diana Hume. "Community and Creativity, An Approach to Teaching the Subject of Aging." 1978 Modern Language Association Special Session—Perspectives on Aging, New York.

Giesen, Carol Boellhoff and Nancy Datan. "The Competent Older Woman." In *Transitions of Aging,* edited by Nancy Datan and Nancy Lohmann. New York: Academic Press, Inc., 1980, pp. 57–72.

Gladney, Margaret Rose. "If It was Anything for Justice." *Southern Exposure* (Winter 1977) 4(4): 19–23.

Glasgow, Ellen. *Barren Ground.* New York: The Modern Library, 1936.

———. *The Sheltered Life.* Garden City, N.Y.: Doubleday, Doran and Co., Inc., 1932.

———. *They Stooped to Folly, A Comedy of Morals.* Garden City, N.Y.: Doubleday, Doran and Co., Inc., 1929.

———. *Vein of Iron*. New York: Harcourt, Brace and Co., 1935.

———. *The Woman Within*. New York: Harcourt, Brace and Co., 1954.

Gluck, Sherna. "What's So Special About Women? Women's Oral History." *Frontiers* (Summer 1977) 2(2):3–13.

"The Goals." *Forum* (Fall 1978) 1(2):1.

Goodman, Charlotte. "Despair in Elderly Women: Katherine Anne Porter's 'The Jilting of Granny Weatherall' and Tillie Olsen's 'Tell Me a Riddle.'" 1978 Modern Language Association Special Session—Perspectives on Aging, New York.

Greenfield, Sidney M. "Industrialization and the Family in Sociological Theory." In *Marriage and the Family: A Comparative Analysis of Contemporary Problems*, edited by Meyer Barash and Alice Scourby. New York: Random House, Inc., 1970, pp. 9–27.

Gross, Irma H., ed. *Potentialities of Women in the Middle Years*. East Lansing, Mich.: Michigan State University Press, 1956.

Growing Numbers, Growing Force. A Report From the White House Mini-Conference on Older Women (The Long Report). San Francisco, Calif.: Western Gerontological Society, and Oakland, Calif.: Older Women's League Educational Fund, 1981.

Gutmann, David L. "Aging among the Highland Maya: A Comparative Study." In *Middle Age and Aging: A Reader in Social Psychology*, edited by Bernice L. Neugarten. Chicago: The University of Chicago Press, 1968, pp. 444–52.

———. "Parenthood: A Key to the Comparative Study of the Life Cycle." In *Life-Span Developmental Psychology: Normative Life Crises*, edited by Nancy Datan and Leon H. Ginsberg. New York: Academic Press, Inc., 1975, pp. 167–84.

———, Jerome Grunes and Brian Griffin. "The Clinical Psychology of Later Life: Developmental Paradigms." In *Transitions of Aging,* edited by Nancy Datan and Nancy Lohmann. New York: Academic Press, Inc., 1980, pp. 119–31.

Hall, G. Stanley. *Senescence: The Last Half of Life*. New York: D. Appleton and Co., 1922.

Hamblen, Abigail Ann. *Ruth Suckow*. Boise, Id.: Boise State University Western Writers Series No. 34, 1978.

Harding, M. Esther. "Introduction." In *Psychological Reflections on the Fresco Series of the Villa of the Mysteries in Pompeii*, by Linda Fierz-David, translated by Gladys Phelan, Zurich, 1957, Kristine Mann Library, C. G. Jung Foundation for Analytical Psychology, Inc., New York, N. Y. pp. 9–10.

———. *The Way of All Women*. New York: G. P. Putnam's Sons for the C. G. Jung Foundation for Analytical Psychology, 1970.

———. *Woman's Mysteries—Ancient and Modern (A Psychological Interpretation of the Feminine Principle as Portrayed in Myth, Story, and Dreams)*. New York: G. P. Putnam's Sons for the C. G. Jung Foundation for Analytical Psychology, 1971.

Hardwick, Elizabeth. *Sleepless Nights*. New York: Random House, 1979.

Harlan, William H. "Social Status of the Aged in Three Indian Villages." In *Middle Age and Aging: A Reader in Social Psychology*, edited by Bernice L. Neugarten. Chicago: The University of Chicago Press, 1968, pp. 469–75.

Harris, Louis, and Associates, Inc. *The Myth and Reality of Aging in America*. Washington: The National Council on the Aging, Inc., 1975.

Hellman, Lillian. "Lillian Hellman on Reading Her Own Work." *The New York Times Book Review*, March 25, 1979, pp. 3, 45.

Hemenway, Robert E. *Zora Neale Hurston: A Literary Biography*. Urbana, Ill.: University of Illinois Press, 1977.

Hendricks, Jon A. "Women and Leisure." In *Looking Ahead: A Woman's Guide to the Problems and Joys of Growing Older*, edited by Lillian E. Troll, Joan Israel, and Kenneth Israel. Englewood Cliffs, N. J.: Prentice-Hall, Inc., 1977, pp. 114–20.

Henry, Jules. *Culture Against Man*. New York: Vintage Books, Random House, Inc., 1963.

Herbst, Josephine. "Hunter of Doves." *Botteghe Oscure* (1954) 13 : 310–44.

Hess, Beth B. "Family Myths." *New York Times*, January 9, 1979, p. A19.

Hessel, Dieter, ed. *Maggie Kuhn on Aging, A Dialogue edited by Dieter Hessel*. Philadelphia: The Westminster Press, 1977.

Hochschild, Arlie Russell. *The Unexpected Community: Portrait of an Old Age Subculture*. Berkeley, Calif.: University of California Press, 1973.

Holden, Constance. "Briefing: Bioethical Reference." *Science* (February 23, 1979) 203(4382) : 729.

Howland, Bette. "Golden Age." In *Blue In Chicago*, by Bette Howland. New York: Harper and Row, Inc., 1978, pp. 119–47.

———. "How We Got the Old Woman To Go." In *Blue In Chicago*, pp. 149–83.

———. "Public Facilities." In *Blue in Chicago*, pp. 67–94.

Hudson, Jean Barlow. "The Double Enemy." *Broomstick* (March 1980) 2(4) : 5.

Hurston, Zora Neale. *Dust Tracks on a Road*. New York: Arno Press and The New York Times, 1969.

———. *Jonah's Gourd Vine*. Philadelphia: J. B. Lippincott, 1934.

———. *Mules and Men*. Philadelphia: J. B. Lippincott Co., 1935.

———. *Seraph on the Suwanee*. New York: Charles Scribner's Sons, 1948.

———. *Their Eyes Were Watching God*. New York: Negro Universities Press, 1969.
"Infant Mortality Highest in Capital." *New York Times*, December 13, 1981, p. 37.

Jackson, Jacquelyne Johnson. "Older Black Women." In *Looking Ahead: A Woman's Guide to the Problems and Joys of Growing Older*, edited by Lillian E. Troll, Joan Israel, and Kenneth Israel. Englewood Cliffs, N.J.: Prentice-Hall, Inc., 1977, pp. 149–56.

Jacobs, Jerry. *Fun City: An Ethnographic Study of a Retirement Community*. New York: Holt, Rinehart and Winston, Inc., 1974.

Jacobs, Ruth Harriet. *Life After Youth: Female, Forty—What Next?* Boston: Beacon Press, 1979.

Janeway, Elizabeth. "Breaking the Age Barrier." *Ms.* (April 1973) 1(10) : 50–51, 53, 109–11.

Jelinek, Estelle C. "Introduction: Women's Autobiography and the Male Tradition." In *Women's Autobiography: Essays in Criticism*, edited by Estelle C. Jelinek. Bloomington, Ind.: Indiana University Press, 1980, pp. 1–20.

Jewett, Sarah Orne. "Aunt Cynthy Dallett." In *The Best Stories of Sarah Orne Jewett*, Gloucester, Mass.: Peter Smith, 1965, pp. 279–306.

———. "The Flight of Betsey Lane." In *The Best Stories of Sarah Orne Jewett*, pp. 22–63.

———. "Going to Shrewsbury." In *The Best Stories of Sarah Orne Jewett*, pp. 90–108.

Johnson, Josephine W. *Seven Houses: A Memoir of Time and Places*. New York: Simon and Schuster, 1973.

Johnson, Sheila K. *Idle Haven: Community Building among the Working-Class Retired*. Berkeley, Calif.: University of California Press, 1971.

Jung, Carl G. *Answer to Job.* Translated by R. F. C. Hull. London: Routledge and Kegan Paul, Ltd., 1954.

————. *Modern Man in Search of a Soul.* Translated by W. S. Dell and Cary F. Baynes. New York: Harcourt, Brace and World, Inc., 1933.

Kalish, Richard A., and Sam Yuen. "Americans of East Asian Ancestry: Aging and the Aged." *The Gerontologist* (Spring 1971, Part II) 11(2):38.

Kallir, Otto. *Grandma Moses.* New York: Harry N. Abrams, Inc., 1973.

Kaminsky, Marc. *What's Inside You It Shines Out of You.* New York: Horizon Press, 1974.

Kamp, Irene Kittle. "Facing A New Face." *New York Times Magazine,* September 9, 1979, pp. 116–19, 130.

Kassel, Victor. "Polygyny after 60." *Geriatrics* (April 1966) 21(4):214–18.

Kastenbaum, Robert, and Sandra E. Candy. "The 4% Fallacy: A Methodological and Empirical Critique of Extended Care Facility Population Statistics." In *Aging in America: Readings in Social Gerontology,* edited by Cary S. Kart and Barbara B. Manard. Port Washington, N. Y.: Alfred Publishing Co., Inc., 1976, pp. 166–74.

Kates, George N. "Willa Cather's Unfinished Avignon Story." In *Five Stories* by Willa Cather. New York: Vintage Books, 1956, pp. 175–214.

Keller, Helen. *Midstream: My Later Life.* Garden City, N. Y.: Doubleday, Doran and Co., Inc., 1929.

Kephart, William M. *Extraordinary Groups: The Sociology of Unconventional Life-Styles.* New York: St. Martin's Press, 1976.

Kethley, Alice J. "Women and Aging: The Unforgivable Sin." In *Women on the Move: A Feminist Perspective,* edited by Jean Ramage Leppaluoto, Joan Acker, Claudeen Naffziger, Karla Brown, Catherine M. Porter, Barbara A. Mitchell, and Roberta Hanna. Pittsburgh, Pa.: Know, Inc., 1973, pp. 39–45.

Klein, Marcus. Introduction. In *My Mortal Enemy* by Willa Cather. New York: Vintage Books, 1926, 1954, pp. v–xxii.

Klemesrud, Judy. "Conference on Aging Views Older Women." *New York Times,* December 1, 1981, p. A28.

————. "For Older Women, Parley Raises Hope." *New York Times,* December 5, 1981, p. 52.

————. "Improving the Self-Image of Older Women." *New York Times,* November 1, 1981, p. B9.

————. "Older Women: No Longer 'Invisible.'" *New York Times,* December 2, 1981, pp. C1, C8–C9.

Kline, Chrysee. "The Socialization Process of Women." In *The Older Woman: Lavender Rose or Gray Panther,* edited by Marie Marschall Fuller and Cora Ann Martin. Springfield, Ill.: Charles C. Thomas, 1980, pp. 59–70.

Knopf, Olga, M.D., *Successful Aging.* New York: The Viking Press, 1975.

Koch, Kenneth. *I Never Told Anybody: Teaching Poetry Writing in a Nursing Home.* New York: Vintage Books, 1978.

Kotz, Mary Lynn. "Georgia O'Keeffe at 90: A Day with Georgia O'Keeffe." *Art News,* (December 1977) 76(10):37–45.

Kramer, Sydelle, and Jenny Masur, eds. *Jewish Grandmothers.* Boston: Beacon Press, 1976.

Krause, Corinne Azen. *Grandmothers, Mothers and Daughters: An Oral History Study of*

Ethnicity, Mental Health, and Continuity of Three Generations of Jewish, Italian, and Slavic-American Women. New York: The Institute on Pluralism and Group Identity of the American Jewish Committee, 1978.

————. "Italian, Jewish, and Slavic Grandmothers in Pittsburgh: Their Economic Roles." *Frontiers* (Summer 1977) 2(2):18–28.

Kreps, Juanita. *Sex in the Marketplace: American Women at Work.* Baltimore: The Johns Hopkins University Press, 1971.

———— and Robert Clark. *Sex, Age, and Work: The Changing Composition of the Labor Force.* Baltimore: The Johns Hopkins University Press, 1975.

Lally, Maureen, Eileen Black, Martha Thornock, and J. David Hawkins. "Older Women in Single Room Occupant (SRO) Hotels: A Seattle Profile." In *The Older Woman: Lavender Rose or Gray Panther,* edited by Marie Marschall Fuller and Cora Ann Martin. Springfield, Illinois: Charles C. Thomas, 1980, pp. 304–16.

Lantero, Erminie Huntress. *Feminine Aspects of Divinity.* Wallingford, Pa.: Pendle Hill Publications, 1973.

Larsen, Stephen. *The Shaman's Doorway: Opening the Mythic Imagination to Contemporary Consciousness.* New York: Harper and Row, 1976.

Lasch, Christopher. "Aging in a Culture without a Future." *Hastings Center Report* (August 1977) 7(4):42–44.

Laslett, Barbara. "The Family as a Public and Private Institution: An Historical Perspective." *Journal of Marriage and the Family* (August 1973) 35(3):480–92.

Lawrence, Josephine. *Years Are So Long.* New York: Frederick A. Stokes Co., 1934.

Lehman, Harvey C. *Age and Achievement.* Princeton, N.J.: Princeton University Press, 1953.

Lehmann, Phyllis. "The Aging and the Arts." *The Cultural Post* (July/August 1977) 12:1, 4–5.

Leslie, Gerald R. *The Family in Social Context.* New York: Oxford University Press, 1967.

LeVine, Robert A. "Intergenerational Tensions and Extended Family Structures in Africa." In *Marriage and the Family: A Comparative Analysis of Contemporary Problems,* edited by Meyer Barash and Alice Scourby. New York: Random House, Inc., 1970, pp. 144–64.

Lewis, Myrna I., and Robert N. Butler. "Why Is Women's Lib Ignoring Old Women?" *Aging and Human Development* (1972) 3(3):223–31.

Lewis, R. W. B. *Edith Wharton: A Biography.* New York: Harper and Row, 1975.

————. "Introduction." In *The Age of Innocence,* by Edith Wharton. New York: Charles Scribner's Sons, 1968, pp. v–xiv.

Lewontin, Richard C., and Lewis Thomas. "Letters: Death of TB." *The New York Review of Books* (January 25, 1979) 25(21 and 22):47–48.

Lienhardt, Godfrey. *Social Anthropology.* London: Oxford University Press, 1966.

Limmer, Ruth. *Journey Around My Room: The Autobiography of Louise Bogan, A Mosaic by Ruth Limmer.* New York: The Viking Press, 1980.

————, ed. *What the Woman Lived: Selected Letters of Louise Bogan 1920–1970.* New York: Harcourt Brace Jovanovich, Inc., 1973.

Linderman, Frank B. *Pretty-Shield, Medicine Woman of the Crows (as told to Frank B. Linderman).* Lincoln, Neb.: University of Nebraska Press, 1932, 1972.

Lindsey, Robert. "Gerontology Comes of Age." *New York Times,* January 8, 1978, Education, p. 11.

Long, Christina. "Social Security: The Right On the Rampage." *Gray Panther Network,* November/December, 1981, p. 6.

Lopata, Helena Znaniecki. *Occupation: Housewife.* New York: Oxford University Press, 1971.

———. *Widowhood in an American City.* Cambridge, Mass.: Schenkman Publishing Co., Inc., 1973.

———. *Women as Widows: Support Systems.* New York: Elsevier North Holland, Inc., 1979.

Loughman, Celeste. "Novels of Senescence." *The Gerontologist* (February 1977) 17(1):79–84.

Lowenthal, Leo. *Literature and the Image of Man.* Boston: The Beacon Press, 1957.

Lowenthal, Marjorie Fiske and Clayton Haven. "Interaction and Adaptation: Intimacy as a Critical Variable." *American Sociological Review* (February 1968) 33(1):20–30.

———, Majda Thurnher, David Chiriboga, et al. *Four Stages of Life: A Comparative Study of Women and Men Facing Transition.* San Francisco: Jossey-Bass, Inc., 1975.

Lucretius. *Of the Nature of Things.* William Ellery Leonard, trans. New York: E. P. Dutton and Co., Inc., 1950.

Lurie, Nancy Oestreich, ed. *Mountain Wolf Woman: Sister of Crashing Thunder, The Autobiography of a Winnebago Indian.* Ann Arbor, Mich.: The University of Michigan Press, 1966.

Lyons, Richard D. "Elderly in U.S. Are Sold Unneeded Health Insurance as Medicare Supplement, Congressional Staff Finds." *New York Times,* November 28, 1978, p. A16.

McCarthy, Mary. *Memories of a Catholic Girlhood.* New York: Harcourt, Brace and Co., 1957.

McClure, Charlotte S. *Gertrude Atherton.* Boise, Id.: Boise State University Western Writers Series, No. 23, 1976.

MacDougall, Allan Ross, ed. *Letters of Edna St. Vincent Millay.* New York: Harper and Brothers, 1952.

McLeish, John A. B. *The Ulyssean Adult: Creativity in the Middle and Later Years.* Toronto: McGraw-Hill Ryerson Ltd., 1976.

Maslow, Abraham. *Motivation and Personality.* New York: Harper and Row, 1970.

Matthews, Sarah H. *The Social World of Old Women: Management of Self-Identity.* Beverly Hills, Calif.: Sage Publications, 1979.

Mead, Margaret. *Blackberry Winter: My Earlier Years.* New York: William Morrow, Pocket Books, 1975.

Meese, Elizabeth A. "Telling It All: Literary Standards and Narratives by Southern Women." *Frontiers* (Summer 1977) 2(2):63–67.

Miller, Jennifer. "Quilting Women." *Southern Exposure* (Winter 1977) 4(4):24–28.

Miller, Luree. *Late Bloom: New Lives for Women.* New York: Paddington Press, Ltd., 1979.

Miner, Horace. "Body Ritual among the Nacirema." *American Anthropologist* (June 1956) 58:503–5.

Mitchell, Margaretta. "Introduction." In *After Ninety,* by Imogen Cunningham. Seattle, Wash.: University of Washington Press, 1977, pp. 9–23.

Moffat, Mary Jane, and Charlotte Painter, eds. *Revelations: Diaries of Women.* New York: Random House, 1974.

Monroe, Harriet. *A Poet's Life (Seventy Years in a Changing World)*. New York: The Macmillan Co., 1938.

Moses, Bob. Review of *The Aging Enterprise* by Carol Estes in "Worth Reading." *The Gray Panther Network* (September/October 1979), p. 10.

Moss, Walter G., ed. *Humanistic Perspectives on Aging: An Annotated Bibliography and Essay*. Ann Arbor, Mich.: The Institute of Gerontology, University of Michigan–Wayne State University, 1976.

"Most Near 65 Are Expected to Retire Voluntarily." *New York Times*, December 31, 1978, p. 20.

Myerhoff, Barbara. *Number Our Days*. New York: E. P. Dutton, 1978.

Neugarten, Bernice L. "The Aged in the Year 2025." In *The Older Woman: Lavender Rose or Gray Panther*, edited by Marie Marschall Fuller and Cora Ann Martin. Springfield, Ill.: Charles C. Thomas, 1980, pp. 332–43.

————. "Age Groups in American Society and the Rise of the Young-Old." *Annals of the American Academy of Political and Social Science* (September 1974) 415:187–98.

———— and David Gutmann, "Age-Sex Roles and Personality in Middle Age: A Thematic Apperception Study." In *Middle Age and Aging: A Reader in Social Psychology*, Bernice L. Neugarten, ed. Chicago: The University of Chicago Press, 1968, pp. 58–71.

————, Vivian Wood, Ruth J. Kraines, and Barbara Loomis. "Women's Attitudes Toward the Menopause." In *Middle Age and Aging: A Reader in Social Psychology*, pp. 195–200.

Neumann, Erich. *Amor and Psyche: The Psychic Development of the Feminine (A Commentary on the Tale By Apuleius)*. Translated by Ralph Manheim. New York: Pantheon, Bollingen Series LIV, 1956.

————. *Art and the Creative Unconscious (Four Essays)*. Translated by Ralph Manheim. New York: Pantheon, Bollingen Series LXI, 1959.

————. *The Great Mother: An Analysis of the Archetype*. Translated by Ralph Manheim. Princeton, N.J.: Princeton University Press, 1963.

———— "The Moon and Matriarchal Consciousness." In *Fathers and Mothers: Five Papers on the Archetypal Background of Family Psychology*, translated by Hildegard Nagel. Zurich: Spring Publications, 1973, pp. 40–61.

Nevelson, Louise. *Dawn + Dusks—taped conversations with Diana MacKown*. New York: Charles Scribner's Sons, 1976.

Nightingale, Benedict. "After Making Nine Films Together, Hepburn Can Practically Direct Cukor." *New York Times*, January 28, 1979, Section 2, p. 29.

Nin, Anaïs. Letter. *Ms.* (July 1974) 3(1):7.

No Longer Young: The Older Woman in America. Ann Arbor, Mich.: The Institute of Gerontology, University of Michigan–Wayne State University, Occasional Papers in Gerontology No. 11, 1975.

No Longer Young: Work Group Reports from the 26th Annual Conference on Aging. With an Introduction by Natalie P. Trager. Ann Arbor, Mich.: The Institute of Gerontology, University of Michigan–Wayne State University, 1974.

"NOW Task Force Presses Reforms for Older Women." *Aging* (April 1975) 246(9):9.

Older Women: The Economics of Aging. Washington, D.C.: The Women's Studies Program and Policy Center at George Washington University, in conjunction with The Women's Research and Education Institute of the Congresswomen's Caucus, 1981.

Olney, James. *Metaphors of Self: The Meaning of Autobiography.* Princeton, N.J.: Princeton University Press, 1972.

Olsen, Tillie. *Silences.* New York: Delacorte Press/Seymour Lawrence, 1978.

———. *Tell Me a Riddle.* New York: Dell Publishing Co., Inc., 1976.

O'Neil, Kate, Recorder. "Economic and Legal Status." In *No Longer Young: Work Group Reports from the 26th Annual Conference on Aging.* Ann Arbor, Mich.: The Institute of Gerontology, University of Michigan–Wayne State University, 1974, pp. 57–61.

Palmore, Erdman. "The Future Status of the Aged." In *The Older Woman: Lavender Rose or Gray Panther,* edited by Marie Marschall Fuller and Cora Ann Martin. Springfield, Ill.: Charles C. Thomas, 1980, pp. 323–31.

———. "United States of America." In *International Handbook on Aging: Contemporary Developments and Research,* edited by Erdman Palmore. Westport, Conn.: Greenwood Press, 1980, pp. 434–54.

Parker, Dorothy. "The Middle or Blue Period." In *The Portable Dorothy Parker,* Harmondsworth, Middlesex, England: Penguin Books Ltd., 1976, pp. 594–97.

Parton, Mary Field, ed. *The Autobiography of Mother Jones.* Chicago: Charles H. Kerr Publishing Co., 1977.

Payne, Barbara, and Frank Whittington. "Older Women: An Examination of Popular Stereotypes and Research Evidence." *Social Problems* (April 1976) 23(4): 488–504.

Peck, Robert C. "Psychological Developments in the Second Half of Life." In *Middle Age and Aging: A Reader in Social Psychology,* edited by Bernice L. Neugarten. Chicago: The University of Chicago Press, 1968, pp. 88–92.

Pepper, Claude. Letter. *New York Times,* February 29, 1980, p. A30.

Pesotta, Rose. *Bread Upon the Waters.* Edited by John Nicholas Beffel. New York: Dodd, Mead and Co., 1944.

Peterson, Virgilia. *A Matter of Life and Death.* New York: Atheneum, 1961.

"Poll Shows Most Workers in U.S. Prefer Jobs to Early Retirement." *New York Times,* March 4, 1979, p. 46.

Pomeroy, Sarah B. *Goddesses, Whores, Wives, and Slaves: Women in Classical Antiquity.* New York: Schocken Books, 1975.

Pope, Elizabeth. "Divorce, Death of Husbands Make Millions 'Displaced' Homemakers." *The Sunday Freeman,* January 1, 1978, p. 16.

Porter, Katherine Anne. Introduction. In *A Curtain of Green,* by Eudora Welty. Garden City, N.Y.: Doubleday, Doran and Co., Inc., 1943, pp. ix–xix.

———. "The Jilting of Granny Weatherall." In *The Collected Stories of Katherine Anne Porter.* New York: New American Library, 1970, pp. 80–89.

———. "The Journey." In *The Collected Stories of Katherine Anne Porter,* New York: New American Library, 1970, pp. 326–40.

———. "The Last Leaf." In *The Collected Stories of Katherine Anne Porter,* New York: New American Library, 1970, pp. 348–51.

———. "The Source." In *The Collected Stories of Katherine Anne Porter,* New York: New American Library, 1970, pp. 321–25.

Quindlen, Anna. "Where the Divorced and Widowed Learn to Cope Again." *New York Times,* February 10, 1978, p. A22.

Ravenscroft, Catherine, Recorder. "Biological Realities and Myths." In *No Longer Young: Work Group Reports from the 26th Annual Conference on Aging.* Ann Arbor,

Mich.: The Institute of Gerontology, University of Michigan–Wayne State University, 1974, pp. 15–22.

Redmond, Rosemary. "Legal Issues Involving the Older Woman." In *The Older Woman: Lavender Rose or Gray Panther,* edited by Marie Marschall Fuller and Cora Ann Martin. Springfield, Illinois: Charles C. Thomas, 1980, pp. 228–33.

"Retirement." *Family Weekly,* April 22, 1979, p. 42.

Riley, Matilda White. "Old Women." *Radcliffe Quarterly* (June 1979), pp. 7–10.

———. "Social Gerontology and the Age Stratification of Society." *The Gerontologist* (Spring 1971, Part 1) 11(2):79–87.

———, Marilyn Johnson, and Anne Foner. "Age Strata in the Society." In *Aging and Society,* Volume 3: *A Sociology of Age Stratification.* New York: Russell Sage Foundation, 1972, pp. 397–452.

——— and Joan Waring. "Age and Aging." In *Contemporary Social Problems,* edited by Robert K. Merton and Robert Nisbet. 4th ed., New York: Harcourt Brace Jovanovich, Inc., 1976, pp. 355–410

Roberts, Steven V. "Growing U.S. Expenditures for the Aged Cause Concern Among Policymakers." *New York Times,* December 27, 1978, p. B8.

———. "How Social Security Penalizes Women." *New York Times,* November 19, 1978, p. 20E.

Robertson, Ian. *Sociology,* 2d ed. New York: Worth Publishers, Inc., 1981.

Robertson, Nan. "Barbara Tuchman: A Loner at the Top of Her Field." *New York Times,* February 27, 1979, p. C10.

Robinson, Anna Hope Gould. *The Evolution of an Idea, a personal research project in Analytical Psychology.* 2 volumes. Kristine Mann Library, C. G. Jung Foundation for Analytical Psychology, Inc., New York, New York.

Roddy, Joseph. "The Treasure on Deck 19." *RF Illustrated, The Rockefeller Foundation* (September 1978) 4(2):1–2.

Roosevelt, Eleanor. *The Autobiography of Eleanor Roosevelt.* New York: Harper and Brothers, 1961.

———. *This Is My Story.* New York: Harper and Brothers, 1937.

Rose, Arnold M. "A Current Theoretical Issue in Social Gerontology." In *Middle Age and Aging: A Reader in Social Psychology,* edited by Bernice L. Neugarten. Chicago: The University of Chicago Press, 1968, pp. 184–89.

Rosenmayr, Leopold, and Eva Kockeis. "Propositions for a Sociological Theory of Aging and the Family." *International Social Science Journal* (1963) 15:410–26.

Rosow, Irving. *Social Integration of the Aged.* New York: Free Press, 1967.

Rouse, Blair, ed. *Letters of Ellen Glasgow.* New York: Harcourt, Brace and Co., 1958.

Rousseau, Ann Marie. *Shopping Bag Ladies: Homeless Women Speak About Their Lives.* New York: The Pilgrim Press, 1981.

Rubin, Lillian B. *Women of a Certain Age: The Midlife Search For Self.* New York: Harper and Row, 1979.

Russ, Lavinia. *A High Old Time or How to Enjoy Being a Woman Over Sixty.* New York: Saturday Review Press, 1972.

Sanger, Margaret. *Margaret Sanger: An Autobiography.* New York: W. W. Norton and Co., Inc., 1938.

Sarton, May. *As We Are Now.* New York: W. W. Norton and Co., Inc., 1973.

———. *Journal of a Solitude.* New York: W. W. Norton and Co., Inc., 1977.

———. "More Light." *New York Times,* January 30, 1978, p. A21.

———. *Mrs. Stevens Hears the Mermaids Singing.* New York: W. W. Norton and Co., Inc., 1975.

———. *Plant Dreaming Deep.* New York: W. W. Norton and Co., Inc., 1968.

———. *A Reckoning.* New York: W. W. Norton and Co., Inc., 1978.

———. *The Small Room.* New York: W. W. Norton and Co., Inc., 1961.

Scarf, Maggie. *Unfinished Business: Pressure Points in the Lives of Women.* Garden City, N.Y.: Doubleday and Co., Inc., 1980.

Scott-Maxwell, Florida. *The Measure of My Days.* New York: Alfred A. Knopf, Inc., 1969.

Scudder, Vida. "The Privileges of Age." *Atlantic Monthly* (February 1933) 151(2):205–11.

Seltzer, Mildred. "Jewish-American Grandmothers." In *Looking Ahead: A Woman's Guide to the Problems and Joys of Growing Older,* edited by Lillian E. Troll, Joan Israel, and Kenneth Israel. Englewood Cliffs, N.J.: Prentice-Hall, Inc., 1977, pp. 157–61.

"Senior Scholars Unite." *Science* (May 11, 1979) 204(4393):596.

Seskin, Jane, and Bette Ziegler. *Older Women/Younger Men.* Garden City, N.Y.: Doubleday and Co., Inc., 1979.

Shabecoff, Philip. "Life in a Rose-covered Cottage Isn't Rosy on $2,485 a Year." *New York Times,* June 25, 1978, p. E3.

———. "Overhaul Is Urged in Jobless Figures." *New York Times,* July 16, 1978, p. 19.

Shanas, Ethel. "Social Myth as Hypothesis: The Case of the Family Relations of Old People." *The Gerontologist* (February 1979) 19(1):3–9.

Shapiro, Joan Hatch. *Communities of the Alone: Working with Single Room Occupants in the City.* New York: Association Press, 1971.

Sheehy, Gail. *Passages: Predictable Crises of Adult Life.* New York: E. P. Dutton and Co., 1976.

Sheppard, Harold L. "The Status of Women, 1993–1998: Financial Aspects." In *No Longer Young: The Older Woman in America.* Ann Arbor, Mich.: The Institute of Gerontology, University of Michigan–Wayne State University, 1975, pp. 107–10.

Silk, Leonard. "Aging, Inflation, and Retirement." *New York Times,* November 22, 1978, p. D2.

Simmons, Leo W. *The Role of the Aged in Primitive Society.* New Haven, Conn.: Yale University Press, 1945.

Singer, June. *Androgyny: Toward a New Theory of Sexuality.* Garden City, N.Y.: Anchor Press/Doubleday, 1977.

———. *Boundaries of the Soul: The Practice of Jung's Psychology.* Garden City, N.Y.: Anchor Press/Doubleday, 1973.

Smith, Catharine Cook. *A Graft from the Golden Bough.* New York: The Dial Press, Inc., 1937.

Smith, Lillian. "On Women's Autobiography." *Southern Exposure* (Winter 1977) 4(4):48–49.

"Social Security and Sex Discrimination." *New York Times,* March 1, 1979, p. A18.

"Social Security Benefits to Be Raised 11.2% in July." *New York Times,* April 24, 1981, p. A18.

"Social Security Cash-Flow Problem Held Possible if U.S. Has Recession." *New York Times*, April 17, 1979, p. B17.

Sohngen, Mary. "The Experience of Old Age as Depicted in Contemporary Novels." *The Gerontologist* (February 1977) 17(1):70–78.

———. "The Selfhood of Aging Women in the Contemporary Novel." 1977 Modern Language Association, Session on Women: Aging and Death in Literature, Chicago.

———. "The Writer as an Old Woman." *The Gerontologist* (December 1975) 15(6):493–98.

Soldo, Beth J. "America's Elderly in the 1980's." *Population Bulletin* (November 1980) 35(4).

Sommers, Tish. "The Compounding Impact of Age on Sex." In *The New Old: Struggling for Decent Aging*, edited by Ronald Gross, Beatrice Gross and Sylvia Seidman. Garden City, N.Y.: Anchor Press/Doubleday, 1978, pp. 123–36.

———. "Cuts to Hit Women Hardest," Moving Right Along, *The Gray Panther Network*, (July/August 1981), p. 9.

———. "My Health and Yours." *The Gray Panther Network* (September/October 1979), p. 4.

———. "On Growing Older Female: An Interview with Tish Sommers." In *The Older Woman: Lavender Rose or Gray Panther*, edited by Marie Marschall Fuller and Cora Ann Martin. Springfield, Ill.: Charles C. Thomas, 1980, pp. 31–34.

——— and Laurie Shields. *Social Security: Adequacy* and *Equity for Older Women*. Oakland, Calif.: Older Women's League Educational Fund, Gray Paper No. 2, 1979.

Sontag, Susan. "The Double Standard of Aging." In *No Longer Young: The Older Woman in America*. Ann Arbor, Mich.: The Institute of Gerontology, University of Michigan-Wayne State University, 1975, pp. 31–39.

Spicker, Stuart F. "Gerontogenetic Mentation: Memory, Dementia and Medicine in the Penultimate Years." In *Aging and the Elderly: Humanistic Perspectives in Gerontology*, edited by Stuart F. Spicker, Kathleen M. Woodward and David D. Van Tassel. Atlantic Highlands, N.J.: Humanities Press, Inc., 1978, pp. 153–80.

———, Kathleen Woodward, and David D. Van Tassel, eds. Foreword. In *Aging and the Elderly: Humanistic Perspectives in Gerontology*, pp. vii–viii.

Spindler, George, and Louise. Foreword. In *Fun City: An Ethnographic Study of a Retirement Community*, by Jerry Jacobs. New York: Holt, Rinehart and Winston, Inc., 1974, pp. v–vi.

Spiro, Melford E. *Kibbutz: Venture in Utopia*. New York: Schocken Books, 1963.

Stafford, Jean. "The Children's Game." In *The Collected Stories of Jean Stafford*. New York: Farrar, Straus and Giroux, 1969, pp. 19–33.

———. "Life Is No Abyss." In *The Collected Stories of Jean Stafford*. New York: Farrar, Straus and Giroux, 1969, pp. 93–112.

Starr, Louis M. "Introduction." In *Columbia University: The Oral History Collection of Columbia University*, edited by Elizabeth B. Mason and Louis M. Starr. New York: Oral History Research Office, 1971, pp. vii–ix.

Stehouwer, Jan. "Relations between Generations and the Three-Generation Household in Denmark." In *Marriage and the Family: A Comparative Analysis of Contemporary Problems*, edited by Meyer Barash and Alice Scourby. New York: Random House, Inc., 1970, pp. 165–92.

Stein, Ellen. "That Civilizing Spirit." *Southern Exposure* (Winter 1977) 4(4):65–69.

Stephens, Joyce. *Loners, Losers, and Lovers: Elderly Tenants in a Slum Hotel.* Seattle, Wash.: University of Washington Press, 1976.

Stern, Paul J. *C. G. Jung: The Haunted Prophet.* New York: George Braziller, 1976.

Stuhlmann, Gunther, ed. *The Diary of Anaïs Nin, 1931–1934,* Volume 1. New York: Harcourt Brace Jovanovich, 1966.

———. *The Diary of Anaïs Nin, 1944–1947,* Volume 4. New York: Harcourt Brace Jovanovich, 1971.

———. *The Diary of Anaïs Nin, 1947–1955,* Volume 5. New York: Harcourt Brace Jovanovich, 1974.

———. *The Diary of Anaïs Nin, 1955–1966,* Volume 6. New York: Harcourt Brace Jovanovich, 1976.

Suckow, Ruth. "A Memoir." In *Some Others and Myself: Seven Stories and a Memoir,* by Ruth Suckow. New York: Rinehart and Co., Inc., 1952, pp. 169–281.

———. "Mrs. Vogel and Ollie." In *Some Others and Myself: Seven Stories and a Memoir,* pp. 35–65.

———. "Sunset Camp." In *Children and Older People,* by Ruth Suckow. New York: Alfred A. Knopf, 1931, pp. 218–31.

Tacha, Athena. "The Process of Aging." *The Village Voice* (February 26, 1979) 24(9):57.

Talmon, Yonina. "Aging In Israel, A Planned Society." In *Middle Age and Aging: A Reader in Social Psychology,* edited by Bernice L. Neugarten. Chicago: The University of Chicago Press, 1968, pp. 461–468.

"TASKFORCE Reports: Who Cares about Older Women . . . Older Women's Task Force at Work." *The Gray Panther Network* (September/October 1979), p. 7.

Thompson, Fred. Introduction. In *The Autobiography of Mother Jones,* edited by Mary Field Parton. Chicago: Charles H. Kerr Publishing Co., 1977, pp. iii–xxxvi.

Trager, Natalie P. Introduction. In *No Longer Young: Work Group Reports from the 26th Annual Conference on Aging.* Ann Arbor, Mich.: The Institute of Gerontology, University of Michigan–Wayne State University, 1974, pp. ix–xv.

Troll, Lillian E. "Issues in the Study of Generations." *International Journal of Aging and Human Development* (1970) 7:199–218.

———, Helen Lycaki, and Jean Smith. "Development of the Cognitively Complex Woman over the Generations." In *No Longer Young: The Older Woman in America.* Ann Arbor, Mich.: The Institute of Gerontology, University of Michigan–Wayne State University, 1975, pp. 81–87.

Turner, Victor. Preface. In *Number Our Days,* by Barbara Myerhoff. New York: E. P. Dutton, 1978, pp. ix–xiii.

Turoff, Barbara Kivel. "Mary Beard: Feminist Educator." *The Antioch Review* (Summer 1979) 37(3):277–92.

Ulanov, Ann Belford. *The Feminine in Jungian Psychology and in Christian Theology.* Evanston, Ill: Northwestern University Press, 1971.

U. S. Department of Commerce, Special Studies Series P23, No. 58. *A Statistical Portrait of Women in the U.S.* Washington, D.C.: U. S. Government Printing Office, 1976.

U. S. Department of Health, Education, and Welfare. *Social Security and the Changing Roles of Men and Women.* Washington, D.C.: U. S. Department of Health, Education, and Welfare, 1979.

U. S. Department of Labor, Bureau of Labor Statistics, Employment Standards Administration, Women's Bureau. *Mature Women Workers: A Profile.* Washington, D.C.: U.S. Government Printing Office, 1976.

Van Hoosen, Bertha. *Petticoat Surgeon.* Chicago: Pellegrini and Cudahy, 1947.

Van Tassel, David D. Preface. In *Aging and the Elderly: Humanistic Perspectives in Gerontology,* edited by Stuart F. Spicker, Kathleen M. Woodward, and David D. Van Tassel. Atlantic Highlands, N. J.: Humanities Press, Inc., 1978, pp. v–vi.

Vickery, Florence E. *Old and Growing: Conversations, Letters, Observations, and Reflections on Growing Old.* Springfield, Ill.: Charles C. Thomas, 1978.

Vining, Elizabeth Gray. *Being Seventy: The Measure of a Year.* New York: The Viking Press, 1978.

Vorse, Mary Heaton. *Autobiography of an Elderly Woman.* Boston: Houghton Mifflin Co., 1911; Reprint Edition 1974 by Arno Press, Inc.

———. *A Footnote to Folly: Reminiscences of Mary Heaton Vorse.* New York: Farrar and Rinehart, Inc., 1935.

Walker, Alice. "In Search of Our Mothers' Gardens." *Southern Exposure* (Winter 1977) 4(4):60–64.

———. "The Welcome Table." In *In Love and Trouble: Stories of Black Women,* by Alice Walker. New York: Harcourt Brace Jovanovich, 1973, pp. 81–87.

Waters, Elinor, and Betty White. "Helping Each Other." In *Looking Ahead: A Woman's Guide to the Problems and Joys of Growing Older,* edited by Lillian E. Troll, Joan Israel, and Kenneth Israel. Englewood Cliffs, N.J.: Prentice-Hall, Inc., 1977, pp. 184–93.

Watriss, Wendy. "It's Something Inside You." *Southern Exposure* (Winter 1977) 4(4):76–81.

Weaver, Rix. *The Old Wise Woman—A Study of Active Imagination.* London: Vincent Stuart Ltd., 1964.

Weaver, Warren, Jr. "House Unit Finds Aged Getting Poorer." *New York Times,* May 2, 1981, p. 10.

———. "House Votes to Keep Minimum Retirement Benefit." *New York Times,* December 17, 1981, p. B16.

Welty, Eudora. "Is Phoenix Jackson's Grandson Really Dead?" In *The Eye of the Story: Selected Essays and Reviews.* New York: Random House, 1978, pp. 159–62.

———. "Must the Novelist Crusade?" In *The Eye of the Story: Selected Essays and Reviews,* pp. 146–58.

———. "Some Notes on Time in Fiction." In *The Eye of the Story: Selected Essays and Reviews,* pp. 163–73.

———. "A Visit of Charity." In *A Curtain of Green,* by Eudora Welty. New York: Doubleday, Doran and Co., Inc., 1943, pp. 219–27.

———. "A Worn Path." In *A Curtain of Green,* pp. 273–85.

West, Jessamyn. *The Woman Said Yes: Encounters with Life and Death (Memoirs.)* Greenwich, Conn.: Fawcett Publications, Inc., 1976.

Westin, Jeane. *Making Do: How Women Survived the 30s.* Chicago: Follett Publishing Co., 1976.

Wharton, Edith. "After Holbein." In *Certain People.* New York: D. Appleton and Co., 1930, pp. 63–101.

———. *A Backward Glance.* New York: D. Appleton-Century Co., Inc., 1934.

———. *The Children.* New York: D. Appleton and Co., 1928.

———. *The Mother's Recompense.* New York: D. Appleton and Co., 1925.

———. *Quaderno dello Studente.* Wharton Archives, Beinecke Library, Yale University, New Haven, Conn.

———. *Twilight Sleep.* New York: D. Appleton and Co., 1927.

"Who Reads in the United States?" *Coda: Poets and Writers Newsletter* (September/October 1979) 7(1):6.

"Widows Would Be Aided under Pension Law Change." *New York Times,* February 7, 1979, p. A16.

Wigginton, Eliot, ed. *The Foxfire Book.* New York: Anchor Press, Doubleday, 1972.

———. *Foxfire 2.* New York: Anchor Press/Doubleday, 1973.

———. *Foxfire 3.* New York: Anchor Press/Doubleday, 1975.

———. *Foxfire 4.* New York: Anchor Press/Doubleday, 1977.

Winfrey, Carey. "At 81, a Blind Teacher Gives a Lesson in Determination." *New York Times,* December 15, 1979, p. 20.

Winslow, Ron. "Elderhostel: A Growing Chain," *New York Times,* September 9, 1979, Education, p. 11.

Winston, Elizabeth. "The Autobiographer and Her Readers: From Apology to Affirmation." In *Women's Autobiography: Essays in Criticism,* edited by Estelle C. Jelinek. Bloomington, Ind.: Indiana University Press, 1980, pp. 93–111.

Wolff, Cynthia Griffin. *A Feast of Words: The Triumph of Edith Wharton.* New York: Oxford University Press, Inc., 1977.

Woodward, Kathleen. "Aging and Disengagement: May Sarton's *As We Are Now* and *Journal of a Solitude.* 1977 Modern Language Association, Session on Women: Aging and Death in Literature, Chicago.

———. "May Sarton and Fictions of Old Age." In *Gender and Literary Voice,* edited by Janet Todd. New York: Holmes and Meier Publishers, Inc., 1980, pp. 108–27.

Wrye, Harriet, and Jacqueline Churilla. "Looking Inward, Looking Backward: Reminiscence and the Life Review." *Frontiers* (Summer 1977) 2(2):98–105.

Yeats, William Butler. "The Countess Cathleen." In *The Variorum Edition of the Plays of William Butler Yeats,* edited by Russell K. Alspach, assisted by Catharine C. Alspach. New York: The Macmillan Co., 1966, pp. 1–179.

Zabel, Morton Dauwen. "Epilogue." In *A Poet's Life: Seventy Years in a Changing World,* by Harriet Monroe. New York: The Macmillan Co., 1938, pp. 459–76.

Zola, Irving Kenneth. "Culture and Symptoms: An Analysis of Patients' Presenting Complaints." In *Perspectives on the Social Order: Readings in Sociology,* edited by H. Laurence Ross. 2nd ed. New York: McGraw-Hill Inc., 1968, pp. 65–82.

Name Index

Subject Index